Criminal Law

THIRTEENTH EDITION

THOMAS J. GARDNER

Attorney at Law

TERRY M. ANDERSON

Creighton University School of Law

Australia • Brazil • Mexico • Singapore • United Kingdom • United States

Criminal Law, **Thirteenth Edition**
Thomas J. Gardner and Terry M. Anderson

Senior Product Director: Marta Lee-Perriard

Senior Product Manager: Carolyn Henderson Meier

Senior Content Developer: Shelley Murphy

Product Assistant: Timothy Kappler

Marketing Director: Mark Linton

Senior Content Project Manager: Christy Frame

Senior Art Director: Helen Bruno

Senior Manufacturing Planner: Judy Inouye

Production Service and Compositor: Lynn Lustberg, MPS Limited

Photo Researcher: Lumina Datamatics

Text Researcher: Rameshkumar Muthuramalingam, Lumina Datamatics

Copy Editor: Barbara LeFleur

Text Designer: Jeanne Schreiber

Cover Designer: Helen Bruno

Cover Image: Brandon Bourdages/ Shutterstock.com

For product information and technology assistance, contact us at
**Cengage Customer & Sales Support, 1-800-354-9706
or support.cengage.com.**

For permission to use material from this text or product, submit all requests online at **www.cengage.com/permissions.**

Unless otherwise noted, all content is © Cengage Learning

Library of Congress Control Number: 2016941535

Student Edition:
ISBN: 978-1-305-96636-9
Loose-leaf Edition:
ISBN: 978-1-305-96640-6

Cengage
200 Pier 4 Boulevard
Boston, MA 02210
USA

Cengage is a leading provider of customized learning solutions with employees residing in nearly 40 different countries and sales in more than 125 countries around the world. Find your local representative at: **www.cengage.com.**

To learn more about Cengage platforms and services, register or access your online learning solution, or purchase materials for your course, visit **www.cengage.com.**

Printed in Mexico
Print Number: 08   Print Year: 2020

Dedicated to Eileen Gardner
January 25, 1925–September 26, 2005

THOMAS J. GARDNER, after earning a Bachelor of Science degree in economics, served three years as a naval officer in the South Pacific during and immediately after World War II. He then attended and graduated from Marquette Law School with a Juris Doctor degree in 1949. During the Korean War he worked in procurement for the Air Material Command. He also earned a Master of Arts degree in political science. His long association with the criminal justice system began as a criminal defense lawyer. He then worked as a prosecutor, as a police legal adviser, and in police in-service legal training. He was a member and president of a police and fire commission. For twenty-eight years, he taught courses in Criminal Law, Criminal Evidence, and Arrest, Search and Seizure at the Milwaukee Area Technical College complex of campuses. He lives in Milwaukee, Wisconsin.

TERRY M. ANDERSON, Professor of Law, is a Professor of Law at Creighton University School of Law in Omaha, Nebraska. He was a Visiting Professor at Denver College of Law for the 2001–2002 academic year, and at the University of New Mexico during the 1980–1981 academic year. He received his Bachelor of Arts degree in 1968 and Juris Doctor degree in 1971 from the University of North Dakota, where he was a member of the Order of the Coif and the Case Editor of the North Dakota Law Review. After earning a Master of Laws degree from Harvard Law School in 1972, he joined the Creighton Law School faculty. He teaches Criminal Law, Contracts, Insurance, and Secured Transactions in Personal Property. E-mail: terryanderson@creighton.edu

Contents in Brief

v

Contents

PART TWO
CRIMES AGAINST THE PERSON

Chapter 10
Homicide   266

Chapter 11
Assault, Battery, and Other Crimes Against the Person   300

PART THREE
CRIMES AGAINST PROPERTY

Chapter 13
Theft 366

PART FOUR
OTHER CRIMINAL CONDUCT

Chapter 19
Immigration Crimes, Contempt, and Other Crimes Against Government   532

Boxed Features

GOALS

The first edition of this text was published more than 30 years ago. Its goal was to introduce law enforcement personnel and others in the criminal justice field to the main principles of American criminal law. In the subsequent editions, including this, the thirteenth edition, we have tried to adhere to that goal and at the same time broaden the scope of the text while also keeping it current. As in past editions, we have included recent court opinions and legislative acts that illustrate the current status of those principles of American criminal law. We have also tried to include information we believe to be helpful to the study of criminal law, taken from governmental reports, empirical studies, and news accounts of current criminal cases and developments. We hope these additions and changes in the thirteenth edition serve to advance our goal for this text.

We make extensive use of court opinions, especially U.S. Supreme Court opinions and case citations in the text. We use these opinions and case citations primarily to illustrate how the majority of courts interpreted and applied criminal statutes within their jurisdiction. We also identify and cite decisions on key points of criminal law so that teachers and students will have a sound basis for doing more extensive research into such points. It has always been our plan to create a text that would prove useful as both a classroom learning tool and a reference book for post-classroom use. We are gratified that users of our text have found that it met that plan in previous editions, and we hope they will conclude the same about this edition.

Features

In this edition we continue to use more detailed case excerpts called Case Close-Ups to examine courts' analyses of difficult or emerging criminal law issues, sometimes including our observations about the possible effect of a court's decision on a particular issue. These case excerpts generally include a more detailed factual statement and a more complete discussion of the court's reasoning than the other case excerpts found in the text. Also, in some chapters we examine an important U.S. Supreme Court case or cases and then discuss lower court cases that apply the rules announced by the Supreme Court. As an example, in Chapter 8 we include an extensive analysis of three U.S. Supreme Court cases involving juvenile life sentences, *Graham v. Florida*, *Montgomery v. Louisiana*, and *Miller v. Alabama*, together with important lower court decisions decided subsequently.

Where possible, we chose U.S. Supreme Court cases for the Case Close-Up features. Given the increase in federal criminal statutes we describe in Chapter 2, it is not surprising this edition has several recent Supreme Court decisions interpreting federal statutes on scienter or other elements of the offense in the statute. In subject areas where the Supreme Court does not ordinarily issue opinions, we chose opinions of the federal circuit courts or the highest state courts. Cases were usually selected because their topics were of current interest, but not necessarily because the opinion represented the majority view on the topic (though in most cases it does). We hope these closer looks at important cases will add substance to our coverage of the issues framed in those cases.

We continue to make references to specific state and federal criminal statutes, as well as illustrations from the Model Penal Code, which we have expanded in this edition. For example, in Chapter 6, we include excerpts from the Florida "Stand Your Ground" statute, including amendments to the statute since the last edition, which has been a model for similar legislation in twenty-nine other states.

In this edition we have retained the chapter-opening vignettes, with new vignettes for most chapters. We also retained the chapter-ending "Case Analysis and Writing Exercises" feature. Most of the cases highlighted in the exercises are new to this edition, though we did retain a small number from the previous edition. In this edition we also continue to use charts, boxes, and lists as supplements to text and case summaries. We intend the textual materials and case summaries to serve as the main exposition of criminal law principles, with the boxes and other tools helping to illustrate specific applications or examples of those principles.

New to This Edition

In addition to the features just discussed, we have made other changes and additions to this edition. While we have always striven to incorporate new cases and statutes into each new edition, in the twelfth edition we did this on a very broad scale. We not only added many cases decided since the eleventh edition was published, we also replaced a substantial number of older cases that illustrated legal principles with more recent cases that accomplish the same result but in a more current setting. There are hundreds of cases cited or discussed in our book; in this thirteenth edition over **300** court decisions will have come from cases decided in the years 2010–2016. With this effort we believe we have made the thirteenth edition as up to date and complete as possible, while at the same time maintaining the clarity and ease of understanding that we hope are the hallmarks of our Criminal Law textbook.

In this edition we have a new feature, called "**You Be the Judge.**" In this feature, which appears throughout the edition, students are asked to consider some of the issues presented to a trial judge (or in a few instances to an appellate judge) in a criminal case. These include motions to dismiss based on a claim the prosecution didn't prove every element of an offense, and the proper jury instruction on the relevant law to be given by the judge to the jury to use when making its fact findings. We hope this feature will help students focus on the elements of a criminal charge and what the prosecution must do to prove those elements.

Finally, we have added the most recent reports available in the many places in the book where we include statistical information. There is commonly a lag between when statistics are gathered and reports are published, and we tried our best to minimize that lag time.

We have always been appreciative of the efforts of those who review our book before we begin work on a new edition. In this edition, as in the past, we have made it a point to incorporate specific suggestions made by our reviewers and others who have taken the time to communicate with us. We thank them and invite all our readers to share their thoughts on the book with us at Terry Anderson's e-mail address, which is listed in the brief biography that appears in the front pages of this edition.

New Content

In addition to the changes discussed above, in the thirteenth edition we have made many substantive additions as well. They include the following:

- **Chapter 1, Criminal Law: Purposes, Scope, and Sources:** In this chapter, as in most others, we changed the approach of the chapter-opening "vignettes." These short features now are used not only to introduce the criminal law issues discussed in the chapter, but also to ask students to think about, as they study the materials in the chapter, what the law should be for the fact situation in the vignette. We continue to examine the constitutional limits on criminal laws, including a new section focused on vagueness and the meaning of "violent felony," as a result of the U. S. Supreme Court's 2015 decision in *Johnson v. United States*. The application of that decision to related issues by lower federal courts will be reviewed by the Supreme Court in 2016.

- **Chapter 2, Jurisdiction:** In response to the growth of federal crimes (and requests from readers), we expanded our discussion of the basis of federal jurisdiction to enact criminal laws. This includes a new section on the Commerce Clauses, interstate, foreign, and the Indian Tribes. We discuss a case before the U.S. Supreme Court in 2016 on the interstate commerce clause and what effect criminal acts must have to trigger federal jurisdiction under the clause. We also discuss the 2015 *Yates* and 2014 *Bond* Supreme Court decisions on the limits of federal jurisdiction. We include two 2015–2016 cases on jurisdiction of tribal courts and federal courts to try cases involving crimes by or against Indian tribe members. We also discuss the decision pending before the Supreme Court in 2016 on the permissible use of prior convictions of Indians in tribal courts for use in federal courts. There, the Court will consider if such tribal court convictions where the defendant did not have appointed counsel may be used under the federal habitual offender statute.

- **Chapter 3, Essential Elements of a Crime:** We continue to focus on the mens rea and scienter requirements in criminal statutes. To that end, we discuss in a "Case Close-Up" the 2015 U.S. Supreme Court decision in *Elonis v. United States* on when Facebook posts become criminal threats. We also have a "You Be the Judge" box on what "knowingly" requires the prosecution to prove under illustrative federal criminal statutes. We have new sections on when "willful blindness" satisfies a statute's scienter requirement, and when (if ever) a defendant may raise a mistake of age defense in a sex with a child crime. In the possession section we added a box on when one "possesses" the stolen gun subsequently used by another person to kill four Lakewood, Washington, police officers.

- **Chapter 4, Criminal Liability:** We added new cases on solicitation to illustrate attempts to persuade another to commit a crime, including a 2015 Illinois case on the impact of a failure of a solicitation communication to reach the person solicited. In the conspiracy section we added recent cases that considered if a federal conspiracy statute has an overt act requirement, since some do and some don't. In the attempt section we again have a new case looking at the availability of an attempt charge where the underlying crime (here felony-murder) does not have a specific intent element. Finally, we expanded the discussion of accomplice liability, especially in light of the Supreme Court's decision in *Rosemond v. United States*. That decision has already influenced lower courts' accomplice liability decisions.

- **Chapter 5, Criminal Responsibility and the Capacity to Commit a Crime:** In the capacity materials, we expanded the section on juvenile courts to include recent cases and statutes that illustrate how criminal charges are transferred from juvenile to adult courts. In the insanity materials we included recent cases and examples discussing the "substantial capacity" test used in the Model Penal Code. We discuss the use of mental illness evidence to prove lack of specific intent in states that have abolished or limited the insanity defense. We added a new box that focuses on the mental illness evidence in the John Holmes, Aurora, Colorado, mass killings trial. Holmes' insanity defense was rejected by the jury, and he was convicted of murder in 2015. The box asks students to compare the expert medical evidence introduced in Holmes' trial to similar evidence introduced in a recent Wisconsin case. We reorganized the intoxication and diminished capacity defense materials, with an expanded discussion of what courts hold constitutes "diminished capacity" and what it means as a defense to a charge of homicide. Finally, we updated the "forced competency" box with a 2015 case on when a defendant can be forced to take medication to achieve competency.

- **Chapter 6, The Law Governing the Use of Force:** In this chapter we include many new cases, examples, and boxed materials to illustrate the use of force in self-defense. This includes updating cases under the "stand your ground" laws and the "castle" doctrine. We also updated the box on the meaning of "unlawful" activity under those laws, with a 2014 Florida case holding the defense available even if a defendant was acting unlawfully, and the subsequent amendment of the Florida statute in response to that case. We also include a "You Be the Judge" box raising a question about the proper application of a "stand your ground" defense to a homicide. The "battered women" defense section was rewritten to delete older cases and add a 2013 case showing the possible use of evidence of "battered woman syndrome." In the use of force by police materials we added a new section, "Police and the Use of Deadly Force." There we include several recent cases illustrating fact patterns where courts found the use of deadly force by police either excessive or reasonable.

- **Chapter 7, Other Criminal Defenses:** In the previous edition we included, for the first time, a 2011 case on legislative immunity under the Speech and Debate Clause of the Constitution. In this edition we added a 2015 case showing the limits of that privilege. In witness immunity, we added a recent Oregon case showing the consequences (for the prosecution) of a violation of an immunity agreement with a suspect in a murder case. We updated the mistake of fact defense materials with four new examples of that defense. To illustrate the borders of the duress defense, we include a "You Be the Judge" box on the duress defense in a robbery/felony-murder case. In the Double Jeopardy section we added the Supreme Court's 2014 affirmation in *Martinez v. Illinois* of the "bright line" rule for when jeopardy attaches. We also include a 2015 Michigan case on double jeopardy as applied to a "double punishment" for a single offense. We completely updated the "Stings, Scams, and Outrageous Government Conduct" box, adding three 2015 cases and one 2013 case on this subject. Finally, we include a 2015 Wisconsin case showing what kind of corroboration evidence is required before a defense that a third person committed the crime may be raised.

- **Chapter 8, Criminal Punishment:** In previous editions we noted the rarity of U.S. Supreme Court decisions, under the Cruel and Unusual Punishment Clause, on the proportionality of non-capital prison sentences. Because states are free to have their own, broader proportionality review of prison sentences, in this edition we added a section titled "Proportionality in State Sentencing Laws," with appropriate recent cases showing how representative sentencing reviews work. The new section includes a discussion of factors a sentencing judge is to consider when deciding when punishments for multiple convictions can be consecutive rather than concurrent. In a related manner, we have a "You Be the Judge" box on sentence enhancement statutes, based on the Supreme Court's 2016 decision in *Lockhart v. United States*. In the capital punishment section we updated all the death sentence/execution statistics, noting the decline of both from previous years. We added Supreme Court death penalty decisions reached since the last edition, and also updated the box on life sentences without parole for juveniles, adding cases showing how resentencing is proceeding since *Miller* and *Graham*, as well as the Supreme Court's decision in *Montgomery v. Louisiana* making the decision in *Miller* retroactive to juveniles whose sentences were final before *Miller* was decided. In the forfeiture as punishment section, we added the 2016 Supreme Court decision in *Luis v. United States*, where the court held "untainted" assets of a defendant could not be seized pretrial. Finally, we added a Case Close-Up of the Supreme Court's 2013 decision in *Descamps v. United States*, establishing a rule on when a prior conviction is a "violent crime" for sentence enhancement under the ACCA.

- **Chapter 9, Free Speech, Public Order Crimes, and the Bill of Rights:** We use the chapter-opening vignette to show the developments in prosecutions under the federal "false valor" statute, part of which was struck down by the Supreme Court in the *Alvarez* case. That case remains a Case Close-Up in this edition. In the "fighting words" section we rewrote the introductory paragraphs to make it clearer how "fighting words" interact with the "clear and present danger" test. We included several recent cases considering when speech constitutes "fighting words." We converted the Case Close-Up discussion of the Supreme Court's decision in *United States v. Stevens* on the overbreadth doctrine to a new box on overbreadth and "crush videos" to show Congress's reaction to the *Stevens* decision, and one court's decision upholding the amended statute aimed at "crush videos." In the section on use of the mail, Internet, or e-mails to threaten another person we added a box titled "Criminal Threats, Harassment, and Social Media," containing several recent decisions on when posts on social media go beyond protected speech and become criminal threats. In the section on gun ownership and regulation, we added (as a subset of gun regulation limitations under the Second Amendment) a "You Be the Supreme Court Justice" box. The Supreme Court granted review in *United States v. Voisine* in 2015, a case presenting the issue of what Congress intended when it passed a statute making it illegal for a person convicted of a "misdemeanor crime of domestic violence" to own a gun. The box asks students to consider the arguments for and against an expansive interpretation of the statute. It is here to supplement a new section in this edition on the federal criminal statute establishing a (often) lifetime ban on gun ownership by persons previously convicted of violent crimes or drug offenses, illegal aliens, or persons subject to a domestic abuse protection order. We note that virtually every court hearing cases under this statute has upheld the statute in the face of Second Amendment claims. Finally, we updated the recent cases in the section on regulating guns after *Heller*.

- **Chapter 10, Homicide:** This chapter was substantially changed in the twelfth edition, in part in response to requests from our users. In this edition we have mainly updated those changes. For example, in the causation section we added a recent California case to illustrate how the presumption in that state's "three years and a day" rule works. In the section on murder, we added a 2015 New York case showing the limits of transferred intent as a vehicle to achieve multiple convictions for the same homicide. We also have a "You Be the Judge" box that raises questions about when a "predicate" felony such as child abuse or neglect can be used to invoke the felony-murder rule. We also note that in a 2015 case the Massachusetts Supreme Judicial Court adopted the agency or "malice" theory for felony-murder convictions, as opposed to the minority "proximate cause" theory followed by some courts. Finally, in the manslaughter section we added a (somewhat unusual) 2014 Georgia case finding "words" to be adequate provocation to change murder to manslaughter.

- **Chapter 11, Assault, Battery, and Other Crimes Against the Person:** We have continued our effort from the twelfth edition to try clarify the elements under the federal assault statutes. To that end, we added a 2016 case that illustrates the broad scope of the federal assault statute, as well as a 2014 and a 2015 case that discuss the meaning of "dangerous weapon" under the federal assault statute. We believe these decisions, though not binding in state assault trials, will have some persuasive authority. We also included a charge under a state aggravated assault statute in a "You Be the Judge" box in the assault materials. We updated the hate crime statistics, and added two new hate crime-related cases. One, the subject of a "Case Close-Up" box, is a 2014 case that focuses on the required relationship under the federal hate crime law between the "hate" and the motive for the criminal acts. The second is a 2015 New Jersey case striking a hate crime statute that made the perception of the victim the basis for criminal assaults being treated as hate crimes. Finally, we added yet another example, here a 2015 California case, of a court struggling with the "movement" requirement in a kidnapping conviction; and (sadly) updated the school shootings box to show some that have occurred since the last edition.

- **Chapter 12, Sexual Assault, Rape, Prostitution, and Related Sex Crimes:** In the previous edition we substantially rewrote the rape materials, including the rape shield laws section, substituting newer cases for older ones. Here, we updated those changes. For example, we added a 2014 case that explains why there are limits in sexual assault prosecutions on the admissibility of evidence of past sexual relations between the victim and the defendant. The Internet and social networks unfortunately provide a fertile ground for child sex predators. Some states have passed laws limiting the access of convicted sex offenders to Internet sites like Facebook, where children can gain access. We added a 2015 North Carolina case upholding such a law, and noted a petition for certiorari was filed in the U.S. Supreme Court in March of 2016. In a related issue, we included the 2016 U.S. Supreme Court decision in *Nichols v. United States* on the registration requirements under SORNA for those who move to a foreign country. In the child pornography materials we noted the effect of the Internet and cell phone technology on prosecutions under child pornography laws. We included two 2014 cases under the federal child pornography statutes, one involving posts on Facebook, and the other involving downloads of photographs from a cell phone to a computer. Also reflecting the growth of the use of the Internet in child sexual abuse cases, we added a new section in this edition titled "The Federal Enticement Statute," with one 2015 and two 2014 cases under that statute. Finally, we added a "You Be the Judge" box to focus on the use of cell phone video and photography technology in state law crimes such as "up-skirting."

- **Chapter 13, Theft:** We have rewritten the theft chapter in previous editions to reflect the way that crime is treated today. In this edition we tried to add materials that "stretch" some of the theft concepts. For example, we added a 2014 case on abandoned property and specific intent in theft prosecutions. In the fraudulent use of credit cards section we included a 2013 Arizona case finding a violation of a credit card fraud statute, followed by an excerpt from the LaFave treatise criticizing such decisions. Finally, we added a box on "The Home Depot Scam," mainly to show how retail fraud scams can be organized and executed.

- **Chapter 14, Robbery, Burglary, and Related Crimes:** In this chapter we updated the materials on robbery, carjacking, and home invasion by adding cases that explore the limits of those crimes. When is "force" part of a theft sufficient to make it robbery, or carjacking? States differ on the answer to those questions, and we therefore showed competing views. In home invasion robberies states also vary on whether perpetrators can be charged with both home invasion and crimes committed once a home has been invaded. We included recent cases on that question as well. In the 2013 case of *Sekhar v. United States* the U.S. Supreme Court decided that extortion convictions under the Hobbs Act required the prosecution to prove the extortionate acts or threats were made to obtain "property," meaning something of value capable of being transferred to another. In the burglary chapter we added 2015 cases illustrating how courts interpret the "breaking and entering" part of a burglary crime. We also included a "You Be the Judge" box raising the question of whether under a state burglary statute the "dwelling house of another" can include the defendant's own house. Finally, as one of the "Case Analysis and Writing Exercises," we ask students to consider the decision of the New Jersey Supreme Court in the *Gibson* defiant trespass case that was the subject of the vignette in the twelfth edition and on appeal to that court when the last edition was published.

- **Chapter 15, White-Collar Crime, Cybercrime, and Commercial Crime:** The mens rea requirement in "white collar" crimes continues to evolve. To illustrate that evolution we added a "Case Close-Up" highlighting the U. S. Supreme Court's 2014 decision in *Loughrin v. United States*. Courts had split on the specific intent required under the federal bank fraud statute, and in *Loughrin* the Court resolved that split. We also added a new section titled "The Meaning of Willful." Most of the federal crimes we discuss in this chapter have a "knowing" or "willful" mens rea requirement. We included significant federal court decisions on the meaning of "willful" in health care fraud charges, and (in a new subsection) criminal copyright infringement. In the Program Fraud section we added a new box, "Kickbacks," illustrating the kind of conduct that violates federal "anti-kickback" statutes. Given the U.S. Supreme Court's recent decision in *Skilling* that "honest services fraud" is limited to "classic" crimes like bribery and kickbacks, we thought it would be useful to see what courts say constitutes a "kickback" under federal statutes. In the bribery section we include a "You Be the Judge" box focusing on a bribery charge against a public official under state bribery law. In financial market frauds we discuss in some detail the decision of the Second Circuit Court of Appeals in *United States v. Newman*. Many believe this decision has important consequences for insider trading prosecutions. Identity theft goes on, so we added recent cases illustrating the scope of identity theft laws. We substantially expanded the "Cybercrime" section by first adding a box with 2015 information from the new F.B.I. "IC3" department on reports of cybercrime. Second, we discuss the 2016 decision of the U.S. Supreme Court in the *Musacchio* case under the federal Computer Fraud and Abuse Act. In the "Case Analysis and Writing Exercises" for this chapter we highlight "financial aid fraud" by a college professor, and environmental violations by an environmental recycling corporation.

- **Chapter 16, Drug Abuse and Alcohol-Related Crimes:** The statistics on illegal drug sale and use are important; as a result, we extensively updated and revised our opening materials on drug abuse and the "war on drugs" to incorporate recent information about both those topics. In the Drug Laws section we used a "You Be the Judge" box to focus on a prosecution under the federal "Controlled Substance Analogue" statute. We then ask students to draft the appropriate jury instruction on the mens rea required under the statute, keeping in mind the rival instructions proposed by U.S. Supreme Court Justices in the 2015 *McFadden v. United States* decision under the statute. The legal medical and recreational use of marijuana continues to grow. We provide the latest information available on state and federal laws relating to that growth, as well as a 2016 Montana case illustrating a state marijuana regulatory scheme. The justice department has stated that it will not prosecute "legal" marijuana use if a state has adequate regulations on its use. Montana's regulatory scheme may prove to be a model for other states. It appears, after the U. S. Supreme Court's 2014 decision in *Burrage v. United States*, that federal and state laws making those who distribute illegal drugs criminally liable for deaths that "result" from use of those drugs differ on the causation connection between the distribution of the illegal drugs and the death that follows.

As a contrast to the *Burrage* conclusion on what "results from" means, we added a 2013 Illinois decision under Illinois's drug-induced death statute. That court said liability attaches if the distributor could foresee the death, even if the illegal drug distributed was not the "but for" cause of the death. We greatly expanded the "Booze It and Lose It" section, mainly because of the U.S. Supreme Court's decision in *Missouri v. McNeeley* that blood tests on a DUI suspect require a warrant. After that decision, courts were flooded with claims that state implied consent laws that contained penalties for refusal to consent were also unconstitutional. We note the Supreme Court will face that issue in 2016.

- **Chapter 17, Terrorism:** Once again, regrettably, the various tables and boxes with statistical information on terrorist attacks and killings have been updated. The sections on "Criminal Charges Against Terrorists" and "The Crime of Terrorizing (Terrorist Threats)" have been combined and reorganized under one heading. We added a new subsection, "Terrorism, Terrorist Threats, and Support of Terrorism." There we included a 2015 federal sabotage prosecution, a 2015 federal prosecution of "material support" of terrorism, and a "You Be the Judge" box on a 2015 prosecution under a state terrorist threat statute.

- **Chapter 18, Organized Crime and Gangs:** The introductory material on criminal gangs has been updated, both by new statistics, and with the inclusion of a new box, "The Latin Kings." Here we focus on the history, internal structure, and criminal activities of a major national criminal gang. We also included a 2015 case showing how RICO is used against the gang's criminal activities. The witness tampering section was expanded to include prosecutions of those who kill potential witnesses before they can communicate with a federal officer about a federal crime. Notwithstanding the U.S. Supreme Court's decision in *Fowler v. United States*, it is not completely clear what intent must be proved in witness tampering prosecutions. In the money laundering section we added a "You Be the Judge" box that addresses the question of the knowledge a defendant must possess to be convicted of money laundering. The prosecution of these cases has a very specific and often difficult burden of proof for the prosecutors. Finally, we updated the box on sports betting to reflect the final court result in the New Jersey sports betting legislation case.

- **Chapter 19, Immigration Crimes, Contempt, and Other Crimes Against Government:** Immigration cases and statutes are still the news in this edition. We begin by discussing lower court decisions after the *Arizona v. United States* decision struck down much of the controversial Arizona immigration law. We then document the state of immigration reform in the U.S. Congress. We added a new subsection in the "Criminal Charges for Illegal Immigration Offenses" section titled "Admission, Removal, and Detention." This subsection looks more closely at each of these fates that aliens, both legal and illegal, might face. We included the 2016 decision of the U.S. Supreme Court in *Torres v. Lynch* on what kind of state conviction qualifies a legal alien for removal, as well as two 2016 lower court decisions holding lengthy detentions of aliens awaiting removal to be violations of Due Process. We note the government filed petitions for review in the U.S. Supreme Court in those cases. In the "Obstruction of Justice" section we added the result in the Barry Bonds case; he successfully appealed his conviction for obstruction of justice in the investigation of the use of steroids in professional sports.

SUPPLEMENTS

A number of supplements are provided by Cengage Learning to help instructors use *Criminal Law*, Thirteenth Edition, in their courses and to aid students in preparing for exams. Supplements are available to qualified adopters. Please consult your local sales representative for details.

MindTap® for Criminal Law The most applied learning experience available, MindTap is dedicated to preparing students to make the kinds of reasoned decisions they will have to as criminal justice professionals faced with real-world challenges. Available for virtually every Criminal Justice course, MindTap offers customizable content, course analytics, an e-reader, and more—all within your current learning management system. With its rich array of assets—video cases, interactive visual summaries, decision-making scenarios, quizzes, and writing skill builders—MindTap is perfectly suited to today's Criminal Justice students, engaging them, guiding them toward mastery of basic concepts, and advancing their critical thinking abilities.

Instructor's Resource Manual with Lesson Plans The manual includes learning objectives, key terms, a detailed chapter outline, a chapter summary, lesson plans, discussion topics, student activities, "What If" scenarios, media tools, and sample syllabi. The learning objectives are correlated with the discussion topics, student activities, and media tools.

Downloadable Word Test Bank The enhanced test bank includes a variety of questions per chapter—a combination of multiple-choice, true false, completion, essay, and critical thinking formats, with a full answer key. The test bank is coded to the learning objectives that appear in the main text, and identifies where in the text (by section) the answer appears. Finally, each question in the test bank has been carefully reviewed by experienced criminal justice instructors for quality, accuracy, and content coverage so instructors can be sure they are working with an assessment and grading resource of the highest caliber.

Cengage Learning Testing Powered by Cognero, the accompanying assessment tool is a flexible, online system that allows you to:

- import, edit, and manipulate test bank content from the text's test bank or elsewhere, including your own favorite test questions
- create ideal assessments with your choice of 15 question types (including true/false, multiple choice, opinion scale/likert, and essay)
- create multiple test versions in an instant using drop-down menus and familiar, intuitive tools that take you through content creation and management with ease
- deliver tests from your LMS, your classroom, or wherever you want—plus, import and export content into other systems as needed.

Online PowerPoint Lectures Helping you make your lectures more engaging while effectively reaching your visually oriented students, these handy Microsoft PowerPoint® slides outline the chapters of the main text in a classroom-ready presentation. The PowerPoint® slides reflect the content and organization of the new edition of the text and feature some additional examples and real world cases for application and discussion.

ACKNOWLEDGMENTS

We would like to thank our reviewers for their helpful comments as we prepared this Thirteenth Edition:

Yury Cheryachukin, California State University, Stanislaus
Megan Cole, Brown College
Howard Jordan, Hostos Community College
Thomas McAninch, Scott Community College
Amy Pinero, Baton Rouge Community College
Robert Simpson, Champlain College
M. Lisa W. Clayton, College of Southern Nevada, Cheyenne Campus
Diane K. Sjuts, Metro Community College
Lisa A. Hoston, Allegany College of Maryland
John C. Kunich, University of North Carolina at Charlotte
Lizbeth P. McManus, Prince George Community College
Peter J. Puleo, William Rainey Harper College

Thomas J. Gardner
Terry M. Anderson

1

Criminal Law: Purposes, Scope, and Sources

LEARNING OBJECTIVES

In this chapter we introduce criminal law and the role it plays in the American legal system. The learning objectives for this chapter are the following:

LO 1. Identify the branches of government, and their relationship to the criminal law.

LO 2. Describe the difference between public law and private law, including the difference between criminal law and tort law.

LO 3. List the reasons people commit crimes, and why they do not.

LO 4. Discuss the four generally recognized goals of the criminal justice system.

LO 5. Explain the meaning of police power.

LO 6. Identify the general limitations on the exercise of the police power by government.

LO 7. Describe the classifications of crimes and the principle of legality.

LO 8. List and describe five specific constitutional limitations on the power to create a criminal law.

LO 9. Define circumstances that would make a criminal law a status crime.

LO 10. Trace the origin of the common law to its place in criminal law today.

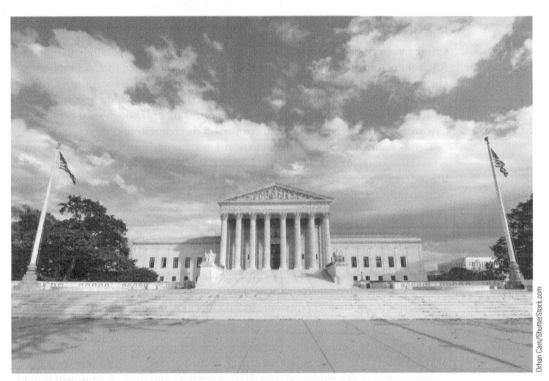

The United States Supreme Court building in Washington, D.C.

Annabel Melongo was a defendant in an Illinois criminal case. Based on her investigation of the court documents in her case, she believed the court reporter wrongly reported that she was present at an arraignment hearing, when in fact she was not present. Melongo attempted to correct this mistake in telephone conversations with the Assistant Court Administrator. Without telling the administrator, Melongo recorded these telephone conversations. Later, she posted transcripts of the conversations on her website.

The State of Illinois charged Melongo with violation of the Illinois Eavesdropping Statute, 720 Ill. Comp. Stat. 5/14-2, which makes it a crime to "knowingly and intentionally" use an eavesdropping device to record "any part of any conversation" without the consent of all parties to the conversation. The statute also makes it a crime to publish such recorded conversations.

Do you think it is proper for Illinois (and most other states as well) to pass a law like this one? If so, do you see a problem with the scope of the law, that is, the type of conduct made criminal by its terms? How should situations like this be resolved? To see how the Illinois Supreme Court addressed the problem, read the 2014 case of *People v. Melongo*.[1] We discuss these issues later in this chapter.

In this chapter we examine the basis for the power of states and the federal government to pass criminal laws, and the constitutional limitations on that power.

IMPORTANT CONCEPTS IN CRIMINAL LAW

Crime has been part of the human condition since people began to live in groups. Ancient documents indicate that conduct we now call murder, theft, or robbery was identified as criminal by civilizations that existed thousands of years ago. Criminal laws regulate human conduct and tell people what they cannot do and, in some instances, what they must do under certain circumstances. Though their content may have differed, all societies have had criminal codes regulating conduct.

Democracies have always sought to translate their basic principles and ideals into achievable goals through a system of laws that balance the rights of individuals with the compelling needs of society as a whole. These goals include public order, domestic tranquility, and protection of the basic rights of individuals.

Because governments in democracies are the servants and not the masters of the people, laws are seen as the product of the will of the people. Criminal justice systems in democracies operate most successfully when the majority of the people believe that laws are fair and that the system can operate efficiently and effectively.[2]

The issue of what laws should be enacted often causes intense public debate. Laws are enacted by elected representatives of the people. They are enforced, administered, and interpreted by civil servants and elected officials in other branches of government.

In the United States, those branches are as follows:

1. *The legislative branch:* Laws (including criminal laws) are enacted by the legislative branch. The chief executive officer participates in the legislative process by signing or vetoing proposed laws. State governors and the U.S. president provide leadership on many proposed laws by either supporting or opposing them and by providing information about proposed laws.

2. *The executive branch:* Agencies within the executive branch of government administer and enforce laws. Law enforcement agencies are found within the executive branch of government and are charged with the enforcement of criminal laws, in addition to the performance of other duties.

3. *The judicial branch:* People who are charged with crimes have a right to be tried before a judge or a jury in a court in the judicial branch of government. Fact finders (jury or judge) determine the issues in cases presented to them, including the issue of guilt or innocence. Judges in the United States have the power of judicial review in determining the constitutionality of laws or ordinances.

In the United States each state and the federal government has its own judicial system. These systems are generally independent of one another. Each state has a tier of trial courts, where jury trials take place. After a defendant has been convicted of a crime, the conviction may be appealed to the state's appellate courts. Many states have a two-tiered appellate court plan: a first tier, generally called the court of appeals, and a top tier, generally called the supreme court. Appeals of convictions for violation of criminal law proceed first in the state's appellate court system.

certiorari A form of review of lower court decisions by the U.S. Supreme Court. Certiorari is discretionary with the Court, and most petitions requesting it are denied. Traditional legal doctrine is that no conclusion can be drawn from a denial of certiorari.

habeas corpus A writ that compels the authority holding a person in confinement to explain the basis for that confinement. Used frequently as a method for state and federal prisoners to attack the constitutionality of their imprisonment. Both the federal government and states have some form of habeas corpus laws, often called post-conviction relief laws.

public law Laws or statutes that apply to all people within a state or nation. Criminal laws in England and the United States are examples of public law.

tort A noncontractual civil wrong.

Once a conviction has been affirmed by the highest state court, it is usually final. However, if the defendant raises an issue about the constitutionality of the conviction, under the U.S. Constitution he or she is entitled to ask the U.S. Supreme Court to review that issue. The defendant would do so by asking the Supreme Court to issue a writ of **certiorari**, a discretionary writ issued by the Court to review the decision of a lower court. Writs of certiorari are infrequently granted. If the writ is denied, the conviction is final. Limited post-conviction review is possible under state post-conviction review laws, and through use of the writ of **habeas corpus**, discussed later in this chapter.

In the federal system, federal district courts serve as trial courts. The United States is divided into eleven judicial circuits, plus the District of Columbia Circuit and the Federal Circuit (which handles special areas such as patent law). The judicial circuits each have a court of appeals, which hears appeals from the federal district courts located in the circuit. Decisions of the circuit courts may be reviewed by the Supreme Court through the certiorari process, though here also such review occurs infrequently.

As discussed more fully later in this chapter, criminal law in the United States traces its beginnings to the criminal law and its development in England. In early England, actions we now define as crimes, such as robbery, murder, or theft, were classified as private matters. As a result, victims were responsible for remedying their own problems. Victims and their families usually responded with violence if they knew or suspected the identity of the offender. They also had the option of bringing the matter before a civil court, but such courts were few and the chances of success minimal. During the reign of Henry II (1154–1189), English law began to recognize that crime was more than a personal affair between the victim and the perpetrator, and that punishment should not be left to individuals.

Today, criminal law in England and the United States is part of each nation's **public law**. The criminal law applies to all persons within each country, and it is enforced by public officials rather than by the victims of criminal conduct. Apprehension and prosecution of criminals are public matters. Public law enforcement agencies, public prosecutors, courts, jails, and correctional institutions make up the criminal justice systems in both countries.

Because the same action can be a violation of the criminal law and a civil wrong known as a **tort**, victims of a crime may bring civil actions in civil courts to seek compensation from the offender. The crimes of sexual assault, battery, theft, and criminal libel are examples of actions that may be prosecuted as crimes under public law, and also serve as a basis for a civil action. If the victim obtains a judgment in the civil action, the victim is responsible for collecting that judgment from the offender. The tort laws governing such a civil action are examples of private law. Private law deals with relationships between individuals in matters such as divorce, contractual issues, real estate law, and private inheritance.

Criminal law in the broadest sense refers to the many laws and statutes that define and regulate prohibited, criminal conduct. These laws and statutes are called substantive criminal law. In addition, criminal law in this sense includes many rules and statutes designed to set out and regulate the steps that are followed from the criminal incident through punishment and release of the offender. This part of criminal law is called criminal procedure. Many of the rights guaranteed by the U.S. Constitution in criminal investigations and prosecutions serve as limitations on the process used by the government in those investigations and prosecutions. For example, the well-known

Miranda rule requiring police to inform a suspect of his rights at the time of arrest stems from the Fifth Amendment. The requirement that police obtain a search warrant based on probable cause is found in the Fourth Amendment; the rights to have the assistance of counsel and confront witnesses against an accused are contained in the Sixth Amendment. There are also many statutory rules in both the federal and state criminal codes regulating the procedures that must be followed in criminal investigations and prosecutions. Because of the immense scope and complexity of criminal procedure rules and principles, it is generally treated as a subject distinct from substantive criminal law. See Gardner & Anderson, *Criminal Evidence* (9th edition, Cengage Learning, 2015). Thus, while this chapter discusses many of the constitutional limitations on the power of governments to define and punish conduct, such as the Ex Post Facto Clause and the "overbreadth" doctrine, it should be remembered that a significant part of the constitutional and statutory limitations on the investigation and prosecution of criminal conduct must be learned by studying criminal procedure.

Criminology and criminalistics are fields that are separate from but related to substantive criminal law. **Criminology** is the sociological and psychological study of the causes of crime, the control of crime, and the conditions under which criminal law developed. Criminalistics, often called **forensic science**, is the professional and scientific discipline directed to the recognition, identification, individualization, and evaluation of physical evidence by application of the natural sciences. Criminology is a branch of sociology; criminalistics is the application of science to criminal investigation, and encompasses forensic science.

criminology The sociological and psychological study of the causes, development, and control of crime, as well as the conditions under which criminal law developed.

forensic science scientific principles and tests used in courts of law.

Substantive Criminal Law

Substantive criminal law is an important branch of public law. It defines the standards of conduct that the society and the community require for the protection of the community as a whole. It establishes the standards necessary to preserve public order and to protect property rights. It seeks to protect the right of individual privacy and the right to move about freely without fear of molestation. It does this primarily by defining conduct that is unacceptable and punishable.

In earlier times in our history people "took the law in their own hands" to punish criminals. With the establishment of a system of laws and the growth of public confidence in the ability of the criminal justice system to preserve ordered liberty, people have generally ceased taking the law into their own hands. Public confidence that the government, as an agent of the people, has the ability and the desire to maintain public order is an indispensable ingredient of a successful criminal justice system.[3]

Not all legal wrongs come under substantive criminal law. Some legal wrongs are only civil violations. A *civil wrong* is a private wrong, such as a tort or a contract violation, done to a person or property, and involves only the private individuals affected by the wrong. A *criminal wrong* is one in which the state and the public have declared an interest. Ordinarily, when a private wrong occurs, only the injured party or the party's representative may seek civil redress in a civil court of law. Nearly every large American community has three or four times as many civil courts, which hear civil cases of alleged private wrongs, as criminal courts, which hear criminal cases involving public wrongs. In cases of public wrong, the state may file a criminal action in a criminal court, seek relief for the alleged public wrong in a civil court, or do both concurrently, as is done occasionally in obscenity, antitrust, or consumer fraud cases.

Criminal Law and Moral Law

Criminal laws are strongest when they reflect the moral and ethical beliefs of the society. Murder, for example, is considered morally wrong, and most people would not murder another person even if it were not a crime. Murder is forbidden not only by the criminal law but also by the moral law. This moral or ethical commitment to the law is important because it compels most people to conform to standards necessary for public order regardless of whether a police officer is watching them. Public order is not possible without that commitment, because not enough police officers are available to enforce criminal law without this moral and ethical backing.

WHY SOME CONDUCT MAY OR MAY NOT BE DESIGNATED AS CRIMINAL

Reasons a Legislative Body Might Designate Specific Conduct as Criminal

- The conduct may be designated as criminal to protect the public from violent or dangerous conduct.
- The conduct may be designated as criminal to protect public health.
- The conduct may be designated as criminal to maintain public order.
- The conduct may be designated as criminal to protect the right of privacy of individuals.
- The conduct may be designated as criminal to protect public morality.
- No other apparent way to promote a desired public policy is available.

Reasons a Legislative Body Might Not Designate Specific Conduct as Criminal

- The government does not have constitutional power to prohibit such conduct.
- The conduct in question is constitutionally protected.
- No influential public or private groups or individuals have demanded the regulation of such conduct.
- Enforcing a law criminalizing such conduct would not be economically feasible.
- Passing a law criminalizing such conduct would not be politically popular.

RIGHTS OF CRIME VICTIMS

A majority of states have amended their state constitutions to include a guarantee of rights for crime victims. This guarantee, which is often posted on courtroom doors, generally includes provisions such as the following:

- The right to notification of all court proceedings related to the offense
- The right to be reasonably protected from the accused offender
- The right to have input at sentencing, such as by offering a victim impact statement
- The right to information about the conviction, sentencing, imprisonment, and release of the offender
- The right to an order of restitution from the offender
- The right to notice of these rights
- The right to enforce these rights

Source: See FS 00301, United States Office for Victims of Crime, April 2002.

DISTINGUISHING CRIME, TORT, AND MORAL WRONG

Type of Wrong		Court Determining Wrong
Crime	A public wrong against society	Criminal court
Tort	A private wrong against an individual	Civil court or individuals
Moral wrong	Violation of a moral or religious code	No punishment unless the moral wrong is also a crime or tort

A crime may also be a tort and a moral wrong. For example, murder is a crime, a tort, and also a moral wrong.

The standards set by moral laws are often higher than those set by criminal laws. Moral law attempts to perfect personal character, whereas criminal law, in general, is aimed at misbehavior that falls substantially below the norms of the community. Criminal conduct is ordinarily unjustifiable and inexcusable.

Criminal law alone cannot bring all conduct into conformity with the standards expected by the community. Society uses many sanctions besides criminal law to encourage people to behave properly. Civil law judgments, licensing regulations and revocations, loss of employment, and simple peer pressure are examples of the ways a society can use sanctions other than the criminal law to control offensive conduct.

GOALS AND PURPOSES OF CRIMINAL LAW

People in all societies have the inherent right to protect their society and those living in that society from acts that threaten either the society or the people. Societies throughout history have exercised this inherent right, through laws either written or unwritten forbidding and punishing acts or omissions considered detrimental to the group or the individual.

From colonial days through World War I, the criminal codes of the various American states were generally limited to those crimes that were considered serious wrongs against the society. Moreover, because criminal laws were used to define and enforce public morality, the traditional attitude of lawyers and judges was that a crime was essentially a moral wrong and should primarily be enforced through family, religious, and social pressures.

The first decades of the twentieth century saw the rapid change of the United States from an agricultural society to an industrial one. This transformation, plus the unbelievable array of economic, social, and political changes that accompanied it, hastened the arrival of the mass industrial society. These changes reduced the influence of American religious institutions, the community, and the home in molding and shaping behavior (particularly of the young) to the standards expected by society. To compensate for this change, many new criminal laws were enacted. The burden of maintaining public order and public safety gradually shifted to local, state,

FACTORS INFLUENCING WHETHER TO COMMIT A CRIME

Why a Person Would Not Commit a Crime	Why a Person Would Commit a Crime
Moral or ethical commitment to obey the law	Insufficient moral or ethical commitment to obey the law
Fear of arrest and punishment	Belief in ability to get away without detection, arrest, and punishment
Social and peer pressures of friends, associates, family, and community	Peer pressure
Fear of embarrassment to self, family, and friends	Belief that detection and associated embarrassment can be avoided
Lack of motive or compelling drive to commit crime (no compelling desire to steal, murder, assault, rape, and so on)	Compelling desire or motive to achieve illegal objective (narcotic addiction, for example, provides motive for a person who would probably not otherwise commit a crime)
Lack of opportunity, or lack of capacity or skill, to commit crime	Opportunity combined with capacity and skill
Fear of economic sanction, such as loss of job or promotion, lawsuit and damages, or loss of license (driver's license, liquor license, credentials for lawyer, doctor, nurse, and so on)	Sees crime as a quick, easy way of obtaining money, drugs, power, or other objectives. (Even if caught, the odds are good that the person will not go to prison. Few persons convicted of nonviolent felonies go to prison.)

and federal governments, so that today the U.S. criminal justice system is both large and complex and assumes a greater role in shaping conduct than ever before.

The U.S. Constitution is the supreme law of the United States. Its preamble states that the purposes of the U.S. Constitution are to "establish Justice, insure domestic Tranquility, . . . promote the general Welfare, and secure the Blessings of Liberty to ourselves and our Posterity." As the U.S. Supreme Court stated in the famous *Miranda* case, the "most basic function of any government is to provide for the security of the individual and his property." *Miranda v. Arizona*, 384 U.S. 436, 539 (1966).

The generally recognized goals and purposes of the criminal justice system are to

- Discourage and deter people from committing crimes.
- Protect society from dangerous and harmful people.
- Punish people who have committed crimes.
- Rehabilitate and reform people who have committed crimes.

The U.S. District Court for the District of Columbia expressed the objective and purpose of criminal law in these terms in the first-degree murder case of *United States v. Watson:*

The object of the criminal law is to protect the public against depredations of a criminal. On the other hand, its purpose is also to prevent the conviction of the innocent, or the conviction of a person whose guilt is not established beyond a reasonable doubt. The Court must balance all these aims of the trial. This view was eloquently stated by Mr. Justice Cardozo in *Snyder v. Commonwealth of Massachusetts*, 291 U.S. 97, 122, 54 S. Ct. 330, 338, 78 L. Ed. 674: ". . . [J]ustice, though due to the accused, is due to the accuser also. The concept of fairness must not be strained till it is narrowed to a filament. We are to keep the balance true."[4]

In forbidding burglary, assault, rape, robbery, and other crimes, criminal laws protect the right of privacy of individuals. The U.S. Supreme Court recognized this important function in the case of *Katz v. United States,* when the Court wrote,

> The protection of a person's general right of privacy—his right to be left alone by other people—is, like the protection of his property and his very life, left largely to the laws of the individual States.[5]

Many factors contribute to the causes and prevention of crimes. The criminal laws passed by the state and federal governments are intended to affect, and do affect, decisions by citizens to commit crimes. Other factors are also present. Statistics collected by the U.S. Bureau of Justice Statistics (BJS) show that the number of violent crimes and major property crimes committed in the United States decreased by over 30% between the years 1994 and 2004. In the FBI Uniform Crime Reports, Violent Crimes Report, released in 2015, the FBI stated that violent crimes declined from 1,251,248 in 2010 to 1,165,383 in 2014. The drop in violent crime since 1994 is likely due not only to more and harsher criminal laws, but also to factors such as the aging of the population and falling unemployment rates during much of that period. Declines in drug and alcohol use also played important roles in lowering the crime rates.

The signing of the U.S. Constitution, the supreme law of the United States.

THE PERMISSIBLE SCOPE OF CRIMINAL LAWS IN THE UNITED STATES

Criminal laws have been used by totalitarian governments, from Hitler's Nazi Germany to the rule of the Taliban in Afghanistan, as a means to control their citizens by brute force and terror. In a government like that of the United States, criminal laws and the criminal justice system are essential parts of the democratic system, serving to strike a balance between maintaining public order and preserving basic freedoms. To prevent misuses of the criminal justice system, in the United States constitutional limits are placed on the power of government to regulate the conduct and lives of its citizens through the use of criminal laws. Some of these constitutional limitations are presented in this chapter. Other limitations are presented in Chapters 5, 6, 7, and 8 of this book.

The Use and Limitations of the Police Power to Maintain Public Order

police power The inherent power of every state and local government, subject to constitutional limits, to enact criminal laws.

Each state is responsible for the maintenance of public order and public safety within that state. To do this, states enact criminal laws and establish a criminal justice system under the police power of that state. The **police power** is an inherent power vested in each state. The Tenth Amendment of the U.S. Constitution provides that "[t]he powers not delegated to the United States by the Constitution, nor prohibited by it to the States, are reserved to the States respectively, or to the people."

The term *police power* refers to the broad legislative power of a state to pass laws that promote the public health, safety, and welfare. The U.S. Supreme Court has stated:

> The police power of a state extends beyond health, morals and safety, and comprehends the duty, within constitutional limitations, to protect the well-being and tranquility of a community. A state or city may prohibit acts or things reasonably thought to bring evil or harm to its people.[6]

Following this reasoning in *Village of Belle Terre v. Boraas*, the U.S. Supreme Court sustained a zoning ordinance restricting land use to single-family dwellings:

> The police power is not confined to elimination of filth, stench, and unhealthy places. It is ample to lay out zones where family values, youth values and the blessing of quiet seclusion, and clean air make the area a sanctuary for people.[7]

In enacting criminal laws through the use of the police power, the state is regulating the conduct of citizens within the state by telling them what they may not do or what they must do. However, the police power is not absolute. In addition to limitations placed on the police power by the U.S. Constitution or state constitutions, the state may not regulate conduct capriciously or arbitrarily.

In enacting criminal law, the state must be able to show

- A compelling public need to regulate the conduct the state seeks to regulate, and that the power to regulate is within the police power of the state. The U.S. Supreme Court held in *Lawton v. Steele* that "it must appear, first, that the interests of the public generally...require such interference; and, that the means . . . are not unduly oppressive upon individuals."[8]
- That the law does not contravene the U.S. Constitution or infringe on any of the rights granted or secured by the U.S. Constitution or the constitution of that state.

- That the language of the statute or ordinance clearly tells people what they are not to do (or what they must do) and that the law prohibits only the conduct that may be forbidden.

To understand these limitations, suppose some of the states create the following offenses as misdemeanors:

- State A enacts a law requiring that all people in the state go to a church of a specific religion every Sunday.
- State B enacts a law forbidding skateboarding.
- State C enacts a law forbidding the sale, use, or possession of any tobacco product.
- State D enacts a law requiring operators of motorcycles and their passengers to wear protective headgear.[9]

State A would violate First Amendment rights to the freedom of religion by passing a law of this nature; furthermore, the statute would not be within the police power of a state because it serves no valid function of government.

Regulation of skateboarding in State B could be done by governmental units, such as cities and school districts, for public safety reasons and to minimize interference with pedestrian and motor vehicle traffic. But no compelling public need exists to completely forbid such conduct because of public health, safety, or morals; therefore, such regulations could hardly stand under attack. The right to be free from interference by government has been described as follows:

> No right is more sacred, or is more carefully guarded, by the liberty assurance of the due process clause than the right of every citizen to the possession and control of his own person, free from restraint or interference by the state. The makers of our Constitution conferred, as against the government, the right to be let alone—the most comprehensive of rights and the right most valued by civilized man.

* * *

However, personal freedoms are not absolute, and the liberty guaranteed by the due process clause implies absence of arbitrary interferences but not immunity from reasonable regulations.[10]

State C could show that its regulation is within the police power of the state because medical studies show that the use of tobacco products does affect people's health. As of 2014, 40 states had adopted some type of ban on smoking that includes public buildings, government buildings, private workplaces, child-care centers, and food service centers. The other 10 states do not have statewide bans, but most have prohibited smoking in some but not all these locations. Those states also commonly have laws that regulate smoking in public buildings, usually by requiring a limited smoking area. There is no general federal law prohibiting smoking in public places, though federal regulations do so in public buildings, airplanes, trains, and so forth. Enforcement of a complete ban on smoking in public and private spaces has not been advocated by any group because it would be difficult if not impossible to enforce. A total ban on smoking could lead to the kind of lawlessness associated with attempts to outlaw alcohol in the 1920s.

THE PRINCIPLE OF "NO PUNISHMENT WITHOUT A LAW FOR IT"

A basic principle of both English and American law is that no one can be lawfully punished for his or her conduct or omission unless that conduct or omission has been clearly made a crime by statutory or common law of that jurisdiction. The Latin maxim **nulla poena sine lege** ("no punishment without law") long ago established this principle.

nulla poena sine lege The principle of legality; no act should be made criminal or punished without advance warning in the form of legislative act.

This principle, generally known as the *principle of legality,* was made part of American law in 1791 by the enactment of the Fifth Amendment of the U.S. Constitution, which provides that "No person shall be . . . deprived of life, liberty, or property without due process of law."[11]

In American jurisprudence the principle of legality has two main tenets: one, it prohibits retroactive definition of criminal behavior by judicial decision, and two, it requires statutory definitions of crimes to be sufficiently clear and precise so as to enable reasonable people to understand what conduct is prohibited. By the end of the nineteenth century, it was generally accepted in this country that courts lacked the power to "create" crimes that had not previously existed under statute or common law (see later in this chapter). Most states have passed statutes similar to section 720 ILCS 5/1-3 of the Illinois Criminal Code, which states:

> Applicability of Common Law. No conduct constitutes an offense unless it is described as an offense in this Code or in another statute of this State.

The second tenet of the principle of legality requires that a statute must define criminal conduct clearly enough that people affected by the statute will receive adequate notice of the behavior prohibited. If the statute is too vague, courts might construe the statute to include conduct not reasonably understood to be prohibited, thus effectively creating a new crime. The "void for vagueness" doctrine is discussed in more detail later in this chapter.

Although the "prior notice" doctrine requires that fair warning be given in language that the ordinary person will understand, it does not require that the statute list in detail the many ways in which a forbidden wrong may be committed. The following example illustrates this:

EXAMPLE   Criminal homicide can be committed by many different unlawful acts such as using a gun, knife, poison, a crowbar, a truck, or another vehicle; pushing the victim off a cliff or a bridge or down stairs; or strangulation. Murder statutes do not have to list the hundred or more ways of committing murder. Such statutes forbid the defined evil and clearly provide notice as to the act or acts forbidden.[12]

Therefore, in view of the principle of "no punishment without a law for it," the following questions must be asked before any person is arrested, charged with a crime, or convicted: What has the person done that violates the statutes of the state? Was the person legally (not just morally) obligated to act, and then failed to perform this legal (not moral) duty?

CLASSIFICATIONS OF CRIMES

Many acts have been designated as criminal offenses in the United States. In 1790, only 20 federal criminal statutes existed. Today, the federal government alone has designated more than 4,500 offenses; 42 of the 51 titles in the federal statutes include listed crimes. A much larger number of state and local offenses exist.[13]

The large number of crimes in the United States may be classified as follows:

- According to their sources, as statutory, common law, administrative, or constitutional crimes (see later in this chapter).
- As felonies or misdemeanors; this determines how the crimes are tried and, in many states, affects the law of arrest for such crimes. Many states classify felonies and misdemeanors as class A, class B, and so forth. In this way, punishment can be standardized, though it is common for each classification to have punishment ranges. As an example, Section 28-105 of the Nebraska Statutes lists a class IA felony as life imprisonment without parole, a class IB felony as 20 years to life, and a class IC felony as 5 to 50 years.

Felony and Misdemeanor

Felony The most serious grade of crime; usually includes possibility of prison sentence.

The felony/misdemeanor classification is the most common and most important classification of crime. A **felony** is the most serious type of crime and generally is punished by one year or more in prison or a penitentiary. As of 2015, thirty-one states and the federal government had laws providing for the death penalty for a few very serious felonies.

Misdemeanor Offenses that carry punishment of a degree less than felonies. Usually misdemeanor crimes do not involve prison sentences.

A **misdemeanor** is a less serious offense and usually carries a sentence of imprisonment for no more than a year, though some states may provide for longer sentences (Figure 1.1). An offense that does not provide for possible jailing or imprisonment is generally not classified as a crime but rather as a civil offense. For example, ordinary speeding is punished by a fine and imposition of points but is not a crime.

Whether a crime is a felony or a misdemeanor is important for the following reasons:

1. Conviction of a felony would, in most states, stand in the way of some types of employment, affect a person's credit rating or ability to adopt a child, and prevent a person from entering the armed forces, becoming a law enforcement officer, or obtaining a license as a nurse, doctor, lawyer, and so on, unless a pardon is obtained.[14] A misdemeanor conviction would not ordinarily have these effects.

 QUALITY-OF-LIFE CRIMES AND THE BROKEN WINDOW THEORY

Many veteran law enforcement officers subscribe to the broken window or quality-of-life theory of crime. This theory holds that small quality-of-life crimes will eventually encourage greater lawlessness. For example, if graffiti and broken windows are tolerated, more serious property damage and other crimes will follow. If prostitution is tolerated, other crimes will follow, since prostitution often fuels illegal drug activity. With prostitution and illegal drug activity come purse snatchings, robbery, theft, burglary, and other felonies.

Law enforcement officers believe a community should be concerned and take action when the first signs of a breakdown in the quality of life appear, such as the abandoned building with broken windows, loud drunken bar patrons out on the street after closing hours, or the presence of street gangs.

FIGURE 1.1 Government May Regulate Conduct by Making the Conduct Either a Criminal or a Civil Offense

[a]Felonies are punished by possible imprisonment for one year or more in state prison. Misdemeanors are usually punished by possible imprisonment for up to one year in a jail or a detention center. Both felonies and misdemeanors may also be punished by fines and forfeitures. Capital felonies can be punished by death in states.

[b]Fill in maximum imprisonment in your state.

2. People charged with felonies have the right to a preliminary hearing or a "presentation or indictment of a grand jury."[15]

3. The law governing making an arrest for a felony differs from the law governing making an arrest for a misdemeanor in the following ways:

   (a) There is broad authority for law enforcement officers to make a felony arrest; however, law enforcement officers in states using the "in presence" requirement cannot arrest for misdemeanors unless the misdemeanor is committed in their presence or unless other statutory or common law authority exists.

   (b) "Citizen's arrest" is generally limited to felonies committed in the presence of the citizen unless the statutes or common law of a state provide additional authority.[16]

GENERAL CONSTITUTIONAL LIMITATIONS ON CRIMINAL LAWS

The U.S. Supreme Court has stated that "[b]roadly speaking, crimes in the United States are what the law of the individual States make them, subject to (constitutional) limitations."[17] States, therefore, have broad authority to create criminal laws.

The authority to enact criminal laws cannot be exercised in a manner that violates the rights of persons guaranteed by the U.S. Constitution or the constitution of a state. In succeeding chapters we discuss some of these rights in detail: States cannot criminalize conduct protected by the First Amendment, including freedom of speech, freedom of religion, and freedom to move about freely (see Chapter 9). Nor may states impose a punishment that violates the Eighth Amendment prohibition against "cruel and unusual punishment" (see Chapter 8). Chapters 6 and 7 on defenses also present other constitutional limitations. The following materials present some of the general, constitutional limitations on criminal laws and the exercise of the police power.

VICTIMLESS CRIMES

The term *victimless crimes* is used to designate crimes that do not directly inflict personal or property harm on another person in the sense that murder, robbery, rape, and theft do. The term is controversial when applied to crimes such as drug violations because the deadly drug trade in the United States results in many victims.

Examples of Victimless Crimes[a]	Examples of Victimless Crimes that Have Been Abolished by Many States	Examples of Crimes that Have Been Declared Unconstitutional
Possession or use of a small amount of a drug such as marijuana	Fornication	Use of contraceptives (even by married couples)—*Griswold v. Connecticut*, 381 U.S. 479 (1965)
Public drunkenness (decriminalized by many states)	Adultery	Drug addiction as a crime in and of itself—*Robinson v. California*, 370 U.S. 660 (1962)
Prostitution	Cohabitation	Possession of or reading obscene material in privacy of one's home—*Stanley v. Georgia*, 394 U.S. 557 (1969)
Gambling (many forms of gambling are now legal)		
Obscenity offenses involving consenting adults		Homosexual relations between consenting adults in privacy of one's home—*Lawrence v. Texas*, 123 S. Ct.2472 (2003)

[a]Some people take the position that society is the victim of many of these offenses.

Ex Post Facto Laws

ex post facto Criminal law made retroactive to punish prior conduct not criminal when done. Prohibited by Article I, Sections 9 and 10, of the Constitution.

Sections 9 and 10 of Article I of the U.S. Constitution forbid the U.S. Congress and all states from enacting **ex post facto** (after the fact) laws. Therefore, no state or the U.S. Congress can create a new crime in November and make the law retroactive so as to punish conduct that was lawful prior to November of that year. Most state constitutions also forbid ex post facto laws. Ex post facto restrictions apply only to criminal laws and not to civil laws such as tax laws. The ex post facto restriction also only limits the power of state and federal legislative bodies; it does not apply to the judicial branch of government. See the U.S. Supreme Court case of *Rogers v. Tennessee*, 532 U.S. 451 (2001). The Ex Post Facto Clause forbids the following:

1. Laws made retroactive so as to make conduct before the enactment of the law a criminal violation.

2. Laws that aggravate a crime retroactively (e.g., making a misdemeanor a felony as of a date six months before the enactment of the legislation).

3. Laws that increase the punishment for a crime retroactively.

4. Laws that alter the legal rules of evidence and permit conviction on less or different evidence than the law required at the time of the commission of the offense.[18]

In 2013 the U.S. Supreme Court discussed the retroactive increased punishment prohibition under the Ex Post Facto Clause as applied to the Federal Sentencing

Guidelines. In *Peugh v. United States*, 133 S. Ct. 2072 (2013), the Court held that use of Federal Sentencing Guidelines amended after the defendants committed the crimes charged violated the Clause. Under the amended guidelines, the range of possible sentences for those crimes was increased substantially over the earlier range for the same crimes. Although the guidelines are not mandatory, the Court held that the higher range of possible sentences created a high risk of increased punishment for the crime, which violates the Ex Post Facto Clause.

The Ex Post Facto Clause does not necessarily apply every time a statute incorporates past behavior into a new designation of criminal conduct. For example, in 1996 Congress enacted the Domestic Violence Offender Gun Act, which amended the 1968 Federal Gun Control Act, 18 U.S.C. § 921. The 1968 Act prohibited convicted felons from owning or possessing firearms. The 1996 amendment made it a violation of the Act for any person convicted of a "misdemeanor crime involving domestic violence" to own or possess a firearm. A person convicted of a domestic violence misdemeanor in 1990, for example, could lawfully possess a firearm prior to the 1996 amendment. After 1996, however, that same person could be convicted under the amended Act. This is not an Ex Post Facto Clause problem because the amendment did not make past conduct criminal; rather, it provides that the future action of possessing a firearm after the amendment's effective date, 1996, by persons convicted of misdemeanor domestic violence crimes would be a crime. Since people are presumed to know the law, those affected by the amendment were under a duty to avoid ownership or possession of firearms after the Act became applicable to them. The U.S. Supreme Court considered the meaning and applicability of the Domestic Violence Offender Gun Ban in *United States v. Hayes,* 129 S. Ct. 1079 (2009), discussed in Chapter 11.

The applicability of the Ex Post Facto Clause to statutes of limitation was discussed by the U.S. Supreme Court in the 2003 case of *Stogner v. California,* 123 S. Ct. 2446. Most crimes, except murder and some other violent crimes, have limitation periods for prosecution. If prosecution does not occur during the statutory period, it is barred. Courts have often held that the Ex Post Facto Clause does not prevent a state from increasing the limitation period for future offenses, or offenses that were not time-barred when the increased limitation period became law. Thus, an offender who committed a crime that had a 5-year limitation period when committed cannot raise an ex post facto objection if the legislature increases the limitations period to 10 years during the initial 5 years after the crime was committed. In *Stogner,* the California legislature increased the limitation period for sexual crimes committed against children and expressly made the increased period applicable to offenses that had become time barred under existing limitation periods prior to the time the statute increasing the limitation was adopted. The Supreme Court held the statute unconstitutional under the second part of the test, concluding the statute aggravated the crime of sexual assault retroactively.

In order to run afoul of the Ex Post Facto Clause a statute must have the effect of retroactively "punishing" an offender. When is a law "penal" and subject to the Ex Post Facto Clause? In the 2003 case of *Smith v. Doe,* 538 U.S. 84, the U.S. Supreme Court held that the Alaska Sex Offender Registration Act (so-called Megan's Law, see Chapter 12) was not punitive in nature, and thus the ex post facto limitations did not apply. The defendants contended that because they committed their crimes before the act was passed, its registration requirements could not be applied to them. The Supreme Court disagreed. Because the act was intended by the Alaska legislature to set up an administrative system to track sex offenders, the Court held it was civil and non-punitive in nature. Though the act did contain information about sex offenders that might "taint" those forced to register, the Court held such forced registration was not a penal law because the information was already a matter of public record.

Bills of Attainder

bill of attainder
Legislative act that inflicts punishment without trial; prohibited by Article I, Sections 9 and 10, of the Constitution.

Article I, Sections 9 and 10, of the U.S. Constitution also forbids Congress and the states from enacting any bill of attainder. A **bill of attainder** is a legislative act that inflicts punishment without the person (defendant) already having had a trial in a court before a judge. In 1965, the U.S. Supreme Court stated the history of the bill of attainder in *United States v. Brown,* 381 U.S. 437:

> The bill of attainder, a parliamentary act sentencing to death one or more specific persons, was a device often resorted to in sixteenth-, seventeenth-, and eighteenth-century England for dealing with persons who had attempted, or threatened to attempt, to overthrow the government. In addition to the death sentence, attainder generally carried with it a "corruption of blood," which meant that the attained party's heirs could not inherit his property. The "bill of pains and penalties" was identical to the bill of attainder, except that it prescribed a penalty short of death, e.g., banishment, deprivation of the right to vote, or exclusion of the designated party's sons from Parliament. Most bills of attainder and bills of pains and penalties named the parties to whom they were to apply; a few, however, simply described them.

In forbidding bills of attainder, the U.S. Constitution and state constitutions limit legislatures to the task of writing laws (making rules). Persons charged with a crime must be brought before a court to determine guilt or innocence.

The Second Amendment and Gun Control

Before 2008 it was unclear whether the Second Amendment to the U.S. Constitution created an individual right to "bear arms," or only a "public" right to keep an armed militia. However, in *District of Columbia v. Heller,* 128 S. Ct. 2783 (2008) the Supreme Court held that the Second Amendment protected an individual's right to own and possess firearms, at least under federal criminal laws. As a result, the Court held that the District of Columbia's prohibition on gun ownership must comply with the Second Amendment's right to bear arms. The *Heller* case and the limits placed on federal gun control laws are discussed in more detail in Chapter 9, as is the opinion of the U.S. Supreme Court in the case of *McDonald v. City of Chicago,* 130 S. Ct. 3020 (2010), on the applicability of the Second Amendment to state laws.

Due Process, "Void for Vagueness," and the "Overbreadth" Doctrine

due process The constitutional guarantee that criminal arrests and trials must meet certain minimum standards of fairness (procedural due process) and that laws not violate constitutional rights (substantive due process).

The Due Process Clause of the Fourteenth Amendment prohibits a state from depriving a person of life, liberty, or property without **due process** of law. In some situations, the Due Process Clause works to prohibit a state from making protected conduct criminal.

For example, it is clear a state could not make it a crime for a person to leave the state, because the right to travel is a protected right. A state could make leaving the state an offense if it aggravated some other crime, such as abandonment of a child. See *Jones v. Helms,* 452 U.S. 412 (1981). In 2003 the U.S. Supreme Court applied the Due Process Clause to invalidate a Texas sodomy statute. In *Lawrence v. Texas,* 123 S. Ct. 2472,

SORNA AND EX POST FACTO CLAIMS

After Congress passed the Sexual Offender Registration and Notification Act, 42 U.S.C. §16901 (SORNA) in 2006, adults and young persons over the age of 14 charged with sexual offenses or adjudicated delinquents under the Federal Juvenile Delinquency Act, 18 U.S.C. §5031, were required to register as sex offenders. The federal statute delegated to the U.S. Attorney General the decision whether to apply the registration requirement to persons who committed sexual offenses before SORNA became effective. The Attorney General promulgated such a rule in February 2007.

Adults

All federal courts of appeals that have considered ex post facto claims by persons who were adults when they committed sexual offenses before SORNA was enacted have rejected that claim.[19] The U.S. Supreme Court has not reached a decision on this issue, though in the 2012 case of *Reynolds v. United States*, 132 S. Ct. 975, it concluded that SORNA did not apply to adults whose offenses occurred before the time the Attorney General determined SORNA was retroactive.

Juveniles

In 2010 the Ninth Circuit Court of Appeals held that the Ex Post Facto Clause prohibited application of SORNA to persons who were juveniles when they committed the sexual offenses that triggered registration under SORNA. The Court concluded the registration burden for juveniles, held not to be punishment in *Smith v. Doe* when applied to adults, was punishment for juveniles and thus retroactive.[20] However, in 2011 the U.S. Supreme Court vacated the Ninth Circuit's decision, holding that because the juvenile had been ordered to register only until he was 21, after he turned 21 the case became "moot."[21]

In a related case under SORNA, the U.S. Supreme Court in 2010 held that a defendant who was convicted of a criminal sexual offense and who traveled in interstate commerce, both of which occurred before SORNA was passed, could not be convicted of failing to register as a sex offender. SORNA states that any convicted sex offender who travels in interstate commerce must register under applicable state sex offender laws. Failure to do so is a federal offense. The defendant traveled to a new state without registering, but did so before SORNA was passed. The Court found the Act inapplicable and reversed the conviction because SORNA by its terms only applied to sex offenders who traveled in interstate commerce after the Act was passed. The Court therefore did not resolve any ex post facto issues raised by a conviction under SORNA for failure to register based on a pre-2006 sex offender conviction. See *Carr v. United States,* 130 S. Ct. 2229 (2010).

two adult men were convicted of engaging in homosexual conduct in the privacy of their home. The Texas statute provided: "A person commits an offense if he engages in deviate sexual intercourse with another individual of the same sex." The statute defined "deviate" sexual intercourse as including contact between the genitals of one person and the mouth or anus of another. The Court held the statute violated the Due Process Clause because it deprived the defendants of their liberty interest under the Fourteenth Amendment: "The State cannot demean their existence or control their destiny by making their private sexual conduct a crime. Their right to Liberty under the Due Process Clause gives them the full right to engage in their conduct without intervention of the government." In doing so, the Court reversed the decision reached in *Bowers v. Hardwick,* 478 U.S. 186 (1986), which upheld a Georgia sodomy statute.

The Due Process Clause of the U.S. Constitution also requires that a legislative body, when writing a criminal statute or ordinance, must use clear and precise language that gives fair and adequate notice of the conduct that is forbidden or required. If the language of a statute or ordinance is vague, it may be held unconstitutional under the **"void for vagueness" doctrine**.

"void for vagueness" doctrine The constitutional law doctrine that invalidates criminal laws written in such a manner as to make it unreasonably difficult for a defendant to know whether or not conduct is prohibited by the law.

The "void for vagueness" test asks whether a statute or ordinance on its face or as applied to a particular defendant "is so vague that men of common intelligence must guess at its meaning and differ as to its application."[22] A vague criminal statute or ordinance creates uncertainty as to what the law requires and may have some or all of the following results:

1. It may trap those who desire to be law abiding by not providing fair notice of what is prohibited.[23]

2. It may cause arbitrary and discriminatory enforcement because those who enforce and apply the law have no clear and explicit standards to guide them.[24]

3. When a vague statute "abut(s) upon sensitive areas of First Amendment freedoms, it operates to inhibit the exercise of (those) freedoms. Uncertain meaning inevitably leads citizens to steer far wider of the unlawful zone . . . than if the boundaries of the forbidden areas were clearly marked."[25]

"overbreadth" doctrine
The constitutional law doctrine that invalidates laws that regulate conduct so broadly that they interfere with individual freedoms.

Criminal statutes and ordinances may also be held to be unconstitutional if the manner in which they are written violates the **"overbreadth" doctrine.** The U.S. Supreme Court has stated that overbreadth "offends [when the words of a statute or ordinance] . . . sweep unnecessarily broadly and thereby invade the area of protected freedoms."[26] A vague statute or ordinance may be overbroad if its uncertain boundaries leave open the possibility of punishment for protected conduct and thus lead people to avoid such protected activity in order to steer clear of violating the uncertain law.[27] However, a clear and precise statute may also be overbroad if it prohibits constitutionally protected conduct.

The "void for vagueness" test and the "overbreadth" test are separate and distinct. However, when First Amendment rights are at issue, the U.S. Supreme Court uses the two tests in a manner that makes them virtually one doctrine. From the cases, it can be stated that statutes and ordinances that regulate conduct must comply with the following requirements:[28]

• Fair and adequate notice must be given of the conduct that is forbidden or required.
• A precise standard of conduct must be specified in terms of results that can reasonably be expected.
• The statute or ordinance cannot permit or encourage arbitrary and discriminatory law enforcement that may result in erratic and arbitrary arrests and convictions.
• The statute or ordinance cannot violate or infringe on rights that are secured or granted by the U.S. Constitution.

Vagueness and the "Violent Felon"   The U.S. Congress has decided that career criminals with a history of convictions for violent crimes pose a greater threat to society than convicted felons lacking such history. Most states have reached similar conclusions. (See Chapter 8.) To that end, in 1984 Congress passed the Career Armed Criminal Act (ACCA), 18 U.S.C. 924. This act increases the punishment for persons who were felons convicted of possession of a firearm, a federal offense, if the person had been convicted of three previous "violent felonies." The Act lists certain crimes as violent, such as murder, robbery or rape, and in its residual clause defines "violent felony" to include any crime that has a "serious potential risk of physical injury to another."

In *Johnson v. United States,* 135 S. Ct. 2551 (2015) the U.S. Supreme Court concluded the residual clause of the ACCA was so unclear and uncertain that it was unconstitutionally vague. In *Johnson* the defendant was convicted of being a felon in possession of a firearm. The prosecution sought enhanced sentencing under the ACCA, claiming the defendant had been convicted of three previous "violent crimes" as defined by the act. One of these convictions was for possession of a short-barreled shotgun, a violation of Minnesota state law. The sentencing court agreed, and sentenced the defendant to 15 years in prison, rather than the 10-year maximum applicable without the ACCA enhancement.

The Supreme Court reversed the lower court's sentencing decision. Noting that the Court had over several years struggled to give meaning to the ACCA's residual clause, without much success, the Court concluded it was too vague as written to give the required constitutional guidance for its application. Among other problems with the clause, the Court said, was its failure to give any guidance on what degree of "potential risk" was enough to make the act applicable in any given case. This vagueness, the Court held, violated due process.

As of early 2016 there already had been significant repercussions in the lower federal courts from the decision in *Johnson*. One question left unanswered in *Johnson* is whether the decision applies retroactively to sentences under the ACCA handed down before *Johnson*. The Federal Circuit Courts of Appeal are split on that question; see *In re Rivero,* 797 F.3d 986 (11th Cir. 2015). In January of 2016 the U.S. Supreme Court granted certiorari to consider that question. *Welch v. United States,* No. 15-6418, I-8-2016.

Another important question involves federal sentencing rules. The Federal Sentencing Guidelines provide enhanced sentences for defendants who have a history of violent felonies. There, "violent felony" is defined virtually identically to the language in the ACCA, which the *Johnson* court found unconstitutionally vague. Some of the Federal Courts of Appeal that have considered the effect of *Johnson* on the sentencing guidelines have held the language in the Guidelines is not unconstitutionally vague. The court in *United States v. Matchett,* 802 F.3d 1185 (11th Cir. 2015), for example, stated that the vagueness doctrine applies to statutes that prohibit conduct or fix punishments, not to guidelines used by sentencing courts as the starting point for determining a sentence. The court in *United States v. Madrid,* 805 F.3d 1204 (10th Cir. 2015) disagreed with the reasoning in *Matchett,* and held the sentencing guidelines language violated the vagueness rule of *Johnson*. The United States Sentencing Commission has proposed changing the language in the Guidelines to be consistent with the holding in *Johnson*.

Finally, many other federal criminal statutes provide for increased punishment if the defendant had been previously convicted of an aggravated or violent felony. For example, 8 U.S.C. § 1326 (b)(2), which provides for a sentence of up to 2 years for illegal re-entry into the U.S. after being deported or excluded, increases the punishment to up 20 years if the defendant committed an "aggravated felony" prior to being deported. An "aggravated felony" is defined as a "violent crime," as defined in 18 U.S.C. § 16(b). That section's definition has a residual clause very similar to the residual clause in the ACCA. In *United States v. Vivas-Ceja*, 808 F.3d 719 (7th Cir. 2015) the court held that the decision in *Johnson* required a conclusion that section 16(b) was also unconstitutionally vague. It reversed the sentence the defendant received and remanded for new sentencing.

Status Crimes

A state may regulate and control the use of such drugs as heroin, cocaine, and crack in a number of ways. The government may and does forbid the importing or manufacturing of the drugs; the law forbids possession and transportation of the forbidden drugs; the sale, use, or possession of such drugs is also forbidden. All of these specific acts (conduct) have been determined to be harmful to others or to the society as a whole. But can a state make addiction to heroin, cocaine, or crack, by itself, a crime?

To do something about its increasing heroin problem in the late 1950s, California passed a law making heroin addiction, by itself, a crime. The issue before the U.S. Supreme Court in the case of *Robinson v. California* was whether a person could be arrested and convicted for what he or she is or was.[29] The U.S. Supreme Court considered the question of whether a state could make a status or a "chronic condition" a crime in itself. This type of crime is referred to as a **status crime**.

status crime Criminal laws that punish a status, such as drug addiction, with no act requirement.

The Court held that a state law that made the "status" of narcotic addiction a criminal offense for which an offender might be prosecuted and imprisoned at any time inflicted a "cruel and unusual punishment" in violation of the Eighth and Fourteenth Amendments to the U.S. Constitution. The Court stated that "even one day in prison would be a cruel and unusual punishment for the 'crime' of having a common cold." In the case of *Powell v. Texas,* the defendant was an alcoholic with approximately 100 arrests for acts of public intoxication.[30] In this case, the defendant argued that because he was compelled to drink and because he could not control his "status," the state did not have the power to punish him for his acts of public intoxication.

The U.S. Supreme Court, however, affirmed Powell's conviction, holding that he was arrested and convicted for what he did (being drunk in a public place) and that Powell was not convicted for what he was (status). In refusing to extend the rule of law that had been established in the case of *Robinson v. California*, the Supreme Court held:

> Traditional common-law concepts of personal accountability and essential considerations of federalism lead us to disagree with appellant. We are unable to conclude, on the state of this record or on the current state of medical knowledge, that chronic alcoholics in general, and Leroy Powell in particular, suffer from such an irresistible compulsion to drink and to get drunk in public that they are utterly unable to control their performance of either or both of these acts and thus cannot be deterred at all from public intoxication.

The *Robinson* status/*Powell* acts distinction is illustrated by two examples. A law making it a crime for a homeless person to sleep on the sidewalk is a status crime, if the act of sleeping on the sidewalk occurred because there was no other shelter available.[31] A law making it a crime for a felon to possess a weapon is not a status crime, because the act of possessing the weapon constitutes the crime, not the status of being a felon.[32]

"VOID FOR VAGUENESS" AND "OVERBREADTH" DOCTRINES

The Due Process Clause of the U.S. Constitution, made binding on states by the Fourteenth Amendment, requires that criminal legislation clearly identify prohibited conduct so as to give a reasonable person fair notice of that conduct. A criminal statute written so broadly as to invade the area of constitutionally protected rights such as free speech is unconstitutional under the "overbreadth" doctrine. This table shows representative cases applying the "void for vagueness" and "overbreadth" doctrines.

Vagueness

Coates v. City of Cincinnati Supreme Court of the United States 402 U.S. 611 (1971)	Ordinance made it illegal for three or more people gathered on a sidewalk to "annoy" passersby. Because what annoys one person may not annoy another, the Court held that "[t]hus the ordinance is vague . . . in the sense that no conduct is specified at all."
Papachristou v. City of Jacksonville Supreme Court of the United States 405 U.S. 156 (1972)	Ordinance making being a "vagrant" a crime and defining vagrants as "rogues and vagabonds," "dissolute persons," or "common night walkers" held unconstitutional. The ordinance did not give fair notice of prohibited conduct.
Warren v. State Florida Supreme Court 572 So.2d 1376 (1991)	Statute making it a crime to keep a "house of ill fame" held unconstitutionally vague.
State v. Lara Kansas Court of Appeals 853 P.2d 1168 (1993)	Statute making criminal "excessive and unusual" motor vehicle noises held not void for vagueness.
State v. Bohannon Washington Court of Appeals 814 P.2d 694 (1991)	Statute making it a crime for causing a minor to engage in "sexually explicit conduct" held not void for vagueness.

Overbreadth

City of Houston v. Hill Supreme Court of the United States 482 U.S. 451 (1987)	Ordinance making it unlawful to "interrupt policeman in execution of his duty" held overbroad, because it made otherwise protected speech a violation of the ordinance. (A citizen who interrupted a police officer to tell the officer of a bank robbery could lawfully be arrested under this ordinance.)

Equal Protection of the Laws

If a state made the crime of burglary in that state applicable only to males, the first man charged with burglary in that state would challenge the statute, arguing that it violated the Fourteenth Amendment requirement of "equal protection of the laws." Women could commit burglary in that state, but for the same conduct a man could be convicted and sent to jail.

The Equal Protection Clause of the Fourteenth Amendment requires that states must treat all people alike, not only in enacting criminal and civil laws but also in enforcing rules. For example, all states have consanguinity laws forbidding marriages between brothers and sisters; most also prohibit marriage between other close relatives, such as first cousins. Consanguinity laws apply to all persons, regardless of status, race, or religion.[33] They represent a valid exercise of the police power of a state because children born to closely related parents are more apt to have abnormalities.

However, a state may not make it a crime (under so-called miscegenation laws) for a black person to marry a white person (or vice versa), as in the past some states did.[34] Such a prohibition would violate the Equal Protection Clause because a black person marrying a white person would be guilty of a crime, whereas a white person marrying another white person would not. Since all persons, black or white, are of the same class when it comes to marrying another person, the law would operate unequally as to some members of the class.

SOURCES OF CRIMINAL LAW

Substantive criminal law can be found in the following sources, each of which is discussed in the next sections:

- Criminal law, on rare occasions, can be found today in the common law of some states.
- Most criminal law is found in the statutes of each state and in the statutes of the federal government.
- Criminal law can also be found in commercial, sanitation, health, financial, and tax administrative regulations that have criminal sanctions. These regulations are enacted by state and federal administrative and regulatory agencies.
- A few sections of state constitutions and one section of the U.S. Constitution contain criminal law. Treason is the only crime defined by the U.S. Constitution. For material on treason, see Chapter 17 on terrorism.

Common Law Crimes

common law The earliest type of law. Common law was created by judges based on custom, usages, and moral concepts of the people. Most law today is statutory law enacted by legislative bodies.

Because the **common law** was the first and earliest source of criminal law, it is presented first here. And, because the historic source of U.S. criminal law lies in the common law of England, a review of the development of criminal law in England and in the American colonies is necessary.

When the English kings gained control of the whole of England in the Middle Ages, royal judges began deciding civil and criminal cases throughout all of England, thus supporting the Crown by preserving the peace and dispensing justice. Few people in those days could read or write, and England was not a democracy. The king, the judges, and the ecclesiastical authorities played important roles not only in creating (sometimes inventing) criminal laws but also in defining the elements and the scope of the criminal offenses. Judges became familiar with the general customs, usages, and moral concepts of the people and based judgments on them. In doing so, the judges determined which customs and moral concepts should prevail as law.

common law crimes Crimes created by judges.

By the early 1600s, the criminal law of England was composed primarily of the mandatory rules of conduct laid down by the English judges, with only a few criminal statutes. In formulating the **common law crimes** of England, the royal judges believed that their decisions represented the best interests of the king and of the country as a whole. These decisions became the common law of England. As authoritative precedents, they were followed and applied in future cases wherever English common law was used and followed.

During this period of development of the criminal law in England, the English Parliament enacted a few criminal statutes, such as embezzlement, false pretense, and incest. The English ecclesiastical courts (religious courts) both defined and punished offenses, such as private acts of fornication, adultery, and seduction, that were held to be violations of the moral code, but were not public offenses. The English settlers who began colonizing North America in the early 1600s brought with them the English common law. This formed the basis of the law in each of the individual colonies. Modifications and adjustments were made to meet the needs of each colony. A great deal of discretion was vested in colonial governors, councils, and judges with respect to the enforcement and scope of offenses and with respect to the creation of new laws. However, for the most part, English common law crimes continued as the common law crimes in each of the American colonies.

During the American Revolution and for some time after it, a great deal of hostility was directed toward the English in America; this hostility extended to the common law. Justice Hugo L. Black of the U.S. Supreme Court referred to this situation in his 1958 dissenting opinion in *Green v. United States*, in which he stated:

> Those who formed the Constitution struck out anew free of previous shackles in an effort to obtain a better order of government more congenial to human liberty and welfare. It cannot be seriously claimed that they intended to adopt the common law wholesale. They accepted those portions of it which were adapted to this country and conformed to the ideals of its citizens and rejected the remainder. In truth, there was widespread hostility to the common law in general and profound opposition to its adoption into our jurisdiction from the commencement of the Revolutionary War until long after the Constitution was ratified.[35]

American lawyers and judges knew the value of many of the English common law principles, which at that point had been developing for more than 200 years. But the public wanted American law for Americans, and many changes were thus made by the new state legislative bodies, which transformed English common law into statutory law.

Common Law Crimes in the U.S. Federal Courts.   In 1812, the case of *United States v. Hudson and Goodwin* came before the U.S. Supreme Court.[36] The defendants were charged with the common law crime of criminal libel because they wrote in a newspaper that the president of the United States and the Congress had secretly voted to give $2 million as a present to Napoleon Bonaparte. No federal statute made libel a crime, but criminal libel was a common law crime.

The Supreme Court pointed out that state courts could punish a person for a violation of the common law crime of libel under their police power if they chose to adopt and incorporate the offense as part of the crimes of that state. But the Supreme Court held that federal courts had only that power and jurisdiction given to them by the U.S. Constitution and the Congress, and had no power to adopt common law crimes. The rule that there are no federal common law crimes has since been affirmed many times over the years. In 1949, Justice Robert H. Jackson wrote that "it is well and wisely settled that there can be no judge-made offenses against the United States and that every federal prosecution must be sustained by statutory authority."[37]

Common Law Crimes in State Courts.   Most states have abolished criminal common law crimes, but many states continue to use common law rules of criminal procedure. Some states, however, have not abolished common law crimes and continue to allow prosecution for common law crimes. In those states, prosecution is rare and not often successful.

IMPORTANT DOCUMENTS OF THE ENGLISH-SPEAKING WORLD

Magna Carta, 1215. A civil war in England forced King John to sign the **Magna Carta** ("great document"), which provided:

- There will be no criminal "trial upon . . . simple accusation without producing credible witnesses to the truth therein."
- "No freeman shall be taken, imprisoned . . . except by lawful judgment of his peers or the law of the land."

The signing of Magna Carta in 1215 was the first step toward democracy in England, because it was the first time that a king relinquished some of his power to the people. Until Magna Carta, English kings ruled with almost absolute power under the concept of "divine right of kings," and the people had only the little freedom the kings chose to give them.

The writ of habeas corpus developed in English common law to protect the new rights of English people under Magna Carta. In 1679, the English Parliament enacted the first habeas corpus statute. The U.S. Constitution of 1788 guarantees and protects the writ of habeas corpus in Article I, Section 9. All of the original thirteen states guaranteed the writ in their original constitutions. Today, people who believe they are being illegally detained can use the writ of habeas corpus to challenge their imprisonment.

Mayflower Compact, 1620. As the *Mayflower* rode at anchor off Cape Cod, some of the passengers threatened to go out on their own, without any framework of government. To avoid this threat of anarchy, the Mayflower Compact agreed that "We . . . doe . . . solemnly and mutually . . . covenant and combine our selves together into a civil body politike for our better ordering and preservation . . . and by vertue hereof to enact . . . such just and equal laws . . . unto which we promise all due submission and obedience."

Magna Carta The document signed by King John in 1215 giving certain rights to his nobles. Successive kings affirmed this charter before Parliament.

For example, Dr. Jack Kevorkian, the medical doctor who championed assisted suicides, was charged in Michigan with the common law crime of assisting two suicides. Angry over being charged with an "unwritten" law, Dr. Kevorkian shouted a number of times in court during his trial, "This is not a trial! This is a lynching! There is no law! No law!" The jury acquitted Dr. Kevorkian of the common law charges. (Later, using the Michigan criminal code, Dr. Kevorkian was charged and convicted of murder in 1999 and sentenced to 10 to 25 years in prison. He was paroled in 2007.)

Because of the difficulties and limited success of prosecuting for common law crimes, prosecutors use the modern statutory crimes that are available in the criminal codes of their state.

Statutory and Administrative Crimes

After the American Revolution, the new state legislatures began converting common law crimes to statutory form. Through the police power of the state, they had the power to amend, affirm, change, extend, abolish, modify, or alter any common law crime or rule.

In many instances, state legislatures kept the common law crime intact by merely restating the law in statutory form. In other instances, legislatures created new crimes by forbidding and punishing conduct that was not a crime in common law.

English Bill of Rights, 1689. Because of numerous attacks on personal liberty, the English Parliament forced King James II to abdicate, and Parliament produced a Bill of Rights. This document served as a guide for Americans and provided:

- "Suspending laws . . . without consent of Parliament is illegal"
- "Keeping a Standing Army within the Kingdom in Time of Peace unless it be with Consent of Parliament is against the law"
- "Election of Members of Parliament ought to be free"
- "Freedom of Speech . . . ought not to be impeached or questioned."

Declaration of Independence, July 4, 1776. After King George declared the American colonies to be in a state of rebellion and the English Parliament forbade all trade with the colonies, an eloquent statement of the American democratic creed was made in the Declaration of Independence:

We hold these truths to be self-evident, that all men are created equal, that they are endowed by their Creator with certain unalienable Rights, that among these are Life, Liberty and the pursuit of Happiness.—That to secure these rights, Governments are instituted among Men, deriving their just powers from the consent of the governed,—That whenever any Form of Government becomes destructive of these ends, it is the Right of the People to alter or to abolish it, and to institute new Government, laying its foundation on such principles and organizing its powers in such form, as to them shall seem most likely to effect their Safety and Happiness.

U.S. Constitution, ratified 1788. Because of the failure to achieve a workable government under the Articles of Confederation, delegates from the American states met in Philadelphia in 1787. George Washington presided for months over the debates and arguments that led to the adoption and ratification of the Constitution that has been used by the United States since that time.

The Bill of Rights. The first ten amendments were made part of the U.S. Constitution in 1791. See the appendix of this book for applicable sections of the U.S. Constitution.

In still other instances, they redefined the common law crime by changing elements of the crime or removing common law limitations and extending the crime to cover conduct not included in the common law crime. If the common law punishment was considered too severe, changes were made in the degree or form of punishment. Attempts were made to clarify areas of doubt or uncertainty in common law crimes.

Practically all criminal laws that are enforced today are statutory laws enacted by legislative bodies. Many of today's statutory crimes were unknown in common law. Most of these criminal laws were enacted to meet the problems of a mass industrial society.

In the early twentieth century Congress began passing laws creating administrative agencies whose responsibility was to adopt and enforce regulations to further the purposes of federal laws. As some of the regulations adopted could be enforced by the imposition of criminal penalties, the question of the authority of administrative agencies to make criminal laws was raised. In 1911, that issue came before the U.S. Supreme Court in the case of *United States v. Grimaud*.[38] Congress had passed a statute authorizing the secretary of agriculture to make regulations to preserve and maintain government forests as forest reserves. Congress made violation of these regulations a criminal offense. The defendant (Grimaud) had continued to graze his sheep on U.S. forest lands without obtaining permits as required under the new regulations. Because the federal courts were divided on the question of whether a violation of such regulations constituted a crime, the government appealed the case to the U.S. Supreme Court.

The Supreme Court held that Congress may constitutionally delegate to an administrative agency the power to make regulations that are enforced by criminal penalties established by that legislative body. The Court stated that the secretary of agriculture does not exercise the legislative power of declaring the penalty or fixing the punishment for grazing sheep without a permit; the punishment is imposed by the act itself. The offense is not against the secretary but, as the indictment properly concludes, is "contrary to the laws of the United States and the peace and dignity thereof."

Today, established practice allows Congress and most state legislatures to delegate to an administrative agency the power to make rules, and the legislature may provide by statute that such rules may be enforced by criminal penalties. In a few states, this procedure has been held to be unconstitutional. But in the majority of states, criminal laws may be created by the legislature establishing the framework and by the administrative agency providing the specific regulation or rule within that framework. The delegation of such authority is constitutional in the majority of the states if

- The legislative act sets forth sufficient standards to guide the administrative agency, and the act provides for criminal penalties for the violation of the administrative regulations created within the guidelines, and
- The administrative agency stays within the guidelines established by the legislative body in creating rules enforced by the criminal penalties, but
- The rules of the administrative agency "must be explicit and unambiguous in order to sustain a criminal prosecution; they must adequately inform those who are subject to their terms what conduct will be considered evasive so as to bring the criminal penalties of the Act into operation,"[39] and
- The determination (adjudication) of whether a violation of the **administrative crime** has occurred is made by a court with proper jurisdiction and is not made by the administrative agency.

Administrative crime Crime created by government administrative agencies under specific authority and guidelines granted to the regulatory or administrative agency by law of that state or the federal government.

COMMON LAW, STATUTORY, AND ADMINISTRATIVE CRIMES

Common Law Crimes (used in the early days of the United States)	Custom, usage, or moral values, and concepts of a community built up over a period of many years	Plus	Adoption by judges of these customs or concepts in court decisions as crimes
Statutory Crimes (make up the vast majority of crimes today)	Enactment of bills by a legislative body	Plus	Signing of the bills by the chief executive officer (governor or president)
Administrative Crimes (used in the fields of health, drugs, stock market, taxation, and other areas the government must regulate)	Enactment of sufficient guidelines by a legislative body that are signed into law by the governor or president	Plus	Authorized regulatory agencies that create rules within the guidelines established by law

WHO WILL POLICE THE POLICE WHEN POLICE COMMIT CRIMES?

The criminal laws, goals, and protections discussed in this chapter depend on many societal elements for success, such as a concerned citizenry and a fair court system. One of the most important elements of the criminal law system is a professional, honest, corruption-free law enforcement body.

In the past, complaints of police misconduct by citizens were reviewed internally by police department officials. However, today in a great many cities civilian review boards have been established to review and in some cities prosecute police misconduct.

A leading example is New York City. New York has over 34,000 sworn police officers. In 2014, about 4778 citizen complaints were made alleging police misconduct. The New York Civilian Complaint Review Board reviews citizen complaints involving four kinds of police misconduct: (1) Force used by police officers; (2) Abuse of authority, such as improper stops or searches of citizens; (3) Discourtesy by police officers; and (4) Offensive language used by officers.

The Board states that it is an independent city agency, and not part of the police department. It has the authority to subpoena witnesses to provide information to assist its investigation of complaints, a power seen by many as necessary to make a review board effective.

In November of 2014 the mayor of Ferguson, Missouri announced the creation of a citizen review board to review and investigate police misconduct complaints. Widespread dissatisfaction with police actions followed the 2014 killing of Michael Brown by a Ferguson police officer. On March 17 2016 the City and the U.S. Justice department signed an agreement on police reforms to be implemented by the city. The agreement addresses many of the citizen complaints about police conduct. The terms of the agreement are extensive; a Justice Department summary can be viewed at www.justice.gov/opa.

At times, police misconduct and corruption may require stiffer measures. The city of New Orleans, Louisiana has experienced extensive police corruption, in particular when and after Hurricane Katrina struck the city. There were many incidents of police misconduct during this period, including one incident where police fired into a crowd crossing a New Orleans bridge during the flooding after Katrina struck, killing two people and wounding four others.

In response to these problems, in 2010 the people of New Orleans, through their newly elected mayor, invited the Justice Department to come to the city and help clean up the 1,300-member police department. At the time Mayor Landrieu stated, "We have a systemic failure."

After hundreds of interviews and ten months of investigation the City and the Justice Department negotiated a far-reaching agreement to overhaul the New Orleans police department so as to improve safety in the city of New Orleans. The investigation showed that corruption and dysfunction existed throughout the NOPD. Evidence showed that police used excessive force on civilians, and that police failed to investigate serious crimes involving sexual assaults on women. The investigation also discovered serious problems of discrimination and lack of accountability for unlawful actions of police officers.

In July 2012 the city and the Justice Department signed a 122-page agreement (known as a "consent decree"). At the time, U.S. Attorney General Eric Holder stated,

> "[T]he ability of a police department to protect the community it serves is only as strong as the relationship it has with the community... Effective policing and constitutional policing go hand in hand."

On January 11, 2013, a federal court approved the consent decree and provided for immediate implementation of its recommendations. *See* Department of Justice, *Justice News*, January 11, 2013.

★ ★

LEARNING OBJECTIVES SUMMARY

LO 1. Identify the branches of government, and their relationship to the criminal law.
In American jurisprudence, legislatures make criminal law, and the judicial branch determines when the criminal law has been violated.

LO 2. Describe the difference between public law and private law, including the difference between criminal law and tort law.
Criminal laws, which are public laws, are applicable generally to every person within the jurisdiction of the law. Private law, such as tort and contract law, applies only to the individuals affected by conduct of other individuals.

LO 3. List the reasons people commit crimes, and why they do not.
The reasons for making conduct criminal are closely tied to the goals of the criminal law, which are to deter prohibited behavior, protect society from dangerous individuals, and both punish and reform those convicted of a crime.

LO 4. Discuss the four generally recognized goals of the criminal justice system.

LO 5. Explain the meaning of police power.

LO 6. Identify the general limitations on the exercise of the police power by government.

The police power of a state can be broadly used to define criminal conduct, but it is subject to many constitutional limitations. Among these limitations are the principle of legality (nulla poena sine lege), the Ex Post Facto Clause, the bill of attainder clause, the "void for vagueness" and "overbreadth" doctrines, and the Due Process and Equal Protection Clauses.

LO 7. Describe the classifications of crimes and the principle of legality.

LO 8. List and describe five specific constitutional limitations on the power to create a criminal law.

LO 9. Define circumstances that would make a criminal law a status crime.
A "status" crime is one that makes a condition or character trait a crime without any requirement of a criminal act. Such a crime inflicts a cruel and unusual punishment in violation of the Constitution.

LO 10. Trace the origin of the common law to its place in criminal law today.
Common law crimes—those without a specific statute defining the criminal conduct—were at one time the predominant source of criminal law. By the twentieth century virtually all criminal law was statutory, and under federal law no conduct may be adjudged criminal without a specific statutory authority.

KEY TERMS

CASE ANALYSIS AND WRITING EXERCISES

1. Most people are aware that using a credit card to purchase merchandise involves a fee paid by the seller to the credit card company. In some cases, the merchant passes this fee on to the purchaser by charging a higher price for merchandise bought using a credit card. In other cases, merchants offer a "discount" for cash purchases.

   Florida passed a law, Sec. 501.0117 of the Florida Statutes, making it a misdemeanor for a merchant to "impose a surcharge on a buyer" for "electing to use a credit card" in a purchase transaction. Another part of the statute states that it is permitted to "offer a discount for payment by cash."

   In *Dana's R.R. Supply v. Att'y Gen.*, 807 F.3d 1235 (11ᵗʰ Cir. 2015), *rehearing denied* January 13, 2016 a federal court of appeals concluded the Florida statute violated the U.S. Constitution, specifically the First Amendment. How did it reach that conclusion?

2. Los Angeles has a substantial population of homeless people. The city has sometimes passed laws making it a crime to engage in conduct that appears to be related to homelessness. One such law is Municipal Code section 85.02. It states that it is a crime to use a vehicle "as living quarters either over-night, day-by-day, or otherwise." Do you see constitutional problems with this law? What might they be? *See Desertrain v. Los Angeles*, 754 F.3d 1147 (2014).

3. As we saw in this chapter, most courts have refused to hold that SORNA sex offense registration provisions, when applied to sex offenders whose crimes pre-dated SORNA, violated the ex post facto clause of the U.S. Constitution. However, states have their own constitutions, many of which include ex post facto clauses similar to the federal clause. In *Doe v. Department of Public Safety and Corrections*, 62 A.3d 123 (Md. 2013) the highest court in Maryland considered the constitutionality of the Maryland sex offender registration laws. How was that court's decision different from decisions under SORNA? [For those interested in the interplay between state and federal sex offender registration laws, *see Department of Public Safety and Corrections v. Doe*, 94 A.3d 791 (Md. 2014)].

4. Is driving while intoxicated (DWI) a "victimless" crime? It is true, is it not, that one can commit the crime without injuring any "victim?" Does that mean statutes that order convicted defendants to pay restitution to their "victims" do not apply to those convicted of DWI? *See Hanna v. State*, 426 S.W.3d 87 (Tex. Crim. App. 2014).

ENDNOTES

1. 6 N.E.3d 154 (Ill. 2014).

2. Polls taken in recent years report that Americans have less confidence in the criminal justice system than they do in other institutions, such as public schools, the medical system, big business, news services, and organized labor. Only 23 percent of white and 25 percent of black respondents expressed confidence in the criminal justice system. By contrast, 61 percent of those polled expressed confidence in the police, and 52 percent felt confident in the Supreme Court. See Pew Research Center Report, May 1, 2012. A 2009 report by the Pew Institute indicated that only 48% of Hispanics and 36% of blacks believed the police would not unfairly use force in confrontations with members of these minorities.

3. Failure to protect citizens breeds crime. When the government fails to protect citizens, some persons are likely to take the law into their own hands. An example of private justice (vigilantism) may have occurred in a New York City subway in December 1984. Bernhard Goetz told New York police that he believed he was about to be robbed and that he produced a gun, shot his presumed assailants, and then left the scene. A New York grand jury would not indict Goetz for the shooting but did indict him for the illegal possession of a handgun. He was convicted and punished for that offense.

4. *United States v. Watson*, 146 F. Supp. 258, 262 (D.D.C. 1956), *judgment reversed*, 249 F.2d 106 (C.A.D.C. 1957).

5. 389 U.S. 347, 350 (1967).

6. *Kovacs v. Cooper*, 336 U.S. 77, 69 S. Ct. 448 (1949).

7. *Village of Belle Terre v. Boraas*, 416 U.S. 1, 94 S. Ct. 1536 (1974).

8. *Lawton v. Steele*, 152 U.S. 133 (1894).

9. State laws that require motorcycle operators and passengers to wear protective headgear have generally been upheld by state and federal courts as being a valid use of the police power of the state. The Supreme Court of Nebraska reviewed these cases in *Robotham v. State*, 488 NW.2d 533

(1992), in which the Nebraska motorcycle helmet law was upheld. However, some motorcycle groups have mounted considerable political opposition to state helmet laws. As a result, though in the 1970s 47 states had mandatory helmet laws, as of April 2012, when Michigan repealed its helmet law for adult riders, only nineteen states had mandatory helmet laws for all riders. The remaining states, except for Iowa, Illinois and New Hampshire, which do not have helmet laws, require helmets for young riders.

10. *Bykofsky et al. v. Borough of Middletown,* 401 F. Supp. 1242, *affirmed* 535 F.2d 1245 (3rd Cir. 1976) *rev. denied* 97 S. Ct. 394 (1976).

11. See the appendix of this text for applicable sections of the U.S. Constitution.

12. See the case of *United States v. Bass,* 404 U.S. 336, 92 S. Ct. 515 (1971), in which the U.S. Supreme Court held that "a fair warning should be given . . . in language that the common world will understand."

13. *Wall Street Journal,* September 27, 2011. "As Federal Crime List Grows, Threshold of Guilt Declines."

14. When good reasons are given, state governors are likely to grant a pardon for a felony or misdemeanor conviction. The pardon will wipe the slate clean for the person. Depending on the law of the state, governors have the authority and power to grant clemency in different ways. They may grant a pardon, or commute or modify a sentence. Such clemency may be conditional if authorized by state law.

15. Fifth Amendment to the U.S. Constitution.

16. Some states authorize store employees to arrest persons for shoplifting, which in most cases is a misdemeanor or is charged as an ordinance violation. The shoplifting statutes of other states authorize the store employees to detain the suspect until the police or sheriff arrives.

17. *Rochin v. California,* 342 U.S. 165, 168, 72 S. Ct. 205, 207 (1952).

18. See the May 2000 U.S. Supreme Court decision in *Carnell v. Texas,* 529 U.S. 513, where the sexual assault conviction of the defendant was reversed because a Texas law retroactively reduced the amount of proof necessary to support the sexual assault conviction in violation of the Ex Post Facto Clause.

19. See *United States v. Leach,* 639 F.3d 769 (7th Cir. 2011). Ten of the eleven federal circuit courts have heard and rejected ex post facto claims by adults.

20. *United States v. Juvenile Male,* 590 F.3d 924 (2010).

21. *United States v. Juvenile Male,* 131 S. Ct. 2860 (2011).

22. *Connolly v. General Construction Co.,* 269 U.S. 385, 46 S. Ct. 126 (1926).

23. See *Papachristou v. City of Jacksonville,* 405 U.S. 156, 162, 92 S. Ct. 839, 843 (1972) and *United States v. Harris,* 347 U.S. 612, 617, 74 S. Ct. 808, 811 (1954).

24. See *Coates v. City of Cincinnati,* 402 U.S. 611, 614, 91 S. Ct. 1686, 1688 (1971); and *Shuttlesworth v. City of Birmingham,* 382 U.S. 87, 90-91, 86 S. Ct. 211, 213-214 (1965).

25. *Grayned v. City of Rockford,* 408 U.S. 104, 109, 92 S. Ct. 2294, 2299 (1972).

26. *Zwickler v. Koota,* 389 U.S. 241, 250, 88 S. Ct. 2294, 2299 (1972).

27. See *Grayned v. City of Rockford,* 408 U.S. 104, 109, S. Ct. 2294, 2299 (1972); *Dombrowski v. Pfister,* 380 U.S. 479, 486, 85 S. Ct. 1116, 1120 (1965).

28. See 119 S. Ct. 1849 (1999).

29. 370 U.S. 660, 82 S. Ct. 1417 (1962).

30. 392 U.S. 514, 88 S. Ct. 2145 (1968).

31. *Jones v. City of Los Angeles,* 444 F.3d 1118 (9th Cir.2006), *vacated* by settlement agreement, 505 F.3d 1006 (9th Cir. 2007). The city's agreement not to enforce a similar ordinance unless public shelter was available saved the ordinance in *Bell v. City of Boise,* 834 F. Supp.2d 1103 (D. Idaho 2011).

32. *Shivers v. State,* 688 S.E.2d 622 (Ga. 2010).

33. State statutes also often provide that marriage licenses may be issued to women beyond childbearing age who wish to marry a close relative. Under such statutes, two first cousins could marry if the woman met the requirements of the state statute. The results of six major medical studies reported in 2002 concluded that only small medical risks are seen in children born to first cousins who marry. The report recommended that the term *incest* should not apply to sexual relations between cousins—only to sexual relations between siblings and between parents and children. (See the *New York Times* article "Few Risks Seen to the Children of First Cousins," April 4, 2002.)

34. *Loving v. Virginia,* 388 U.S. 1 (1967). It is reported that there are now more than 1 million married interracial couples living in the United States. For example, U.S. Supreme Court Justice Clarence Thomas is a black man and is married to a white woman.

35. *Green v. U.S.,* 356 U.S. 165, 78 S. Ct. 632 (1958).

36. *U.S. v. Hudson and Goodwin,* 11 U.S. (7 Cranch) 32, 3 L. Ed. 259 (1812).

37. *Krulewitch v. U.S.,* 336 U.S. 440, 69 S. Ct. 716 (1949).

38. *U.S. v. Grimaud,* 220 U.S. 506, 31 S. Ct. 480 (1911).

39. *M. Kraus & Bros., Inc. v. U.S.,* 327 U.S. 614, 66 S. Ct. 705 (1946).

2

Jurisdiction

OUTLINE

JURISDICTION OF THE FEDERAL GOVERNMENT TO ENACT CRIMINAL LAWS

The Commerce Clauses

Other Federal Jurisdictional Powers

Federal Crimes Frequently Used to Support State and Local Enforcement

The Federal Domain—One-Third of America

The Expanding Federal Criminal Code

NATION-TO-NATION JURISDICTION

International Criminal Law

Jurisdiction of the Sea Approaches to the Continental United States

The Crimes of Piracy, Felonies Committed on the High Seas, and Offenses Against the Law of Nations

THE MILITARY, MARTIAL, AND WAR POWERS JURISDICTION OF THE FEDERAL GOVERNMENT

Jurisdiction of Military Courts

When U.S. Citizens or Military Are in a Foreign Country

The Use of National Guard Troops and Curfews to Assist Police with Riots and Disorders

The Crime of the Improper Use of National or State Guard Troops

INDIAN TRIBES WITHIN THE UNITED STATES

LEARNING OBJECTIVES

In this chapter we discuss the basis of the power of a court to try a defendant charged with a crime. The learning objectives for this chapter are as follows:

LO 1. Explain why a state has general power to make criminal laws and to prosecute those who violate the law.

LO 2. List four of the specific powers granted to the federal government to make criminal laws.

LO 3. Identify the boundaries of congressional power under the Commerce Clause to regulate actions through criminal laws.

LO 4. Explain the basis for an international court to claim jurisdiction over a person charged with a violation of international law.

LO 5. Describe the "Federal Domain."

LO 6. Identify the jurisdiction of military courts.

LO 7. Describe the jurisdiction of Indian tribal courts.

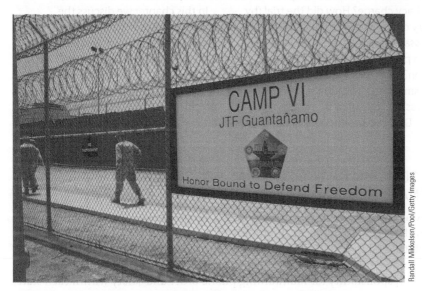

Detainees at the Guantanamo Naval Base detention center, Guantanamo Bay, Cuba. 780 people have been detained over the years at "Gitmo." 647 have been released or transferred. 3 have been tried and convicted by Military Commissions. One has been tried in U.S. courts. Four have died in detention since 2009. As of January 21, 2016, 91 enemy combatants or suspected terrorists remain at "Gitmo."
Source: Human Rights First, January 21, 2016.

Following the terrorist attack on 9/11/2001, Congress passed various pieces of legislation designed to combat terrorism. (See Chapter 17 for a more detailed discussion of these laws.) Among those was the 2006 Military Commissions Act (MCA),[1] which gave jurisdiction to Military Commissions to try any crime punishable by federal statute or the "law of war," committed by an unlawful alien combatant "before, on or after September 11, 2001."

Ali Hamza al Bahlul ("Bahlul") was a personal assistant to Osama bin Laden before and after 9/11. He participated in the preparation and planning of the 9/11 attacks. He was captured in Pakistan three months after 9/11, brought to the United States, and

detained at the U.S. Naval Base at Guantanamo Bay, Cuba. Bahlul was ultimately charged with conspiracy to commit war crimes and providing material support to terrorists. He was tried and convicted pursuant to the MCA on these charges by a military commission, and sentenced to life in prison.

Bahlul appealed his conviction to the D.C. Circuit Court of Appeals, claiming the military commission did not have lawful jurisdiction to try him for the charges filed against him, and that if Congress conferred that jurisdiction in the MCA it violated the ex post facto clause of the Constitution. In *Bahlul v. United States* 767 F.3d 1 (D.C. Circuit 2014) the court held the conspiracy to commit war crimes charge was properly within the jurisdiction of the military commission, but not the charge of material support of terrorism. What was the court's reasoning on the conspiracy charge? How did the trial (by military commission) of the conspirators who assassinated President Abraham Lincoln provide support for the court's decision? Why was the support of terrorism charge outside the military commission's jurisdiction? Finally, what did the D.C. Circuit sitting en banc do when it reviewed the panel decision discussed above? Which court do you think was correct? See Bahlul v. United States, 792 F.3d 1 (D.C. Cir. 2015).

In this chapter we discuss the various jurisdictions in the United States with the power to make criminal laws and apply them to persons who act in violation of those laws. In some situations, one jurisdiction may "assimilate" criminal laws passed by another jurisdiction.

JURISDICTION OF THE FEDERAL GOVERNMENT TO ENACT CRIMINAL LAWS

The American criminal justice system is a huge, complex system serving over 300 million people living in thousands of cities, counties, and parishes in the fifty states and in U.S. territories. As we saw in Chapter 1, under the American system of federalism, states have, through the exercise of the "police power," the primary responsibility for maintaining public order and safety within each state, including passing criminal laws. The federalism system thus gives general power to the states to make and enforce criminal laws, while the federal government must rely on a specific grant of power in the Constitution to pass criminal laws.

The states' power to pass criminal laws is extremely broad. The U.S. Supreme Court has stated, ". . . crimes in the United States are what the law of the individual state makes them, subject to (constitutional) limitations."[2] The federal government, however, does not have an inherent "police power,"[3] and its **jurisdiction** is thus limited to enacting criminal laws pursuant to the powers granted to the federal government in the U.S. Constitution. Every federal criminal statute must trace its jurisdictional origin to one of those powers. Some of the most important powers enumerated in the Constitution are the Commerce Clauses.

The Commerce Clauses

Article I, Section 8 of the U.S. Constitution contains 17 clauses, each specifically conferring on Congress enumerated powers. Clause 18 authorizes Congress to pass any laws "necessary and proper" to carry out those powers. For criminal laws, one important clause is clause 3, which states that Congress has the power "To regulate Commerce with foreign Nations, and among the several States, and with the Indian Tribes."

The power to regulate "Commerce . . . among the several States," is the source of a great part of the authority the federal government uses to enact criminal laws. If an activity (e.g., legal or illegal drug trade) involves more than a single state, Congress may regulate it by either criminal or civil laws.

On the other hand, an activity that is solely within a single state (e.g., maintenance of local public schoolyards) can be regulated by the state or local communities, but not by the federal government.

jurisdiction Power to create and enforce laws. The federal government has power to create laws under the U.S. Constitution; each state has the legislative power to create laws effective within the state; city and village police departments have the power to enforce the laws; and local and state courts have power to sit in judgment of those accused of violating the laws.

EXAMPLE   The conviction under a federal statute of a Texas schoolboy for carrying a gun in a Texas schoolyard was held invalid by the U.S. Supreme Court in the case of *United States v. Lopez*.[4] Schoolyards are not ordinarily part of interstate commerce, and thus the U.S. Congress may not enact criminal laws regulating them. Texas and the school may punish Lopez for carrying a gun in a schoolyard, but the federal government may not. Most states make this conduct a specific crime.

Historically, the legislative power granted in the interstate commerce clause has been interpreted by the U.S. Supreme Court in the context of federalism: Congress's power "must be considered in the light of our dual system of government." Thus, while the commerce clause gives Congress power to regulate activity that "substantially" affects interstate commerce, the Supreme Court in cases like *Lopez* has been careful not to overstep state powers.[5]

The other commerce clauses in Article I have not always been interpreted by courts in the same manner, and as a result the "foreign commerce" clause and the "commerce with the Indian Tribes" clause may be read to give Congress broader power than the more commonly invoked interstate commerce clause.

The Supreme Court has interpreted the Indian Commerce clause very broadly. In *United States v. Lara*, 541 U.S.193, 200 (2004) the Court said that the "central

 YOU BE THE JUDGE

Defendant has been charged with robbery under the federal Hobbs Act (see Chapter 14), which makes it a crime to engage in a robbery that affects interstate commerce. He is a member of the "Southwest Goonz," a group of robbers headquartered in Roanoke, Virginia that targets known drug dealers for robbery, anticipating they will recover cash and drugs in such robberies. In an armed home invasion in Virginia of a known drug dealer, defendant made off with some jewelry, two cell phones, $40, and one marijuana cigarette. These would all be crimes under Virginia state law.

The federal prosecutor charged defendant with violation of the Hobbs Act. You are the federal district court judge hearing the case. The defendant has moved for a dismissal of the case, contending the Commerce Clause does not give Congress the power to make the Hobbs Act applicable to his conduct, because there is no showing it "affects" interstate commerce. You are aware that in *Gonzales v. Raich*, 545 U.S. 1 (2005) the U.S. Supreme Court held that the Commerce Clause gave Congress the power to regulate purely intrastate illegal drug sales under the federal Controlled Substances Act (see Chapter 16), because of the impact such in-state sales have on the illegal drug trade nationwide.

Does stealing one marijuana cigarette affect interstate commerce? Or is that the wrong question? What is your decision on the jurisdiction to charge the defendant under the Hobbs Act? See **United States v. Taylor, 754 F.3d 217 (4th Cir. 2014). The U.S. Supreme Court granted certiorari, 136 S. Ct. 26 (2015), and heard oral arguments on February 23, 2016. (Oral arguments in the Supreme Court may be heard at this location: http://www.supremecourt.gov/oral-arguments/argument-audio.aspx**

function of the Indian Commerce Clause is to provide Congress with plenary power to legislate in the field of Indian Affairs."

The U.S. Supreme Court has not stated its views on the scope of the Foreign Commerce clause as a source of power for Congress to pass criminal laws that have an extra-territorial effect. As a result, lower federal courts differ on how that clause is interpreted. That difference is illustrated by the following 2015 judicial decisions:

Bollinger, a Lutheran minister, supervised a children's charitable house in Haiti. He was indicted under 18 U.S.C. §2423(c) for alleged "non-commercial illicit sexual conduct" with young girls that occurred exclusively in Haiti. (This section is part of the PROTECT Act; see Chapter 12, page 356.) Should the Foreign Commerce clause give power to Congress to punish conduct by U.S. citizens done exclusively in a foreign country? Why or why not? See *United States v. Bollinger*, 798 F.3d 201 (4th Cir. 2015), *cert filed* December 16, 2015. [Yes] Compare *United States v. Al-Maliki*, 787 F.3d 784 (6th Cir. 2015), *cert denied* 136 S. Ct. 204 (2015). [Probably not.]

Other Federal Jurisdictional Powers   In addition to the Commerce Clause, Federal power to pass criminal laws can be divided into the following three general classes:

1. Crimes committed in places beyond the jurisdiction of any state. These include crimes committed in the District of Columbia and crimes committed overseas by the military or on U.S.-controlled ships or aircraft.

2. Crimes that interfere with the activities of the federal government.[6] Because the federal government's scope of activities is broad, this category of federal crimes is broad. It includes fraud by use of the U.S. mails, robbery of federally insured banks or savings and loan associations, violation of the federal income tax laws, and attempted overthrow of the U.S. government.

3. Crimes committed against federal officers.

As examples of the above, the following are some situations in which the federal government has jurisdiction over a criminal homicide:[7]

- Within the special maritime and territorial jurisdiction
- When death results from terrorism, sabotage, or certain cases of reckless or negligent destruction of federal transportation facilities
- When the victim is the president of the United States, the vice president, or successors to the office of the president
- When the victim is engaged in performing federal functions
- When the victim is killed "on account of the performance of his official duties"
- When death occurs in connection with a federally punishable bank robbery
- When the homicide occurs during an offense defined by the Civil Rights Act of 1968 (18 U.S.C.A. § 245)
- When an American citizen is killed anywhere in the world under the Comprehensive Crime Control Act of 1984

Federal Crimes Frequently Used to Support State and Local Enforcement

The power of state and local law officers generally can be exercised only within their borders. Federal law officers, however, are not limited to the borders of a state. For example, a child is missing and may have been kidnapped. If the child is not recovered after a few days, the FBI will presume that the child has been transported to another state, which will give the FBI jurisdiction to become involved in the case. In such cases, federal laws and agencies serve as important forces in complementing state and local law enforcement.

The following are some of the many federal crimes that are of particular and frequent interest to state law enforcement officers.

Unlawful Flight Statute (Fugitive Felon Act) (18 U.S.C.A. § 1073): This law permits federal agencies to assist in locating state fugitives who may have fled from one state to another. The fugitive may be seeking to avoid prosecution for a felony or may be a potential witness in a felony case. If apprehended by a federal agency, the person will be returned to the state from which he (or she) fled. There is seldom federal prosecution under this law.

Federal Kidnapping (18 U.S.C.A. § 1201): Kidnapping or abduction of any person for reward or ransom when interstate transportation or use of special maritime or territorial jurisdiction of the United States is involved.

Federal Conspiracy (18 U.S.C.A. § 371): The federal crime of conspiracy makes it illegal for two or more persons to "combine or conspire" either to commit any offense against the laws of the United States or to defraud the government of the United States. As there are a vast number of "laws of the United States" on the books, this covers a vast amount of territory. See Chapter 4 for material on the law of conspiracy.

RICO (Racketeer Influenced and Corrupt Organizations) (18 U.S.C.A. §§ 1963 and 1964): See Chapter 18 for the history and wide use of this federal statute. State RICO statutes are commonly called "Little RICOs."

The Federal Domain—One-Third of America

The federal government owns and controls up to one-third of all of the land in the United States in the form of territories and federal enclaves.[8] The U.S. Constitution (Art. IV, Sec. 3) states that "In the Territories of the United States, Congress has the entire dominion and sovereignty . . . and has full legislative power over all subjects. . . ."

For example, the District of Columbia (Washington, D.C.) is one of the territories of the United States, and Congress thus has full police power to enact a full criminal code necessary to maintain public order and security in this large American city.

federal enclaves
Federally owned and controlled lands.

Federal Enclaves, Territories, and the Assimilative Crimes Act   **Federal enclaves** are federally owned and controlled lands. They can be found in all states. Military installations—such as Army posts, Navy yards, Air Force bases, Coast Guard stations, and Marine bases—are enclaves if they are within the borders of states. National parks and forests and federal buildings, such as post offices, federal court buildings, and federal office buildings, can under certain circumstances also be enclaves.

Before 1948, some of the enclaves had a degree of autonomy, which created some problems throughout the United States. In 1948, Congress passed the Assimilative Crimes Act (ACA) (18 U.S.C.A. § 13), which incorporates by reference the state criminal law of the surrounding state in force at the time of the defendant's conduct. In the case of *United States v. Sharpnack,* the U.S. Supreme Court held that the ACA was constitutional.[9] In that case, the defendant, who was a civilian, was convicted of committing sex crimes involving two boys at the Randolph Air Force Base, a federal enclave in Texas. In affirming the conviction, the Court stated:

> There is no doubt that Congress may validly adopt a criminal code for each federal enclave. It certainly may do so by drafting new laws or by copying laws defining the criminal offenses in force throughout the State in which the enclave is situated. As a practical matter, it has to proceed largely on a wholesale basis. Its reason for adopting local laws is not so much because Congress has examined them individually as it is because the laws are already in force throughout the State in which the enclave is situated. The basic legislative decision made by Congress is its decision to conform the laws in the enclave to the local laws as to all offenses not punishable by any enactment of Congress. Whether Congress sets forth the assimilated laws in full or assimilates them by reference, the result is as definite and as ascertainable as are the state laws themselves.

extradition The surrender of an accused criminal under the provisions of a treaty or statute by one authority to another having jurisdiction.

The ACA will generally not operate to incorporate a state law making conduct a crime if the federal government has already passed a statute or regulation that makes the same conduct a federal crime. For example, in *Lewis v. United States*,[10]

USE OF EXTRADITION TO BRING FUGITIVES BEFORE COURTS

Extradition

Extradition is the removal of a person from one jurisdiction to another so that he or she can face charges in the requesting jurisdiction.

International Extradition

The United States has more than eighty treaties in force with foreign countries that allow for extradition of fugitives between sovereign nations. A compilation of these treaties can be found in the notes following 18 U.S.C.A. § 3181. Whether or not a person can be extradited, either to or from the United States, depends on the terms of the treaty.

Extradition Permitted

In 1997 Arthur Patterson was a teenager living in South Korea with his father, an American service member stationed there. Patterson was involved in the killing of a Korean citizen, and ultimately convicted in a South Korean court of destruction of evidence, and served about one year in prison. On his release Patterson returned to the United States. 20 years later South Korea charged Patterson with the murder of the person killed in 1997, and sought extradition to South Korea for trial on the charges. The State department, acting on the request for extradition, issued an arrest warrant for Patterson. Patterson objected to the extradition on the grounds that because of the time elapsed he could not be prosecuted for the crime in this country. He also objected based on the Status of Forces Agreement reached between South Korea and the U.S., because that agreement stated service personnel and their dependents cannot be subjected to double jeopardy. The Federal court hearing the extradition case held that even if Patterson was correct in his claims of time limitations and double jeopardy, he must still be extradited. *Patterson v. Wagner*, 785 F.3d 1277 (9th Cir. 2015).

the Supreme Court reversed a conviction of defendants for first-degree murder of a child under Louisiana law, which the federal district court held was applicable under ACA. Because Congress had passed a second-degree murder statute that would apply to the murder of a child on an Army base in Louisiana, the Supreme Court said that law should have been the basis for the defendants' conviction and sentencing.

A federal statute must be of "general applicability" to prevent assimilation of a state criminal law. Thus, in the 2010 case of *United States v. Dotson*[11] the court upheld the conviction of civilians working on a military base for selling liquor to minors in violation of a state statute. While military regulations prohibited the same conduct, these regulations were not applicable to civilians working on the military base, and thus the state statute could be assimilated.

The Expanding Federal Criminal Code   The federal government has, as we saw above, constitutional authority to enact criminal laws only in identified areas. Over the years, the number of federal criminal laws has increased. Although the number of federal crimes grew significantly since the end of the

---

Extradition Not Permitted

In 1977 Roman Polanski, a famous Hollywood film director, was charged with drugging and raping a 13-year-old girl. He pleaded guilty to lesser charges but fled to France prior to his sentencing. After being a fugitive for years, he was taken into custody in 2010 by Swiss authorities on an international arrest warrant, pending extradition requested by Los Angeles prosecutors. After holding Polanski for several months of house arrest, the Swiss authorities refused to extradite Polanski, and declared him a free man. Polanski returned to his native France, a country that refuses to extradite its citizens. The arrest warrant on Polanski still exists, which effectively prevents him from traveling to the United States.

Rendition and the War on Terror

"Extraordinary rendition" is the practice of seizing foreign nationals (mainly suspected terrorists) in one country and transporting them to another country for questioning or prosecution. The C.I.A. has been authorized to use this tactic by Presidents Clinton, Bush, and Obama, though President Obama has authorized this practice only for transportation to a jurisdiction that has authority to prosecute the person rendered. At least twenty-eight countries have served as hosts for suspected terrorists who have been transported under this practice.

Interstate Extradition. Article IV, Section 2 of the Constitution, as well as 18 U.S.C.A. § 3182 and the Uniform Criminal Extradition Act,[a] provide that fugitives who flee to another U.S. state can also be extradited to the original state for trial.

[a]Courts in the United States have held that the Uniform Criminal Extradition Act (adopted in many states) has changed the common law. Bail bond agents and law enforcement officers can be sued civilly for violations in failing to comply with the Uniform Criminal Extradition Act in forcing a person to return to another state without that person's consent. For cases involving bail bond agents, see *State v. Lopez,* 105 N.M. 538, 734 P.2d 778 (App. 1986), *review denied* 107 S. Ct. 1305 (1987), and *Loftice v. Colorado* (Colo. Ct. App. 1988), *review denied* 490 U.S. 1047, 109 S. Ct. 1957 (1989). However, in many states bail bond agents continue to have greater arrest power than private citizens. See *Shiffiett v. State,* 319 Md. 275, 572 A.2d 167 (1990).

In a 1998 unanimous decision, the U.S. Supreme Court held that states have essentially no discretion and must extradite as long as proper procedures are followed and the wanted person's identity and fugitive status are confirmed. See *New Mexico v. Reed,* 118 S. Ct. 1860 (1998).

Civil War, more than half of that growth occurred since 1970. There are now over 4500 federal crimes; about 400 of those crimes were enacted between 2008 and 2013. (Wall Street Journal, A-10, January 3, 2015).

Many of the recent additions to the federal criminal code involve so-called "white collar" crimes. (See Chapter 15.) These include corporate crimes, fraud, environmental crimes, and health care fraud. Many of these crimes lower the required mental state needed to violate the statute, making it difficult for ordinary people to know they are breaking the law. (See Chapter 3.)

While Congress ultimately is responsible for adopting (or repealing) federal criminal laws, how courts interpret criminal statutes can play a role in limiting the impact of the statute. Two cases decided by the U.S. Supreme Court in 2014 and 2015 illustrate this limiting function of courts:

Yates v. United States, 135 S. Ct. 1074 (2015) Yates was indicted and convicted under 18 U.S.C. § 1519, commonly known as the Sarbanes–Oxley Act (SOA), for throwing undersized red grouper fish overboard to prevent federal authorities from using the fish to prove he violated fishing regulations. SOA was passed to respond to acts taken by corporate officers that were designed to shred, hide, or destroy documents that would be important in criminal prosecutions.

The Supreme Court in *Yates* held that the federal law did not apply to discarded fish. Rather, the Court said, only destruction of tangible objects intended to store or record information were crimes under the act. It accordingly reversed Yates' conviction under section 1519.

Bond v. United States, 134 S. Ct. 2077 (2014). Bond was indicted and convicted under 18 U.S.C. § 229 (a) (1), a federal statute that makes it a crime to possess or use a toxic "chemical weapon." Bond used toxic chemicals in an attempt to make

---

 ## HATE CRIMES I

In 2009 Congress enacted the Matthew Shepard and James Byrd Jr. Hate Crimes Prevention Act, 18 U.S.C. § 249(a)(1). It makes it a federal crime to commit an assault, which would normally be within a state's jurisdiction, against a person because of the victim's race. In *United States v. Cannon*, 750 F.3d 492 (5th Cir. 2014), *cert. denied* 135 S. Ct. 709 (2014) defendants were charged under the federal hate crimes law with an assault on an African-American victim. The defendants had initially been charged with misdemeanor assault under Texas state law, but that charge was dropped when federal prosecutors charged them under the federal law.

The defendants contended the hate crimes statute exceeded Congressional authority under the Constitution. The Hate Crimes statute states that the authority for the act comes from the Thirteenth Amendment's "enabling clause," which authorizes Congress to make any law necessary to enforce the Amendment.

Do you think the hate crimes statute is "necessary" to enforce the anti-slavery provisions of the Thirteenth Amendment? Do you agree with the court's decision in *Cannon*? Why or why not? Other issues pertaining to the scope of the federal Hate Crime Law (and also state hate crime laws) are discussed in Chapter 11.

her husband's lover uncomfortable by causing a rash to that person's hands when she touched her car, her mailbox, and similar surfaces. Because the term "chemical weapon" was defined broadly in the statute that would include many common household chemicals, the prosecution contended Bond violated the statute. The Supreme Court disagreed. Noting that the statute was passed as part of an international convention aimed at chemical warfare, it held Congress did not intend to make the statute applicable to a "local assault" that would be under "traditional state authority."

NATION-TO-NATION JURISDICTION

Nations long ago realized that the world could not afford criminal jurisdictional gaps between nations. An alarming situation would exist, for example, if a person could commit a murder in the middle of the Atlantic or Pacific Ocean, with no nation having criminal jurisdiction. Because of this, the jurisdiction of each nation was extended to follow its ships over the high seas. The English common law gave jurisdiction to English courts over crimes committed on British ships and over crimes committed by British subjects on foreign ships.

Today, statutes in both the United Kingdom and the United States give each country jurisdiction over crimes committed not only on ships but also on aircraft controlled by each country. By virtue of the international convention ratified by the Tokyo Convention Act of 1967, the courts of any country in the world may try individuals accused of piracy (armed violence at sea committed on a surface ship or an aircraft), even though the piracy was not committed within that country's territorial waters.[12] In addition to piracy, international conventions of nations have sought the elimination of slave trading, war crimes, hijacking and sabotage of civil aircraft, genocide, and terrorism.

Because of the statutes giving many nations jurisdictions over crimes, situations could exist in which a number of nations had concurrent jurisdiction (that is, the same crime could be tried in the courts of multiple nations).

EXAMPLE   A Romanian man was on an American airplane flying from Europe to New York City. While in the air, the man placed his hand on the genitals of a 9-year-old Norwegian girl. It was held that jurisdiction existed to try the man for sexual assault in a New York federal court under the federal "special aircraft jurisdiction."[13]

International Criminal Law

Article I, Section 8, clause 9 of the U.S. Constitution provides that "The Congress shall have Power . . . to define and punish Piracies and Felonies committed on the high Seas, and Offenses against the Law of Nations." Over the years, the United States has participated with the other nations of the world to define international criminal law—*offenses against the law of nations*—by international treaties and international conventions. In 1928, sixty-three nations, including Germany and Japan, outlawed aggressive warfare by signing and agreeing to the Kellogg-Briand Pact. The brutalization of civilians and the deportation of people from their homelands to slave labor camps were defined and forbidden by the Geneva Convention of 1897.

After the end of World War II, the Allied nations tried some of the Nazi and Japanese military and civilian leaders for war crimes in trials held at Nuremberg, Germany,[14] and Tokyo, Japan. Special temporary criminal courts were created to try these leaders for crimes like ethnic cleansing, deportation of thousands of people to slave labor camps, use of slave labor in German and Japanese war factories, and killing millions of people.

Other temporary criminal courts were established in 1993 to sit at The Hague, Netherlands, to try persons charged with crimes committed during the civil war in the former Yugoslavia (Bosnia).[15] A similar court was established in Africa in 1994 after the slaughter of half a million Tutsi and Hutu people.[16]

The Treaty of Rome, which was ratified in July 2002, created the world's first permanent war crimes court, the International Criminal Court (ICC), which sits at The Hague. This court has the power to investigate and prosecute people accused of genocide, war crimes, and crimes against humanity. The court's jurisdiction extends to all countries that ratified the treaty and to crimes committed in countries that ratified the treaty. The United States did not ratify the treaty and is currently negotiating for immunity from prosecution by the ICC for the U.S. military.

The ICC has issued only two verdicts in its 10-year history, both in 2012. In December of 2012 the court acquitted Mathieu Ngudjolo of charges he led a Congolese militia that raped and killed 200 people in a Congo village in 2003. Earlier in 2012 the ICC convicted Thomas Lubango of using children as soldiers in Congo battles. He was sentenced to 14 years in prison.

In 2015 the ICC reported that there were 23 cases being prosecuted before the court based on "situations" in several countries brought to the court. ICC, Situations and Cases, 2015.

Jurisdiction of the Sea Approaches to the Continental United States

Each nation has established territorial jurisdiction in the waters and airspace around it. In 1983, the United States claimed sovereignty over waters extending 200 nautical miles from the United States and its possessions.[17] Vessels within

---

 CRIMES AGAINST SHIPS AND AIRCRAFT

Piracy or Hijacking	The seizure of a ship or aircraft while it is underway. This is a federal crime and also a crime against the law of nations.
Mutiny	When the crew (or some of the crew) seizes an aircraft or ship and revolts against lawful authority, the crime of mutiny is committed. In military law, the crime also includes an insurrection of soldiers against lawful authority.
Barratry or Barretry	Unlawful acts committed by the captain or officers of a ship that are contrary to their duties. The term is also used for the offense of frequently exciting and stirring up quarrels or lawsuits.

these waters or on the high seas may be stopped under any of the following circumstances:

1. When there is reasonable suspicion or probable cause to believe that contraband such as illegal drugs exists or other criminal activity is occurring,[18] or

2. If a ship or vessel is without nationality (stateless) or "a vessel on the high seas whose nationality (is) unclear,"[19] or

3. With consent or a statement of no objection from the foreign nation where the vessel is registered, *United States v. Bustos-Useche*, 273 F.3d 622 (5th Cir. 2001), or if the ship meets the statutory definition of a "hovering vessel," *United States v. Gil-Carmona*, 497 F.3d 52 (1st Cir. 2007).

maritime jurisdiction
Jurisdiction of the United States over actions within territorial waters of the United States on U.S. ships, or stateless vessels on the high seas.

Under **maritime jurisdiction**, criminal laws can be created to govern the conduct of persons (either Americans or aliens) aboard American ships or aircraft in the territorial waters, on the high seas, or elsewhere. The United States has jurisdiction of crimes committed on aircraft or vessels of whatever nationality in its internal waters and territorial seas and waters, including "stateless vessels," that is, vessels not operating under the authority of any nation.

The Crimes of Piracy, Felonies Committed on the High Seas, and Offenses Against the Law of Nations

When the U.S. Constitution was written, the Barbary Pirates were a problem that led the United States government to send the U.S. Marines to " . . . the shores of Tripoli" (memorialized in the Marine Hymn). The authority for this action is found in Article I, Section 8 of the U.S. Constitution, which provides, "The Congress shall have Power . . . to define and punish Piracies and Felonies committed on the high Seas, and Offenses against the Law of Nations."

Since around 2003, pirates operating off the coast of Somalia have plagued international shipping by seizing ships and holding their crews and passengers for ransom. At the height of these piracy attacks in 2008, hundreds of millions of dollars in ransom had been paid to the pirates. However, starting in 2009 many countries, including the NATO members, begin policing the seas near Somalia. While pirates took forty-six ships in 2009, and forty-seven in 2010, in 2011 only twenty-five were successfully attacked by the pirates. NATO reported in December 2012 that only five successful pirate attacks occurred in 2012, and none in the second half of the year. At that time, 140 persons were still being held hostage by pirates. The IMB, a division of the International Chamber of Commerce, reported that there were no piracy attacks off the coast of Somalia in 2015.

To combat the international drug trade, in 2006 Congress passed the Maritime Drug Law Enforcement Act (MDLEA), 46 U.S.C. § 70501 et. seq. It makes it a federal crime to possess or distribute a controlled substance "on board" a "covered vessel," which includes a U.S. vessel, any vessel in U.S. waters, or any stateless vessel.

Federal courts appear to be split on the applicability of the MDLEA to defendants who engaged in illegal drug transactions but were not "on board" a "covered vessel." In *United States v. Bellaizac-Hurtado*, 700 F.3d 1245 (11th Cir. 2012) the court said MDLEA could not apply to conduct that occurred in the territorial waters of another country. However, in *United States v. Ballestas*, 795 F.3d 138 (D.C. Cir. 2015), *cert denied* 136 S. Ct. 1229 (2016), the court held that the MDLEA applied to conduct of a defendant in Colombia who was part of an illegal drug conspiracy that used stateless vessels to transport illegal drugs to the United States, even though the defendant never went on board the vessels. The court found authority for the statute under the "felonies committed on the High Seas" clause in Article I, Section 8 of the Constitution.

THE MILITARY, MARTIAL, AND WAR POWERS JURISDICTION OF THE FEDERAL GOVERNMENT

The Constitution and Congressional acts give the federal government the power to raise and maintain a military force, to declare and conduct war, and in certain circumstances to use military forces within the several states. Incident to this power is the need for federal laws and courts to oversee the military forces and those associated with the military forces.

Jurisdiction of Military Courts[20]

A person who enters U.S. military service becomes subject to the Uniform Code of Military Justice.[21] Over the years, hundreds of thousands of military personnel have been tried for many offenses, ranging from "military" crimes such as desertion, unauthorized absences, willful disobedience of orders, and drunkenness on duty, to "civilian" crimes such as rape, murder, and drug violations that took place on leave.

Article I, sec. 8, cl. 14 of the U.S. Constitution gives Congress the power to "make Rules for the Government and Regulation of the land and naval Forces." From 1866 to 1960 the only requirement for military court jurisdiction over a defendant charged with a crime was the military status of the accused. The U.S. Supreme Court in 1969 held as an additional requirement that the offense charged must be "service connected" before a military court had jurisdiction; however, this limitation was eliminated by the Court in the 1987 case of *Solorio v. United States*.[22] It is now the law that the military justice system has jurisdiction to try a member of the armed service for *any* crimes committed (on- or off-base) as long as the accused was a member of the military service at the time of the alleged offense.

Civilians working with military units can also be subject to the Code of Military Justice. In 2011 the Army Court of Criminal Appeals upheld the court-martial of a civilian interpreter assigned to a combat unit engaged in "Operation Iraqi Freedom."[23]

When U.S. Citizens or Military Are in a Foreign Country

Americans who commit crimes in foreign countries, whether they are military personnel or tourists, are subject to prosecution before foreign courts. U.S. civilians have been sentenced to serve long prison terms in Turkey, Mexico, and other countries for narcotics violations—a grim reminder that sentences in some countries are quite severe.

U.S. military personnel are stationed in many countries throughout the world. A service person who commits a crime while off base, while off duty, and in a foreign country is subject to the jurisdiction of the laws of that country. Under a status of forces agreement (SOFA), or visiting forces agreement, which many countries have with the United States, the military person could be tried by the courts in the host country.[24] However, in many instances the prosecutor in the foreign country waives jurisdiction and turns the offender over to the U.S. military authorities for trial before a military court.

Examples of crimes that American service personnel have been charged with are murder of a West German taxi driver and desertion *(Plaster v. United States)*,[25] rape of a South Korean girl,[26] and rape of a German woman *(Bell v. Clark)*.[27]

Because foreign countries in the past generally wanted a continued U.S. military presence, they often waived criminal prosecution. However, in November 1995, Japan did not waive jurisdiction to try three U.S. servicemen for the rape of a 12-year-old schoolgirl on the island of Okinawa. Before a Japanese court, one serviceman pleaded guilty, and the other two admitted assisting in the rape. Thousands of Okinawans demonstrated to demand the removal of U.S. military bases from Okinawa and removal of the 47,000 U.S. troops from Japan.[28] In 2006, the governments of the Philippines and Italy asserted their right to try American military personnel for crimes committed in their countries.

The Use of National Guard Troops and Curfews to Assist Police with Riots and Disorders

Military forces have been used many times in the history of our country to maintain public order and enforce laws. In 1787, the year when the Constitution was formulated, the governor of Massachusetts used the militia to cope with Shays' Rebellion. President Washington sent federal troops into Pennsylvania to suppress the Whiskey Rebellion of 1794. Federal troops were used by President Lincoln to prevent the withdrawal of the southern states from the Union and to maintain public order. Federal troops remained in the South until the 1880s. During some of this time, **martial law** was in effect in the southern states where federal troops remained.

martial law A state of military control over civilian populations as declared by state or federal government.

Federal troops were used by President Eisenhower to secure compliance with Supreme Court school desegregation orders in Arkansas in 1957 and by President Kennedy in Mississippi in 1962 and in Alabama in 1963. In the 29-month period between January 1968 and the end of May 1970, National Guard troops were called upon 324 times to cope with urban riots and disorders and unrest on college campuses. In all the incidents in the 1950s, 1960s, and 1970s, troops and National Guard units provided assistance to civilian law enforcement agencies that had the primary responsibility for preserving public order. People arrested or taken into custody were brought before federal and state courts, where they were advised of their constitutional rights.

The Crime of the Improper Use of National or State Guard Troops

National Guard troops can lawfully be used in disaster assistance, search and rescue missions, domestic terrorist events, civil disturbances, and other specific circumstances when they are needed to protect constitutional rights, to support a request from a state, or to enforce federal authority. However, the 1878 **Posse Comitatus** Act makes it a federal offense to use military forces to execute the law without specific congressional authorization.[29]

posse comitatus Latin, meaning "power of the country." In the United States, it traditionally has referred to the military forces.

The December 2001 *FBI Law Enforcement Bulletin* article "Military Support of Domestic Law Enforcement: Working Within Posse Comitatus" (http://www.fbi.gov) lists specific circumstances where U.S. military forces may be called upon to directly perform domestic law enforcement duties.

Figure 2.1 illustrates the power that stands behind the neighborhood police officer in the United States.

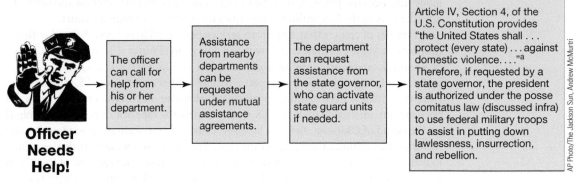

FIGURE 2.1 Who Backs Up the Police Officer on the Street?

[a]States may not maintain armed forces without the consent of the U.S. Congress: Article I, Section 10, of the U.S. Constitution provides that "No State shall, without the Consent of Congress . . . keep Troops, or Ships of War in Time of Peace." (See the appendix of this text for applicable sections of the U.S. Constitution.)

INDIAN TRIBES WITHIN THE UNITED STATES

Of the almost 1.5 million Native Americans in the United States, more than half live on reservations located mainly in seventeen states. The U.S. Supreme Court has pointed out that the 310 recognized Indian tribes in the United States "possess those aspects of sovereignty not withdrawn by treaty or statute, or by implication as a necessary result of their dependent status."[30]

In 1975 and again in 1977, the U.S. Supreme Court held that

> Indian tribes are unique aggregations possessing attributes of sovereignty over both their members and their territory, *Worcester v. Georgia*, 31 U.S. 6 Pet. 515, 557 (1832); they are "a separate people" possessing the power of regulating their internal and social relations. *United States v. Mazurie*, 419 U.S. 544, 557, 95 S. Ct. 710, 717 (1975).[31]

Indian tribal governments have Indian tribal courts and Indian police. However, criminal jurisdiction in Indian Country (the term used to identify areas of Indian Territory) and on Indian reservations is complex. Some crimes are the exclusive jurisdiction of tribal courts, while others are under federal or state jurisdiction. As a general statement, crimes by non-Indians against non-Indians are within the jurisdiction of the state where the crimes occurred, even if that happened to be on an Indian reservation. However, the Indian Country Crimes Act (ICCA), 18 U.S.C. § 1152 gives federal jurisdiction over any crime where either the defendant or the victim is an Indian, but not if both are Indians. Crimes by Indians against Indians occurring in Indian Country are within tribal court jurisdiction, if the crimes are not punishable by more than three years' imprisonment or a $15,000.00 fine.

Absent a federal statute limiting the states' criminal jurisdiction over Indians, Indians who commit crimes while not on or within their reservation or Indian Country are subject to the laws of the state or government where the crime was committed. It is not clear, because Congress has not passed a specific statute addressing the question, if Tribal Courts may exercise criminal jurisdiction over member Indians who commit crimes against other member Indians outside of Indian Country. One court, in *Kelsey v. Pope*, 809 F.3d 849 (6th Cir. 2016) has held such jurisdiction exists. The defendant, a tribal council member, was charged with misdemeanor sexual assault against another tribal member after a meeting of the tribal council. The meeting and the alleged assault did not occur on Indian Territory. The court said the tribal court still had jurisdiction because Congress had not explicitly or implicitly divested tribes of that jurisdiction in cases that substantially affected the tribe's ability for self-governance.

Major crimes committed by Indians within Indian Country, whether against another Indian or a non-Indian, are under the exclusive jurisdiction of the federal courts. 18 U.S.C. § 1153, generally known as the Indian Major Crimes Act, lists the crimes covered by the act. They include crimes like murder, rape, felony assault, and child sexual assault.

The Act by its terms is limited to defendants who are Indians. However, it does not define "Indian," and courts have needed to create their own definition for coverage under the Act. The current definition is illustrated by the court's opinion in the 2015 case of *United States v. Zepeda*, 792 F.3d 1103 (9th Cir. 2015).

Zepeda was indicted under section 1153 and charged with felony assault with a deadly weapon. He objected to the court's jurisdiction, contending the government failed to prove he was an "Indian" under the Act. He was convicted, and appealed his conviction.

On appeal the court agreed that the government had to prove Zepeda was an "Indian" for the Act to apply. This required, the court said, two prongs: (1) that Zepeda had the required "quantum of Indian blood" and (2) that he was a member of a recognized Indian tribe. The court said that the "Enrollment Certificate" issued by the Gila River Indian Community showing Zepeda was a member of that tribe satisfied the first prong, and it was uncontested the Gila River Tribe was a recognized Indian Tribe. The court therefore found that the government proved Zepeda was an "Indian" and covered by the Act. It affirmed his conviction and sentence. On April 25, 2016, the Supreme Court denied certiorari. 2016 WL 1618270.

One area where the relationship between tribal courts and federal laws is unclear is the application of 18 U.S.C. § 117, the Habitual Domestic Violence Offender statute. The statute applies, among other areas, to domestic assault convictions in "Indian Country," where the defendant had two or more prior convictions in "Federal, State, or Indian Tribal Court." In *United States v. Bryant*, 769 F.3d 671 (9th Cir. 2015) the court considered the effect of tribal convictions under the habitual offender statute.

Bryant was charged in federal court with domestic abuse by a habitual offender under section 117, based on two prior domestic abuse convictions in the Northern Cheyenne Tribal Court. Bryant contended use of the tribal convictions violated his 6th Amendment rights because he was not given assistance of counsel in the tribal courts, notwithstanding his request for counsel. Bryant's convictions in the tribal courts were not in violation of the Constitution: The 6th Amendment has been held not to apply to tribal courts, because the Constitution does not generally apply to Indian territory or tribes, as sovereign nations when the Constitution was adopted; see *Santa Clara Pueblo v. Martinez*, 436 U.S. 49 (1978). However, Congress requires tribal courts to appoint counsel for indigent defendants where the punishment for the crime could exceed one year. See the TLOA, discussed in this chapter. In any state or federal court criminal prosecution Bryant would have been given assistance of counsel under the 6th Amendment, and Bryant argued that as a result only Indians can be convicted under section 117 without assistance of counsel.

THE TRIBAL LAW AND ORDER ACT (TLOA) OF 2010

Some of the more than 500 recognized Indian tribes are prosperous, owing to casino operations or because valuable mineral or oil deposits exist on their land. But many Indian tribes, particularly those located in the Southwest and the Northern Plains, are very poor. Crime has always been a problem in these poor tribal areas. The May 2012 *FBI Bulletin* entitled "Indian Country and the Tribal Law and Order Act of 2010" states that criminal victimization of Indians living in Indian country is 2.5 times greater than that of other ethnic or racial groups. Speaking to this problem, U.S. Senator Byron Dorgan of North Dakota stated that because of budget cuts and increased criminal caseloads, prosecutors decline to prosecute more than 50% of the murders in Indian country, and 75% of rapes and sexual assaults. (See *N.Y. Times*, 8/2/2012, "Tribal Law and Order.")

In response to these problems, Congress passed the TLOA in 2010. It provides, in part, that

- Federal departments and agencies (FBI, DEA, ATF, Justice Department, and others) "shall coordinate" with their tribal counterparts on the status of investigations and the use of relevant evidence in tribal courts. This is hoped to make it easier to obtain convictions in murder, rape, and other serious crimes.
- Tribal courts may now sentence convicted persons to up to 3 years in prison per offense, with a maximum of 9 years for multiple-offense convictions. There is a $15,000 limit on fines. Previously, tribal courts could only prosecute misdemeanors.
- Native Americans sentenced for felony convictions may now be imprisoned in tribal facilities (if approved by the Bureau of Indian Affairs) or federal facilities at federal expense under a pilot program that allows up to 100 inmates.
- Tribal law enforcement must now be notified whenever a prisoner convicted of a sex offense, drug trafficking, or a violent crime is released into Indian country. This was not previously required.
- If crimes are not prosecuted because of a lack of funds or interest, tribes may seek federal intervention and federal prosecution.

Bryant was convicted, and on appeal the court reversed his conviction. The court agreed that Bryant's convictions in tribal court could not be used in federal court prosecutions under section 117. The U.S. Supreme Court reversed that decision in 2016, holding the use of the prior convictions violated neither the Sixth Amendment nor the Due Process Clause. 2016 WL 3221519.

LEARNING OBJECTIVES SUMMARY

LO 1. Explain why a state has general power to make criminal laws and to prosecute those who violate the law.
Each state has general power to make criminal laws. The federal government has only the power delegated to it in the U.S. Constitution.

LO 2. List four of the specific powers granted to the federal government to make criminal laws.
The federal government has specific power to make laws including criminal laws under parts of the Constitution such as 1) the Commerce Clause, 2) the power to make criminal laws

for federal territories, enclaves, military posts, 3) the power to pass laws to prohibit conduct that harms federal activities, such as the U.S. Mail and Internal Revenue laws, and 4) the power to punish crimes against federal employees or officers.

LO 3. **Identify the boundaries of congressional power under the Commerce Clause to regulate actions through criminal laws.**
The Commerce Clause gives the federal government power to regulate actions by use of criminal laws only if the actions involve or affect interstate commerce.

LO 4. **Explain the basis for an international court to claim jurisdiction over a person charged with a violation of international law.**
International conventions, treaties, and other agreements between nations can confer power on the federal government to make criminal laws. All countries, including the United States, have the power to regulate their shores and the sea area around those shores.

LO 5. **Describe the "Federal Domain."**
The federal domain consists of substantial land areas within the United States, Puerto Rico, and other territories and enclaves. It also includes sea and air approaches to the United States.

LO 6. **Identify the jurisdiction of military courts.**
U.S. citizens serving in the military may be prosecuted for crimes in military courts, including when they are serving in foreign countries.

LO 7. **Describe the jurisdiction of Indian tribal courts.**
Indian tribal courts have power to try Indians charged with crimes on an Indian reservation. Crimes committed by Indians outside a reservation are subject to state or federal prosecution.

KEY TERMS

jurisdiction, p. 36

federal enclaves, p. 39

extradition, p. 40

maritime jurisdiction, p. 45

martial law, p. 47

posse comitatus, p. 47

CASE ANALYSIS AND WRITING EXERCISES

1. The U.S. Supreme Court has routinely held that Congressional statutes do not have "extraterritorial" application unless the statute clearly shows a contrary intent. Under that rule, the Court has decided that the U.S. Securities laws do not have extraterritorial application, unless (1) the case involves a purchase of a security listed on an American stock exchange, or (2) the purchase or sale occurs in the United States. Does a purchase or sale "occur" in the United States when the buyer/sellers use brokerage accounts located outside the United States but use a "market maker" to complete the transaction? (A "market maker" is a specialist who facilitates stock transactions). See *United States v. Georgiou*, 777 F.3d 125 (3rd Cir. 2015), *cert denied* 136 S. Ct. 401 (2015).

2. After the Supreme Court's decision in *United States v. Bond*, discussed in this chapter, when does use of a toxic chemical become more than a "purely local" crime? In *United States v. Levenderis*, 806 F.3d 390 (6th Cir. 2015) the court held the manufacture of homemade ricin, a dangerous toxic chemical, for use by a defendant to injure firefighters who might enter his home to combat a fire was not a "purely local" crime, and as a result Congress in 18 U.S.C. § 175(a) intended the defendant's actions to be covered by the statute. Why was *Bond* different from this case? Were the statutes involved in each case the same? If not, were they similar in origin? If so, why did that matter?

3. May police officers sitting in a New Jersey "listening post" monitor cell phone conversations under the New Jersey Wiretapping Surveillance law, when those conversations occurred in other states? May the state then use the conversations as evidence in a murder trial in New Jersey? See *State v. Ates*, 86 A.3d 710 (N.J. 2014), *cert denied* 135 S. Ct. 377 (2014).

4. Does the Uniform Code of Military Justice confer jurisdiction on military courts to try charges of forgery of travel reimbursement forms by an army reserve member? If so, when? *United States v. Morita*, 74 M.J. 116, 2015 WL 1837200 (2015).

ENDNOTES

1. 10 U.S.C. § 948d(a). This statute was passed to specifically give jurisdiction for certain crimes to Military Commissions after a decision of the U.S. Supreme Court that concluded Congress had not done so in other statutes. See *Hamdan v. Rumsfeld*, 548 U.S. 557 (2006).

2. *Rochin v. California*, 72 S. Ct. 204 (1952).

3. "[T]he Constitution . . . withholds from Congress a plenary police power." *United States v. Lopez,* 514 U.S. 549, 566. (1995).

4. 514 U.S. 549 (1995).

5. In United States v. Lopez, supra, the U.S. Supreme Court stated that

   > We have identified three broad categories of activity that Congress may regulate under its commerce power. . . . [First] "[T]he authority of Congress to keep the channels of interstate commerce free from immoral and injurious uses has been frequently sustained, and is no longer open to question." Second, Congress is empowered to regulate and protect the instrumentalities of interstate commerce, or persons or things in interstate commerce, even though the threat may come only from intrastate activities.
   >   . . . [F]or example, the destruction of an aircraft (18 U.S.C. § 32), or . . . thefts from interstate shipments (18 U.S.C. § 659). Finally, Congress' commerce authority includes the power to regulate those activities having a substantial relation to interstate commerce, Jones & Laughlin Steel, 301 U.S., at 37, that is, those activities that substantially affect interstate commerce. 514 U.S., at 558.

6. If federal property is intentionally damaged or destroyed, the federal government ordinarily has jurisdiction over the matter. When state property is intentionally damaged or destroyed within that state, the state government has jurisdiction. What about a situation in which the property is internationally owned, such as the United Nations building in New York City? In the 1976 case of *People v. Weiner (*85 Misc. 2d 161, 378 N.Y.S.2d 966), the defendant was charged with criminal mischief for having sprayed red paint on the outside wall of the UN headquarters. The New York Criminal Court held that it had jurisdiction over the person of the defendant and the offense.

7. This material was presented in the *Working Papers of the National Commission on Reform of Federal Criminal Laws,* vol. 2, p. 832.

8. The *National Geographic* magazine article "To Use or to Save" (October 1996) states that the federal domain "covers a third of the nation, more than 700 million acres, a public trust unmatched in the world."

9. 355 U.S. 286, 78 S. Ct. 291 (1958).

10. 118 S. Ct. 1135 (1998).

11. 615 F.3d 1162 (9th Cir. 2010).

12. Indeed, under international law, piracy has always been viewed as every nation's problem: "A pirate, under the laws of nations, is an enemy of the human race. Being the enemy of all, he is liable to be punished by all." *United States v. Ali*, 2012 WL 2870263 (D.D.C. 2012), quoting Chief Justice John Marshall.

13. *United States v. Georgescu*, 723 F. Supp. 912 (1989). The "special aircraft jurisdiction" also gives federal courts concurrent jurisdiction with a state over which an aircraft was flying when a crime is committed aboard the aircraft. *United States v. Moradi*, 706 F.Supp.2d 639 (D. Md. 2010).

14. See the *New York Times* article "Trying to Make Sure That War Crimes Aren't Forgotten or Go Unpunished," September 22, 1997.

15. The first person convicted for Balkan war crimes was a Croat. See the *New York Times* article "Croat Is First to Be Convicted (in The Hague) by Balkan War Crimes Panel," June 1, 1997. The article points out that of seventy-six people charged with Balkan war crimes, only nine were in custody.
    A Bosnian Serb who returned to live in Germany was sentenced to life imprisonment by a German court for war crimes committed in Bosnia. After the man was arrested in Germany, the German government agreed to try him under German law because the United Nations War Crimes Tribunal in The Hague stated it was overburdened. See the *New York Times* article "Bosnian Serb Is Sentenced to Life Term for Genocide," September 27, 1997.

16. The United Nations established the United Nations Tribunal for Rwanda in 1994. It was responsible for prosecuting persons suspected of committing the crime of genocide.

17. During Prohibition in the 1920s (when the consumption and sale of alcoholic beverages were illegal in the United States), European ships would sell liquor to Americans in "Rum Row," international waters off the East Coast of the United States. The U.S. Supreme Court upheld a Coast Guard vessel coming alongside Lee's ship and observing illegal whiskey on the deck. Lee's conviction was affirmed in the case of *United States v. Lee*, 47 S. Ct. 746 (1927).

18. *Singleton v. United States,* 789 F. Supp. 492 (D. Puerto Rico 1992).

19. Article I, Section 8, of the U.S. Constitution provides (in part) that

The Congress shall have Power . . .To define and punish Piracies and Felonies committed on the high Seas, and Offenses against the Law of Nations; To declare War . . . and make Rules concerning Captures on Land and Water; To raise and support Armies; . . . To provide and maintain a Navy; To make Rules for the Government and Regulation of the land and naval Forces; To provide for calling forth the Militia to execute the Laws of the Union, suppress Insurrections and repel Invasions; . . . To make all Laws which shall be necessary and proper for carrying into Execution the foregoing Powers, and all other Powers vested by this Constitution in the Government of the United States, or in any Department or Officer thereof.

Article II of the U.S. Constitution provides in part that

Section 1. The executive Power shall be vested in a President of the United States of America. . . . Section 2. The President shall be Commander in Chief of the Army and Navy of the United States, and of the Militia of the several States, when called into the actual Service of the United States.

20. 10 U.S.C.A. §§ 801–940 (Supp. V. 1970) amending 10 U.S.C.A. §§ 801–940 (1964).

21. 395 U.S. 258, 89 S. Ct. 1683 (1969).

22. 483 U.S. 435, 107 S. Ct. 2924 (1987).

23. *United States v. Ali,* 70 M.J 514 (Army Ct. Crim. App. 2011).

24. The best-known SOFA (status of forces agreement) is that with the NATO countries, where there has been a large U.S. military commitment since 1945 in a continuous effort to keep the peace.

25. 720 F.2d 340 (4th Cir. 1983).

26. The military magazine "Stars and Stripes" reported in 2011 that military authorities were permitting Korean courts to prosecute soldiers charged with rape and other offenses, and that in 2011 a military curfew was reinstated in South Korea.

27. 437 F.2d 200 (4th Cir. 1971).

28. See the *New York Times* article "One Pleads Guilty to Okinawa Rape; 2 Others Admit Role," November 8, 1995.

29. 18 U.S.C. § 1385 (1878).

30. 430 U.S. 641, 645 (1977).

31. *United States v. Antelope,* 430 U.S. 641, 645 (1977).

3

Essential Elements of a Crime

LEARNING OBJECTIVES

In this chapter we examine the acts or states of mind that constitute elements of a crime. The learning objectives for this chapter are the following:

LO 1. Explain the meaning of and difference between *actus reus* and *mens rea*.

LO 2. Identify when a criminal statute includes a requirement of a specific intent.

LO 3. Write a simple criminal charge that does not have as an element a specific intent.

LO 4. List the Model Penal Code degrees of culpability and their accompanying mental states.

LO 5. Distinguish between motive and intent.

LO 6. Identify some of the similarities of strict liability crimes.

LO 7. Explain why the year-and-a-day rule is a rule of proximate cause.

LO 8. Identify the relationship between use of presumptions in the prosecution's case and the Due Process Clause.

LO 9. Explain why a conclusive presumption is prohibited.

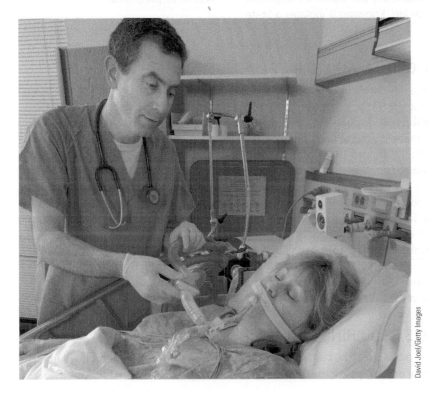

David Joel/Getty Images

Victims of criminal assaults who lose essential brain functions may be kept alive by artificial means. Although the artificial means may be removed by physicians or family members, the death of the victim may still be treated as caused by the assault, resulting in a charge of murder.

Brian Bishop was a Foreign Service Officer working at the U.S. embassy in Amman, Jordan. In 2011 Bishop, pursuant to a State Department policy permitting shipment of "personal effects" overseas, packed over 300 pounds of ammunition for various guns and weapons into crates and delivered the crates to a government shipping contractor for shipment to him in Jordan. The shipper discovered the ammunition, and informed the State Department. Bishop was subsequently indicted and convicted under 22 U.S.C. § 2778, the Arms Export Control Act (AECA). That statute prohibits the export of specified weapons or ammunition from the U.S. without a license. Section 2778 (c) makes it a crime for any person to "willfully violate" any provision of the act. On appeal Bishop contended his actions were not "willful" violations because he did not know the ammunition he was shipping was on the prohibited list, or that he needed a license to ship it. His conviction was affirmed in *United States v. Bishop*, 740 F.3d 927 (4th Cir. 2014).

Consider, as you study the materials in this chapter, whether Bishop violates the AECA if:

1. He puts the ammunition in crates, addresses it to ship to Jordan, but does not ship it;

2. Same as (1), but without his knowledge his son delivers the crates for shipment;

3. He addresses the crates to go to Ammon, Mississippi, but they are sent by mistake to Jordan;

4. He addresses the crates for shipment to Jordan, knowing it violates a State Department rule, but does not know about the AECA;

5. He knows about the AECA, but not the license requirement.

TRUE CRIMES AND STRICT LIABILITY CRIMES

From the development of common law until modern times, all crimes had two essential elements: (1) the physical act or omission and (2) a mental requirement known as criminal intent or purpose. Some writers refer to such crimes as *true crimes*. Today, true crimes continue to make up a considerable number of crimes in any criminal code.

In the 1920s and 1930s, state legislatures began creating criminal laws that did not require the mental element essential to true crimes. This relatively new type of crime is called a *strict liability crime,* or regulatory offense. Strict liability crimes can be found in criminal laws pertaining to traffic violations, narcotics, liquor, sanitation, hunting, and pure-food requirements. In strict liability crimes, the government does not have to prove intent or purpose and must show only that the accused performed the act or omission charged or brought about the results that are alleged and shown. Most crimes have some form of mental requirement as an element of the crime. The various forms of mental requirement found in those crimes are discussed in the following section.

CRIMES REQUIRING PROOF OF MENTAL FAULT

reasonable doubt
Proof beyond a reasonable doubt means that it is not enough to prove it was more likely than not that an element of the crime was true. The proof must be such that a reasonable person could not conclude the element was not true.

actus reus The criminal act.

mens rea The criminal intent or state of mind.

Before a person may be convicted of a crime that requires proof of mental fault, the government must prove the following elements beyond a **reasonable doubt:**

- *The external physical act:* That the conduct or act forbidden by the law of the jurisdiction was in fact committed by the defendant.
- *The internal mental element:* That the act or omission was accompanied by a state of mind required by the criminal statute.

The Latin term ***actus reus*** ("guilty act") is used by courts and writers to describe the essential physical act, and the term ***mens rea*** ("guilty mind") is used to describe the essential mental requirement. State statutes vary on how they define the degrees of criminal intent. That is, with respect to an element of the offense, the mental state of the defendant as to that element can have various formulations. For example, to be convicted of the crime of possession of stolen property, almost all state statutes require that the defendant have knowledge that the property was stolen. The *actus reus* is the physical possession of the property; the *mens rea* is the intent to possess the property; the scienter (knowledge) element is knowledge that the property was stolen. (Scienter is discussed later in this chapter.) Other crimes might require only that the defendant was negligent about an element of the crime. For example, in most states the crime of vehicular homicide can be established by proof that the defendant unintentionally caused the death of another, while operating a motor vehicle recklessly or with gross negligence.

Model Penal Code (MPC) Proposed criminal law developed by the American Law Institute, a group of lawyers, judges, and teachers. Many states have modeled their criminal codes on the Model Penal Code.

The **Model Penal Code (MPC)** is a proposed criminal code drafted by the American Law Institute, a group of lawyers, judges, and law professors. Many states have used parts of the MPC when drafting their own criminal codes. Section 2.02 of the MPC suggests the following formulation of the mental element:

> *Minimum Requirements of Culpability.* Except as provided in Section 2.05, a person is not guilty of an offense unless he acted purposely, knowingly, recklessly, or negligently, as the law may require, with respect to each material element of the offense.

The U.S. Supreme Court has never created or announced a doctrine requiring proof of *mens rea* in all crimes and in all cases before an accused can be held accountable for his or her acts.[1] Therefore, the states are generally free to create criminal laws that do not require proof of *mens rea* or to create criminal laws requiring different degrees of mental fault or mental guilt. But if a degree of mental guilt is made an element of the crime by law, the prosecutor must then prove this essential element of the crime, as well as prove the acts taken together with this mental element.

Thinking of committing a crime without performing a criminal act is not a crime. If a person with criminal thoughts does nothing to carry out those thoughts, no crime has occurred. Government cannot punish thoughts alone. To show that a true crime has occurred, the state must show that the external physical act and the internal mental state essential to that crime occurred at the same time. Even crimes such as conspiracy, in which two or more people share their thoughts about a crime, generally require that the conspirators do at least one physical act in furtherance of the conspiracy (see Chapter 4).

In some instances, an act without the required mental state (guilty mind) is no crime. For example, a person incapable of entertaining the required criminal mind because of legal insanity has not committed a crime. A student who picks up someone else's book or briefcase by mistake has performed a physical act, but without the guilty or criminal state of mind necessary for the crime of theft, no crime has been committed. However, suppose that the student keeps the book or briefcase for two days and then, realizing the mistake, decides to keep the property. The taking and keeping of the property for two days has been a continuous act in the eyes of the law. The crime of theft occurred when the intent to deprive the true owner of permanent possession concurred with the act of taking and retaining possession.

Concurrence The requirement in crimes requiring proof of mental intent that the forbidden act and guilty mind must occur at the same time or otherwise be linked. For example, trustees, guardians, or lawyers might have possession of another person's money (physical act). However, for the crime of embezzlement to occur they must intentionally and wrongfully misappropriate this money (forbidden act and guilty mind).

The requirement that the mental fault and prohibited act must both be present in crimes requiring mental fault is usually called "concurrence." **Concurrence** requires a connection between the mental fault and the forbidden act, in the sense that the mental fault "drives" or "actuates" the forbidden act. For example, a person innocently enters a residence of another, but once inside decides to steal the occupant's property. While the crime of theft has been committed, the person cannot under most state statutes be convicted of burglary, because that crime requires the mental intent to enter the house for the purpose of committing a crime. The forbidden act occurred, but there was no concurrence of the required mental fault. Or, a person may both desire and make plans for the death of another, but if he subsequently and inadvertently kills that person in an automobile accident he cannot be guilty of murder. His mental state of wanting to kill the other person did not "drive" or "actuate" the act that caused the death.

Although the forbidden act and the guilty mind must concur, the resulting harm need not take place at the same time.

EXAMPLE	While A is on vacation, X rigs a spring gun to A's front door (forbidden act), setting it with the intention that A be killed when he opens the door (guilty mind). Two weeks after the spring gun is set in place, A returns from vacation and is shot and killed when he opens his door.

> In the example given, the *actus reus* and the *mens rea* concurred, but the results did not occur until A opened the door two weeks after the act with intent to kill was performed.

Actus Reus: The Forbidden Act or Omission

Most criminal laws forbid specific acts, and a few punish the failure (omission) to carry out a legal duty. The act forbidden or commanded by the law is described in the definition of each particular offense, usually in terms of the prohibited conduct and the harm or the wrong that occurs. In the crime of murder, the death of the victim caused by the defendant's forbidden act or omission is the harm and the wrong. In the crime of larceny, the loss of personal or movable property caused by the defendant's wrongful taking and carrying away is the harm and the wrong.

The manner in which the harm or wrong can be caused varies considerably. A murder can be committed by use of a gun, a knife, a blow, poison, or by any one of many other acts. The harm or the wrong done usually varies from crime to crime, but sometimes two crimes embody the same harm or wrong.

All criminal homicides share the same harm or wrong, which is the death of a person. Homicides differ from one another primarily because of the differing states of mind of the offenders at the time they cause the harm or wrong, which is the death of another person. Both murder and manslaughter involve the death of a person, but because of the different mental states required for a conviction, they are different crimes.

Just as different mental states may result in different crimes charged, so too may different acts be made criminal where more than one person is a party to a crime. As a result, the *actus reus* may be different for each party's involvement in the crime. A *party to a crime* could be (1) a person who actually and physically commits the crime, (2) a person who conspires in the planning of the crime or orders that the crime be committed, or (3) a person who aids and assists in the commission of the crime. All state criminal codes define parties to a crime and make each of the parties to a crime equally liable for the crime (see Chapter 4).

The different *actus reus* for parties to a crime are illustrated by the following example:

EXAMPLE	A hires B and C to murder X. A tells B and C how and where she wants X to be murdered. B is the vehicle driver and lookout while C commits the murder. A hired and ordered the killing.

> C's act in killing X is the *actus reus* of the direct commission of the crime, murder. B's acts (driver and lookout) are the *actus reus* of aiding and abetting murder. A jury could easily find that all three parties (particularly A) conspired and agreed in the planning of the murder, which is the *actus reus* of the crime of conspiracy.

ELEMENTS OF A CRIME: *ACTUS REUS*

Virtually every crime is defined in a statute. The statute describes the prohibited conduct, and in many cases also describes a prohibited result. The conduct (or omission) and result specified are the *actus reus* elements of the crime, and must be proved by the prosecution. In some cases, the statute may designate circumstances that accompany the prohibited conduct. These usually are called "attendant circumstances," and can also be elements of the crime.

EXAMPLE: A statute makes "discharging a gun in a public place" a crime. The conduct is discharging a gun, and "in a public place" is an attendant circumstance; both are elements of the crime and must be proved.

EXAMPLE: A statute makes it a crime to "drive a vehicle negligently so as to cause the death of another person." The result, the death of another person, is an element of the crime, and is part of the *actus reus* of the crime.

In addition to the *actus reus* elements of a crime, many statutes also require a particular mental state as part of the crime. In such cases, the required mental state must also be proved. The mental state requirement is discussed later in this chapter.

The state has the burden of proving beyond a reasonable doubt the *actus reus* element of every offense, and the jury must unanimously agree that the state has proved the *actus reus* elements before they may find a defendant guilty.

The criminal acts must be volitional; that is, the act must be the product of conscious thought. Sleepwalking, experiencing a seizure, and many reflexive actions are not volitional and thus don't satisfy the *actus reus* requirement. This requirement of volition differs from *mens rea*, discussed below. Consider this example: A woman's arm lifts up and strikes another person. If the arm moved as a reflexive action, or during a seizure, or if another person caused the arm to move, the woman has not performed a conscious act, and the movement of her arm cannot satisfy the *actus reus* requirement of a criminal statute. However, if the woman made the conscious decision to raise her arm, she has acted volitionally, and satisfied any *actus reus* requirement. The *mens rea* requirement, if any, would depend on her mental state that accompanied her act in raising her arm. Did she intend to strike another person? Did she raise her arm in a crowded elevator, in reckless disregard of others? Or, did she reasonably believe she was alone in a room? These are *mens rea* questions.

A 2012 decision of the Washington Supreme Court illustrates a troublesome aspect of the volitional requirement. The prosecution must prove all the elements of a crime charged. In the example above, this would seem to mean the prosecution cannot simply prove the woman's arm *was raised*. It must prove the woman *raised her arm*. However, in *State v. Deer*[2] this was not the result. In that case, a woman was charged with having sex with a boy under the age of 16, a strict liability crime in Washington (and elsewhere). The woman did not contend the sexual acts did not occur, but asserted she was asleep during the sexual acts, and that thus the sexual acts were not volitional. The Washington Supreme Court agreed that proof she was asleep would make the sexual acts non-volitional; however, the court rejected her claim that the state was required to prove she was not asleep. All the state needed to prove, the court said, was that the sexual acts occurred. The woman's contention that she was asleep was an affirmative defense, the court said, and she carried the burden of proof on that defense.

Mens Rea: The Guilty Mind

A cardinal principle of criminal law pertaining to true crimes was long ago expressed in Latin as *actus non facit reum nisi mens sit rea* ("an act does not make a person guilty unless the mind is guilty").

The term *mens rea* means evil intent, criminal purpose, and knowledge of the wrongfulness of conduct. It is also used to indicate the mental state required by the crime charged, whether that is **specific intent** to commit the crime, recklessness, guilty knowledge, malice, or criminal negligence.

Criminal liability usually requires "an evil-meaning mind [and] an evil-doing hand."[3] However, while the phrase *evil-meaning mind* suggests an evil purpose for doing the evil act, a mind can be "guilty" without such evil purpose. For example, doing an act recklessly, but without the "evil" intent to harm another, may lack the *mens rea* for one crime but nonetheless satisfy the *mens rea* requirement of another. One's state of mind can range from being "purposeful"—that is, intending a particular result or consequence—to merely negligent—that is, failing to be aware of the probable results or consequences of an act. Figure 3.1 illustrates the degrees of mental fault.

> **specific intent** The intent necessary for one or more elements of an offense. Murder, for example, requires the specific intent that the act be done intentionally or purposely.

 WHEN FAILURE TO ACT IS A CRIME

State and federal criminal codes usually identify and prohibit specific, affirmative actions, called crimes of commission. Examples of these crimes are the prohibitions against murder, robbery, and similar crimes where the crime consists of taking defined actions.

A small percentage of crimes in criminal codes are crimes of omission—failure to act when a duty or obligation is imposed upon persons under certain circumstances. The following are examples of crimes of omission that can be found in state criminal codes. Using the statutes from your state's criminal code, find a section that defines and makes criminal the following crimes of omission:

1. Failure to report the death of a child
2. Failure to report the location of a human corpse
3. Failure by a parent or guardian to provide adequate food, clothing, shelter, or medical care to a child under the person's care and supervision
4. Failure to submit to a Breathalyzer or other similar test when lawfully requested to do so by a police officer
5. Failure of one involved in an accident to remain at the scene
6. Homicide by omission.

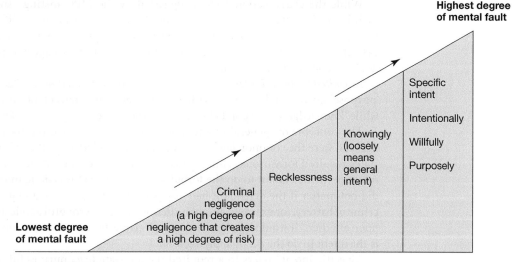

FIGURE 3.1 Degrees of Mental Fault

*All definitions are from § 2.02 of the Model Penal Code

The following example illustrates situations in which the harm done is the same in all cases, but the mental element varies. Consider the likely mental state of X in each situation:

EXAMPLE

X, a construction worker, is working on the fourth floor of a building under construction in the downtown area of a city. His conduct caused the death of W, who was hit on the head by a crowbar as she was walking on the sidewalk past the building.

1. X deliberately dropped the heavy crowbar so as to hit W on the head.

2. X did not want to kill anybody but wanted to see the people scatter when he dropped the crowbar to the sidewalk.

3. X threw the crowbar at another worker in a fight, but missed. The crowbar fell, killing W on the sidewalk below.

4. X came to work drunk and accidentally pushed the crowbar off the edge of the building, killing W.

5. Another worker called for the crowbar and X threw it to him, but the throw was bad and the crowbar hit W on the sidewalk below.

6. X was knocked unconscious when a crane collapsed, causing him to drop the crowbar, which hit and killed W.

Assuming a jurisdiction uses the mental fault classification similar to that suggested by the MPC, i.e., purposely, knowingly, recklessly, or negligently, what homicide crimes, if any, could X be charged with in each of these examples?

While the classification system suggested by the MPC distinguishes between each level of mental state, the distinction does not always make a difference. See *United States v. U.S. Gypsum Co.,* in which the U.S. Supreme Court stated that in the case of most crimes, "the limited distinction between knowledge and purpose has not been considered important."[4]

In *United States v. Bailey,* the U.S. Supreme Court stated that in a "general sense, 'purpose' corresponds loosely with the common-law concept of specific intent, while 'knowledge' corresponds loosely with the concept of 'general intent.'"[5]

The concepts of "general intent" and "specific intent" referred to in the *Bailey* decision were the common law's attempt to isolate and identify the different mental states required for various crimes. At common law, "general intent" referred to the intent of the defendant to do the forbidden act. If the act was done intentionally, it did not matter if the defendant had any particular purpose for doing the act. The crime of battery, for example, might be defined as the "wrongful application of force upon another." It would be a "general intent" crime, because the only intent required is the intent to do the act of applying force.

"Specific intent" refers to a required mental state (e.g., purposeful or reckless), which must be proved to have accompanied the prohibited acts. Thus, if a statute defined aggravated battery as "wrongful application of force upon another with the intent to cause fear or apprehension," the crime requires proof of the defendant's mental state when the force was applied.

"Specific intent" is thus understood today as referring to the intent that must accompany the forbidden act, over and above the intent to do the forbidden act. For example, the crime of burglary not only required the general intent to do the forbidden act of unlawfully entering the premises of another, but also the specific intent to steal or otherwise commit a felony within the premises. Other illustrations of the difference between general intent and specific intent might include the crime of "indecent exposure," which requires only the intent to do the forbidden act. It does not require the specific intent that any particular person should see the act. The crime of false pretenses requires not only the general intent to make a false statement, but also the specific intent to use the false statement to defraud another person of money or property.

For the most part, crimes are no longer classified as either "general intent" or "specific intent" crimes.[6] Rather, as the U.S. Supreme Court did in the following Case Close-Up, courts determine what elements of a crime charged require proof of a specific intent.

Proving Criminal Intent or Criminal State of Mind

When criminal intent or another mental element is an essential element of a crime, the state has the burden of proving the required *mens rea*. Proof of the mental element may be made by

- Showing the acts of the defendant and the circumstances that existed at the time of the crime. Because most people know what they are doing and also know the natural and probable consequences of their acts, a judge or jury may reasonably infer that the defendant intended the natural and probable consequences of his or her deliberate acts.[7] Thus, a person who pointed a loaded gun at another person

CASE CLOSE-UP

Elonis v. United States

United States Supreme Court
135 S. Ct. 2001 (2015)

Anthony Elonis had a Facebook page, with many "friends," including some at his workplace. After his wife left him, Elonis began posting inflammatory comments and photographs on his Facebook page, usually written as "rap" lyrics from his new Facebook name, "Tone Dougie." These lyrics included statements like "Did you know it is illegal to say I want to kill my wife?," and "Hell hath no fury like a crazy man in a Kindergarten class." After his posts led to his getting fired from his job, he posted a photograph of himself holding a toy knife to the neck of a co-worker with the caption "I wish." When she saw these posts, Elonis' estranged wife stated they put her in fear for her life, and she obtained a restraining order against Elonis. Notwithstanding the restraining order, and even a visit by an F.B.I. Agent, Elonis continued to make similar crude and violent sounding posts on his Facebook page.

Ultimately, a grand jury indicted Elonis for violation of 18 U.S.C. § 875(c). That statute makes it a crime to transmit in interstate commerce "any communication containing any threat to kidnap any person or any threat to injure the person of another."

Elonis was tried and convicted of four counts under this statute, and sentenced to three years and eight months in prison. The Court of Appeals affirmed Elonis' conviction, rejecting his argument that the government failed to prove he intended to make threats in his Facebook posts.

The U.S. Supreme Court reversed the conviction, holding that the prosecution failed to prove Elonis possessed the mental state required by section 875(c). The Court first stated that although section 875(c) does not specify any required mental state, unless Congress has made it clear none was required, criminal statutes generally are not read to dispense with some degree of criminal intent. Moreover, any criminal intent requirement included in the statute must apply to each element of the crime. Here, the Court said, the elements of the crime were making a communication, and the threatening nature of the communication. The statute's required mental state was the issue in the case, the Court said.

Had the prosecution proved Elonis made the Facebook posts for the purpose of issuing a threat, or with knowledge it would be perceived as a threat, the mental state requirement of section 875(c) would have been satisfied, the Court said. However, the trial judge instructed the jury that it must convict Elonis if it found a "reasonable person would foresee that the statement would be interpreted by those to whom it was communicated" as a threat to do serious harm. The Supreme Court said the use of "foreseeability" in the instruction amounted to a negligence standard. Under this instruction, the jury could convict the defendant even if it concluded he did not know or intend his statements would be perceived as threats. The Court said "we have long been reluctant to infer that a negligence standard was intended in criminal statutes," and concluded that was not the mental state intended by Congress in section 875(c). It therefore reversed Elonis' conviction, and remanded the case to the trial court.

If Elonis is retried under section 875(c), what must the prosecution prove? That he intended to threaten his ex-wife or former co-workers? That he made the Facebook posts knowing they would be perceived as threats of violence? That he acted in reckless disregard of the effect of his Facebook posts?

and pulled the trigger knew what he or she was doing and desired the natural and probable consequences of the acts.

- Producing evidence to show the statements of the defendant at the time of the crime, as well as statements made after the crime. Statements of a defendant before or after a crime may be incriminating and may include admissions or a confession of guilt.

Only rarely is written evidence of the intent or purpose of a defendant available to the state. The following jury instruction on intent was approved by the Fifth Circuit Court of Appeals in the case of *United States v. Durham*:

> It is reasonable to infer that a person ordinarily intends the natural and probable consequences of his knowing acts. The jury may draw the inference that the accused intended all the consequences that one standing in like circumstances and possessing like knowledge should reasonably have expected to result from any intentional act or conscious omission. Any such inference drawn is entitled to be considered by the jury in determining whether or not the government has proved beyond a reasonable doubt that the defendant possessed the required criminal intent.[8]

Although one can reasonably infer that a person ordinarily intends the natural and probable consequences of his or her knowing and deliberate acts, one cannot extend that inference to conclude that a person intends results that are not the natural, reasonable, or probable consequences of a voluntary act. Moreover, this inference has sometimes been rejected as a basis for convicting a defendant who is charged with accomplice liability, such as aiding and abetting another in the commission of a crime, if the underlying crime requires a showing of specific intent. (Vicarious liability of aiding and abetting is discussed in Chapter 4.) Courts have held that convicting one who aids another person who has committed a crime that has a specific intent, like murder, based only on the inference that the accomplice could foresee the other person might commit the specific intent crime, is not permitted, unless it is shown the accomplice intended to further the commission of the specific intent crime. In *People v. Chiu*, 325 P.3d 972 (Cal. 2014), the California Supreme Court reversed the conviction for first-degree murder of a defendant convicted of aiding and abetting the murder. The court held the "natural and probable consequences" rule should not apply to aiders and abettors in first degree murder cases. Rather, the government must prove the aider had the specific intent to kill required by the statute, the court said.

The crime of murder generally requires proof of premeditation, which means not only that the killing was intentional, but also that the killer deliberated the killings for some (however short) period of time. In the tragic December 2012 killings by Adam Lanza in Newtown, Connecticut, and William Spengler in Webster, New York, premeditation could be inferred from their actions prior to the killings. Lanza killed his mother before going to the Sandy Hook school, destroyed his computer's hard drive, arrived at the school wearing a camouflage vest and clothing, and killed most of his twenty-six victims with multiple bullet wounds. Spengler left a note indicating his intent to burn down his neighborhood and "do what he liked doing best: kill people." The firefighters shot by Spengler when they answered the fire alarm to put out the fire Spengler started were likely, it could be inferred, shot by Spengler to further his plan to burn his entire neighborhood.

INNOCENT ACTS THAT, IF DONE WITH FORBIDDEN INTENT, ARE CRIMES

Innocent Acts	Forbidden Intent	Resulting Crimes
Possessing a tool or other instrumentality	To use such a device to break into a depository or building and steal therefrom	Possession of burglary tools
Traveling in interstate or foreign commerce	To avoid prosecution for a state felony or to avoid giving testimony in such a prosecution	Fugitive felon or witness violation; 18 U.S.C.A. §§ 1073 & 1074 (a)
Traveling in interstate or foreign commerce	For the purpose of engaging in non-marital sexual activity with a person under 18 years of age (21 countries now permit police to arrest for this offense in an effort to stamp out the sex trade in children between nations)	Mann Act; 18 U.S.C.A. § 2423
Traveling in interstate or foreign commerce	With intent to incite a riot (statute requires an overt act, but such act could be a lawful act)	18 U.S.C.A. § 2101 (a)(1)
Using U.S. mail, telephone, or interstate wire facilities	To participate through racketeering in a criminal enterprise	RICO violation; 18 U.S.C.A. §§ 1961–1968 (see Chapter 18)
Using U.S. mail	To advance a fraudulent scheme	Mail fraud; 18 U.S.C.A. § 1341
Using a fictitious name or address	To further a fraudulent mail scheme	18 U.S.C.A. § 1342
Association with other people or organizations	Knowing they advocate the overthrow of our government and that they intend to use force or violence to bring it about	18 U.S.C.A. § 2385
Entering a train	With intent "to commit any crime or offense against a person or property thereon"	18 U.S.C.A. § 1991
Going on "any military, naval, or Coast Guard reservation, post, fort, arsenal, yard, station, or installation"	"For any purpose prohibited by law or lawful regulation"	18 U.S.C.A. § 1382
Teaching or demonstrating the use, application, or making of a firearm, or making of a firearm, explosive, or incendiary device, or a technique capable of causing injury or death	"Intending that the same will be unlawfully employed for use in, or in furtherance of, a civil disorder which may in any way or degree obstruct, delay, or adversely affect commerce" or the performance of any federally protected function	18 U.S.C.A. § 231(a)(1)

Proving intent to kill under offenses like "assault with intent to kill" can be more difficult and often requires circumstantial evidence. As an example, in *State v. Wilds*[9] a defendant was convicted of assault and battery with intent to kill (ABIK) when he severely injured a victim he dragged under his car. An appeals court held that the jury could infer the required "malice aforethought" based on evidence the defendant knew the victim was in front of his car but accelerated anyway, repeatedly swerved the car with the victim under the car, and was observed laughing during the time the victim was being dragged.

The Requirement of Scienter

Scienter A form of specific intent requiring a showing that the actor knew of the existence of certain facts. For example, one cannot be guilty of possession of stolen property if one does not know property is stolen.

Scienter is sometimes made an essential element of a crime that the state must prove beyond a reasonable doubt. **Scienter** is a legal term meaning possession of a degree of knowledge about facts material to a conviction of a crime. If a statute requires knowledge about the existence of a fact, that knowledge must be proved by the prosecution. Examples of crimes in which state statutes most often require scienter include the following:

- In battery or assault on a law enforcement officer, knowledge that the victim is a law enforcement officer
- In refusing to aid a law enforcement officer, knowledge that the person requesting assistance is a law enforcement officer
- In obstructing a law enforcement officer, knowledge that the person obstructed is a law enforcement officer
- In receiving stolen property, knowledge that the property received is stolen property
- In possession of obscene material, knowledge of the nature of the material
- In bribery of a public official or a juror, knowledge that the person is a public official or juror
- In harboring or aiding a felon, knowledge that the person aided is a felon

Whether or not a criminal statute has a scienter requirement depends on how the statute is written. In addition, it often matters whether a fact is an essential element of the offense, or whether the existence of the fact serves as the basis for sentence enhancement upon conviction of an underlying offense. For example, Georgia's aggravated assault statute, § 16-5-21, states that "A person who knowingly commits the offense of aggravated assault upon a peace officer . . . [while the officer is performing official duties]" is guilty of a felony. Because "knowingly" is made part of the offense, the statute has been held to require proof the defendant knew the person assaulted was a police officer.[10]

An example of a statute that does not require such knowledge is a California statute, Cal. Pen. Code § 12022 (a)(1). It states that "any person who is armed with a firearm in commission of a felony . . ." shall receive an additional one-year sentence. Because it is a sentence-enhancement statute, it does not require proof that all persons involved in the crime had knowledge one of them was armed with a firearm, it has been held.[11]

Most state[12] and federal courts[13] have reached similar conclusions interpreting so-called "schoolyard" laws, which provide for imposition of additional sentences for certain crimes, such as sale of illegal drugs, committed near or on a schoolyard.

These statutes generally have been interpreted as sentence enhancement statutes, with no requirement of knowledge that the schoolyard was located near the place where the crime occurred.

A statute can of course add a scienter requirement by appropriate language. In *United States v. Thomas*[14] a defendant was charged with violation of 10 U.S.C.A. § 911, 912(a), which makes it a crime to "wrongfully introduce" illegal drugs into a military installation. The prosecution did not prove the defendant knew he was entering a military installation, but contended that knowledge was not required, citing the schoolyard cases discussed above. The court of military appeals disagreed, finding that while Congress intended strict liability in some federal statutes, such as the schoolyard drug-free zone statute, by adding the requirement of "wrongful" to 10 U.S.C.A. § 911, 912(a), Congress intended to make knowledge an element of the offense. The court thus held the statute applied only to those who knew they were introducing illegal drugs to a military installation.

Statutes can also dispense with the requirement of scienter as applied to an element of an offense. In such a case, with respect to that element the statute becomes one of "strict liability" (discussed more fully below). An example of such a statute is

 YOU BE THE JUDGE

Assume you are the district court judge in the trial of Don Defendant. Don has been charged with two counts of violations of federal statutes: (1) Violation of 18 U.S.C. § 39 (A) (a), and (2) Violation of 18 U.S.C. § 32(a) (5). In pertinent part, those statutes state as follows:

Section 39(A) (a): "Whoever knowingly aims the beam of a laser pointer at an aircraft, . . ." violates the statute.
Section 32(a) (5): Any person who "interferes with or disables, with intent to endanger the safety of any person or in a reckless disregard for human life, anyone engaged in the authorized operation . . ." of any aircraft violates the statute.

The facts are not in dispute. Don was in his back yard playing with his new laser pointer. Don did not know how high the pointer would project the laser beam, so he pointed it at a commercial airplane flying high overhead. The pilot of the airplane radioed local police, informing them her cockpit had been illuminated by a laser beam. Police traced the beam to Don, who admitted he was pointing the laser at the airplane.

To convict him under section 39 (A) (a) Don contends the prosecution must prove he knew his laser could hit the aircraft; the prosecution agrees Dan lacked such knowledge. The prosecution contends the only thing Don needed to know is that it was an aircraft at which he was pointing his laser.

To convict him under section 32 (a) (5) Don contends the prosecution must prove he knew the laser pointer would hit the airplane and endanger the pilot. The prosecution contends all it needed to prove was that Don intentionally pointed the laser at the aircraft.

***What is your decision on these arguments?* See United States v. Rodriguez, 790 F.3d 951 (9th Cir. 2015),** *and* **United States v. Smith,** *756 F.3d 1070 (8th Cir. 2014),* **cert denied 135 S. Ct. 948 (2015)**

the federal assault statute, 18 U.S.C.A. § 111, which makes it an offense to "forcibly assault" a federal officer. In *Feola v. United States*[15] the U.S. Supreme Court held that the prosecution need not prove the defendant had knowledge the victim was a federal officer. All the statute required was proof of the intent to assault, not the intent to assault a federal officer, the Court held.

The "Willful Blindness" Rule

If a criminal statute has a scienter requirement, such as knowledge of facts that are elements of the crime, when does lack of such knowledge provide a defense? May a defendant avoid criminal liability by ignoring the facts? Cases where defendants have raised this lack of knowledge as a defense have resulted in the "willful blindness" rule, sometimes called the "ostrich instruction." Under this rule, the trial judge can instruct the jury to find "knowledge" if it finds the defendant deliberately avoided learning the facts, much like the mythical ostrich burying its head in the ground to avoid danger. (They really don't do that!)

The U. S. Supreme Court has held that under that rule, for willful blindness to serve as a substitute for actual knowledge "(1) the defendant must subjectively believe that there is a high probability that a fact exists and (2) the defendant must take deliberate actions to avoid learning of that fact." *Global Tech Appliances v. SEB S.A.*, 131 S. Ct. 2060, 2070 (2011) the Court noted that such a formulation of the willful blindness rule adequately separates it from the lesser mental states of recklessness or negligence.

An example of willful blindness is the actions of the defendant in *United States v. Hansen*, 791 F.3d 863 (8th Cir. 2015). There, Hansen, the general partner of a hedge fund, made representations about the fund to investors that turned out to be untrue, resulting in losses of millions of dollars to the investors. Hansen was charged with various mail and wire fraud crimes (see Chapter 15) under federal law, all of which require knowledge of the fraud for conviction. Hansen said he lacked such knowledge. However, the evidence showed he was aware reports he was receiving from subordinates did not accurately show the hedge fund's assets, but he repeatedly refused to accept information or reports that would have disclosed the true state of those assets. The court confirmed his conviction for mail and other frauds and his sentence of 108 months in prison and fines of 17 million dollars.

The court in *United States v. Macias*, 786 F.3d 1060 (7th Cir. 2015) concluded the "ostrich instruction" should not have been given in that case. There, the defendant, a resident of Mexico, had a bus company that moved legal immigrants from Mexico to the U.S. He was approached by another person and asked to use his buses to move money from the U.S. to Mexico. The defendant was not told, nor did he ask, where the money originated. In fact, the money was from sales of illegal drugs, and the defendant was charged with conspiracy to distribute illegal drugs. (Conspiring to move the money from illegal drug sales would usually make the conspirator liable for the drug crimes as well. See Chapter 4.)

The defendant argued he did not know the money he carried was from illegal drug sales. The prosecution argued that the defendant should have known the amount of money involved came from illegal activities, and he should have made an attempt to discover the source. The trial court agreed, and gave the willful blindness "ostrich" instruction. The jury convicted the defendant, and he was sentenced to 25 years in prison on that charge. (The defendant did not appeal his conviction for conducting an unlicensed money-transmitting business in violation of 18 U.S.C. § 1960.)

On appeal the court held the instruction should not have been given. The evidence did not show the defendant took deliberate steps to avoid learning about the drug sales, the court said. Rather, the court said, based on the "ostrich" instruction the jury might have convicted him because "he wasn't curious enough to discover the source of the illegal funds." Suppressing curiosity is not the same as deliberate avoidance of the facts, the court held, and reversed the conspiracy conviction.

The Motive for Committing a Crime

Intent and *motive* are sometimes thought of as being one and the same. However, the law contains a clear distinction between the two. **Intent** is the mental purpose or design to commit a specific act (or omission), whereas **motive** is the cause, inducement, or reason why an act is committed.

Intent The mental purpose or design to commit a specific act (or omission).

Motive The cause, inducement, or reason why an act is committed.

Intent is an essential element of many crimes and must be proved beyond reasonable doubt when required. Motive is seldom made an essential element required for a criminal conviction. However, motive evidence can be used by the prosecution as an aid in obtaining a conviction or to rebut a defense offered by a defendant. For example, in the 2012 case of *State v. Laswell*,[16] the Arkansas Supreme Court held evidence that the defendant had expressed to a witness his desire to "live the thug life" was admissible to show the defendant's motive in robbing and killing the victim, and also to rebut the defendant's claim that he had no intent to rob the victim when he entered the victim's residence.

STRICT LIABILITY CRIMES

In enacting statutes to enforce rules having to do with public safety—such as traffic, liquor, purity of food, hunting, and narcotics offenses—modern legislative bodies often choose not to create "true" crimes, but rather to enact statutes that do not require any proof of *mens rea*. In these areas, the legislature's interest in promoting public safety justifies strict regulation of acts that threaten that public safety. In such cases, the statute may dispense with the need to prove a defendant was aware his or her actions violated the statute or regulation. These statutory crimes are usually called **strict liability crimes**. Except for narcotics offenses, the penalties for strict liability offenses are usually lighter than those for "true" crimes. The offenders are often not considered "criminals" in the full sense of the word, and the state is not required to carry the burden of proving criminal intent or other mental fault. The defendant is liable based only on the acts taken, regardless of his or her state of mind at the time of the acts.

Strict liability crime Crime that does not require proof of the mental element essential to true crimes.

The motor vehicle codes, hunting regulations, and food and liquor laws of most states contain strict liability statutes that require no showing of any particular mental intent. Thus, a bartender cannot ordinarily use as a defense the fact that the person to whom he sold liquor looked 22 when in fact the person was only 17; the driver of an overweight truck cannot argue that the company scales were faulty; nor can an adult male, in most states, argue that he did not know the age of the 15-year-old girl with whom he had sexual intercourse.

In referring to strict liability crimes in these areas, the U.S. Supreme Court pointed out that "Congress has rendered criminal a type of conduct that a reasonable person

ESSENTIAL ELEMENTS OF A TRUE CRIME

To obtain a conviction, the state must prove the following essential elements when charging a *true crime*:

- *The act element:* The forbidden act (or failure to act).
- *The mental element:* The state of mind required for the crime (the guilty mind); usually proven by use of inferences drawn from the acts of the defendant.
- *The harm element:* The wrong done (killing, physical injury, property damage, loss, and so on). Note that not all crimes have a harmful result element. For example, vehicular homicide requires proof that a person was killed; by contrast, drunk driving does not require proof of any harmful result be proven.
- *The cause element:* The harm done was the natural and probable result of the wrongful act.

Some crimes require proof of additional essential elements, such as scienter and possession (actual or constructive).

should know is subject to stringent public regulation and may seriously threaten the community's health or safety."[17]

The following list shows laws that commonly have strict liability terms:

Firearms	Unregistered hand grenades
	Unregistered machine guns
	The offense of carrying a concealed weapon
Motor vehicle safety laws	Defective headlight
	Running a red light
Intoxicating liquor or beer	Sale to underage person
Drug-related deaths	A number of states have enacted so-called Len Bias laws that make people who illegally manufacture, distribute, or dispense illegal drugs strictly liable for drug-related deaths.
Public health laws	Corporation officers can be convicted of Federal Food and Drug Act violations even when "consciousness of wrongdoing [is] totally wanting."
Other laws	Prior to discharge from service, an Air Force colonel negotiated for a civilian job and was involved in contract negotiations that violated the laws against taking government action while having conflicting financial interest.

In the case of federal criminal statutes, the U.S. Supreme Court has stated that strict liability crimes are not preferred and that Congress must make it clear if it intends to eliminate the *mens rea* requirement from a criminal statute. For example, in *Staples v. United States*[18] the Court held that in a prosecution under the National Firearms Act (26 U.S.C. § 5801), which requires registration of automatic weapons that meet the definition of "firearms" under the act, the prosecution must prove that a defendant knew the weapon he or she possessed constituted a firearm under the act. The defendant was in possession of an automatic rifle, which qualified as a firearm that must be registered under the act.

The prosecution argued that because the statute stated simply that it was a crime to possess or receive a firearm that was not registered, the prosecution did not have to prove the defendant knew the weapon in his possession qualified as a firearm under the act. The Supreme Court disagreed. It held that where the act—possession of a rifle—was not clearly dangerous, the statute should be construed as requiring that the defendant know the weapon in his possession was one that must be registered. The Court distinguished cases involving firearms like hand grenades, on the basis that any person would know that a grenade was something inherently dangerous and liable to be the subject of regulations. That is not the case, the Court reasoned, for more standard weapons.

The maxim "ignorance of the law is no excuse" is generally applicable to most crimes. The U.S. Supreme Court has said that unless a statute provides otherwise, the use of a term such as "knowingly" in a statute refers only to knowledge of facts, not knowledge that conduct is illegal.[19]

In strict liability crimes, which often involve conduct that is not inherently "bad" or wrongful, that maxim may not always be applicable, and knowledge that an act is unlawful may be an element of the crime. This was the case in *Liparota v. United States*.[20] There the U.S. Supreme Court held that for a defendant to be convicted under 7 U.S.C.A. § 2024(b)(l) for the unlawful use of food stamps, the prosecution must prove the defendant knew that his use of food stamps was not authorized under the statute.

The result in *Liparota* is not the norm.[21] More common is the result in the 2012 case of *United States v. Zhou*.[22] There a research assistant at U.C.L.A. Health Systems accessed patients' (mainly celebrities') health records after he had been terminated from employment, and thus was not authorized to access those records. There was no evidence the defendant intended to use or sell the records in any manner. He was convicted of a violation of the federal Health Insurance Portability and Accountability Act (HIPAA), which makes it a crime for a person "who knowingly and in violation" of HIPAA accesses patient health information.

The defendant appealed, contending the prosecution failed to prove he "knew" his actions violated the HIPAA statute. The court rejected that argument, holding that the only knowledge required under the statute was knowledge the defendant was obtaining individual patient health records.

Strict Liability Laws That Seek to Protect Children

The age of a minor is an essential element of such crimes as SIWAC (sexual intercourse with a child), contributing to the delinquency of a child, violating liquor laws or child pornography laws, and giving or selling a minor a pistol, drugs, cigarettes, and so on. Such laws seek to protect children. To provide further protection to children, many states take away the defense of "mistake of age" from some or all of the offenses that seek to protect children. When this defense is taken away, defendants cannot argue that they made an honest mistake about the age of a child. (See Chapter 7 for a discussion of the defenses of honest mistake of law or fact.)

Stockbyte/Getty Images

If the young people shown here are not old enough to be drinking alcoholic beverages under the state laws setting the minimum drinking age, the bar or store that sold them the alcohol could be criminally liable under the state underage drinking laws, even if the bar did not know the young people were underage and even if the young people presented false identification showing them to be of drinking age. Underage drinking laws are examples of strict liability laws, which have no requirement that the person charged with violation of the law possess any particular mental state.

By taking away the defense of honest mistake as to the age of a child, the state makes the offense a strict liability offense, and defendants can be proved guilty by showing only that they committed the forbidden act.

The "Honest Mistake" Defense   Some states have passed statutes that make a "mistake of age" defense available to a defendant who is charged with sexual conduct with a child under the legal age (usually around 18), but above a certain age. Pennsylvania, as an example, has such a statute, 18 Pa.C.S.A. § 3102. It provides for a mistake of age defense if the child victim is over the age of 14.

The federal statutes aimed at protecting children from sexual abuse have varied responses to the mistake of age defense. The aggravated sexual abuse law, 18 U.S.C. § 2241 (c) & (d), makes it a crime to have sex with a child under 12 or, under specified circumstance, under the age of 16. It states that in the prosecution for sexual abuse of a child the prosecution "need not prove that the defendant knew [the victim] had not attained the age of 12 years." The language of the statute suggests that the mistake of age defense might be available if the age of the child is between 12 and 16; the statute requires a "knowing" violation, and thus a defendant could contend that it must be shown the defendant knew the age of a victim who is over 12 years of age.

However, it seems more likely a court would interpret "knowingly" in the statute to refer only to the sexual act, not the victim's age.

A related federal statute that addresses sexual abuse against children, 18 U.S.C. § 2243 (c), specifically states that a reasonable belief that the "other person" was age 16 or older is a defense under the statute. This is a defense that the defendant must prove; the statute states the prosecution need not prove the age of the "other person." 18 U.S.C. § 2243 (d).

The federal Sex Trafficking of Children statute, 18 U.S.C. § 1591, is aimed at those who exploit children under 18 for sexual commercial purposes. It has a limited mistake of age defense. While the statute generally requires proof that a defendant "knowingly" (and for certain acts, in reckless disregard of the child's age) violated its terms, section 1591 (c) states that if the defendant had a "reasonable opportunity to observe the person" being exploited, the prosecution need not prove the defendant had knowledge the exploited person was under 18 years of age. Thus, while a mistake of age defense might be available to some defendants under the statute, it will not be available to those who had an opportunity to observe the children. See *United States v. Robinson*, 702 F.3d 22 (2nd Cir. 2012), *cert denied* 133 S. Ct. 1481 (2013).

PROXIMATE CAUSE OR CAUSATION

The material elements of crimes include conduct that is forbidden or required, and often the mental state existing at the time of the forbidden act or omission. In some crimes the result (the harm done or the wrong that occurs) of the conduct can also be a material element that must be proved by the prosecution.

In these crimes, the state must prove that the defendant's wrongful act or omission was the cause of the harm that resulted. In many cases this is an easy task. The harm to the victim could occur immediately, such as a bloody nose resulting from a blow to the face or death from being shot at point-blank range. In other instances, making the causal connection between the prohibited conduct and the harmful result of that conduct can be more difficult. This can be the case in homicide prosecutions, where the prosecution must prove the prohibited acts caused the resulting death. These causation problems are resolved by use of the **proximate cause** doctrine.

proximate cause The ordinary and probable cause of a result.

Causation problems in homicide crimes can occur when a substantial time gap exists between the criminal acts and the victim's death, or other factors contribute to the death. In these cases, the state must prove beyond a reasonable doubt that the unlawful and wrongful act of the defendant was the proximate cause of the death that resulted. The following cases illustrate court rulings in which the victim's death did not occur immediately or involved other factors that contributed to that death:

- In the 2010 case of *People v. Amigon*[23] the Illinois Supreme Court affirmed a murder conviction where the victim died 5 years after being shot by the defendant. The shooting caused the victim to be paralyzed from the shoulders down, and 5 years later he died from bacterial pneumonia, a condition common in paralyzed victims. The court said the pneumonia was an ordinary, probable result of the defendant's wrongful acts.
- In the 2011 case of *State v. Fox*[24] the Iowa Court of Appeals upheld a conviction of motor vehicle homicide where the victim chose to end life-support systems.

"PROXIMATE CAUSE" AND "CAUSE-IN-FACT"

Both the civil and criminal laws distinguish between "cause-in-fact" causation and "proximate cause." "Cause-in-fact" causation means the result would not have happened "but for" the prohibited conduct. Proximate cause (sometimes called "legal cause") refers to the ordinary and probable consequences that follow from actions.

EXAMPLE: A slashes B's tires, stranding B on a highway. While B is waiting for help, C comes along and kills B. A's act of slashing B's tires is the cause-in-fact of B's death, because "but for" that act B would not have been stranded and subsequently killed by C. However, under the proximate cause doctrine, A is the legal cause of B's death only if B's death was the ordinary and probable result of A's action. Here, the actions of C would likely be called an "intervening" or "superseding" cause, and not the ordinary consequence of slashing a car's tires.

The victim was paralyzed in an auto accident caused by defendant while defendant was intoxicated. After several days on life-support systems, the victim, who could communicate only by blinking his eyes, asked to have the life-support systems removed. They were, and he died at once. The court said the accident was the proximate cause of the death because the decision to terminate life support was an ordinary and foreseeable consequence of the accident.

- The court in the 2002 case of *State v. Kirby*[25] affirmed a conviction of second-degree murder where the victim of a terrible beating died while receiving medical treatment from personnel who did not discover damage to some of the victim's internal organs. The court said the beating was the proximate cause of the death because ordinary negligence of medical personnel treating a victim is not a superseding cause. Only gross negligence acts as a superseding cause.

The proximity between the distribution of illegal drugs such as cocaine or heroin and drug overdose deaths has led in to the enactment in some states of criminal statutes making the person who distributed the illegal drugs responsible for the resulting overdose death. For example, section 782.04(l)(a)(3) of the Florida Statutes (2001) states that a person who distributes illegal drugs that cause death by overdose of the drugs is guilty of first-degree murder. In *Armuller v. State*[27] a drug distributor convicted of murder under this statute contended his actions were not the proximate cause of the overdose death because he sold the drugs (heroin) to friends of the victim, who then helped the victim to inject the drug. The court rejected his "intervening cause" argument, holding that the defendant initiated the distribution of the heroin, and that was sufficient under the statute to satisfy the causation requirement.

The Ancient Year-and-a-Day Murder Rule

The response by the common law to a significant lapse of time between the criminal act and the victim's death was the "year and a day" rule. Under this rule, death of the victim must occur within a year and a day of the criminal act in order to be the "cause" of the death. The rule goes back hundreds of years, perhaps as early as the

MULTIPLE CAUSES OF DEATH IN HOMICIDE PROSECUTIONS

When a victim dies and there can be shown multiple causes of that death, application of the "but for" cause-in-fact test can be difficult in theory.

EXAMPLE: A stabs V, inflicting a non-mortal wound that by itself would not cause V's death. Acting independently, B shoots V in the leg, causing a similar non-mortal wound. However, the two wounds combined cause V's death. Viewed independently, in theory neither A nor B was the "but for" cause of V's death, since V would not have died as a result of either independent wound.

EXAMPLE: A stabs V, causing a mortal wound that will cause V's death. Before V dies, B independently shoots V in the head, which also inflicts a mortal wound from which V will die whether or not A had stabbed him. In theory, neither A nor B is the "but for" cause of V's death, since it cannot be said with respect to either A or B that V would not have died "but for" their actions.

EXAMPLE: A stabs V, inflicting a mortal wound that will cause V's death in 30 minutes. Before that time ends, B shoots V in the leg, inflicting a non-mortal wound. The increased bleeding from B's wound causes V to die 20 minutes faster. While A's mortal wound is the "but for" cause of V's death, in theory B's actions are not.

Courts usually resolve these multiple "but for" causation problems as follows:

- **Joint action.** In many of these kinds of cases the defendants act in concert, and thus the actions of each are attributed to the other, making the "but for" applicable to each of them.
- **Concurrent causes.** In the first example, A and B, though acting independently, are concurrent causes of V's death, since V would not have died "but for" the combined actions of A and B. Both can be charged with murder.
- **Substantial factor.** In the second example, courts would hold that A and B are each the "but for" cause of V's death because their actions were each a substantial factor in that death. Both can be charged with murder.
- **Accelerated cause.** In the third example, courts would hold B also as the "but for" cause of V's death, because that death occurred earlier than it would have but for B's actions.[26] Both can be charged with murder.

1300's, when medical science was primitive.[28] Before the American Revolutionary War, Sir William Blackstone described the rule as follows: "In order . . . to make the killing murder, it is requisite that the party die within a year and a day after the stroke (blow) received, or cause of death administered; in the computation of which the whole day upon which the hurt was done shall be reckoned the first."[29]

When the colonies became states, they all adopted the common law of England, which included the year and a day rule. Because of changes in medical science, making it easier to show the relationship between an injury and a death that occurs much later, many, perhaps most, states, either by statute[30] or by court decision,[31] have abandoned the year and a day rule. A few courts have rejected requests by defendants to judicially abrogate the rule, stating that is a legislative function. It appears Alabama still follows the common law rule: In *Ex parte Key*,[32] the Alabama Supreme Court held that the rule was still in effect until the legislature abolishes the rule.

CASES OF UNINTENDED HARM RESULTING FROM A MISDEMEANOR OR OTHER MINOR OFFENSE

In the following cases the defendants were convicted of manslaughter or negligent homicide based on unintended deaths that occurred during or following the defendants' unlawful actions. Courts there held that the defendants' unlawful actions were the cause of the death of the victims.

- *Kin Yiu Cheung v. Com., 753 S.E.2d 854 (Va. App. 2014).* Defendant recklessly drove a passenger bus into a ditch, killing four passengers. Involuntary manslaughter convictions upheld.

- *State v. Rodriguez*, 804 N.W.2d 844 (Iowa 2011). Defendant permitted intoxicated brother to drive a car after brothers fled from a gas station without paying for gas. Brother hit motorcycle, killing driver. Conviction for vehicular homicide affirmed.

- *State v. Rivera*, 291 P.3d 512 (Kan. App. 2012). Mother left 4-year-old child with boyfriend, despite her knowledge that boyfriend abused the child. The child died after boyfriend's abuse, and mother was charged with involuntary manslaughter based on a death that occurred while mother was violating child endangerment statute, a misdemeanor. Conviction for involuntary manslaughter upheld.

- *State v. Small*, 100 So3d 797 (La. 2012). Mother left 6-year-old child in apartment while she went out drinking. Accidental fire started, killing the child. Conviction for negligent homicide affirmed.

In those states that abolished the rule by judicial decision, defendants have on occasion contended that retroactive application of such a change in the law violates the ex post facto clause. In *Rogers v. Tennessee*, 532 U.S. 451 (2001) the U.S. Supreme Court held that because the ex post facto clause prohibits only legislative acts, retroactive application of judicial changes in the law violate due process only when they are unexpected or indefensible. It held retroactive abolition of the year and a day rule by the Tennessee Supreme Court did not violate due process because the rule was not a well-recognized rule in Tennessee.

California has developed a hybrid version of the rule: Cal. Penal Code § 194 (West 2007) states that there is a rebuttable presumption that a death that occurs more than three years after an injury was not caused by the injury. The state must then bear the burden of proving that causation.

POSSESSION ALONE AS A CRIME

All states make the possession of certain objects a criminal offense. Examples of such crimes are possession of illegal drugs, carrying a concealed weapon, possession of an instrument of a crime, possession of stolen property (vehicles, credit cards, and so on), and possession of graffiti instruments (in some cities and states). The following jury instruction defining *possession* is used in federal courts:

[T]he law recognizes different kinds of possession. A person may have actual possession or constructive powssession. . . . A person who has direct physical control of something on or around his person is then in actual possession of it.

A person who is not in actual possession but who has both the power and the intention to later take control over something . . . is in constructive possession of it. . . . Whenever the word "possession" has been used in these instructions it includes actual as well as constructive possession.[33]

Because of public safety, virtually all states forbid carrying an unauthorized concealed weapon (see Chapter 9). *Carrying* requires a showing of actual possession. If a pistol is in the trunk of the car and not within the immediate reach and control of a person, it is not within actual possession.

Illegal drugs could be in actual possession of a defendant, or a defendant could have constructive possession of the drugs. The term *constructive possession* is used to indicate control over property and objects that the defendant does not have in actual possession. The object may be in his or her car parked two blocks away, in a home or office desk drawer, or in a suitcase stored somewhere for which he or she has a baggage claim check or key. Constructive possession would not be sufficient to sustain a conviction for carrying a concealed weapon, as a showing of actual possession is necessary. However, constructive possession would sustain a conviction for the possession of contraband, such as narcotics.

The mental element that must be proved in possession offenses is generally that of intention or "knowledge." These mental elements are usually easy to prove, because a person with a loaded revolver or a bag of marijuana in his pocket cannot argue convincingly that he did not know that the contraband was in his actual possession. The intent to possess, then, is a state of mind existing at the time the person commits the offense. In seeking to determine the state of mind of the alleged offender in order to decide whether an intent existed, the jury or the court may base its decision on the defendant's acts, conduct, and other inferences that can be reasonably deduced from all the circumstances.

Possession is one of the rights of ownership of property. Criminal statutes do not require that ownership be proved. A person who possesses heroin may or may not be the owner of the heroin. Possession of personal property is presumptive evidence of ownership, and possession accompanied by the exercise of complete acts of ownership for a considerable time is strong evidence of ownership. In the absence of evidence showing otherwise, the presence of objects and articles in a vehicle, dwelling, or business place leads to a strong inference that they are in the constructive possession of the person controlling the vehicle, dwelling, or business place. Therefore, heroin found in an apartment searched under the authority of a search warrant is in the constructive possession of the person controlling and occupying the apartment, unless the person can show otherwise (also see Chapter 16 on drug abuse).

The Possession of Illegal Contraband Inference

A strong inference of possession of illegal contraband (such as cocaine or an illegal gun) can be made when the contraband is found (1) under the front seat of a car driven by the owner of the vehicle, (2) in the home of a person who is the sole occupant of the house or apartment, or (3) in other situations in which a reasonable inference of possession can be drawn.

However, unless a statute has eliminated the scienter requirement and made possession a strict liability offense, some knowledge of the nature of the things possessed

WHEN IS A STOLEN GUN POSSESSED?

On November 29, 2009 Maurice Clemmons shot and killed four police officers in a Lakewood, Washington, coffee shop. Clemmons stole the police pistol from the fourth officer he killed, but only after the officer had shot and wounded Clemmons. Clemmons then went to a friend's house, Eddie Davis, and after telling him he had killed four police officers asked to be driven to another friend's house. Davis agreed, and drove Clemmons to the house. There, Clemmons received fresh clothes and some medical aid from the friend. While at the house, the friend placed the stolen gun in a shopping bag. When Davis and Clemmons left the house, Clemmons asked, "Where is the gun?" Davis told Clemmons it was in the shopping bag, and Davis handed him the bag. On December 1, 2009, Clemmons was killed by a Seattle police officer as he attempted to draw the stolen gun on the officer.

Davis was charged with and convicted of rendering criminal assistance, and possession of a stolen gun. Davis appealed the stolen gun conviction, contending insufficient evidence existed to prove he possessed the stolen gun. What do you see as the arguments for either side on the possession conviction? If you find disagreement with others on those arguments, note that the Washington Supreme Court did as well. See *State v. Davis*, 340 P.3d 820 (Wash. 2014).

must be shown. The U.S. Supreme Court in *United States v. X-Citement Video, Inc.*[34] used the following examples to illustrate this requirement, noting that innocent persons could be charged with possession without some knowledge requirement:

- A Federal Express courier delivers a box containing the illegal contraband.
- A new resident of an apartment receives mail (containing contraband) for the prior resident and stores the mail unopened.
- A retail druggist returns an uninspected roll of developed film to a customer, unaware that the film contains illegal sexually explicit child photographs.

In the 2013 case of *Commonwealth v. Romero*[35] the Massachusetts Supreme Judicial Court reversed a conviction for carrying a firearm without a permit. The defendant was the driver of a car carrying a passenger, who had placed a gun in his lap after the car was stopped for a traffic violation. The lower courts had held that the driver had "constructive possession" of the gun because of his proximity to the gun and his operation of the car. The Supreme Judicial Court reversed, holding that the state must prove the defendant exercised some control over the gun beyond the simple fact he owned and operated the car in which the passenger possessed the gun. Drivers are not strictly liable for all contraband brought into their cars, the court said.

THE USE OF PRESUMPTIONS AND INFERENCES IN CRIMINAL LAW

Presumptions and inferences have long been hailed as a "staple of our adversary system of fact-finding."[36] Presumptions and inferences enable a fact finder to conclude that because some facts have been proved (usually called *predicate facts*), other facts may be inferred or presumed to be true. For example, if it is proved that a contractor failed to order materials needed to perform a home repair contract, it might logically be presumed or inferred that the contractor never intended to perform the home improvement contract.

In criminal prosecutions, use of presumptions and inferences can present due process problems, if the jury is permitted or required to find facts necessary to a conviction based only on inferences or presumptions drawn on other facts. Because the Due Process Clause requires the prosecution to prove every element of a crime beyond a reasonable doubt, the use of inferences or presumptions can violate that clause if the facts establishing the element of the crime are the result of a presumption or inference.

The Supreme Court of the United States has generally permitted the use of permissive inferences and permissive presumptions, because the fact finder need not reach the presumed conclusion. As a result, the prosecution continues to bear the burden of proof beyond a reasonable doubt, and the Due Process Clause is not violated. However, mandatory presumptions have been treated differently. Mandatory presumptions, generally referred to as *irrebuttable* or *conclusive* presumptions, can be unconstitutional under the Due Process Clause because such a presumption allows the prosecution to avoid proving an element of the crime charged.[37]

Some presumptions direct the fact finder to reach conclusions in favor of the defendant. The best-known presumption, and probably the oldest, is the presumption of innocence until proven guilty. The presumption of innocence until proven guilty is a *rebuttable* presumption, which means it may be overcome by evidence proving otherwise. The presumption of innocence may be overcome by evidence showing that a defendant is guilty beyond a reasonable doubt.

Sometimes a conclusive presumption is stated as a rule of substantive law that cannot be overcome with evidence showing otherwise. Of the few conclusive presumptions of this type, perhaps the best known is the rule of law that a person under a certain minimum age, usually 7 years, has not reached the age of reason and therefore is not capable of committing a crime. (Infancy as a limit on criminal responsibility is discussed more fully in Chapter 4.)

Figure 3.2 illustrates the different elements that may be essential to the proof of a crime.

Functions of Presumptions and Inferences

Both presumptions and inferences play an important role in trials. Presumptions are created to permit orderly civil and criminal trials.[38] The Supreme Court of Pennsylvania and the Supreme Court of Indiana defined the function and legal significance of presumptions as follows:

> A presumption of law is not evidence nor should it be weighed by the fact finder as though it had evidentiary value. Rather, a presumption is a rule of law enabling the party in whose favor it operates to take his case to the jury without presenting evidence of the fact presumed. It serves as a challenge for proof and indicates the party from whom such proof must be forthcoming. When the opponent of the presumption has met the burden of production thus imposed, however, the office of the presumption has been performed; the presumption is of no further effect and drops from the case.[39]

FIGURE 3.2 Essential Elements of Crimes

State statutes can require as essential elements:
– proof of the harm done (death, etc.)
– proof of the age of the victim
– other essential elements required by statute

Possession (either actual or constructive) can be an essential element of a crime.

Scienter can be made an essential element of a crime.

Actus reus (a forbidden act or omission) is an essential element of all crimes.

Mens rea (the guilty mind) can be made an essential element of a crime.

Motive is rarely made an essential element of a crime, but is always admissible evidence and may be used by the state to help prove the guilty mind requirement of many crimes.

presumption A rule of law that the trier of fact shall assume the existence of a state of facts without evidence being produced. Presumptions are either rebuttable or irrebuttable.

A **presumption** is an assumption that the law expressly directs that the trier of fact (jury or judge) make. Because most presumptions may be disputed, they may be outweighed or overcome with evidence showing otherwise. Unless a presumption is overcome with other evidence, judges and jurors *must* accept the presumption as true. It is this aspect of presumptions that creates due process problems in criminal cases, since placing the duty on a defendant to overcome a presumed fact can operate to relieve the prosecution from its duty to prove every element of a crime beyond a reasonable doubt.

The purpose of civil and criminal trials is to determine the truth of the issues presented to the fact finder. Criminal trials commence with the presumption that the defendant is innocent. To overcome this presumption, the state must present evidence proving the guilt of the defendant beyond a reasonable doubt in the minds of the jury. Each essential element of the crime charged must be proved beyond a reasonable doubt.

inference A conclusion or deduction that a jury or judge may draw from a fact or a group of facts presented to them.

An **inference** is a conclusion or deduction that juries or judges *may* draw from a fact or a group of facts presented to them. Fact finders must use good common sense and their knowledge of everyday life. In their reasoning process, juries and judges must use inferences. A common inference used in criminal trials is that persons intend (desire) the natural and probable consequences of their deliberate acts. The following example illustrates this.

EXAMPLE	X is charged with either attempted assault with a deadly weapon or attempted murder. X is a strong 30-year-old man who did the following:

Conduct of X	Inferences That Can Logically Be Drawn from X's Conduct
Reliable witnesses testify that X repeatedly attempted to hit Y on or about Y's head with a baseball bat. Bystanders stopped X. A rolled-up newspaper to strike at Y.	Fact finders can easily conclude that a baseball bat is a deadly weapon in the hands of a strong man who exhibited an intent to kill or seriously injure. Fact finders cannot logically conclude that a rolled-up newspaper is a deadly weapon or that the defendant exhibited intent to kill; therefore, neither charge could stand.

The Presumption That All Persons Are Sane, Normal, and Competent

An important presumption is that all adults are sane, normal, and competent. Thus, adult witnesses in civil and criminal cases are assumed to be sane, normal, and competent. However, attorneys in civil or criminal proceedings may challenge this presumption if necessary, and show otherwise. Furthermore, before young children can testify, the trial judge questions them (*voir dire*) and then rules as to whether they meet these requirements of a witness.

California statutes, like those of most states, provide that defendants in criminal cases are presumed to be competent to stand trial. Thus, in most states a defense lawyer challenging this presumption has the burden of coming forward with evidence to prove that a defendant is incompetent and cannot be tried. In a very few states, the prosecution must prove by "clear and credible evidence" that the defendant is competent. See, e.g., Wis. St. Ann., § 971.14(4)(b). The U.S. Supreme Court held in *Medina v. California*[40] that it was not a constitutional violation for a state to use the presumption of competency. The defendant in *Medina* was convicted of three murders committed during robberies and shooting sprees. The U.S. Supreme Court followed the ruling of the California Supreme Court in holding that California Penal Code Section 1369(f), which makes a defendant prove incompetence by a preponderance of the evidence, does not violate any right granted or protected by the U.S. Constitution. However, in *Cooper v. Oklahoma*,[41] the Court reversed a conviction because an

Oklahoma law required a defendant to prove incompetence by "clear and convincing" evidence, rather than the lesser standard of "preponderance of the evidence."

★★★
LEARNING OBJECTIVES SUMMARY

LO 1. Explain the meaning of and difference between *actus reus* and *mens rea*.
Actus reus describes the physical acts making up the crime, while *mens rea* refers to any mental requirement for conviction of the crime.

LO 2. Identify when a criminal statute includes a requirement of a specific intent.
Not all crimes require proof that a defendant had a specific intent to achieve a specific end. In some cases, all that is required is that the defendant intended to do the prohibited act, sometimes known as general intent.

LO 3. Write a simple criminal charge that does not have as an element a specific intent.
An example of a crime that does not require a specific intent is second-degree murder, which under many state statutes does not require that the defendant act with the specific intent to cause death.

LO 4. List the Model Penal Code degrees of culpability and their accompanying states.
The Model Penal Code, which some states have followed, lists the mental states for criminal liability as purposely, knowingly, recklessly, and negligently. If a statute requires a showing that the defendant acted purposely or knowingly, the defendant's mental state (intent or knowledge) is an element of the offense.

LO 5. Distinguish between motive and intent.

Motive is the reason a defendant took action; intent is simply the mental state leading to the action taken.

LO 6. Identify some of the similarities of strict liability crimes.
Strict liability crimes generally involve areas where a government has a strong interest in regulating conduct to promote public safety, such as food laws, or protect certain persons, such as school children.

LO 7. Explain why the year-and-a-day rule is a rule of proximate cause.
The year-and-a-day rule in murder cases, though no longer followed in many jurisdictions, is a rule of proximate causation that sets a limit on how far removed in time a death can be from acts causing harm to the victim and still be treated as a murder.

LO 8. Identify the relationship between use of presumptions in the prosecution's case and the Due Process Clause.
Since the Due Process Clause requires the prosecution to prove every element of an offense beyond a reasonable doubt, a presumption that operated to mandate a jury finding on an element of an offense without such proof would violate the Due Process Clause. A conclusive or mandatory presumption is one that may not be rebutted by the defendant.

LO 9. Explain why a conclusive presumption is prohibited.

KEY TERMS

reasonable doubt, p. 56
actus reus, p. 56
mens rea, p. 56
Model Penal Code (MPC), p. 57
concurrence, p. 57

specific intent, p. 60
scienter, p. 66
intent, p. 69
motive, p. 69
strict liability crime, p. 69

proximate cause, p. 73
presumption, p. 80
inference, p. 81

CASE ANALYSIS AND WRITING EXERCISES

1. Every state has a statute making it a crime to "cause" another person's death if the defendant was operating a vehicle while intoxicated. What exactly must the prosecution prove to make the causal connection between one element of the crime, intoxicated, and the victim's death? Is it enough to show (1) the defendant was driving the vehicle that struck the victim and (2) the defendant was intoxicated? Or does the prosecution have to show a causal connection between the intoxication and the death? What did the Supreme Court of Iowa decide was the answer to the causation question? Do you agree? See *State v. Adams*, 810 N.W.2d 365 (Iowa 2012). [For those interested in how the "ineffective assistance of counsel" issue was ultimately resolved, see *State v. Adams*, 2015 WL 2089646 (2015).]

2. It is a crime in most states to "possess burglary tools." What does "possession" require the state to prove? Do the tools have to be used in a burglary? Does the defendant in possession have to be convicted of burglary to be convicted of the possession charge? In *State v. Platt*, 154 So.3d 1200 (Fla. App. 2015) the defendant was convicted under the Florida burglary tools statute, 810.06 Fla. Stat. The jury did not find the defendant guilty of burglary, but did find him guilty of the possession charge. After the verdict, the trial judge granted the defendant's motion for acquittal on the possession charge, and the state appealed. Was the trial judge correct to overrule the jury verdict on the possession charge? Why or why not? [Note that the case was remanded to the trial court. When you study the defense of double jeopardy in Chapter 7, determine why the remand in *Platt* wasn't a case of double jeopardy.]

3. As we note in this chapter, at times failure to act can be a crime. Child abuse can go undetected and unpunished if only the victim is relied upon for reporting the abuse. Children are often incapable of understanding the need to tell others about such abuse. As a result, it is common to have statutes making certain persons who encounter children on a regular basis "mandated reporters." It is also common to make it a crime for a mandated reporter who learns, or even suspects, a child has been sexually abused to fail to report as mandated. An example of such a statute is Ark. Code Ann. § 12-18-201. High school teachers are typically mandated reporters. What did the high school teacher fail to do as a mandated reporter under Arkansas law in *Griffin v. State*, 454 S.W.3d 262 (Ark. App. 2015)? There, one teacher learned that another teacher had a sexual relationship with a 16-year-old student. She learned this after the student turned 18, and thus was no longer covered by the child abuse statutes. What was her argument that she did report the abuse in that case? What reason did she give for believing the facts she learned did not trigger her duty to report? Why were her arguments rejected? Do you think she was a "bad" person? Does that matter?

4. Under 26 U.S.C. § 5861(d) it is a crime to possess certain kinds of "unregistered" firearms, such as sawed-off shotguns or machine guns. The term includes "destructive devices," such as grenades or "flash bang" devices. The crime is thus being in possession of a covered firearm without registering that possession with the appropriate federal agency. In *United States v. Berres*, 777 F.3d 1083 (10th Cir. 2015) the defendant was convicted under this statute of carrying a flash bang device in his back pack. On appeal the defendant contended he could not be convicted for failure to register the device, because the registration statute did not permit him to register the device. Is that a good argument?

ENDNOTES

1. *Powell v. Texas*, 392 U.S. 514, 535, 88 S. Ct. 2145 (1968).

2. 287 P.3d 539 (Wash. 2012), *cert denied* 133 S.Ct. 991 (2012).

3. *Morissette v. United States*, 342 U.S. at 252.

4. 438 U.S. 422 (1978).

5. 444 U.S. 394, 404 (1980).

6. The Court noted in the *Bailey* case that the use of the general intent-specific intent distinction had "been the source of a good deal of confusion." 444 U.S.394 (1980).

7. See 22 *Corpus Juris Secundum Criminal Law,* Sections 30–36.

8. 512 F.2d 1281 (5th Cir. 1975).

9. 584 S.E.2d 138 (S.C. App. 2008).

10. *Fedd v. State*, 680 S.E.2d 453 (Ga. App. 2009). Most states have similar statutes requiring knowledge that the person assaulted is a police officer.

11. *People v. Overton*, 34 Cal. Rptr. 2d 232 (Cal. App. 1994).

12. See *State v. Herman*, 474 N.W.2d 906 (Wis. App. 1991), *review denied*, 477 N.W.2d 286 (Wis. 1991), interpreting a Wisconsin statute similar to the federal "schoolyard" statute, 21 U.S.C. § 860.

13. See *United States v. Harris*, 313 F.3d 1228 (10th Cir. 2002).

14. *65* M.J. 132 (2007).

15. 420 U.S. 671 (1975). Congress amended the assault statute after the *Feola* decision, which some lower federal courts have regarded as limiting some aspects of the *Feola* decision. However, the scienter part of the decision does not seem to have been changed.

16. 2012 WL 1630878 (Ark. 2012).

17. See pages 242–250 of LaFave and Scott, *Criminal Law,* 2nd ed. Belmont, CA: West/Wadsworth (1986).

18. 511 U.S. 600 (1994).

19. *Dixon v. United States*, 548 U.S. 1 (2006).

20. 471 U.S. 419 (1985).

21. Indeed, in *Bryon v. United States*, 524 U.S. 184 (1998) the Supreme Court indicated the result in *Liparota* was required by the way Congress phrased the statute.

22. 678 F.3d 1110 (9th Cir. 2012).

23. 940 N.E.2d 63 (Ill. 2010).

24. 810 N.W.2d 888 (Iowa App. 2011).

25. 39 P.3d 1 (Kan. 2002).

26. A good discussion of these causation issues can be found in *State v. Jackson*, 697 S.E.2d 757 (Ga. 2010).

27. 944 So. 2d 1137 (Fla. App. 2006), *rev denied* 956 So. 2d 455 (2007).

28. See *People v. Stevenson*, 416 Mich. 383, 331 N.W.2d 143 (1982).

29. Blackstone, *Commentaries,* 197.

30. See *e.g.,* Fla. Stat. § 782.035 (2007).

31. See *e.g., State v. Fairbanks,* 842 N.W.2d 297 (Minn. 2014).

32. See *Ex Parte Key*, 890 So.2d 1056 (Ala. 2003).

33. See *United States v. Winchester* (916 F.2d 601 (11th Cir. 1990)), having to do with people who cannot possess a firearm under the Federal Gun Control Act of 1968.

34. 115 S. Ct. 464, 467 (S. Ct. 1994).

35. 984 N.E.2d 853 (Mass. 2013).

36. *County Court v. Allen*, 442 U.S. 140 (1979).

37. *Sandstrom v. Montana*, 442 U.S. 510 (1979).

38. Because taxpayers have possession of their tax records, the burden of proof is on the taxpayers to prove the accuracy of their tax returns. Federal courts have held for many years that rulings of the commissioner of the Internal Revenue Service are presumed to be correct. See *Welch v. Helvering,* 290 U.S. Ill at 115 (1933). During the debate on the new federal tax code in 1998, changes were urged by members of Congress, and many writers predicted that this presumption and burden of proof would be changed in the new tax law. However, the 1998 Tax Reform Act modifies the old rules only slightly, and the presumption and burden of proof remain practically the same as they have been for many years.

39. *Commonwealth v. Vogel*, 440 Pa. 1, 17, 268 A.2d 89, 102 (1970); *Sumpter v. State*, 261 Ind. 471, 306 N.E.2d 95 (1974).

40. 505 U.S. 432 (1992).

41. 517 U.S. 348 (1996).

4

Criminal Liability

LEARNING OBJECTIVES

In this chapter we examine the manner in which criminal liability is assessed, in particular for liability based upon acts and the relationship of those acts to crimes. The learning objectives for this chapter are the following:

LO 1. Identify when conduct has crossed the line between thinking about committing a crime and attempting to commit a crime.

LO 2. Explain the function of and need for corroborating evidence in solicitation prosecutions.

LO 3. Identify the steps that must be taken before one can be guilty of a conspiracy.

LO 4. Explain when, if ever, impossibility of committing the completed crime is a defense to a charge of attempt.

LO 5. Identify the circumstances when abandonment of the criminal purpose can have an effect on liability for an attempt, or liability for criminal acts done in a conspiracy.

LO 6. Explain the rule for liability of one conspirator for actions of another.

LO 7. List the parties who can be treated as principals for purposes of criminal liability.

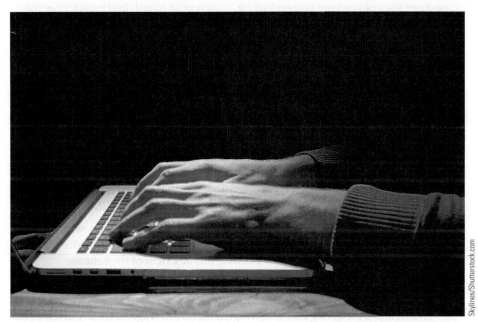

Yes, computers are everywhere. Unfortunately that includes use of the internet by adults soliciting children for illegal sexual contact. In this chapter, and in others that follow, we discuss the role of computers in crimes, in particular crimes against children

Ronald Everett was in a Clackamas County, Oregon, jail awaiting trial on charges he tried to run over a deputy sheriff with his car. In jail Everett met Piatt, a member of the Outsiders Motorcycle Club, who Everett believed was a club "enforcer." Everett asked Piatt to murder the deputy sheriff, once Piatt was released from jail. Instead, Piatt informed the police that Everett asked him to murder the deputy.

Still in jail, Everett discovered Piatt's actions. He then asked another inmate, Van Alstine, to tell Outsider members that Piatt had "ratted" him out, once Van Alstine was released from jail. Everett believed the Outsiders would act on that information by "taking care of" Piatt. Van Alstine did not go to the Outsiders upon his release. Instead he went to the police. As a result, Everett was charged with two counts of solicitation to commit aggravated murder under the Oregon solicitation statute, Ore. § 161.435 (1).

As you read the materials in this chapter, consider the charges against Everett. It is clear, is it not, that Everett can be convicted of solicitation based on his conversations with Piatt? Can he be convicted of solicitation based on his conversations with Van Alstine? Was he soliciting Van Alstine to commit a crime? What crime? See *State v. Everett*, 330 P.3d 22 (Ore. 2014). Read the Court's footnote 5: Did the lawyer for Everett make a strategic mistake?

Criminal laws have long recognized that a person's conduct prior to or leading up to a substantive crime is often by itself blameworthy, even if the substantive crime is not committed. The same is true of actions taken after a crime that in some way aid the criminal, or obstruct law enforcement officers in their efforts to identify and apprehend the criminal. This chapter discusses many of these crimes and the elements that must be proved in the prosecution of them. Crimes such as solicitation, conspiracy, and attempt can be committed and punished quite independently from prosecution and punishment of the crime that was the intended outcome.

We discuss many of the limitations on these crimes that have developed over the years, and continue to develop.

In some actions involving two people, such as an illegal drug transaction, the two parties may have earlier agreed between themselves that they would commit that crime. That agreement suggests they have also committed the crime of conspiracy, but as we will see, the Wharton rule prevents them from being convicted of that crime. We learn about this and other limiting doctrines in this chapter.

PRELIMINARY, ANTICIPATORY, AND INCHOATE CRIMES

Professor Wayne LaFave, in his treatise on criminal law, uses the following example to illustrate the varieties of criminal charges that might result from criminal behavior, with the nature of the charge depending on the extent of the behavior:

> Suppose A wants B to kill C. If A hires B to do so, and B does kill C, B is guilty of murder, and so is A, either as an accessory, or as a principal. If B tries to kill C, but fails, A and B are both guilty of attempted murder. If B agrees with A to kill C, but does not attempt the murder, A and B are guilty of conspiracy to commit murder. However, even where B refuses A's request to kill C, and thus cannot be liable for any crime, A can be liable for solicitation.[1]

In this chapter we examine the basis for criminal liability, including liability for the preliminary crimes illustrated in the example above. In prosecutions for preliminary crimes it is not required that the underlying criminal act occur; it is the planning or attempt to commit that crime that the law makes criminal.

Preliminary crimes are not always present when an underlying crime occurs, because not all crimes are planned in advance. Some crimes are committed impulsively, with the decision to commit the crime being made on the spur of the moment or almost simultaneously with the commission of the offense. Nor are all crimes completed. In some instances, the person who has carefully planned to commit a crime decides, for one reason or another, not to do so. Crimes are sometimes not completed because of events that prevent their completion. The problem in prosecuting preliminary crimes is determining when sufficient planning or attempt has occurred to justify the conclusion a crime has been committed.

In most situations, a person who has formulated the intent to commit a crime, but has taken no actions in furtherance of the crime, has not yet violated any law. He or she may even in some instances vocally express the intention to commit a crime without committing an offense. However, in some instances, such a person may be subject to arrest or to detention for expressing such intentions. One example we saw in Chapter 1 involved threats upon the life of the president of the United States.

It is possible for a person to commit a crime based on a statement of intention even though that person only intended a joke or hoax. For example, 18 U.S.C. § 35(b), the so-called Bomb Hoax statute, makes it a crime to make a false statement about the presence of a bomb in a civil aircraft. A person making such a statement can be convicted under the act, even if the person never intended to place a bomb on an aircraft, so long as the statement was made maliciously.[2]

The examples above illustrate areas where the simple statement of an intention is regarded as sufficiently dangerous or intrusive to justify criminal sanctions. They also demonstrate the need to prevent serious social harm before it occurs. To accomplish this goal, courts long ago created the three separate and distinct common law crimes of solicitation, conspiracy, and attempt. Although these offenses are crimes in themselves, each of these acts is **preliminary** or **anticipatory** to a more serious crime that the offender has in mind. These anticipatory crimes are commonly referred to as **inchoate crimes**.

In considering the preliminary offenses, the following questions always arise:

preliminary, anticipatory, and inchoate crimes
Criminal acts that lead to or are attempts to commit other crimes.

1. Where and when does non-criminal conduct become criminal conduct by a further act of the suspect?
2. Which of the preliminary offenses, if any, has the suspect committed?
3. When does the commission of the principal offense begin, so as to allow the state to charge either the preliminary offense or the principal offense?

Solicitation or Incitement to Commit a Crime[3]

By the early 1800s, English and American courts had recognized solicitation as a misdemeanor under the common law.[4] *Solicitation* may be defined as an attempt to get another person to commit a crime. It may also be described as an attempt to conspire to commit a crime. The solicitation does not have to be successful. The crime of **solicitation** or **incitement** (as it is called in England) is committed even if the person solicited refuses to cooperate and repudiates the proposal. It is also immaterial, in most instances, whether payment or reward is offered and whether it is accepted or refused. Evidence of the offer of payment or reward, however, can be important in proving solicitation.

solicitation or incitement crimes
Attempting to get another to commit a crime.

States commonly have both specific solicitation statutes—such as solicitation of prostitution or bribery—and general solicitation statutes applicable to other conduct. An example of a general solicitation statute is Wisconsin Statutes Annotated, Section 939.30, which states:

(1) Except as provided in sub. (2) and § 961.455, whoever, with intent that a felony be committed, advises another to commit that crime under circumstances that indicate unequivocally that he or she has the intent is guilty of a Class H felony.

Prosecutions under solicitation statutes require a showing that the defendant has done more than make a casual suggestion that a crime be committed. In many cases the defendant's intent is shown by eliciting incriminating statements that are overheard by the police. For example, in a case prosecuted under the Wisconsin statute cited above, a defendant was charged with solicitation to commit murder. She told a friend that she had hired a co-worker to kill her ex-boyfriend. The friend permitted a police officer to listen in on a telephone conversation with the defendant, where she repeated those statements. Her conviction was upheld based on the testimony of the friend and the police officer, even though the defendant subsequently told the "hit man" not to go through with the crime.[5]

Some state statutes have specific corroboration requirements in the general solicitation statutes. For example, the Texas Penal Code Annotated, Section 15.03(b), states in part that "A person may not be convicted under this section on the uncorroborated testimony of the person allegedly solicited . . ." The federal solicitation to commit a crime of violence statute, 18 U.S.C. § 373, requires evidence that is "strongly corroborative" of the accused's intent to solicit the other person to commit the underlying crime.

The following cases further illustrate the crime of solicitation:

- A prison inmate mailed letters from prison to a friend on the outside, urging him to murder a certain drug addict. The mail was intercepted by prison officials, and never reached the friend. The inmate was charged with solicitation under the Illinois general solicitation statute. He argued the crime of solicitation cannot occur if the communication never reaches the person being solicited. The Illinois Supreme Court agreed, but held the inmate was lawfully convicted of attempted solicitation under the Illinois general attempt statute. *People v. Boyce*, 27 N.E.3d 77 (Ill. 2015). Note that MPC § 5.02 (2) specifically states that failure to communicate to the person solicited is immaterial to solicitation.
- A defendant was convicted of solicitation to commit murder after he offered another man money to kill the main witness against the defendant in a fraud case. The conviction was upheld even though, in a subsequent "tapped" phone conversation with the other man, the defendant stated he "didn't need" to go through with the planned murder because "he had a good case." *People v. Houthoofd*, 790 N.W.2d 315 (Mich. 2010).
- In the two previous examples, the defendant was soliciting another to commit a crime as a perpetrator. Solicitation under specific-crime solicitation statutes can also apply to attempts by a defendant to involve a victim in illegal activity. In *State v. Arave*, 268 P.3d 163 (Utah 2011) the solicitation conviction of a man who offered an 11-year-old boy $20 to let the man perform oral sex on him was upheld.[6]

Conspiracy to Commit a Crime[7]

conspiracy An agreement between two or more persons to engage in unlawful acts.

The crime of **conspiracy** is the oldest of the preliminary crimes. It received some legislative recognition as early as 1292, but it was not until the early 1600s that the English Court of the Star Chamber developed the crime of conspiracy into an offense of wide scope, capable of extensive application. This court was created in the late 1500s to try certain high crimes without a jury. Because of the ruthless methods used, the court is sometimes referred to as "the infamous Star Chamber." Modern critics of the crime of conspiracy sometimes recall the ancient unsavory use of the crime of conspiracy, as did former U.S. Supreme Court Justice Robert H. Jackson in his concurring opinion in *Krulewitch v. United States*:

> The crime comes down to us wrapped in vague but unpleasant connotations. It sounds historical undertones of treachery, secret plotting and violence on a scale that menaces social stability and the security of the state itself. "Privy conspiracy" ranks with sedition and rebellion in the Litany's prayer for deliverance. Conspiratorial movements

do indeed lie back of the political assassination, the coup d'état, the putsch, the revolution and seizure of power in modern times, as they have in all history.[8]

The federal government (18 U.S.C.A. § 371) and all states have enacted statutes making conspiracy a crime in their jurisdictions. The reasoning behind such legislation generally is that when two or more persons plan a crime together, (1) the extent of potential harm to the society is often increased considerably, (2) the possibility of the abandonment of the criminal plan is greatly reduced, (3) the chances of success in the criminal venture are greater than if only one individual were involved, and (4) their actions can be more difficult to detect than an individual's preparation to commit a crime.

The purpose, then, of criminal conspiracy statutes is to prevent and punish criminal partnerships in crime and to stop, if possible, such criminal combinations of people before attempts to commit substantive crimes are made.

Each state has its own definition of conspiracy, but most have language similar to that found in the Texas Penal Code: "A person commits criminal conspiracy if, with intent that a [crime] be committed: (1) he agrees with one or more persons that they or one or more of them engage in conduct that would constitute the offense; and (2) he or one or more of them performs an overt act in pursuance of the agreement" (V.T.C.A., Penal Code, § 15.02).[9]

Because conspiracy was looked on as a partnership in crime, the traditional view, known as the "bilateral approach," was that the state must prove the involvement of *two or more* guilty persons in the conspiracy.[10] One consequence of the bilateral approach was that if A and B were charged with conspiracy to murder and a jury found A guilty and B not guilty, the traditional view was that the conviction against A could not stand. The reasoning for the dismissal of the charge and conviction against A was that A could not conspire alone and that two or more guilty persons are necessary for the conviction to stand.

Influenced by § 5.03 of the Model Penal Code, a substantial number of states have limited or rejected the "two or more guilty persons" requirement for the crime of conspiracy.[11] The "bilateral" approach of conspiracy has largely been replaced by the "unilateral" approach. Section 5.03 (1) of the M.P.C. states a person is "guilty of conspiracy with another person" if the person "(a) agrees with such other person or persons that they or one of them will engage in conduct . . ." that constitutes the agreed crime. The unilateral approach has two main differences from the bilateral approach: First, the crime is committed if the defendant agrees with another person, even if that other person is only feigning agreement, or lacks the capacity to make agreement; second, the person with whom the defendant agreed (such as an undercover police officer) need not be guilty in order to convict the defendant.

EXAMPLE	A defendant used an Internet chat room to reach "agreement" with a woman to meet and have sex with the woman and her 13-year-old daughter. The woman was an undercover police officer, and there was no daughter. When the defendant arrived for the meeting he was arrested and charged with conspiracy to commit sexual assault on a child. In affirming his conviction, the Colorado Court of Appeals held in 2012 that the Colorado conspiracy statute adopted the "unilateral" approach, and thus it was not a defense that the other party to the agreement was an undercover officer.[12]

A conspiracy does not end if one of the conspirators dies before the object of the conspiracy is obtained or an overt act occurs.[13] Conspiracy can also be proved even if the co-conspirator cannot be found or cannot be identified. See *United States v. Thomas.*[14] (All that was required for a conspiracy conviction is that the existence of a co-conspirator is alleged and proved, even if he cannot be identified.)

A conspiracy, even under the "unilateral" approach, does require the agreement of two natural persons. Thus, an officer of a corporation acting for the corporation cannot be convicted of a conspiracy with the corporation. On the other hand, as long as another natural person was part of the agreement, even if not identified, conspiracy can be proved.[15]

The Requirement of an Overt Act

Under the common law conspiracy rules, proof of the criminal partnership was all that was required to prove the crime of conspiracy. There was no requirement that the prosecution prove that some overt act was done in furtherance of the conspiracy. Today, most states have written into their criminal conspiracy statutes the requirement of proof of an overt act by a defendant. The Model Penal Code, section 5.03(5) states that a conviction for conspiracy requires proof of an overt act, unless the underlying crime is a "felony of the first or second degree."

Virtually any act in furtherance of the conspiracy will satisfy this requirement. Moreover, the overt act need not be itself illegal. For example, making a telephone call[16] or obtaining guns to be used in a robbery[17] can satisfy the overt act requirement. However, some overt act must be alleged and proved. The agreement itself cannot be the overt act. In the 2012 case of *United States v. Lockhart*[18] the court dismissed an indictment charging conspiracy to sell prescription drug samples because the government failed to allege any overt act taken in furtherance of the conspiracy.

The overt act requirement exists in some federal conspiracy statutes, but not others. The general federal conspiracy statute, 18 U.S.C. § 371, expressly requires proof of an overt act done in furtherance of the criminal conspiracy that is charged. However, Congress has enacted specific conspiracy statutes that do not contain express overt act requirements. For example, 21 U.S.C.A. § 846, which applies to a conspiracy to violate federal drug laws, has no requirement of proof of an overt act, but only proof of a criminal conspiracy. The U.S. Supreme Court held in the case of *United States v. Shabani*[19] that the federal drug conspiracy statute was constitutional, stating: "[T]he language (of the federal statutes does not) require that an overt act be committed to further the conspiracy, and we have not inferred such a requirement from congressional silence in other conspiracy statutes."

Conspiracy prosecutions under the Federal Racketeer Influenced and Corrupt Organizations Act (RICO), 18 U.S.C. § 1962, have presented some problems in the overt act requirement. The RICO Act (discussed in Chapter 18) punishes persons who form criminal enterprises. Convictions under § 1962(c) require the prosecution to prove that a defendant committed at least two "predicate acts," that is, actions that were themselves criminal violations, in furtherance of the enterprise. When a defendant is charged under § 1962(d) with conspiracy to violate the RICO laws, the federal circuit courts were initially split on the need for proof that the defendant agreed to commit the two predicate acts.

However, in *Salinas v. United States,*[20] the U.S. Supreme Court held that § 1962(d) did not require proof that the defendant committed or agreed to commit the two predicate acts needed for conviction under § 1962(c). Salinas, a deputy sheriff, and his superior, the sheriff, were charged with accepting bribes in violation of the federal bribery law, 18 U.S.C. § 666; violation of the RICO law, § 1962(c); and conspiracy to violate the RICO law, § 1962(d). Salinas was acquitted of the substantive violation, but convicted under the conspiracy section. On appeal Salinas contended that because the jury did not find that he committed the two predicate acts needed for conviction under § 1962(c), and the prosecution did not prove he agreed to commit such acts, he could not be convicted of conspiracy.

The Supreme Court rejected his argument, noting first that § 1962(d), unlike the general conspiracy statute, had no overt act requirement. As a result, a person could be convicted of the conspiracy without having taken any acts, so long as he agreed to participate in the underlying crime. The Court said that while the underlying crime, the RICO violation, required two predicate acts, Salinas could be convicted under § 1962(d) without personally committing or agreeing to commit those two predicate acts:

> In the case before us, even if Salinas did not accept or agree to accept two bribes, there was ample evidence he conspired to violate subsection (c). The evidence shows that (the sheriff) committed at least two acts of racketeering activity when he accepted numerous bribes and that Salinas knew about or agreed to facilitate the scheme. This is sufficient to support a conviction under § 1962(d) (522 U.S. at 66).

In *Whitfield v. United States,* 543 U.S. 209 (2005) the Supreme Court held that 18 U.S.C. § 1956(h), the money-laundering statute, required no overt act for a conspiracy conviction. In discussing whether a statute has an overt act requirement, the Court in *Whitfield* stated that if the congressional statute was "modeled on 18 U.S.C. § 371" (the general conspiracy statute) it had an overt act requirement, but if it was "modeled on the Sherman Act, 15 U.S.C. § 1" (the antitrust statute) it dispensed with such a requirement.

Based on this distinction, federal courts have held that the following conspiracy statutes do not have an overt act requirement:

> 18 U.S.C. § 1958 (a) the federal murder for hire statute; *United States v. Johnson,* 624 F. Supp. 2d 903 (W.D. Tenn. 2009)

> 18 U.S.C. § 1951 the extortion statute (Hobbs Act-see Chapter 14); *United States v. Salahuddin,* 765 F.3d 329 (3rd Cir. 2014), *Cert denied,* 135 S. Ct. 2309 (2015)

> 18 U.S.C. § 1349 the wire and bank fraud act; *United States v. Roy,* 783 F.3d 418 (2nd Cir. 2015)

Overt acts are often very convincing evidence of the sincerity of a conspiracy agreement, and almost all strong conspiracy cases have evidence of overt acts.

Wharton rule The requirement that crimes needing more than one person for commission, such as bigamy, require three or more people for a conspiracy conviction.

The Wharton Rule Some crimes cannot be committed alone, but instead require two or more people. Examples of such crimes are dueling, bigamy, gambling, adultery, incest, pandering for prostitution, receiving a bribe, and distributing illegal drugs. As the crime of conspiracy punishes partnerships in crime because of increased danger to society, the **Wharton rule**, named after Francis Wharton, the author of an early treatise on criminal law, states that the crime of conspiracy cannot be charged if the number of people involved include only those necessary to commit the crime. In *Ianelli v. United States*,[21] the U.S. Supreme Court explained the place of the Wharton rule in federal conspiracy prosecutions. The Court stated that it applied, but only to those crimes that required multiple participants for their commission, and subject to clear legislative intent that Congress intended both prosecutions to be permitted. The Court in *Ianelli* held that Congress did intend prosecutions for conspiracy to violate federal gambling statutes, which require the participation of five persons, to be maintained together with prosecutions for the underlying crime.

EXAMPLE	To distribute illegal drugs, there must be both a deliverer and a person receiving the drugs. Under the Wharton rule, if two persons engage in a one-time sale of a small quantity of an illegal drug, the seller and buyer cannot be charged with conspiracy.[22]

Most states and the federal government use the Wharton rule and will not permit a conspiracy charge when only the people necessary to commit the crime are named as defendants. However, if more people than the number necessary to commit the crime were charged with conspiracy, the Wharton rule would not apply. For example, if three people conspire to sell illegal drugs all three can be charged with the conspiracy crime and also the underlying drug offense, if completed.

In the example given above of the drug deal, the Wharton rule could also be defeated if sufficient evidence showed that the buyer and seller have a long-standing criminal relationship involving repeated sales of large quantities of illegal drugs. The evidence would have to show an agreement beyond a simple one-time transaction. Most states would then permit substantive drug charges in addition to the conspiracy charge.

Impossibility, Abandonment, and Withdrawal   What effect, if any, should the impossibility of committing the criminal object of a conspiracy, the abandonment of the conspiracy by all the conspirators, or the withdrawal from the conspiracy of one conspirator have on the conspiracy charge?

In the case of impossibility, the U.S. Supreme Court in 2003 rejected a federal court of appeals ruling that included an impossibility defense. In *United States v. Jimenez Recio*[23] the Court reversed a Ninth Circuit Court of Appeals decision that conspirators could not be convicted of the crime if the "object of the conspiracy had been defeated" before the defendants had joined the conspiracy. In *Jimenez,* police officers seized a truck carrying illegal drugs and convinced the truck driver to lure the defendants to the scene. When they arrived and drove away with the truck, the police arrested them. The defendants argued that since the object of the conspiracy, possession of illegal drugs, was made impossible by the drug seizure by the police, the conspiracy was over before it began. The Ninth Circuit Court of Appeals agreed, but the Supreme Court did not. The Court stated that the essence of the crime is the agreement to commit a crime, not the crime to be committed. Citing the LaFave treatise and the Model Penal Code, it rejected the notion that impossibility is ever a defense to a conspiracy charge.

In the 2013 case of *United States v. Min*[24] the Fourth Circuit Court of Appeals rejected an impossibility defense to a conspiracy charge, where the defendants were charged with conspiracy to rob what they believed was a criminal "stash house" for illegal drugs. In fact, the house was part of an FBI sting operation aimed at drug dealers. The defendants contended it was impossible to complete the crime because the "stash house" didn't exist. The court rejected that argument, noting that the conspiracy crime is complete when the agreement is made, and thus it did not matter that the purpose of the agreement could not be realized.

The same reasoning applies to abandonment of the conspiracy or withdrawal by one conspirator. Even if the conspiracy is abandoned or one conspirator withdraws, the crime of conspiracy is nonetheless complete; "since the crime is complete with the agreement, no subsequent action can exonerate the conspirator of that crime."[25] However, if one conspirator withdraws from a conspiracy outside the limitations period for prosecution of the conspiracy, the withdrawal bars conviction. In the 2013 case of *Smith v. United States*[26] the U.S. Supreme Court held that the defendant carried the burden of proving he withdrew from a conspiracy prior to the limitation period. Under federal law, most prosecutions must commence within 5 years of the criminal acts. In *Smith*, the defendant was part of the conspiracy, but spent the 6 years prior to commencement of the prosecution in federal prison, which the defendant contended amounted to withdrawal from the conspiracy. The Court said it was the defendant's duty to prove that withdrawal, not the prosecution's duty to prove the defendant had not withdrawn.

The Model Penal Code provides a defense to a conspiracy charge where a conspirator "thwarted the success of the conspiracy, under circumstances manifesting a complete and voluntary renunciation of his criminal purpose." A few states have similar provisions. The New York Penal Code, Section 40.10 (4) states: "In any prosecution for criminal solicitation . . . or for conspiracy . . . in which the crime solicited or the crime contemplated by the conspiracy was not in fact committed, it is an affirmative defense that, under circumstances manifesting a voluntary and complete renunciation of his criminal purpose, the defendant prevented the commission of the crime."

The Crime of Attempt

Attempt is the most frequently charged of the three preliminary crimes, because "near" victims and witnesses generally report attempted rapes, robberies, murders, and other crimes to the police. Moreover, such victims and witnesses are generally more cooperative about appearing in court to testify to the attempted crimes.

Actus Reus of Attempt Crimes   States can differ on how the act requirement in **attempt crimes** is defined, though as the box below notes, the "substantial step" test is probably the majority view. One method of defining the act requirement in attempt, which usually imposes a higher burden on the prosecution, is illustrated by the New York Criminal Code, which provides that "a person is guilty of an attempt to commit a crime when, with intent to commit a crime, he engages in conduct which tends to effect the commission of such crime."[27] New York courts have held under this statute that the state must show that the defendant performed acts that carried the "project forward within dangerous proximity of the criminal end to be attained."[28]

attempt crimes Acts that are a substantial step toward the commission of a crime that is not yet completed.

Bad thoughts alone cannot be charged as attempt or any other crime. The prosecution must show that the defendant attempted to commit the crime charged, and this requires showing an overt act or acts. The following cases illustrate conduct that courts ruled to be attempts to commit the crime charged:[29]

- Building a pipe bomb intended to blow up the car owned by the husband of the woman the defendant was involved with was a sufficient substantial step for attempted murder, whether or not the pipe bomb was attached to the car by defendant. *United States v. Heyn*, 605 Fed. Appx. 801 (11th Cir. 2015).
- Contacting potential accomplices, touring bank, and recruiting "getaway" driver were substantial steps for attempted robbery conviction. *United States v. Wesley*, 417 F.3d 612 (6th Cir. 2005).
- Defendant was stopped by police in possession of cold pills and ammonia, two of the six ingredients needed to "cook" methamphetamine. A container in his car also contained minute traces of meth residue. The court held that was enough to show a "substantial step" for attempted manufacture of methamphetamine. *State v. Stensaker*, 725 N.W.2d 883 (N.D. 2007).
- Defendant entered a convenience store and went into the bathroom, where he smoked some cocaine. He then exited the bathroom and walked to the front of the store carrying a knife. When he reached the cashier he swiped the knife in the air, but then collapsed in a corner, where he was subsequently arrested. In affirming the defendant's conviction of attempted armed robbery, the court said his actions were sufficient overt acts under the state's attempt statute. The court said an act need not be the "last requisite" act, but only must go beyond "mere preparation." *State v. Legins*, 645 S.E.2d 835 (N.C. App. 2007), *affirmed*, 653 S.E.2d 144 (N.C. 2007).

Mens Rea of Attempt   One element of most states' attempt statutes is the intent to commit a crime. Thus, even if a person engages in conduct that could

THE ACTUS REUS OF ATTEMPT IN STATE AND FEDERAL COURTS

For many years courts differed greatly on the definition of the *actus reus* in attempt crimes. Terms such as "dangerous proximity test" (see below), "probability of desistence test," and "fragment of the crime test" as well as other terms were used by courts to describe the act requirement. That has changed. In the 2011 case of *United States v. Hernandez-Galvanithe*[30] the court noted that "The modern trend is a shift toward the 'substantial step' test from the Model Penal Code, which is now the majority view among the states and federal courts." Section 5.01 of the MPC states the requisite elements of attempt:

1. an intent to engage in criminal conduct, and
2. conduct constituting a "substantial step" toward the commission of the substantive offense that strongly corroborates the actor's criminal intent.

"Substantial step" means conduct that is strongly corroborative of the actor's criminal purpose. MPC § 5.01 (2). Later in this chapter we present several examples of "substantial steps" sufficient to support a conviction for an attempt.

result in the completed crime, coupled with that conduct must be the intent to complete that crime. In part, this is because the focus of attempt crimes is the dangerousness of the actor, and not the conduct, which need not by itself be illegal or criminal. Thus, an otherwise legal act can satisfy the "substantial step" test.

What relevance, if any, does the kind of intent required by the completed crime have to a conviction for the attempt of that crime? That is, if the completed crime requires a specific intent, must the person charged with attempt have the same specific intent? The answer seems to be a qualified "yes."

As an example of this, courts have usually held that despite the fact that one could be convicted of the completed crime of murder even though one intended only to inflict serious bodily harm on the victim, one could not be convicted of attempted murder if the victim did not die. That is because "attempted murder" requires the intent to bring about the result described in the completed crime of murder, which is the death of a person, and not merely serious bodily harm.[31]

This rule has led to inconsistent holdings in attempt convictions of crimes that do not have a specific intent. For example, the crime of voluntary manslaughter, and in many jurisdictions the crime of second-degree murder, do not require proof that the defendant intended death to occur. As a result, some courts have held that there can be no crime of attempted manslaughter or attempted second-degree murder, because attempt crimes all require the intent to commit the base crime (death of another).[32] Others have held that proof that the defendant committed an act that would have resulted in death and was evidence of a "depraved mind" (the usual definition of second-degree murder—see Chapter 10), constituted proof of attempted second-degree murder.

 OVERT ACTS: CONSPIRACY VERSUS ATTEMPT

As we have seen, both conspiracy (under many statutes) and attempt require an "overt act" or "substantial step" before the crime is complete. Are the requirements for what constitutes the necessary act the same for both crimes? Based on what you know about conspiracy, is proof of the necessary "overt act" in conspiracy prosecutions easier or harder than proof of the necessary "substantial step" in attempt prosecutions? Why or why not? Consider the following two cases from the same jurisdiction, and decide if they are consistent.

1. Defendant stated to others that he planned to kill his estranged wife. Shortly after that, police found defendant in his car, parked in his wife's workplace parking lot near the door she used to exit the building. In his car he had an ice pick, a box cutter, and binoculars. Is he guilty of attempted murder? See *Collier v. State*, 846 N.E.2d 340 (Ind. App. 2006), *review denied*, 860 N.E.2d 585 (Ind. 2006).
2. Defendant and another person were arrested and charged with sale of illegal drugs. The two men discovered the name of the witness who turned them in, and agreed to kill her. They had a third person, a sister of one of the men, go to the witness's home and conduct surveillance so as to come up with a plan for killing the witness. Assuming the agreement to kill the witness was made, have the defendants taken the "overt act" needed for a conspiracy conviction? Would that act constitute a "substantial step" under attempt law? See *Conn. v. State*, 948 N.E.2d 849 (Ind. App. 2011).

In the 2014 case of *State v. Nolan*, 25 N.E.3d 1016 (Ohio 2014) the Ohio Supreme Court held that "attempted felony murder" is not a cognizable crime in Ohio. The Ohio attempt statute requires proof that the defendant intended to commit the attempted crime, the Court said, while the felony murder statute applies to unintended deaths. The court concluded that it is "impossible to purposely or knowingly cause an unintended death," and thus there can be no crime of attempted felony murder.

In the case of strict liability crimes (see Chapter 3), it would seem logical to conclude that one cannot be convicted of strict liability attempt, because attempt is defined as doing an act with the intent to commit a crime. In strict liability, one can be convicted of the crime without either knowledge or intent to commit a crime if one engages in conduct that is made criminal. Merely attempting to engage in that conduct, the reasoning goes, cannot be an attempt crime, because it lacks the required intent.

In at least one kind of strict liability crime, unlawful sex with a child, courts have upheld attempt convictions. While statutes aimed at adults having sex with children have a variety of names (generally grouped under the name "statutory rape"), they all share one element: If the defendant had sexual intercourse with the victim, he could be convicted of the crime, even though he may have not known the victim was under age. These statutes thus require no intent with respect to the age of the victim.

Most courts uphold convictions of attempted sexual contact with a child, holding that all the state must prove is that the defendant intended to have sex with the victim.[33] In the 2012 Internet "sting" case of *State v. Washington*[34] the court held that where the defendant was attempting to have sexual contact with a police officer who was pretending to be a child, the state must prove the defendant believed the victim was a child.

Impossibility in Attempt Cases

Courts formerly categorized impossibility defenses in attempt cases into two classes: factual impossibility and legal impossibility. Attempting to pick an empty pocket is an example of factual impossibility. The only thing that prevents the crime from being completed is the fact that the pocket is empty. Attempting to receive stolen goods that were not stolen has been characterized as an example of legal impossibility. Even if the defendants completed the intended act, they would not be guilty of a crime.

Most state courts and the federal courts have abandoned the distinction between factual and legal impossibility and have rejected the defense in both situations.[35] The Model Penal Code, Section 5.1, also rejects the impossibility defense, whether factual or legal, concluding that the culpability of the defendant should be judged by the circumstances as the defendant viewed them. Thus, in the examples above, the pickpocket believed he would find something in his victim's pocket, and the person receiving the goods believed they would be stolen property. Had their beliefs been correct, they would have committed the completed crime. As a result, they can be convicted of attempting that crime.

One form of the impossibility defense in attempt cases remains viable. If a defendant plans to engage in conduct that he believes to be a crime, but the conduct as planned is not a crime, the defendant is not guilty of an attempt.

EXAMPLE Assume an adult male plans to have sex with a female, believing her to be 16 years old, and also believing the age of consent in his state is 18 years of age. In fact, the age of consent is 16, so that having consensual sex with the female is not a crime. The man cannot be convicted of an attempt, even though he believed he was committing a crime.

LaFave, in *Criminal Law,* states that under the principle of legality (discussed in Chapter 1 of this text), "the defendant did not intend to do anything which had been made criminal, and what is not criminal may not be turned into a crime after the fact by characterizing his acts as an attempt."[36] For the same reason, one cannot be convicted of a conspiracy to commit a crime if the agreed objective is not criminal. See *In re Sealed Case,* 223 F.3d 775 (D.C. Cir. 2000).

Abandonment of the Criminal Purpose In attempt, conspiracy, and solicitation, a person usually has time to change his or her mind and decide not to go ahead with the intended crime. The Model Penal Code, Section 501.04, states that it is a defense to the crime of attempt that the actor abandoned the attempt under circumstances "manifesting a complete and voluntary renunciation of his criminal purpose."

Many states now have statutes in their criminal codes on abandonment of a criminal effort. Important questions concerning abandonment of a criminal intent include these: Has a preliminary crime already been committed (how far along is the criminal effort)? Was the abandonment voluntary or involuntary? What was the reason for the abandonment (did the victim scream or police arrive at the scene or a burglar alarm go off)? The following cases illustrate:

- A liquor store video camera caught the defendant putting three bottles under his coat. The store manager then followed the defendant, who went into a bathroom where other men were located. The defendant was overheard saying "They're on us. We need to get out of here." He then left the bottles on the bathroom floor and exited the bathroom, where he was detained and arrested. His conviction of attempted theft was affirmed, the court stating that the Indiana statute on abandonment of criminal purpose, which applies to attempt and conspiracy crimes, requires the abandonment to be completely voluntary, based only on a change of mind not caused by external circumstances. Here, the renunciation was the result of fear of getting caught, which is not a proper basis for the abandonment defense. *Mumford v. State,* 923 N.E.2d 11 (Ind. App. 2011).
- A defendant and three other high school students went to police and informed them that another student, Kerns, was planning a Columbine-style attack at their high school. The police searched Kerns's home, and found explosives and other information showing the intent to bomb the high school. The information also showed the defendant had agreed to be a part of the attack. The defendant was convicted of conspiracy to commit murder. On appeal the court rejected his claim that he had abandoned the conspiracy and renounced his criminal intention, because when he went to the police he did not tell them he was part of the conspiracy, and had renounced because of his fear of Kerns. *Commonwealth of Massachusetts v. Nee,* 935 N.E.2d 1276 (Mass. 2010).[37]

ATTEMPT CRIMES AND INTERNET CHAT ROOMS

One of the unfortunate side effects of the Internet boom is the use of so-called chat rooms by pedophiles to communicate with children. These sex-related communications are, by themselves, harmful to children and present the real possibility that the conversation could lead to actual contact between the adult pedophile and the child. As a result, states have passed legislation aimed at this conduct, generally making it criminal to entice a child into having unlawful sexual relations. As an example, Section 18.2-374.3 of the Virginia Code Annotated makes it a crime to use a communication system, including a computer, for the purpose of promoting unlawful sex with a child.

Police officers often enter these chat rooms and pass themselves off as young children to others using the chat room. When an adult pedophile connects with the officer, the officer engages in conversations that frequently lead to the arrest of the adult for attempted violations of these enticement statutes.

Two issues often arise in these cases. First, the defense of legal impossibility is often raised by these defendants. Courts virtually always reject that defense, as the courts in the following cases did:

- *U.S. v. Murrell,* 368 F.3d 1283 (11th Cir. 2004), *cert. denied,* 125 S. Ct. 439 (2004). Defendant was convicted of attempt to entice a child into having unlawful sexual relations. An investigator posed as the father of a minor child in chat room conversations with the defendant, although in fact no minor child existed. The defendant contended that he could not be convicted because he never communicated with a minor child. The court rejected this argument, saying the attempt crime required only that the government prove the defendant tried to entice a child into having sexual relations. It did not matter that no child ever heard those enticements.
- *State v. Patel,* 242 P.3d 856 (Wash. 2010). The defendant was convicted of attempted rape of a child under the age of 14. After chat room conversations in which the defendant proposed having sex with the "child," an undercover officer posing as a 13-year-old girl, the defendant agreed to meet the "child"

- The defendant approached a "hit man," actually an undercover police officer, and asked him to kill her ex-husband. The hit man agreed, and they discussed how it could be accomplished. Later, the defendant telephoned the hit man, and said, "Let's just hold off for a while." She was arrested and charged with solicitation to commit murder. Before trial, she moved to dismiss the charges, based on Alabama's abandonment statute, which states it is a defense if the defendant proves a "complete and voluntary renunciation of [his] criminal intent." The trial court agreed, and dismissed the charges, but the state appealed (generally permitted for dismissals before jeopardy attaches—see Chapter 7). On appeal, the court held that because the defendant did not clearly renounce all intention to have her husband killed, it was a jury question whether the abandonment defense was available. The case was remanded for trial on the solicitation to commit murder charge. *State v. Cromwell,* 33 So. 3d 31 (Ala. 2009).

PARTIES TO THE PRINCIPAL CRIME

At the time of the American Revolution, more than 200 crimes were punished by death in England. Application of the death penalty depended on the degree of criminal participation in the completed crime. The following four common law at her apartment. When he arrived, police arrested him. The court rejected his argument that he could not be convicted of the crime of attempted rape of a child under the age of 14, holding that it did not matter that he never actually communicated with a child. It was sufficient, the court held, that he was attempting to do so.

Second, the question of the "substantial step" requirement is often involved in these attempt crimes, since getting close to the "completed act" is logically difficult because there is no child involved. The following two cases considered the proper substantial step requirement in Internet attempt prosecutions:

1. The defendant entered into Internet conversations with "Emily," who stated she was 14, though she was in fact a police officer. After several Internet conversations where defendant "groomed" Emily ("grooming" refers to recognized procedures pedophiles use to gain the confidence of their victims), defendant agreed to meet Emily at a motel to have sex. The defendant went to the motel, and later to a nearby park where he believed Emily was waiting, where he was arrested. His conviction was affirmed, the court saying his actions satisfied the substantial step requirement for attempted incitement of a child. *United States v. Young*, 613 F.3d 735 (8th Cir. 2010).
2. An Internet conversation by itself has been held insufficient to constitute an overt act. In *United States v. Winckelmann*, 70 M.J. 403 (U.S. Armed Forces 2011), an army officer was convicted of attempted enticement of a child. An adult believed the officer was a pedophile, and entered an Internet chat room that she knew the officer visited. Passing herself off as a 15-year-old boy, the adult had several sexually explicit conversations with the officer. At the end of one chat the officer asked "u free tonight," the adult said "yes," and they signed off. In reversing the officer's conviction for attempted enticement of a child the court said the Internet chat messages did not satisfy the substantial step requirement.

parties to the principal crime Under common law, persons who either committed the crime, or aided or abetted the commission of the crime or the persons who committed the crime.

categories were used to determine the penalty that would be applied after conviction to the **parties to the principal crime**:

1. *Principal in the first degree* was the person (or persons) who actually committed the crime, and would receive the death penalty if applicable.
2. *Principal in the second degree* was a person who was present at the commission of the crime, was not involved in the planning of the crime, but aided and abetted in the actual commission of the crime. Under the common law this offender could not be tried until the actual perpetrator had been apprehended and convicted of the offense.
3. *Accessory before the fact* was a person who, knowing that a crime was to be committed, aided in the preparation for the crime but was not present at the time the crime was committed.
4. *Accessory after the fact* was a person who knew that the crime had been committed and gave aid or comfort to the person who committed the crime. Neither an accessory before the fact nor an accessory after the fact could be tried until after the conviction of the principal in the first degree.

Today, most states have done away with the four common law categories, as has the federal government. Under 18 U.S.C. § 2, in prosecutions for violation of federal law any person who "commits" the crime or "aids or abets" commission of the crime may be convicted "as a principal." The Model Penal Code, § 2.06 (3), calls this "accomplice" liability. The **accomplice** to a crime has liability that derives from the actions of the principal, and can be prosecuted for the same crimes committed by the principal. Persons who aid a person after a crime has been committed are no longer treated as parties to the crime, and thus have no derivative liability. These persons can be charged with other crimes, such as Model Penal Code § 243.2, Hindering Apprehension or Prosecution.

accomplice One who aids another in the commission of a crime. An accomplice is generally treated the same as a principal.

The majority of jurisdictions have statutes that create the following two categories of criminal liability and make all principals or parties to the crime liable to the same punishment:

1. All people who knowingly are involved in or connected with the commission of a crime either before or during its commission are known as *principals, accomplices, or parties to the crime,* regardless of their connection. This category is a combination of the common law principal in the first and second degree and the accessory before the fact.

2. The person or people who render aid to the criminal after the crime has been committed were previously known under the common law as *accessories after the fact.* Legislative bodies have statutes identifying the criminal offenses in this category. This category is discussed in the section on post-crime offenses in this chapter.

The rule has been abolished that neither the principal in the second degree nor the accessories before or after the fact could be forced to trial before the trial of the principal in the first degree. Any participant in a crime may be tried and convicted, even though the person who actually committed the crime has not been apprehended and tried or even identified.[38]

Theories of Criminal Liability

Defendants may be charged as principals or parties to violations of criminal laws either because they committed the forbidden acts themselves, or because some other person did so and they are in some way liable for the acts of the other person. The following sections discuss the various ways one can incur criminal liability based on actions of another person.

Criminal Liability as an Aider and Abettor   A person can be liable for the conduct of another if he or she is an **aider and abettor** to a person who committed a crime. Aiding and abetting, or accomplice liability, requires both an act and a mental state. The act is conduct undertaken that in some way encourages or facilitates the crime. In virtually all states, and the federal criminal code, the mental state requirement is that the accomplice intends to facilitate the principal in committing the underlying crime.

aider and abettor One who provides help to the person who commits a crime, either before or after the crime is committed.

In the 2014 case of *Rosemond v. United States,* 134 S. Ct. 1240 the U. S. Supreme Court considered the intent requirement under the federal accomplice statute, 18 U.S.C. § 2. In *Rosemond,* the defendant and two others went to meet two buyers of illegal drugs the men wished to sell. The defendant was actively involved in the illegal drug transaction. When the buyers showed up, they punched one of the sellers, grabbed the drugs, and ran off. One of the sellers (for purpose of the case the Court assumed it was not the defendant) pulled a gun and shot at the robbers. Police subsequently arrested the three sellers. The defendant was charged as a principal in the drug offense, and also as an aider and abettor in violation of 18 U.S.C. § 924 (c), which makes it a crime to use a gun in an illegal drug transaction. He was convicted of both offenses, and appealed.

The Supreme Court reversed the conviction for aiding and abetting the violation of 924(c). It said that the accomplice liability statute requires the prosecution to prove the defendant knew in advance that one of his cohorts was bringing a gun to the drug deal. It rejected the government's argument that continued participation in the drug deal after the gun was fired satisfied the intent requirement. Rather, the knowledge must be acquired when the defendant still had a realistic opportunity to withdraw from the crime, the Court said.

The Court's decision in *Rosemond* has influenced lower courts in accomplice liability cases. For example, in *United States v. Encarnacion-Ruiz*, 787 F.3d 581 (1st Cir. 2015) the court held, based on *Rosemond*, that even though a principal could be convicted of violating the federal child pornography statute, 18 U.S.C. § 2251, without knowledge a child was used in a pornographic video, an accomplice could not. The court held the prosecution needed to prove the accomplice knew the person being filmed in the pornographic video was a minor.

Some states have duel theories of culpability as an aider and abettor. In addition to showing the accomplice intended to facilitate an offense, some states make the accomplice liable for any other crime that was "the natural and probable consequence" of the crime the accomplice intended to aid and abet. Even in those states, however, the doctrine has limits. For example, in *People v. Chiu*, 325 P.3d 972 (Cal. 2014) the California Supreme Court held that an aider and abettor cannot be guilty of premeditated murder under the "natural and probable consequences" rule. The prosecution must prove the accomplice aided and abetted the crime with the intent that the victim be murdered. Thus, if the accomplice aided and abetted another to commit an assault, and the principal intentionally killed the victim, the accomplice could be convicted of second or third degree murder under the natural consequences rule, but not first degree premeditated murder, the court said.

It isn't clear if the "natural and probable consequences" doctrine applies in federal prosecutions based on aiding and abetting, although in *Gonzales v. Duenas-Alvarez*, 549 U.S. 183, 191 (2007) the U.S. Supreme Court noted that many federal circuits used "some variation" of the doctrine. In *Rosemond*, it should be said, the Supreme Court noted (in footnote 7) that some authorities follow the natural and probable consequences doctrine as "an exception" to the mental intent requirement, while others say the better view is to reject the doctrine in accomplice liability prosecutions. The Court said it expressed "no view on the issue" because no one contended that a violation of the gun use statute was a natural and probable consequence of an illegal drug transaction.

conspirator A person who is a party to an agreement to commit an unlawful act.

Criminal Liability Under the Common Design or Common Plan Rule

Under the common design rule, when people have a common plan to do an

common design or plan Scope of liability of persons who are party to a conspiracy or other agreement to do an unlawful act.

unlawful act, whatever is done in furtherance of the **common design or plan** is the act of all, and they can all be punished for that act.

Thus, if one of the parties to an armed robbery wore a mask, then all the parties to the robbery wore a mask, and all are subject to the penalties of committing the crime of armed robbery while concealed. If one of the parties to a drug-trafficking offense carried a gun, then all the parties are subject to the penalties of carrying a loaded gun while trafficking illegal drugs.

A common design is a spoken or unspoken conspiracy to commit an unlawful act. Any member of the conspiracy (plan) could be held liable as a principal for any offense committed in the furtherance of the plan or conspiracy while he or she is a member of it. Latecomers cannot be convicted as principals for offenses that were committed before they joined the conspiracy or after they withdrew from the conspiracy.[39]

what one did, they all did The rule that all parties to a conspiracy or other agreement to perform an unlawful act are liable for every action taken by any party in furtherance of the conspiracy or agreement.

The following cases are illustrations of the principle **"what one did, they all did"**:

- The defendant told two friends a woman he knew was holding drugs and money for a local drug dealer. The three men agreed to go to the woman's house, and have the defendant gain entry by greeting the woman at the front door, which he would then leave unlocked. The other two men would then enter the home, and steal the drugs and money. They did as planned, and when they entered one of the men shot and killed the woman. The defendant claimed that he did not know the killing was planned, but the court affirmed his conviction for murder.[40]
- Defendant Watts guarded the parents of a teenage girl while his two friends raped the girl. Watts was convicted of two counts of rape in concert because he aided and abetted both rapes. In affirming the California convictions for these and other crimes, the Federal Court of Appeals wrote,

  We hold that no violation of due process has occurred in this case. . . . The ancient and universally accepted principle of accomplice liability holds a defendant legally responsible for the unlawful conduct of others that he aids and abets.[41]

- In a 2009 case[42] the court upheld the manslaughter conviction of a defendant who had left an apartment he and two other men had entered with the intent to rob the occupant. After the defendant and one man found drugs and money, they ran out of the building. The remaining man shot at and killed the occupant of the apartment. Defendant's conviction was affirmed because the man who killed the victim stated prior to entering the apartment that he would use the shotgun he was carrying "if he needed to." The defendant could thus foresee that a killing might occur in the robbery.

Liability for Crimes Other than the Planned and Intended Offense: Conspiracy

Pinkerton rule The rule followed in federal courts that one conspirator is liable for crimes committed by another conspirator, if foreseeable and done in furtherance of the conspiracy.

When the evidence demonstrates a common design or conspiracy to commit an unlawful act to which all the defendants agreed, whatever is done in the furtherance of the criminal plan is the act of all, if it is a natural and probable consequence of the intended crime. In prosecutions under the various federal conspiracy laws, courts commonly apply the so-called *Pinkerton rule*, taken from the Supreme Court's decision in *Pinkerton v. United States*, 328 U.S. 640 (1946). Under the *Pinkerton* rule a co-conspirator can be held liable for crimes committed by another conspirator, even if the co-conspirator did not know about the other crime, and did not agree to commit the other crime, so long as the crimes were committed in furtherance of the conspiracy and were foreseeable. Thus, the "natural and probable consequences" doctrine, which might have limited applicability for accomplice liability, quite clearly applies to conspiracies.

EXAMPLE   Several men agreed to enter into an illegal drug distribution conspiracy. When they were caught dealing drugs, one of the men was carrying a concealed weapon, which the other men claimed they did not know existed. They were all convicted of possessing a firearm while distributing illegal drugs. The court affirmed the conviction, stating that it is foreseeable that one member of an illegal drug conspiracy would be armed. *United States v. Vasquez-Castro*, 640 F.3d 19 (1st Cir. 2011).

Some but not all[43] state courts apply rules similar to the *Pinkerton* rule. For example, if guns are carried and a shot is fired by one member of the group, that shot is fired by all the defendants, and all of them must answer for the results.[44]

In *People v. Jones,* the California courts held that an accused who knew that his co-defendants were armed was responsible for all the consequences when a night watchman was killed in a robbery.[45] The defendant in the *Jones* case was unarmed.

The definition of the natural and probable consequences of the intended crime varies somewhat from jury to jury and court to court. The following example illustrates the problem:

EXAMPLE   X and Y conspire to burglarize a residence. X is the lookout and getaway driver while Y is in the house committing the burglary. Y commits the following additional crimes. For which of the crimes committed by Y may X be convicted?

1. Y is surprised by the homeowner and, in an attempt to get away, kills the man.
2. Y is surprised by an 11-year-old boy who lives in the house and needlessly kills the boy.
3. In addition to stealing, Y comes upon a woman in bed and rapes the woman.
4. After stealing from the house, Y sees a gallon of gasoline in the back hall of the house, spills the gasoline around the house, and burns it down.

Prosecutors could charge X as a co-conspirator with all the additional crimes, but whether X would be convicted would depend on whether the finder of fact determined that the additional acts were a natural and probable consequence of the burglary.

X's defense could be that some of the offenses are not the natural or probable consequence of the intended crime of burglary, and therefore X would not be criminally liable for those offenses. In all cases, X would be charged with and convicted of the crime of burglary.[46]

Can Criminal Liability Result from an Accident?   Criminal liability can result from intentional, reckless, or grossly negligent conduct. However, can criminal liability result from accidental conduct? Criminals also have accidents. U.S. Supreme Court Chief Justice Roberts noted in the 2009 case of *United States v. Dean,* 129 S. Ct. 1849, "Accidents happen. Sometimes they happen to individuals committing crimes with loaded guns."

The famous English lawyer and writer Sir William Blackstone answered the question of criminal liability from accidents in his *Commentaries*, written in 1769, as follows:

> [I]f any accidental mischief happens to follow from the performance of a lawful act, the party stands excused from all guilt: but if a man be doing anything unlawful and a consequence ensues which he did not foresee or intend, as the death of the man or the like, his want of foresight shall be no excuse . . . he is criminally guilty of whatever consequences may follow from the first misbehavior.

In the *Dean* case a defendant entered a bank carrying a weapon, intending to rob the bank. In the process, the firearm he carried discharged. The defendant was charged with violation of 18 U.S.C. § 924(c)(1)(A), carrying a firearm during the commission of a violent crime. Conviction under that statute results in a 5-year minimum sentence, which is increased to 7 years if the firearm is discharged. The defendant argued the discharge was an accident, but the Court said the enhanced sentence was still proper: "It is unusual to impose criminal punishment for the consequences of purely accidental conduct. But it is not

 IF THE STATE CAN PROVE ONE OF THE FOLLOWING BEYOND REASONABLE DOUBT, A PERSON CAN BE HELD CRIMINALLY LIABLE

For a preliminary or anticipatory crime:

- Solicitation
- Conspiracy
- Attempt

For the planned and intended crime (if completed):

- As the person who committed the crime, or
- As a person who intentionally aids and abets the person who committed the crime, or
- As a conspirator who advises, hires, counsels, or otherwise procures another to commit the crime

For a post-crime offense relating to the planned and intended crime:

- Party to a crime, in which the state would have to prove each person participated in one of the preceding categories
- Common design or plan
- Criminal liability under the complicity, accountability, or accomplice rules

unusual to punish individuals for the unintended consequences of their unlawful acts."

post-crime offenses Actions taken after a crime has been committed, with knowledge that the crime was committed, which provide aid to the person who committed the crime.

POST-CRIME OFFENSES

Today, all states and the federal government have enacted many statutes regarding **post-crime offenses**. These statutes are meant to assist law enforcement officers in performing their duty of investigating crimes and apprehending criminals. Some statutes punish people who knowingly give police false information with the intent to mislead them. Other statutes are designed to permit the proper and efficient functioning of the courts and the criminal justice system. Some of these offenses existed under the common law, whereas others have been created in modern times. Examples are the following:

- Refusing to aid an officer while the officer is doing any act in his or her official capacity
- Obstructing or resisting an officer while the officer is doing any act in his or her official capacity (interfering with an officer)[47]
- Obstructing justice
- Compounding a crime: the making of an agreement (for a consideration) to withhold evidence of, or to abstain from prosecuting, a crime of which the accused has knowledge[48]
- Making false reports to an officer or law agency[49]
- Misprision of a felony (failure to report or prosecute a known felon)[50]

 ## STRICT LIABILITY DISTINGUISHED FROM VICARIOUS LIABILITY

Strict Liability

When a criminal statute imposes liability without requiring proof of mental fault, the offense is called a strict liability offense. If a statute requires proof of a mental element, the offense is not a strict liability offense.

To prove a strict liability offense, the state need prove only that the defendant did the forbidden act. The state does not have to prove a mental fault (*mens rea*). For example, in most states, it is not necessary for the state to prove a defendant knew the age of a victim of statutory rape.

Vicarious Liability

When a person becomes liable for the criminal act (or acts) of another, the liability is vicarious. Section 2.06 of the Model Penal Code lists the following categories of vicarious liability:

- Causing innocent or irresponsible people to do a criminal act
- Becoming a criminal accomplice of another person by:

  a. Soliciting the person to do a criminal act
  b. Aiding the other person in planning or committing the act
  c. Having a legal duty to prevent the act and failing to take reasonable steps to prevent the act
  d. Falling into a class of persons whose complicity for the crime is expressly established by statute

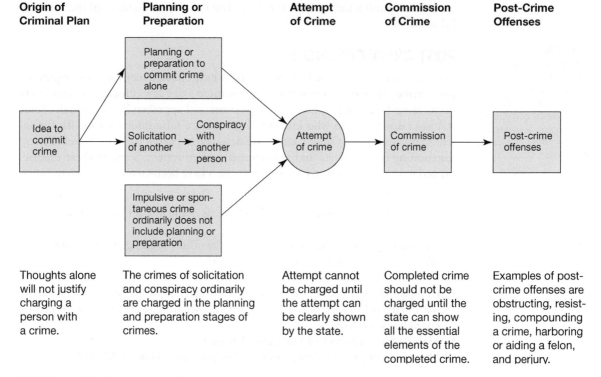

FIGURE 4.1 The Various Stages of Crimes

- Harboring or aiding felons
- Committing perjury
- Escaping from custody
- Bribing witnesses
- Jumping bail
- Communicating with jurors with the intent to influence them

Figure 4.1 illustrates the various stages of crimes, from the original idea of the crime to the offenses that can occur after the crime.

★★★

LEARNING OBJECTIVES SUMMARY

LO 1. Identify when conduct has crossed the line between thinking about committing a crime and attempting to commit a crime.
Thoughts alone are not crimes. However, when actions are taken that are steps toward completing a crime, or persuading another to commit the crime, criminal liability is possible.

LO 2. Explain the function of and need for corroborating evidence in solicitation prosecutions.
In solicitation charges, corroboration is important to show the defendant unequivocally intended to convince another person to engage in criminal conduct.

LO 3. Identify the steps that must be taken before one can be guilty of a conspiracy.
A conspiracy conviction requires as a minimum that two or more people agree to commit actions that are criminal. Most conspiracy statutes require the additional step of an overt act taken in furtherance of the conspiracy, but many federal conspiracy statutes have no overt act requirement.

LO 4. Explain when, if ever, impossibility of committing the completed crime is a defense to a charge of attempt.
The fact that the completed crime could not have occurred, the impossibility defense, is generally not a defense to an attempt charge, unless what was being attempted was not a crime at all.

LO 5. Identify the circumstances when abandonment of the criminal purpose can have an effect on liability for an attempt, or liability for criminal acts done in a conspiracy.
Because the crimes of conspiracy, solicitation, or attempt are complete whether or not

the underlying crimes ever are committed, abandonment of the conspiracy or attempt is generally not a defense. Some states provide an abandonment defense if a defendant prevents the underlying crime from occurring.

LO 6. Explain the rule for liability of one conspirator for actions of another.
One conspirator can be held liable for acts of another conspirator, including other crimes, if they are committed in furtherance of the conspiracy. The fact that one conspirator did not know of or agree to the commission of other crimes does not matter unless the other crimes were unforeseeable.

LO 7. List the parties who can be treated as principals for purposes of criminal liability.
Both those who commit the acts constituting the crime and thus who act to facilitate commission of the crime can be convicted as principals in the crime.

KEY TERMS

CASE ANALYSIS AND WRITING EXERCISES

1. Assume that the defendant is riding in a car being driven by a person who is clearly intoxicated. Nonetheless, the defendant urges the driver to exceed the speed limit and ignore traffic signs. The driver does so, and smashes the car into a building, injuring another passenger. Can the defendant be charged, under accomplice liability, for driving while intoxicated? Vehicular assault (the auto accident)? See *People v. Childress*, 363 P.3d 155 (Colo. 2015). What is the mental state requirement in Colorado for conviction or driving while intoxicated? Vehicular assault, while intoxicated? What is the mental state requirement for accomplice liability?

2. Illinois police became concerned about the number of high-powered rifles Olutosin Oduwole, a student at Southern Illinois University, had ordered on the internet. The purchase order came shortly after the killings at Virginia Tech in 2007. After monitoring Oduwole's conduct, officers found a written note in Oduwole's car (left unattended on campus) that said "send $2 to this PayPal account" or another "murderous rampage similar to the VT shooting will occur at another highly populated university. THIS IS NOT A JOKE!" Police subsequently found that Oduwole had recently opened a PayPal account. Oduwole was charged with attempted terrorist threat under the Illinois terrorist threat statute. Should he be convicted? See *People v. Oduwole*, 985 N.E.2d 316 (Ill. App. 2013), *review denied*, 39 N.E.3d 565 (Ill. 2013).

3. The defendant, Brantley, was driving a car with her boyfriend, a convicted felon, when she was stopped by police for a traffic violation. When the two police officers began questioning the boyfriend, he got out of the car, pulled a gun, and killed both officers. He then ran away. The defendant drove away from the crime scene, and the two exchanged various text messages. Brantley was charged with misprision of felony under 18 U.S.C. § 4. What did Brantley do that violated the misprision statute? What crime did she conceal: the murders? Another crime? *United States v. Brantley*, 803 F.3d 1265 (11th Cir. 2015).

4. Allen, a volunteer fire fighter in Vermont, and some of his other fire fighters, believed the lack of fire calls was "like kind of getting boring." So, they decided to set some fires in uninhabited grasslands, so they could respond to a fire call at the fire station. Some of the fires were set in federally owned parklands. Allen was charged and convicted of conspiracy to violate 18 U.S.C. § 1855, which makes it a crime to "willfully" set on fire timber or grass on any land owned or managed by the United States. Allen claims the prosecution failed to prove he knew the grass land was owned by the United States. Should his conviction be reversed? *United States v. Allen*, 788 F.3d 61 (2nd Cir. 2015).

ENDNOTES

1. See Section 11.1, Wayne LaFave, *Criminal Law*, 4th ed. (Belmont, CA.: Thomson/West, 2003).

2. See *United States v. Hassouneh*, 199 F.3d 175 (4th Cir. 2000).

3. In the United States, the crime is generally called "solicitation"; in England the crime is called "incitement," as the term *solicitation* is used there for solicitation for prostitution. See *Moriarty's Police Law (Law and Regulations for the Use of Police Officers)*, 21st ed. (London: Butterworths, 1972).

4. The English parliament enacted the Incitement to Mutiny Act (English armed forces) in 1797. See *Moriarty's Police Law*, p. 12.

5. *State v. Hauk*, 652 N.W.2d 393 (Wis. 2002). Since the crime of solicitation is complete when the solicitation occurs, it does not matter if the defendant later recants the solicitation. Also, as the *Hauk* court held, the usual rule that one cannot be convicted of a crime based only on a confession is inapplicable where the confession is not made to the police, but to a friend. See page 219, Thomas Gardner and Terry Anderson, *Criminal Evidence*, 6th ed. (Belmont, CA: Thomson/ Wadsworth, 2007).

6. The defendant was also convicted of attempted sodomy on a child, but the Utah Supreme Court reversed that conviction, stating that "Solicitation alone cannot constitute a substantial step toward commission of a crime." 268 P.3d at 168.

7. In 1925, Judge Learned Hand called conspiracy the "darling of the prosecutor's nursery," as prosecutors were using conspiracy as a weapon against organized crime and illegal business practices. See *Harrison v. United States* (7 F.2d 259, 263, 2d Cir. 1925). Today, the federal and state RICO statutes are much more effective in this type of criminal prosecution. See Chapter 18 for a discussion of the RICO statutes.

8. 336 U.S. 440, 445, 69 S. Ct. 716, 719 (1949).

9. The Texas conspiracy statute is actually limited to agreements to commit a *felony*, as opposed to a *crime*. In that respect, Texas is in the minority; most states have statutes making the crime of conspiracy applicable to an agreement to commit any crime. For those states retaining the common law definition of conspiracy, the agreement need only be to achieve some "unlawful purpose." See *Commonwealth v. Hunt* (45 Mass. (4 Mete.) Ill, 123 (1842)).

10. Under the old common law, a husband and wife were one person, with the wife being subject to the control and discipline of the husband. (See the discussion on the defense of duress and coercion in Chapter 7.) Because of this relationship, the common law rule held that *because* the husband and wife were one person, they could not conspire together and be charged as the two persons to a conspiracy.

   This old common law rule was rejected by the U.S. Supreme Court in the 1960 case of *United States v. Dege* (80 S. Ct. 1589), in which the Court held that a wife is a person like anyone else and therefore is capable of entering into a criminal conspiracy with her husband or another person. Today, all states would follow this reasoning if the question were before a state court.

11. The general federal conspiracy statute, 18 U.S.C.A. § 371 retains the "bilateral" approach to conspiracy, and thus there must be two or more guilty persons before a conspiracy is formed.

12. *People v. Vecellio*, 2012 WL 866421 (Colo. App. 2012), *review denied*, 2012 WL 5384641 (Colo. 2012).

13. See *Alleyne v. California,* 98 Cal. Rptr. 2d 737 (2000), *cert, denied* 532 U.S. 958 (2001).

14. 348 F.3d 78 (5th Cir. 2003), *cert denied,* 540 U.S. 1207 (2004).

15. See *United States v. Giuseppe Bottiglieri Shipping Co. S.P.A.,* 2012 WL 1899844 (S.D. Ala. 2012).

16. *United States v. Fellabaum,* 408 F.2d 220(7th Cir. 1969).

17. *Burk v. State,* 848 P.2d 225 (1993).

18. 2012 WL 5866672 (E.D. Ky. 2012).

19. 115 S. Ct. 382 (1994).

20. 522 U.S. 52 (1997).

21. 420 U.S. 770 (1975).

22. See *United States v. Delutis,* 722 F. 2d 902 (1st Cir. 1983). The Wharton rule was held not to apply to the crime of possession with intent to distribute illegal drugs, as one person alone can commit this crime. See *Johnson v. State,* 587 A.2d 444 (Del. 1991).

23. See *United States v. Cohen,* 260 F.3d 68 (2d Cir. 2001).

24. 704 F.3d 314 (4th Cir. 2013).

25. LaFave, *Criminal Law,* 4th ed., p. 652 (Belmont, CA: Thomson/West, 2003).

26. 133 S. Ct. 714 (2013).

27. Section 110.00, McKinney's *Consolidated Laws of New York, Annotated,* Book 39.

28. *People v. Warren,* 489 N.E.2d 240 (N.Y. 1985).

29. Examples of conduct that was mere preparation and did not amount to conduct to attempt to commit the crime charged include the following:
    • In *Comm. v. Bell,* 917 N.E.2d 740 (Mass. 2009) the court reversed an attempted rape conviction. The defendant had arranged to meet a woman, actually an undercover police officer, to discuss paying her to have sex with her "child." The defendant met the woman in a parking lot, and they agreed to meet later with the child. The defendant was then arrested, and later convicted of attempted rape. The Court of Appeals reversed, holding that under Massachusetts law an overt act must be either the "last act" before completion of the crime, or only a "narrow gap" must exist between the overt act and the completed crime.
    • In *United States v. Thornton,* 539 F.3d 741 (7th Cir. 2008) the court reversed a conviction for attempted bank robbery. The defendant was seen attempting to enter the bank's door, wearing a mask and dressed to disguise his appearance. The court said those acts were not a "substantial step" toward completion of the crime.

30. 632 F.3d 192, 198 (5th Cir. 2011).

31. See Wayne, *Criminal Law,* 4th ed. Section 11.3b, p. 584. (Belmont, CA.: Thomson/West, 2003).

32. Cases from many jurisdictions are collected in *State v. Gutierrez,* 172 P.3d 18 (Kan. 2007). More recent decisions, at least for attempted voluntary manslaughter and second-degree murder, hold there can be attempts of these crimes. See *Mendenhall v. State,* 82 So. 3d 1153 (Fla. App. 2012).

33. See *People v. Reyes,* 908 N.Y.S. 2d 14 (N.Y.A.D. 2010); *Maxwell v. State,* 895 A.2d 327 (Md. App. 2006); *State v. Sorabella,* 891 A.2d 897 (Conn. 2006), *cert denied,* 549 U.S. 821 (2006).

34. 270 P.3d 591 (Wash. 2012).

35. See page 38 of LaFave and Scott, *Criminal Law,* 2nd ed. (Belmont, CA.: West/Wadsworth, 1986). Legal writers distinguish between legal and factual impossibility. However, the Supreme Court of Pennsylvania states that no American court has recognized factual impossibility as a defense to an attempt charge (*Commonwealth v. Henley,* 474 A.2d at 1116).

    In addition to legal and factual impossibility, some courts write of "inherent impossibility." The committee drafting the revised Illinois Criminal Code in 1961 wrote this comment on the defenses of impossibility (Chapter 38, p. 513):

    > It is the intent of section 8-4(b) to exclude both factual and legal impossibilities as defenses to prosecution for attempt. However, inherent impossibility (attempts to kill by witchcraft such as repeatedly stabbing a cloth dummy made to represent the person intended to be killed) is not intended to be excluded as a defense. [Emphasis in original]

36. LaFave, *Criminal Law,* 4th ed., p. 600 (Belmont, CA.: Thomson/West, 2003).

37. The court stated that it was not adopting an abandonment defense, which it said must be created by the legislature. It simply said that even if such a defense existed, the defendant would not be entitled to the defense. In Missouri, which has a conspiracy renunciation statute, the court held that the defense would not be available in attempt crimes until the legislature said so. *State v. Rollins,* 321 S.W.3d 353 (Mo. App. 2010).

38. In the 1980 case of *Standefer v. United States* (447 U.S. 10, 100 S. Ct. 1999) the U.S. Supreme Court held that a defendant may be convicted of aiding and abetting the commission of a federal crime, even though the person who actually committed the crime had been acquitted of the offense. Model Penal Code § 2.06 (7) has a similar provision.

39. The New Jersey accountability and accomplice liability law is presented in the 1992 case of *State v. Bryant,* 607 A.2d 1343 (N.J. 1992), as follows:

    > N.J.S.A. 2C:2-6a provides that a person is guilty of an offense "if it is committed by his own conduct or the conduct of another person for which he is legally accountable, or both." N.J.S.A. 2C:2-6b provides in part: b. A person is legally accountable for the conduct of another person when:* * *

    (3) He is an accomplice of such other person in the commission of an offense; or
    (4) He is engaged in a conspiracy with such other person.

2C-2-6c provides that: A person is an accomplice of another person in the commission of an offense if:
(1) With the purpose of promoting or facilitating the commission of the offense, he
  (a) Solicits such other person to commit it;
  (b) Aids or agrees or attempts to aid such other person in planning or committing it; or
  (c) Having a legal duty to prevent the commission of the offense, fails to make proper effort so to do; or
  (d) His conduct is expressly declared by law to establish his complicity.

40. *State v. Turner*, 130 P.3d 1154 (Nev. 2009).

41. *Watts v. Bonneville*, 879 R2d 685 (9th Cir. 1989).

42. *State v. Coward*, 972 A.2d 691 (Conn. 2009).

43. *State v. Nevanez*, 130 P.3d 1154 (Idaho App. 2005); *State v. Roberts*, 14 P.3d 713 (Wash. 2000).

44. *People v. Bracey*, 249 N.E.2d 224 (1969).

45. 29 P.2d 902 (1934).

46. In the 1991 case of *Ward v. State* (567 N.E.2d 85), no evidence showed that the defendant knew anything about the planned robbery. The defendant drove three men to the store they planned to rob and then left the area. Another car arrived carrying the weapons and ski masks used. During the robbery, a store clerk was killed. The Supreme Court of Indiana reversed the defendant's conviction of felony murder, pointing out that the defendant was not shown to have participated in either the planning or carrying out of the robbery, that he did not remain as a lookout but left the area, that he did not return to aid in the escape, and that he did not receive any proceeds of the robbery.

In the case of *Mumford v. Maryland*, 313 A.2d 563 (Md. App. 1974), a rape and murder occurred during a burglary. The defendant (a 15-year-old girl) stated that she was elsewhere on the premises when the rape and murder occurred and that she did not know these crimes were being committed. In reversing her conviction for first-degree murder (felony murder) and ordering a new trial, the court stated:

> There must be a direct causal connection between the homicide and the felony. Something more than mere coincidence in time and place between the two must be shown; otherwise, the felony-murder rule will not be applicable.

(See Chapter 10 for material on the felony murder rule.)

47. Obstructing or interfering with an officer sometimes occurs during an accident or public disaster. Newspaper photographers were convicted in the following cases for seeking to obtain photographs of accidents after being repeatedly told to stay in the area where the general public was permitted. In both disasters, police had cleared the area so that emergency fire and medical vehicles could enter the area, control fire and explosions, and render aid to the injured and dying.

In the case of *State v. Peruta*, 591 A.2d 140 (Conn. App. 1991), a fatal car accident had occurred. The photographer was convicted of "interfering with an officer" because he repeatedly interfered with rescue efforts.

In the case of *City of Oak Creek v. King*, 436 N.W.2d 285 (Wis. 1989), a commercial airline had crashed, causing many deaths and injuries. King was convicted of disorderly conduct because he would not stay behind police lines. The Supreme Court of Wisconsin pointed out that reporters do not have special rights that the general public does not have and must obey reasonable police orders at the scene of a public emergency.

48. The South Dakota statute of compounding a crime is as follows:

Any person who accepts or offers or agrees to accept any pecuniary benefit as consideration for

1. Refraining from seeking prosecution of an offender; or

2. Refraining from reporting to law enforcement authorities the commission or suspected commission of any crime or information relating to a crime; is guilty of compounding. Compounding a felony is a Class 6 felony. Compounding a misdemeanor is a Class 1 misdemeanor.

49. For a false report case that went to the U.S. Supreme Court, see *United States v. Rogers*, 466 U.S. 475 (1984).

50. The drafters of the Model Penal Code state, "In general, our society does not use penal sanctions to compel reporting of crime" (§242.5, Comment at pp. 251–252, 1980).

5

Criminal Responsibility and the Capacity to Commit a Crime

OUTLINE

LEARNING OBJECTIVES

In this chapter we consider when a person has the capacity for criminal responsibility. The learning objectives for this chapter are

LO 1. Discuss when a child can be held responsible for violation of a criminal law.

LO 2. Differentiate between the method of imposing criminal liability upon a child under age 7 and a child of age 14.

LO 3. List the two prongs of the *M'Naghten* rule.

LO 4. Distinguish the "cognitive" approach to insanity from the "volitional" approach.

LO 5. Describe the difference between the *M'Naghten* rule and the "substantial capacity" test.

LO 6. Identify the extent, if any, to which the voluntary use of drugs or alcohol may be used as an insanity defense or diminished capacity defense.

LO 7. Distinguish the "not guilty by reason of insanity" verdict from the "guilty but mentally ill" verdict.

LO 8. List factors that may present issues of a criminal defendant's competency to be tried on criminal charges.

LO 9. Explain why a defendant of questionable competency should not be tried for a criminal violation.

James Holmes, convicted mass killer in Aurora, Colorado, after sentencing. A jury rejected Holmes' insanity defense, and in August 2015 he was sentenced to 11 life terms, plus 3,318 additional years for the persons he injured. He will never be paroled.

Andre Leteve and his wife Laurie were going through a divorce proceeding in Arizona. After engaging in various retaliations against Laurie for instituting the divorce action, in March of 2010 Leteve shot and killed the couple's two children; Alex, age 6, and Asher, age 2. Leteve also attempted to kill himself, but was unsuccessful. He was charged with first degree murder for both killings, was convicted of both, and sentenced to death.

On appeal Leteve contended the trial court erred by refusing to permit a defense witness, a psychologist, to testify that Leteve had a character trait of acting impulsively. Leteve argued this evidence was admissible as "observational evidence" and relevant to whether he possessed the necessary premeditation for first degree murder. Arizona,

like many states, does not permit the "diminished capacity" defense. Thus, evidence of a mental disorder is only admissible to prove insanity, not the absence of a required mens rea. The Arizona Supreme Court agreed with Leteve that the trial court erred by excluding the psychologist's testimony, but held the error was harmless. The court said the overwhelming evidence showed "no reasonable juror could have concluded that Leteve had not reflected on the killings before he committed them." His death sentence was affirmed. *State v. Leteve*, 354 P.3d 393 (Az. 2015), *cert denied* 136 S. Ct. 898 (2016)

As you study this chapter's materials on aspects of a defendant's "mental condition," consider why the Arizona Supreme Court held that the psychologist's evidence was admissible in *Leteve*, and when similar evidence about a defendant's mental condition might not be admissible in a state, like Arizona, that rejects the diminished capacity defense.

In this chapter we examine the rules that determine when persons can be held criminally responsible for their actions. We also learn about the evolution of the insanity defense and its place in criminal law today.

ANCIENT CONCEPTS OF CRIMINAL RESPONSIBILITY

The law has undergone many changes over the centuries regarding how to determine criminal responsibility and how to assess who has the capacity to commit a crime. At the time of the Norman Conquest of England (1066), for example, trial by ordeal and trial by battle were commonly used to determine criminal responsibility. If a person was of noble birth or was titled, he could demand trial by battle if accused of a crime. In trial by battle, if the suspect or accused came out second, it was then determined that he was guilty of the offense with which he was charged. However, the question of guilt or innocence could become moot, because the accused might be killed or badly injured.

trial by ordeal A test used to determine criminal responsibility in ancient England involving subjecting the individual to a torturous ordeal. These ordeals were essentially appeals to God; surviving the ordeal was viewed as God's judgment of innocence.

In determining criminal responsibility in a **trial by ordeal,** the accused often was required to take a pound weight of red-hot iron into his hands or to plunge his hand, up to the wrist, into boiling water. Ordeal by fire and ordeal by water were also used. Sir James Stephen described trial by ordeal in his *History of the Criminal Law of England,* published in 1883:

> It is unnecessary to give a minute account of the ceremonial of the ordeals. They were of various kinds. The general nature of all was the same. They were appeals to God to work a miracle in attestation of the innocence of the accused person. The handling of hot iron and immersion of the hand or arm in boiling water were the commonest. The ordeal of water was a very singular institution. Sinking was the sign of innocence, floating the sign of guilt. As anyone would sink unless he understood how to float, and intentionally did so, it is difficult to see how anyone could ever be convicted by this means. Is it possible that this ordeal may have been an honorable form of suicide, like the Japanese happy dispatch? In nearly every case the accused would sink. This would prove his innocence, indeed, but there would be no need to take him out. He would thus die honorably. If by accident he floated, he would be put to death disgracefully.[1]

Another form of superstition involved the concept that individuals deliberately became witches or practiced witchcraft. These individuals were thought to be capable of causing great social harm, such as crop failure, as well as causing serious injuries or illnesses and death to others. Witchcraft first became a crime under the Roman Empire. During the sixteenth, seventeenth, and eighteenth centuries, thousands of people were tried and put to death because they were believed to be either witches or to practice witchcraft. For example, Joan of Arc was charged with being a witch and condemned to death. She was burned at the stake in France in 1431.

Prosecution of such people in the American colonies occurred in Massachusetts, Connecticut, and Virginia. These trials reached a high point in 1692 in Salem,

Massachusetts, where 19 persons were executed as witches, and 150 more were sent to prison. The Salem trials were the last American witchcraft trials; the last English witchcraft trials took place in 1712. In 1735, Scotland repealed all laws that made witchcraft a crime in that country.

Today the lack of criminal responsibility and capacity are generally seen as potential excuses for the commission of acts that would ordinarily be criminal, as opposed to defenses to criminal liability. That is, if one who commits criminal acts can show he lacked responsibility or capacity, his actions are excused from criminal liability. In this chapter we examine the specifics of the traditional tests for determining responsibility and capacity, mainly as they apply to infancy and insanity. In later chapters we examine the circumstances where one accused of criminal acts might have a defense to criminal liability.

The capacity and criminal responsibility doctrines discussed in this chapter are often labeled affirmative defenses, though if proved they serve not as justification for actions, but as excuse of responsibility. In the case of infancy most states have adopted various presumptions about a child's criminal responsibility, as the materials below discuss. In the case of adults, in most states a defense of insanity requires the defendant to prove insanity by a **preponderance of the evidence**. The U.S. Supreme Court has long held that to require a defendant to prove insanity or other lack of criminal responsibility does not violate the Constitution.[2]

> **preponderance of the evidence** The greater weight of the evidence, though not necessarily the amount needed to remove every reasonable doubt. It is proof sufficient to incline a reasonable person toward one side of an issue rather than the other.

In only a very few states the prosecution must prove the presence of capacity or sanity, usually beyond a reasonable doubt. Most states treat lack of capacity or sanity as affirmative defenses, which must be proved by the defendant. However, in some of those states once some evidence of insanity has been introduced, the burden shifts to the prosecution to prove sanity. See *e.g., People v. Grenier*, 200 P.3d 1062 (Colo. 2008). Those states may have been influenced by the Model Penal Code, § 112 (1) and (2) (a), which requires the prosecution to prove an affirmative defense that relates to an element of the crime, once some evidence showing the defense has been introduced.

One aspect of criminal responsibility has seen recent developments. The U.S. Supreme Court held in *Atkins v. Virginia*, 536 U.S. 304 (2002), discussed in Chapter 8, that a mentally retarded person could not be subject to the death penalty. Following that decision, many states passed statutes establishing procedures for determining when a defendant is mentally retarded and thus not subject to the death penalty. Virtually all states placed the burden of proof of mental retardation on the defendant. While many state statutes only require proof by a preponderance of the evidence, others require proof by "clear and convincing" evidence. In *Stripling v. State*, 711 S.E.2d 665 (Ga. 2011), the Georgia Supreme Court held that the Georgia statute required the defendant to prove mental retardation by proof beyond a reasonable doubt.

> **infant (child)** Under the civil law, a person who has not yet reached the age of majority, whether that age is 18, 19, 20, or 21, as determined by the law of each jurisdiction.

Infancy and Criminal Responsibility

Under the civil law, an **infant (child)** is a person who has not yet reached the age of majority, whether that age is 18, 19, 20, or 21, as determined by the law of each jurisdiction. Although infants, with some exceptions, are not able to enter into contracts, make wills, or vote, the law on children's criminal responsibility for their acts differs from the law governing the children's civil capacity.

The question of the criminal responsibility of children first came before courts in Western Europe in the Middle Ages. By the fourteenth century, the common law had determined that children under the age of 7 did not have the capacity to commit a crime. By that time, 7 had been established as the "age of reason" under ecclesiastical law and also as the age of responsibility under Roman civil law. In establishing the age of 7 as the lowest age of criminal responsibility, the common law concluded that a child under the age of 7 did not have the mental capacity to formulate the intent to commit a crime and that, therefore, for children under 7, the threat of punishment would not serve as a deterrent against crime.

Many states have codified some version of the common law rules on children's criminal capacity, though they vary on the age limits adopted.[3] An example of a typical state statute determining children's criminal responsibility is Section 9A.04.050 of the Washington Statutes, which provides in part:

> Children under the age of eight years are incapable of committing crime. Children of 8 and under 12 years of age are presumed to be incapable of committing crime, but this presumption may be removed by proof that they have sufficient capacity to understand the act or neglect, and to know that it was wrong.

The age selected by the jurisdiction as the minimum age for a child's criminal responsibility creates a conclusive presumption that a child under that age lacks the capacity to commit a crime. As the presumption is conclusive, evidence to the contrary may not be presented. People over a certain age—in most states, around 14 years of age—are inferred to be capable of formulating the necessary mental frame of mind to commit a crime. Evidence showing otherwise, however, can be used to show incapacity. Moreover, such children may be prosecuted through the juvenile court system, rather than in adult court.

A rebuttable presumption exists under most state statutes and the common law that children between the minimum age (usually around 7) and the maximum age (usually around 14) are presumed to be without criminal capacity to commit a crime. This presumption, however, may be overcome by the presentation of evidence by the state showing that the child has the mental capacity and the ability to formulate the necessary criminal intent.[4]

The U.S. courts look to a variety of factors when the capacity presumption is at issue, and they usually hold that the younger the child, the stronger must be the evidence of mental capacity. The Washington Supreme Court considered the presumption contained in the statute cited above in the case of *State v. Ramer.*[5] There, an 11-year-old boy was charged with first-degree rape of a child, a 7-year-old boy. The state unsuccessfully attempted to prove the child had the capacity to understand the nature of his acts and that the acts were wrong. In reviewing the trial court's decision, the Washington Supreme Court said,

> We have identified seven factors to consider in determining capacity: (1) the nature of the crime, (2) the child's age and maturity, (3) whether the child evidenced a desire for secrecy, (4) whether the child told the victim (if any) not to tell, (5) prior conduct similar to that charged, (6) any consequences that attached to that prior conduct, and (7) whether the child had made an acknowledgment that the behavior is wrong and could lead to detention.[6]

The court also noted that in sexual charges against children, it is difficult to overcome the presumption, because it is hard to tell if children understand prohibitions on sexual behavior. Based on the testimony of two psychologists, who both stated the child did not understand that his conduct was wrong, the court agreed that the state failed to overcome the presumption of incapacity.

The Juvenile Court System

All states have enacted statutes governing the jurisdiction of children's (juvenile) courts. These courts deal with children who are delinquent and in need of supervision or with children who are neglected and dependent. "Delinquency" is usually defined by statute as conduct by a child that, if committed by an adult, would be a violation of the criminal code of that state. States vary on the maximum age for the jurisdiction of juvenile courts but usually set a limit around 18 years of age. State statutes also generally provide that juvenile courts may waive jurisdiction to the adult courts of children otherwise under the jurisdiction of the juvenile court.

The primary goal of juvenile courts, as compared to adult courts, is the rehabilitation of delinquent youths. To that end, dispositions in juvenile court are viewed not as punishment for a crime, but steps designed to help the delinquent child mature into a law-abiding adult. However, the rise of serious, violent juvenile crime in the 1980s and 1990s created an atmosphere of anxiety and fear among the general public. These events caused many state legislatures to modify the juvenile court system, mainly to make it easier for a juvenile to be waived out of the system and into adult court. These modifications took two forms. In one form, states' statutes listed crimes committed by juveniles over a designated age, usually 16, for which the juvenile courts had no jurisdiction. Typically those crimes are murder, sexual assault, use of a firearm in a crime, or any felony that results in death or serious bodily harm.

Under the other form of modification, states began expanding the circumstances under which a juvenile could be transferred from juvenile court to adult court. At least 40 states now have some form of transfer statute, and the age of youths eligible for transfer has dropped significantly. For example, the Ohio transfer statutes, Ohio R.C. § 2152.10 and .12 make transfer mandatory where the crime charged is a category one crime (murder or attempted murder) and the child is 16 or 17. It also provides for mandatory transfer of a child who is 14 or 15 and has previously been declared delinquent in a category one or two (e.g., armed robbery) crime. For other crimes and younger offenders, transfer is discretionary and a hearing in juvenile court must occur. *State v D.W.*, 978 N.E.2d 894 (Ohio 2012)

An example of such a hearing in juvenile court can be found in *In re J.C.N.-V*, 342 P.3d 1046 (Or. App. 2015). There, a 13-year-old boy participated, with a 20-year-old friend, in the planned murder and robbery of a victim. There was no question of the juvenile's involvement with the acts leading to the victim's death. The state moved to remove the case from juvenile to adult court, as provided by ORS 419C.349 and 352. Under those statutes, a juvenile under the age of 15 may be transferred to adult court if the juvenile court determines the juvenile possessed "sufficient sophistication and maturity" to appreciate the nature of the criminal conduct. If that determination is made, the court must consider the best interests of the juvenile and society, taking into account factors like the severity of the offense, amenability of the juvenile to treatment, and prior offenses and treatments.

The juvenile court determined transfer was proper, and granted the state's request for transfer to adult court. The juvenile appealed that order, contending that the juvenile court erred in determining he possessed the requisite "sophistication and maturity" under the transfer statute. The court of appeals affirmed the juvenile court's order. It stated that the evidence introduced in the transfer proceedings showed the juvenile possessed the sophistication and maturity of an average 13 year-old, and that was all the statute required. It rejected the juvenile's contention that the statute required a showing he possessed the sophistication of a person who could be tried as an adult, which is presumably greater than that possessed by an average 13-year-old child. The Oregon Supreme Court agreed to review the decision, 357 Or. 324 (2015).

THE INSANITY DEFENSE

No subject in criminal law has received as much attention and debate as the insanity defense. The questions of what degree of insanity, mental defect, or mental disease renders a person blameless for acts or omissions and what **insanity tests** should be used in determining legal and moral liability have been debated for years.

insanity tests Tests to determine legal and moral liability.

Defense lawyers seldom use the insanity defense for minor criminal charges.[7] It is most often used in murder cases and for other serious felony charges in which the evidence against a defendant may be so strong that no other defense is available.

Studies have shown that the insanity plea is usually not an easy way out for criminal defendants and that only about 2 percent of defendants charged with serious crimes use the insanity plea.[8] The success rate among defendants using the insanity plea is not high when medical doctors differ as to the sanity of a defendant. Terrible and gross crimes by themselves are not likely to convince a jury to make a finding of "not guilty by reason of insanity."

In most jurisdictions the burden is on the defendant to prove the insanity defense, usually by a preponderance of the evidence.

Insanity at the Time of the Criminal Incident

The question of insanity (mental disease or defect) may be raised at specific stages during the criminal proceedings. If a defendant is found insane at the time the crime occurred, the court enters a judgment of not guilty by reason of insanity, and the defendant may never again be tried for that offense.

A defendant who is found not guilty by reason of insanity is almost always committed to a mental institution under the laws of that state (or the federal government). Such state and federal laws provide for the length of stay and the conditions under which the person may be eligible for release.[9]

In the case of *Foucha v. Louisiana*,[10] the defendant was found not guilty of burglary by reason of insanity. After four years in a state psychiatric hospital, a doctor at the hospital stated that Foucha was no longer mentally ill, but declined to certify that the defendant was no longer a danger to himself or others. Under Louisiana law at that time, Foucha had the burden of proving that he was no longer dangerous in order to earn his release from the hospital.

The U.S. Supreme Court held that the Louisiana law violated due process: "the State must establish insanity and dangerousness by clear and convincing evidence in order to confine an insane convict beyond his criminal sentence, when the basis for his original confinement no longer exists." The Court stated that since the State conceded Foucha was no longer insane, the only basis for holding him was his dangerousness. While "dangerousness" by itself can sometimes be a basis for confining a person, the Court said, it must be proved by the State, not disproved by the person confined.

The holding in *Foucha,* where the State conceded the defendant was no longer insane, should be contrasted to the burden of proof required for the release of a person committed after a finding of not guilty by reason of insanity. It is common for commitment statutes to place the burden of proving a person committed is no longer insane on that person, not the government. For example, in *United States v. Weed,*[11] a defendant was found not guilty by reason of insanity of the murder of a postal worker, a federal offense. Under the federal commitment statute, 18 U.S.C. § 4243, after such a verdict a hearing is held to determine if the defendant should be confined in a mental institution or released "because no longer dangerous" to others. At that hearing, section 4243(d) requires the defendant to prove by "clear and convincing" evidence that his mental condition does not present a risk to others. The court held that since the defendant had the benefit of a jury trial in which it was found he was insane, sufficient reason existed to confine him, and that it thus became his burden to show that the reason no longer existed.

TESTS USED TO DETERMINE INSANITY

If a state permits a defense to criminal charges based on insanity, it remains to be determined how the insanity decision is made. In *Clark v. Arizona,* 126 S. Ct. 2709 (2006), the U.S. Supreme Court reviewed the kinds of tests traditionally used to make that determination, and listed the states using the various tests. It noted that states are free to define insanity as they think proper. The Court found that the insanity tests have historically followed one or more of four approaches: (1) cognitive incapacity, (2) moral incapacity, (3) volitional incapacity, and (4) the product of mental illness.

Numbers (1) and (2) combined are the *M'Naghten* rule, number (3) is commonly called the "substantial capacity" rule, and number (4) is usually referred to as the "product" rule. The *Clark* Court stated that seventeen states and the federal government have adopted the *M'Naghten* rule. One state has adopted only the "cognitive incapacity" approach, and ten have adopted only the "moral incapacity" approach. Fourteen states have adopted the "volitional incapacity" approach, most using the Model Penal Code's "substantial capacity" as a model. Two states combine the *M'Naghten* rule with "substantial capacity." Only one state, New Hampshire, has adopted the "product-of-mental-illness" approach. The following materials in this section discuss those rules in more detail. The verdict of "guilty but mentally ill" is also discussed in this section, while the "diminished capacity" test appears in the next section.

The *M'Naghten* Case and the "Right and Wrong" Test

It was not until the 1800s that English and American courts considered the question of whether insanity, mental disease, and mental defect should be factors in determining the criminal responsibility of people charged with crimes. The **"right and wrong" test**, which became the most widely used test to determine the question of

"right and wrong" test An insanity test that claims that defendants are not legally responsible for their acts if, due to a defect of the mind, at the time of the crime they were unable to understand the difference between right and wrong.

legal insanity in the United States, was developed in 1843 in the aftermath of the famous English murder case of *Rex v. M'Naghten,* House of Lords, 1843.[12]

Daniel M'Naghten lived in London in the 1840s and believed that the British Home Secretary, Sir Robert Peel, was the head of a conspiracy to kill him. (Peel was the widely recognized founder of the British police, who thus received the nickname "bobbies.") In 1843, M'Naghten shot and killed Edward Drummond, private secretary to Peel, because he mistook Drummond for Peel. At his trial, the defense argued that M'Naghten was insane at the time of the shooting and that he should not be held responsible because his mental delusions had caused him to act as he did. The British jury agreed, and M'Naghten was found not guilty because of insanity.

The "right and wrong" test that emerged from the *M'Naghten* case has become the prevailing standard and test for insanity in U.S. courts. Under the *M'Naghten* rule, defendants are not legally responsible for their acts if at the time they were "laboring under such a defect of reason, from disease of the mind, as not to know the nature and quality of the act he was doing, or, if he did know it, that he did not know that what he was doing was wrong." 8 Eng. Rep. at 722 Under this rule, insanity is present when a person, because of mental illness, either has "cognitive incapacity," that is, does not know what actions he is taking, or "moral incapacity," that is, he does not know the actions taken were wrong.

M'Naghten rule The insanity defense rule requiring proof that because of mental disease or defect defendants did not know the scope or character of their actions.

The *M'Naghten rule* established the burden of proof as follows:

> Every man is presumed to be sane and to possess a sufficient degree of reason to be responsible for his crimes, until the contrary be proved to (the jury's) satisfaction; and that to establish a defense on the ground of insanity, it must be clearly proved.

The "Product-of-Mental-Illness Rule" and "Irresistible Impulse"

After courts had for some time used the *M'Naghten* rule to determine insanity, many were critical of the rule. According to its critics, the principal fault of the *M'Naghten* rule was its narrowness and its restricted application to only a small percentage of the people who are mentally ill. The rule does not, critics said, recognize that mental illness is not limited to an inability to *know* that one is doing wrong, but includes an inability to control one's acts even if known to be wrong. In response to this criticism, a few states adopted a form of "volitional incapacity" called the "irresistible impulse" and added it to the *M'Naghten* rule.[13] Under this test, defendants must prove that even if they knew what they were doing was wrong, mental illness prevented them from controlling their conduct.[14]

The irresistible impulse rule has not been widely adopted, mainly because courts and legislators have concluded that it lacks precision on the question of what an impulse is and when it is irresistible.

The "product-of-mental-illness" approach has had very limited adoption. In 1954, a form of this approach called the *Durham* product test was adopted by the U.S. Court of Appeals for the District of Columbia in the case of *Durham v. United States.*[15] The court stated that "an accused is not criminally responsible if his unlawful act was the product of mental disease or defect." The *Durham* case established a test for insanity based on a *substantial* lack of mental capacity rather than a complete lack of capacity. It has been criticized on the grounds that it is too broad and gives psychiatrists, rather than the jury, too much discretion in determining the legal issue of insanity. "Criminal responsibility is a legal not a medical question."[16]

In 1984 Congress passed the Insanity Defense Reform Act, 18 U.S.C. § 17. This act established a rule for federal criminal prosecutions that is virtually identical to the *M'Naghten* rule. The Act was designed to abolish both the "irresistible impulse" rule and the *Durham* test. Section 17 states:

> It is an affirmative defense to a prosecution under any Federal statute that, at the time of the commission of the offense, the defendant, as a result of severe mental illness or defect, was unable to appreciate the nature and quality or the wrongfulness of his acts. Mental disease or defect does not otherwise constitute a defense.

The federal rule may differ from the *M'Naghten* rule in one important respect. While it is a solely "cognitive" rule like *M'Naghten*, an inability to "appreciate" the nature or wrongfulness of conduct may be a lower standard than "know" the nature or wrongfulness of conduct.

Congress also addressed the criticism that "criminal responsibility" is not a medical question by providing in Rule 704(b) of the Federal Rules of Evidence that a medical expert may not render an expert opinion on the ultimate question of a defendant's sanity under the statute. Most states that considered the "product-of-mental-illness" test ultimately adopted a test modeled on the "substantial capacity" test discussed next.

The Model Penal Code "Substantial Capacity" Test

About a year after the adoption of the *Durham* test by a few jurisdictions, the American Law Institute proposed still another test for determining criminal responsibility. In proposing the new test, the following comment was made:

> No problem in the drafting of a penal code presents larger intrinsic difficulty than that of determining when individuals whose conduct would otherwise be criminal ought to be exculpated (freed of guilt) on the grounds that they were suffering from mental disease or defect when they acted as they did. What is involved specifically is the drawing of a line between the use of public agencies and public force to condemn the offender by conviction. . . . [T]he problem is to discriminate between the cases where a punitive-correctional disposition is appropriate and those in which a medical-custodial disposition is the only kind that the law should allow.[17]

"substantial capacity" test A test to determine criminal responsibility based on whether the defendant could (1) distinguish between right and wrong or (2) conform his or her conduct to the requirements of law.

The final draft of the American Law Institute (ALI) **"substantial capacity" test,** found in Section 4.01 of the Model Penal Code, states:

1. A person is not responsible for criminal conduct if at the time of such conduct as a result of mental disease or defect he lacks substantial capacity either to appreciate the criminality (wrongfulness) of his conduct or to conform his conduct to the requirements of law.

2. As used in the Article, the terms *mental disease* or *defect* do not include an abnormality manifested only by repeated criminal or otherwise antisocial conduct.

The Model Penal Code test (or the ALI "substantial capacity" test) reportedly has now been adopted by about half the states.

The *M'Naghten* rule requires a defendant to show total mental incapacity; an impairment that prevents the defendant from "knowing" either what he is doing, or that it is wrong. The MPC test puts less of a burden on defendants. Under the "substantial capacity" test, the "cognitive" part of the rule is satisfied even if defendants "knew" what they had done, but lacked the "substantial capacity" to appreciate that what they had done was wrong. The rule does not require a showing of total incapacity. The "volitional" part of the rule, the ability to control one's conduct even if it is known to be wrong, also requires only a showing of lack of substantial capacity. To that extent the MPC rule incorporates some aspects of the "irresistible impulse" rule.

EXAMPLE   Vincent Vento, a man with a history of mental illness, violently attacked a neighbor and caused serious injuries. He was charged with substantial battery under Wisconsin law. Vento was initially determined not to be competent to participate in his trial, but with medication was later found competent. Before trial he raised the insanity defense under Wisconsin's statute, which uses the "substantial capacity" version of the insanity defense. The trial court concluded Vento failed to prove he lacked substantial capacity to control his conduct, and convicted him of the battery.

On appeal, the Wisconsin Court of Appeals reversed the trial judge, and ordered a new trial. It noted that while the trial court agreed Vento had severe psychotic delusions, and may have been suffering from one at the time of the attack on the neighbor, the trial court also concluded Vento was able to generally "maintain himself in the community." The appeals court said this amounted to a requirement that Vento prove there "was no other possible explanation for his behavior." That, the court held, is not the correct meaning of the "substantial capacity" test. *State v. Vento*, 833 N.W.2d 873 (Wis. App. 2013)

Because of the publicity surrounding many recent uses of the insanity defense, some states that have used the Model Penal Code "substantial capacity" test have returned to the stricter standards of the *M'Naghten* rule. In addition, five states—Idaho, Montana, Kansas, Nevada, and Utah—have passed legislation that abolished the insanity defense.

The Montana Supreme Court has held that the abolition of the insanity defense did not violate the Constitution *(Montana v. Cowan)*.[18] The U.S. Supreme Court denied certiorari.[19] The Supreme Courts of Idaho, Kansas, and Utah[20] all reached the same result. However, in 2001 the Nevada Supreme Court reached the opposite conclusion and held the Nevada statute abolishing the insanity defense unconstitutional.[21] Nev. Rev. Stat. § 194.010 (2004) now follows the *M'Naghten* rule.

The U.S. Supreme Court has never expressly held that a state may abolish the insanity defense. In *Clark v. Arizona*, 126 S. Ct. 2709 (2006) the Court affirmed a lower court's decision that Arizona legislation that narrowed the insanity defense to apply only to the second prong of the *M'Naghten* rule, proof a defendant did not know what he was doing was wrong, did not violate due process. It also upheld Arizona's court rule that expert evidence of a defendant's mental illness was not admissible on the question of the required mens rea of a crime.

The states listed above that have abolished the insanity defense reject the idea that mental illness can serve as basis for excusing the criminal conduct of a defendant. It does not follow from that rejection, however, that mental illness is never admissible

Andy Cross-Pool/Pool/Getty Images

Robert Dear, who in 2015 killed three persons at a Colorado Springs, Colorado, Planned Parenthood center. In 2016, a trial judge ruled Dear incompetent to stand trial.

in a criminal prosecution. Idaho's statute abolishing the insanity defense, as an example, states that expert evidence of a defendant's mental condition is admissible to show the defendant lacked a specific intent required by the statute. Idaho Code Ann. § 18-207 (3) The distinction is between using the evidence to completely excuse the criminal act (insanity), and using the evidence (like any other type of evidence) to rebut the prosecution's burden to prove all the elements of a crime, including any specific intent.

EXAMPLE   The crime of burglary has a specific intent, i.e. to enter premises of another with intent to commit a crime therein. The prosecution must prove each element of the crime, including the intent to commit a crime once entry has occurred. Consider the following rebuttal evidence from the defendant: (1) The defendant thought it was his house; (2) the defendant was drunk; and (3) the defendant suffered from a mental condition that caused him to believe "God told me all property belongs to me." Each of these evidentiary offerings, if believed, rebuts the specific intent requirement of the statute. In a state like Idaho, each would in theory be admissible.

The perceived effect of the Idaho statute abolishing the insanity defense but retaining the "mens rea" use of evidence of mental illness has caused three Justices of the U.S. Supreme Court to doubt the wisdom of the statute. In *Delling v. Idaho*, 133 S. Ct. 504 (2012) the Court refused to grant certiorari to review an Idaho Supreme Court decision upholding the constitutionality of the Idaho statute that abolished the insanity defense in that state. In a dissent joined by two other Justices, Justice Breyer used the following example to illustrate what he considered the unfairness of the Idaho statute: A person who because of mental illness shot and killed another person, believing that person to be a wolf, would not be convicted of murder because it requires proof of the specific intent to take a human's life. But a person who shot and killed another person because his mental illness made him believe a supernatural wolf commanded him to do so would be convicted of murder. The second person possesses the required specific intent for the crime of murder, even though his mental illness made it impossible for him to perceive his conduct was wrong, Justice Breyer said. The dissenting Justices would have granted the petition to determine if the Idaho law was constitutional.

The Plea and Verdict of Guilty but Mentally Ill[22]

guilty but mentally ill A defendant may be found guilty but mentally ill if all the following are found beyond a reasonable doubt: (1) defendant is guilty of the offense; (2) defendant was mentally ill at the time the offense was committed; and (3) defendant was not legally insane at the time the offense was committed.

The incidence of people who are found not guilty because of insanity and who then go on to commit other violent crimes after release from mental hospitals has caused thirteen states to adopt the plea and verdict of **guilty but mentally ill**.[23] (Statutes authorizing this plea and verdict are often called "GBMI" laws.) The Michigan legislature was the first to do so in 1975, when it enacted Mich. Comb. Laws § 768.36 after several defendants found not guilty of earlier murders because of insanity committed additional murders.

The public outcry over the insanity defense can be illustrated by events arising in an insanity defense case in Illinois. In that case, Thomas Vanda killed a girl when he was 18 years old. While undergoing psychiatric treatment in Chicago, he was released and killed another girl. He was found not guilty because of insanity. When doctors concluded that his psychosis had disappeared, he was again released over objections from the trial judge and his own defense attorney. In 1978, when he was 25 years old, Thomas Vanda was again charged with murder. The third victim was a 25-year-old woman.

Illinois enacted a guilty but mentally ill statute in 1981. Former Illinois Governor James R. Thompson described the new statutory procedure as follows:

> Under this procedure, when an insanity defense is raised, the court, if the evidence permits, may instruct the jury on the alternative verdict of guilty but mentally ill.

When a person is not legally insane, he or she may be found guilty but mentally ill if, at the time of the offense, he or she suffered from a disorder of thought or mood that does not represent a condition amounting to insanity in the legal sense. When a guilty but mentally ill verdict is returned, the court may impose any sentence that could have been ordered for a conviction on the crime charged. However, the prison authorities must provide necessary psychiatric or psychological treatment to restore the offender to full capacity in an appropriate treatment setting. If the mental illness is cured, the offender must be returned to prison to serve out his or her sentence.

The guilty but mentally ill verdict does not abolish the insanity defense. It simply recognizes that there are gradations in the degree of mental impairment; it provides accountability, promotes treatment, and eliminates the need to manipulate the system.

 ## WHEN DOES MENTAL ILLNESS BECOME INSANITY?

On July 20, 2012 James Holmes entered an Aurora, Colorado, movie theater showing the premier of the Batman movie "The Dark Knight Rises." Armed with a rifle, shotgun and pistol, Holmes fired his weapons into the theater audience at random, killing 12 people and injuring more than 50 others. He then left the theater and surrendered to police.

At his murder trial (after a determination he was competent to stand trial) Holmes raised the insanity defense. Under Colorado law, which defines insanity as a mental disease or defect that makes the defendant incapable of "distinguishing right from wrong" or unable to form the "culpable mental state" (mens rea) of the crime, once some evidence of insanity is introduced by the defendant, the presumption of sanity is gone. The prosecution must then prove sanity, as well as the other elements of the crime, beyond a reasonable doubt.

It was undisputed that Holmes suffered from bouts of schizophrenia; he had been experiencing homicidal thoughts since he was 12, he wrote in a notebook sent to a Colorado University counsellor just hours before the theater killings. The culmination of that struggle, Holmes said, was to put him on a "mission" to kill as many people as possible. Defense psychiatrists testified that Holmes was delusional at the time of the killings, and could not distinguish right from wrong.

Prosecution psychiatrists testified that Holmes was able to distinguish right from wrong. They stated that in interviews with Holmes he told them it was legally wrong to kill, and that one gets punished for killing people. The prosecution argued that the extensive planning done by Holmes before the shooting spree, as well as the fact he peacefully surrendered to police, were signs of a rational mind, not a delusional one. Under the Colorado version of the *M'Naghten* rule, Holmes could be found insane only if he had "cognitive" disability caused by his mental illness, that is, that he did not know the difference between right and wrong. His behavior and statements after the shooting spree, the prosecution argued, showed that Holmes knew what he was doing, and that it was wrong. Moreover, the state argued, his extensive planning showed he possessed the required mens rea of premeditated murder.

The jury rejected Holmes' insanity defense, and found him guilty of 12 murders. However, it could not agree on the death penalty. On August 27, 2015 Holmes was sentenced to life in prison for each person he killed, plus 3,318 years for the other crimes he committed. Holmes will never be eligible for parole.

Is it possible a court or jury would reach a different result in Holmes' case in a state that uses the "substantial capacity," "volitional," test? Consider the similarities and differences compared to Holmes' case in the murder conviction and insanity defense in *State v. Kucharski*, 866 N.W.2d 697 (Wis. 2015)

Most important, it is designed to protect the public from violence inflicted by people with mental ailments who previously slipped through the cracks in the criminal justice system.[24]

In most states, the statute authorizing a GBMI verdict allocates the burden of proof as follows: First, the prosecution must prove beyond a reasonable doubt that the defendant committed the crime charged. Second, the jury must determine if the defendant was legally insane. Typically, the defendant must prove insanity by a preponderance of the evidence standard, though a few states place the burden of proving sanity on the prosecution. If the jury finds the defendant was not legally insane, it must determine if the defendant was mentally ill—that is, whether the defendant suffered from some mental impairment that affected his ability to control or understand his behavior, but that did not amount to insanity. In most jurisdictions, the prosecution must prove mental illness beyond a reasonable doubt. See, e.g., Ga. Code Ann. § 17-7-131. A few jurisdictions demand only proof by a preponderance of the evidence. See, e.g., *Commonwealth v. Rabold,* 951 A2d 329 (Pa. 2008).

Defendants convicted with GBMI verdicts have frequently attacked the GBMI statute as unconstitutional under the Due Process Clause, contending the presence of the GBMI option permits the prosecution to effectively convict a defendant without proving guilt beyond a reasonable doubt. To date, no court has declared a GBMI statute unconstitutional. See 2 *Wharton's Criminal Law* § 105 (15th ed. 2007).

Opponents of the guilty but mentally ill verdict argue that it is nothing but a nice name for "guilty and going to prison." The National Alliance for the Mentally Ill opposes such legislation "because it would stigmatize insane offenders with a criminal conviction, compounding the handicaps already faced by those persons in obtaining employment and social acceptance."[25]

MENTAL CONDITIONS THAT DO NOT SATISFY THE INSANITY DEFENSE

Many mental conditions do not rise to the level of "insanity" and thus do not provide a defense to criminal conduct. For example, the battered woman syndrome, discussed in Chapter 6, has rarely been successfully raised as a mental disease. Nor have claims like television intoxication, premenstrual syndrome, or so-called cultural defenses.

Defendants have tried to use compulsive gambling as a defense against criminal charges such as theft, bank robbery, and embezzlement. They argue they would not have committed such crimes but were compelled to do so because of their gambling urges.[26] For example, in the case of *United States v. Lynch,* the defendant stole $7.5 million and unsuccessfully asserted compulsive gambling in an attempt to be found not guilty on his insanity plea.[27]

In all the reported cases, defendants using compulsive gambling as a defense have failed to be found not guilty because of insanity. There is no showing of acceptance in the mental health field that a compulsive gambler is unable to resist the impulse to steal or to commit other crimes.

Prosecutors argue that accepting compulsive gambling as an insanity defense could set a dangerous precedent. In any state that would allow such a defense, thieves could claim kleptomania as a defense, arsonists could claim pyromania, perjurers could claim pathologic lying, drunk drivers could claim alcoholism, and prostitutes could claim nymphomania.

Voluntary Intoxication   Voluntary intoxication or drug abuse can sometimes lead to the same mental impairment that constitutes the classic insanity defense: A person drunk or high might not "know" what he is doing. Though voluntary intoxication might establish the diminished capacity defense by eliminating the defendant's ability to form a required specific intent (see Chapter 7), virtually all states reject such voluntary intoxication or drug abuse acts as a sufficient basis for the insanity defense. For example, in the 2011 case *State v. Hotz*, 795 N.W.2d 645 (Neb. 2011), the court held that a defendant who suffered a psychotic episode caused by ingesting hallucinogenic drugs could not use that mental state as proof of the insanity defense. Citing cases in other states, the court noted that some states permit the insanity defense where voluntary intoxication or drug use has created a "settled" psychotic mental state, that is, where prolonged use of drugs or alcohol has permanently altered the defendant's mental condition. The court did, however, permit evidence of the defendant's mental state on the issue of his diminished capacity to form the specific intent required under the Nebraska murder statute.

Some states permit evidence of intoxication or drug abuse to be used in an insanity defense, if it is shown the intoxication or abuse triggered a preexisting mental illness that would satisfy the insanity defense. In *Com. v. Rivera*, 979 N.E.2d 1112 (Mass. App. 2012), *rev. denied* 984 N.E.2d 295 (Mass. 2013) the court reversed a defendant's conviction for armed assault with intent to murder a police officer. The defendant suffered from severe paranoid schizophrenia that caused serious delusions, but which could be somewhat controlled by medications. However, stopping the medications and ingesting alcohol, as the defendant did for several days before the assault, triggered the mental illness and accompanying violent delusions. The jury convicted the defendant of assault with intent to murder, but on appeal the court ordered a new trial to determine if the existing mental illness by itself satisfied the "substantial capacity" test for insanity. If it did, and it was triggered by the voluntary intoxication, the defendant was not criminally responsible, the court said. The court also said that on remand the jury must consider whether the defendant knew the use of alcohol would trigger his mental illness. In such a case, the insanity defense would not apply, the court said.

THE DEFENSE OF DIMINISHED CAPACITY

diminished capacity defense A defense for criminal responsibility based on the fact that because of mental or emotional conditions, the defendant did not possess the required *mens rea* for conviction of crime charged.

In some states a defendant is permitted to assert what is usually called the **diminished capacity defense.** It applies when a defendant has introduced evidence of mental incapacity that does not satisfy the requirement for a finding of insanity under the relevant statute. A court may consider the evidence on the issue of the defendant's requisite *mens rea* for crimes that require a specific intent. Under this defense, it is possible that a defendant was not insane at the time he committed the crime charged, but that his mental condition made it impossible to entertain some specific intent required for conviction. This basis for this defense and its consequences were discussed in the case of *United States v. Fishman* as follows:

> The defense of "diminished capacity" is simply a label that identifies evidence introduced by a defendant to support a claim that he did not commit the crime charged because he did not possess the requisite *mens rea*. A diminished capacity defense varies from a legal insanity defense in several important respects. Whereas following a successful legal insanity defense the court retains control of the defendant and may order involuntary commitment, a successful diminished capacity defense results in a complete acquittal of the crime charged.[28]

The diminished capacity defense under the Federal Insanity Defense Reform Act, 18 U.S.C. § 17, is generally permitted in federal prosecutions. Section 17(a) of the Act adopts a test for insanity that is essentially the *M'Naghten* rule, and identifies it as an affirmative defense, which under § 17(b) the defendant must prove by clear and convincing evidence. Section 17(a) also states that except as set forth for the insanity defense, "Mental disease or defect does not otherwise constitute a defense." Courts applying this sentence to the diminished capacity defense generally conclude that Congress intended only to exclude evidence of mental incapacity as proof of any other test for insanity. Congress did not intend to exclude evidence of mental incapacity less than legal insanity on other issues, such as the absence of the required *mens rea* in a crime. Thus, diminished capacity is in fact not a "defense" at all, since it cannot be used to excuse a defendant, as a true insanity defense could. It is better seen as an evidentiary rule, permitting a defendant to introduce evidence of diminished capacity as relevant to the presence or absence of any required specific intent in a statute.

A number of states that retain the insanity defense have decided, either by statute or by court rule, that the diminished capacity defense is not available to rebut the prosecution's proof of a mens rea requirement. In those states the insanity defense is an "all or nothing" defense. If the defendant is found not to be insane, then no further expert evidence about his mental condition is permitted. See *Clark v. Arizona*, discussed earlier in this chapter. However, even in those states, so-called non-expert, "observation evidence" about a defendant's actions that tend to show the defendant lacked the ability to form the required knowledge or intent under a statue is usually permitted.

It is commonly said that the concept of "diminished capacity" is not clearly and uniformly understood and applied in all state and federal courts. See E. Nevins-Saunders, *Not Guilty as Charged: The Myth of Mens Rea for Defendants with Mental Retardation* 45 U. C. Davis L. Rev. 1419, 1456 (2012). In the 2014 case of *State v. Congress*, 114 A.3d 1128 (Vt. 2014), *cert denied* 136 S. Ct. 83 (2015) the Vermont Supreme Court announced its decision to clear up confusion among trial courts and juries on the proper use of "diminished capacity" in homicide cases.

In *Congress* the defendant was convicted by a jury of second degree murder in the stabbing death of her niece. At her trial she offered evidence from psychologists that she suffered from "acute stress disorder." Based on what had been the practice in Vermont murder trials, the defendant's lawyer requested instructions to the jury that it could find the defendant (1) not guilty because of insanity, (2) guilty of involuntary manslaughter if her impaired mental state made it impossible to possess the specific intent to kill as required by murder (the traditional diminished capacity instruction), and (3) guilty of voluntary manslaughter, treating her impaired mental state as an extenuating circumstance similar to provocation, the usual basis for lowering a murder to voluntary manslaughter. (See Chapter 10.)

The trial court refused to give the requested third instruction, and the defendant was convicted of second degree murder. The Vermont Supreme court, noting that "we have sent mixed signals on the question" of using diminished capacity to reduce a murder charge to voluntary manslaughter, held that the trial judge was correct in refusing to give the third instruction. Mental illness, the court said, can either excuse the homicide under the insanity defense, or eliminate proof of specific intent, resulting at most in a conviction for involuntary manslaughter. Diminished capacity cannot be used to reduce a murder charge to voluntary manslaughter, since that crime, like murder, has a specific intent requirement, the court held.

 TESTS OR PROCEDURES USED TO DETERMINE CRIMINAL RESPONSIBILITY

Test or Procedure	Year When First Used	Type of Test	Current Extent of Use
M'Naghten "right and wrong" test	1843	Based on ability of defendant to know the difference between right and wrong.	Used by practically all U.S. courts until the 1970s. Now used, with variations, by about half of the states.
Model Penal Code "substantial capacity" test	1955	Did defendant have the "substantial capacity" to (1) distinguish between right and wrong or (2) conform his or her conduct to the requirements of law?	Used in some states, though California and the federal courts have returned to use of the *M'Naghten* rule.
Guilty but mentally ill alternative verdict and plea	1975	Defendant may be found guilty but mentally ill if all the following are found beyond a reasonable doubt: (1) defendant is guilty of offense; (2) defendant was mentally ill at time offense was committed; and (3) defendant was not legally insane at time offense was committed.	Used in thirteen states with either the *M'Naghten rule* or the "substantial capacity" test.
Diminished capacity defense	1957	Defense seeks to introduce evidence showing that because of mental or emotional conditions, the defendant did not possess the required *mens rea* for conviction of crime charged.	A finding that the state failed to prove the *mens rea* for the crime charged could result in a finding of not guilty of the more serious offense, but guilty of a lesser offense.

SEXUAL VIOLENT PREDATOR LAWS AND INVOLUNTARY CIVIL COMMITMENT LAWS

Type of Law	Examples
Sexual violent predator laws used to detain persons likely to be sexually violent	Sexual violent predators are persons who have been convicted of a sexual violent crime. Once released from confinement, such persons often revert to their previous actions. In May 2010 John Gardner, a convicted sexual offender released on parole in California, was sentenced to life imprisonment for the rapes and murders of Chelsea King, 17, and Amber DuBois, 14. In response to cases like this, most states have adopted Sexual Violent Predator Laws (SVP laws) that permit states to bring civil commitment proceedings against the offender based on a showing the person is a sexual violent offender, and poses a substantial risk of future violent sexual actions. In *Crane v. Kansas*, 534 U.S. 407 (2002), the U.S. Supreme Court held that in civil commitment proceedings under SVP statutes the state must prove not only that the person is a sexual violent offender who is a danger to others, but also that the offender lacks significant control over his actions. In *United States v. Comstock*, 130 S. Ct. 1949 (2010), the U.S. Supreme Court held that Congress possessed the power to pass a law permitting federal officials to bring civil commitment proceedings to keep dangerous sex offenders confined after their prison sentences have been served. In the 2013 case of *United States v. Kebodeaux*, 133 S. Ct. 2496, the U.S. Supreme Court held federal courts possessed jurisdiction to hear charges that defendants who had been released from federal custody after serving prison terms for sex offenses violated SORNA registration provisions. The U.S. Supreme Court has repeatedly affirmed state sexual violent predator laws that permit a state to hold for an indefinite period of time anyone "who has been convicted or charged with a sexual violent offense and who suffers from a mental abnormality or personality disorder which makes the person likely to engage in predatory acts of sexual violence." *Kansas v. Hendricks*, 117 S. Ct. 2072 (1997). If such laws are civil and not criminal, and not punitive in nature, they do not violate the *Due Process, Ex Post Facto,* or *Double Jeopardy* clauses. As treatment is not a constitutional requirement for civil commitment, such laws do not have to provide for treatment. See also *Allen v. Illinois*, 106 S. Ct. 2988 (1986).
Emergency mental detention laws and civil commitment to mental hospital laws	States have emergency mental detention laws under which persons who appear dangerous to themselves or others or are unable to care for themselves may be detained for mental observation for a short period of time, as provided by the statutes of that state. For example, a person who has attempted to commit suicide could be detained for medical observation for a time as provided by the statute of that state.

THE REQUIREMENT OF COMPETENCY TO STAND TRIAL

competency to stand trial Defendants must have the ability to cooperate with their attorneys and the ability to understand the charges and proceedings against them.

A defendant must be competent (mentally fit) before the government can force him or her to go to trial on criminal charges. The U.S. Supreme Court has stated:

> A person whose mental condition is such that he lacks the capacity to understand the nature and object of the proceedings against him, to consult with counsel, and to assist in preparing his defense may not be subjected to a trial.[29]

The test for **competency to stand trial** originated in the common law and now has been codified in state and federal statutes. For example, 18 U.S.C. § 4241 provides procedures for determining competency for persons charged with federal crimes. When either the defendant or the prosecution requests, the court may order the defendant to submit to examination to determine competence. If the court finds by a preponderance of the evidence that the defendant lacks competence to stand trial, the defendant can be hospitalized for up to four months to try to restore competence. If that does not happen, the defendant may be hospitalized for a longer period under 18 U.S.C. § 4246(d). Under that section, the court must find by clear and convincing evidence that the defendant has a mental defect that creates a substantial risk that the defendant might harm another person. If so, the defendant may be confined until he no longer presents such a risk.

The U.S. Supreme Court has repeatedly held that it is a violation of due process to try to convict a mentally incompetent person. Because most states place the burden on the party challenging the presumption of competency, the standard of proof on defendants to prove incompetency is that of the "preponderance of the evidence."[30]

A translator or an attorney who can speak the language of a defendant could solve the problem of a defendant who does not understand English. People skilled in sign language could communicate for a deaf person. But a defendant with the mental ability of a 5-year-old child or a defendant who is mentally disabled because of excessive use of drugs or alcohol presents more difficult problems. If a defendant does not understand the charges and proceedings against him or her and cannot cooperate with the defense lawyers, that individual cannot be determined to be competent to stand trial. In such cases the criminal proceedings must be suspended.[31]

A criminal defendant found to be incompetent might remain so either for a short time, or indefinitely. Under most state statutes, a defendant may be placed in an appropriate institution for treatment for a period of time to determine if he or she can become competent. For example, the Ohio statute, R.C. § 2945.38, provides that if the court determines that it is probable the defendant can be restored to competency within a year, the defendant can be sent to a treatment facility. However, if it is unlikely that competency will be restored within a year, either the defendant must be discharged, or the state must start civil commitment procedures.

Statutes like the Ohio law discussed above are patterned after the decision in *Jackson v. Indiana*, where the U.S. Supreme Court held that defendants could not be held for longer than a "reasonable period of time" to determine whether they will regain their competence and capacity to stand trial.[32] After this period of time, the state has these options:

- Try the defendant, if he or she is found competent and capable of standing trial.
- Dismiss the charges.
- Commence civil proceedings against the person for the purpose of committing him or her to a mental institution if he or she remains incompetent and cannot be tried criminally.[33]

THE CRIMINAL LIABILITY OF CORPORATIONS

A corporation is a legal entity created under the laws of a state or the federal government. Although a corporation is not a living person and thus would seem to lack the capacity to commit a crime, it acts through human beings. Thus, for a crime committed by a person to be attributable to the corporation, the person must be in control of the corporation's affairs or in the employment of the corporation.

MAY THE GOVERNMENT FORCE A DEFENDANT'S COMPETENCY?

In federal and state prosecutions, a defendant who has been found to be incompetent to stand trial because of his or her mental condition can be transferred to a medical facility for a reasonable time for examination and treatment.[a] If the defendant has a condition that is treatable by medications, may the government force the defendant to take those medications in order to render the person competent to stand trial?

In *Sell v. United States*, 539 U.S. 166 (2003), the U.S. Supreme Court held that although a defendant has a constitutional right to be free of involuntary medical treatment, medications can be forced on a defendant to render him or her competent if (1) the treatment is medically appropriate, (2) the medications will not have side effects that undermine the fairness of the trial, and (3) the medications are necessary to advance an important government interest.

The following two cases illustrate how the *Sell* rule is applied in federal courts. In *United States v. Hardy*, 878 F. Supp.2d 373 (E.D. N.Y. 2012), the court ordered a defendant charged with murder to be involuntarily medicated to make him competent to stand trial. The court concluded that the medicine for treating the defendant's condition, paranoid schizophrenia, was appropriate and successful for most patients; that the medicine had no unmanageable side effects; and that prosecuting the defendant on the murder charge was an important government interest. The defendant had a history of violence and had assaulted medical personnel during treatment.

In *United States v. Grigsby*, 712 F.3d 964 (6th Cir. 2013), the court refused to order the involuntary medication of a defendant charged with bank robbery. The defendant was shown to suffer from a severe case of schizophrenia, and if not prosecuted for the robbery charges would very likely be civilly committed to a mental health facility for a substantial period, the court found. Given that the defendant raised a substantial insanity defense claim, the court concluded under *Sell* that it was not appropriate to force the defendant to take antipsychotic drugs.

State courts also must comply with the *Sell* requirements; so-called "*Sell* orders" are issued from a trial judge when a defendant is found to be incompetent to stand trial, but medical evidence indicates the proper medication will restore the defendant to competency. The meaning of "medically appropriate" was at issue in *Oregon State Hosp. v. Butts*, 359 P.3d 1187 (Or. 2015). There, a defendant charged with murdering a police chief was sent to the Oregon State Hospital (OSH) for examination to determine competency and treatment. Doctors, one independent and one from OSH, concluded the defendant was not competent but could be treated with antipsychotic drugs, and the trial court issued a *Sell* order for treatment without defendant's consent. However, OSH refused to administer the approved medication, and appealed the trial judge's order to the Oregon Supreme Court.

The Supreme Court held that the trial judge had the final authority to issue and compel compliance with the *Sell* order. OSH did not, the court held, have a "veto" power to refuse to administer the drugs. OSH contended that forcing it to administer medication would present ethical problems for its physicians; but the court noted that OSH physicians had approved the medication plan, and there was no evidence they would not administer the medication once OSH's objections were overruled.

[a] 18 U.S.C. Section 4241 (d) has a 4-month limit; most states have similar limits, up to one year.

criminal liability of corporations The rules for making corporations liable for actions taken by officers, directors, or employees. Corporations can be vicariously criminally liable for actions of their agents if the offense is minor, a duty is specifically assigned to a corporation, a statute explicitly creates vicarious criminal liability, or the person committing the crime is acting in the interest of the corporation and is a high managerial agent.

Regarding the **criminal liability of corporations,** Sir William Blackstone wrote in his eighteenth-century *Commentaries* that "a corporation cannot commit treason or felony or other crime in its corporate capacity, though its members may in their distinct individual capacities."[34] Blackstone's statement reflected the early common law thinking that because a corporation had no mind of its own, it could not formulate a criminal intent, and because it had no body, it could not be imprisoned or executed. The early common law view was understandable because relatively few corporations existed in those days, and other ways were available to handle crimes that were committed in the names of corporations. The corporate officers (or employees) who committed the act (or acts) could be criminally charged. The corporation was civilly liable for the acts of its officers and employees, and therefore civil suits for damages could be brought. In addition, a corporation that had committed *ultra vires* acts (acts that are beyond the scope of the corporate charter or that violate the laws of the state) could have its corporate charter revoked by the state.

This common law view changed as corporations became more numerous and as it became apparent that corporations should be made criminally responsible for some types of criminal acts. Today, corporations may be charged with many but not all crimes. The Model Penal Code, Section 2.07(l)(a)–(c), provides that corporations can have criminal liability for (1) specific duties assigned to a corporation, (2) violations of minor offenses that carry only a fine, and (3) an offense authorized or performed by a "high managerial agent."

Many states have reached similar conclusions. As an example, in *People v. Hock Shop,*[35] a corporation was charged with the crime of knowingly selling a firearm to a convicted felon. An employee of the corporation sold a firearm to a person known by the employee to be a convicted felon. The Michigan Court of Appeals held that though the corporation was a "person" for purposes of the criminal law, it could not have vicarious criminal liability for the acts of an employee who was not a high management agent unless the statute specifically imposed such liability, or the board of directors authorized or permitted the employee's acts. The state statute did not provide for criminal liability for violation of the firearm law, and the corporation's board of directors was not aware of the sale of the firearm to the felon, so the court affirmed a dismissal of the criminal charges.

Where a corporation can be criminally liable for violation of a statute, the only penalty that can be imposed must involve payment of a fine. Corporation cannot go to jail! In an unusual case, the trial court in a case involving a corporation's violation of a state environmental law regulating discharge of pollutants did just that. Finding the corporation guilty of 15 counts under the statute, it sentenced the corporation to two years of hard labor on each count. However, the prison term was suspended, but the corporation was placed on supervised probation for 5 years and ordered to pay heavy fines. On appeal, the court vacated the sentences against the corporation, agreeing with the defendant that corporations cannot be sentenced to prison. *State v. Jones,* 101 So.3d 1083 (La. App. 2012)

Even if a state permits criminal liability for corporations based on authorized acts of employees, courts have held that the prosecution must prove an individual employee could be liable for the offense with which the corporation is charged. In *Com. v. Life Centers of America,* 926 N.E.2d 206 (Mass. 2010), a nursing home corporation was charged with involuntary manslaughter in the death of a nursing home resident. The elderly resident wheeled her wheelchair through the home's entrance doors, and fell down eight steps to her death. The victim had a history of trying to exit the home, and physicians had placed orders on her chart that she must wear a "WanderGuard" device that automatically would lock exit and entrance doors when approached by the wearer. Due to a combination of factors, including staff changes and unclear directives about auditing residents' charts, the duty nurses on the night in question did not know the resident was supposed to be wearing the safety device. As a result, the resident was able to exit the home, with the resulting fatal fall.

The prosecution did not charge any individual employee of the nursing home with involuntary manslaughter, conceding that no one person had been anything more than negligent in performing his or her duties. However, the prosecution charged

---

 ## CORPORATE LIABILITY FOR ENVIRONMENTAL CRIMES

Many corporations conduct business operations that have an impact on the environment. They are thus required to conform their operations to rules and regulations protecting the environment, including the criminal laws adopted to accomplish environmental goals. Many environmental crimes applicable to corporations include only fines as punishment for violations, and are often classified as misdemeanors. These statutes usually are aimed at some harm that an environmental interest suffered based on actions of the corporation. However, even though it can be shown the corporation's actions caused the environmental harm, attaching criminal liability for those actions can be unclear. The following cases involving criminal prosecutions under the federal Migratory Bird Treaty Act (MBTA) illustrate the difficulty.

The MBTA prohibits the "taking" (killing, catching, or causing death) of certain protected, migratory birds without a permit. As applied to corporations, it is a class B strict liability misdemeanor, providing fines for violations. The application of the act to commercial operations of corporations has had varied results.

In *United States v. Citgo Petroleum Corp.*, 893 F. Supp.2d 841 (S.D. Tex. 2012), the court held the act did apply to commercial activities that were not intended to kill or capture protected birds. There, the defendant corporations maintained open-air oil tanks in which migratory birds became entrapped and died. The court said the act applied because the corporations were the proximate cause of the birds' deaths, even though the commercial activity was not intended to cause those deaths.

On the other hand, in *United States v. Brigham Oil & Gas Co.*, 840 F. Supp.2d 1202 (D. N.D. 2012), the court held the act inapplicable to corporate commercial actions not intended to cause the death of the migratory birds. There, the defendants maintained oil reserve pits that were used to hold chemicals and other residue from oil drilling operations. Migratory birds landed in and died in the pits. The court dismissed prosecutions under the MBTA, saying the act applied only to intentional killing of migratory birds.

Courts have recognized the difficulty of applying environmental crime laws to corporate commercial activity that indirectly harms the protected environmental goals. An example of a court attempting to fairly apply these environmental crime laws to commercial activity is *United States v. Apollo Energies, Inc.*, 611 F.3d 679 (10th Cir. 2010). In that case the court affirmed corporate convictions under the MBTA where it was clear the corporation had knowledge that its equipment carried the probability of killing migratory birds, but reversed convictions of a corporation that lacked such knowledge.

the corporate owner of the nursing home on the theory of "collective knowledge" of all the employees. Under that theory, the liability of a corporation can be based on aggregating the knowledge and actions of multiple employees.

The Massachusetts Supreme Judicial Court held that the corporation could not be liable under the collective knowledge theory. The Court reasoned that since involuntary manslaughter was a crime that required "wanton or reckless" conduct, unless at least one individual acted in such a fashion, the corporation could not be liable. While many of the nursing home employees were negligent in connection with the death, multiples of simple negligence to not constitute "wanton or reckless" conduct, the court concluded. If no individual employee could be convicted of involuntary manslaughter, the court held, neither could the corporation.

LEARNING OBJECTIVES SUMMARY

LO 1. Discuss when a child can be held responsible for violation of a criminal law.
Children below a certain age, usually 7 or 8, cannot be convicted of a crime. Children between the minimum age and about 12–14 are presumed to lack capacity to commit a crime, but the presumption may be overcome.

LO 2. Distinguish between the method of imposing criminal liability upon a child under age 7 and a child of age 14.
A child under the minimum age may not be convicted of a crime regardless of the evidence of his mental state. A child of 14 can be convicted if it can be shown the child had the mental ability and understanding to formulate the required criminal intent.

LO 3. List the two prongs of the *M'Naghten* rule.
The first prong of the M'Naghten rule requires a showing the defendant did not know what he was doing (the cognitive capacity prong); the second prong requires a showing that the defendant did not know what he was doing was wrong (the moral incapacity prong).

LO 4. Distinguish the "cognitive" approach to insanity from the "volitional" approach.
Cognitive rules examine what a defendant knew about his actions, and if those actions are wrong. Volitional rules examine the ability of a defendant to control her conduct.

LO 5. Describe the difference between the *M'Naghten* rule and the "substantial capacity" test.
The M'Naghten rule differs from the substantial capacity test primarily on the magnitude of the defendant's understanding of events that made up the crime charged. The M'Naghten rule applies only if the defendant did not "know" the nature of his acts and that they were wrong. The substantial capacity test applies whenever the defendant cannot "appreciate" the nature of his acts, or that they were wrong, a lesser requirement. The MPC rule also includes a second, volitional test.

LO 6. Identify the extent, if any, to which the voluntary use of drugs or alcohol may be used as an insanity defense or diminished capacity defense.
Voluntary intoxication or drug use is almost never the basis for the successful assertion of the insanity defense. However, in most states the defendant's intoxication or drug use may serve as the basis for a claim for diminished capacity.

LO 7. Distinguish the "not guilty by reason of insanity" verdict from the "guilty but mentally ill" verdict.
A verdict of not guilty by reason of insanity results in an acquittal of the defendant; a verdict of guilty but mentally ill is a

conviction, but the defendant must be given treatment during his confinement.

LO 8. **List factors that may present issues of a criminal defendant's competency to be tried on criminal charges.**
Mental illness, mental retardation, and many forms of physical illness may be the basis for finding a person incompetent to stand trial. Unless the condition is cured, the defendant cannot be tried for a crime. Defendants may be confined while competency is determined and treated.

LO 9. **Explain why a defendant of questionable competency should not be tried for a criminal violation.**
A person who lacks competency does not have the ability to understand what is happening at trial, and thus lacks the ability to participate in his own defense. Due process requires persons charged with crimes to be given an opportunity to consult with counsel, and assist in their own defense. Lack of competency makes that impossible, and thus trials of incompetent persons violate their due process rights.

KEY TERMS

trial by ordeal, p. 116
preponderance of the evidence, p. 117
infant (child), p. 117
insanity tests, p. 120

"right and wrong" test, p. 121
M'Naghten rule, p. 122
"substantial capacity" test, p. 123
guilty but mentally ill, p. 126
diminished capacity defense, p. 129

competency to stand trial, p. 132
criminal liability of corporations, p. 135

CASE ANALYSIS AND WRITING EXERCISES

1. Can a defendant prevent a court from entering a verdict of "Guilty but Mentally Ill" (GBMI)? Assume a defendant is charged with attempted murder. While there is evidence she suffered from serious mental impairments, she did not raise an insanity defense, nor did she contend she had "diminished capacity." A jury convicted her of attempted murder. The state then filed a motion to have her found GBMI, which the trial judge granted, finding that the defendant was mentally ill. Are there problems with this procedure? See *State v. Clifton*, 315 P.3d 694 (Alaska App. 2013).

2. Many states bifurcate the guilt/insanity portions of a trial, so that a jury first must determine beyond a reasonable doubt that a defendant is guilty of committing the crime charged. If a guilty verdict is returned, the second phase begins. In some states the burden remains on the state to prove sanity, but more commonly it becomes the defendant's duty to prove insanity. In those states, must the defendant always introduce medical evidence of mental illness? Or can lay testimony be sufficient? What about the defendant's own testimony? Consider the case of *State v. Magett*, 850 N.W.2d 42 (Wis. 2014). The defendant testified he could not remember the criminal incident (attack on prison guard) because he was unconscious, and thus in his unconscious state he lacked the substantial capacity to appreciate the wrongfulness of his conduct. Why did the Wisconsin Supreme Court find this evidence insufficient?

3. When the Pennsylvania legislature passed its Juvenile Act, setting procedures for juvenile courts, it abolished the infancy defense. Does that mean there is no infancy defense in adult courts? That was the position of the state in *Com. v. Martz*, 118 A.3d 1175 (Pa. Super. 2015). Was it correct? What did the state contend based on the age of the defendant (28) when he was charged with crimes committed when he was under 14? If the infancy defense remains in Pennsylvania, who has the burden of proving the defendant lacks the required capacity to be tried in adult court? What did the trial court do wrong? The appellate court decision is pending review in

the Pennsylvania Supreme Court. What do you think will be decided there?

4. Assume a defendant is convicted of murder under a state felony-murder statute. (See Chapter 10.) The underlying crimes were rape and burglary. The defendant contended he was "high" on Quaaludes and alcohol and had no memory of committing

the crime. Assuming the state had a "diminished capacity" defense available at the time the crime was committed (California subsequently abolished the defense), what mens rea can be rebutted by the defense? The killing of the victim? The burglary? The rape? See *People v. Vasquez*, 2015 WL 8297698 (Cal. App. 2015).

ENDNOTES

1. Sir James Fitzjames Stephen, A *History of the Criminal Law of England*, vol. 1 (Macmillan & Co., 1883), p. 73.

2. *Leland v. State*, 343 U.S. 790 (1952).

3. An example of a state statute that codifies the common law is Mississippi Code Annotated, Section 43-21-151. This statute provides that no child under the age of 13 can be charged with a crime. Children over that age can be so charged, and apparently there is no presumption about their lack of capacity. See *Clemens v. State*, 733 So. 2d 266 (S. Ct. 1999), where a 14-year-old boy was convicted of killing three people and was given two life sentences, to run consecutively.

4. In 1994, a 10-year-old boy became the youngest child in a maximum-security juvenile prison when he and an 11-year-old were found to have thrown a 5-year-old out of the fourteenth floor of a Chicago housing project building. The 5-year-old, who died in the fall, had refused to steal candy for the older boys.

   See the 1991 case of *In re Devon T.*, 584 A.2d 1287 (Md. App. 1991), for a discussion of this law. Devon T. was almost 14 years old and a middle-school student in Baltimore when twenty plastic bags of heroin were found on his person. The Maryland courts held that the state produced sufficient evidence permitting a reasonable inference that Devon knew the difference between right and wrong and knew the wrongfulness of his acts.

5. 86 P.3d 132 (Wash. 2004).

6. 86 P.3d at 136–137.

7. A defense lawyer who entered an insanity plea for a client in a minor charge could find the client committed to an institution for a much longer time than if the client were found guilty of the offense charged.

   In *Lynch v. Overholser*, 369 U.S. 705, 82 S. Ct. 1063 (1962), a municipal court refused to accept a former mental patient's plea of guilty to a minor check forgery charge. Instead, the court found the defendant not guilty by reason of insanity. Because the defendant was a first offender, he would probably have not received a jail sentence. After the defendant served two years in a mental institution, the U.S. Supreme Court reversed the trial court's decision, holding that the trial court was not justified in committing the defendant to a mental institution on bare reasonable doubt concerning past sanity.

   Also note that prosecutors sometimes find that it is in the state's best interest to seek a civil commitment of a person when evidence shows that the individual is dangerous to him- or herself or others and in need of treatment.

8. The 1990 study done by Policy Research Associates of Delmar, New York, is one such study.

9. The federal Insanity Defense Reform Act of 1984 (the "Act") provides that a federal criminal defendant found not guilty by reason of insanity may not be released onto the streets. Justice Stevens of the U.S. Supreme Court summarized the act as follows in *Frank v. United States*, 113 S. Ct. 363 (1992):

   > It (the federal Act) provides that "the Attorney General shall hospitalize the person [found not guilty by reason of insanity] in a suitable facility" until a state assumes responsibility for his care and treatment or the Attorney General finds that his release would not create a risk of harm to people or property in 18 U.S.C. § 4243(e). The question presented by the petition for certiorari is whether a defendant who has pleaded not guilty by reason of insanity is entitled to a jury instruction explaining the effect of this statute. If such an instruction is not given, there is a strong possibility that the jury will be reluctant to accept a meritorious defense because of fear that a dangerous, mentally ill person will go free.

10. 112 S. Ct. 1780 (S. Ct. 1992).

11. 389 F.3d 1060 (10th Cir. 2004).

12. 10 Cl. & R 200, 8 Eng. Rep. 718.

13. See, e.g., Georgia Code Annotated, Section 16-3-3; *Vann v. Commonwealth*, 544 S.E.2d 879 (Va. 2001).

14. The "irresistible impulse" rule became well known because of the book and film *Anatomy of a Murder*. There, a soldier escapes punishment for the death of his wife by pleading that an irresistible impulse caused him to act.

15. 94 U.S. App. D.C. 228, 214 R2d 862 (1954).

16. *Sauer v. United States*, 241 F.2d 640, 648 (9th Cir. 1957).

17. Commentary to Section 4.01, Model Penal Code.

18. 260 Mont. 510, 861 P.2d 884 (Mont. 1993).

19. 114 S. Ct. 1371 (1994).

20. Idaho: *State v. Searcy*, 798 P.2d 914 (Idaho 1996); Kansas: *State v. Bethal*, 66 P.3d 804 (Kan. 2003), *cert. denied*, 540 U.S.

1006 (2003); and Utah: *State v. Herrera*, 895 P.2d 359 (Utah 1995).

21. *Finger v. State*, 27 P.3d 66, (Nev. 2001) *cert, denied* 534 U.S. 1127 (2002).

22. An heir to the du Pont fortune, John E. du Pont, was found guilty of third-degree murder but mentally ill. World-class wrestlers were using du Pont's Pennsylvania estate for training. John du Pont shot Olympic gold medalist David Schulz three times at point-blank range without any apparent provocation. The defendant was found to be "actively psychotic" and was ordered to be treated in a mental hospital until cured, after which he will be sent to a prison for the remainder of his sentence. Du Pont was the wealthiest murder defendant in the history of the United States.

23. In 1998, the Federal Court of Appeals for the Tenth Circuit upheld the guilty but mentally ill law of New Mexico in the case of *Neely v. Newton* (1998 WL 33423). The court held that in clarifying the distinction between those individuals who are not guilty by reason of insanity and those who are mentally ill yet criminally liable, the law serves a legitimate state interest. State court decisions upholding the constitutionality of guilty but mentally ill laws are found in *State v. Neely*, 819 P.2d 249 (New Mex. 1991).

However, in 1997 an Illinois appellate court held that the Illinois guilty but mentally ill law encouraged compromised verdicts in violation of due process and that the law seduced juries into settling on a middle ground between guilty and not guilty when in fact there is no middle ground. See *People v. Robles*, 1997 WL 342483 (111 App. 2 Dist. 1997). In *People v. Lantz*, 712 N.E.2d 314 (111. 1999) the Illinois Supreme Court reversed the Appellate Court, and found the GBMI act constitutional.

24. *The Journal of Criminal Law and Criminology* 73 (1982), pp. 867–874, contains the entire text of former Governor Thompson's remarks as co-chair of the National Violent Crime Task Force. Governor Thompson stated that "the insanity defense has been described as the chronic scandal of American criminal law."

25. "The Insanity Defense: Ready for Reform?" *Wisconsin Bar Bulletin*, December 1982.

26. A 1997 study conducted by the Harvard Medical School and financed by the gambling industry concluded that 1.29 percent of adults in Canada and the United States have compulsive gambling disorders. However, the percentage of problem gamblers among people with alcohol or drug abuse problems or mental disorders was found to be 14.29 percent.

The need for money to gamble could cause compulsive gamblers to steal from employers, family, friends, and others.

Compulsive gamblers also borrow money from other people, including loan sharks. Children of compulsive gamblers are often deprived of necessities needed for their well-being and education. (See the *New York Times* article "Compulsion to Gamble Seen Growing: Study Finds Legality Spreads the Problem," December 7, 1997.)

27. 699 F.2d 839 (7th Cir. 1982).

28. 743 F. Supp. 713 (N.D. Cal. 1990). It should be noted that many specific intent crimes, such as murder, have lesser offenses like manslaughter that have no specific intent requirement. A defendant using the diminished capacity defense may avoid the murder charge, but be convicted of the manslaughter charge.

29. See *Drope v. Missouri*, 420 U.S. at 171, 95 S. Ct. at 903–04 (1975) and *Pate v. Robinson*, 383 U.S. at 378, 86 S. Ct. at 838 (1966).

30. See the 1996 U.S. Supreme Court case of *Cooper v. Oklahoma*, 517 U.S. 348 (1996), in which the Supreme Court invalidated laws in Oklahoma, Connecticut, Rhode Island, and Pennsylvania and required these states to place the burden on defendants to prove incompetency by a "preponderance of the evidence." Laws in these states had previously used the higher burden of "clear and convincing evidence."

31. The U.S. Supreme Court has held that persons mentally competent have a right to represent themselves in criminal trials.

32. 406 U.S. 715, 92 S. Ct. 1845 (1972).

33. A made-for-television movie aired in 1979 about Donald Lang, an 18-year-old totally illiterate deaf-mute. Lang could not talk, write, read lips, or understand sign language. In 1965, he was charged with the murder of a Chicago prostitute (Cook County criminal case #65-3421). Because he could not hear, speak, read, or write, he was declared incompetent to stand trial and was placed in a state mental hospital. After Lang was held for five years, the Illinois Supreme Court ordered him tried or released. Because witnesses were no longer available, he was released. In 1973, Lang was charged with killing another woman. After a conviction for the second murder, he was held to be incompetent and was committed in 1979 to a mental hospital. In 1992, Lang again was found unfit to stand trial and was denied release from the Illinois institution to which he was committed. See *People v. Lang*, 587 N.E.2d 490 (Ill. App. 1992).

34. 18 *Commentaries*, section 12.

35. 681 N.W.2d 669 (Mich. App. 2004).

6

The Law Governing the Use of Force

LEARNING OBJECTIVES

In this chapter we consider the rules governing the use of force by private persons or police officers. The learning objectives for this chapter are

LO 1. Identify the three key points for determining when force is justified.

LO 2. Describe the "castle" doctrine and explain what it says.

LO 3. Determine how "stand your ground" laws affect the general rules for using force and the effect such laws have on the "castle" doctrine.

LO 4. List the circumstances that justify a police officer using non-deadly force in making an arrest.

LO 5. Explain why the Fourth Amendment applies to use of force by a police officer.

LO 6. Identify the circumstances that would justify the use of deadly force by a police officer.

LO 7. List the people who may use force in the discipline of children.

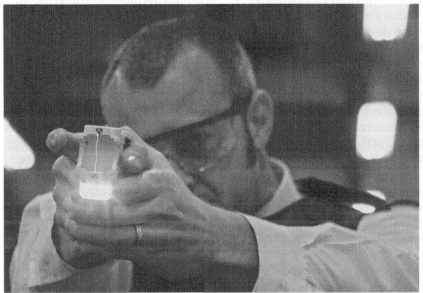
CARL DE SOUZA/AFP/Getty Images

A police officer fires a Taser device, which propels wires carrying an electrical charge of over 1,200 volts. The wires are attached to darts, which can penetrate a suspect's clothing to cause temporary paralysis.

Police officers carry weapons, and with these weapons can apply deadly force to suspects. When deadly force is used by a police officer against a suspect, questions arise about the legality of the officer's decision. Police officers, like ordinary citizens, must use restraint when considering the use of deadly force. As we will see in this chapter, there are a variety of tests that go into a determination of the legality of an officer's use of deadly force. However, the application of these tests to the facts of a case is often difficult. Consider the case of Officer Thomas White, an Ottawa Hills, Ohio, police officer.

Officer White observed a rider on a motorcycle violating various traffic laws, and began following the motorcycle in his cruiser. A few minutes later the motorcyclist appeared to look back, see the cruiser, and accelerate away from the cruiser. Officer White activated his lights and siren, radioed his actions in to headquarters, and began pursuit. The motorcyclist stopped his bike. Officer White drew his weapon, and ordered the rider to dismount and put his hands up. The rider did not do so at once. Officer White stated that the rider began a motion with his right hand that appeared to White to be the rider reaching for a weapon. Officer White fired one round into the back of the rider, paralyzing him.

A jury convicted Officer White of felonious assault with a firearm specification. Under Ohio law, the specification adds several years to a prison sentence if a defendant uses a weapon in an assault. Ultimately, the Ohio Supreme Court reversed the conviction, and remanded the case to the trial court. *State v. White*, 29

N.E.3d 939 (Ohio 2015) As you study the materials in this chapter on use of force by police officers, consider what standards should be used by the factfinder to evaluate Officer White's decision to fire his weapon at the rider. What did the trial court do wrong? Should the firearm sentence enhancement law apply to police officers?

In this chapter we discuss the rules governing the use of force, including the force law enforcement officers may use to arrest or control criminal suspects.

The use of force by one person against another is a violation of the criminal law unless some justification for the use exists. Justification means that the person using the force had a legally sufficient reason for doing so. Whether or not the use of force is justified often depends on the kind of force used, the person using the force, and the circumstances leading up to the use of force.[1] For example, the rules justifying the use of deadly force are different from those that apply to non-deadly force. The rules justifying the use of force in the protection of property differ from those that justify force to protect persons. Also, the rules justifying the use of force by law enforcement officers reflect the duties and risks facing such officers. As you study the materials in this chapter, consider how they apply to the following hypothetical situation:

A, the owner of a house, throws a graduation party for his daughter, D. B, an uninvited acquaintance of D, "crashes" the party by entering A's house. A orders B to leave the house, but B refuses, and starts knocking over party decorations. A twists B's arm behind his back, drags him out of the house, and throws B into the street. Incensed, B goes to his car and grabs a tire wrench, and runs at A. A, mistakenly believing the wrench is a machete, pulls a pistol and shoots B in the arm. B runs off as a police officer arrives at the scene. The officer orders B to stop, and when B refuses the officer fires his service revolver at B, hitting B in the leg.

Force has been used by each of the actors in this hypothetical situation. As you study the materials in this chapter, try to determine which, if any, use was justified.

self-defense   The elements to evaluate whether an act of force for self-defense is justified include the unlawfulness of the other's action, the necessity to defend oneself immediately, and the reasonableness of the act of self-defense under the circumstances.

defense of another   The elements to evaluate whether an act of force for defense of another is justified include the unlawfulness of the action toward the other, the necessity to defend the other immediately, and the reasonableness of the act of defense under the circumstances.

SELF-DEFENSE AND THE DEFENSE OF OTHERS

Section 3.04 of the Model Penal Code provides that force can be used in self-protection "when the actor believes that such force is immediately necessary for the purpose of protecting himself against the use of unlawful force by such other person on the present occasion." In their criminal codes and in their court decisions, all states and the federal government have rules for the use of force. The state of New York, for example, provides in Public Law 35.15 that "one may use physical force upon another when and to the extent he reasonably believes necessary to defend himself or a third person from what he reasonably believes to be the imminent use of unlawful physical force by such other persons." The key points in determining the lawfulness of force in **self-defense** or the **defense of another** are

- *Unlawfulness:* Is what the other person doing unlawful? If the other's behavior is not unlawful, force is not justified.
- *Necessity:* Force must be immediately *necessary* to protect the person or another from the use of *unlawful* force or interference by another.

- *Reasonableness:* The amount of force used in self-defense or defense of another must be *reasonable* under the circumstances that exist.

In determining what force is reasonable in self-defense, a court or a jury will take into account the size and age of the parties in relation to one another, the instruments or weapons used, and the aggressiveness of the assault made. Ordinarily, if fists were used in the attack and the parties were about the same size and strength, then fists and the strength of arms and body would be the maximum force that could be used in defense.

Also, so long as the belief is reasonable, it does not need to be correct. Someone who reasonably believes another person is reaching for a weapon to use against her or him may respond with force, even if in fact the aggressor was reaching for something else.

EXAMPLE	A 70-year-old, 100-pound woman becomes angry with a 25-year-old, 200-pound man and begins to hit him with an umbrella. The man may defend himself by taking the umbrella away from the woman, but because he has such physical control of the situation, the amount of force that he would be justified in using against her ends there.

The rules for defense of another person mirror the rules for self-defense. A person may come to the aid of another and use necessary and reasonable force to defend the other person against unlawful force or interference. The person coming to the assistance or defense of another must reasonably believe that the facts are such that the third person would be privileged to act in self-defense and also must reasonably believe that his or her intervention is necessary to protect the third person against unlawful force or interference.

Good Samaritan laws Laws that encourage people to come to the aid of another or to defend another against unlawful force or interference.

Many states have enacted **Good Samaritan laws** that encourage, but do not require, people to get involved when they witness an assault. As an example, the Maryland statute states, "Any person witnessing a violent assault upon the person of another may lawfully aid the person being assaulted by assisting in that person's defense" (Art. 27, § 12A). Under these statutes a person may use force to protect another only if the threat of violence is occurring or imminent. Thus, in the 2011 case of *State v. Clinch*, 335 S.W.3d 579 (Mo. App. 2011) the court affirmed a murder conviction, holding that the defendant's belief that the victim would abuse the defendant's grandchildren once given visitation rights did not warrant a "defense of others" instruction to the jury.

Some states have enacted statutes that require people witnessing an assault to take limited action, such as calling the police. Violations of these laws usually are punished by a small fine.

deadly force Force that is likely to cause or is capable of causing death or serious bodily injury.

The Use of Deadly Force in Self-Defense or the Defense of Others

The rules providing justification for the use of deadly force generally are similar to those governing the use of non-deadly force, with some important differences. **Deadly force** is force that is likely to cause or is capable of causing death or serious bodily injury. Firing a weapon at a person is the use of deadly force, whether the intent is to kill or to wound.

All people, including law enforcement officers, may use deadly force, but only if such force is necessary to prevent imminent death or great bodily harm to themselves or others. Moreover, unlike the use of non-deadly force, where there is no duty to retreat, some states impose such a duty where deadly force is used. Section 3.04 (b)(ii) of the Model Penal Code, for example, states that deadly force is not justified if the actor knows he or she can retreat with "complete safety." (See Chapter 10 for a discussion of imperfect self-defense where unlawful force has been used in self-defense.)

Under the common law, and some state statutes, a person was not permitted to use deadly force if retreat from an attack was reasonably possible and safe. Thus, even if an unlawful attacker threatened death or serious bodily harm, the law instructed the victim of the attack to "retreat to the wall" before employing deadly force against the attacker.

The Florida "Stand Your Ground" Law   Perhaps because it was dissatisfied with the duty to retreat, in 2005 the Florida legislature passed this country's first **"stand your ground" law.** The original version of the Florida law states:

"stand your ground" laws   Recent laws passed in many states that permit using deadly force in response to an unlawful attack, in contrast to the traditional "duty to retreat" policy.

> A person who is not engaged in an unlawful activity and who is attacked in any other place where he or she has a right to be has no duty to retreat and has the right to stand his or her ground and meet force with force, including deadly force if he or she reasonably believes it is necessary to do so to prevent death or great bodily harm to himself or herself or another or to prevent the commission of a forcible felony.[2]

Section 776.032 of the Florida law provides for immunity from prosecution if force, even deadly force, is used as authorized by this statute. Immunity means that if a judge determines a defendant used force under circumstances authorized by the statute, self-defense is not a jury question and the charges must be dismissed. In *State v. Gallo*, 76 So.3d 407 (Fla. App. 2011), the court affirmed a dismissal of second-degree murder charges against a defendant engaged in a gunfight "reminiscent of the 'Shootout at the OK Corral'" because the trial court determined the defendant was using lawful force under the statute.

In the 2009 case of *Hair v. State*, 17 So.3d 804 (Fla. App. 2009), the court held that a passenger in a car who shot and killed a person who unlawfully and forcibly entered the car could not be charged with a crime under the Florida "stand your ground" law, because the law states that any person making such a forcible entry is presumed to present a threat of imminent harm to the occupants of the car. The court also held that it did not matter that at the time the passenger fired the handgun the intruder was backing out of the car. After a highly-charged Florida trial, in July 2013, a six-person jury found George Zimmerman not guilty of murder or manslaughter in the death of teenager Trayvon Martin. Zimmerman argued he was acting in self-defense when he shot and killed the unarmed Martin.

Since the Florida statute was passed, at least twenty-nine other states have passed similar laws or are considering such laws. These laws have been criticized as "giving more rights to use deadly force than we give police officers"[3] and are really "shoot first" with a "license to kill."[4]

YOU BE THE JUDGE

Is the prosecution's evidence admissible? Why or why not? Is the defendant correct that under the "stand your ground" law all that she must show is that she actually believed she was being threatened by deadly force? If not, should you instruct the jury on lesser offenses, such as reckless homicide? See **Commonwealth v. Hasch, 421 S.W.3d 349 (Ky. 2013)**

The defendant before you has been charged with murder. No one disputes that she shot her husband between the eyes, killing him instantly. She contends that under the state's "stand your ground" law, she was justified in using deadly force. The statute, which is similar to the Florida statute, specifically says there is no duty to retreat when one is in a place she has a right to be. Defendant's husband, who had a history of domestic abuse, was threatening her in the couple's bedroom, she contends, and she believed he would take the hand gun she was holding away from her and use it on her.

The prosecution contends the defendant had been in similar situations in the past, and knew she could simply leave the house and avoid any serious injury. As a result, the prosecution wants you to permit it to introduce evidence of past domestic assaults, and the fact the defendant safely retreated from those assaults. The prosecution argues such evidence would be relevant to the jury for its determination of whether the defendant "reasonably believed it is necessary to do so to prevent death or great bodily harm."

The defendant contends the jury should be instructed it could either convict her of murder, or find her not guilty of murder by reason of self-protection, based on her actual belief her husband was threatening her with deadly force. The self-protection law, she contends, requires only that she actually believed she was threatened with deadly force, even if that belief was unreasonable. Thus, she claims, she cannot be convicted of any lesser crime, like manslaughter or reckless homicide.

Loss of Self-Defense Privilege for a Wrongdoer or an Aggressor

The right of a person to use force in self-defense arises from the unlawful force or activity encountered by that person. If the person asserting self-defense is engaged in unlawful activity such as the commission of a crime, or is himself the unlawful aggressor, the right of self-defense does not exist.

EXAMPLE	V, the owner of a car, discovers D unlawfully breaking into the car. V grabs D and tries to restrain him. To escape, D punches V and runs away. Since V was using reasonable force to protect his property, V was acting lawfully. As a result, D's use of force against V was unlawful.
EXAMPLE	D wrongfully starts a fight with V, pushing him to the ground. V fights back, striking D with his fists. To defend himself, D kicks V in the knee, severely injuring him. D was the initial aggressor and thus had no right to use force in self-defense against V's use of force.

State statutes and court decisions recognize two situations in which the aggressor or wrongdoer can regain the right of self-defense:

1. A wrongdoer (X) begins an encounter with the unlawful use of his or her fists or some non-deadly weapon. The victim, however, unlawfully uses deadly force, which, under the circumstances, is unnecessary and unreasonable. Now, X may use force in self-defense but is not privileged to resort to the use of force intended or likely to cause death unless he or she has exhausted

   • every means of escape (under the duty to retreat) and
   • every means of avoiding death or great bodily harm to herself or himself.

2. A wrongdoer who is the initial aggressor may regain the right of self-defense by withdrawing in good faith from the use of force and giving adequate notice of that withdrawal to the victim. If the initial victim continues to use force, the victim becomes the aggressor, and the initial aggressor reacquires a right of self-defense.

The "Castle" Doctrine and the Minority Duty-to-Retreat Exception to That Doctrine

It has long been the law that people who have been assaulted in their homes by a trespasser have no duty to retreat or flee but instead may stand their ground and use

---

 ### "STAND YOUR GROUND" AND UNLAWFUL ACTIVITY

The "stand your ground" laws all apply to force used by "A person who is *not engaged in an unlawful activity*…" This language raises two questions: (1) what does "unlawful activity" include and (2) what rule applies if the defendant uses force while engaged in an unlawful activity? Two 2014 decisions from states with "stand your ground" laws addressed these questions.

• *Dawkins v. State*, 252 P.3d 214 (Okla. App. 2011). Defendant was in a friend's home when the friend's former boyfriend entered the home and began hitting another occupant. Defendant had a sawed-off shotgun, and shot the former boyfriend. When he was charged with manslaughter, the defendant invoked the "immunity" provision of the Oklahoma "stand your ground" law. The appeals court affirmed his conviction, holding that because the sawed-off shotgun was illegal, defendant was "engaged" in illegal activity and thus lost the right to use deadly force under the statute. The court said the illegal activity did not have to relate to use of force, but did not include mere "technical" violations of the law.

• *Rios v. State*, 143 So.3d 1167 (Fla. App. 2014). An appeals court held a defendant was entitled to the "stand your ground" defense under § 776.012 of the Florida statutes. The court said that unlike the stand your ground defense in § 776.013, the 2005 version of § 776.012 did have an exception for persons engaged in unlawful activity. Thus, even though the defendant was carrying a concealed weapon and thus engaged in unlawful activity, the defense under § 776.012 was available to him, the court held. The court reversed his conviction for murder and remanded the case for a new trial. In response to decisions like *Rios*, the Florida legislature amended § 776.012 in 2014. That section, like the other stand your ground defense in § 776.013, now has an exception for a defendant engaged in unlawful activity.

"castle" doctrine The doctrine permitting people who have been assaulted in their homes by a trespasser to stand their ground and use such force as is necessary and reasonable to defend themselves.

"make my day" rules Rules adopted by some states that put no limits on the use of deadly force by the occupant of a dwelling in response to a trespasser.

such force as is necessary and reasonable to defend themselves or others. Because a person's home is his or her "castle," the privilege not to retreat in one's home is known as the **"castle" doctrine.** Even states that require retreat before using deadly force exempt dwellings from the duty, as does the Model Penal Code (see § 3.04(b)(ii)(A)). The U.S. Supreme Court decided long ago in the case *of Beard v. United States*[5] that under federal law a homeowner had no duty to retreat in the face of an unlawful assault in his home or on his property.

Also, some states have adopted **"make my day" rules**, which put no limits on the use of deadly force by the occupant of a dwelling. In *State v. Anderson,*[6] the court interpreted the Oklahoma statute (Tit. 21, § 1289.25) as intended to remove any requirement that the force used must be "reasonable" under the circumstances. An occupant who reasonably believes the intruder who has wrongfully entered a residence intends to use some force, however slight, is privileged to use any force, including deadly force.

> **EXAMPLE**
>
> D trespassed in V's apartment, and V ordered him to leave. D did, but returned and jiggled V's doorknob. V followed D back to D's apartment, and entered without D's knowledge. D then came out of his bedroom with a machete, and injured V. D was convicted of first-degree assault. The appeals court reversed, saying that if the jury found that V was wrongfully in D's apartment, D would be entitled to the "make my day" defense. *People v. Zukowski*, 260 P.3d 339 (Colo. App. 2011), *cert. denied,* 2011 WL 3855726 (Colo. 2011).

Florida's "stand your ground" law, discussed above, also changes the law on the force permitted under the "castle" doctrine.[7] The Florida law creates a presumption that a homeowner has a reasonable fear of imminent peril or death whenever another person unlawfully and forcefully enters the dwelling. Under this law it is no longer necessary for the homeowner (or other legitimate occupant) to prove the intruder presented the threat of death or serious bodily harm.

> **EXAMPLE**
>
> D and V are strangers. V breaks into D's house, planning only to find something to eat. D sees V, who advances towards D in a hostile manner. D shoots V dead. Under the original castle-doctrine, D's decision to use deadly force was unreasonable, because V did not threaten deadly force. In "make my day" states, D may use any force on the intruder, even if the intruder did not threaten deadly force. In "stand your ground" states, there is a presumption an intruder presented a threat of death or serious bodily harm, thereby justifying use of deadly force.

The "castle" doctrine does not require a lawful occupant of a home to retreat when confronting a trespasser or a person who does not reside in the home. However, state laws vary when the wrongdoer is also a co-occupant of the home (such as a spouse or domestic partner, housemate, or family member). The Florida "stand your ground" law, for example, states that the presumption that a person forcefully entering a residence will use deadly force does not apply if that person has a right to be there, such as a co-occupant.

HOW RULES ON USE OF FORCE EVOLVED

The common law rules on the use of force have evolved over time, mainly by statutory changes. In these columns we compare the common law rules to current rules on the use of force.

Common Law	Current Statutes
Non-deadly force: Reasonable force in response to unlawful force or activity. No duty to retreat.	Same
Deadly force: Only in response to unlawful, deadly force; duty to retreat.	"Stand your ground" laws: Only in response to deadly force or to prevent forcible felony; no duty to retreat.
In dwellings: Deadly force if intruder threatens deadly force; no duty to retreat.	Castle doctrine: Deadly force if intruder threatens deadly force; no duty to retreat. "Make my day" laws: Deadly force in response to any force by intruder. No duty to retreat. "Stand your ground" laws: Presumption that intruder in dwelling threatens deadly force, so deadly force permitted against any intruder. No duty to retreat.

EXAMPLE   D and V are co-owners of a house. After an argument, V leaves the house and stays in a hotel. The next night, V forces his way into the house, and appears to be drunk and violent. D shoots V. D is not entitled to the presumption that she has a reasonable fear of deadly force, even though V forcefully entered the house. D will be entitled to claim self-defense only if in fact V was threatening her with deadly force.

EXAMPLE   Assume the same facts as above, except that V is threatening D with a knife, and D is standing by the open back door. In most states D has no duty to retreat (the "castle doctrine"), and may use deadly force to defend herself.

In a few states the "castle" doctrine has a duty to retreat. The Supreme Court of New Jersey pointed out in the case of *State v. Gartland*[8] that New Jersey is now among the minority of states that require a lawful co-occupant to retreat (if possible) before using deadly force against another co-occupant. In the *Gartland* case, a trial court convicted the wife of manslaughter because she failed to retreat before shooting her husband, who was assaulting her in a bedroom of their home. The appeals court reversed the conviction and ordered a new trial, stating that although a duty to retreat existed, the jury did not consider if retreat was possible:

Exactly where could she retreat? As we understand the record, there was no other way out of the bedroom other than the doorway where her assailant stood. The (jury) charge should have asked whether, armed with a weapon, she could have safely made her way out of the bedroom door without threat of serious bodily injury to herself.

Battered Women and Domestic Homicides

The National Clearinghouse for the Defense of Battered Women states that every year 500 to 750 women kill men who abused them and that "our prisons are filled with women with long histories of abuse, linked to the crimes they're in prison for."[9] The clearinghouse also estimates that a woman is abused in the United States every 13 seconds.

These estimates indicate the high levels of anger, fear, hatred, and humiliation in the households where such conditions prevail. Battered women (and those who allege they were abused) can be found in the prisons of every state. They are serving sentences ranging from assault and battery to voluntary manslaughter and first-degree murder.

To lawfully use deadly force in self-defense, a real or reasonable fear of imminent death or great bodily harm must exist. If no immediate threat is present, then, it is assumed that the abused woman has lawful alternatives to force, such as going to a shelter for battered women or going to a family member for help.

EXAMPLE	A woman is terrified as her husband comes toward her in a rage, screaming that he will use the knife in his hand to kill her. Witnesses state that the woman had no opportunity to retreat but was able to grab a gun, which she used to kill the man. Her action would be held to be lawful use of force in self-defense.

EXAMPLE	After years of beatings and many other abuses, the defendant kills her husband with a handgun as he is taking a nap. Her husband has been drinking for two days, and the defendant believed he would beat her again, as he had often done in the past, when he finished his nap and resumed drinking. In most states a claim of self-defense would fail, because the fear of bodily harm was not imminent. (The killing might be held to be "imperfect self-defense," and the defendant charged with voluntary manslaughter rather than murder. See Chapter 10.

battered woman defense Evidence of past abuse offered by women charged with violence against their abusers to show its psychological effects as part of their claim of self-defense.

While courts have rejected the **battered woman defense** as a complete defense in the absence of a reasonable belief that the abuser presented an immediate threat of death or serious bodily harm, it does not mean the history of abuse is irrelevant to assertions of self-defense. In *State v. Frei*, 831 N.W.2d 70 (Iowa 2013), the court noted that many states use the battered woman defense as a factor in evaluating a claim of self-defense. It said:

As applied to a battered woman, an appropriately specific reasonableness inquiry might consider objective facts about the batterer, any history of violence, any failed

After 25 years of life with her abusive husband who was also a former police officer, Barbara Sheehan shot him 11 times with her husband's gun, killing him. At her murder trial, Sheehan contended she was in fear of her life when she shot her husband. Sheehan introduced evidence of past abuse in her defense. While the "battered-woman" defense does not serve as an excuse for killing an abusive spouse, evidence of past abuse is relevant to whether the battered spouse reasonably believed she was under imminent threat of serious physical harm, the requirement for self-defense using deadly force. Sheehan was acquitted of the murder charge but convicted of the illegal use of a gun.

attempts to escape abuse, and any other facts relevant under the circumstances. Further, expert testimony can aid in cautioning jurors that the behavior of battered women should not be lightly determined (sic) as inherently unreasonable.

The *Frei* court rejected, however, the defendant's contention that she need only show she subjectively believed she was in danger. The test remains a reasonable one, the court said, but jurors should judge reasonableness from the perspective of the battered woman.[10]

THE USE OF FORCE IN THE DEFENSE OF PROPERTY

A person is privileged to threaten to or intentionally use non-deadly force to protect property that is lawfully in his or her custody or care. The interference with the property must be unlawful. Force may be used only when necessary to terminate the interference, and the amount of force must be reasonable under the circumstances.

WHEN FORCE CANNOT BE USED

Force in self-defense or in the defense of another person cannot be used under the following circumstances:

- The force is not immediately necessary to protect against unlawful force.
- The amount of force used is unreasonable compared to the unlawful force threatened.
- In states without a "stand your ground" law, the force is deadly and the person using deadly force had an opportunity to retreat.
- The person using the force is the aggressor or is acting unlawfully.
- The other person's actions are lawful.
- The force used cannot be based on a fear that another person means to do harm sometime in the future if there is no immediate fear of harm.
- Force cannot be used to punish or to retaliate for past harm or past injury, such as a sexual assault in the past.

EXAMPLE   Y, a store employee, sees X snatch merchandise and run out of the store. Y may use *necessary* and *reasonable* force to prevent the *unlawful* taking of merchandise by X.

EXAMPLE   X snatches W's purse and runs off. Y, who observed the crime, would be justified in using necessary and reasonable force to recover the purse. Theft from the person (or robbery, if force is used) is a felony in most, if not all, states, which would authorize Y, in most states, to make a citizen's arrest. Force could also be used under these circumstances under the state law governing the use of force in making an arrest.

Deadly force was at one time commonly used to protect property. On the American frontier, farmers and ranchers often used deadly force to prevent the theft of their horses, cattle, or farm equipment. This force was necessary in those times, because law enforcement officers were seldom readily available. Today all states forbid the use of deadly force in the defense of property.

The rule that a person cannot use deadly force to protect property applies whether the owner is present or uses an automated device, such as a spring gun, that is triggered by opening a door or otherwise engaging a spring attached to the property. Indeed, some U.S. jurisdictions, such as Oregon and Wisconsin, and some countries, such as England, go so far as to punish separately the mere setting of a spring gun.

EXAMPLE   A farmer who becomes exasperated because melons are being stolen from his fields is not justified in shooting the thieves with a shotgun. Neither can he set up a shotgun that is discharged when a thief brushes a wire attached to the trigger mechanism.

SECTIONS OF THE U.S. CONSTITUTION CONTROLLING THE USE OF FORCE BY LAW ENFORCEMENT OFFICERS

Provision of the U.S. Constitution	Limit on Force Used
The Fourth Amendment forbids "unreasonable searches and seizures;" a "seizure" includes the use of unreasonable force.	The use of force, including deadly force by law enforcement officers, must be "objectively reasonable in light of the facts and circumstances confronting (the officer) . . . judged from the perspective of a reasonable officer on the scene. . . ." *Graham v. Connor*, 490 U.S. 386, 390 (1989).
The Eighth Amendment forbids "cruel and unusual punishment."	Once convicted and incarcerated, any use of force against an inmate is viewed as punishment and thus subject to the "cruel and unusual punishment" clause. Where force is used to maintain order in jails or prisons, the question becomes "whether force was applied in a good faith effort to maintain order . . . or maliciously and sadistically for the very purpose of causing harm." *Whitley v. Albers*, 475 U.S. 312, 320–321 (1986).
The Due Process Clauses of the Fifth and Fourteenth Amendments forbid governments from depriving any person of "life, liberty, or property without due process of law."	The U.S. Supreme Court has limited the use of the "due process" guarantee to those circumstances where there is no other source "of constitutional protection against a particular sort of intrusive governmental conduct." *Graham v. Conner*, 490 U.S. 386 at 395 (1989).

Virtually all states permit owners of real estate to use non-deadly force to evict trespassers from their property or protect the real estate from imminent harm. Most state statutes require the property owner to request that the trespassers leave the property before force is used. In the 2011 case of *State v. Starke*[11] the appeals court reversed a conviction for terrorist threats because the trial court failed to instruct the jury on the defendant's right to use force to protect his premises. The defendant, a 79-year-old man, ordered two men, whom he had paid to do some work, to leave his house, and when they refused the defendant threatened them with a handgun, a use of "force" under that state's law. The appeals court remanded the case for a new trial because a jury might find that the defendant had a reasonable belief the men would refuse to leave and damage his property.

THE USE OF FORCE IN MAKING AN ARREST

Force may not be used legally in making an arrest unless the arrest is a lawful, custodial arrest made in good faith. This does not mean that the arrested person must be found guilty of the charge; however, it does mean that probable cause (reasonable grounds to believe) must exist to authorize the arrest.

In most arrests, force is unnecessary because the person arrested complies with instructions and offers no resistance. If force in making arrests should be necessary because of resistance or an attempt to escape, the officer may use only such force as is reasonably believed necessary to

1. Detain the offender, make the arrest, and conduct lawful searches.
2. Overcome any resistance by the offender.
3. Prevent an escape and retake the offender if an escape occurs.
4. Protect the officer, others, and the offender, if necessary.

The tests used in determining whether excessive force was used by a law enforcement officer in making an arrest were established by the U.S. Supreme Court in the case of *Tennessee v. Garner,* discussed below for the use of deadly force, and the case of *Graham v. Connor.*[12] In *Graham* the U.S. Supreme Court held:

> Today we make explicit what was implicit in *Garner*'s analysis, and hold that *all* claims that law enforcement officers have used excessive force—deadly or not— in the course of an arrest, investigatory stop, or other "seizure" of a free citizen should be analyzed under the Fourth Amendment and its "reasonableness" standard, rather than under a "substantive due process" approach. Because the Fourth Amendment provides an explicit textual source of constitutional protection against this sort of physically intrusive governmental conduct, that Amendment, not the more generalized notion of "substantive due process," must be the guide for analyzing these claims.
>
> Determining whether the force used to effect a particular seizure is "reasonable" under the Fourth Amendment requires a careful balancing of "the nature and quality of the intrusion on the individual's Fourth Amendment interests" against the countervailing governmental interests at stake. (Citations omitted.) Our Fourth Amendment jurisprudence has long recognized that the right to make an arrest or investigatory stop necessarily carries with it the right to use some degree of physical coercion or threat thereof to effect it.[13]

The question of what force is reasonable in making an arrest must make allowance for the fact that the police are making judgments in volatile situations. Common uses of force courts find reasonable include forceful application of physical restraints, like handcuffs; force used to place a suspect on the ground to be handcuffed; and force used to take away a weapon on the suspect's person. One area where courts differ is the use of Taser guns to make arrests, a subject discussed later in this chapter.

Using Reasonable Force to Obtain Evidence of Drunk or Drugged Driving

A 2015 report from the National Highway Traffic Safety Administration (NHTSA) revealed that in 2014, 9,967 people were killed in alcohol-related traffic accidents. In 2014 32,675 traffic deaths occurred, so that alcohol or drug use was involved in about 31 per cent of total traffic deaths. NHTSA estimates the annual cost to Americans for alcohol or drug-impaired driving to be $45 billion. On October 2, 2012, the Centers for Disease Control and Prevention reported that although more than 1.4 million people were arrested for driving under the influence (DUI) in 2010, it estimated that there were over 112 million episodes that year where drivers operated vehicles while under the influence of alcohol or drugs.

All states make driving under the influence of alcohol or drugs a crime and have laws that require a driver to submit to breath, blood, or urine analysis when police officers have reasonable grounds to believe the driver is impaired. These laws have been upheld as reasonable regulation of an important and potentially dangerous activity. As these courts frequently point out, driving on public streets is a privilege, not a right.

In recent years an increasing number of drivers have refused to submit to standard breath tests. While all states have "refusal to consent" criminal statutes, the penalties for failure to consent are generally less than for a DUI conviction, and defense lawyers might believe that defending a refusal to consent charge presents fewer obstacles than defending a DUI charge.

It is difficult, as a practical matter, to force an uncooperative driver to submit to a breath or urine test. As a result, police and prosecutors have begun taking forced blood samples from these uncooperative drivers. The U.S. Supreme Court upheld the constitutionality of taking a blood sample without the consent of a suspect in *Schmerber v. California*[14] but stated that the sample must be taken under reasonable circumstances. It should be noted that while the police did not have a warrant to draw the blood sample in *Schmerber*, the Supreme Court stated the warrant was not needed under the "exigent circumstances" exception to the Fourth Amendment's warrant requirement. (See Gardner & Anderson, *Criminal Evidence*, p. 426 (9th ed., 2016).) However, in the 2013 case of *Missouri v. McNeeley*[15] the U.S. Supreme Court held that the fact that alcohol in the bloodstream dissipates over time is not by itself "exigent circumstances" that justify drawing blood without consent or a warrant. Absent other facts that make it imperative for the blood sample to be taken before police obtain a warrant, the Fourth Amendment requires them to obtain the warrant.

Standards for the Use of Deadly Force Established by the U.S. Supreme Court

Deadly force is force that is likely to cause death or serious bodily injury. The law regarding the use of deadly force in making an arrest varies somewhat from state to state.

Police department regulations also vary in the language used to regulate and instruct officers as to the use of deadly force. State laws and police regulations must conform, however, to the requirements established by the U.S. Supreme Court in the case of *Tennessee v. Garner* (which follows) and the case of *Graham v. Connor* (discussed above).

The question of the reasonableness of the use of deadly force by a law enforcement officer can arise as a defense to criminal charges against the officer. If a police officer uses excessive deadly force, murder or manslaughter charges can be filed by state prosecutors. The reasonableness question also frequently arises in a "1983" action, a civil action brought under 42 U.S.C. § 1983. That statute makes state officials, including police officers, liable if they violate a person's civil or constitutional rights. In the case of deadly force in an arrest, the representative of a person killed or an injured person may assert a cause of action against the officer employing the deadly force under the Fourth Amendment, since the use of force is a "seizure" and violates the Fourth Amendment if it is unreasonable. That was the claim in *Tennessee v. Garner,* which follows:

CASE CLOSE-UP

Tennessee v. Garner

Supreme Court of the United States
(1985) 471 U.S. 1, 105 S. Ct. 1694

At about 10:45 p.m. on October 3, 1974, Memphis police officers were dispatched to answer a "prowler inside call." Upon arriving at the scene, they saw someone run across the backyard. The fleeing suspect, Edward Garner, stopped at a six-foot-high chain-link fence at the edge of the yard. With the aid of a flashlight one of the officers was able to see Garner's face and hands. He saw no sign of a weapon. Garner was 17 or 18 years old and about five feet five inches or five feet seven inches tall. While Garner was crouched at the base of the fence, the officer called out "police, halt" and took a few steps toward him. Garner then began to climb over the fence. Convinced that if Garner made it over the fence he would elude capture, the officer shot him. The bullet hit Garner in the back of the head, killing him.

In using deadly force to prevent the escape, the officer was acting under the authority of a Tennessee statute and pursuant to police department policy. The statute provides that "[i]f, after notice of the intention to arrest the defendant, he either flee or forcibly resist, the officer may use all the necessary means to effect the arrest" (Tenn. Code Ann. § 40-7-108 (1982)). The department policy was slightly more restrictive than the statute but still allowed the use of deadly force in cases of burglary. The incident was reviewed by the Memphis Police Firearms Review Board and presented to a grand jury. Neither took any action.

Garner's father then brought this action in the U.S. District Court for the Western District of Tennessee, seeking damages under 42 U.S.C. § 1983 for asserted violations of Garner's constitutional rights. The complaint alleged that the shooting violated the Fourth, Fifth, Sixth, Eighth, and Fourteenth Amendments to the U.S. Constitution.[16] The District court dismissed the case. The Supreme Court said this about the Court of Appeals decision reversing the District Court:

> *It reasoned that the killing of the fleeing suspect was a "seizure" under the Fourth Amendment and thus constitutional only if reasonable. The court concluded that the Tennessee statute failed to distinguish between degrees of felonies, and in the present case the use of deadly force was unreasonable.*

On review the U.S. Supreme Court affirmed the conclusion of the Court of Appeals that "the facts, as found, did not justify the use of deadly force" and further held:

> *While we agree that burglary is a serious crime, we cannot agree that it is so dangerous as automatically to justify the use of deadly force. The FBI classifies burglary as a "property" rather than a "violent" crime. See Federal Bureau of Investigation, Uniform Crime Reports, Crime in the United States 1 (1984). Although the armed burglar would present a different situation, the fact that an unarmed suspect has broken into a dwelling at night does not automatically mean he is physically dangerous. This case demonstrates as much . . . . In fact, the available statistics demonstrate that burglaries only rarely involve physical violence. During the 10-year period . . . 1973–1982, only 3.8 percent of all burglaries involved violent crime.*

Police and the Use of Deadly Force   No question today seems more pressing in the relationship between the police and citizens than the proper use of deadly force by police when apprehending suspects. This is even more compelling when the victim of deadly force is a member of a minority group. The deaths in 2014 of Michael Brown in Ferguson, Missouri, Tamir Rice in Cleveland, and Laquan McDonald in Chicago, Freddie Gray in Baltimore, Maryland in 2015, and LaVoy Finicum in Oregon in 2016 have drawn national attention to the use of deadly force by police officers. Moreover, the failures of state or federal prosecutors to bring criminal actions against the police officers involved in the Tamir Rice, Michael Brown and LaVoy Finicum deaths have raised questions about the confidence citizens have in the police and those who supervise the police. While an officer was indicted for murder in the Laquan McDonald case, the indictment took more than a year to be obtained, and then formally charged only a few hours before a video of the killing was made public. The prosecution in Maryland of the six officers involved in the death of Freddie Gray was stalled, due to a hung jury in December of 2015 in the first trial against one of the officers. However, on March 8, 2016, the Maryland Court of Appeals ordered that officer to testify against the other five officers under a grant of limited immunity given by the prosecution.

Charges against police officers for wrongful use of deadly force do go to trial, however. This can be in a state or federal criminal prosecution, or in a civil case for damages as an **unreasonable seizure** that violated the Fourth Amendment rights of the victim. The meaning of "excessive force" for police actions is the same in either kind of case. The following cases illustrate some recent deadly force decisions:

unreasonable seizure   A seizure made by a government officer that is unreasonable under the circumstances and thus violates the Fourth Amendment.

Deadly Force was Excessive: *United States v. Pagen-Ferrer.*[17] In a 2013 case a federal court affirmed the conviction of four San Juan, Puerto Rico police officers in the 2003 death of a handcuffed suspect the officers kicked to death. No actions were brought against the officers by Puerto Rico authorities. In 2008 the officers were indicted under federal law for perjury, obstruction of justice, and violation of the victim's civil rights. The federal court of appeals affirmed the officer's convictions and sentences ranging from 57 months in prison for one officer, to 360 months in prison for the supervising officer.

Contreras v. Los Angeles[18]   Police investigating a drive-by shooting arrested a suspect. The suspect, who was not carrying a weapon, attempted to flee from the police. After just 20 seconds of flight, the officers shot him four times in the back. In a 2015 decision a federal court of appeals affirmed a $5.75 million judgement in a 1983 action against the officers.

Deadly Force was Not Excessive   *Davis v. Romer*[19] Fort Worth, Texas police officers stopped a car after observing the driver violate traffic laws. While questioning the driver, the police discovered he was wanted on several other traffic warrants. The driver refused to exit the car, and began accelerating away from the officers. One officer was standing on the vehicle's running board, and ordered the driver to stop. He refused, and started driving the vehicle towards a freeway entrance. The officer shot the driver, who died. The driver's children filed a 1983 action, contending the police officer used excessive force because it was unreasonable for him to jump on to the running board and put himself in danger. In a 2015 case the appeals court affirmed a dismissal of the action, saying the only question was the reasonableness of the officer's decision to use deadly force when he pulled the trigger. At that time, the court said, the driver's actions posed a threat to the officer and the public generally.

Plumhoff v. Rickard, 134 S. Ct. 2012 (2014) A West Memphis, Arkansas police officer stopped a car observed to have only one working headlight. When asked to show his driver's license, the driver refused and sped away. There followed a police pursuit by five police cruisers, at speeds up to 100 MPH, on I-40 and residential streets. Twice the fleeing vehicle bumped police cars trying to stop him. Once, the driver forced an officer to jump out of the way to avoid being run over. After being trapped by one cruiser, with officers approaching the vehicle, the driver did a 180 degree turn and accelerated away. Officers fired 15 shots at the vehicle, which went out of control and crashed into a building. The driver and his passenger died from a combination of gunshot wounds and injuries suffered in the crash. The U.S. Supreme Court reversed the judgment of the trial court and held the police did not use excessive force. It was reasonable, the court said, for the police to perceive the driver

THE SEARCH FOR NONLETHAL WEAPONS

Device	Description
Stun guns, stun shields, and stun belts	Devices deliver electrical charge meant to subdue without killing. The M26 Taser electric stun pistol shoots darts that stick to clothing and deliver up to 50,000 volts of electricity. Law enforcement agencies often use Tasers to incapacitate people without physical restraint. There is usually no long-term injury, though death has occurred in rare occasions.
Chemical sprays such as pepper spray, mace, and tear gas	Devices used to repel but not kill an assailant. Most states permit any person over age 18 to carry these products.
Crowd control devices	Water cannons and tear gas are commonly used; American law enforcement agencies are reluctant to use rubber bullets, which can be lethal under some circumstances. A new device known as the "Active Denial System" uses concentrated electromagnetic waves to control crowds. The waves, which can reach subjects from as far as a mile away, cause extreme temperature increases—as much as 122 degrees Fahrenheit—in the clothes and outer skin of those hit by the waves. The heat increase causes the person hit to move away at once, called "the goodbye effect." The waves can cause second-degree burns, but no permanent injury unless handled improperly.

as posing a "grave public safety risk," and thus "acted reasonably in using deadly force to end that risk."

Use of Force in Resisting an Unlawful Arrest

Under the common law, a person had a legal right to forcibly resist an unlawful arrest. This rule developed hundreds of years ago in England, when safeguards to protect a person from unlawful arrest did not exist. Today, there are many safeguards, and the old rule has been changed by court decisions and statutes in most states. California Penal Code, Section 834a, and Connecticut Statutes, Sections 53a-23, are examples of such statutes. The Connecticut statute is as follows: "A person is not justified in using physical force to resist an arrest by a reasonably identifiable police officer, whether such arrest is legal or illegal." A few states, however, retain the common law rule. For example, in 2012 the Michigan Supreme Court held that the common law right to resist a police officer who had entered a defendant's home unlawfully to search for another suspect still existed. The court reversed a conviction for felony obstruction of a police officer. *People v. Moreno*, 814 N.W.2d 624 (2012).

The Use of Tasers and Other Force in Traffic Stops

When a motorist is stopped by police for a traffic violation, the common procedure is for the police to inform the motorist of the violation, issue a ticket, and obtain the motorist's signature showing receipt of the ticket. However, when this common, usually peaceful transaction becomes a confrontation, officers sometimes use force on the motorist to compel the motorist to comply with the officer's commands. What level of force is permitted in these situations?

In 2009 and 2010, the Ninth Circuit Court of Appeals had occasion to consider two cases where officers used Taser guns to subdue persons stopped for traffic violations. Taser guns use compressed nitrogen to propel aluminum darts (probes), which are connected to wires that deliver a very painful, 1,200-volt electrical charge into the muscles of the person hit, causing pain and temporary paralysis in muscles hit. Subsequently, both motorists brought actions against the officers under 42 U.S.C. § 1983, the civil rights statute. The officers would have been liable only if the force they used was "excessive" under the principles discussed earlier in this chapter, so the court was required to evaluate the reasonableness of using Tasers in those cases.

In *Bryan v. McPherson*, 590 F.3d 767 (9th Cir. 2009), the court held that the police use of a Taser gun was excessive force. There, the motorist, Bryan, was stopped by a California police officer for failure to wear a seat belt. Bryan exited his car, wearing only boxer shorts and tennis shoes, and began slapping his thighs, yelling gibberish, and acting agitated. Bryan did not attack the officer, but the officer fired his Taser gun from about 20 to 26 feet away and struck Bryan, who fell to the ground and fractured four teeth. One of the Taser's probes had to be removed with a scalpel. The court found the use of the Taser to be excessive, noting that "traffic violations generally will not support the use of a significant level of force."

In *Brooks v. City of Seattle*, 599 F.3d 1018 (9th Cir. 2010), the court concluded that use of a Taser in a traffic stop was not excessive. There, a motorist, Brooks, was stopped

USE OF PHYSICAL RESTRAINTS

When law enforcement officers come in contact with a suspect or a person who might become violent, they may decide to use some form of physical restraint to protect themselves or the person restrained. Use of such restraints can in some circumstances be an unreasonable use of force, as the following materials illustrate.

Use of neck choke holds	Could be held to be unreasonable and excessive use of force	The FBI Law Enforcement Bulletin article "Physiological Effects Resulting from Use of Neck Holds" (July 1983) states, Because of the organs involved, neck holds must be considered potentially lethal whenever applied. Officers using this hold should have proper training in its use and effects. Police officers should have continual in-service training and practice in the use of the carotid sleeper. They should not use or be instructed in the use of the chokehold other than to demonstrate its potential lethal effect. Officers should recognize that death can result if the carotid sleeper is incorrectly applied.
Use of handcuffs	When an arrest is made	Generally upheld as reasonable
Use of handcuffs	When an investigative stop is made	Would be held reasonable if circumstances justified use
Use of handcuffs	In transporting mental patients	Would be unreasonable if there was no need to handcuff, but would be justified when there was a reasonable concern for safety

by Seattle police for speeding in a school zone. When presented with a ticket, Brooks refused to sign the ticket and tried to grab her driver's license away from the officer. The officer called his supervisor, who came to the scene and instructed Brooks to comply with the officer's commands. Brooks again refused, refused to turn off her car, and refused to exit her vehicle. The officers opened the driver's door and exerted pressure on Brooks's left arm to gain compliance, but Brooks resisted efforts to remove her from the vehicle. The officers then stated they were going to use a Taser gun, but Brooks again refused, informing the officers she was pregnant. The officers then applied the Taser to Brooks's thigh, removed her from her vehicle, and arrested her.

The District Court found the officers had used excessive force. The Court of Appeals reversed, stating that under the circumstances the use of the Taser was not excessive. The court distinguished the *Bryan* case by noting that here, unlike in *Bryan,* the Taser was used in "drive-stun" mode, and applied directly to Brooks's body, causing only temporary, localized pain. In that mode, the court noted, the effect of the Taser was considerably less than in the "dart" mode used by the officer in *Bryan.* The court also noted that the Seattle Police Department Use of Force

Training Guideline identified use of a Taser in "drive-stun" mode as a "level 1 Tactic." Since the officers were acting reasonably in arresting Brooks for obstruction, the use of "level 1" force was not excessive.

In the 2011 case of *McKenney v. Harrison*[20] the court held that use of a Taser by an officer to prevent a suspect wanted on misdemeanor charges from jumping out a window was not excessive, even though the suspect died when the Taser incapacitated him.

In a small, informal survey of ten police departments in five states, published in the September 2007 *FBI Law Enforcement Bulletin* and titled "The Dynamic Resistance Response Model—A Modern Approach to the Use of Force," the author who conducted the survey found that while most police departments require motorists to sign for tickets, all ten responded "no" to the question, "Would you use a Taser on a motorist who refused to sign a ticket?" Most of the officers stated that their practice was to hold the driver's license, but let the motorist go, assuming the motorist had no outstanding warrants and had proof of registration and insurance.

DISCIPLINING CHILDREN

Under common law, parents and people who take the place of parents *(in loco parentis)* have a natural right to the custody, care, and control of their children. They have a duty to provide food, clothing, shelter, and medical care to the children and to educate and discipline them. Under the common law, a parent or a person *in loco* may use a reasonable amount of force in disciplining a child.

A 2001 study[21] reported that the majority of American families discipline their preschool children by using occasional mild to moderate spanking. The study reported no negative effects on children. However, the study also showed that 4 to 7 percent of parents fell into the "red zone" (danger zone) because they disciplined their children frequently and impulsively by such means as verbal punishment, using a paddle, hitting their children in the face or body, or throwing or shaking their child. These children were more likely to have behavioral problems or experience anxiety or depression.

All states have laws requiring school officials, health professionals (nurses, doctors, and therapists), and law enforcement officials to report suspected child abuse. In determining the crime of child abuse, the following factors have to be considered:

- The age, size, and health of the child, as force used on a baby or a sick or helpless child is much different than the same force used on a healthy 14-year-old boy.
- The reason for the discipline, because spanking a child for unintentional bed-wetting or throwing up could lead to the conclusion that the parent was out of control and not rational.

The question of what amount of force is reasonable was presented to the Texas Court of Appeals (Houston) in the case of *Teubner v. State.*[22] The court held:

> Texas Penal Code section 9.61 permits the use of force against a child under a "reasonable belief" standard. However, force going beyond that which is necessary for discipline is prohibited. The question in this case is whether the appellants reasonably believed their use of force was necessary to discipline their child.

SUMMARY OF THE LAW ON THE USE OF FORCE

Situation	Less than Deadly Force	Deadly Force
In self-defense or in the defense of others	"The use of (reasonable) force upon or toward another person is justified when the actor (reasonably) believes that such force is immediately necessary for the purpose of protecting himself or herself (or another) against the use of unlawful force by such other person on the present occasion."[a]	"The use of deadly force is not justified unless such force is necessary to protect against death, serious bodily harm, kidnapping, or sexual intercourse compelled by force or threat."[b]
In the defense of property	"One may use physical force, other than deadly force such as may be necessary to prevent or terminate the commission or attempted commission of larceny or of criminal mischief with respect to property other than premises."[c]	Under the old common law, deadly force could be used in the defense of property. All states now forbid the use of intentional deadly force in the defense of property.
To apprehend a person who has committed a crime	"When an officer is making or attempting to make an arrest for a criminal offense, he is acting for the protection of public interest and is permitted even a greater latitude than when he acts in self-defense, and he is not liable unless the means which he uses are clearly excessive."[d]	Misdemeanor: Never. Fleeing felon: Deadly force could be used when officers "have probable cause to believe that the suspect (has committed a felony and) poses a threat to the safety of the officers or a danger to the community if left at large" (*Tennessee v. Garner*).
To stop a person for investigative purposes when only "reasonable suspicion" exists	Only such force that is reasonable and necessary under the circumstances that then exist.	Never
Disciplining children (corporal punishment)	Only parents and other people having a status of *in loco parentis* to a child may use reasonable force "reasonably believed to be necessary for (the child's) proper control, training, or education."[e] Other persons (such as strangers or neighbors) may not discipline a child.	Never

[a]Sections 3.04(1) and 3.05(1) of the Model Penal Code.
[b]Section 3.04(2) (b) of the Model Penal Code.
[c]State of New York, Public Law 35.25.
[d]*Restatement of Torts*, § 132(a).
[e]*Restatement of Torts*, § 147(2), as quoted by the U.S. Supreme Court in *Ingraham v. Wright*, 429 U.S. 975, 97 S. Ct. 481(1976).

From the evidence presented, no reasonable person could possibly believe the conduct was justifiable. The child was subjected to a savage beating with a leather belt on two successive nights. On the first night, Victoria Teubner took over the whipping when her husband tired himself. On the second night, they gagged their daughter to stifle her crying. The photographs admitted into evidence offer a grim record of the effects of the beating. The appellants could not have reasonably believed that the degree of force used was necessary for disciplinary purposes. Appellants' second point of error is overruled.

Besides the parents, any person taking the place of the parents and thus classified as ***in loco parentis*** may reasonably discipline a child in his or her care. This category includes legal guardians, foster parents, and public school teachers.

in loco parentis (Latin; "in place of the parents") Any person taking the place of the parents has the duties and responsibilities of the parents and may reasonably discipline a child in his or her care. This category includes legal guardians, foster parents, and public schoolteachers.

Because of the threats of lawsuits and pressure from anti-paddling groups, many states have forbidden corporal punishment in public schools within those states. In the states that continue to permit corporal punishment, many school boards forbid or limit the use of corporal punishment of students within the school district. The U.S. Supreme Court held in the case of *Ingraham v. Wright* that under common law, "a teacher may impose reasonable but not excessive force to discipline a child."[23] The U.S. Supreme Court noted:

> Where the legislatures have not acted, the state courts have uniformly preserved the common law rule permitting teachers to use reasonable force in disciplining children in their charge.

Law enforcement officers, neighbors, and other adults who see children misbehave may not discipline a child (or children), although they may use reasonable force to prevent damage to property or injury to other persons or themselves.

Reasonable force to maintain order (as distinguished from discipline) may be used by personnel on airplanes, ships, trains, or buses and by ushers at theaters, sporting events, and other public gathering places. A disorderly child or adult may be ordered to leave if he or she is disturbing other people or has failed to pay the fare or admission fee. The test, again, is that of reasonableness. Did the provocation justify the action taken? Was the force reasonable under the circumstances?

LEARNING OBJECTIVES SUMMARY

LO 1. Identify the three key points for determining when force is justified.
Use of force is justified only if (1) reasonable, (2) necessary, and (3) in response to unlawful actions by another.

LO 2. Describe the "castle" doctrine and explain what it says.
The "castle" doctrine states that a person in his home is justified in using reasonable force, including deadly force, in response to an assault in his home. There is no duty to retreat under this doctrine.

LO 3. Determine how "stand your ground" laws affect the general rules for using force and the effect such laws have on the "castle" doctrine.
The "stand your ground" laws generally give persons the absolute right to refuse to retreat and to respond to an attacker with reasonable force, including deadly force. Such laws change the "castle" doctrine in many states by adopting a presumption that a homeowner has a fear of imminent peril whenever he is attacked in his home.

LO 4. List the circumstances that justify a police officer using non-deadly force in making an arrest.
A police officer may use non-deadly force to detain a suspect, prevent his escape, overcome resistance to arrest, or protect the officer or others from harm.

LO 5. Explain why the Fourth Amendment applies to use of force by a police officer.
Actions by police officers using force to arrest a suspect are "seizures" of the suspect, and thus under the Fourth Amendment must be reasonable. State laws or regulations stating how and when police officers may use force must also comply with the Fourth Amendment.

LO 6. Identify the circumstances that would justify the use of deadly force by a police officer.
A police officer may, as may any person, use deadly force when faced with the threat of death or serious bodily harm to the officer or another. A police officer may also use deadly force to prevent the escape of a suspect in serious, violent felony arrests if the officer reasonably believes the escaped suspect presents a serious danger to the public.

LO 7. List the people who may use force in the discipline of children.
Parents, guardians, and those in loco parentis may use reasonable force in disciplining children in their charge.

KEY TERMS

self-defense, p. 144
defense of another, p. 144
Good Samaritan laws, p. 145
deadly force, p. 145

"stand your ground" laws, p. 146
"castle" doctrine, p. 149
"make my day" rules, p. 149
battered woman defense, p. 151

unreasonable seizure, p. 158
in loco parentis, p. 164

CASE ANALYSIS AND WRITING EXERCISES

1. Was the use of force justified in the following situation? Defendant was awakened around midnight by noise in the hallway of his apartment building. He walked into the hall, where he saw a man loudly knocking at a neighbor's door. Defendant told the man to leave, and after an exchange of words, Defendant claims the man threw a punch at him. Defendant then struck the man, knocking him down a flight of stairs. At Defendant's trial for assault he contends he was privileged to use force because the other man was in Defendant's "castle." As a result, Defendant contends, he had no duty to retreat. Is Defendant correct? See *State v. Devens*, 852 N.W.2d 255 (Minn. 2014). Would it change your answer if this had happened in a "stand your ground" state?

2. When a police officer is charged with assault based on force used by the officer during a lawful arrest, how should the jury be instructed to evaluate the officer's claim that the force used was not excessive? Does the officer have to consider other options to the use of force, such as a duty to retreat? Is it relevant the victim was resisting arrest? To what extent? See *Comm. v. Asher*, 31 N.E.3d 1055 (Mass. 2015).

3. Police officers were summoned to a residence by a 911 call which said a person there was having seizures. Police and emergency medical personnel entered the premises, and determined the person should be taken to a hospital for observation. The person resisted, kicked out at the officers and medical personnel, and refused to be strapped into an EMT transport chair. Ultimately, a police sergeant used a Taser to subdue the person. Subsequently, the person sued the officer and city, alleging excessive force had been used. How should a court evaluate the officer's decision to use the Taser? *Pacheco v. City of New York*, 104 A.3d 548 (N.Y. App. 2013)

4. Three members of a street gang, La Sierra Brown Nights, went looking for members of a rival gang,

Tiny Winos, intending to confront the other gang over harassment by that gang. They found seven members of Tiny Winos, and asked them, "Where you from?", which in gang custom is a challenge to the other gang. Fistfights immediately broke out, and several Tiny Winos' "double-teamed" the La Sierra members. At one point one of the La Sierra members believed a Tiny Wino had pulled a gun, so he pulled his gun and shot the Tiny Winos member, who died.The La Sierra members were charged with murder. At their trial they asserted a defense of self-defense. Were they entitled to assert that defense? If so, what did the trial court (and the prosecutor) do wrong? *People v. Ramirez*, 233 Cal. App. 4th 940 (Cal. App. 2015)

ENDNOTES

1. When cases go before a criminal court, most states place the burden of proving there was no justification for the force (such as self-defense) upon the state. The U.S. Supreme Court pointed out in the 1987 case *of Martin v. Ohio* (480 U.S. 228, 107 S. Ct. 1098) that only two states continue to follow the common law "that affirmative defenses, including self-defense, were matters for the defendant to prove." Forty-eight states require "the prosecution to prove the absence of self-defense when it is properly raised by the defendant." Ohio and South Carolina continue to follow the common law rule. The Supreme Court held that the rule used in Ohio and South Carolina is constitutional. The Court pointed out that "the Constitution (does not) require the prosecution to prove the sanity of a defendant who pleads not guilty by reason of insanity."

2. Florida Statutes Section 776.013(3). In 2014 the Florida stand your ground statutes were amended to include within their protection persons who threaten to use force. The original language in §776.013 (3) is now consolidated in §§ 776.012, 776.013, and 776.031. § 776.012 was also amended to include the requirement found in 776.013, that the defendant not be engaged in unlawful activity.

3. Paul Logli, president of the National District Attorney's Association.

4. See the *New York Times* article, "15 States Expand Victim's Rights on Use of Deadly Force," August 7, 2006.

5. 158 U.S. 550 (1895).

6. 972 P.2d 32 (Okla. Cr. 1998).

7. Florida Statutes Section 776.013 (1).

8. 694 A2d 564, 574 (N.J. 1997).

9. See the *New York Times* article, "More States Study Clemency for Women Who Killed Abusers," February 2, 1991.

10. 831 N.W.2d, at 75.

11. 800 N.W.2d 705 (N.D. 2011).

12. 490 U.S. 386, 109 S. Ct. 1865.

13. 490 U.S. at 395–396.

14. 384 U.S. 757 (1966).

15. 2013 WL 1628934 (2013).

16. The police officers in the U.S. Supreme Court case of *Tennessee v. Garner* could use the defense known as "qualified immunity." Under this defense, police officers or other public officials who are sued for violating someone's constitutional rights cannot be held liable if either the law at the time of the incident was unclear or they (the police officers) reasonably believed at the time that their conduct was lawful.

17. 736 F.3d 573 (1st Cir. 2013), *cert denied* 134 S. Ct. 2839 (2014).

18. 603 Fed. Appx.530 (9th Cir. 2015), *cert denied* 136 S. Ct. 688 (2015).

19. 600 Fed. Appx. 926 (5th Cir. 2015).

20. 635 F.3d 354 (8th Cir. 2011).

21. See the *New York Times* article, "Finding Gives Some Support to Advocates of Spanking: Adding Fuel to Bitter Debate on Child Care," August 25, 2001.

22. 742 S.W.2d 57 (Tex. App. 1987).

23. 430 U.S. 651, 97 S. Ct. 1401 (1977).

7

Other Criminal Defenses

OUTLINE

AFFIRMATIVE DEFENSES

IMMUNITY AS A DEFENSE

Diplomatic Immunity

Legislative Immunity

Witness Immunity

MISTAKE OR IGNORANCE OF FACT AS A DEFENSE

Strict Liability Crimes and the Defense of Mistake

Mistake or Ignorance of Criminal Law

INTOXICATION OR DRUGGED CONDITION AS A DEFENSE

DURESS, COERCION, OR COMPULSION AS A DEFENSE

NECESSITY OR CHOICE OF EVILS DEFENSE

CAN ONE KILL TO SAVE ONESELF?

ALIBI AS A CRIMINAL DEFENSE

Alibi Notice Statutes

THE DEFENSE THAT THE DEFENDANT WAS ACTING UNDER THE AUTHORITY, DIRECTION, OR ADVICE OF ANOTHER

THE DEFENSE OF DOUBLE JEOPARDY

The Times When Jeopardy Attaches

Prosecution by Both State and Federal Governments

The Meaning of "Separate Offense"

ENTRAPMENT AND OUTRAGEOUS GOVERNMENT CONDUCT AS DEFENSES

THE DEFENSE THAT ANOTHER PERSON COMMITTED THE CRIME

THE RIGHT TO A SPEEDY TRIAL AS A DEFENSE

THE STATUTE OF LIMITATIONS AS A DEFENSE

LEARNING OBJECTIVES

In this chapter we present several defenses a defendant may assert in a criminal prosecution. The learning objectives for this chapter are the following:

LO 1. Identify the kinds of immunity to criminal prosecution available, and their limits.

LO 2. Determine when, if ever, a mistake of fact or law may provide a defense.

LO 3. Distinguish between the defenses of duress and necessity.

LO 4. Explain why the Double Jeopardy Clause prohibits successive prosecutions for the same crime.

LO 5. Distinguish between a prosecution for the same offense and one for a separate offense.

LO 6. Define "acquittal" for purposes of the Double Jeopardy Clause.

LO 7. Identify the tests that determine when government inducements become entrapment.

LO 8. List the factors that determine when a speedy trial violation has occurred.

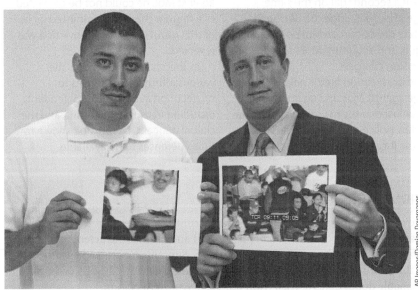

Juan Catalan was charged with murder in a homicide that occurred in San Fernando Valley, California, and served 5 months in jail after his arrest. He maintained that he and his 6-year-old daughter were attending a Los Angeles Dodgers–Atlanta Braves game at Dodger Stadium, 20 miles away from the murder site, at the time the victim was killed. Here, Catalan and his attorney hold prints from film of the TV show *Curb Your Enthusiasm*, which was shooting scenes during the Dodgers-Braves baseball game. The time-coded film showed Catalan and his daughter at the game, confirming his alibi. We examine other criminal defenses in this chapter, including alibi defenses like the one successfully raised by Catalan.

One of the defenses we study in this chapter is the defense of double jeopardy. The defense is based on the belief that once a defendant has been placed at risk for a conviction of a crime but has been acquitted, the government should not be allowed a second trial on the same charge. One corollary of that belief is a doctrine called "collateral estoppel," which sometimes applies in criminal prosecutions to effectively prevent second trials even when the defendant has not been acquitted in a first trial. The prosecution discovered that in the 2015 case of *In re Moi*, 30 P.3d 811 (Wash. 2015).

Someone shot and killed Keith McGowan in 2006. Police found the gun that was used in the shooting, and believed it belonged to Matthew Moi. Moi was charged with murder and illegal possession of a gun, based on convictions when Moi was a juvenile. Moi successfully moved to sever the two charges, because he didn't want the jury to be prejudiced by evidence of his earlier convictions.

The prosecution introduced evidence to the jury on both the murder charge and the gun charge, although the prosecution and defendant agreed the judge would decide the gun charge. The jury could not reach a verdict on the murder charge, and the judge declared a mistrial. (A hung jury does not normally prevent a second trial on the same charge.) The trial judge did decide that the state did not prove Moi possessed the gun, and acquitted Moi of the illegal possession charge.

The prosecution filed a new murder charge against Moi, and again proved the gun used in the murder was the gun found by police and tied to Moi. This time the jury convicted Moi of murder.

On appeal, the court said that because Moi had already been acquitted of the gun possession charge, and because that fact was part of the prosecution's case against Moi, he could not be convicted of a murder that was committed by use of that gun. His murder conviction was reversed.

In this chapter we discuss the various affirmative defenses to prosecution available to a defendant, including immunity defenses, and the circumstances that must be shown for those defenses to be available.

AFFIRMATIVE DEFENSES

corpus delicti   In all criminal cases, the government must prove that the crime charged was committed (corpus delicti) and that the defendant was party to the crime (committed the crime or was an accomplice).

To prove the guilt of a person charged with a crime, the state must present evidence (1) that a crime was committed (**corpus delicti**) and (2) that the defendant committed or was a party to the crime charged. The U.S. Supreme Court has repeatedly held that "the requirement that guilt of a criminal charge be established by proof beyond a reasonable doubt dates at least from our early years as a Nation."[1]

Defendants in criminal cases may, if they wish, sit quietly and place on the government the burden of coming forward with evidence proving guilt beyond a reasonable doubt. If the government does carry this burden, a defendant may then produce evidence showing actual innocence, justification, or other defenses, usually called affirmative defenses.

affirmative defense
A defense to a criminal charge in which the defendant generally admits doing the criminal act but claims an affirmative defense such as duress (he or she was forced) or entrapment.

An **affirmative defense** is any defense that assumes the complaint or charges to be correct but raises other facts that, if true, would establish a valid excuse or justification or a right to engage in the conduct in question. An affirmative defense does not concern itself with the elements of the offense at all; it concedes them. In effect, an affirmative defense says, "Yes, I did it, but I had a good reason."

Defenses to a criminal charge provide either an excuse for the criminal conduct or a justification for that conduct. The insanity defense, for example, if proved, excuses the behavior that would otherwise be criminal. Self-defense, on the other hand, doesn't excuse the force used; if proved, the defense provides a justification for the use of the force. The distinction between excuse and justification is not of great importance, and the term "affirmative defense" is commonly used to refer to both kinds of defense.

It is generally agreed that a state may place the burden of proof for the establishment of an affirmative defense on the defendant. In *Leland v. Oregon*,[2] discussed in Chapter 3, the Supreme Court upheld a law that required a defendant to prove the defense of insanity beyond a reasonable doubt. Not all states do so; in the case of the insanity defense, a few states require the prosecution to prove the defendant was sane when the crime was committed.

It is also generally agreed that a state may not shift the burden of proof on an element of the crime to the defendant by designating the element as an affirmative defense.[3] However, it is not always clear that the state has made this improper designation. If the state has the power, as states usually do, to define what conduct is criminal, a statute that defines a crime broadly, and then makes affirmative defenses to the crime the burden of the defendant, is not a violation of the burden of proof principle. For example, in many states it is a strict liability crime to sell impure food; the prosecution need only prove that the food sold was impure. It would be permissible for a state to make it an affirmative defense that the seller used reasonable efforts to inspect the food sold, and then place the burden of proof on the defendant to prove the defense. On the other hand, a state would probably be prohibited from defining, as an example, first-degree burglary as any unprivileged entry of a dwelling, and then placing the burden on the defendant to show as an affirmative defense that the entry was not made at night, and thus only a second-degree felony. The fact "at night" is an element of the crime that makes the burglary a more serious crime (as it is in some jurisdictions; see Chapter 14). As a result, the state must bear the burden of proving that element.

Affirmative defenses come from various sources. Some, such as immunity or the alibi defense, are the product of state or federal statutes. Others, such as self-defense and duress, have evolved from the common law. Finally, a few affirmative defenses are mandated by the U.S. Constitution. The double jeopardy and speedy trial defenses are examples of defenses with their roots in the Constitution. In this chapter we identify the requirements for many of the affirmative defenses available in state and federal criminal prosecutions.

IMMUNITY AS A DEFENSE

Under some circumstances, persons who have committed crimes are exempt from prosecution for their actions, either temporarily or permanently. The basis for their claim to immunity might come from a federal or state statute, an international agreement, or in one case from the U.S. Constitution. The principal forms of immunity are discussed in this section.

Diplomatic Immunity

In 1972 the United States ratified the Vienna Convention on Diplomatic Relations, an international agreement on the status of diplomats stationed in a foreign country. More than a hundred other countries have ratified this Convention. Article 31.1 of the Convention states that a "diplomatic agent" shall enjoy full **immunity** from the criminal jurisdiction of the receiving state. (In international law conventions, the word *state* means a "nation or country.") Article 37.1 extends this immunity to members of the diplomat's family. U.S. law (22 U.S.C. § 254(d)) states that any action brought against a person entitled to diplomatic immunity must be dismissed. Two federal cases illustrate the scope and limit of diplomatic immunity.

In the case of *United States v. Kuznetsov*,[4] a federal district court denied diplomatic immunity to a Russian citizen employed by the United Nations in New York City. Although the defendant was at one time certified as a member of the Russian Federation Mission, and therefore entitled to immunity, when he became chairman of a UN committee the Russian Mission informed the State Department that the defendant was no longer part of the Mission. The court thus concluded that even

immunity An exemption from criminal prosecution based on the U.S. Constitution, statutes, or international agreements.

though the defendant regarded himself as a "career Russian diplomat," during the years he worked for the UN, when the crimes he was charged with occurred, he was not a "diplomatic agent" and not entitled to immunity. The court also held that the defendant lacked immunity under the United Nations Convention on Privileges and Immunities. That convention applies only to "visiting foreign officials." The court concluded the defendant was not simply "visiting" the UN, but rather was a full-time employee. As a result, the only immunity the defendant enjoyed under the Convention was immunity for acts done in his official capacity. This immunity can be waived by the secretary general of the UN, who did so in this case.

In the case of *United States v. Al-Hamdi,*[5] a federal court of appeals held that the diplomatic immunity given to members of a diplomat's family ends at age 21. The Vienna Convention leaves it to member states to determine the extent of the family immunity, the court held, and since the State Department issued a regulation setting the 21 years of age limit (23 if enrolled in school), that regulation was conclusive on the issue. The defendant, 26 years old when indicted, was thus convicted of being a nonimmigrant alien in possession of a firearm.

Diplomatic immunity may be waived by the diplomat's home country, and in the case of serious crimes, the U.S. government frequently requests that waiver. An example of this waiver can be seen in *Van Den Borre v. State,*[6] in which Belgium waived immunity for a diplomat who was then convicted of a double murder.

Immunity for consular officers is not absolute, as it is for diplomats. Article 43 of the Vienna Convention provides that "consular officers . . . shall not be amenable to the jurisdiction of [the host nation] in respect to acts performed in the exercise of consular functions." Criminal acts not so performed expose the consular offices to prosecution. For example, in *United States v. Cole,*[7] a consular officer was successfully prosecuted for smuggling money out of the United States in a diplomatic pouch. The court said the officer was not exercising consular functions.

Legislative Immunity

Article I, Section 6, of the U.S. Constitution provides that U.S. senators and representatives "shall in all Cases except Treason, Felony and Breach of the Peace, be privileged from Arrest during their Attendance at the Session of their respective Houses, and in going to and returning from the same." Most state constitutions extend the same or similar privileges to state legislators while the state legislature is in session.

Representatives, senators, and state legislators thus have a limited degree of temporary immunity while their legislative bodies are in session. Charges, however, could be held until the legislative body adjourns. Also, state legislators enjoy no immunity from prosecution for federal crimes.[8]

Article I, Section 6 also contains the "speech and debate clause," which provides that members of Congress may not be "questioned" for any "speech or debate" in their respective houses, which has been interpreted to bar prosecution for all "legislative acts" taken by a member and part of the "legislative process." This protection is limited. In the 2011 case of *United States v. Renzi,*[9] the court held that the clause did not bar prosecution of corruption charges against a House of Representatives member who promised to introduce legislation in exchange for a payment of money. The negotiations for the proposed legislation were not "legislative acts," the court held.

Moreover, the clause creates no privilege to refuse to surrender records, not otherwise privileged, to state or federal investigators. In the 2015 case of *In re Fattah*, 802 F.3d 516 (3rd Cir. 2015) the court said the speech and debate clause did not create a privilege in a U.S. House of Representative Member to refuse to surrender e-mails from his G-mail account to Department of Justice investigators looking into a corruption charge against the Member.

Witness Immunity

Federal and state prosecutors have the power to subpoena witnesses to give testimony to aid the prosecutors in investigations of crimes. Legislative bodies have a similar power. Under the Fifth Amendment, a witness cannot be compelled to testify against himself. A witness summoned to testify may thus refuse to testify by invoking his Fifth Amendment right. To resolve this conflict, both the federal government and the states have passed various immunity statutes, under which a witness can be given immunity from prosecution, thereby protecting his Fifth Amendment right, and be compelled to answer questions that might be incriminating.

The principal federal immunity statute is 18 U.S.C. § 6002, which requires a witness to testify if called before a court, federal agency, or legislative body, on the condition that his or her testimony may not be used against him in a criminal prosecution. Because of statements made by the Supreme Court in the early case of *Counselman v. Hitchcock*,[10] earlier versions of section 6002 had been interpreted as grants of total or **transactional immunity**. Under transactional immunity the witness cannot be prosecuted for any offense related to the subject matter of his or her testimony.

Congress was concerned that total immunity hampered federal efforts to combat crime. In 1970 Congress enacted the current version of section 6002, which grants only **use immunity**. Under use immunity, the statements made by the witness may not be used in subsequent prosecutions, but the witness can be prosecuted for the crimes about which the witness testified if other evidence is used to convict the witness. The U.S. Supreme Court upheld the constitutionality of section 6002 in *Kastigar v. United States*,[11] holding that the statute gives the same protection as the Fifth Amendment, and that is all the protection Congress is required to give a witness.

Many states have enacted both transactional and use immunity statutes, with the prosecution deciding which immunity to request. For example, Illinois has a transactional immunity statute, 725 ILCS 5/106-1, which provides that after a request by the state a court "may order" a witness to testify by granting immunity from prosecution for the crimes about which the witness testifies. The use immunity statute, 725 ILSC 5/106-2.5, provides that after a request by the State, the court "shall order" a witness to testify with immunity from use of his testimony. In *People v. Ousley*, 919 N.E.2d 875 (Ill. 2009), the Illinois Supreme Court held that the prosecution's request to a court for an order granting use immunity was mandatory on the court.

In many cases, the grant of immunity is the result of an agreement between a prosecutor and a potential witness or defendant. The scope of the resulting immunity may then turn on the meaning of the agreement. In *Oatney v. Premo*, 2015 WL 8316856 (Or. App. 2015), the court reversed a murder conviction because evidence introduced at the defendant's murder trial should have been barred under

transactional immunity Total or full immunity for the criminal offense to which compelled testimony relates.

use immunity Prohibits prosecutorial authorities from using compelled testimony in a criminal prosecution, but does not make the witness totally immune from prosecution based on evidence other than the witness's testimony and not derived from that testimony.

an immunity agreement reached with the prosecutor prior to trial. The defendant agreed to talk with police about a murder after the prosecutor agreed that nothing he said would be used against him. The defendant implicated another man, Johnston, in the murder. The police read the defendant's statement to Johnston, who then said the two committed the murder together. Johnston agreed to testify against the defendant in exchange for an agreement the state would not seek the death penalty in his case. The defendant was convicted of the murder and sentenced to death. On appeal the court reversed his conviction, holding the immunity agreement barred the use of any evidence derived from the defendant's statements, which included the testimony of Johnston.

MISTAKE OR IGNORANCE OF FACT AS A DEFENSE[12]

At times, a mistake of fact can serve as a defense to criminal liability. For example, suppose a man walking out of a restaurant takes the wrong coat from the coat rack. A few minutes later, the true owner of the coat angrily complains to a police officer. The officer stops the man with the wrong coat blocks away and brings him back to the restaurant. Investigation shows that the man does have a coat similar to the coat that he walked away in. Has the man committed a theft, or has he made an honest mistake of fact?

The common law rule is that an honest mistake or ignorance of fact is a defense if it negates the existence of a state of mind essential to the crime. A material element of the crime of theft is taking property of another with intent to deprive the owner of the property. Did the man take the coat with intent to deprive the owner of possession of his coat? If his honest mistake negated that intent, he is not guilty of the crime.

Other kinds of mistake of fact do not provide a defense. For example, the mistaken belief that property taken belongs to person A, when in fact it belongs to person B, does not serve as a defense to the crime of theft. That is because even if the circumstances were as believed, the person taking the property would be guilty of the crime.

One of the most often cited cases for the mistake defense is the case of *Morissette v. United States*,[13] where the U.S. Supreme Court reversed a conviction for theft of government property. The defendant asserted the defense that he believed spent bomb casings on a government bombing range had been abandoned by the government, based on their condition and the fact that the defendant and other people routinely used the area for hunting. The Court said the jury should have been allowed to consider whether the defendant had the requisite "evil-meaning mind" necessary to convict him of theft.

The following cases are examples of application of the honest mistake of fact rule.

Mistake of fact defense allowed:

- *People v. Andrews*, 234 Cal. App. 4ᵗʰ 590 (Cal. App. 2015): Defendant's honest and reasonable belief that female victim consented to sexual activity negated specific intent necessary for conviction of misdemeanor sexual battery.
- *Commonwealth v. Liebenow*, 20 N.E.3d 242 (Mass. 2014): Defendant's honest belief that scrap metal on private construction site was abandoned negated specific intent to steal, even if the belief was unreasonable because of a "no trespassing" sign on property.

Mistake of fact defense not allowed:

- *Chavers v. State*, 991 N.E.2d 148 (Ind. App.2013): Mistaken belief that protection order had been cancelled based on statements of protected person who obtained order was not reasonable, because the same day defendant contacted protected person his probation officer told him the order was still effective.
- *People v. Braslow*, 183 Cal. Rptr. 3d 575(Cal. App. 2015): Honest belief that intoxicated victim had capacity to give consent to sex not enough. Belief must also be reasonable.

Strict Liability Crimes and the Defense of Mistake

When a state legislature or the Congress of the United States creates a strict liability crime, the defense of mistake of fact cannot be used, because criminal liability comes from simply doing the forbidden act without any requirement for the state or government to prove any mental fault (see Chapter 3). Examples include the following:

- *Fleming v. State*, 455 S.W.3d 577 (Tex. App. 2014), *cert denied* 135 S. Ct. 1159 (2015): Defendant could not use defense of honest but mistaken belief as to the age of the victim in a charge of sexual assault of child under 14. The court said that while mistake of fact is a defense to a crime that requires specific intent, the sexual assault of a child has no specific intent requirement.[14]
- In assaulting a federal officer, the defendant cannot use the honest but mistaken belief that he or she did not know the victim was a federal officer: *United States v. Feola,* 420 U.S. 671; 95 S. Ct. 1255 (1975); *United States v. Goldson*, 954 F.2d 51 (2d Cir. 1992).
- Shooting deer because defendant believed they were eating feed intended for his cattle, and thus justified, not a defense to violation of the statute making shooting big game out of season a strict liability offense. *State v. Kleppe*, 800 N.W.2d 311 (N.D. 2011).

Mistake or Ignorance of Criminal Law

The full scope of the Latin maxim *Ignorantia legis neminem excusat* ("Ignorance of the law excuses no one") may have caused Blackstone to change the phrase in his *Commentaries* (4 *Commentaries, 27*) to "Ignorance of the law which every one is bound to know, excuses no man." Blackstone's statement is a far better expression of the law, because courts will not allow a defendant who has committed an offense that is generally well known to the public to argue ignorance or mistake of that law. Serious offenses, such as murder, rape, robbery, and theft, are violations not only of the statutory law but also of moral and ethical laws. Courts would not seriously consider a defense of mistake or ignorance of such laws. Nor would courts ordinarily permit a person charged with a traffic violation in the state in which he or she is licensed to drive to argue ignorance of the traffic laws of that state. It is presumed that the holder of a license knows the traffic laws when the license is received or renewed.

But what of the hundreds of criminal laws that are not well known? In a now-famous publication, the President's Commission on Law Enforcement and Administration of Justice reported in *The Challenge of Crime in a Free Society* that the federal government alone has defined more than 2,800 crimes and observed that state and local governments have defined even more numerous offenses (p. 18). The following U.S. Supreme Court cases illustrate the complexity and great numbers of laws that exist today:

Cheek v. United States

Supreme Court of the United States (1991),
498 U.S. 192, 111 S. Ct. 604

Mr. Cheek was an airline pilot who did not file federal income tax returns for six years. Cheek argued that he did not "willfully" fail to file income tax returns and that he honestly believed his failure to file returns was lawful.

Because of the complexity of the U.S. tax laws, the Supreme Court held that the "willfully" requirement of the criminal charge against Cheek could not be met if the alleged violator was honestly confused about the meaning of the law.

Other courts now view this case as an exception to the general rule that ignorance of the law is no excuse. (See the 2009 case of *State v. Casper*, 297 S.W.3d 676 (Tenn. 2009), reviewing court decisions.)

Lambert v. California

Supreme Court of the United States (1957),
355 U.S. 225, 78 S. Ct. 240

The defendant was charged with and convicted of failing to register as required under a Los Angeles municipal ordinance that requires "any convicted person" who is in the city for longer than five days to register with local authorities. The defendant had been convicted of forgery and had lived in Los Angeles for more than seven years without registering. In a 5–4 decision, the U.S. Supreme Court held that the registration provision of the ordinance violated the due process requirement of the Fourteenth Amendment.

Justice William O. Douglas, writing for the majority, stated:

The rule that "ignorance of the law will not excuse" ... is deep in our law, as is the principle that of all the powers of local government, the police power is "one of the least limitable." ... On the other hand, due process places some limits on its exercise. Engrained in our concept of due process is the requirement of notice. Notice is sometimes essential so that the citizen has the chance to defend charges. Notice is required before property interests are disturbed, before assessments are made, before penalties are assessed. Notice is required in a myriad of situations where a penalty or forfeiture might be suffered for mere failure to act. ...

This appellant on first becoming aware of her duty to register was given no opportunity to comply with the law and avoid its penalty,

> *even though her default was entirely innocent. . . . Where a person did*
> *not know of the duty to register and where there was no proof of the*
> *probability of such knowledge, he may not be convicted consistently with*
> *due process. Were it otherwise, the evil would be as great as it is when*
> *the law is written too fine or in a language foreign to the community.*

mistake of law A claim by a defendant that the defendant did not know the action taken violated the criminal law.

Sometimes what appears to be a **mistake of law** may nonetheless provide a defense. For example, in *United States v. Smith*,[15] a government employee was charged with violating the federal Espionage Act. That act makes it a crime to reveal classified information with the intent to cause injury to the United States. The defendant revealed classified information to two individuals the defendant believed were CIA officials. The defendant claimed he believed he was authorized by law to reveal the information to CIA officials, though in fact he was not authorized to do so. The court said his defense, if believed, negated the "intent to harm the United States" element of the crime, and could be raised.

The mistake of law in the *Smith* case provided a defense because the defendant's mistaken belief negated a required mental state, the "intent to harm" the United States. Where the mistake of law is simply that the defendant did not know the actions he or she took were against the criminal law, but the defendant otherwise had the required mental state, it is rare for the mistake to provide a defense.

INTOXICATION OR DRUGGED CONDITION AS A DEFENSE

Voluntary intoxication or drugged condition as a defense to the commission of criminal acts is frequently raised unsuccessfully. Crimes that require only a general intent, that is, only the intent to do the act, do not permit an intoxication defense. For example, in the case of *United States v. Sewell*,[16] a defendant charged with robbery attempted to defend himself by offering evidence that he was high on crack cocaine when he committed the robbery. The court concluded that robbery was a general intent crime and rejected the defense.

Crimes that require a specific intent as to one or more elements of the crime do permit a defense based on voluntary intoxication or drugged condition. To assert the intoxication defense, the defendant must be charged with a specific intent crime, such as intentional murder, kidnapping, or arson. The degree of intoxication must be so great "as to render (the defendant) incapable of purposeful or knowing conduct."[17]

Even if the intoxication defense successfully negates a specific intent, the defendant may still be convicted of a lesser offense requiring only general intent. For example, although defendants may lack the specific intent to commit murder, they could be convicted of a lesser general intent crime, such as second-degree murder or manslaughter.[18]

A few states have eliminated the defense of voluntary intoxication entirely. Montana not only did away with the defense of intoxication but also prohibited any consideration of the defense of intoxication by a fact finder (judge or jury). The Montana law was challenged before the U.S. Supreme Court in 1996. In the case of

Montana v. Egelhoff, the Supreme Court found that the Montana law did not violate due process protections of the U.S. Constitution.[19]

The involuntary intoxication or drugged condition can be a defense to a criminal charge if the defendant can prove that (1) he or she did not voluntarily take the drug or intoxicant and instead was tricked or forced into taking the substance and (2) the defendant became so intoxicated or drugged that he or she was not able to mentally form the specific intent necessary for the crime charged but was physically able to commit the crime.

DURESS, COERCION, OR COMPULSION AS A DEFENSE

If a person charged with a crime can show his or her actions were the result of duress, coercion, or compulsion, under some but not all situations, a valid defense may be raised. In attempting to use the defense, defendants must admit that they committed the offense charged but assert that they were forced to do so to avoid death or serious bodily injury to themselves or others. Defining **duress** and **coercion** in *People v. Sanders,* the court stated:

> In order for duress or fear produced by threats or menace to be a valid, legal excuse for doing anything, which otherwise would be criminal, the act must have been done under such threats or menaces as show that the life of the person threatened or menaced was in danger, or that there was reasonable cause to believe and actual belief that there was such danger. The danger must not be one of future violence, but of present and immediate violence at the time of the commission of the forbidden act. The danger of death at some future time in the absence of danger of death at the time of the commission of the offense will not excuse. A person who aids and assists in the commission of the crime, or who commits a crime, is not relieved from criminality on account of fears excited by threats or menaces unless the danger be to life, nor unless that danger be present and immediate.[20]

One area where duress or coercion is offered as a defense involves escape from prison or other custody. The Supreme Court of Delaware has held that the general rule is that "intolerable conditions" were not by themselves justification for escape from prison, and that defendants must introduce other evidence for such justification to exist.[21] The court stated that the tests used by California courts to determine if sufficient duress existed to justify an escape were useful in determining justification.

The California tests, established in *People v. Lovercamp,* hold that justification is available as a defense to the charge of escape from prison only when

1. The prisoner is faced with a specific threat of death, forcible sexual attack, or substantial bodily injury in the immediate future.

2. There is no time for a complaint to the authorities or there exists a history of futile complaints that make any result from such complaints illusory.

3. There is no time or opportunity to resort to the courts.

4. There is no evidence of force or violence used toward prison personnel or other "innocent" persons in the escape.

5. The prisoner immediately reports to the proper authorities when he or she has attained a position of safety from the immediate threat.[22]

duress A defense to criminal prosecution on the grounds that the defendant was forced to commit the criminal act.

coercion A person who forces (coerces) another to commit a crime can be charged and convicted of the crime committed in addition to other offenses.

The U.S. Supreme Court ruled as follows in the escape case of *United States v. Bailey*:

> We therefore hold that, where a criminal defendant is charged with escape and claims that he is entitled to an instruction on the theory of duress or necessity, he must proffer evidence of a bona fide effort to surrender or return to custody as soon as the claimed duress or necessity had lost its coercive force. We have reviewed the evidence examined elaborately in the majority and dissenting opinions below, and find the case not even close, even under respondents' versions of the facts, as to whether they either surrendered or offered to surrender at their earliest possible opportunity. Since we have determined that this is an indispensable element of the defense of duress or necessity, respondents were not entitled to any instruction on such a theory. Vague and necessarily self-serving statements of defendants or witnesses as to future good intentions or ambiguous conduct simply do not support a finding of this element of the defense.[23]

Duress or coercion is generally not a defense to a charge of murder. Under the common law, the defense of duress was not available to a defendant in a murder or treason charge. Blackstone stated that the reason for this was that a man under duress "ought rather to die himself than escape by the murder of an innocent."[24] This apparently is the common law today in more than half the states and in the United Kingdom. About twenty states define the defense of duress by statute, and most do not allow the defense in murder cases (and sometimes in other serious crimes). A few states allow the defense in murder cases: *MacKool v. State*, 213 S.W.3d 618 (Ark. 2005); *State v. Heinemann*, 920 A.2d 278 (Conn. 2007). This is also the rule in the Model Penal Code, § 2.09. Finally, in a few states the defense of duress in a murder charge may be proved for the purpose of reducing the charge of first-degree murder to manslaughter.[25]

Even in those states that do not permit the defense of duress or coercion in murder cases, the defense is generally available to a charge of felony murder (see Chapter 10). In the treatise *Criminal Law* (2nd ed., West/Wadsworth, 1980 § 5.3 b, pp. 435–436), La Fave and Scott state, "The law properly recognizes that one is justified in aiding a robbery if he is forced by threats to do so to save his life; he should not lose the defense because his threateners (*sic*) unexpectedly kill someone in the course of the robbery and thus convert a mere robbery into a murder." In *McMillan v. State*, 51 A.2d 623 (Md. 2012), the court held that although Maryland does not permit the duress defense in murder cases, where the murder charge is based on the felony-murder rule the defendant may prove duress forced him or her to participate in the underlying felony. The court reasoned that if the duress would be a complete defense to the underlying felony (robbery), it would lead to "absurd results" if the defendant could then be convicted of murder. The *McMillan* court also concluded that the threat of imminent harm made by gang members who forced the defendant to help them secure entry for a home invasion was sufficient proof of the "imminent" threat to life required for the duress defense.

necessity A defense to criminal prosecution on the grounds that the harm to be avoided outweighed the harm caused by the crime committed. Necessity will not justify taking another person's life.

NECESSITY OR CHOICE OF EVILS DEFENSE[26]

A person who, because of necessity, performs an act that otherwise would constitute a crime may use the justification of **necessity** as a defense if the "harm or evil sought

YOU BE THE JUDGE

Should you give the duress instruction? Was the kidnapping "over" when the murder occurred? See **United States v. Zayac, 765 F.3d 112 (2nd Cir. 2014), cert denied 135 S. Ct. 2858 (2015)**

At his trial for kidnapping, robbery and felony-murder, Defendant testified that on the night of the murder he and another man, Gonzales, picked up the victim in Defendant's car to complete a drug deal. Gonzales, sitting in the front seat with Defendant, first ordered the victim, sitting in the back seat, to bind his own wrists with zip ties. Gonzales then shot and killed the victim. Gonzales told Defendant to be "happy it was not him" who was shot. The two men then drove to an isolated location, and while Defendant waited in his car, Gonzales dragged the victim down to the bottom of a hill and left the body there.

You are the trial judge. All the evidence is in and the case is ready to go to the jury. Defendant requests that you give the jury a duress instruction on the kidnapping and robbery charges. Defendant contends that he was forced to participate in the robbery and kidnapping, and thus the murder that occurred after the kidnapping was over should not be charged to him under the felony-murder rule.

to be avoided by such conduct is greater than that sought to be prevented by the law defining the offense charged."[27]

EXAMPLE   An airplane crashes at night in an isolated area. It is very cold and rescue is not likely until daylight, so the survivors break into a summer cottage and use the food and blankets in the cottage to comfort the injured and sustain themselves until help arrives. In this example, the necessity of breaking into the cottage is obvious and serves as a justification for breaking into the cottage. It is likely the survivors would openly admit what they had done, and the owner of the cottage would be assured of compensation for the damages. Law enforcement officers and the prosecutor would not consider criminal charges, and the matter would not receive further attention.

While the common law recognized the necessity defense, and was thus incorporated into the law of most states, the existence of the defense in federal prosecutions is unclear. In *United States v. Oakland Cannabis Buyers' Co-op*, 532 U.S. 483, 490 (2001), the U.S. Supreme Court stated: "[W]e note that it is an open question whether federal courts ever have authority to recognize a necessity defense not provided by statute." There, the Court did not decide the question, simply holding that even if available, the necessity defense was incompatible with the Controlled Substances Act, and thus not available. A few lower federal courts have held that the defense is available in prosecutions under the felon-in-possession charge under 18 U.S.C. § 922(g), though the statute does not expressly state that such a defense exists. See *United States v. Alston*, 526 F.3d 91 (3d Cir. 2008). In *United States v. Fraser*, 47 F.3d 1242 (10th Cir. 2011), the court doubted a defense of necessity was available in a federal charge of being a felon in possession of a gun. The defendant said he needed the gun to protect himself from a threatened attack by another man, who the defendant subsequently killed during that attack. The court said that even if the necessity defense existed, the defendant did not show he had no lawful alternative to possessing the gun.

Most courts that recognize a common law defense of necessity state the requirements for the defense to contain some or all of the following elements:

1. The emergency or threat of imminent harm must not have been caused by the defendant.
2. The situation must present the immediate and imminent threat of serious harm to the defendant or another.
3. There must be no reasonable alternative available to avoiding the harm other than breaking the law.
4. The harm to be avoided must be greater than the harm to be prevented by the law prohibiting the conduct.

State statutes that have codified the necessity defense generally have similar requirements, though they do not always include all four elements listed above. The Texas statute, VTCA Penal Code § 9.22, requires only that the actor reasonably believe the conduct is necessary to avoid immediate harm, the harm to be avoided "clearly outweighs" the harm sought to be prevented by the prohibited conduct, and a legislative purpose to exclude the defense does not plainly appear. The Illinois statute requires that the defendant not have caused the circumstances that created the threat of imminent harm, that it was reasonable to believe serious harm was imminent, and that the harm to be avoided is greater than the harm to be prevented by the statute prohibiting the conduct.[28]

The necessity defense, like the duress and coercion defense discussed above, is not available to justify the death of another person.

CAN ONE KILL TO SAVE ONESELF?

The question of whether a person can kill to save his or her own life came before courts many years ago in the following famous cases:

United States v. Holmes
Court of Appeals of the United States
(1842), 26 Fed. Cas. 360

The defendant was a member of the crew of a ship that sank, leaving him and many others in an overcrowded lifeboat. Because the ship's mate feared that the boat would sink, he ordered the male passengers thrown overboard, leaving the women and the ship's crew. The defendant assisted in throwing sixteen of the men out of the boat to their deaths. A grand jury refused to indict him for murder, so he was charged with and convicted of manslaughter.

Rex v. Dudley and Stephens
Queen's Bench Division (1884), 14 Q.B.D. 273

The defendants and another man and a boy were shipwrecked and adrift in an open boat for eighteen days. After seven days without food or water, the defendants suggested that the men kill the boy, who was then very weak. When the other man refused, the defendants killed the boy, and all the men fed on the boy's body. Four days later, they were rescued. The jury, by a special verdict, found that the men would probably have died within the four days had they not fed on the boy's body. The jury also found that the boy would probably have died before being rescued. However, the defendants were convicted of murder, with the sentence commuted to six months' imprisonment.

These two cases have been debated by judges, lawyers, and law students throughout the English-speaking world for years. Few people urge that the doctrine of necessity be expanded to full forgiveness instead of the partial forgiveness of manslaughter used in both the cases given. In commenting on the problem, former U.S. Supreme Court Justice Benjamin N. Cardozo observed: "Where two or more are overtaken by a common disaster, there is no right on the part of one to save the lives of some, by killing of another. There is no rule of human jettison."[29]

The attitude of the British courts today is probably reflected by the 1971 case of *Southwark London Borough v. Williams:*

[T]he law regards with the deepest suspicion any remedies of self-help, and permits these remedies to be resorted to only in very special circumstances. The reason for such circumspection is clear—necessity can very easily become simply a mask for anarchy.[30]

ALIBI AS A CRIMINAL DEFENSE

alibi A defense to criminal prosecution on the grounds that the defendant physically could not have committed the crime because at the time the crime was committed, he or she was at another place.

In using the defense of **alibi,** the defendant is asserting that he or she physically could not have committed the crime, because at the time the crime was committed, he or she was at another place.

EXAMPLE   X is charged with robbery and has been identified by two witnesses and the victim as the man who robbed a liquor store. X uses the defense of alibi and argues that it was physically impossible for him to rob the store because he was at his mother's home 100 miles away at the time of the robbery. His mother and his wife corroborate X's story, stating that they were there also.

Because an alibi can be easily fabricated, it must be carefully investigated. Many states have statutes requiring defendants who plan to use an alibi defense to serve

THE USE OF THE DUDLEY CASE IN ETHICS CLASSES TODAY

The *Dudley* case discussed earlier, while decided in 1884, continues to be used in classrooms throughout the United States today. In 2009, a public broadcasting program featured the case in an ethics discussion with several hundred Harvard University students. The various choices open to the shipwrecked sailors in the lifeboat were discussed, including the ethical and legal implications of each choice.

Using the criminal code of your state, would police and prosecutors likely seek criminal charges today for the following choices made by the persons in the lifeboat?

1. A lottery was suggested in the *Dudley* case, but not used. Suppose the lottery idea was adopted, and the loser was killed. Would the remaining persons be subject to criminal charges? Would it matter if they did or did not feed on the dead person's body?
2. Suppose the boy (or another person) agreed to be killed in order to save the others. Would the others be charged with a crime?
3. Based on the facts of the *Dudley* case, should all the persons on board the lifeboat be charged, or only those who actually killed the boy?

notice on the prosecutor before trial. These statutes are meant to safeguard against the wrongful use of alibis, as they give law enforcement agencies and prosecutors necessary notice and time to investigate the merits of the proposed alibi.

Alibi Notice Statutes

Alibi notice statutes require defendants to make disclosures regarding their cases. Such disclosures include the place where the defendant claimed to have been at the time the crime was committed and the names and addresses of witnesses to the alibi, if known.

In the case of *Wardius v. Oregon,* the U.S. Supreme Court held that when a defendant is compelled to disclose information regarding his or her case, the state must also make similar disclosures. The U.S. Supreme Court held:

> [In] the absence of a strong showing of state interests to the contrary, discovery must be a two-way street. The State may not insist that trials be run as a "search for truth" so far as defense witnesses are concerned, while maintaining "poker game" secrecy for its own witnesses. It is fundamentally unfair to require a defendant to divulge the details of his own case while at the same time subjecting him to the hazard of surprise concerning refutation of the very pieces of evidence which he disclosed to the State.[31]

Alibi notice statutes now require disclosure by prosecutors as well as defendants.

An alibi presented to and believed by a jury constitutes a complete defense to the crime charged. Even if the alibi raises only a reasonable doubt in the mind of a jury, it becomes a good defense because the jury cannot convict if a reasonable doubt exists. If only two or three of the jurors believe the alibi, a hung jury may result. The burden is not on the defendant to show that he or she was not at the scene of the crime; it is on the state to show beyond reasonable doubt that the defendant *was* at the scene and committed the crime. Charges of perjury, solicitation to commit perjury, or subornation of perjury have resulted when it has been shown that alibi witnesses testified falsely or that attempts were made to persuade people to testify falsely.

THE DEFENSE THAT THE DEFENDANT WAS ACTING UNDER THE AUTHORITY, DIRECTION, OR ADVICE OF ANOTHER

A person who commits an act that is obviously criminal, such as arson or murder, and then attempts to use as a defense the fact that he or she was acting under the direction of a superior officer or on the advice of an attorney or another person would ordinarily be held fully liable for such an offense. The general rule is that one who performs a criminal act under the advice, direction, or order of another cannot use such a defense.

However, because hundreds of crimes are not well known to the general public, the U.S. Supreme Court quoted with approval a jury instruction stating that when a person

> [f]ully and honestly lays all the facts before his counsel, and in good faith and honestly follows such advice, relying upon it and believing it to be correct, and only intends that his acts shall be lawful, he could not be convicted of crime which involves willful and unlawful intent; even if such advice were an inaccurate construction of the law. But, on the other hand, no man can willfully and knowingly violate the law and excuse himself from consequences thereof by pleading that he followed the advice of counsel.[32]

Where the advice that contemplated conduct would be legal comes from a government official, the defense called "entrapment by estoppel" (also known as "official misleading") has developed in federal prosecutions.[33] The following two U.S. Supreme Court cases are often cited as the origin of the defense:

Cox v. Louisiana

Supreme Court of the United States (1965), 379 U.S. 559, 85 S. Ct. 476

Among other charges, the defendant was convicted of demonstrating "in or near" a courthouse in violation of a Louisiana law modeled after a 1949 federal statute. The U.S. Supreme Court reversed the conviction, stating:

> *The highest police officials of the city, in the presence of the Sheriff and Mayor, in effect, told the demonstrators that they could meet where they did, 101 feet from the courthouse steps, but could not meet closer to the courthouse. In effect, appellant was advised that a demonstration at the place it was held would not be one "near" the courthouse within the terms of the statute.*[34]

> ### *Raley v. Ohio*
> **Supreme Court of the United States (1959),**
> **360 U.S. 423, 79 S. Ct. 1257**
>
> The U.S. Supreme Court held "that the Due Process Clause prevented conviction of persons for refusing to answer questions of a state investigating commission when they relied upon assurance of the commission, either express or implied, that they had a privilege under state law to refuse to answer, though in fact this privilege was not available to them." The Court stated that this would be to sanction an indefensible sort of **entrapment** by the State—convicting a citizen for exercising a privilege that the State had clearly told him was available to him.

entrapment The defense that a law enforcement officer used excessive temptation or urging to wrongfully induce the defendants to commit a crime they would not have ordinarily committed.

The requirements for the defense of entrapment by estoppel are (1) the official giving the opinion on legality is "empowered to render" that opinion, (2) the official knew all the facts giving rise to the request for the opinion, (3) the opinion was "affirmatively misleading," and (4) the defendant's reliance on the opinion was reasonable.[35]

In the 2007 case of *People v. Chacon,*[36] the California Supreme Court held that the defense of entrapment by estoppel was recognized in California, but was not available in the case before the court. The defendant, a city councilwoman, was charged with criminal conflict of interest. She alleged she relied on the advice of the city attorney that she was not in a conflict of interest situation. The court rejected the defense, holding that the city attorney was not in a position to render that advice.

THE DEFENSE OF DOUBLE JEOPARDY

The Fifth Amendment of the U.S. Constitution provides that "no person . . . shall . . . for the same offense . . . be twice put in jeopardy of life or limb." In the case of *United States v. Scott,* the U.S. Supreme Court, quoting other Supreme Court cases, held that the Double Jeopardy Clause ensures

> that the State with all its resources and power should not be allowed to make repeated attempts to convict an individual for an alleged offense, thereby subjecting him to embarrassment, expense and ordeal and compelling him to live in a continuing state of anxiety and insecurity, as well as enhancing the possibility that even though innocent he may be found guilty.[37]

double jeopardy A defense, stated in the Fifth Amendment, to prosecution on the grounds that the defendant has been tried before on the same charge, and acquitted.

Therefore, **double jeopardy** means that a person who has been acquitted by a judge or a jury may not be tried again, even if subsequent investigation reveals evidence that proves conclusively that the defendant is guilty. If a defendant is found not guilty because of insanity, the person may not be tried again for the same crime, even if the person is later found sane and normal.

The Times When Jeopardy Attaches

In the case of *Press-Enterprise Co. v. Superior Court of California, Riverside County,*[38] the U.S. Supreme Court pointed out that jeopardy attaches when a jury is sworn.[39]

THE MEANING OF ACQUITTAL

Michigan v. Evans
United States Supreme Court (2013),
133 S. Ct. 1069

Lamar Evans was charged with arson under a Michigan statute that applied to burning "other real property"; another statute applied to burning real property that was a dwelling. Penalties were higher for burning a dwelling than for burning "other real property." After the prosecution rested the case against Evans, Evans moved for a directed judgment of acquittal. He contended the prosecution was required to prove, as an element of the offense, that the building burned was not a dwelling, and that the only proof introduced by the prosecution was evidence that the building was a dwelling. The trial court agreed, and entered a verdict of acquittal.

On appeal, the Michigan Supreme Court reversed and remanded the case for a new trial. That court held, and Evans agreed, that the trial court erred in holding that an element of the statute included proof that the burned building was not a dwelling house. The court rejected Evans's double jeopardy argument, holding that the trial judge's "acquittal" was based on an error of law that "did not resolve any factual element of the charged offense."

The U.S. Supreme Court granted review, and reversed the Michigan Supreme Court. It held that the trial court's judgment of acquittal, even though based on an erroneous interpretation of the statute, was nonetheless an "acquittal" for purposes of double jeopardy. Unlike a dismissal on a procedural ground, which does not generally present a double jeopardy issue, here the trial court evaluated the evidence and found it insufficient to prove the crime charged. The Court said that even though the trial court did so erroneously, it was still a resolution of the guilt or innocence of the defendant. Such a resolution can only occur once under the Double Jeopardy Clause, the Court said.

In March of 2016 the Supreme Court agreed to review the conviction in *United States v. Bravo-Fernandez*, 790 F.3d 41 (1st Cir. 2015). The question to be reviewed was whether an appellate court's order vacating a conviction as unconstitutional had the same preclusive effect as an "acquittal" under the Double Jeopardy Clause.

In a nonjury trial, the Court stated that jeopardy attaches when the first witness is sworn.[40] Thus, if the defendant is acquitted of the charges after jeopardy attached, he cannot be tried again on the same charge, or on a lesser included crime.

Questions about the meaning of "acquitted" were raised before the U.S. Supreme Court in the 2012 case of *Blueford v. Arkansas*.[41] In that case a defendant was charged with capital murder, and the jury was instructed to consider lesser included charges such as manslaughter if it could not agree on the capital murder charge. After deliberating for some time, the jury told the judge it could not reach a verdict, because although it unanimously voted "not guilty" on the capital murder charge, it could not reach a decision on any lesser charge. As a result, the trial court declared a mistrial.

When the state filed new charges of capital murder, the defendant claimed the double jeopardy clause barred the prosecution because he was "acquitted" on the capital murder charge in the first trial. The U.S. Supreme Court rejected that claim. It said that in the case of a mistrial the double jeopardy clause does not bar another prosecution, because there has been no final decision by the jury. That was the case here, the Court held, because although the jury said it had voted not guilty on the capital murder charge, that was not final, and the jury could have gone back to deliberations and changed its mind. As a result, the defendant had not been acquitted of the charge of capital murder, and could be retried.

The U. S. Supreme Court reaffirmed the "bright line" rule that jeopardy attaches when a jury is sworn in the 2014 case of *Martinez v. Illinois*, 134 S. Ct. 2070. In that case the prosecution obtained several delays to the start of trial because two chief witnesses could not be located. When trial was finally scheduled to begin, and after the jury was sworn, the prosecution still could not find the witnesses. The trial judge insisted the case should proceed, but the prosecution repeatedly said it "will not be participating in the trial," and introduced no evidence. The trial judge therefore directed a verdict of not guilty.

The state appealed. (The state normally cannot appeal a verdict of not guilty.) The Illinois Supreme Court permitted the appeal, saying that the trial judge's directed verdict was not a "true acquittal" because the defendant "was never at risk of conviction." The U.S. Supreme Court reversed the Illinois Supreme Court. It said that the rule that jeopardy attaches when a jury is sworn is absolute, for it is at that point the defendant is now at risk of conviction. How the case ends, once jeopardy attaches, can have a bearing on a claim of double jeopardy, the Court said. A mistrial or a hung jury may not bar a retrial, but an acquittal will, the Court said. Since an acquittal includes any ruling that the prosecution's case is insufficient to prove liability for the crime charged, the trial judge's directed verdict of not guilty was an acquittal, the Court concluded.

Prosecution by Both State and Federal Governments

Dual Sovereignty Doctrine A doctrine that different governments may each file separate criminal actions for the same criminal act.

Because most crimes are crimes only against a state, only the state may prosecute. Some crimes, however, are offenses against not only the state but also the federal government. The **Dual Sovereignty Doctrine** permits both the state and federal governments to prosecute a defendant for the same crime. The robbery of a federally insured bank or savings and loan association is an example.

The question of whether the state and federal governments may both prosecute for such offenses has come before the U.S. Supreme Court more than a dozen times. Justice Oliver Wendell Holmes, in noting that both state and federal prosecution in such cases is not in violation of the Fifth Amendment, stated that the rule "is too plain to need more than a statement."[42] The reasoning is presented in the case of *Bartkus v. Illinois* as follows:

> Every citizen of the United States is also a citizen of a State or territory. He may be said to owe allegiance to two sovereigns, and may be liable to punishment for an infraction of the laws of either. The same act may be an offense or transgression of the law of both. That either or both may (if they see fit) punish such an offender cannot be doubted. Yet it cannot be truly averted that the offender has been twice punished for the same offense; but only that by one act he has committed two offenses, for each of which he is justly punishable. He could not plead the punishment by one in bar to a conviction by the other.[43]

WHEN IS A NEW TRIAL A "SECOND TRIAL" FOR DOUBLE JEOPARDY?

A criminal prosecution can "end" in a variety of ways: conviction, acquittal, dismissal of charges, mistrials, or hung jury. Moreover, the result in a trial may be changed on appeal. When any of these happen, can the government bring new charges, or would it amount to a "second trial," barred by the Double Jeopardy Clause? The following rules address some of these situations.

I. Re-prosecution after conviction, where conviction reversed on appeal.
   (A) Retrial not permitted if reversal was for failure to grant defendant's motion for judgment of acquittal.
   (B) Retrial permitted if reversal is for any other trial error.
II. Re-prosecution after "acquittal."
   (A) Pretrial: The government may appeal pretrial dismissal, because effect of reversal would not be a "second trial."
   (B) Mid-Trial

   1. Dismissal
      (a) The government may not appeal a verdict of not guilty or a pre-verdict grant of motion for judgment of acquittal, because effect of reversal on appeal would be a second trial after a determination of factual guilt/innocence.
      (b) The government may appeal a mid-trial dismissal on any grounds other than factual guilt/innocence. A retrial would not be a "second trial."
   2. Mistrials
      (a) Where the government moves for a mistrial, a retrial is permitted only if it shows a "manifest necessity" for mistrial.
      (b) Where the defendant moves for a mistrial, a retrial is permitted unless the government intended to provoke the mistrial motion.
   3. Hung jury
      (a) If the jury is unable to reach a decision and the case is dismissed, a retrial is permitted.
      (b) Post-trial.

   The government may appeal a post-trial dismissal of the charges because the effect of the reversal on appeal is simply reinstatement of the verdict of conviction, and does not require a second trial.

In *Bartkus v. Illinois,* the defendant was tried in a federal court and acquitted of robbing a federally insured bank. He was then indicted by an Illinois grand jury and convicted on substantially the same evidence used in the federal court. The Illinois court sentenced him to life imprisonment under the Illinois Habitual Criminal Statute. The U.S. Supreme Court affirmed the conviction, holding that the second trial did not violate the Fifth Amendment of the U.S. Constitution.

Since *Bartkus v. Illinois,* however, many states, including Illinois, have passed legislation that forbids prosecution after another jurisdiction has prosecuted the defendant for the same crime. In such states, the law of the state, and not the Double Jeopardy Clause, forbids prosecution after prosecution in another jurisdiction.[44]

The Meaning of "Separate Offense"

Double jeopardy does not bar successive prosecutions of a defendant convicted of one offense if the subsequent prosecution involves a different or separate offense. The meaning of *separate* adopted by the U.S. Supreme Court has changed over time. In *Blockburger v. United States,* the Court adopted the following "different offense" rule:

> The applicable rule is that where the same acts or transaction constitutes a violation of two distinct statutory provisions, the test to be applied to determine whether there are two offenses or only one is whether each provision requires proof of an additional fact which the other does not.[45]

This rule prevented, among other things, prosecutions for so-called lesser included offenses, that is, offenses whose elements were included in the greater offense. In a related manner, double jeopardy also prohibits double punishments for the same acts. For example, in the 2015 case of *People v. Miller,*[46] the Michigan Supreme Court reversed a conviction for both drunken driving and drunken driving that caused serious injury. The double jeopardy clause applied because the same act (drunken driving) constituted the *actus reus* for both crimes, and the legislature had not stated separate punishments for each crime were permitted.

In the early 1990s, the Supreme Court in *Grady v. Corbin* appeared to modify the *Blockburger* "same element" test, holding in one case that successive prosecutions arising out of the "same conduct" were barred by the Double Jeopardy Clause.[47] If the same conduct violated two criminal statutes, successive prosecutions were barred, even though the statutes had different elements. Such a rule would prevent some prosecutions that would be possible under *Blockburger.*[48] However, in 1993, the Supreme Court reversed *Grady v. Corbin* and the "same conduct" rule.[49] It held that the *Blockburger* "same element" test determined double jeopardy questions.

ENTRAPMENT AND OUTRAGEOUS GOVERNMENT CONDUCT AS DEFENSES

The defense of entrapment was recognized by the U.S. Supreme Court in the case of *Sorrells v. United States.*[50] In *Sorrells,* the Supreme Court ruled that entrapment occurs "when the criminal design originates with the officials of the government, and they implant in the mind of an innocent person the disposition to commit the alleged offense and induce its commission in order that they (the Government) may prosecute." The defense of entrapment therefore has two elements: (1) improper government inducement of the crime and (2) lack of predisposition on the part of the defendant to engage in the criminal conduct.

Defendants seeking to use the defense of entrapment carry the initial burden of coming forward with evidence of both the government's improper inducement and the defendant's lack of predisposition to commit the alleged offense. If a defendant makes a showing of improper inducement by the government and lack of predisposition by the defendant, the burden then shifts to the government. The government must then show "readiness" on the part of the defendant and that the "defendant was poised, was likely, to engage in criminal activity."[51]

The U.S. Supreme Court ruled in the case of *Mathews v. United States*[52] that a defendant "is entitled to an entrapment instruction (to a jury) whenever there is sufficient evidence from which a reasonable jury could find entrapment."

Courts throughout the United States have long recognized that law enforcement officers (or their agents) can properly create ordinary opportunities for a person to commit an offense if the criminal intent or willingness originated in the mind of the defendant. The fact that the officer afforded the opportunity or the facility for the defendant to commit the crime in order to obtain evidence does not constitute entrapment. In *Hampton v. United States*,[53] the Court held the entrapment defense was not available to a defendant who sold illegal drugs to undercover police officers, even though a government informer, acting for the government, supplied the drugs sold. The Court said the defendant must prove he did not have the criminal intention until it was implanted by the agent.

A sting operation is not improper inducement to commit a crime if it merely provides an opportunity to commit a crime. Thus, the Supreme Court held in *United States v. Russell* that infiltration into a drug ring, and supplying some of the items needed to produce the illegal drugs, does not amount to entrapment.[54] However, proof of a sting operation that includes additional conduct by police may amount to sufficient evidence to meet a defendant's burden. For example, in *Jacobson v. United States*,[55] the Supreme Court held that repeated attempts by government agents to entice a defendant to purchase child pornography through the mail constituted entrapment. Entrapment occurs, the Court said, "when the Government's quest for convictions leads to the apprehension of an otherwise law abiding citizen who, if left to his own devices, likely would have never run afoul of the law."

Although law enforcement officers may create and present the usual and ordinary opportunities for a person to commit a crime, they may not use excessive urging, inducement, temptation, or solicitation to commit a crime. For example, in the early case of *Sherman v. United States*,[56] the Court held that actions by a government informant to entice a drug addict to return to drug use and supply drugs to the informant constituted entrapment.

The Supreme Court quoted another court as follows in the *Sorrells* case:

> It is well settled that decoys may be used to entrap criminals, and to present opportunity to one intending or willing to commit crime. But decoys are not permissible to ensnare the innocent and law-abiding into the commission of crime. When the criminal design originates, not with the accused, but is conceived in the mind of the government officers, and the accused is by persuasion, deceitful representation, or inducement lured into the commission of a criminal act, the government is estopped by sound public policy from prosecution therefore.

States Are Free to Write Their Own Rules for Entrapment   The U.S. Supreme Court has held that the defense of entrapment is not of constitutional dimension. Therefore, the U.S. Congress and state legislative bodies may "adopt any substantive definition of the defense that [they] may desire."[57]

Some states have enacted statutes that define entrapment. Most states, however, use common law definitions created by their courts as the entrapment rules to be used within that state.

Most states and the federal courts use the "origin of intent" test in determining whether the defendant was predisposed to commit the crime charged. The test seeks to determine whether the defendant had the willingness and readiness to commit the crime *and* whether the police or a government agent only provided what appeared to be a favorable opportunity.

Denying the Criminal Act While Using the Defense of Entrapment

Until 1988, most states would not permit defendants to plead innocence, while at the same time using an affirmative defense such as entrapment. The innocent plea generally means, "I didn't commit the crime," whereas in the entrapment defense, the defendant is pleading, "I wouldn't have committed the crime if it had not been for the improper conduct of the police."

In the case of *Mathews v. United States,*[58] the U.S. Supreme Court pointed out that such inconsistent defenses have historically been permitted in federal prosecutions. But because it is not a constitutional issue, the Supreme Court held that it is up to each state to determine whether inconsistent defenses would be permitted.

In response to the *Mathews* decision, many states now permit inconsistent defenses (such as entrapment and denying the criminal act), and other states continue to require that criminal defenses be consistent.

A defendant who cannot claim entrapment may still be able to invoke the defense of outrageous government conduct. The U.S. Supreme Court first raised the concept of outrageous police conduct in the case of *United States v. Russell* (discussed earlier in this chapter), in which the Court stated:

> [W]e may some day be presented with a situation in which the conduct of law enforcement agents is so outrageous that due process principles would absolutely bar the government from invoking judicial processes to obtain a conviction. . . . [59]

In the case *of Hampton v. United States,* Justice Powell stated that "police over-involvement in crime would have to reach a demonstrable level of outrageousness before it could bar conviction."[60] Thus, even if it is found that the government conduct was wrong or illegal, before dismissing charges based on that conduct a court must determine that the outrageous conduct violated due process rights of the defendant.

Outrageous Government Conduct That Violated the Due Process Rights of Defendants

The following conduct was held to fall within the shock-the-conscience or outrageous conduct exception so as to cause dismissal of the criminal charge:

- Using a defendant's attorney to gather information against him was held to violate not only due process but also the defendant's Sixth Amendment right to an attorney.[61]
- Manufacture of crack cocaine by the police for use in a reverse sting[62] operation caused dismissal of charges by the Supreme Court of Florida.[63]
- For two and a half years, government agents supplied many materials and showed defendants how to manufacture illegal alcohol, which the agents said they would buy. *Greene v. United States.*[64]

STINGS, SCAMS, AND OUTRAGEOUS GOVERNMENT CONDUCT

The U.S. Supreme Court stated long ago that American "courts have uniformly held that in waging war against crime . . . traps, decoys and deception (may be used) to obtain evidence of the commission of the crime." *United States v. Sorrells,* 287 U.S. 435, 454 (1932).

Exactly when government deception becomes so outrageous that it violates due process is not always clear, as the following sting cases illustrate:

United States v. Black, 733 F.3d 294 (9th Cir. 2013), *cert denied,* 135 S. Ct. 267 (2014) ATF officers in "Operation Gideon" paid a confidential informant (CI) $100 per day to recruit persons to rob fictional drug stash houses of drugs and money. The CI solicited 4 men to do so by going to "bad bars" in "bad parts of town," and seeking recruits. When the robbery was planned and ready to be executed, the 4 men were arrested and charged with conspiracy to commit various drugs and weapons offenses. The court rejected the defendant's claim of entrapment/outrageous government conduct. While the court was troubled by the fact the CI was not told to focus on persons suspected of this kind of criminal behavior, the court concluded the inducement was not persistent, the government did not actively participate in the criminal activity, and the defendants readily accepted the offer to rob the stash houses.

United States v. Barta, 776 F.3d 931 (7th Cir. 2015) Barta owned a business that managed prescription benefit programs for various parties, including some city health plans. Because of Barta's friendship with a man the FBI believed was a criminal, Barta was approached by "Castro," an undercover FBI agent, with a proposal to bribe a fictional Los Angeles city official to get business for Barta. Ultimately Barta wrote a check for $6500 to pay the fictional official, and he was then arrested for conspiracy to commit bribery. The trial court rejected his defense of entrapment, and he was convicted of conspiracy to commit bribery.

On appeal the court reversed his conviction. It said Barta was entrapped "as a matter of law," based on the repeated, persistent attempts by the undercover agent to get Barta to agree to the bribe. The court noted that in the month before Barta finally agreed to pay the bribe, the undercover agent emailed Barta multiple

Conduct Held Not to Be Outrageous So as to Violate Defendant's Due Process Rights   In the following cases, courts held that the conduct was not so outrageous as to violate the defendant's due process rights:

- A civilian working with a police department had sex with a woman to obtain evidence necessary to convict her of prostitution. The Supreme Court of Hawaii affirmed the conviction, holding that it was not outrageous conduct, but it was also not the "ethical standards which law enforcement officials should be guided by."[65]
- Paying a defendant's former girlfriend's living expenses while she assisted in building a criminal case against the defendant was held not to be outrageous conduct.[66]
- In a 2011 decision, a California court held that while it was undoubtedly a serious misconduct for a prosecutor to give false testimony in a hearing involving a criminal trial, the false testimony did not violate the defendant's due process rights. The court reversed a trial court's dismissal of the criminal charges against the defendant.[67]

times, saying Barta needed to get on board or the deal would go away. Barta did not respond to any of these emails, the court said. In addition, the court said, the undercover officer on two occasions "sweetened" the deal for Barta in an attempt to get him to commit. This finally wore down Barta's resistance, the court said, and amounted to entrapment as a matter of law. The court not only reversed the conviction, but took the unusual step of ordering Barta released from jail a few days after oral argument was held in the case.

United States v. Gonzales-Perez, 778 F.3d 3 (1st Cir. 2015), *cert denied*, 135 S. Ct. 1911 (2015) Defendant, a former police officer in San Juan, Puerto Rico, was recruited by a CI in an FBI sting called "Operation Guard Shack." The sting was aimed at uncovering corruption in the PRPD. The CI recruited Defendant to serve as armed security in staged drug deals. Defendant did so, and was charged with 15 drug and arms related crimes. The trial court refused to give the jury an entrapment instruction, and Defendant was convicted on all counts.

On appeal, the court held that the entrapment defense was unavailable as a matter of law. The court said that even if the CI called the Defendant several times to get him to agree to the deal, the number of calls is not the basis of a finding of persistent inducement. The Defendant's reluctance to go forward, the court said, was only "logistical" in nature, having to do with how he would get a weapon and how he would be paid. The court affirmed his conviction.

Outrageous government conduct can occur after arrest as well, which can taint a conviction. In *United States v. Bowen*, 799 F.3d 336 (5th Cir. 2015) five New Orleans police officers were charged with various crimes involving shootings and cover-ups in the aftermath of Hurricane Katrina. During their trial, but after they were found guilty, it was discovered that federal prosecutors, using false names, had made numerous posts on internet web sites castigating the defendants and the New Orleans police department, as well as other insulting comments about the defense team representing the defendants. Based on this conduct, which the trial court discovered over the denials by the prosecution, the trial court ordered a new trial. On appeal by the government, the court of appeals agreed that the government's actions were so shocking that the defendants could not have received a fair trial in the "online 21st century carnival atmosphere" that surrounded the trial. It affirmed the grant of a new trial.

THE DEFENSE THAT ANOTHER PERSON COMMITTED THE CRIME

There are a number of ways of proving the wrong person has been charged with or convicted of a crime. Providing exculpatory evidence to the prosecution or investigating officers is the easiest way to accomplish this result, in particular if the evidence is convincing, such as DNA evidence. Showing that an eyewitness wrongly identified the defendant or committed perjury can also be good exculpatory evidence. The Innocence Project, a national organization that works to free wrongfully convicted persons, estimates that 62 percent of single-witness identifications are incorrect. See the Innocence Project, "Eyewitness Misidentifications," http://www.info@innocenceproject.org.

Another defense that can be used is evidence that another person committed the crime. Courts generally require something more than just the uncorroborated claim by the defendant that another person did it. For example, in *State v. Wilson*, 864 N.W.2d 52 (Wis. 2015), *cert denied* 2016 WL 854244, the Wisconsin Supreme Court rejected a defendant's claim that he should have been permitted to offer evidence a third party killed the victim he was convicted of murdering. The court said that before such evidence may be admitted it must be shown the third party had the motive, opportunity, and "direct connection" to the crime so that the evidence is more than mere speculation. There, the court found that the third party identified by the defendant as the actual killer had no opportunity to commit the murder, either directly or indirectly. It reversed a court of appeals decision ordering a new trial, and affirmed the murder conviction.

To deal with this situation, many states have rules similar to Rule 804(b) (3) of the Federal Rules of Evidence. That rule states that before a witness can be allowed to offer evidence to exculpate a defendant, there must be evidence of corroborating circumstances that clearly indicate the trustworthiness of the statement.

THE RIGHT TO A SPEEDY TRIAL AS A DEFENSE

The Sixth Amendment of the U.S. Constitution provides that "in all criminal prosecutions, the accused shall enjoy the right to a speedy and public trial."[68] Most defendants charged with a serious crime do not wish either a speedy or a public trial, but unless the right to a speedy trial is waived with the consent of the trial court, the constitutional mandate of a speedy trial must be followed.

The four-factor balancing test used to determine whether a speedy trial violation has occurred was established by the U.S. Supreme Court in the case of *Barker v. Wingo*.[69] The factors that are weighed are (1) the length of the delay, (2) the reason for the delay, (3) the defendant's assertion of his or her right, and (4) the prejudice resulting from the delay.

In holding that the right to a speedy trial commences when a person "is indicted, arrested, or otherwise officially accused," the U.S. Supreme Court held in *United States v. Marion* that

> The protection of the Amendment is activated only when a criminal prosecution has begun and extends only to those persons who have been "accused" in the course of that prosecution. These provisions would seem to afford no protection to those not yet accused, nor would they seem to require the Government to discover, investigate, and accuse any person within any particular period of time.[70]

The Court stated that the purpose and "interests served by the Speedy Trial Clause" are as follows:

> Inordinate delay between an arrest, indictment, and trial may impair a defendant's ability to present an effective defense. But the major evils protected against by the speedy trial guarantee exist quite apart from actual or possible prejudice to an accused's defense. To legally arrest and detain, the Government must assert probable cause to believe the arrestee has committed a crime. Arrest is a public act that may seriously interfere with the defendant's liberty, whether he is free on bail or not, and that may disrupt his employment, drain his financial resources, curtail his associations, subject him to public obloquy, and create anxiety in him, his family and his friends.[71]

The U.S. Constitution does not identify a specific number of days necessary to satisfy the speedy trial requirement. Therefore, the federal government and states have enacted statutes establishing their own standards. For example, the federal government in the Speedy Trial Act, 18 U.S.C. § 3161(c)(1), requires that a person indicted for a felony be tried within 70 days unless the defendant waives his or her right to a speedy trial. Failure to try the person within that time could cause dismissal of the criminal charge if it were shown that the delay prejudiced the defendant under the *Barker v. Wingo* factors. In the 2010 case of *Bloate v. United States,*[72] the Court held that time delays caused by filing pretrial motions are not automatically excluded from calculating the 70-day period, but can be excluded if the trial court makes a specific finding that the time should be excluded.

Defendants already incarcerated in one state often have pending charges in another state. Obtaining a speedy trial under those circumstances can be difficult, and determining if a Speedy Trial Clause violation has occurred can also be a problem. To deal with this situation most states are party to the Interstate Agreement on Detainers Act. Under this Act, if a person detained in one state makes a request that charges against him pending in another state be brought to trial, the other state must bring the prisoner to trial within 180 days of the request. If that does not occur, the charges must be dismissed. The dismissal court has the discretion to make the dismissal with or without prejudice, depending on the circumstances. In the 2011 case of *United States v. Ferraira,*[73] the Sixth Circuit Court of Appeals reversed a trial court's decision that a dismissal should be without prejudice, so that the government could file new charges. The appeals court concluded that the 3-year delay in requesting transfer of the defendant to the district court for trial violated the defendant's Sixth Amendment right to a speedy trial, and that the appropriate remedy was dismissal of the indictment with prejudice.

THE STATUTE OF LIMITATIONS AS A DEFENSE

The old English common law adopted the doctrine that "no lapse bars the King"; therefore, statutes limiting the time for criminal prosecutions are rare in England.

statute of limitations A defense to a criminal prosecution based on a statute that sets the maximum time the government has to prosecute a violation of a criminal law.

However, criminal **statutes of limitations** appeared in America as early as 1652. The federal government adopted time limits for the prosecution of most federal crimes in 1790, and the majority of the states have enacted statutes of limitations for most crimes.

The speedy trial requirements are constitutional mandates and therefore are imposed on all states. Statutes of limitations on criminal prosecutions are optional legislative enactments. Reasons given for limitations on criminal prosecutions are as follows:

A limitation statute is designed to protect individuals from having to defend themselves against charges when the basic facts may have become obscured by the passage of time and to minimize the danger of official punishment because of acts in the far-distant past.[74]

The Speedy Trial Clause and the limitations statutes work in tandem to prevent pretrial delay: the statutory period insures against pre-accusation delays and the

Sixth Amendment controls the post-indictment time span. . . . Both provisions shield defendants from endless anxiety about possible prosecution and from impairment of the ability to mount a defense. By encouraging speedy prosecution, they also afford society protection from unincarcerated offenders, and insure against a diminution of the deterrent value of immediate convictions, as well as the reduced capacity of the government to prove its case.[75]

Statutes of limitation generally permit a longer period for the prosecution of felonies than for the prosecution of misdemeanors. No time limit is generally placed on prosecution for murder. As discovery of some theft offenses may occur years after the theft, extensions of time are generally given, based on the time of discovery of the offense. The running of time under a criminal statute of limitation could be halted by

- Issuance of an arrest warrant or summons, an indictment, filing of information, or the commencement of prosecution.
- Statutory requirement that the person must be a public resident of that state for the time to toll.
- Acts by the suspect to avoid or to frustrate legal proceedings against him or her.

 SPEEDY TRIAL, DOUBLE JEOPARDY, AND STATUTES OF LIMITATIONS AS DEFENSES

Double jeopardy and the requirement of a speedy trial are both mandated by the U.S. Constitution and must be complied with.

Speedy trial	Because the U.S. Constitution does not specify the time period within which a defendant must be tried, federal law or the law of each state establishes this time period. Defendants, however, often waive their right to a speedy trial. This is done in open court and most often in writing and signed by the defendant and the defense lawyer.
Double jeopardy	A criminal defendant cannot be retried if jeopardy has attached to the crime with which the defendant has been charged. The U.S. Supreme Court has held that jeopardy attaches when a jury is sworn and, in a non-jury case, when the first witness is sworn.
Statutes of limitation	These are not required by the U.S. Constitution and are optional state legislative enactments. The states of South Carolina and Wyoming have no criminal statutes of limitation.[a]

[a]"The Statute of Limitation in Criminal Law," 102 U. Pa. L. Rev. 630.

★ ★

LEARNING OBJECTIVES SUMMARY

LO 1. Identify the kinds of immunity to criminal prosecution available, and their limits.
Diplomatic immunity is limited to recognized diplomats and certain members of their families. Legislative immunity applies only to active legislators, and only during the time the legislature is in session. Witness immunity can be given to overcome the Fifth Amendment privilege a witness has. The immunity can be for prosecution for any charges related to the witness's testimony, or only for use of that testimony.

LO 2. Determine when, if ever, a mistake of fact or law may provide a defense.
A mistake of fact provides a defense when the mistake is honest and reasonable and nullifies a specific intent necessary for conviction of the crime charged. A mistake of law rarely provides a defense, unless the criminal law defining the offense is generally not known to reasonable people.

LO 3. Distinguish between the defenses of duress and necessity.
Duress is a defense if the defendant was compelled by life-threatening coercion; necessity is a defense based on a reasonable decision to commit a lesser crime to prevent the occurrence of a more serious crime.

LO 4. Explain why the Double Jeopardy Clause prohibits successive prosecutions for the same crime.
The Double Jeopardy Clause serves as a limitation on the power of government to use its resources to subject a citizen to repeated exposure to the criminal laws, and it also guards against the conviction of innocent persons.

LO 5. Distinguish between a prosecution for the same offense and one for a separate offense.
Two offenses are the "same" for double jeopardy purposes if the same facts serve as a basis for each offense. If one offense requires proof of a fact that was not part of the other offense, each charge can be prosecuted. Prosecutions based on the same actions under both a state and a federal statute are not prosecutions for the "same" offense under the Double Jeopardy Clause.

LO 6. Define "acquittal" for purposes of the Double Jeopardy Clause.
Acquittal under the Double Jeopardy Clause means a judgment of dismissal or not guilty made by the fact finder (judge or jury) based on an evaluation of the evidence and a finding that it was insufficient to prove the crime charged.

LO 7. Identify the tests that determine when government inducements become entrapment.
Government inducements become entrapment when the actions of law enforcement officers are improper and the defendant had no predisposition to commit the crimes made the subject of the improper inducements.

LO 8. List the factors that determine when a speedy trial violation has occurred.
A speedy trial violation has occurred when there has been an excessive delay (made specific in statutes but not in the Constitution), no good reason for the delay exists, the defendant has asserted the right to a speedy trial, and the delay has caused prejudice to the defendant.

KEY TERMS

corpus delicti, p. 170
affirmative defense, p. 170
immunity, p. 171
transactional immunity, p. 173
use immunity, p. 173

mistake of law, p. 177
duress, p. 178
coercion, p. 178
necessity, p. 179
alibi, p. 182

entrapment, p. 185
double jeopardy, p. 185
"dual sovereignty" doctrine, p. 187
statute of limitations, p. 195

CASE ANALYSIS AND WRITING EXERCISES

1. Assume a defendant is observed by police officer A walking down the street carrying a weapon. A few moments later, the defendant is observed by police officer B walking down another street carrying the same weapon. Defendant, a convicted felon, is arrested and charged two counts of illegal possession of a weapon. Has he committed two crimes, or one? If only one, the Double Jeopardy clause prohibits two convictions for the same offense. If you conclude only one offense has occurred, how did the state convince the court otherwise in *Commonwealth v. Horne*, 995 N.E.2d 773 (Mass. 2013)?

2. Where should the entrapment line be drawn on government "sting" inducements that persuade the recruited person to commit a crime? For example, suppose a confidential informant (CI) working for the FBI is told to find "disaffected Moslems who might be harboring terrorist designs in the United States." The CI finds the defendant, a Moslem who is an impoverished, small-time criminal who worked nights at a Walmart store and made about $14,000.00 per year. The defendant undeniably hated Jews and Americans, and professed a wish to die as a martyr. After months of cultivating the relationship, the CI offers the defendant $250,000.00 to fund attacks on an airport and synagogues in New York. The defendant agrees, and recruits a "team" to help him. The CI provides the team with fake bombs and Stinger missiles, and shows the team how to use them. When the team prepares to use them the FBI arrests them and charges them with conspiracy to commit terrorist acts. Have they been entrapped? *United States v. Cromitie*, 727 F.3d 194 (2nd Cir. 2013), *cert denied* 135 S. Ct. 53 (2014)

3. In this chapter we note that if a defendant seeks and obtains a mistrial, the prosecution ordinarily may retry the defendant with no Double Jeopardy restraints. If it is the prosecution that obtains the mistrial, Double Jeopardy requires that the prosecution show the mistrial was necessary as "the only reasonable alternative to insure justice." What if the trial judge, on her own motion (called "sua sponte") declares a mistrial because she believes she can no longer be objective in her role as trial judge? Can the prosecution retry the defendant on the same charges? Who has the burden to suggest alternatives to the trial judge before she declares a mistrial? See *State v. Manatau*, 322 P.3d 739 (Utah 2014)

4. Defendant was required under Kentucky law to register as a convicted sex offender. The registration statute stated that a registrant must register a new address before moving from the current address. The state police are required to send a change of address registration form to persons required to register every 90 days. When defendant moved a few miles from his parents, where he was registered as residing, to start work on a new job, he did not send a registration notice to the local parole office as required. When, two months later, he was discovered residing at his new residence (his girlfriend's house) he was charged with violation of the registration law, which makes it a crime to "knowingly" fail to register a new address. Defendant states as his defense that he thought he was supposed to wait for the next address verification to be sent to him, and only then register at his new address. Is this a good defense? Should it be? See *Lawson v. Com.*, 425 S.W.3d 912 (Ky. App. 2014)

ENDNOTES

1. *In re Winship*, 90 S. Ct. 1068, 1071 (1970).
2. 343 U.S. 790 (1952).
3. *Mullaney v. Wilbur*, 421 U.S. 197 (1975).
4. 442 F. Supp. 2d 102 (S.D. New York 2006).
5. 356 F.3d 564 (4th Cir. 2004).
6. 596 So.2d 687 (Fla. App. 1992).
7. 717 F Supp. 309 (E.D. Pa. 1989).
8. *United States v. Gillock*, 445 U.S. 360 (1980); *U.S. v. Gonzalez De Modesti*, 145 F. Supp. 2d 171 (D.P.R. 2001).
9. 651 F.3d 1012 (9th Cir. 2011).
10. 142 U.S. 47 (1895).
11. 406 U.S. 441 (1972).
12. The fact that a law enforcement officer made an honest mistake about an important fact in making an arrest would

not necessarily invalidate the arrest. In the 1971 U.S. Supreme Court case of *Hill v. California,* 401 U.S. 797, 91 S. Ct. 1106, police made an "honest mistake" in arresting the wrong man. In the 1980 case of *United States v. Allen,* 629 F.2d 51 (D.C. Cir.), the appellate court held that "the case law establishes that an arrest based on actual assumptions later found erroneous may be valid if there is adequate basis in the record to determine the reasonableness of the officer's conduct in making the arrest." The U.S. Supreme Court heard another honest mistake case in 1987. In *Maryland v. Garrison,* 480 U.S. 79, 107 S. Ct. 1013, police officers obtained a search warrant for the third floor of a building, believing that there was only one apartment on that floor. Before they discovered that there were two apartments on that floor, police found heroin and drug paraphernalia in the apartment of another man (Garrison). The Supreme Court held that the evidence was lawfully obtained, adding another case to what is known as the *honest mistake exception.*

The following three examples are found in the New York Criminal Code Annotated Practice Commentary to Section 15.20, Effect of Ignorance or Mistake Upon Liability:

- A police officer having a warrant for the arrest of A mistakenly arrests B, who resembles A, and holds him in a police station for an hour before ascertaining his mistake and releasing him. The officer is not guilty of "unlawful imprisonment" (Section 135.05) because his mistake of fact "negatives a culpable mental state necessary for the commission of the offense," namely, "knowledge that the restriction is unlawful" (Section 135.00(1)).
- M has sexual intercourse with F, a mentally ill woman whose condition is not always apparent and is not known to or realized by M. Although M would be guilty of third-degree rape if he had realized F's condition, his unawareness is, by statute, expressly made a defense to the charge (Section 130.10).
- During a heated argument between A and B, B, a man with a reputation for violence and rumored to carry a pistol on occasion, suddenly places his hand in his bulging pocket, and A strikes him in the face and breaks his nose. Although B did not have a pistol and was merely reaching for a cigarette, A is not guilty of assault because his factual mistake was of a kind that supports a defense of justification. Section 35.15 (1).

13. 342 U.S. 246 (1952).

14. In a minority of states the defense of mistake of a victim's age in statutory rape charges is allowed. Some states make the defense available in all statutory rape cases; see, e.g. K.R.S. § 510.030. In other states the defense is good only in cases where the underage victim made reasonable declarations that her age was over the statutory minimum for consent; see, e.g., R.C.W.A. 9A.44.030. In still other states, the mistake of age defense is available only for lesser sexual offenses where the age of the victim is over 16, and the defendant is no more than four years older than the victim.

15. 592 F. Supp. 424 (E.D. Va. 1984).

16. 252 F3d 647 (2d Cir. 2001).

17. *State v. Cameron,* 514 A2d 1302 (1986).

18. *State v. Souza,* 72 Haw. 246, 813 P.2d 1384 (1991).

19. 116 S. Ct. 2013 (1996).

20. 82 Cal. App. 778, 785, 256 P. 251, 254 (1927).

21. *Johnson v. State,* 379 A.2d 1129 (Del. 1977).

22. 43 Cal. App. 3d 823, 118 Cal. Rptr. 110 (1974).

23. 444 U.S. 394, 100 S. Ct. 624 (1980).

24. Blackstone, 4 *Commentaries,* 30.

25. See Wisconsin Statute 939.46.

26. In the 1980 case of *United States v. Bailey* (444 U.S. 394 100 S. Ct. 624), the U.S. Supreme Court pointed out the distinctions between the defenses of duress and necessity as follows:

> Common law historically distinguished between the defenses of duress and necessity. Duress was said to excuse criminal conduct where the actor was under an unlawful threat of imminent death or serious bodily injury, which threat caused the actor to engage in conduct violating the literal terms of the criminal law. While the defense of duress covered the situation where the coercion had its source in the actions of other human beings, the defense of necessity, or choice of evils, traditionally covered the situation where physical forces beyond the actor's control rendered illegal conduct the lesser of two evils. Thus, where A destroyed a dike because B threatened to kill him if he did not, A would argue that he acted under duress, whereas if A destroyed the dike in order to protect more valuable property from flooding, A could claim a defense of necessity. See generally LaFave and Scott, *Criminal Law,* 2nd ed. (Belmont, Ca.: West/Wadsworth, 1986), pp. 374–384.

27. Model Penal Code, Section 3.02 (Justification Generally).

28. 720 ILCS 5/7-13

29. *Selected Writings of Justice Cardozo,* 390.

30. 2 All E.R. at p. 181 (1971).

31. 412 U.S. 470, 93 S. Ct. 2208 (1973).

32. *Williamson v. U.S.,* 207 U.S. 425, 453, 28 S. Ct. 163, 173 (1908).

33. *United States v. Batterjee,* 361 F.3d 1210 (9th Cir. 2004)(Fla. App. 1975).

34. The defense lawyer missed the boat on this case. He or she could have also had the statute declared invalid as being "void for vagueness." Everybody has to guess about what is meant by "near." Modern statutes now forbid demonstrations "in" a courthouse or within 200 or 300 feet of a courthouse. Such statutes do not violate "void for vagueness" (see Chapter 1).

35. *Id,* 361 F.3d at 1216.

36. 150 P.3d 755 (Cal. 2007).

37. 437 U.S. 82, 98 S. Ct. 2187 (1978).

38. 464 U.S. 501, 104 S. Ct. 819 (1984).

39. *Downum v. U.S.,* 372 U.S. 734, 83 S. Ct. 1033 (1963).

40. *Wade v. Hunter,* 336 U.S. 684, 69 S. Ct. 834 (1949).

41. 132 S. Ct. 2044 (2012).

42. *Westfall v. U.S.* 274 U.S. 256, 47 S. Ct. 629 (1927).

43. 359 U.S. 121, 79 S. Ct. 676 (1959).

44. In 1993, the United States prosecuted several Los Angeles police officers for civil rights violations arising out of a beating they gave Rodney King. In a previous, very controversial state prosecution, the same officers were acquitted of state criminal charges. Two of the officers, Koon and Powell, were convicted, and two were acquitted. The Double Jeopardy Clause did not prevent those convictions because of the dual sovereignty rule.

    The famous videotape of the King beating, which showed that beating in great detail, was extensively used by the federal court in its sentencing decision. See *U.S. v. Koon,* 833 F. Supp. 769 (C.D. Cal. 1993). Koon and Powell were sentenced to 30 months in prison, based on various sentencing guidelines that indicated a downward departure from the 80- to 87-month sentence guidelines for their convictions.

    The Ninth Circuit Court of Appeals reversed the downward departure made by the federal district court (see 34 F.3d 1416), but the U.S. Supreme Court essentially restored the original sentences. See *Koon v. United States,* 518 U.S. 81 (1996).

45. *Blockburger v. United States,* 284 U.S. 299, 304 (1932). Thus, a prosecution for auto theft barred prosecution for the lesser offense of joyriding, and vice versa. See *Brown v. Ohio,* 432 U.S. 161 (1977).

46. 243 P.3d 556 (Wash. App. 2011), *review denied* 253 P.3d 393 (Wash. 2011).

47. *Grady v. Corbin,* 495 U.S. 508 (1990).

48. Ibid.

49. *United States v. Dixon,* 509 U.S. 688 (1993).

50. 287 U.S. 435, 454, 53 S. Ct. 210, 217 (1932), separate opinion.

51. *Jacobson v. United States,* 503 U.S. 540 (1992).

52. *Mathews v. United States,* 485 U.S. 58 (1988).

53. 425 U.S. 484 (1976).

54. *United States v. Russell,* 411 U.S. 423 (1973).

55. 503 U.S. 540 (1992).

56. 356 U.S. 369 (1958).

57. *U.S. v. Russell,* 411 U.S. 423 (1973).

58. 485 U.S. 58, 108 S. Ct. 883 (1988). Examples of inconsistent defenses that were permitted when the evidence justified it are the following:

    • In an 1896 murder case arising out of a gunfight in Indian Territory, the defense of self-defense was used, along with an instruction on manslaughter. Killing in the heat of passion is inconsistent with self-defense. *Stevenson v. United States,* 162 U.S. 313, 16 S. Ct. 839 (1896).

    • In a 1970 rape case, the defendant was permitted to argue that the act did not take place and that the victim consented. *Johnson v. United States,* 426 F.2d 651 (D.C. Cir. 1970), *cert. granted,* 400 U.S. 864(1970), *cert. dismissed,* 401 U.S. 846 (1971).

59. 93 S. Ct. at 1642–43.

60. 425 U.S. at 495, n. 7.

61. *United States v. Marshank,* 777 F.Supp. 1507 (N.D. Cal. 1991).

62. A reverse buy or reverse sting scheme is one in which the government sells or attempts to sell an illegal drug rather than buy it. Because this conduct by the police could cause defense lawyers to use the entrapment or outrageous government conduct defenses, great caution should be used by law enforcement officers.

63. *Metcalf v. State,* 635 So. 2d 11 (Fla. 1994).

64. 454 F.2d 783 (9th Cir. 1971).

65. *State v. Tookes,* 699 P. 2d 983 (1985).

66. See *United States v. Miller,* 891 F.2d 1265 (7th Cir. 1989). One area where such operations are used by police is Internet chat rooms, where police officers present themselves as children in order to lure adults attempting to initiate sexual meetings with children into the police net. These operations have commonly been upheld as appropriate government conduct.

67. *People v. Uribe,* 132 Cal. Rptr. 3d 102 (Cal. App. 2011).

68. In the 1992 case of *State v. James* (484 N.W.2d 799), an undercover officer was standing in an area known for high drug activity and "sold" crack only to people who approached him. Eight such locations were used in Minneapolis to discourage buyers who came into high drug activity areas to buy drugs. The Minnesota Court of Appeals affirmed the defendant's conviction, pointing out that the state carried the burden of showing predisposition by the defendant and that the officer did not solicit or encourage the defendant in any way. See also the case of *United States v. Cea,* 963 F.2d 1027 (7th Cir. 1992).

69. The Federal Speedy Trial Act (18 U.S.C.A. 3161) sets a 70-day limit, which begins to run on the date of indictment (§3161(c)(l)). See *Henderson v. United States,* 476 U.S. 321, 106 S. Ct. 1871 (1986).

70. 407 U.S. 514 (1972).

71. 404 U.S. 307, 92 S. Ct. 455 (1971).

72. 130 S. Ct. 1345 (2010).

73. 665 F.3d 701 (6th Cir. 2011).

74. *Ibid.* at 320, 92 S. Ct. at 463.

75. See *Toussie v. U.S.,* 397 U.S. 112, 114–115, 90 S. Ct. 858, 859–60 (1970).

8

Criminal Punishments

LEARNING OBJECTIVES

In this chapter we examine the kinds of punishments that may be imposed for violation of a criminal law and some limitations on those punishments. The learning objectives for this chapter are the following:

LO 1. Describe the text of the Cruel and Unusual Punishment Clause.

LO 2. Explain the relationship between the Sixth Amendment and sentencing provisions that permit a judge to determine when an enhanced sentence should be given a criminal defendant.

LO 3. Discuss the present status of the Federal Sentencing Guidelines.

LO 4. Identify the procedures a school official must follow before imposing corporal punishment on a student.

LO 5. Explain why the death penalty was declared unconstitutional in *Furman v. Georgia*.

LO 6. Identify at least three groups of persons who cannot be given the death penalty.

LO 7. Explain the present rule on the imposition of life without parole sentences for juveniles.

LO 8. Describe the kinds of evidence that must be produced if the prosecution seeks imposition of the death penalty after a jury has found the defendant guilty of the crime charged.

LO 9. Define "three strikes" laws and list the common characteristics of such laws.

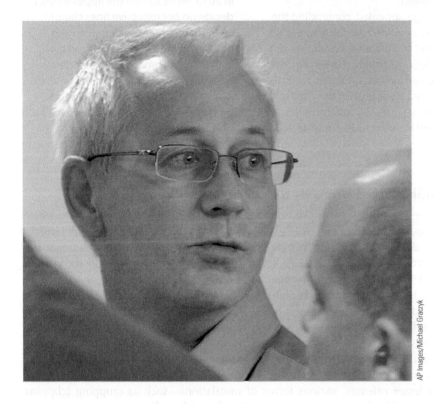

Oscar Ray Bolin, convicted killer of three women in 1986, was executed in Florida by lethal injection in January 2016. Witnesses at Bolin's execution included his defense attorney, Rosalie Martinez, who married Bolin in 1996 while Bolin was on death row.

In 2005 Annie George and her husband made an offer to Valsamma Mathai, at a promised salary of $1000.00 per month, to work for them and reside in their home. Mathai, a citizen of India in the United States on a limited visa, agreed. Mathai's visa did not permit her to work outside New York City, and thus her decision to work for and live with the Georges made her an undocumented, illegal alien. It is a federal crime to harbor an illegal alien. George knew Mathai was an illegal alien.

Mathai worked for George from 2005 to 2011. She cared for George's 5 minor children, as well as performed household tasks. She worked 7 days a week, usually from 5:30 AM to 11:30 PM. Although promised payment of $1000.00 per month, for the 66 months she worked for George she was paid a total of about $25,000.00. George did not file required W-2 or 1099 forms, and actively encouraged Mathai to tell strangers she was a "guest" of George.

In 2011 Mathai's son living in India became concerned for his mother, and contacted federal authorities, who removed Mathai from the George house in 2011. George was charged with harboring an illegal alien. She was convicted in a jury trial. In 2013 the trial judge sentenced her to five years' probation, with eight months' home confinement.

The judge also ordered forfeiture of George's home under 18 U.S.C. § 982 (a)(6)(A). The home was valued at $1.8 million.

George appealed, contending the forfeiture violated the Excessive Fines Clause of the Eighth Amendment to the U.S. Constitution. (Forfeiture orders are treated as fines for purposes of the excessive fines clause in the Eighth Amendment; see discussion in this chapter.) How should a court decide when a forfeiture is "excessive"? What factors in the George case are relevant to that decision? Her appeal was decided in 2015. What should the appeals court decide on her excessive fines claim? [1]

In this chapter we learn the rules governing the imposition of various kinds of punishments, from simple fines to the death penalty. We will also learn some of the limitations the U.S. Constitution places on punishments for violation of criminal laws.

PUNISHMENTS USED IN EARLY ENGLAND

The criminal punishments used hundreds of years ago in England and elsewhere in Europe were very severe. In England alone, more than 200 offenses were punishable by death. Condemned criminals were usually hanged, although occasionally they were beheaded, quartered, or drawn (dragged along the ground by the tail of a horse). Until 1790 burning continued to be the punishment inflicted on women for treason, high or petty (which later included not only the murder by a wife of her husband and the murder of a master or mistress by a servant but also several offenses against the king). In practice, women were strangled before they were burned; this, however, depended on the executioner. In one notorious case, a woman was actually burned alive for murdering her husband, the executioner being afraid to strangle her because he was caught by the fire.[2]

For lesser offenses, various forms of mutilations—such as cropping (clipping of the ears), blinding, amputation of the hand, and branding—were common. The whipping post and the pillory were often used, as were fines and imprisonment. The pillory is a frame erected on a post. The offender's head and hands are placed in the open holes, and the top board is then moved into place, immobilizing the offender in a standing position.

Practices Used in England to Avoid Severe Penalties

benefit of clergy A medieval limit on capital punishment. People convicted of a capital crime entitled to claim the benefit of clergy (by the fifteenth century, anyone who could read) could not be executed for their offense. By the end of the eighteenth century, the privilege had been eliminated for most crimes.

For various reasons, including the severity of penalties, England developed procedures to avoid severe penalties. By usage and custom, the following came into practice.

Benefit of Clergy[3]   In the twelfth century, a controversy arose about whether priests accused of felonies should be tried by the royal courts or the ecclesiastical courts. It was decided that the royal courts could try priests but could not put them to death for the first felony conviction. This privilege was known as the **benefit of clergy**, and by the end of the Middle Ages, it was extended to all laypeople who could read.

The test to determine who could claim the privilege of benefit of clergy was a person's ability to recite the first verse of Psalm 51: "Have mercy upon me, O God,

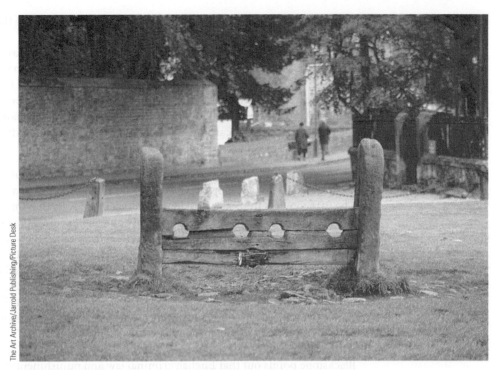

The Art Archive/Jarrold Publishing/Picture Desk

Colonial Americans followed the lead of the English in terms of punishment. As punishment for lesser offenses, various forms of mutilation, such as cropping (clipping of the ears), blinding, amputation of the hand, and branding were common. The whipping post and the pillory were often used, as were fines and imprisonment. Stocks like the one shown here were situated in very public places so that shame and ridicule by the community were a strong part of the punishment.

after Thy great goodness." This came to be known as the *neck verse* because it saved the accused from hanging. The only punishment that could then be inflicted was imprisonment for one year and an *M* branded on the brawn of the left thumb to prevent the criminal from claiming the privilege again. For many years, only three crimes were excluded from benefit of clergy (high treason, highway robbery, and the willful burning of a house), but in 1769, Blackstone noted that "among the variety of actions which men are daily liable to commit no less than 160 have been declared by Act of Parliament to be felonies without benefit of clergy."[4]

The Law of Sanctuary and the Right of Asylum In the Middle Ages, **sanctuary** was common. The place of sanctuary was generally a church or other religious place. Criminals who were permitted to take refuge in a church or monastery could not be removed from it. Even after sanctuary as an institution was abolished, a system developed in England by which the refugee took an oath of abjuration before a coroner, admitted guilt, and swore to leave the country for life to an agreed-upon place (often the American colonies or, later, Australia). Sanctuary was abolished in England in 1623; however, a modified form reportedly continued in England for another century.[5] Sanctuary never

Sanctuary In the Middle Ages in England, a sanctuary was a religious place where criminals could take refuge. The concept of sanctuary later broadened to include asylum for refugees.

became part of the legal system of the American colonies or of the newly formed United States of America.

The United States, however, recognizes and grants right of asylum to refugees from other countries if they can show a "well-founded fear of persecution."[6] Over the last fifty years, the United States has granted asylum to many thousands of refugees. The United States Citizenship and Immigration Service manages requests for asylum by persons physically in the U.S. (even if illegally) who claim persecution in their home countries because of (1) race, (2) religion, (3) nationality, (4) membership in a particular social group, or (5) political opinion.

Transportation People convicted of crimes in England could be pardoned if they agreed to be transported to a colony to do hard labor for a number of years. The first convicts were sent abroad to America in 1655. By the time of the American Revolution, England was sending overseas some 2,000 convicts a year.

After the American Revolution, Australia became the principal place to which prisoners were sent under the condition of the pardon. Over the years, approximately 100,000 prisoners were sent to America and an equal number to Australia.[7] Australia and other British colonies strongly objected to the practice of transporting convicts, which was gradually abolished between 1853 and 1864. Imprisonment in England and hard labor on public works were then substituted as punishment.[8]

Punishment Used in Early America

Blackstone points out that English criminal law and punishments before the American Revolution were fairly civilized by comparison with those of the rest of Europe. U.S. Supreme Court Justice Thurgood Marshall made the following observations in comparing **capital punishment** in the American colonies with its use in England:

> Capital punishment was not as common a penalty in the American Colonies. "The Capitall Lawes of New-England," dating from 1636, were drawn by the Massachusetts Bay Colony and are the first written expression of capital offenses known to exist in this country. These laws make the following crimes capital offenses: idolatry, witchcraft, blasphemy, murder, assault in sudden anger, sodomy, buggery, adultery, statutory rape, rape, man stealing, perjury in a capital trial, and rebellion. Each crime is accompanied by a reference to the Old Testament to indicate its source. It is not known with any certainty exactly when, or even if, these laws were enacted as drafted; and, if so, just how vigorously these laws were enforced. We do know that the other Colonies had a variety of laws that spanned the spectrum of severity.

By the eighteenth century, the list of crimes became much less theocratic and much more secular. In the average colony, there were 12 capital crimes. This was far fewer than existed in England, and part of the reason was that there was a scarcity of labor in the Colonies.[9]

THE CONSTITUTIONAL LIMITATION ON PUNISHMENT

The Eighth Amendment of the U.S. Constitution, ratified in 1791 as part of the Bill of Rights, provides that "excessive bail shall not be required, nor excessive fines imposed, nor cruel and unusual punishments inflicted." Two members of Congress opposed passage of this amendment. One stated,

capital punishment Inflicting deadly injury as punishment for criminal conduct.

What is meant by the term excessive bail? Who are to be the judges? What is understood by excessive fines? It lies with the court to determine. No cruel and unusual punishment is to be inflicted; it is sometimes necessary to hang a man, villains often deserve whipping, and perhaps having their ears cut off; but are we in the future to be prevented from inflicting these punishments because they are cruel? If a more lenient mode of correcting vice and deterring others from the commission of it could be invented, it would be very prudent in the Legislature to adopt it; but until we have some security that this will be done, we ought not be restrained from making necessary laws by any declaration of this kind.[10]

cruel and unusual punishment Under the Eighth Amendment, a limitation on punishment for criminal conduct.

About **cruel and unusual punishment**, Justice William J. Brennan stated in 1972,

[T]he Cruel and Unusual Punishments Clause, like the other great clauses of the Constitution, is not susceptible of precise definition. Yet we know that the values and ideals it embodies are basic to our scheme of government. And we know also that the Clause imposes upon this Court the duty, when the issue is properly presented, to determine the constitutional validity of a challenged punishment, whatever that punishment may be.[11]

proportionality An objective evaluation of the appropriateness of a punishment for a particular crime.

The basis courts have used to evaluate the "constitutionality of a challenged punishment" historically has been the **proportionality** principle. In the case of *Pulley v. Harris,* the U.S. Supreme Court defined the manner of evaluating the appropriateness or proportionality of a punishment for a particular crime:

Traditionally, proportionality has been used with reference to an abstract evaluation of the appropriateness of a sentence for a particular crime. Looking to the gravity of the offense and the severity of the penalty, to sentences imposed for other crimes, and to sentencing practices in other jurisdictions, this Court has occasionally struck down punishments as inherently disproportionate, and therefore cruel and unusual, when imposed for a particular crime or category of crime. See, e.g., *Solem v. Helm,* 463 U.S. 277 (1983); *Enmund v. Florida,* 458 U.S. 782 (1982); *Coker v. Georgia,* 433 U.S. 584 (1977). The death penalty is not in all cases a disproportionate penalty in this sense.[12]

The *Solem* case cited above by the Supreme Court appeared to have held that the Cruel and Unusual Punishment Clause required courts to conduct a proportionality review in all cases, including those in which there was an imposition of a non-capital sentence. Such a review, *Solem* said, included considerations of (1) the gravity of the offense and the harshness of the penalty, (2) sentences imposed for similar crimes in the same jurisdiction, and (3) sentences imposed for the same crime in other jurisdictions.

Decisions of the U.S. Supreme Court since *Solem* was decided cast some doubt on the status of the proportionality test set forth in that case. In *Harmelin v. Michigan*[13] and *Ewing v. California*[14] the Supreme Court expressed disagreement on the continued force of the *Solem* holding. Two members of the Court in each case took the position that the Eighth Amendment did not require proportionality review in non-capital cases. The other justices disagreed with that position, stating that a sentence that is "grossly disproportionate" to the crime runs afoul of the Eighth Amendment. Those Justices agreed that before the tests adopted in *Solem* can be applied to a non-capital sentence, a court must first determine that the sentence meets the "grossly disproportionate" test. Only if the sentence is "grossly disproportionate" is it then subjected to the tests set forth in *Solem.* Moreover, in *Harmelin* the Court also held that courts reviewing non-capital sentences need not make the kind of inter-jurisdiction comparison suggested by the Court in *Solem.*

Since the decision in *Solem,* decisions reversing prison sentences under a proportionality review have been rare, and none have been issued by the U.S. Supreme Court. For example, in the 2014 case of *United States v. Cobler,* 748 F.3d 570 (4th Cir. 2014) the court reviewed a sentence of 120 years for a 28-year-old man who was convicted of possessing child pornography and sexually assaulting a 4-year-old child. The court said that the crimes committed by the defendant were "at least as grave as the drug offense in *Harmelin,*" where the Supreme Court upheld a similar sentence as not "grossly disproportionate" to the crime. It affirmed the sentence.

The Supreme Court in 2010 and again in 2012 reversed life sentences imposed on juvenile offenders under an Eighth Amendment analysis; however, it did not base the decisions on proportionality. See *Graham v. Florida,* 130 S. Ct. 2011 (2010), and *Miller v. Alabama,* 132 S. Ct. 2455 (2012), discussed later in this chapter. As a result, though *Solem* has not been reversed, its continued viability is unclear.

Proportionality in State Sentencing Laws
All sentences imposed in state criminal trials are subject to the Eighth Amendment's Cruel and Unusual Punishment Clause. For non-capital, prison term sentences, the "grossly disproportionate" test is all that is required under the Eighth Amendment. However, some states, though perhaps not a majority, require a sentencing judge and an appellate court in review of a sentence to follow a more detailed proportionality review.

In 10 states the state constitution has explicit mandates to judges to conduct a proportionate sentence review of all sentences. As an example, Article 1, § 9 of the Maine Constitution states that "all penalties and punishments shall be proportionate to the offense."

In many other states the highest state court has interpreted the state constitution's "Cruel and Unusual Punishment" clause as requiring specific proportionality review. Kansas, for example, has interpreted the Kansas Constitution's Cruel and Unusual Punishment Clause as requiring a sentencing judge and reviewing court to evaluate the sentence under three factors: (1) the nature of the offense and the character of the defendant, (2) comparison of the sentence to the sentences in other, more serious offenses, and (3) comparison to sentences in other jurisdictions for similar crimes. *State v. Funk,* 349 P.3d 1230 (Kan. 2015)

A few states have multiple forms of proportionality review. Maine, for example, not only has the Maine Constitution provision quoted above, which looks to the excessiveness of a sentence, but also by statute requires appellate review of sentences for their "propriety." The factors in the statute to be used by the court go to notions of fairness and comparability of sentences. Maine also by statute (as do many states) requires judges to apply various factors to the decision to make sentences run consecutively rather than concurrently. *State v. Stanislaw,* 65 A.3d 1242 (Me. 2013). (See discussion below.)

A few states have specific statutory limits on review by appellate courts of prison sentences, beyond the Eighth Amendment's requirements. In *State v. Moore,*

24 N.E.3d 1197 (Ohio App. 2014) the court stated that the Ohio legislature had limited judicial review of sentencing decisions to "errors of law," meaning only sentences that are outside the maximum permitted for the offence committed. A sentence given that falls within a trial court's discretion is not normally reviewable for proportionality, the court said.

Many states, however, simply limit proportionate review of prison sentences to the "grossly disproportionate" standard under the U.S. Constitution. In those states, unless a prison sentence is "grossly disproportionate," it will not be disturbed on appeal. In *State v. Traversia*, 2016 WL 929333 (S.D. 2016) the court held a 50-year sentence for assault on a police officer was not "grossly disproportionate" under the Eighth Amendment.

One aspect of a prison sentence that is reviewable in most states is the decision of the trial judge to make sentences run concurrently or consecutively. Where a defendant has been convicted of multiple crimes from the same criminal incident, each offence will carry a sentence. For example, a defendant could kidnap a victim, assault the victim, and rob the victim, all in the same "course of criminal conduct." If convicted of all three crimes (kidnapping, assault, and robbery) the trial judge will sentence the defendant on all three convictions.

Most states have by statute given trial courts discretion to make the sentences in multiple offenses run at the same time (concurrent) or one after another (consecutive). However, before a judge makes the decision to have the sentences run consecutively, the statute will require the judge to apply stated criteria, such as whether the multiple offenses came from separate conduct or the same conduct; whether the defendant has a criminal history of similar conduct; the age of the victim; or the seriousness of any injury inflicted on the victim. A few states limit the discretion of a trial judge to give consecutive sentences for multiple convictions where one of the offences is a predicate offence to the main crime. Thus, in those states conviction of one count of conspiracy to commit robbery, and one count of robbery, could result in two prison terms, but they could not be ordered to run consecutively. In federal courts, the Federal Sentencing Guidelines permit consecutive sentences for the substantive crime and conspiracy to commit that crime. See *United States v. Escobar*, 462 Fed. Appx. 58 (7th Cir. 2012), *cert denied* 133 S. Ct. 235 (2012).

Sentencing and Jury Trials

In 2000, the U.S. Supreme Court decided the case of *Apprendi v. New Jersey* (530 U.S. 466). In *Apprendi,* the Court held that any fact that increases the penalty for the crime charged must be submitted to the jury and proven beyond a reasonable doubt. It thus held unconstitutional a New Jersey hate crime statute that permitted the trial judge to increase the sentence of a convicted defendant if the judge found by a preponderance of the evidence that the defendant acted in a manner intended to intimidate the victim. The *Apprendi* opinion caused many changes in sentencing procedures and also resulted in many reversals of sentences handed down by trial judges. Many state sentencing systems, as well as the Federal Sentencing Guidelines, permitted a judge to make fact findings on questions that determined whether the sentence for the crime charged would be enhanced or reduced. After *Apprendi,* judges could make fact findings, but only if they were "sentencing factors" used to determine a sentence within a range provided in the statute establishing the minimum and maximum sentences that could be imposed for the crime charged: "… judge-found sentencing factors cannot increase the maximum sentence a defendant might otherwise receive based purely on the facts found by the jury." *United States v. O'Brien*, 130 S. Ct. 2169, 2175 (2010).

In *O'Brien* the U.S. Supreme Court stated that a fact was a "sentencing factor" only if it was not an "element" of the offence charged. In *O'Brien* defendants were charged with four counts in violation of 18 U.S.C. § 924(c), which prohibits the use or carrying of a firearm in a crime of violence or drug trafficking offense. The minimum sentence for a violation is 5 years in prison. However, § 924(c)(1)(B)(ii) provides that if the firearm is a "machine gun," the minimum sentence is 30 years in prison. The prosecution dismissed one of the counts, the count that alleged use of a machine gun. After the defendants pled guilty to the remaining counts, the prosecution contended the fact that the defendants used a machine gun could be determined by the judge as a "sentence enhancement" factor, and if found by the judge would make the 30-year minimum sentence applicable. The trial judge disagreed, and sentenced the defendants within the 5-year minimum statute.

The prosecution appealed, but the Supreme Court agreed with the trial court. It held the "fact" of the use of a machine gun was an "element" of the offense, and not merely a "sentencing factor." The Court found that the immense danger of a machine gun, the moral depravity of a person choosing to use such a weapon, and the substantial increase in the maximum possible sentence meant the use of a machine gun was an element of the offense, and must be proved by the prosecution beyond a reasonable doubt. 130 S. Ct. at 2175.

Finally, in a June 2013 decision, the Supreme Court used the reasoning of the *Apprendi* decision to reverse *Harris v. United States*, 536 U.S. 545 (2002), which had held that facts that increase the mandatory minimum sentence, but not the maximum sentence, could be treated as "sentencing factors" and found by the trial judge, not the jury. In *Alleyne v. United States*, 133 S. Ct. 2151, the Court held that a fact that increases the mandatory minimum sentence (in *Alleyne* "brandishing" a weapon during a robbery), but not the maximum sentence possible, must be determined by the jury using the reasonable doubt standard.

Blakely v. Washington, 124 S. Ct. 2531 (2004) applied the reasoning of *Apprendi*, which involved specific statutory language that permitted a judge to find facts that increased the maximum sentence for a crime, to state sentencing systems. In *Blakely*, a defendant pled guilty to second-degree kidnapping and use of a firearm. After 3 days of hearings before the trial judge, the defendant was sentenced to a prison term more than 3 years longer than the maximum sentence for the crime charged, based on the trial judge's finding that the defendant acted with "deliberate cruelty." Under Washington State sentencing guidelines, a finding of deliberate cruelty permitted the sentencing judge to increase the sentence. The Washington Court of Appeals affirmed the conviction and sentence (47 P.3d 149). The Supreme Court granted certiorari.

The Supreme Court held the sentence was invalid under the Sixth Amendment, because the sentence imposed exceeded the maximum sentence possible based solely on the facts found by the jury. The Court held that the defendant was entitled to a jury trial on the facts supporting the finding that he acted with deliberate cruelty.

Because the trial judge, rather than the jury, made the finding that the defendant acted with deliberate cruelty, the resulting sentence was invalid, the Court held.

In 2005 the Supreme Court decided the case of *United States v. Booker*, 125 S. Ct. 738. In *Booker*, the Court held that under the holdings of *Apprendi* and *Blakeley*, the Federal Sentencing Guidelines violated the Sixth Amendment's right to jury trials in criminal cases.

A majority of the Court concluded that the mandatory provisions of the Guidelines, which required judges to enhance sentences when certain facts were found by the judge, such as the quantity of the drug possessed by a defendant in a drug case, were unconstitutional. A different majority held, however, that federal judges could use the non-mandatory provisions of the Guidelines as reference points to help reach a sentencing decision.

As a result, sentences may raise a problem under *Blakely* or *Booker* in either of two ways: in one, the sentencing judge may use facts found only by the judge to

YOU BE THE JUDGE

You are a federal district judge. Under federal sentencing guidelines, the prison term that may be given for a conviction of various crimes can be "enhanced" based on factors involving the crime or the defendant. Some examples of enhancement factors include:

- The crime is a hate crime, or the victim is elderly or handicapped.
- The person is a repeat offender (habitual criminal statute).
- A dangerous weapon is used in committing the crime.
- A bulletproof garment is used in committing the crime.
- Concealment of identity (such as a mask) is used.
- Drugs or a weapon are used or sold within 1,000 feet of a school.

The defendant before you has been convicted of possession of child pornography. The appropriate sentence for that crime, you conclude, is 60 months in prison. However, the prosecutor contends that the defendant is subject to a mandatory, ten-year prison term sentence enhancement under 18 U.S.C. § 2252 (b) (2). The section states that the mandatory ten-year enhanced sentence is required if the defendant has a prior conviction for "aggravated sexual abuse, sexual abuse, or abusive sexual contact involving a minor or ward." Eleven years ago the defendant was convicted for sexual assault of his then-53-year-old girlfriend.

Are you required to give the defendant the 10-year minimum sentence enhancement? What are the arguments for or against the prosecution's position? Is the enhancement statute ambiguous? See **Lockhart v. United States, 136 S. Ct. 958 (2016).** *What is the "Rule of Lenity," and why didn't the Supreme Court apply the rule in* **Lockhart?**

enhance the defendant's sentence; in the other, the judge may use the Federal Sentencing Guidelines as mandatory rather than discretionary. The first result is unconstitutional under *Blakely*; the second is prohibited by *Booker*. See, for example, *Villafranco v. United States*, 2006 WL 1049114 (D. Utah 2006).

Lower courts have addressed one question left open in *Booker*, namely, the extent the decision applied retroactively to sentences handed down before *Booker* was decided. While the Court held that the decision was applicable to all sentences that were not final when the decision was handed down, it did not decide what application the decision had for other sentences. Most courts considering the constitutionality of sentences that were final before *Booker* was decided have held the decision was not applicable to such sentences when collateral review was sought under statutes like 28 U.S.C. § 2255, the federal post-conviction relief statute. Generally speaking, when the Supreme Court announces a new rule of constitutional dimension like that in *Apprendi* or *Booker*, unless the Court holds that the rule is retroactive, it is not applicable to cases already final when the rule was announced.

CORPORAL PUNISHMENT

corporal punishment Inflicting nondeadly physical injury as punishment for criminal conduct

Corporal punishment was used as criminal punishment in the early history of the United States. Mutilations, such as cutting off ears and various types of branding, were discontinued many decades ago. Whipping, however, continued in some states into the early 1900s. The Eighth Circuit Court of Appeals observed that in 1968 only two states permitted the use of the strap as punishment. As a result of the Eighth Circuit Court's decision in the case of *Jackson v. Bishop*, whipping as a form of punishment was discontinued in the remaining two states. In the *Jackson* case, the court held:

> We have no difficulty in reaching the conclusion that the use of the strap in the penitentiaries of Arkansas is punishment which, in this last third of the 20th century, runs afoul of the Eighth Amendment; that the strap's use, irrespective of any precautionary conditions which may be imposed, offends contemporary concepts of decency and human dignity and precepts of civilization which we profess to possess; and that it also violates those standards of good conscience and fundamental fairness enunciated by this court in the *Carey* and *Lee* cases.[15]

The Use of Corporal Punishment in Schools

In the case of *Ingraham v. Wright,* the U.S. Supreme Court considered the relationship between the Cruel and Unusual Punishment Clause and the use of corporal punishment in public schools. The Court first observed that no general rule prohibited corporal punishment in schools: "The prevalent rule in this country today privileges such force as a teacher or administrator 'reasonably' believes to be necessary for [the child's] proper control, training or education."[16]

In holding that the Eighth Amendment's Cruel and Unusual Punishment Clause is not applicable to the use of corporal punishment for disciplinary purposes in the public schools, the Court held:

> The schoolchild has little need for the protection of the Eighth Amendment. Though attendance may not always be voluntary, the public school remains an open institution. Except perhaps when very young, the child is not physically

restrained from leaving school during school hours; and at the end of the school day, the child is invariably free to return home. Even while at school, the child brings with him the support of family and friends and is rarely apart from teachers and other pupils who may witness and protest any instances of mistreatment.

The openness of the public school and its supervision by the community afford significant safeguards against the kinds of abuses from which the Eighth Amendment protects the prisoner. In virtually every community where corporal punishment is permitted in the schools, these safeguards are reinforced by the legal constraints of the common law. Public school teachers and administrators are privileged at common law to inflict only such corporal punishment as is reasonably necessary for the proper education and discipline of the child; any punishment going beyond the privilege may result in both civil and criminal liability.... As long as the schools are open to public scrutiny, there is no reason to believe that the common law constraints will not effectively remedy and deter excesses such as those alleged in this case.

We conclude that when public school teachers or administrators impose disciplinary corporal punishment, the Eighth Amendment is inapplicable.

Ingraham continues to be the law today, and corporal punishment continues to be meted out in schools. Eighteen states continue to permit the use of corporal punishment, usually paddling with a wooden or plastic paddle. The most recent state to abolish the practice, New Mexico, did so in 2011. The U.S. Department of Education, Office for Civil Rights, collected data for 2011-2012, and estimates that about 167,000 children are subjected to corporal punishment in public schools each year.

In *Sandin v. Conner*,[17] the U.S. Supreme Court stated that although the Eighth Amendment may not apply to school punishments, where children are sent to public schools "arbitrary corporal punishments represents an invasion of personal security." Since that decision, some lower federal courts have interpreted the *Ingraham* decision as applying only to Eighth Amendment cruel and unusual punishment claims. Other claims based on Fourteenth Amendment procedural and substantive due process may be possible, these courts hold. See, e.g., *Preschooler II v. Clark County Bd. of Trustees*,[18] where the court held that a teacher's slapping of an autistic child could qualify as excessive force and a violation of the Fourth and Fourteenth Amendments.

procedural due process A claim under the Fourteenth Amendment that there is an absence of fair procedures regulating state conduct.

Procedural due process claims under the Fourteenth Amendment are based on the absence of fair procedures regulating state conduct. For example, if a school district permitted corporal punishment without a prior determination of some violation of school rules by the student, the student's procedural due process rights would be violated.[19] Moreover, even if the school had fair procedures regulating such punishment, procedural due process could be violated if the state had no adequate means for a student to seek redress from a school or teacher who violated those procedures.[20]

substantive due process A claim under the Fourteenth Amendment that state conduct is so brutal, demeaning, and harmful as to shock the conscience.

Substantive due process claims under the Fourteenth Amendment are based on state conduct that is so brutal, demeaning, and harmful as to shock the conscience.[21] Almost all the federal courts of appeal have concluded that excessive corporal punishment by a school official can give rise to a Fourteenth Amendment substantive due process claim.[22]

An example of a substantive due process claim can be found in *Neal v. Fulton County Board of Education*, a decision of the Eleventh Circuit Court of Appeals. In

Neal, a student was seriously injured when the varsity football coach struck him in the eye with a metal weight lock as punishment for fighting with another student. The court concluded that the coach intentionally used an excessive amount of force that presented a reasonably foreseeable risk of serious bodily injury.[23]

In *Garcia v. Miera,* the U.S. Court of Appeals for the Tenth Circuit summarized the law concerning school punishments:

> We thus envision three categories of corporal punishment. Punishments that do not exceed the traditional common law standard of reasonableness are not actionable; punishments that exceed the common law standard without adequate state remedies violate procedural due process rights; and finally, punishments that are so grossly excessive as to be shocking to the conscience violate substantive due process rights, without regard to the adequacy of state remedies.[24]

The Use of Corporal Punishment in Prisons

The use of corporal punishment against inmates of prisons is subject to Eighth Amendment cruel and unusual punishment claims. Unlike school students, prison inmates have none of the "community and legal constraints" that provide safeguards against the sort of abuses the Eighth Amendment prohibits.[25]

Eighth Amendment claims by prison inmates have both objective and subjective requirements. The inmate must show that the punishment failed the Eighth Amendment's proportionality test (the objective test) and also that the official administering the punishment possessed the requisite mental intent (the subjective test).[26] An example of such a punishment can be found in *Hope v. Pelzer,*[27] where the U.S. Supreme Court held that chaining a prisoner to a hitching post for seven hours without a water break or bathroom break violated the Eighth Amendment. The Court held that safety concerns were not present once the inmate had been subdued, and that the conduct of the guards supervising the punishment showed the gratuitous infliction of wanton and unnecessary pain.

CAPITAL PUNISHMENT

The death penalty was widely accepted at the time the U.S. Constitution and the Bill of Rights were ratified. The only reference to capital punishment in the Constitution is found in the Fifth Amendment, which reads: "No person shall be held to answer for a capital, or otherwise infamous crime, unless…." In the 1972 case of *Furman v. Georgia,* death penalty laws in all states were struck down as "arbitrary and capricious" by the U.S. Supreme Court.[28] The Court found that the imposition of the death sentence varied greatly from case to case, and that it was being administered without any reasonable standards for determining when it would be imposed. The Court stated that states wishing to use the death penalty must establish objective standards for determining when the death penalty will be imposed.

By 1976, when the Supreme Court upheld the death penalty statute passed by the Georgia legislature, thirty-five states had enacted capital punishment statutes, and in one state, California, the voters adopted a constitutional amendment authorizing capital punishment. The state statutes enacted responded to *Furman v. Georgia* by addressing these issues:

- The state statute must determine which crime (or crimes) may be punished by the death penalty, whether it will be the trial judge or jury who will make the decision to impose it, by what method it will be inflicted, and the appellate process used to review the sentence.
- The statute must require juries or judges considering the death penalty to make findings of statutory **aggravating circumstances** to justify the imposition of the death penalty and also make findings of the **mitigating circumstances** that would weigh against the imposition of the death penalty.

aggravating circumstances A consideration in imposing the death penalty that judges and juries must make a finding of statutory aggravating circumstances to justify the penalty.

mitigating circumstances A consideration in imposing the death penalty that judges and juries must make findings of the mitigating circumstances that would weigh against the imposition of the death penalty.

Death Penalty Laws After *Furman v. Georgia*

Furman v. Georgia invalidated death penalty statutes in forty-one states, as well as the death penalty in federal crimes for which the death penalty could then be imposed. In a 1984 case, the U.S. Supreme Court observed that

> In responding to (*Furman v. Georgia*), roughly two-thirds of the States promptly redrafted their capital sentencing statutes in an effort to limit jury discretion and avoid arbitrary and inconsistent results. All of the new statutes provide for automatic appeal of death sentences. Most, such as Georgia's, require the reviewing court, to some extent at least, to determine whether, considering both the crime and the defendant, the sentence is disproportionate to that imposed in similar cases. Not every State has adopted such a procedure. In some States, such as Florida, the appellate court performs proportionality review despite the absence of a statutory requirement; in others, such as California and Texas, it does not.[29]

In 1976, the U.S. Supreme Court reviewed the new death penalty statutes of Georgia,[30] Florida,[31] and Texas.[32] In the 1984 California death penalty case of *Pulley v. Harris*,[33] the U.S. Supreme Court quoted from its 1976 *Jurek v. Texas* decision in affirming the death penalty procedure used by California:

> Texas' capital sentencing procedures, like those of Georgia and Florida, do not violate the Eighth and Fourteenth Amendments. By narrowing its definition of capital murder, Texas has essentially said that there must be at least one statutory aggravating circumstance in a first-degree murder case before a death sentence may even be considered. By authorizing the defense to bring before the jury at the separate sentencing hearing whatever mitigating circumstances relating to the individual defendant can be adduced, Texas has ensured that the sentencing jury will have adequate guidance to enable it to perform its sentencing function. By providing prompt judicial review of the jury's decision in a court with statewide jurisdiction, Texas has provided a means to promote the evenhanded, rational, and consistent imposition of death sentences under law. Because this system serves to assure that sentences of death will not be "wantonly" or "freakishly" imposed, it does not violate the Constitution.

Since states restored the death penalty in 1976, 1431 people have been executed in the United States. In that same period 142 inmates have been exonerated based on proof of innocence. Forty-three prisoners were executed in 2013, and 35 in 2014; the highest number was ninety-eight in 1999. While California has the highest number of

IMPORTANT RECENT U.S. SUPREME COURT DEATH PENALTY DECISIONS

- In *Ring v. Arizona*, 536 U.S. 584 (2002), the Court held that a state capital sentencing procedure that permitted the sentencing judge to make the factual determination of the aggravating and mitigating circumstances present violated the Sixth Amendment's right of trial by jury. Factual questions bearing on the imposition of the death sentence or life imprisonment must be decided by the jury, the Court held.

- Based on its holding in *Ring*, in *Hurst v. Florida*, 136 S. Ct. 616 (2016) the Court held the Florida capital sentencing scheme unconstitutional. In Florida, a jury hears the mitigating-aggravating circumstances evidence in deciding to impose the death penalty or life imprisonment. However, once the jury hears the evidence, it sends its decision to the trial judge, who makes the final decision on life imprisonment or the death penalty. The jury determination on that question is thus advisory. The Court said this procedure is invalid under the Sixth Amendment: the jury must make the final determination of the facts necessary to sentence a defendant to death. It reversed the sentence of death and remanded to case for resentencing.

- In *Smith v. Spisak*, 558 U.S. 139 (2010), the Court stated the procedure to be followed when deliberating the death sentence: The jury must unanimously find that the prosecution proved each aggravating circumstance beyond a reasonable doubt, but each juror may consider any relevant evidence of mitigating factors. The jury must then unanimously find the aggravating circumstances proved outweigh the mitigating circumstances.

- In *Kansas v. Carr*, 136 S. Ct. 633 (2016) the Court held that a Kansas trial court did not violate the Eighth Amendment by failing to instruct the jury that while the prosecution must prove aggravating circumstances beyond a reasonable doubt, the defendant does not have to prove mitigating circumstances by the same standard. Mitigating circumstances are subject to each juror's judgment, the Court said, and the jury need not be instructed on any particular standard of proof on mitigating circumstances. The Kansas Supreme Court had concluded otherwise, and reversed the defendant's death sentences. The U. S. Supreme Court reversed and remanded the case to the Kansas courts.

- In *Ford v. Wainright*, 477 U.S. 399 (1986), the Court held that the Eighth Amendment prohibits the execution of a prisoner who is insane at the time of the execution.

Courts differed on what constitutes "insane" for Eighth Amendment purposes, though most followed a two-part test referenced in *Ford*: a defendant is not competent to be executed unless (1) he is aware of the punishment he is about to suffer, and (2) he knows why he is to suffer the punishment. In *Panetti v. Dretke*, 448 F.3d 815 (5th Cir. 2006), the Fifth Circuit Court of Appeals held that a defendant on Texas's

prisoners on death row, 724, it has executed only 13 since 1976. Texas has 304 prisoners on death row, and has executed 536 since 1976. The United States government has executed three people since 1976.[34]

Although polls show that the American public continues to generally support the death penalty, the number of death sentences handed out by juries has declined markedly since 1998, when 294 people were sentenced to death. In 2015, 49 people were sentenced to death. 28 inmates were executed in 2015, the lowest number since death row was not insane, even though he suffered from severe paranoid delusions and believed the state really wanted him executed as punishment for preaching the Gospel. The Court concluded *Ford* did not require that the defendant "rationally understand" the reason for his execution. It is enough, the Court said, that he was "aware" of those reasons. The Supreme Court reversed, holding that the District Court should have considered the defendant's claims of delusions before concluding he was competent and sane. See *Panetti v. Quarterman*, 127 S. Ct. 2842 (2007).

- In *Atkins v. Virginia*, 536 U.S. 304 (2002), the Court held that the Cruel and Unusual Punishment Clause of the Eighth Amendment prohibited imposition of the death penalty on defendants with mental retardation.[a] In 2004, the Court held in *Tennard v. Dretke* (124 S. Ct. 2562) that evidence of mental retardation is inherently mitigating in a capital case, whether or not the defendant has shown a nexus between his mental capacity and the crime committed.

- In *Baze v. Rees*, 553 U.S. 35 (2008), the Court upheld the validity of the lethal injection method of execution. The thirty-seven states using the lethal injection method all use a three-step "cocktail" for the execution. The first drug is an anesthetic, the second causes muscle paralysis, and the third causes cardiac arrest.

- In *Sattazahn v. Pennsylvania*, 537 U.S. 101 (2003), the Court held that the Double Jeopardy Clause does not bar a state from imposing the death sentence after a defendant convicted of murder and sentenced to life imprisonment appeals the conviction and gets the conviction reversed. On retrial and subsequent conviction, the death sentence may be imposed.

- In *Kennedy v. Louisiana*, 128 S. Ct. 2641 (2008), the Supreme Court invalidated a Louisiana statute permitting imposition of the death penalty for the rape of a child. Because the rape did not result in death, and was not intended to cause death, the Court said the cruel and unusual punishment did not permit imposition of the death penalty. The Court noted that since Louisiana adopted the statute in 1995, only six other states followed suit, indicating a national consensus existed against use of the death penalty in such cases.

[a] The *Atkins* court did not determine Atkins was retarded. Rather, it remanded the case to Virginia state court for a factual hearing on that issue. Atkins committed the murder for which he was sentenced to death in 1996, when he was 18 and had just dropped out of high school, having failed for the third time to pass the tenth grade. When Atkins was tested during his first trial in 1998 he scored 59 on an IQ test used in Virginia criminal cases, well below the cutoff score of 70 used for determination of retardation. However, when tested in November 2004 he scored 76 on the prosecution's test and 74 on the defense's test. Atkins's mental competency was submitted to a jury in 2005, and the jury concluded he was not retarded. In 2006 the Virginia Supreme Court reversed that decision, finding that the trial court erred by admitting improper expert testimony by the prosecution's expert witness, and by telling the jury the consequence of finding Atkins retarded would be to overturn a decision of another jury to give Atkins the death sentence. The case was remanded for another hearing on Atkins's competency. See *Atkins v. Com.*, 631 S.E.2d 93 (2006). A circuit judge subsequently commuted Atkins's sentence to life imprisonment, which was upheld on appeal.

1991. Only six states carried out executions in 2015, and three states (Texas, Missouri, and Georgia) accounted for 86% of those executions.[35]

State legislatures and courts have also limited the use of the death penalty. The Nebraska legislature abolished the death penalty in 2015, and the Connecticut Supreme Court declared the death penalty unconstitutional in 2015. Several states had put the use of the death penalty on hold as of 2015: Oregon, Pennsylvania, Arkansas, and Ohio.

FEDERAL CRIMES FOR WHICH THE DEATH PENALTY CAN NOW BE APPLIED

When President Clinton signed the 1994 Violent Crime Control and Law Enforcement Act, the number of federal crimes for which the death penalty could be applied increased significantly. The following is the 1994 list of federal death penalty crimes:

Assassination of the president, vice president, a member of Congress, cabinet member, or Supreme Court justice

Drug trafficking of large amount of drugs

First-degree murder on federal land or property

Genocide

Gun murders during federal crimes of violence and during drug trafficking crimes

Killing a person in a federal witness protection program

Killing (or attempted murder) by a drug kingpin of a public officer or a juror to obstruct justice

Murder at a U.S. international airport

Murder by a federal prisoner or escaped prisoner who is (or was) serving a life sentence

Murder for hire (when a federal crime)

Murder in aid of racketeering activity (federal)

Murder in a federal facility involving a firearm

Murder of federal witness, victim, or informant

Murder of a state correctional officer by an inmate

Murder of a U.S. citizen abroad by another U.S. citizen

Murder of a court officer or juror

Murder of a federal law enforcement official

Murder of a foreign official or internationally protected person on U.S. soil

Murder of a state or local official assisting federal law officers

Murder within the special maritime and territorial jurisdiction of the United States

Treason and espionage

Where death results:

- Aircraft hijacking (domestic or international)
- Alien smuggling
- Carjacking (federal)
- Destroying federal property with explosives
- Destruction of aircraft, motor vehicles, or their facilities (federal)
- Drive-by shooting (federal)
- Hostage taking (federal)
- Kidnapping (federal)
- Mailing injurious articles (such as explosives)
- Robbery of a federally insured bank
- Sexual abuse (federal)
- Sexual exploitation of children (federal)
- Torture (federal)
- Train sabotage (federal)
- Transporting explosives with intent to kill
- Use of weapons of mass destruction (poison gas, biological, and so on)
- Violating federally protected rights based on race, religion, or national origin

IMPRISONMENT AS PUNISHMENT

Under early Roman law, imprisonment was illegal as punishment and was used for detention only.[36] Imprisonment is as old as the law of England, but only rarely did statutes in early England provide for imprisonment as punishment for crime. Nearly every English court had its own particular prison, and the right of keeping a gaol (jail) in and for a particular district was a franchise the king granted to certain people, just as he granted other rights connected with the administration of justice in England. In addition to the franchise prisons were the Fleet, the prison of the Star Chamber, and the prison of the Court of Chancery.[37]

Because of the filthy, unsanitary conditions of the early English prisons and the corruption and brutality that arose from the franchise system, reform movements began in England as early as 1773, when John Howard became sheriff of Bedfordshire. When he saw the disgraceful conditions in his jail, he proposed that salaried jailers [well, in 1773 this is what they called jailers. Up to you to make them current] replace the franchise system. The condition of U.S. prisons has also been the subject of many reform movements, and the use of prisons for the purpose of punishment has been subject to much debate.

While conditions in prisons in the United States have improved over these early models, one severe problem is overcrowding. The Government Accountability Office reported in September 2012 that the federal prison system is 39 percent over capacity. In June of 2015 the GAO reported that the Department of Justice spent over $7 billion on prisons in 2014. It announced a new program called "Smart on Crime Initiative" that is intended to cut costs and reduce prison populations. While there are many reasons for the increase in the number of prisoners, drug-related crimes are at the core of the problem. At the end of 2014 there were 210,567 prisoners in federal prisons; 48 percent of these inmates were there on drug charges.[38]

State prisons face similar overcrowding problems. In the 2011 case of *Brown v. Plata*[39] the U.S. Supreme Court found that California state prisons, which were designed to hold 80,000 inmates, had double that number incarcerated. Finding this violated the Eighth Amendment, the Court ordered California to reduce the prison population to 137 percent of design capacity by the middle of 2013. By the end of 2015 California had reduced the prison population by 30,000 inmates, in part by "realignment" of lower level inmates from prisons to county jails, and eliminating jail sentences for lesser offenses that would previously have resulted in jail time.

Can Indigents Be Held in Jail to Work Off Their Money Fines?

In the case of *Williams v. Illinois*,[40] the question of whether a person who was indigent (without money) could be imprisoned for the inability to pay a fine was presented to the U.S. Supreme Court. In the *Williams* case, the Illinois courts had ruled that Williams would be held in prison and work off his fine at the rate of $5 per day. Williams asked to be released so he could get a job and pay the fine and court costs.

In the case of *Tate v. Short*[41] the indigent defendant owed fines of $425 on nine traffic offenses and was ordered to serve 85 days in a Texas prison farm to work off the fines at the rate of $5 per day.

The U.S. Supreme Court held that other ways of collecting fines are available and that permitting a person with money to pay fines, but requiring a person without money to work off a fine in jail or prison violates the Equal Protection Clause of the U.S. Constitution.[42]

LIFE IMPRISONMENT WITHOUT PAROLE FOR JUVENILE DEFENDANTS

The Cruel and Unusual Punishment Clause of the U.S. Constitution has a "proportionality" principle, but the U.S. Supreme Court has generally used that principle only in reviewing capital punishment cases. Where the sentence was a term of years, or life imprisonment, the Court has been reluctant to reverse a sentence because it was out of proportion to the crime committed, or to sentences imposed in similar cases.

In two recent cases involving juvenile defendants the Supreme Court declared that sentences of life imprisonment without possibility of parole (LWOP) for juvenile defendants violated the Cruel and Unusual Punishment Clause. The first case was *Graham v. Florida*, 130 S. Ct. 2011 (2010).

In 2003, at the age of 16, Terrance Graham and two friends attempted to rob a restaurant in Jacksonville, Florida. Graham was arrested, and tried as an adult for attempted robbery. He pled guilty, and was sentenced to 3 years of probation, the first year of which was to be spent in jail. In December 2004, 6 months after his release from jail and while still on probation, Graham and two friends undertook a home invasion, where they assaulted the homeowner, holding a pistol against his chest while the home was ransacked. Later that night Graham and his friends attempted another robbery, during the course of which one of the friends was shot. Graham took the friend to a hospital, and was subsequently arrested and charged with armed robbery. At the time, Graham was 34 days short of his 18th birthday.

Because Graham was on probation, a court held a hearing on the state's claim that Graham had violated his probation by engaging in criminal conduct and possessing a weapon. The court held him in violation of probation, finding Graham committed the crimes charged. Based on these charges, the judge could impose a sentence from 5 years to life. Although the pre-sentence report prepared by the probation office suggested a 4-year prison sentence, the judge sentenced Graham to life in prison. Because Florida had dropped its parole system, see Fla. Stat. § 921.002, this sentence amounted to a sentence of life without possibility of parole. That meant the only chance for Graham to be released was executive clemency. The Florida appellate courts affirmed the sentence. The U.S. Supreme Court granted certiorari, and reversed.

The Court first stated that some sentences for a juvenile should be reviewed using the "categorical" approach. This approach considers "the particular type of sentence," either the nature of offense and the sentence imposed or the characteristics of the defendant. An example of this kind of review is review of the death penalty for juveniles or the mentally retarded, where the Court has said "categorically" the death penalty violates the Eighth Amendment.

The Court then said sentences of life without any possibility of parole for juvenile offenders in non-homicide cases categorically violated the Eighth Amendment. The Court said that the undeveloped maturity of a juvenile made him less culpable than an adult who committed the same crime, and a juvenile's

FINES AND FORFEITURE AS PUNISHMENT

Money fines payable by the convicted offender are frequently used as an alternative to incarceration or together with incarceration. In most states, the maximum fine for any designated criminal act is set by statute. Also, it is common to limit the amount of a fine each level of court within a state may assess against a defendant. A municipal court that handles minor offenses has a lower fine limit than a district court with the jurisdiction to hear major crimes.

Fines must not be excessive. The Eighth Amendment to the U.S. Constitution prohibits "excessive fines imposed" as punishment. Generally, analysis of punishment greater capability for rehabilitation made the denial of any chance of parole more damaging. It therefore reversed the decisions below and remanded the case for resentencing. In 2012, Graham was re-sentenced to 25 years in prison. He could be released in 13 years under the Florida "Gain-time" prison rules.

In the second case, *Miller v. Alabama*, 132 S. Ct. 2455 (2012), the Court held that a mandatory sentence of life without possibility of parole for a juvenile violated the Eighth Amendment even in homicide cases, an area that the Court in *Graham* was careful to exclude from its holding in that case.

In *Miller* and a companion case, 14-year-old boys were involved in robberies where the victim was killed. Each boy received a sentence of life imprisonment without any possibility of parole, which under state law was the mandatory sentence the judge was required to impose with no discretion to do otherwise. The Supreme Court held that mandatory life sentences without any chance for parole in homicide cases "categorically" violated the Eighth Amendment for the same reasons stated in *Graham*. It therefore reversed the cases for resentencing.

One significant difference between *Graham* and *Miller* is the resentencing that will occur. Juveniles sentenced to life without parole for non-homicide crimes must be resentenced with some realistic possibility they will not spend the rest of their lives in prison. Courts after *Graham* have differed on the application of that case's rule to very long sentences of juveniles in non-homicide cases. Some courts have concluded such sentences are tantamount to life without parole, and declared them invalid. *State v. Boston*, 363 P.3d 453 (Nev. 2015) [100-year sentence of 16-year-old held invalid]. Others, like *Angel v. Commonwealth*, 781 S.E.2d 920 (Va. 2016), have held that it is permissible for courts to sentence juveniles to "stacked" non-parole terms for multiple offenses that are in total longer than the juvenile's expected life [133-year sentence for 16-year-old convicted of multiple crimes including rape upheld].

Juveniles in homicide cases given a mandatory sentence of life without possibility of parole also must be resentenced, but they may still be sentenced to life without the possibility of parole if the sentencing judge determines that is the proper sentence, taking into account the fact that the defendant is a juvenile. An example of such a sentence can be found in *People v. Gutierrez*, 147 Cal. Rptr. 3d 249 (Cal. App. 2012), where the court affirmed a sentence of life without parole for a 17-year-old juvenile who murdered his aunt with "special circumstances" (aggravating circumstances).

Finally, in *Montgomery v. Louisiana*, 136 S. Ct. 718 (2016) the U.S. Supreme Court resolved a question left unanswered in *Miller*: Does the holding apply to juveniles whose sentences to LWOP were final before *Miller* was decided? The Court said its decision in *Miller* was retroactive. The defendant in *Montgomery* killed a police officer in 1963, when he was 17. He was sentenced to life without parole. The Supreme Court reversed his sentence under *Miller*, but made it clear Louisiana could remedy the "*Miller* violation" by making the defendant eligible for a parole hearing. The state did not have to resentence the defendant.

under the Cruel and Unusual Punishment Clause requires application of the proportionality test. In excessive fines cases, that means comparing the fine assessed with the nature of the offense charged. In *United States v. Bajakajian*, 524 U.S. 321 (1998) the U.S. Supreme Court said that only fines that are "grossly disproportionate" to the crime violate the Excessive Fines Clause. Factors to be considered, the Court said, are (1) the essence of the crime, that is, the criminal conduct, (2) whether the defendant was within the class the statute was aimed at, (3) the maximum sentence or fine that could be imposed, and (4) the nature of the harm caused by the criminal conduct.

FINES, FACT-FINDING, AND THE SIXTH AMENDMENT

Corporations can only be punished for criminal violations by fines. In the case of violations of environmental crimes, computing the fine can require findings of fact that have the potential for greatly increasing the punishment. In *Southern Union Co. v. United States*, 132 S. Ct. 2344 (2012), the U.S. Supreme Court considered the requirements of the Sixth Amendment when fines as punishment are determined.

The defendant corporation was convicted of violating the federal Resource Conservation and Recovery Act by storing hazardous waste without a permit. The statute provides for a fine of $50,000 for each day the defendant violated the statute. The jury convicted the defendant on one count, but made no finding of exactly how many days the violation lasted. The trial judge imposed a $6 million fine and a "community service obligation" of $12 million. The corporation appealed, contending the Sixth Amendment was violated because the jury must make every factual finding that increases a criminal punishment.

The U.S. Supreme Court agreed, and reversed the conviction and fine. It held that since the potential fine facing the defendant was serious enough to require a jury trial under the Sixth Amendment, the *Apprendi* line of cases (discussed earlier in this chapter) required the jury to find facts that determine the severity of the fine.

Forfeiture Going back to early English law, the concept and use of seizing the property that was used to commit a crime.

The concept and use of **forfeiture** go back to early English law. Seizing the property that was used to commit a crime is a strong deterrent to crime. Seizing the profits of crime is also a deterrent in crimes committed for profit.

Forfeiture was first used in customs violations such as smuggling. In addition to the traditional criminal punishments of death and fines, the economic sanction of forfeiture was imposed through seizure of ships, implements, and the goods being smuggled.

Forfeiture not only punished the wrongdoers by depriving them of ships (or boats), implements, and goods, but also rewarded the king and government, who benefited from the use and sale of these items.

The concept of forfeiture came to America with English common law. It was used over the years in various forms. During Prohibition, forfeiture was used extensively to deter and discourage the manufacture, sale, and use of illegal alcohol.

While forfeiture is not "punishment" for many purposes, such as application of the Double Jeopardy Clause, it remains an important part of law enforcement's efforts to combat crime. Federal statutes today authorize the forfeiture not only of contraband property but also of instrumentalities used in narcotics, gambling, and untaxed alcohol and tobacco. For example, Section 55 of the Uniform Controlled Substance Act, which has been adopted by many states and the federal government, provides for forfeiture not only of controlled substances in violation of the law but also of all raw materials, all vehicles "used, or intended for use," weapons, records and books, and all property, "including money" and profits. Section 55.5 of the act details forfeiture proceedings.[43]

Important U.S. Supreme Court and other federal court cases regarding civil forfeitures are as follows:

- *United States v. Ursery,*[44] The Supreme Court held that "*in rem* civil forfeitures are neither 'punishment' nor criminal for the purposes of the Double Jeopardy

Clause"; therefore, the government can commence both a criminal action and a civil forfeiture action without violating double jeopardy.

- *Austin v. United States*,[45] The Supreme Court held that the civil forfeiture provision of 21 U.S.C. § 881(a)(4), providing for forfeiture of property used in drug transactions, was "punishment" for purposes of the Eighth Amendment excessive fines clause. Whether termed civil or criminal, the Court stated a forfeiture provision is a "punishment" if it has a purpose other than remedial action.

- *Bennis v. Michigan*,[46] In this case, the Supreme Court held that a state forfeiture law could provide for forfeiture (seizure) of property from an owner who was unaware of the illegal use of the property. (Bennis was convicted of a sex act with a prostitute in a car owned by Bennis and his wife, who was unaware of the illegal use of the car.) The U.S. Supreme Court held that under such a state statute, "the innocence of an owner (Bennis's wife) has almost uniformly been rejected as a defense to forfeiture."

- *United States v. 785 Nicholas Ave.*[47] Under 21 U.S.C.A. Section 881(a)(7), the federal government may seize real estate being used for illegal activity such as drug dealing. To defend against such a forfeiture action, the owners must demonstrate a lack of consent to the illegal activities and that they did all that reasonably could be expected to prevent the illegal activities once they learned of them.

18 U.S.C.A. § 983(d)(1), the Civil Asset Forfeiture Act, now provides an "innocent owner" defense applicable in all federal forfeiture cases. The owner must show either lack of knowledge of the illegal activity in which the property was involved, or that the owner did all that reasonably could be done to prevent the use of the property in the illegal activity.

Under federal law today and under the provisions of the forfeiture statutes of many states, the following can now be seized under court order:

- Instrumentalities of the crime (vehicles, watercraft, and the like used in the commission of the crimes)
- Profits of the crime (money from drug dealing, stolen goods, and so on)
- Proceeds of the illegal acts (farms, yachts, cars, homes, and other luxury goods purchased with profits of illegal acts)

The Internal Revenue Service can also seize under court order the property of people charged with or convicted of crimes. Because people involved in the sale of marijuana, cocaine, and narcotics often make huge profits without paying proper taxes, tax liens may be filed against them. Property belonging to such people may be seized for payment of taxes, including homes, furniture, cars, stereo equipment, video games, gems, and real estate.

Under the Mandatory Victims Restitution Act, 18 U.S.C. § 3663A, Federal judges must order restitution as part of the sentence in certain crimes, such as crimes of violence or fraud, where an identifiable person has suffered a loss. In *Dolan v. United States,* 130 S. Ct. 1047 (2010), the Supreme Court held that while the Act requires a judge to determine the amount of restitution to be paid no later than 90 days after sentencing, the 90-day limit may be extended if the judge determines restitution will be ordered, but cannot within the time limit determine the exact amount to be ordered.

One question that has split lower courts is the power of governments to freeze a defendant's assets prior to trial, when the assets are not the fruit of the alleged criminal activity but "untainted" assets. The federal general criminal forfeiture statute, 18 U.S.C. § 982, provides for "substitution" of untainted assets for those assets that were traceable to the crime but cannot now be found. Defendants contend freezing untainted assets violates the Sixth Amendment right to counsel, since they could as a result of the seizure lack the funds needed to employ an attorney. In *Luis v. United States*, 546 Fed. Appx. 493 (11th Cir. 2014) the court rejected that argument. However, in March, 2016 the U.S. Supreme Court reversed the 11th Circuit, and held that untainted assets could not be seized prior to trial. A majority of the court believed such a seizure violated the Sixth Amendment. The court did agree that tainted assets could be seized. *Luis v. United States*, 136 S. Ct. 1083 (2016)

CAREER CRIMINALS AND THE REPEAT OFFENDER

Law enforcement priorities are most often determined by the crime itself. High priority is most often given when crimes involve injury or death or when important aspects of public interest are involved.

Attention is focused on the person committing the crime rather than on the crime when it is determined that the person is a career criminal or a repeater (or habitual criminal). Recidivism is a major problem in the United States. In a 2009 report published by the Office of Justice Program, Bureau of Statistics, titled "Re-Entry Trend in the United States: Recidivism," statistics showed that nationwide 67.5 percent of persons released from prison in 1994 were rearrested within 3 years of their release, and 51.8 percent of those released were back in prison within 3 years.

By taking such offenders off the street, the incidence of crimes can be considerably lessened. Many cities and states have created career-criminal programs. Such programs ordinarily

- Operate under statutes providing additional and longer sentences for repeat offenders.
- Establish special career-criminal units in the offices of police and prosecutors that vigorously investigate frequently committed crimes or crimes following patterns.
- Speed up prosecution of career criminals.
- Discourage plea bargaining, which could lessen prison terms, unless the suspect incriminates associates.

Recidivist One who is a habitual criminal.

Several repeater (**recidivist**) cases have come before the U.S. Supreme Court in recent years, with different results. One of the earliest cases was the 1980 Texas case of *Rummel v. Estelle*. In that case a defendant had received a life sentence under the Texas repeater statutes for three nonviolent crimes that netted the defendant a total of $230. The Court affirmed the conviction and sentence, holding that the sentence did not violate the Eighth Amendment.

In the case of *Solem v. Helm*[48] the U.S. Supreme Court decided another recidivism case. Helm lived in South Dakota and had a serious problem with alcohol. By 1975, he had committed six nonviolent felonies. In 1979, he pleaded guilty to uttering (passing) a "no account" check for $100 (his seventh felony). Under the South

Dakota recidivist statute, his crime was classified as a "class I" felony, and he was sentenced to life imprisonment.

Unlike the Texas statutes in the *Rummel* case, South Dakota statutes forbade parole in recidivist cases. Murderers and rapists were eligible for parole in South Dakota, but Helm would never be eligible for parole. The Supreme Court held that the sentence violated the Eighth Amendment, stating

> The Constitution requires us to examine Helm's sentence to determine if it is proportionate to his crime. Applying objective criteria, we find that Helm has received the penultimate sentence for relatively minor criminal conduct. He has been treated more harshly than other criminals in the State who have committed more serious crimes. He has been treated more harshly than he would have been in any other jurisdiction, with the possible exception of a single State. We conclude that his sentence is significantly disproportionate to his crime, and is therefore prohibited by the Eighth Amendment.

The absence of the possibility of parole appeared to be the basis for the distinction between *Solem* and *Rummel*; the defendant in *Rummel* could be eligible for parole in 12 years, whereas the defendant in *Solem* would never be paroled. However, in *Ewing v. California*, 538 U.S. 11 (2003), the Court upheld a sentence of 25 years to life under the California "Three Strikes" law (discussed in the next section). The statute provided that parole could not be considered until the 25-year term had passed, but the Court did not identify the possibility of parole as the basis of its decision. Rather, the Court held that a state has a legitimate interest in incarcerating repeat offenders who have demonstrated an inability to conform to the criminal laws.

In *Lockyer v. Andrade* (discussed in the next section) a companion case to *Ewing,* the Court upheld a sentence of two consecutive 25-years-to-life terms under the California three strikes law. While dissenting justices noted that a 50-year minimum sentence for a 37-year-old defendant amounted to life without parole, the majority did not make the presence or absence of parole the basis for its decision.

"Three Strikes" Laws

For many years, most states and the federal government have had laws that provide for increased punishment for multiple felony convictions. For example, The Armed Career Criminal Act, 18 U.S.C. § 924(e)(1) (ACCA), mandates a sentence of 15 years in prison for any felon convicted of violation of 18 U.S.C. § 922(g)(1), the felon in possession of a firearm statute, if the felon had three previous convictions for drug offenses or "violent crimes." In *Begay v. United States,* 453 U.S. 137 (2008) the U.S. Supreme Court held that "violent crimes" under § 924(e)(1) did not include previous fourth-offense convictions for drunken driving, even though they were treated as felonies under state law. The Court reasoned that Congress intended to limit the kind of prior felonies that resulted in the increased sentence to crimes that were in their nature violent or created the possibility of violence. For similar reasons, the Supreme Court held in *Johnson v. United States,* 130 S. Ct. 1265 (2010), that a conviction under the Florida battery statute, which defines the crime as "actually and intentionally touching" another person, was not a violent felony under the ACCA.

CASE CLOSE-UP
THE MEANING OF "VIOLENT CRIME"

Descamps v. United States

United States Supreme Court (2013)
133 Supreme Court 2276

In *Deschamps v. United States*, the court introduced a "hard line" rule on how "violent crime" was to be applied under the ACCA for crimes that covered a broad range of conduct, some of which was not "violent." In *Descamps* the defendant was convicted of being a felon in possession of a weapon in violation of 18 U.S.C. § 922(g). That conviction carried a maximum prison sentence of 10 years. The government moved for an enhanced sentence under the ACCA, which has a 15-year minimum sentence if applicable. The enhanced sentence was based on the defendant's conviction of burglary (a "predicate offense" under the ACCA) under California state law. Burglary is one of the crimes included in the list of "violent crimes" that trigger the sentence enhancement under the ACCA. However, California defines burglary very broadly, and is not limited to breaking and entering to commit a crime. One who enters a store through the front door intending to shoplift could be prosecuted under the California statute, the Court noted.

It had become the practice in lower courts for judges, when such broadly written statutes were involved, to look at the facts of the case to determine if the crime qualified as a crime of violence under the ACCA. The trial judge did so in *Descamps*, and because the defendant had in fact broken into a grocery store, the trial judge applied the enhanced sentence under the ACCA, and sentenced the defendant to 262 months in prison, more than double what he would otherwise have been given.

The Supreme Court held that it was improper to look at the facts to determine if the "predicate" offense was a crime of violence under the ACCA. Since the California statute did not divide the crime of burglary into separate, alternate offenses based on the manner in which the burglary occurred, the Court said it was "indivisible." Since the statute thus covered some conduct that wouldn't qualify as an act of violence, the burglary conviction could not be used to trigger the sentence enhancement under the ACCA, the Court held. It reversed the defendant's sentence.

The *Descamps* ruling affects other areas where "three strike" violent crimes can result in increased prison terms. In *United States v. Brown*, 765 F.3d 185 (3rd Cir. 2014) the court held that under *Descamps* the "three strikes" provision of the Federal Sentencing Guidelines did not apply to a conviction under a Pennsylvania Terrorist threat statute. The court said that because the state crime included conduct that would not qualify as a violent crime, it could not be used to trigger the three-strike sentence enhancement under the Guidelines.

In the mid-1990s laws called "three strikes and you're out" laws gained prominence when the U.S. Congress incorporated a "three strikes" provision into the Violent Crime Control and Law Enforcement Act of 1994. Many states followed suit.[50]

In November 1994, California voters adopted Proposition 184, a "three strikes" law, in part as a response to the murder of Kimberly Reynolds, an 18-year-old

PRISONS AND JAILS IN THE UNITED STATES

Every year thousands of inmates are released from U.S. prisons. Unfortunately, many of these inmates are back in prison within a few years of their release. This result, called *recidivism,* has for years been a serious problem in the United States. The causes of this high recidivism rate have been debated for years in Congress and in the states. There is general agreement that two of the major factors contributing to that high rate are the serious mental health problems of about one in six inmates and the scarcity of programs for helping an ex-convict find a job and start a new life.

Because states must spend nearly $30 billion each year to maintain prisons, new efforts are being made to deal with the recidivism problem.

During the 40 years from 1969 to 2009, prison and jail populations have grown every year in the United States, to a present total of about 2 million prisoners. This is far more than the combined total number of inmates incarcerated in the thirty-six European countries.[a]

At present, each year about 650,000 inmates are released from prisons, but unfortunately between one-half and two-thirds of these inmates are back in prison within a few years of their release. Recidivism continues to be a very serious problem in the United States, and state and federal officials are very concerned about that problem. U.S. Attorney General Eric Holder stated before the American Bar Association in 2009 that "[t]here is no doubt that we must be tough on crime. But we must also commit ourselves to being smart on crime … we need to adopt what works."[b]

At the end of 2015 there were 1,561,500 inmates in state and federal prisons.[49] Based on yearly recidivism rates, about 40% of these inmates, once released, will be returned to prison within three years of their release.

[a]See the *New York Times* article of April 23, 2008, entitled "U.S. Inmate Count Far Exceeds Those of Other Nations."
[b]See the *New York Times* op-ed article of August 15, 2009, entitled "Getting Smart on Crime."

"three strikes" laws Laws that impose increased penalties for multiple felony convictions.

fashion student, by a paroled drug dealer with a long history of violent crime. California's law is among the harshest **"three strikes" laws** for three reasons: (1) the third or "trigger" conviction may be any felony, not necessarily one for a violent crime; (2) the first two strikes may be convictions for any "serious" felony, though not necessarily a violent crime; and (3) a sentence of 25 years to life must be assessed on each count, with multiple counts served consecutively. Parole may not be considered until the entire mandatory sentence is served.[51]

In 2003 the U.S. Supreme Court decided *Lockyer v. Andrade,* 538 U.S. 63. Andrade was convicted under California's "three strikes" law and sentenced to two terms of 25 years to life, meaning Andrade would not be eligible for parole until 2046. The crimes Andrade committed to invoke the "three strikes" law were mainly minor theft crimes, not crimes of violence. The Ninth Circuit Court of Appeals found the "three strikes" statute unconstitutional, because the sentence was so disproportionate to the crimes committed it violated the Eighth Amendment. The Supreme Court reversed the Ninth Circuit, holding that under established law the sentence was not so grossly disproportionate as to violate the Eighth Amendment.

The *Andrade* decision provides no clear answer to the "gross disproportionality" problem for sentences under "three strikes" laws. However, the last paragraph in the majority opinion suggests the approach the Supreme Court will take to that problem when presented again: "The gross disproportionality principle reserves a constitutional violation for only the extraordinary case."

State courts may, notwithstanding the holding in *Lockyer v. Andrade*, overturn a sentence under state constitutional provisions. California, as an example, has a "cruel or unusual" prohibition in its state constitution, Article 1, section 17. In *People v. Carmony*, 26 Cal. Rptr. 3d 365 (2005), the court held a 25-to-life sentence imposed under the California three-strikes law for defendant's failure to register as a sex offender within 5 days of his birthday violated the state constitution.

★★★

LEARNING OBJECTIVES SUMMARY

LO 1. Describe the text of the Cruel and Unusual Punishment Clause.
The text of the Eighth Amendment prohibits excessive bail, excessive fines, and cruel and unusual punishment.

LO 2. Explain the relationship between the Sixth Amendment and sentencing provisions that permit a judge to determine when an enhanced sentence should be given a criminal defendant.
The Sixth Amendment requires that factual findings made for the purpose of enhancing a sentence must be made by a jury.

LO 3. State the present status of the Federal Sentencing Guidelines.
The Federal Sentencing Guidelines are no longer mandatory, but federal courts imposing sentences must consider the guidelines and the factors stated in the Federal Sentencing Act, 18 U.S.C.§ 3553 when imposing a sentence.

LO 4. Identify the procedures a school official must follow before imposing corporal punishment on a student.
School officials may impose corporal punishment on a student only if (1) it is not excessive, and (2) it follows a prior determination that the student violated a school rule.

LO 5. Explain why the death penalty was declared unconstitutional in *Furman v. Georgia.*

Furman v. Georgia held that imposition of the death penalty without an established procedure to determine which defendants should live and which die was arbitrary and capricious, and thus a violation of the Eighth and Fourteenth Amendments. It was not the death penalty that was unconstitutional, but rather the "lightning-like" way in which it was imposed.

LO 6. Identify at least three groups of persons who cannot be given the death penalty.
Mentally retarded defendants, juveniles under the age of 18, and insane persons may not be given the death penalty.

LO 7. Explain the present rule on the imposition of life without parole sentences for juveniles.
Juveniles may never be given life without possibility of parole for non-homicide crimes. For homicide crimes juveniles may not be given mandatory life sentences without possibility of parole, but a sentencing court may in its discretion do so after considering all relevant factors, including the fact that the defendant was a juvenile.

LO 8. Describe the kinds of evidence that must be produced if the prosecution seeks imposition of the death penalty after a jury has found the defendant guilty of the crime charged.
State statutes must identify aggravating circumstances, and the jury must find such

circumstances exist, before the death penalty may be imposed. Jurors must also be instructed on mitigating factors to be integrated into the decision to impose the death penalty.

LO 9. Define "three strikes" laws and list the common characteristics of such laws.

"Three-strikes" laws provide for the automatic enhancement of a prison sentence, often to life imprisonment, upon the conviction of a third felony or violent crime. Parole generally is not available until the minimum term of years is served.

KEY TERMS

benefit of clergy, p. 204
sanctuary, p. 205
capital punishment, p. 206
cruel and unusual punishment, p. 207

proportionality, p. 207
corporal punishment, p. 212
procedural due process, p. 213
substantive due process, p. 213
aggravating circumstances, p. 215

mitigating circumstances, p. 215
forfeiture, p. 222
recidivist, p. 224
"three strikes" laws, p. 227

CASE ANALYSIS AND WRITING EXERCISES

1. Cases involving sexual abuse of children pose a special problem for a proportionality analysis under the Eighth Amendment's Cruel and Unusual Punishment Clause. Such crimes inflict the immediate damage of the criminal conduct, but also the likelihood of lifetime emotional injury. On the other hand, a crime of "offensive touching" a child is not the same as rape or murder of that child. In *Hanf v. State*, 182 S0. 2d 704 (Fla. App. 2015) the defendant was sentenced to life in prison for lewd and lascivious molestation of a child under 12 years of age. (Florida has eliminated parole for most crimes.) The criminal conduct was "unwanted touching" of the child's breast. The appeals court affirmed the sentence, holding that it was not "grossly disproportionate" to the crime. What are the relevant facts to consider when making such a determination? Is the dissent correct?

2. The defendant, when he was 16 years-old, and another juvenile gunned down a man outside a Chicago park. The defendant did the shooting; the other juvenile handed him the gun. The other juvenile pled guilty to second degree murder, and was sentenced to 17.5 years in prison. The defendant was tried for first degree murder and use of a weapon in the murder, and convicted by a jury. He was sentenced to 50 years in prison for the murder, and 50 years for the weapon offense, the

sentences to be consecutive. He would thus not be released until he was 117, or died. Does *Miller v. Alabama* require resentencing of the defendant? Why or why not? See *McKinley v. Butler*, 809 F.3d 908 (7th Cir. 2016).

3. It is a federal crime to possess a firearm if one has been convicted of a "misdemeanor crime of domestic violence." 18 U/S/C/ § 922(g)(9) Defendant was convicted in Tennessee state court of "intentionally causing physical injury" to the mother of his child. He was then charged with violation of § 922(g)(9). He contended the Tennessee statute did not qualify as a "misdemeanor crime of domestic violence" because it could apply to a simple touching of a victim. Under *Johnson v. United States*, discussed in this chapter, he contended a "misdemeanor crime of domestic violence" required the use of "physical force" equivalent to "violent" force. The trial court agreed, and dismissed the charges. A court of appeals affirmed. The U.S. Supreme Court granted review. What should it decide? Does this case present the same problem as was presented in *Johnson*? What kind of "physical force" was at issue in that case? Is that what "physical force" means in the statute that prohibits gun possession for a conviction of a misdemeanor crime of domestic violence? See *United States v. Castleman*, 134 S. Ct. 1405 (2014).

4. For the Excessive Fines Clause of the Eighth Amendment, we saw that the U. S. Supreme Court has held that a fine was excessive only if it was "grossly disproportionate' to the crime. *United States v. Bajakajian*, discussed in this chapter. Are the factors identified by the Supreme Court in *Bajakajian* exclusive, or can some other factors be used by a court to determine "grossly disproportionate"? What about the effect of a defendant's future ability to earn a livelihood? See *United States v. Viloski*, 557 Fed. Appx. 28 (2nd Cir. 2014), *cert denied*, 135 S. Ct. 1698 (2015).

ENDNOTES

1. *United States v. George*, 779 F.3d 113 (2nd Cir. 2015).

2. *A History of the Criminal Law of England* (three volumes) by Sir James Fitzjames Stephens, Judge of High Court of Justice, Queen's Bench Division (England 1883) 1: 477.

3. In 1996, John Silber, president of Boston University, wrote an op-ed article for the *New York Times* titled "Students Should Not Be Above the Law: Judging Crimes Is a Job for Courts, Not Colleges" (May 9, 1996). He pointed out that colleges and universities are "circumventing the courts (to) bury serious criminal cases in their own judicial systems." Because crime victims are talked out of reporting their cases to the police, students are receiving special treatment, just as people did who qualified under the "benefit of clergy" exception centuries ago. Silber cited as an example a man who graduated in 1996 from Miami University in Ohio, a private university. After the man was accused of sexually assaulting an 18-year-old freshman as she was sleeping, the man was allowed to graduate on "student conduct probation" instead of having Ohio police and prosecutors handle the matter.

4. Blackstone 4 *Commentaries,* 18.

5. *A History of the Criminal Law of England*, chapter 13, pp. 491–492.

6. The treatment of refugees from Cuba, Haiti, Mexico, Central America, and other parts of the world has been a continuing problem in the United States. The Immigration and Naturalization Service (INS) most often concludes that the refugees are fleeing from poverty in their countries and thus are not eligible for legal entry into the United States. Transporting, smuggling, or harboring aliens in violation of the Refugee Act of 1980 (Public Law 96-212) is a criminal offense. The defendants in the case of *United States v. Aguilar et al.,* 871 F.2d 1436 (9th Cir. 1989), *opinion amended and suspended* 883 F.2d 662 (9th Cir. 1989), ran a "modern-day underground railroad" that smuggled Central Americans across the border between Mexico and Arizona. The defendants in the *Aguilar* case were convicted of violations of the immigration laws (smuggling, transporting, and harboring aliens) arising from their participation in a "sanctuary movement."

7. Radzinowicz, *A History of English Criminal Law and Its Administration* (London: Stevens, 1948); Chute and Bell, *Crime, Courts, and Probation* (New York: Macmillan, 1956).

8. "Transportation" was used by a number of countries. The Roman Empire transported prisoners to Romania; the Soviet Union transported hundreds of thousands of political prisoners to Siberia. In addition, people fleeing from the law or political trouble have always used the frontiers of the world as a refuge.

9. *Furman v. Georgia*, 408 U.S. 238, 92 S. Ct. 2726 (1972).

10. Annals of Congress, 782 (1789).

11. *Furman v. Georgia*, 408 U.S. 238 at 258, 92 S. Ct. 2726 at 2736 (1972).

12. *Pulley v. Harris*, 465 U.S. 37, 104 S. Ct. 871 (1984).

13. 501 U.S. 957 (1991).

14. 538 U.S. 11 (2003).

15. 404 F.2d 571 (8th Cir. 1968), where the court presents reasons why whipping is unconstitutional as a punishment.

16. 429 U.S. 975, 97 S. Ct. 481 (1977).

17. 515 U.S. 472 (1995).

18. 479 F.3d 1175 (9th Cir. 2007).

19. Most school districts that permit corporal punishment require it to be administered only after the principal has approved it, in the presence of another adult, and not with an instrument that could cause physical injury to the student.

20. See *Garcia v. Miera*, 817 F.2d 650, 656 (10th Cir. 1987).

21. *County of Sacramento v. Lewis*, 523 U.S. 833 (1998).

22. *Neal v. Fulton County Board of Education*, 229 F.3d 1069, 1075 (11th Cir. 2000).

23. *Ibid*, at 1076.

24. 817 F.2d 650, 656.

25. *Ingraham*, 429 U.S. 975 (1977).

26. Because of state and federal sentencing guidelines, a convicted defendant is very unlikely to be sentenced by a court to receive corporal punishment. Such a sentence would be judged solely by the objective proportionality test of the Eighth Amendment. Other unusual sentences likewise can run afoul of the Eighth Amendment. For example, in *Williams v. State,* 505 S.E.2d 816 (Ga. App. 1998), a convicted sex offender was required to walk in the area where he committed his crime while wearing a sign that said, "BEWARE HIGH CRIME AREA." The appellate court said

this sentence constituted cruel and unusual punishment because the defendant was put in harm's way from other criminals frequenting the designated area.

27. 536 U.S. 730 (2002).

28. 408 U.S. 238, 92 S. Ct. 2726 (1972).

29. *Pulley v. Harris*, 465 U.S. 37, 44. In *Pulley v. Harris* the Supreme Court also defined and explained the use of proportionality. *Id.* at 42–43.

30. *Gregg v. Georgia*, 428 U.S. 153, 96 S. Ct. 2909 (1976).

31. *Proffitt v. Florida*, 428 U.S. 242, 96 S. Ct. 2960 (1976).

32. *Jurek v. Texas*, 428 U.S. 262, 96 S. Ct. 2950 (1976).

33. 465 U.S. 37, 104 S. Ct. 871 (1984).

34. Report, Death Penalty Information Center, March 23, 2016.

35. *Id*, based on Bureau of Justice Statistics.

36. Rubin, *The Law of Criminal Corrections* (St. Paul, MN.: West, 1963).

37. England also had debtors' prisons in which people who owed civil debts could be imprisoned until the civil debt was paid. England abolished the practice of debtors' prisons in 1869. Such imprisonment would not be lawful under the U.S. Constitution, and some state constitutions specifically forbid this form of imprisonment. Most of the democratic world has abolished the practice.

38. Department of Justice, Bureau of Statistics, NCJ 248955, September, 2015.

39. 131 S. Ct. 1910 (2011).

40. *Williams v. Illinois*, 90 S. Ct. 2018 (1970).

41. 915 S. Ct. 668 (1971).

42. In footnote 19 of the *Williams* case, the Court stated: "We wish to make clear that nothing in our decision today precludes imprisonment for willful refusal to pay a fine or court costs. See *Ex parte Smith*, 97 Utah 280, 92 P.2d 1098 (1939)." Therefore, a person who has money or an income may be imprisoned for refusal to pay either a fine or court costs.

43. Other federal statutes that have forfeiture provisions are the Controlled Substance Act, 21 U.S.C.A. § 881; Organized Crime Control Act of 1970, 18 U.S.C.A. §§ 1963 and 1955(d); Copyrights Act, 17 U.S.C.A. §§ 506(b) and 509(a); and Child Protection Act of 1984, 18 U.S.C.A. §§ 2253 and 2254.

44. 116 S. Ct. 2135 (1996).

45. 509 U.S. 602 (1993).

46. 116 S. Ct. 994 (1996).

47. 983 F.2d 396, *review denied*, 113 S. Ct. 2349 (1993).

48. 463 U.S. 277.

49. Bureau of Justice Statistics, Department of Justice, September 17, 2015.

50. Between 1993 and 1995, twenty-four states enacted "three-strikes" laws. See *State v. Oliver,* 745 A.2d 1165, 1169 (N.J. 2000).

51. California Penal Code § 1170.12.

9

Free Speech, Public Order Crimes, and the Bill of Rights

LEARNING OBJECTIVES

In this chapter we examine the extent to which the Bill of Rights, mainly the First Amendment, serves as a limit on the power of government to make criminal laws regulating conduct, such as speaking or assembling in public places. The learning objectives for this chapter are the following:

LO 1. State and discuss the First Amendment.

LO 2. Identify the difference between fighting words and merely rude language.

LO 3. Define a "clear and present danger."

LO 4. List the circumstances that permit government to regulate speech based on content.

LO 5. Define obscenity.

LO 6. State when a threat becomes a "true threat."

LO 7. Describe some ways one person might stalk another person in violation of a criminal law.

LO 8. Identify when an assembly becomes unlawful.

LO 9. State the basis for the Supreme Court's decision that the Second Amendment is binding on the states.

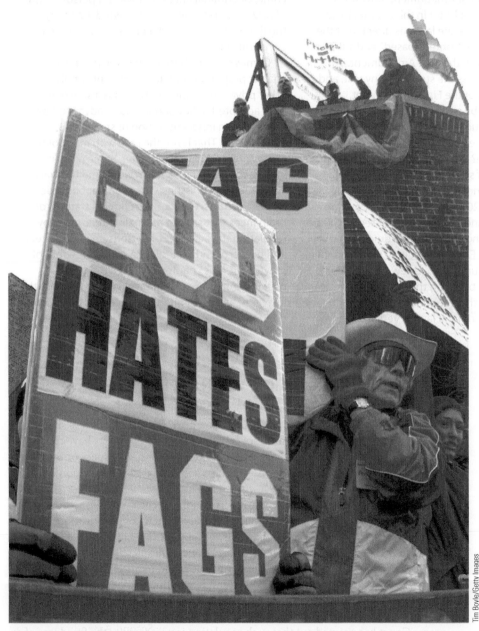

Fred Phillips, founder of the Westboro Church, which leads anti-gay pickets at military funerals. Phillips died in 2014.

In *United States v. Alvarez*, the U.S. Supreme Court held that a federal law that made it a crime to falsely represent that one had been awarded a military medal violated the First Amendment. (*Alvarez* is discussed in more detail later in this chapter.) The Court said that because the law was directed at the false statement, it was "content-based" and subject to strict scrutiny under the First Amendment. The federal law did not pass the strict scrutiny test, and was thus a violation of the First Amendment.

Should the same be said about another section of the federal law struck down in *Alvarez*, one that makes it a crime to *wear* unearned military medals with the intent to deceive? Can wearing a military medal constitute speech? If so, does that make the federal law prohibiting wearing unauthorized military medals "content-based"? In 2016 the Ninth Circuit Court of Appeals said it did, and struck down that section of the federal law as violating the First Amendment. *United States v. Swisher*, 811 F.3d 299 (9th Cir. 2016) Do you think the U.S. Supreme Court should review that decision?

The relationship between the rights of free speech—as well as the freedom of assembly, privacy, and religion—and criminal laws is very important but very complicated. In this chapter we learn about the extent to which governments can pass laws that make certain kinds of speech or assembly a crime, or criminal laws that invade a person's rights of privacy or religion. Also discussed are many of the limits placed on such criminal laws by the U.S. Constitution.

Crimes such as those against the person, or against property rights, rarely present conflicts with other private or public goals. That is, there generally is no accepted policy or goal that is advanced by assaulting an innocent person or stealing his or her property. That is not the case with many of the crimes presented in this chapter. Some of them involve the written or spoken word, and thus raise First Amendment issues. Others are "public order crimes"—that is, violations of criminal statutes or ordinances that seek to maintain public order by regulating the activities of persons on public streets and property and that rub against the freedom of movement. This chapter examines the power of government to use the criminal laws to regulate these activities, and the limitations placed on that power by the U.S. Constitution.

BELIEF—SPEECH—ACTION: WHEN SPEECH MAY BE REGULATED

The First Amendment of the U.S. Constitution provides that "Congress shall make no law ... abridging the freedom of speech, or of the press." Courts have repeatedly pointed out that "freedom to speak one's mind is not only an aspect of individual liberty—and thus a good unto itself—but also is essential to the common quest for truth and the vitality of society as a whole."[1]

Human communications take many forms. Pure speech includes words spoken face to face or through one of the many media. Written communication includes books, magazines, newspapers, billboards, bumper stickers, and so on. Picketing, protest marches, and boycotts are also forms of communication. Symbolic speech such as uniforms, religious garb, black armbands, and hand gestures express messages and ideas and are protected by the First Amendment.

Speech and other forms of communication are not absolute rights, as they can seriously clash with the rights of others and the need for public order. The U.S. Supreme Court has pointed out that such regulation is necessary or the freedoms of an organized society could be "lost in the excesses of unrestrained abuse."[2]

In creating the "narrowly limited classes of speech" that can be forbidden and punished, the U.S. Supreme Court has repeatedly stated that "the line between speech unconditionally guaranteed and speech which may be regulated, suppressed, or punished is *finely drawn.*"[3] *The following are five categories of speech that the First Amendment does not protect:*

1. Obscenity, which when properly identified can be punished as a crime.

2. Fighting words.

3. Inciting or urging unlawful conduct (including "true" threats that clearly and unequivocally threaten the life or safety of another person).

4. Defamation (libel or slander).

5. Public nuisances, which require a "showing that substantial privacy interests are being invaded in an essentially intolerable manner"[4] (for example, loud noises in the middle of the night while others are sleeping).

Criminal statutes that have some effect on speech raise First Amendment issues. Generally speaking, if a statute is directed at the *content* of the speech (e.g., banning a book, a film, or a photograph), the statute is presumptively invalid under the First Amendment, and subject to strict scrutiny. Under strict scrutiny, the state must show a "compelling interest" served by the statute, and that the means used to achieve that interest are the "least restrictive" possible.

However, if the statute is "content neutral," it violates the First Amendment only if the government lacks a substantial interest in adopting the statute. For example, so-called adult movies and books generally cannot themselves be outlawed because of the limitations of the obscenity test. A statute banning specific books or videos would be directed at the content of those books or videos, and be subjected to strict scrutiny. However, reasonable regulations on the location or number of adult bookstores or theaters could be content neutral, and not a violation of the owners' First Amendment rights.[5]

THE "CLEAR AND PRESENT DANGER" TEST

"clear and present danger" test One of the tests used to judge government restrictions on speech.

One of the principal tests used to judge government restriction of speech based on its content is the **"clear and present danger" test**. Local, state, and federal governments in the United States cannot forbid or suppress speech and punish the speaker unless the speech is likely to bring harm to people or property. Justice Oliver Wendell Holmes announced the "clear and present danger" doctrine in the 1919 case of *Schenck v. United States:*

> The most stringent protection of free speech would not protect a man in falsely shouting "Fire" in a crowded theater, causing panic. It would not even protect a man from an injunction against uttering words that may have all the effect of force. The question in every case is whether the words are used in such circumstances that are of such a nature as to create a clear and present danger that they will bring about the substantive evils that Congress has a right to protect. It is a question of proximity and degree. When a nation is at war many things that might be said in time of peace are such a hindrance to its efforts that their utterances will not be endured so long as men fight and that no court could regard them as protected by any constitutional right.[6]

Using Justice Holmes's example, one could yell "fire" in an open field or a public park without fear of prosecution, because anyone hearing the words would feel no need for panic. The words would thus not present a "clear and present danger" of harming anyone. On the other hand, communicating a threat to take the life of the president is inherently dangerous, so much so that Congress passed 18 U.S.C. § 871(a), which makes it a federal crime to knowingly threaten the life of the president.[7]

Fighting Words

disorderly conduct
Loud, obnoxious, or other offensive conduct in a public place.

fighting words Speech which, because it will likely incite immediate violence, is not protected by the First Amendment.

All states and cities have enacted laws and ordinances that are aimed at speech or conduct that may cause public disturbances. Called disorderly persons, **disorderly conduct**, breach of the peace, or disturbance of the peace laws, they forbid speech or conduct that either causes a public disorder or tends to cause a public disorder. As a corollary of the "clear and present danger" test, when these laws are applied only to speech, they can be upheld only if the speech qualifies as "fighting words." **Fighting words** are communications that are likely to cause an immediate public disorder or other "breach of the peace" in response to the communication.

In 1942 the U.S. Supreme Court in *Chaplinsky v. New Hampshire* defined *fighting words* as "those words which by their very utterance . . . tend to incite an immediate breach of the peace."[8] Since that case was decided, the Supreme Court has not upheld a conviction based on the "fighting words" doctrine.[9] However, some state courts have done so.

Where a criminal charge is based only on a communication, most courts have applied the "fighting words" doctrine only where the communication is made "face-to-face." Examples of convictions for disorderly conduct or use of abusive language that were reversed include:

State v. Dugan[10] In a 2013 decision, the Montana Supreme Court rejected the government's claim that a telephone call in which the defendant called the woman speaking with him a "f****** c***" constituted fighting words. The court held words spoken over a telephone cannot be fighting words because the person hearing the words can simply hang up the phone and cool off.

State v. Smith, 855 N.W.2d 493 (Wis. App. 2014); Defendant was convicted of disorderly conduct based on a posting by him on a village police department's official Facebook page that said, in part, the police were "f****** racist basturds (sic)." On appeal the court reversed the conviction because it was not made face-to-face. It rejected the state's argument that the words, directed at the police in a racially-charged environment, might cause others to breach the peace. Inciting violence is not protected by the First Amendment, the court said, but it must be shown the language was urging immediate violence. That was not shown, the court said.

State v. Drahota[11] The Nebraska Supreme Court reversed a conviction for breach of the peace based on e-mails sent by the defendant to a former teacher that called the teacher a "traitor" and "Al Qaeda sympathizer."

When Does Vulgar, Insulting Language to a Police Officer Constitute Fighting Words?

Many state courts have imposed higher standards for "fighting words" directed at police officers, reasoning that police officers are expected to exercise greater

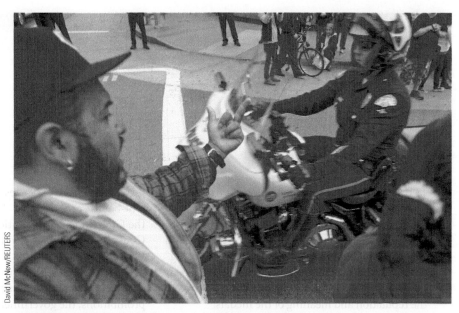

David McNew/REUTERS

While obscene gestures like the one pictured here are vulgar and in bad taste, rarely do gestures alone result in arrests or prosecutions. Such gestures are not generally seen as "fighting words."

restraint when foul, insulting language is directed toward them. After reviewing hundreds of state cases, the *FBI Law Enforcement Bulletin*[12] listed the following generally accepted concepts to assist law enforcement officers in deciding whether to arrest for speech directed at them:

1. Direct threats to the safety of an officer "generally constitute 'fighting words' unprotected by the first amendment." However, if the speech falls short of a direct, outright threat and is only harassing and nasty, state courts have held that such communications do not fall under the threat exception.

2. When a crowd is present and the *speech is likely to incite the crowd* (or some of the people in the crowd) to violence, state courts will hold that such speech is not constitutionally protected.

3. Speech that obstructs and hinders police in the performance of their duty generally has been held to justify an arrest. Probably all states have codified the common law crime of obstructing and hindering police officers in the performance of their public duty. However, state statutes vary considerably in defining the crime of obstruction. A few states limit the crime to "resisting." Other states use the words *resist, obstruct,* or *oppose,* and still other states use *resist, obstruct,* or *abuse.*

The following four cases all involved convictions based only on words spoken to a police officer, and no physical confrontation. Two convictions were upheld on appeal and two were not.

CASE CLOSE-UP

United States v. Alvarez

Supreme Court of the United States,
132 S. Ct. 2537 (2012)

18 U.S.C. § 704(b), The Stolen Valor Act (the "Act"), was enacted by Congress in 2006. Senate and House Reports supporting the adoption of the statute stated that fraudulent claims about military medals and decorations damaged the "reputation and meaning" of the decorations, and that legislative action was needed to permit law enforcement officers to protect the reputation and meaning of the medals.

In 2007 Xavier Alvarez attended his first meeting of a water commission in California, to which he had just been elected. At that meeting, he publicly stated he had been awarded the Congressional Medal of Honor in 1987. This claim was quickly discovered to be false, and Alvarez was indicted and charged with violating the Stolen Valor Act. He pled guilty in the district court, but reserved the right to appeal his conviction based on his claim that the Act violated the First Amendment. The Ninth Circuit Court of Appeals agreed with him, and reversed his conviction. In part because another federal court of appeals subsequently upheld the Act in a similar case, the Supreme Court agreed to review the *Alvarez* decision.

The first words of the Supreme Court's opinion (there was no consensus majority opinion; six justices believed the Act was unconstitutional, but only four joined in the opinion written by Justice Kennedy) disclosed the Court's view of the defendant's conduct: "Lying was his habit," referring to other brazen lies told by the defendant, such as that he played hockey with the Detroit Red Wings. However, the Court said, that did not end the inquiry.

Because the Act was directed to the content of the defendant's false statements, the Court said it must meet the strict tests used to uphold content-based prohibitions. It specifically rejected the Government's contentions on this point: "The Court has never endorsed the categorical rule the Government advances: that false statements receive no First Amendment protection."

Under strict scrutiny applied to content-based prohibitions, the government must show a compelling reason for the statute, and that it is not overly restrictive of speech. The Court held that while the goal of the statute in upholding the importance and meaning of military decorations was clearly appropriate, the government made no showing the outright prohibition of speech was necessary to achieve that goal. The Court noted that within days of the defendant's false statement the local press uncovered his lie, and publicly condemned him as contemptible. This public condemnation protected the medal's reputation, the Court said: "The remedy for speech that is false is speech that is true."

The Court also found the statute to have an improper "chilling effect" on speech, since on its terms it applied to false statements "whether shouted from the rooftops or made in a barely audible whisper." The Court feared that giving such authority to the government would lead to a long list of subjects about which a false statement would lead to criminal sanctions. Such a result, the Court said, was exactly the "chill" the First Amendment was designed to avoid.

Finally, the Court did say that the decision placed no limits on prohibiting false statements designed to commit fraud or secure illegal ends. In those cases it is not the speech that is prohibited but the speech's illegal purpose.

Convictions Upheld

- Defendant was attempting to enter an anti-immigration rally. Because of the expected large crowds, police had posted "no parking" notices in some areas. The defendant parked in such an area, and when told to leave called the African-American police officer a "n-----" and engaged in loud and abusive language. His conviction for disorderly conduct was affirmed. *State v. Mitchell*, 343 S.W.3d 381 (Tenn. 2011), *cert. denied*, 132 S. Ct. 244 (2011).
- Defendant was crossing a crowded street at midnight. The defendant called a police officer sitting in a nearby parked car a "f------ pig." After the defendant finished crossing the street, the officer went to the defendant and asked what the problem was. The defendant said "f---off asshole." Police arrested the defendant and he was convicted of disturbing the peace. His conviction was affirmed, the court holding the words were "fighting words" and not protected speech. *State v. Robinson*, 82 P.3d 27 (Mont. 2003), *cert. denied*, 541 U.S. 1037 (2004).

Convictions Overturned

- A police officer sitting in his police vehicle saw a woman videotaping him. The officer ran a license check on an automobile next to the woman, and then exited his vehicle to ask her who owned the car. She stated her grandfather owned the car. The officer returned to his vehicle, and the defendant approached its passenger-side open window and asked why the officer ran the license check. The officer said he "could run a check if he wanted to," and the defendant walked away, hurling profanities at the officer. The officer exited his vehicle and arrested the defendant for disorderly conduct. A resulting search uncovered crack cocaine in the defendant's pocket. He was convicted of possession of cocaine and disorderly conduct.

On appeal, the court reversed both convictions. It held the abusive language was not accompanied by any threat of "public harm," and did not put the officer in any fear for his safety. Moreover, the court said, the officer was trained to deal with emotional situations such as this and was expected to respond with reserve. The disorderly conduct charge was reversed, and because the search that uncovered the cocaine was the result of an improper arrest, the cocaine should not have been admitted at the defendant's trial. *People v. Baker*, 984 N.E.2d 902 (NY 2013).

- National Park Service rangers were attempting to arrest a suspect in Yosemite National Park. A crowd gathered, and hurled insults at the rangers. The defendant, when told to disperse, said "f--- you" and refused to leave the area. The next day he was arrested and charged with violation of the federal disorderly conduct statute. He was convicted and appealed. The Ninth Circuit Court of Appeals reversed the conviction for disorderly conduct, holding the words were not "fighting words," nor were they likely to incite the crowd to violence. *United States v. Poocha*, 259 F.3d 1077 (9th Cir. 2001).

OBSCENE COMMUNICATIONS

Obscenity is not protected by the First Amendment and may be forbidden by government. Defining obscenity, however, has been the subject of many court

obscenity
Communication that the average person, using contemporary community standards, would find appeals to the prurient interests or depicts sexual conduct in a patently offensive manner and, taken as a whole, lacks serious artistic, literary, political, or scientific value.

VERBAL OFFENSES

Type of Verbal Offense	To Constitute the Verbal Offense, There Must Be
Fighting words[a]	1. Insulting or abusive language 2. Addressed to a person face to face 3. Causing a likelihood that "the person addressed will make an immediate violent response"
Obscenity	1. A communication that, taken as a whole, appeals to the prurient (lustful) interest in sex 2. And portrays sexual conduct in a patently offensive way 3. And the communication, taken as a whole, does not have serious literary, artistic, political, or scientific value
Inciting or urging unlawful conduct	1. Language or communication directed toward inciting, producing, or urging 2. Imminent lawless action or conduct, or 3. Language or communication likely to incite or produce such unlawful conduct
Obstruction of a law enforcement officer or of justice	1. Deliberate and intentional language (or other communication) that hinders, obstructs, delays, or makes more difficult 2. A law enforcement officer's effort to perform his or her official duties (the scienter element of knowledge by the defendant that he or she knew the person obstructed was a law enforcement officer is required) 3. Some states require that "the interference would have to be, in part at least, physical in nature" (see the New York case of *People v. Case*)
Abusive, obscene, or harassing telephone calls	1. Evidence showing that the telephone call was deliberate 2. And made with intent to harass, frighten, or abuse another person 3. And any other requirement of the particular statute or ordinance
Loud speech and loud noise	1. Cities and states may: 2. Forbid speech and noises meant by the volume to disturb others, and 3. Forbid noise and loud speech that create a clear and present danger of violence

[a]Many state courts apply a higher fighting words standard to law enforcement officers.

rulings and debates. The U.S. Supreme Court established the following guidelines for American courts to define obscenity in the famous case of *Miller v. California*[13]:

- Whether "the average person applying contemporary community standards" would find that the work, taken as a whole, appeals to the prurient interest.[14]
- Whether the work or communication depicts or describes, in a patently offensive way, sexual conduct specifically defined by the applicable state law.
- Whether the work or communication, taken as a whole, lacks serious literary, artistic, political, or scientific value.

INCITING AND URGING UNLAWFUL ACTS

inciting The offense of urging another to commit an unlawful act.

Inciting or urging another person to commit a crime or perform an unlawful act was a misdemeanor at common law. The offense is committed even though another person does not commit the suggested act. The First Amendment does not protect speech and other forms of communication that encourage others to commit crimes. To be unlawful, the speech or other communication must be "directed to inciting or producing *imminent* lawless action and [must be] likely to produce such action."[15]

The U.S. Supreme Court cases of *Hess v. Indiana*[16] and *Brandenberg v. Ohio*[17] involved convictions for inciting violence based on statements to crowds that seemed to urge others to commit violent acts ("we'll take the f------ streets later"; "there might have to be some revenge taken"). The U.S. Supreme Court held that the words of the defendants in both cases did not urge imminent (immediate) lawless action, and therefore neither defendant could be convicted of disorderly conduct or inciting. In neither case did the words of the defendant constitute a clear and present danger.

Defamation: Libel and Slander

The crime and the civil offense of defamation go back more than 700 years in the law. As early as 1275, the English Parliament enacted a libel statute that forbade false news and tales. The colonies and the original thirteen states undoubtedly all had laws concerning libel and slander. Over the years, the laws of England and the United States developed into the libel, slander, and defamation laws of today.

defamation The offense of injuring the character or reputation of another by oral or written communication of false statements. Defamation consists of libel (written offense) or slander (oral offense).

Defamation is the offense of injuring the character or reputation of another by oral or written communication of false statements. Defamation consists of the twin offenses of *libel* and *slander*. Libel is generally a written offense, whereas slander is generally an oral offense. Although most states probably have one or more criminal defamation or libel statutes, charges under these statutes are rarely filed, in part because of the First Amendment conflicts and the Supreme Court's decision in *Garrison v. Louisiana*,[18] which struck down a Louisiana criminal libel statute as unconstitutional. A recent case illustrates some aspects of the problems with filing criminal libel prosecutions.

Colorado has a criminal libel statute, Colo. Rev. Stat. § 18-13-105, which makes it a class 6 felony to utter false statements about a person with the intent to damage his reputation or hold the person up to public ridicule or contempt. In *Mink v. Suthers*,[19] a college student was arrested based on a complaint that the student had violated this statute by publishing rude and false stories about a professor in the student's Internet magazine. Because of First Amendment concerns, the state prosecutor decided not to prosecute the student, although the prosecutor did authorize the issuance of a search warrant. The Court of Appeals upheld the student's right to bring a case for damages against the district attorney for her decision to authorize a search warrant to seize the student's computer.

States have sometimes repealed criminal libel statutes after a court has found the statute to be overbroad. In *Parmelee v. O'Neil,* 186 P.3d 1090 (Wash. App. 2008), a court of appeals held the Washington Criminal Libel statute, RCW p.58.010, unconstitutional as overbroad and a violation of the First Amendment. In 2009 the Washington legislature repealed the statute.

As stated earlier, the "fighting words" doctrine is primarily limited to face-to-face confrontations involving a communication that either causes violence or tends to cause a violent reaction by the person to whom the words are addressed. The law of defamation requires that the communication be made to people other than the victim and that the victim's reputation be lowered in the esteem of any substantial and respectable group. It is possible that words spoken could be not only fighting words but also the basis for civil libel and slander suits.

Law enforcement officers and other public officials carry a heavier burden if they file a lawsuit for defamation. Law enforcement officers have been defined by case law as public officials. To succeed as plaintiffs in a defamation proceeding, as public officials they must plead and prove that the person or newspaper publishing the defamation did so with a reckless disregard as to the truth or falsity of the statements.[20]

SYMBOLIC SPEECH AND THE FIRST AMENDMENT

Symbols, along with gestures, conduct, and speech, have always been used to communicate between human beings. The symbol can be used alone or with other forms of communication.

Uniforms and the way people dress are types of symbols. People often communicate by their dress who they are, what their lifestyles are, and, to some extent, what they think and believe. The following seminal **symbolic speech** case came before the Supreme Court in 1969.

symbolic speech
Nonverbal expressions that convey a belief or idea.

During the Vietnam War, a group of Iowa students wished to communicate their opposition to the war by wearing black armbands in school. However, the high school principal forbade the armbands, which led to the lawsuit *Tinker v. Des Moines Independent Community School District.*[21] Because the black armbands did not disrupt classes or school, the U.S. Supreme Court in *Tinker* sustained the students' action, holding

> The wearing of an armband … was closely akin to pure speech, which we have repeatedly held is entitled to comprehensive protection under the First Amendment. Students or teachers [do not] shed their constitutional rights of freedom of speech or expression at the schoolhouse gate.

Flag Burning and Cross Burning as Symbolic Speech

Flags are symbols. The American flag has symbolic meanings that are cherished by most Americans. This, however, has sometimes caused protesters and demonstrators seeking to make a political statement to burn or otherwise defile an American flag in an attempt to communicate the message.

In past years, states had statutes that made this type of defilement of the American flag a crime. If the demonstrators burned their own flag as a means to communicate a political message, the symbolic act was held to have the protection of the First Amendment in the two U.S. Supreme Court cases of *Texas v. Johnson,*[22] and *United States v. Eichman.*[23]

In response to the Supreme Court's decision in *Texas v. Johnson*, the Texas legislature passed a new flag-destruction law that was limited to actual physical destruction of the national or Texas state flag. The statute only applied to flags that could be flown on a staff, and specifically exempted flags on clothing or on a document like a poster. In a 2015 decision, the Texas Court of Criminal Appeals overturned a conviction for flag destruction under this statute, holding that it violated the First Amendment because it still permitted prosecution for flag destruction made as "expressive conduct." *State v. Johnson*, 475 S.W.3d 80 (Tex. App. 2015).

Cross burning can also be a symbolic act that seeks to communicate a message, and therefore it can also have First Amendment protection. A statute that prohibited all forms of cross burning would be unconstitutional. In the case of *R.A.V. v. St.*

 ## FIRST AMENDMENT, OVERBREADTH, AND "CRUSH VIDEOS"

In *United States v. Stevens* 130 S. Ct. 1577 (2010) the defendant was charged with violation of 18 U.S.C. § 48, which makes it a crime for anyone who knowingly "creates, sells, or possesses a depiction of animal cruelty" if done for commercial gain. A depiction of animal cruelty is defined in the act as one "in which a living animal is intentionally maimed, mutilated, tortured, wounded, or killed" if the act violates state or federal law. The legislative history of the statute makes it clear Congress was intending to punish those who create, sell or possess so-called "crush videos," where women are filmed while crushing small animals such as cats, monkeys, or mice with either their bare feet or wearing high heels. Such videos were often accompanied by the sounds of anguish emitted by the animals, or dominatrix patter by the women.

Stevens was convicted of violating § 48 based on sales he made of videos showing pit bull dogfights, and attacks made by pit bulls on other animals. The trial court dismissed Stevens's claim that the statute violated the First Amendment, holding that depictions defined in § 48, just as in the case of child pornography and obscenity, were not protected by the First Amendment. On appeal, the Third Circuit Court of Appeals reversed the conviction, holding that the conduct covered by § 48 was covered by the First Amendment.

On appeal, the Supreme Court affirmed. It rejected the government's argument that animal cruelty depictions should be treated the same as child pornography, and not protected by the First Amendment. (See Chapter 12.) The Court decided the case based on the "overbreadth" doctrine. The Court stated that Stevens's objection to the statute was based on its "facial" overbreadth, that is, that the statute as written can be applied to conduct that is clearly lawful and ordinary, and by making such conduct a crime violates the overbreadth doctrine. The Court agreed, noting that under the statute a depiction of any "killing" or "wounding" of an animal would be a violation, so long as the conduct was unlawful in the state where the sale or possession of the depiction occurred. The statute does not require that such "killing" or "wounding" be done cruelly. As a result, the Court said, the statute would make criminal the "humane slaughter" of a stolen cow, or a video depicting killing an animal during recreational hunting that was legal in the state where the killing occurred, but illegal where the depiction was sold or possessed.

In response to the decision in *Stevens* Congress amended the statute to make it a crime to create or distribute an "animal crush video." That was defined as any depiction of any "nonhuman" animal actually being crushed, burned or otherwise seriously injured, and is obscene. In *United States v. Richards*, 755 F.3d 269 (3rd Cir. 2014) the court upheld the conviction of defendants who filmed a woman mutilating kittens and a puppy while scantily clad and making obscene statements. The court said those limitations in the statute cured the overbreadth problem in its predecessor. The U. S. Supreme Court denied certiorari, 135 S. Ct. 1547 (2015).

Paul, Minnesota, the U.S. Supreme Court struck down a St. Paul ordinance making it a crime to burn a cross[24] with an intent to communicate a hate message. The Court found the ordinance invalid because the ordinance forbade the symbolic conduct "based on its [the ordinance's] hostility to the underlying (hate) message."

However, in the case of *Virginia v. Black,*[25] 538 U.S. 343 (2003), a majority of the U.S. Supreme Court held that a Virginia statute that made it criminal to burn a cross on public property or property of another "with the intent of intimidating any person or group of persons" was not unconstitutional on its face. The Court distinguished *R.A.V.* because there the focus of the ban on cross burning was the content of the message intended to be communicated by the burning. In *Black* the ban on cross burning focused on the intended intimidating effect the burning had on people, regardless of the content of the message the cross burners intended. Taking action, even though it might involve symbolic speech, with the intent to intimidate another is not a protected activity. The Court also concluded, however, that the Virginia statute was unconstitutional as applied, because the statute contained a provision that made burning a cross prima facie evidence of an intent to intimidate another person. This provision, the Court said, invites a jury to punish based solely on the fact of the cross burning, without specifically finding an intent to intimidate.

THREATS OF VIOLENCE AS CRIMES

A threat becomes a crime if it is explicit and likely to result in imminent lawless action. Threats can be charged as various crimes, such as disorderly conduct, inciting violence, or even racketeering if made repeatedly (see Chapter 18). If accompanied by "physical menace," the Model Penal Code, Section 211.1(l)(c), makes **threats of violence** an assault.

threats of violence
Statements or actions that unequivocally convey the message that violent actions will be taken.

Many states have specific statutes making "terroristic threats" a crime.[26] The First Amendment provides no protection for threats of violence because the purpose of the speech is not to communicate ideas but to put another person in fear of imminent physical harm.

true threat A serious expression of an intent to inflict bodily harm.

In the following examples courts considered if speech was a **true threat** and not protected by the First Amendment, or protected speech:

- *Threats against public officials:* In particular, threats against the president of the United States. Such threats are a violation of federal law (18 U.S.C § 871). That statute requires only that the threat be made, and does not require proof that the defendant had the ability or intent to carry out the threat. In the 2013 case of *United States v. Turner,* a federal court of appeals held that blog postings advocating the murder of federal judges were not protected speech.[27] Most states have laws making it a crime to threaten a state official, and require proof similar to the federal statute. In *Abbott v. State,* 989 A.2d 795 (Md. App. 2010), the court reversed a conviction under Md. C. L. § 3-708, threats against public officials. The defendant sent a threatening e-mail to the website maintained by the governor of Maryland, which solicited comments from citizens. The court found that the trial court did not properly instruct the jury on whether a reasonable person would have believed the threat was serious.
- *Threats by schoolchildren against teachers or other students:* Because of the number of school killings in recent years, officials have begun taking students' threats very seriously. However, to be the basis of a criminal conviction (as opposed to

school discipline), the threat must be a "true threat." In *In re Douglas D.,*[28] the Wisconsin Supreme Court overturned the conviction of a high school student under Wisconsin's disorderly conduct statute. The student wrote an essay in class in which the main character (clearly the student) stated he would come to school the next day and cut off the teacher's head. The court held the essay was not a true threat, because the student could not reasonably understand that a reasonable person would view the statement as a serious expression of intent to inflict bodily harm, which is the definition of a "true threat."

- In *Fogel v. Collins,* 531 F.3d 824 (9th Cir. 2009) the court held that painting a sign on the back of a van that said "I am a f——g suicide bomber communist terrorist" was not a true threat, and thus was protected speech. The court stated that a reasonable person viewing the van, which was covered with clearly political statements, would not find the "threat" to be a serious expression of intent to inflict bodily harm.

- *Terrorist threats:* Since the events of September 11, 2001, state and federal governments take terrorist threats seriously. The Model Penal Code, Section 211.3, makes it a third-degree felony to make threats designed to cause the evacuation of public buildings or public conveyances. Many states have also passed "false bomb report" laws, which make it a crime to give a false statement to a police officer or airline employee about concealing a bomb. In *Levin v. United Airlines,*[29] the court held that Cal. Penal Code § 148.1 was constitutional and required only that a person making a false statement about a concealed bomb do so knowing the statement was false. The court stated that "true threat" rules did not apply, because the statute was not directed to the content of the statement, but simply made the *act* of making the false statement a crime. The statute in effect was a codification of Justice Holmes's famous example of yelling "fire" in a crowded theater, the court said.

- *Violations of restraining orders:* Restraining orders directed against former spouses, boyfriends, girlfriends, and family members are routinely issued in an attempt to prevent violence and harassment. Violation of a restraining order can subject the violator to a contempt charge or other criminal liability. In *Cobble v. State,*[30] a defendant was convicted under the Georgia terroristic threat statute when he stood outside his former girlfriend's house and yelled obscenities directed at her. When the police arrived and subdued him, the defendant stated that as soon as he was released, he would return and kill the girlfriend. Even though the girlfriend did not hear those threats, the court found the defendant guilty under the terroristic threat statute.

Using the U.S. Mail, Telephones, the Internet, or E-Mail to Threaten Another Person

Whether speech constitutes a threat is usually a question of state law. However, when the threat is made by U.S. mail, telephones, the Internet, or other interstate communication devices, the threat can also result in a federal charge. Such threats include the following:

Telephone threats   The defendant, a member of the White Aryan Peoples Party, was convicted in 2004 of knowingly transmitting a threat in interstate commerce when he telephoned three synagogues and left a threatening voicemail message: "We're going to blow up your f------ synagogue this coming week and send you f-----s to the gas chambers." He was convicted of three counts of violating 18 U.S.C. § 844(e).[31]

U.S. Mail threats   In 2006 two defendants were convicted of violating 18 U.S.C. § 876 by mailing threatening communications to judges hearing litigation claims the defendants were asserting in the judges' courts. The letters sent included references to Judge Joan Lefkow, a judge whose family had been murdered by a disgruntled litigant, with the note "Be Aware Be Fair." The court of appeals affirmed the conviction, rejecting defendants' claim that they did not intend to threaten the judges. The court said that the statute does not require the government to prove intent, only that the letter was threatening, and that it was sent knowingly.[32]

E-mail and Internet threats   Using e-mail or the Internet to express a threat of violence is also a federal crime. In 2012 a defendant was convicted of violating 18 U.S.C. § 875(c) by posting a music video on YouTube and a Facebook link. The video was addressed to the judge hearing a child custody case in which the defendant was involved. The video's lyrics included the words "Take my child and I'll take your life." The appeals court affirmed the defendant's conviction, rejecting his claim that he didn't really mean the words. The court said the statute does not have a subjective intent requirement; all the government had to prove is that a reasonable observer would regard the video as a true threat.[33]

Many states have passed statutes making it a crime to use e-mails or the Internet to harass a person. In *Massimo v. State*,[34] a defendant was convicted of violation of Texas Penal Code Section 42.07(a)(2), unlawful harassment by electronic communication, when she sent repeated e-mails to a former friend threatening to kill her and her children.

Bullying: Not a Crime, but It Can Consist of Criminal Conduct

In 2010 the State of New York became the forty-third state to enact an "anti-bullying" law. This law requires schools to ban bullying practices, train their staffs to combat bullying, and to formulate anti-bullying programs. While bullying itself is not a crime, the conduct associated with bullying can be criminal.

The U.S. Department of Justice, Office of Community Oriented Policing Services (COPS), defines bullying as having two components:

1. Repeated harmful acts which involve physical, verbal, or psychological attacks of intimidation
2. Directed against victims who cannot properly defend themselves because of size or strength, or because they are outnumbered or less psychologically resilient.

The director of COPS stated that while bullying was once viewed as harmless adolescent behavior, it is now known that bullying can have a long-term effect on both the bully and the victim, and can lead to other forms of violence. The increased use of the Internet has also created cyberbullying, which can exacerbate consequences. In the legislative history to § 814, McKinney's New York Education Statutes (2008), the New York legislature cited a U.S. Department of Justice survey that found one

CRIMINAL THREATS, HARASSMENT, AND SOCIAL MEDIA

The federal government and all states have statutes making threats of violence and certain kinds of harassment crimes. Increasingly, people are using social media like Facebook or Craigslist as a medium to make threats or to harass others. As a result, prosecutions for such use of social media have increased. The following examples illustrate some of the issues that arise in the use of social media for these purposes:

Elonis v. United States, 135 S. Ct. 2001 (2015): As discussed in Chapter 3, in this case the U. S. Supreme Court said that a conviction under a federal statute for posting threatening comments on social media required proof that the defendant either intended to make a threat of violence, or knew the communication would be understood as a threat of violence or physical harm.

Commonwealth v. Johnson, 21 N.E.3d 937 (Mass. 2014): Conviction for criminal harassment through cyber harassment affirmed. Defendants caused false information to be posted on Craigslist on multiple occasions in order to harass a neighbor. They also had another person file a false report of child abuse by the neighbor to a child abuse hotline. The court said the defendants intended to harass the victims, and thus their speech was an integral part of their intended acts, and not protected.

United States v. Sayer, 748 F.3d 425 (1st Cir. 2014): Over a period of years the defendant, after the victim ended her relationship with him, posted sexually revealing online videos and photographs of the victim, with statements that the victim was interested in meeting sexual partners. After countless strangers arrived at her address (even after she moved her residence to another state) defendant was charged and convicted under the federal cyberstalking statute, 18 U.S.C. § 2261A. On appeal the court rejected the defendant's First Amendment claims, stating his actions intentionally caused "substantial emotional distress" as defined in the cyberstalking statute. Speech intended to have a criminal effect is not protected by the First Amendment, the court said.

State v. Craig, 112 A.3d 559 (N.H. 2015): Defendant posted messages to the victim on defendant's public Facebook page. Earlier, the victim had obtained a "no contact" order against the defendant. Many of the messages posted contained threatening language directed to the victim. The victim was not a "friend" on the defendant's Facebook page, but learned of the threatening messages only after she looked for them on his page. The defendant was convicted of criminal threatening and stalking. On appeal the court rejected the defendant's argument that his messages were protected speech, because not directly addressed to the victim. The court said the defendant knew and intended that the victim would search his Facebook page for her own safety and protection.

United States v. Wheeler, 776 F.3d 736 (10th Cir. 2015): Defendant, while vacationing in Italy, posted various messages on his Facebook page addressed to his "religious followers," instructing them to "kill cops" and "drown them in the blood of thier (sic) children." Defendant had no religious followers, and stated he thought he had deleted all his "friends" from his Facebook account. The court of appeals said that the defendant could be convicted under the federal threat statute if it was proved a reasonable person would believe the posts were intended to be acted upon by persons reading the posts, even if those persons did not in fact exist. (The defendant's conviction was reversed for a new trial based on faulty jury instructions on the requisite intent needed for conviction under the federal threat statute. The *Elonis* decision now requires proof that the defendant either intended to issue a threat, or knew the communication would be understood as a threat by those who get the communication.)

out of every five children ages 10 to 17 received sexual exploitation advances over the Internet. The survey also quoted findings by I-SAFE, a non-profit youth Internet safety organization, that 42 percent of children using the Internet have been subjected to bullying when online.

Municipal and county law enforcement offices regularly respond to calls from local schools, and they often place officers within schools to monitor student conduct and enforce state laws. Under the U.S. Supreme Court ruling in *Tinker v. Des Moines School District,* discussed in this chapter, schools may impose discipline on students when the student's speech or conduct, including bullying behavior, substantially interferes with the school's educational mission. However, schools cannot control the bullying that occurs outside of school, or on the Internet.

The consequences of a combination of in-school bullying and Internet harassment can be deadly. On January 14, 2010, Phoebe Prince, a 15-year-old student at South Hadley (Massachusetts) High School, hanged herself after months of bullying at school and over the Internet. Five of her classmates pled guilty to criminal harassment, and received sentences of probation and community service. In March 2010 Alexis Skye Pilkington, a 17-year-old Long Island, N.Y. high school student, killed herself after receiving vicious attacks on the social networking website FormSpring. me. In April of 2016 Aileen Jiminian, a 17-year-old student at Manhattan Village Academy in New York, left school at the lunch hour and jumped in front of a subway train. Students at her school said Aileen was the victim of extensive bullying.

Additional material on bullying in schools can be found on the U.S. Department of Justice COPS website at http://cops.usdoj.gov.

LOUD NOISE OR NUISANCE SPEECH

The U.S. Supreme Court has stated that "it can no longer be doubted that government has a substantial interest in protecting its citizens from unwelcome noise" in *Ward v. Rock Against Racism.*[35] The *Ward* case upheld a New York City regulation that gave city officials broad authority to regulate sounds from Central Park performances.

City ordinances regulating private parties often present both First Amendment and overbreadth problems. In the 2011 case of *U.R.I. Students v. Town of Narragansett*[36] a federal court of appeals upheld a town ordinance that imposed criminal penalties on owners and users of private property where loud or drunken parties were held. Students at the nearby University of Rhode Island often rented housing in Narragansett, and then had loud parties. The city council passed an ordinance that provided that once a property had been "posted" for a loud gathering, a subsequent "loud gathering" on the property was a crime punishable by a fine. The landowners and student renters claimed the ordinance violated their First Amendment and due process rights, but the court of appeals disagreed. It said the ordinance was valid because it required as a precondition to liability a showing that persons at a gathering had violated some other law, such as public intoxication or public urination.

In *Kovacs v. Cooper,* the U.S. Supreme Court upheld a city ordinance that prohibited the use of sound trucks that emitted "loud and raucous" noise on city streets:

City streets are recognized as a normal place for the exchange of ideas by speech or paper. But this does not mean the freedom is beyond all control. We think it is a permissible exercise of legislative discretion to bar sound trucks with broadcasts of public interest, amplified to a loud and raucous volume, from the public ways of municipalities.[37]

REGULATING THE USE OF PUBLIC AND PRIVATE PLACES

The First Amendment guarantees "the right of the people peacefully to assemble and to petition the Government for a redress of grievances." First Amendment freedoms and the rights of expression in public places, however, are not absolute. They may be limited or restricted in order to insure public safety and order. Figure 9.1 illustrates the balance that must be maintained between First Amendment freedoms and public welfare.

When a city, state, or federal agency restricts or limits conduct, it must show the following:

1. The government has significant interest (or good reason) based on the nature of the property or some other source.

2. The restriction or limitation can be no greater "than is essential to the furtherance of that (substantial) interest." See *United States v. O'Brien.*[38]

3. A government (federal or state) may regulate property "under its control for the use for which it is lawfully dedicated" *Adderley v. Florida,*[39] where defendants trespassed in an area of a jail closed to the public.

4. Where there is communication (for example, yelling at a basketball game in a public arena as distinguished from yelling in a library or during a city council meeting), the U.S. Supreme Court has said, "[T]he crucial question is whether the manner of expression is basically incompatible with the normal activity of a particular place at a particular time." See *Grayned v. City of Rockford.*[40]

Under these guidelines, governments may regulate picketing, whether it be at a city hall, a factory, or an abortion clinic; demonstrations, whether against some government action or in celebration of winning the World Series, parades;[41] and

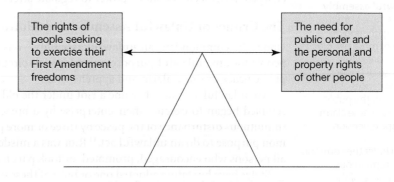

Conflicting rights and needs must be balanced

FIGURE 9.1 Balancing Tests Used by Courts to Determine the Limits of First Amendment Freedoms

PERJURY, SUBORNATION OF PERJURY, AND THE FEDERAL FALSE STATEMENT ACT

The crime of perjury consists of knowingly and materially testifying falsely while under oath. It applies to false statements made under oath to judicial courts, grand juries, or legislative bodies such as the U.S. Congress. The crime of subornation of perjury is committed when a person induces, urges, or knowingly permits another to testify falsely.

People who lie to a federal investigator can be charged with a crime under the Federal False Statement Act, even if they are not under oath. In the case of *Brogan v. United States*,[42] federal investigators from the Labor Department and the Internal Revenue Service asked Brogan during an investigation whether he had received any illegal cash or gifts in the matter they were investigating. Brogan was not in custody, nor did the federal agents intend to take him into custody. But the federal agents did know and had evidence that Brogan had received illegal payments.

When Brogan denied receiving illegal payments and said "no" to the question of the federal investigators, his lie became the basis for federal prosecution under the Federal False Statement Act, which forbids "false, fictitious, or fraudulent statements or representations." Brogan's statement was found to be a deliberate falsehood, and he was convicted of violating the act.

In another case, celebrity Martha Stewart was questioned by federal investigators in regard to her sale of stock just prior to the collapse of the stock's price. Based on her answers, she was charged with the crime of making false statements to the investigators. In 2004, she was convicted of that crime, and sentenced to five months in prison, five months of home confinement, and a $30,000 fine.

In 2011 baseball player Barry Bonds was convicted of obstruction of justice based on false statements he made to a grand jury investigating the use of steroids in professional sports. He was acquitted of a charge of perjury. Bonds was sentenced to 30 days of house arrest, 2 years of probation, and 250 hours of community service. Bonds convictions were overturned on appeal; see Chapter 19.

---

unlawful assembly
Under the common law, a gathering of three or more people for any unlawful purpose or under such circumstances as to endanger the public peace or cause alarm and apprehension.

riot Under the common law, a tumultuous disturbance of the peace by three or more people assembled with a common purpose to do an unlawful act.

door-to-door canvassing and passing out handbills, whether for political or commercial purposes. The next sections in this chapter discuss some of the crimes charged under a city or state's power to regulate streets and public places.

The Crimes of Unlawful Assembly and Rioting

Under the common law, an **unlawful assembly**[43] was a gathering of three or more people for any unlawful purpose or under such circumstances as to endanger the public peace or cause alarm and apprehension.

An unlawful assembly became a **riot** under the old common law when those assembled began to execute their enterprise by a breach of the peace. A riot was a tumultuous disturbance of the peace by three or more people assembled with a common purpose to do an unlawful act.[44] Riot was a misdemeanor at common law, and all persons who encouraged, promoted, or took part in a riot were criminally liable.

States have by statute adopted one or both of these common law crimes. The state of New York, for example, has enacted the following offenses:[45]

- Section 240.10 Unlawful assembly (class B misdemeanor)
- Section 240.08 Inciting to riot (class A misdemeanor)

OBEYING LAWFUL POLICE ORDERS

Failure to obey a lawful, valid police order is punished as an offense in all states. For example, Section 843.02 of the Florida Criminal Code forbids resisting an officer: "Whoever shall obstruct or oppose any such officer … in the execution of legal process or in the lawful execution of any legal duty … shall be guilty of a misdemeanor of the first degree." The following cases illustrate the rule:

Case	Facts of Case	Ruling
City of Oak Creek v. King, Wisconsin Supreme Court, 436 N.W.2d 285 (1989)	When a commercial airline crashed near an airport, the site was sealed off so that emergency equipment and personnel could assist the injured and dying. The defendant and other employees of a newspaper were repeatedly ordered to leave the area, but the defendant wanted to take pictures of the crash site and stated that he would not leave unless he was arrested. The defendant was arrested and convicted of disorderly conduct (not the charge of refusal to obey the police order). The Wisconsin Supreme Court affirmed his conviction and $40 fine.	"We conclude that the appellant's repeated refusal to obey Detective White's reasonable order, combined with his continued penetration into a nonpublic restricted area in the presence of the general public, was conduct of a type which tends to cause or provoke a disturbance, under the circumstances as they then existed. Therefore, we affirm the decision of the circuit court finding the appellant guilty of disorderly conduct."
Georgia v. Storey, Court of Appeals of Georgia, 351 S.E.2d 502, review denied, 107 S. Ct. 1895 (1987)	The defendant and others disrupted the Georgia legislature by shouting opposition to the death penalty. They then refused to obey orders of police and security persons to leave the state capitol building.	Convictions for disrupting the legislature and refusal to obey orders were affirmed, and the U.S. Supreme Court denied review.
State v. Jaramillo, New Mexico Supreme Court, 498 P.2d 687 (1972)	The defendants sat and lay on the floor in the governor's waiting room. They refused to leave when the office closed at 5:00 P.M., and again refused to leave when the building closed at 6:00 P.M. They were convicted under the New Mexico "wrongful use of public property" statute.	The convictions were affirmed, and the statute was held to be constitutional. The court stated: "There is no question but that a State may regulate the use and occupancy of public buildings."
Daniel v. Tampa, Florida, Federal Court of Appeals, 11th Cir., 38 F3d 546, *review denied*, 115 S. Ct. 2557 (1995)	Because of serious crime problems in public housing projects, canvassing was forbidden. Defendant was warned and refused to leave the building. Conviction for trespass was affirmed.	Florida's trespass-after-warning statute was sustained, and because this was a neutral restriction on speech, it was held to be a reasonable means of combating crime in the public housing project. No First Amendment violation occurred.

- Section 240.06 Riot in the first degree (class E felony)
- Section 240.05 Riot in the second degree (class A misdemeanor)

The present federal riot control statute, § 2102, Title 18, United States Code Annotated, provides in part as follows:

> As used in this chapter, the term "riot" means a public disturbance involving (1) an act or acts of violence by one or more persons part of an assemblage of three or more persons, which act or acts shall constitute a clear and present danger of, or shall result in, damage or injury to the property of any other person or to the person of any other individual or (2) a threat or threats of the commission of an act or acts of violence by one or more persons part of an assemblage. . . . where the performance of the threatened act or acts of violence would constitute a clear and present danger of, or would result in, damage or injury to the property of any other person or to the person of any other individual.

In *United States v. Markiewicz*,[46] a federal court of appeals upheld the conviction under the Riot Act of six members of the Oneida Indian tribe. The defendants gathered on tribal lands to confront other tribal members over control of a bingo parlor on tribal property, and subsequently burned down the parlor.

OBSTRUCTION OF THE LAW ENFORCEMENT PROCESS

The crime of obstruction can be committed in many different ways. Failure to identify oneself when there is a legal obligation to do so is a frequent problem. In 2004 the U.S. Supreme Court upheld a state statute that required individuals to identify themselves when they were the subjects of a lawful investigative detention or police stop. There, a police officer who was investigating a report of an assault on a woman asked the suspect, Hiibel, to identify himself eleven times. When Hiibel, who appeared intoxicated, refused to do so, he was arrested and later convicted of the crime of "willfully resisting, delaying, or obstructing a public officer in discharging … any duty of his office." The U.S. Supreme Court held that "stop and identify" laws go back hundreds of years and were a staple of English and American law. In affirming Hiibel's conviction, the Court stated that it had never had an obstruction of justice case come before it in which disclosure of a person's name would violate the Fifth Amendment right to remain silent.[47]

The following are some of the many incidents that could result in a charge of obstruction or other similar crime:

- A witness to a felony or serious accident refusing to identify himself when questioned by the police investigating the crime or accident.
- Making false material statements or providing false information to a law enforcement officer or other investigation (18 U.S.C. § 1038 makes this a federal crime).
- Tampering with a witness, victim, or informant (a federal crime under 18 U.S.C. § 1512).
- Giving false identifying information to an officer that obstructs a computer records search.
- Obstructing a crime scene, such as by destroying evidence (e.g., erasing fingerprints), planting false evidence, or altering evidence to make the incident appear to be an accident.

- Failing to identify a known offender. For example, a Wisconsin attorney had a friend drive her home in her car from a late-night party because she had been drinking. The friend drove the car on a sidewalk, and when police spotted the car, the friend drove off at high speeds to evade arrest, a felony. The friend ultimately ran off, and the attorney refused to identify him. However, when faced with a contempt charge, the attorney identified the driver, who was arrested and convicted of fleeing from the police.

PUBLIC NUISANCES AS CIVIL OR CRIMINAL OFFENSES

Under common law, a public nuisance was a civil offense. More than 200 years ago Blackstone, the famous English lawyer, described *nuisances* as "anything that unlawfully worketh hurt, inconvenience, or damage" (Blackstone 3 *Commentaries,* 216).

Today, cities and states continue to use the civil law of public nuisances to correct problems. By going into a civil court and filing a civil lawsuit, a city can petition the court to declare a public problem to be a nuisance and urge civil remedies. Public nuisance laws have been used to

- Seize and tear down crack houses and property owned by slumlords who allow their properties to be used by gangs or drug dealers.
- Seize and take title to the motor vehicles of people who commit offenses such as having sex with a prostitute on a public street.[48]
- Obtain court orders against repeat offenders, such as people who blocked the entrances to abortion clinics. After some people were arrested more than fifty times, a Wisconsin court issued a court order forbidding this conduct and made violations of the court order punishable by a fine of up to $5,000 and a jail sentence of up to 1 year.
- Obtain court orders against prostitutes with five or more convictions, ordering them not to loiter in specific areas of a city or to flag down cars. Violation of the court order is a much more serious offense than the conviction for prostitution or loitering for the purpose of prostitution and can be punished by a larger fine and longer jail sentences.
- An apartment building, a bar, or other building can be declared a "chronic nuisance" if law officers are repeatedly called to quell a disturbance at the premises. Many ordinances permit the city to bill the owner of the building for the cost of the police calls and other necessary city or county services performed.

THE CRIME OF STALKING AND VIOLATION OF PROTECTIVE ORDERS

stalking A crime involving activities such as spying on the victim, following the victim, or attempting to communicate with the victim through the telephone or mail. Cyberstalking through the Internet is also a crime.

Stalking has become a serious problem in the United States and in Europe. Stalkers have attacked musician John Lennon, tennis star Monica Seles, and some former U.S. presidents. Margaret Mary Ray, the woman who for years stalked TV host David Letterman, committed suicide in 1998 by kneeling in front of a speeding train. Often stalking involves offenders who had a previous relationship with the victim. Stalking has now been made criminal in most states, whether or not the stalker ever commits some other crime against the victim, such as assault or battery. Activities such as spying on the victim, following the victim, or attempting to communicate with the victim through the telephone or mail can be charged as stalking.[49]

Authorities encourage victims to carefully document the stalker's activities, such as in a daily log or journal. This makes it possible for the police to conclude a crime is being committed and gives evidence to the prosecution to satisfy its burden to prove to a court the crime was committed.

The federal government has a general stalking statute, 18 U.S.C. § 2261, which prohibits crossing state lines to intimidate or threaten a person. Part B of the statute applies to cyberstalking, which prohibits using the mail or any computer service, such as the Internet, to place another in fear of his life or serious bodily injury. In the 2010 case of *United States v. Grob*[50] the defendant was convicted under this statute when over the course of several weeks he sent twenty-two e-mails and fifty text messages to a former girlfriend stating he would track her down and make her pay for ending the relationship and having a miscarriage.

State courts have the power to issue protective orders in the appropriate circumstances, such as in a divorce case where one spouse will not leave the other spouse alone. Stalking or harassing a person would be another appropriate situation where a protective order could be obtained. Some states have passed statutes specifically directed at stalking, such as the Kansas Protection from Stalking Act, which permits a person who proves the elements of stalking or harassment set out in the statute to obtain a protective order

In the California case of *People v. Grams*,[51] a court had issued a protective order against Grams. Grams was charged with violating the order by stalking his estranged girlfriend. The California law provided that protective orders remained enforceable, notwithstanding the acts of the parties, until the order was changed by the order of the court. Grams argued that he could be entrapped if his girlfriend invited him over and then called the police. The California appellate court held that the California legislature could reasonably provide that only the court could lift the order, as the victim's consent is often misguided. (For further material on harassment and protective orders, see Chapter 11.)

CRIME ON CITY STREETS

City governments, understandably enough, wish to minimize the amount of street crimes that occur. The use of criminal laws directed at conduct or persons believed to be related to criminal acts is common, but they must be tailored to avoid infringing on individual rights. Some such laws include the following:

- *Anti-cruising laws:* Fines for prohibited cruising—driving cars on designated routes on certain streets during late-night hours—can be as high as $1,000 in some places and may also include short jail sentences. The *Milwaukee Journal Sentinel* reported on April 24, 2007, that the city's new anti-cruising laws resulted in the issuance of 658 tickets and 86 arrests in one weekend. Four shootings occurred on that same weekend.
- *Truancy arrests or detentions:* State laws vary on the treatment of truancy, but in many states authorities are authorized to detain a school-age child not attending school and in some cases obtain criminal convictions of the child's parents.

Enforcement of truancy laws has been shown to cut down on crimes such as burglary, criminal damage to property, theft, and criminal graffiti.

- *Juvenile curfew laws:* Daytime curfew laws are aimed at keeping children in school, while nighttime curfews seek to minimize teen drinking, drug use, fighting, vandalism, and gang activities. Such curfews have generally been upheld if they are not overbroad, that is, written to prohibit conduct that is permitted, like attending school or church events in the evening.

- *Laws directed at homeless persons:* There are close to a million homeless persons on our cities' streets. Some of their conduct can violate criminal laws, such as disorderly conduct, public drinking, and unlawful panhandling. Laws directed specifically at homeless persons—such as prohibitions against sleeping on public streets or parks or in public buildings such as libraries—are generally upheld. (See Chapter 1 for material on homeless persons and status crimes.)

GUN OWNERSHIP AND REGISTRATION LAWS

The federal government, the states, and local governments all have power, to some degree, to regulate the ownership, registration, and use of guns, including through the criminal law. All have done so. For example, 28 U.S.C. § 5841 requires the registration of weapons with silencers, sawed-off shotguns, and similar weapons, on the reasoning that these weapons are much more likely to be involved in crimes than other, more ordinary, guns. Violation of this statute can result in a prison sentence of up to 10 years. California Penal Code § 12280(b) bans ownership of assault weapons. District of Columbia Code § 7-2502.02(a)(4) bars registration of handguns, except by retired D.C. police officers.

Prior to 2008 there was uncertainty in courts and legislatures about the limits, if any, on state or federal power to regulate firearms by the Second Amendment to the U.S. Constitution. That amendment states, "A well regulated Militia, being necessary to the security of a free State, the right of the people to keep and bear arms shall not be infringed." Some regarded this as a private right available to all citizens, while others viewed it as a public right, available only to state governments.

Terry Ashe/The LIFE Images Collection/Getty Images

An AK-47 assault rifle, the weapon of choice for many of the mass killers we identify in this book.

In *District of Columbia v. Heller,* 128 S. Ct. 2783 (2008), the U.S. Supreme Court held that the Second Amendment was a private right, and that as a result the District of Columbia could not ban the home possession or ownership of handguns. The Court stated, however, that the District of Columbia could pass reasonable regulations on firearms, such as barring convicted felons from possessing firearms, or passing laws aimed at controlling the sale of firearms.

In *McDonald v. City of Chicago,* 130 S. Ct. 3020 (2010), the Court held that the Second Amendment applied to the states under the Fourteenth Amendment, because the right to bear arms was "firmly rooted" in our nation's history, and was

 ## YOU BE THE SUPREME COURT JUSTICE

Did Congress intend that a person convicted of reckless domestic violence should be barred from possessing a gun? It is your task to interpret the federal statute as you understand Congressional intent. To see how the Supreme Court decided this case go to 2016 WL 3461559.

You are a U. S. Supreme Court Justice. Earlier in 2015, your Court granted certiorari to review a decision of the First Circuit Court of Appeals, *United States v. Voisine,* 778 F.3d 176 (2015). The conviction was for gun possession by a person convicted of a "misdemeanor crime of domestic violence." 18 U.S.C. § 922 (g) (9)

In 1968 Congress passed legislation making it a federal crime for a person convicted of a felony to possess a gun. In 1996 Congress amended that statute to include gun possession by one who has been convicted of a "misdemeanor crime of domestic violence." A crime qualifies as a crime of domestic violence if it includes the "use of physical force," committed by a parent or current or former spouse of the victim, one who lives with the victim, or has a child with the victim.

In the case before you, the prior conviction (the "predicate" crime) was for a domestic assault under Maine state law. The defendant in that assault conviction got drunk and slapped his girlfriend. Under Maine law, one can be convicted of a domestic assault if one "intentionally, knowingly or recklessly" causes bodily injury or offensive physical conduct. Your Court granted certiorari solely to consider whether a conviction for "recklessly" causing bodily injury or offensive touching in a domestic setting qualified as a predicate crime under the federal statute. 136 S. Ct. 386 (2015)

Last term, in *United States v. Castleman,* 134 S. Ct. 1405 (2014), your Court held that an intentional act of "domestic violence" served as a predicate crime under 922(g) (9), even though the act did not meet the definition of "use of physical force" for purposes of the Armed Career Criminal Act, which also defines prior crimes as those in which the predicate crime involved "use of physical force." Earlier, in *United States v. Johnson,* 130 S. Ct. 1265 (2010), your Court had concluded the term "use of physical force" meant "violent force" under the ACCA. *Castleman* held that a conviction for any intentional "use of physical force," violent or otherwise, qualified as a predicate crime under 922 (g) (9).

The present case asks whether reckless, non-intentional acts constitute "use of physical force" for a prior conviction to be a crime of domestic violence under 922 (g) (9). The Maine statute defines the offense to include reckless injury or offensive conduct.

thus a "fundamental right" made binding on states by the Due Process Clause. The Court struck down a Chicago ordinance that (1) banned possession of a firearm without a registration certificate, and then (2) prohibited virtually all citizens from registering handguns. The *McDonald* Court reiterated the statements in *Heller* that reasonable regulation of gun use and ownership was permitted. Because of its virtual prohibition of gun ownership, the Chicago ordinance was not reasonable, the Court said.

Regulating Guns After *Heller*

The federal government, states, and cities have continued to try to regulate ownership and possession of guns after the *Heller* and *McDonald* cases were decided. Some degree of regulation is permitted, since in both cases the Supreme Court was careful to say the Second Amendment right is not unlimited. Certain aspects of the opinion in *Heller* have served as guidelines for courts considering the constitutionality of gun regulations.

First, the actual holding in *Heller* was this: "We hold that the District's ban on handgun possession *in the home* violates the Second Amendment." (Emphasis added) 554 U.S., at 635. Thus, strictly speaking the decision does not address regulations effective *outside* the home. However, lower courts have noted that the first sentence in the Supreme Court's opinion in *McDonald* was that in *Heller* "[w]e held that the Second Amendment protects the right to keep and bear arms for the purpose of self-defense..." This suggests a broader reach than just possession in the home, they conclude.

Second, while the Court said it was not conducting an "exhaustive analysis" of the Second Amendment right, it made it clear that nothing in its decision should cast doubt on prohibitions such as (1) possession of guns by felons and the mentally ill, (2) carrying guns in "sensitive" places like schools and government buildings, (3) placing conditions on the commercial sale of guns, and (4) possession of "unusual weapons" that are not in common use.

Third, the Court said about gun regulations: "And whatever else it leaves for future evaluation, it surely elevates above all other interests the right of law-abiding responsible citizens to use arms in the defense of hearth and home." 554 U.S., at 635.

The following cases applied *Heller* and the Court's statements set out above to claims that gun regulations violated the Second Amendment that were made after *Heller* and *McDonald* were decided.

- *Moore v. Madigan*, 702 F.3d 933 (7th Cir. 2012). The court held the Second Amendment right extended to ownership and possession of guns outside the home. It also held that the Illinois law that prohibited most persons other than police and security guards from carrying "ready-to-use" firearms violated the Second Amendment, because the law was not based on reasonable limitations that satisfy a legitimate governmental interest.
- *United States v. Masciandaro*, 638 F.3d 458 (4th Cir. 2011), *cert. denied,* 132 S. Ct. 756 (2011). The court upheld a conviction under a federal law that made it a crime to carry a loaded gun in a car in a national park. The court held that outside the home the Second Amendment right is subject to regulation, and

that such regulations were to be judged by "intermediate scrutiny," not strict scrutiny. All the regulation need do is to regulate the use or possession of guns consistent with a legitimate government purpose. Here, the court said, safety of the general public using a national park was sufficient to justify the limit on the defendant's Second Amendment right. The Fourth Circuit reached a similar decision in the 2013 case of *Woollard v. Gallagher*, 712 F.3d 865 (4th Cir. 2013), where it upheld a Maryland regulation that required citizens to show a "good and substantial reason" for a permit to carry a gun in public for personal protection.

- *Kachalasky v. Westchester County, N.Y.*, 701 F.3d 81 (2nd Cir. 2012), *cert. denied* 133 S. Ct. 1806 (2013). The court upheld New York State's requirement that any person seeking a license to carry a handgun must "demonstrate a special need for self-protection distinguishable from that of the general community." The court said that while Second Amendment protections are at "their zenith" within the home, they do extend outside the home. However, outside the home the government may pass reasonable restrictions. Using "intermediate scrutiny," the court said that limiting the right to carry a concealed gun in public to people who have an actual, not speculative, need for self-defense is a reasonable method to achieve the state's legitimate interest in public safety. The U. S. Supreme Court denied certiorari: 1333 S. Ct. 1806 (2013).

- *United States v. Marzzarella*, 614 F.3d 85 (3rd Cir. 2010), *cert. denied* 131 S. Ct. 958 (2011). The court upheld a federal law making it a crime to possess a gun, in or out of a home, with an obliterated serial number. The court said that while the law applied to the defendant's possession of a gun in his home, it did not bar him from possessing *any* gun, as was the case in *Heller*, but only certain kinds of guns. The court said this was not a prohibition of the core right of the Second Amendment. As a result, the court said intermediate scrutiny was appropriate, and agreed that the government's legitimate interest in being able to trace and identify dangerous articles like guns made the law permissible.

- *National Rifle Association of America v. McCraw*, 719 F.3d 338 (5th Cir. 2013). The court upheld a Texas law that barred most persons under the age of 21 from obtaining a concealed handgun permit because age limitations were one of the "longstanding limitations" courts have upheld.

Forty-nine states permit law-abiding residents to carry concealed handguns. Most do so by requiring applicants to obtain permits, though three states allow residents to carry without a permit. Illinois was the only state with a complete ban on ordinary citizens carrying concealed handguns, and that law was struck down in 2012 (see above). The Seventh Circuit Court gave the Illinois legislature until June 2013 to pass a law consistent with the Second Amendment rights. On July 10, 2013, the Illinois legislature overrode the Illinois Governor's veto of legislation permitting ordinary citizens to carry concealed handguns.

Section 922 (g)(9) and the Second Amendment   18 U.S.C. § 922 (g) (1-9) makes it a federal crime for any person falling within the coverage of that section to possess a firearm. It is thus in many cases effectively a lifetime ban on the right of such persons to "bear arms," subject to a very limited right to seek relief from that ban under § 925 (c). The statute pre-dates the decisions in *Heller* and *McDonald*, and after those decisions defendants' contended that the lifetime ban under § 922 (g) violated the Second Amendment. Virtually every court hearing those claims upheld the constitutionality of § 922 (g). Those decisions include:

United States v. Meza-Rodriguez, 798 F.3d 664 (7th Cir. 2015); Second Amendment right to bear arms applies to illegal aliens, but § 922 (g)(5) was a reasonable attempt by Congress to regulate the possession of firearms by people who live outside the law and "are harder to trace," the court held. Other courts have held the Second Amendment is limited to "citizens," which excludes illegal aliens. See *e.g. United States v. Carpio-Leon*, 701 F.3d 974 (4th Cir. 2012), *cert denied* 134 S. Ct. 58 (2013).

Schrader v. Holder, 704 F.3d 980 (D.C. Cir. 2013), *cert denied* 134 S. Ct. 512 (2013); Every court that has addressed the issue has held that § 922 (g) may constitutionally bar convicted felons from firearm possession. See *e.g. United States v. Moore*, 666 F.3d 313 (4th Cir. 2012). As the Supreme Court said in *Heller*, nothing in its decision casts doubt on prohibitions against firearm possession by felons. In *Schrader*, the court upheld a lifetime ban on a person who had been convicted of a misdemeanor assault in 1968, involving a simple street fight. The court said that § 922 (g)(1) applies to any person convicted of a crime that could be punished by imprisonment for more than one year. That was the case with Schrader's misdemeanor crime, and thus Congress could constitutionally prohibit him from firearm ownership.

United States v. Chapman, 666 F.3d 220 (4th Cir. 2012); Upheld the conviction under § 922(g)(8) of a defendant in possession of a firearm while subject to a domestic abuse protection order.

United States v. Carter, 750 F.3d 462 (4th Cir. 2014), *cert. denied* 135 S. Ct. 273 (2014); Held it was reasonable for Congress to prohibit illegal drug users from possession of firearms, since that would serve the Congressional goal of protecting the public from gun violence by keeping guns out of the hands of those who are impaired by use of illegal drugs.

United States v. Chovan, 735 F.3d 1127 (9th Cir. 2013), *cert. denied* 135 S. Ct. 187 (2014); Lifetime ban on firearm possession by defendant convicted of a misdemeanor crime of domestic violence under § 922 (g)(9) upheld. The court said it was reasonable for Congress to conclude that persons convicted of domestic violence crimes are likely to commit similar crimes in the future, and if they possess firearms make such crimes more dangerous to the victims.

THE FREE EXERCISE OF RELIGION

The U.S. Supreme Court stated in 1990: "We have never held that an individual's religious beliefs excuse him from compliance with an otherwise valid law prohibiting conduct that the State is free to regulate." [52]

Freedom to believe is absolute; freedom to act is not. The U.S. Supreme Court has stated that it has never held that an individual's religious belief excuses compliance with an otherwise valid law regulating conduct. When a statute forbids a specific action or conduct, one who engages in that action or conduct because of a religious belief may be prosecuted for the violation. The following chart illustrates some of the conduct not protected by the Freedom of Religion clause:

CONDUCT NOT PROTECTED[53]	CASE
Multiple marriages in violation of state polygamy laws (crime of bigamy).	*Reynolds v. United States,* U.S. Supreme Court (1879) 98 U.S. 145, 25 L. Ed. 244.
Handling poisonous snakes in a public place in violation of the state law[54] as part of a religious ceremony.	*State v. Massey,* North Carolina Supreme Court (1949) 229 N.C. 734, 51 S.E.2d 179.
Requirements at airports, state fairs, and so on that religious, political, and other groups distribute or sell literature only from booths provided for that purpose.	*Heffron v. International Society for Krishna Consciousness,* U.S. Supreme Court (1981) 452 U.S. 640, 101 S. Ct. 2559.
Violation of child labor laws. Religious order used 9-year-old child to distribute religious pamphlets.	*Prince v. Massachusetts,* U.S. Supreme Court (1944) 321 U.S. 158, 64 S. Ct. 438.
An Air Force officer continued to wear his yarmulke (Jewish skullcap) after repeated orders to remove it. He was dropped from the service. Judgment for Air Force affirmed.	*Goldman v. Weinberger,* U.S. Supreme Court (1986) 475 U.S. 503, 106 S. Ct. 1310.
Members of the Old Order Amish, who do not use motor vehicles but travel in horse-drawn buggies, would not obey a state law requiring reflecting triangles on the rear of all slow-moving vehicles. Held not exempt from complying with this highway safety law.	*Minnesota v. Hershberger,* U.S. Supreme Court (1990) 495 U.S. 901, 110 S. Ct. 1918, *vacating* 444 NW.2d 282 (Minn. 1989).

THE RIGHT OF PRIVACY

The U.S. Constitution has no explicit right of privacy. However, the Supreme Court has in various cases found such a right to exist by implication from notions of personal liberty found in the Constitution. Where a right to privacy exists, governments may not pass criminal laws that impinge upon the right, unless the laws have a reasonable, legitimate government purpose and are tailored to advance that interest with the least restriction on the right. In other words, like the freedom of speech, the right of privacy is not absolute.

Some criminal laws have been found to unlawfully impinge on the right of privacy. In *Griswold v. Connecticut,*[55] the case where the right of privacy was first articulated, the Court struck down a state statute that prohibited providing medical information on birth control to a married woman. In *Lawrence v. Texas,*[56] the Court struck down a Texas statute that made criminal consensual homosexual acts done in private, holding that the statute violated the concepts of personal liberty in the Fourteenth Amendment.

The right of privacy or personal liberty also resulted in the famous abortion decision *Roe v. Wade*,[57] 410 U.S. 113, 153 (1973). In that case the Court declared a state abortion law unconstitutional as a violation of a woman's right of privacy. It said,

> This right of privacy, whether it be founded in the Fourteenth Amendment's concept of personal liberty and restrictions on state action, as we feel it is, or, as the District Court determined, in the Ninth Amendment's reservation of rights to the people, is broad enough to encompass a woman's decision whether or not to terminate a pregnancy.

The Court also held, however, that the right was not absolute: "We, therefore, conclude that the right of personal privacy includes the abortion decision, but this right is not unqualified and must be considered against important state interests in regulation."

The Court then held that during the first trimester of a pregnancy the abortion decision was solely up to the woman; after the first trimester and before viability the state could regulate the abortion procedures, but could not ban abortions; and after viability the state could ban abortions, so long as an exception was made for the mother's health.

LEARNING OBJECTIVES SUMMARY

LO 1. State and discuss the First Amendment.
The First Amendment protects freedom of religion, freedom of speech, free assembly, freedom of the press, and the right to petition the government for redress of grievances.

LO 2. Identify the difference between fighting words and merely rude language.
Fighting words differ from ordinary rude language because they carry the possibility of inciting another to violence. It is not enough that the words cause injury.

LO 3. Define a "clear and present danger."
A clear and present danger is the possibility that some speech or conduct will bring harm to people or property immediately, not some time in the future.

LO 4. List the circumstances that permit government to regulate speech based on content.

Laws directed at the content of speech are subjected to strict scrutiny, meaning the government must have a compelling interest in achieving some goal, and that the limit on the speech is necessary.

LO 5. Define obscenity.
Obscenity is speech or other communication that appeals to a reasonable person's prurient interest, describes in an offensive manner specific defined sexual conduct, and has no redeeming social value.

LO 6. State when a threat becomes a "true threat."
A true threat is a threat that a reasonable person would believe was a serious expression of the intent to take violent, unlawful actions.

LO 7. Describe some ways one person might stalk another person in violation of a criminal law.
A person can stalk another by physically intruding into the other person's life, by

sending harassing messages, or through telephone conversations or the Internet.

LO 8. Identify when an assembly becomes unlawful.
An assembly becomes unlawful when three or more people gather and make a public disturbance that includes acts that present a clear and present danger of harming people or property.

LO 9. State the basis for the Supreme Court's decision that the Second Amendment is binding on the states.
The basis for finding the Second Amendment binding on the states was the Due Process Clause of the Fourteenth Amendment. Under the Supreme Court's incorporation rules, a right that was deeply embedded in our nation's history and was a fundamental right is made binding on the states.

KEY TERMS

"clear and present danger" test, p. 235
disorderly conduct, p. 236
fighting words, p. 236
obscenity, p. 239

inciting, p. 241
defamation, p .241
symbolic speech, p. 242
threats of violence, p. 244
true threat, p. 244

unlawful assembly, p. 250
riot, p. 250
stalking, p. 253

CASE ANALYSIS AND WRITING EXERCISES

1. Massachusetts has a law that makes it a crime to possess a "stun gun" in public. The defendant was convicted under this law for carrying a stun gun in her purse. She said she needed it to protect herself from an abusive former boyfriend. On appeal she contended the total ban of stun guns violated the Second Amendment. The appeals court disagreed, reasoning that (1) the Second Amendment only protects possession of weapons that were in common use when the Amendment was adopted, (2) stun guns are a "thoroughly modern invention," and (3) are not adaptable for military use, like ordinary firearms are. It therefore affirmed the defendant's conviction. Is this decision consistent with *Heller*? Why or why not? See *Caetano v. Massachusetts*, 2016 WL 1078932 (2016) for the U. S. Supreme Court's opinion of those reasons.

2. As we will see in Chapter 12, courts routinely uphold the constitutionality of state laws that target on-line attempts to solicit sex with a minor child. That is because speech intended to achieve an illegal purpose is not protected by the First Amendment. It is the illegal conduct, not the speech, that is made criminal. Texas has a law that makes it a crime to communicate on-line in a "sexually explicit" manner with a minor if the communication

is intended to "gratify anyone's sexual desire." Does that law violate the First Amendment? Is it directed at "content" or "conduct"? How does a court consider First Amendment claims that a criminal law is directed at speech content? See *Ex Parte Lo*, 424 S.W.3d 10 (Tex. Ct. of Crim. App. 2013).

3. 49 U.S.C. § 46302(a) attaches civil penalties for conveying false information of a bomb threat on an airplane. § 46507 (1) makes it a felony to convey a false bomb threat on an airplane if it is done "willfully and maliciously." A flight attendant, upset with the ground workers servicing the American Airlines plane she was working, tried to get them "in trouble" by writing on the back of a storage compartment door in one of the plane's bathrooms "Bomb on Board! BOS-Mia." She was charged under § 46507 with "maliciously" making the bomb hoax. The judge charged the jury that it should convict her if she acted "with an evil purpose or motive, or improper motive." She was convicted, and appealed. Should her conviction be reversed? Did she do what Congress decided constituted a felony bomb hoax? See *United States v. Gray* 780 F.3d 458 (1ˢᵗ Cir. 2015).

4. A high school student did the following in a short period of time: (1) Asked a teacher what she

would do if he came to school wearing a bomb vest; (2) drew a picture of a stick figure wearing a bomb vest, with the word "soon" written below the stick figure, and showed the picture to other students, and (3) in reply to a Facebook post by another student, who suggested he would bring a "blow-up doll" to the prom, the student posted "fill the doll with 20 pounds of explosives." Are these statements sufficient to constitute the crime of making bomb threats to persons or places? See *Com. v. Grenga*, 2015 WL 6956766 (Mass. Sup. Ct. 2015).

ENDNOTES

1. *Hustler Magazine v. Falwell,* 485 U.S. 46 (1988), quoting *Base Corp. v. Consumers Union,* 466 U.S. 485 (1984).

2. *Cox v. New Hampshire,* 312 U.S. 569 (1941).

3. *Speiser v. Randall,* 357 U.S. 513 (1958).

4. *Hustler v. Falwell.*

5. *City of Los Angeles v. Alameda Books, Inc.,* 535 U.S. 425 (2002).

6. 249 U.S. 47 (1919).

7. *Watts v. United States,* 394 U.S. 705 (1969).

8. *Chaplinsky v. New Hampshire,* 315 U.S. 568 (1942).

9. See *State v. Drahota,* 788 N.W.2d 796, 803 (Neb. 2010), citing "Demise of the *Chaplinsky* Fighting Words Doctrine," 106 Harv. L. Rev. 1129 (1993).

10. 303 P.3d 755, *cert denied,* 134 S. Ct. 220 (2013)

11. 788 N.W.2d 796 (2010).

12. *FBI Law Enforcement Bulletin,* "The Fighting Word Doctrine," April 1992.

13. 92 S. Ct. 2607 (1973).

14. The term *prurient interest* is generally defined as appealing "to a shameful, unhealthy, unwholesome, degrading … interest in sex." *County of Kenosha v. C&S Management Inc.,* 588 N.W.2d 236 (1999).

15. *Brandenburg v. Ohio,* 89 S. Ct. 1827 (1969).

16. 94 S. Ct. 326 (1973).

17. 89 S. Ct. 1827 (1969).

18. 379 U.S. 64 (1964).

19. 482 F.3d 1244 (10th Cir. 2007).

20. See *New York Times v. Sullivan,* 376 U.S. 254 (1964).

21. 89 S. Ct. 733 (1969).

22. 109 S. Ct. 2533 (1989).

23. 110 S. Ct. 2404 (1990).

24. 112 S. Ct. 2538 (1992). Many communities have ordinances regulating the manner and time in which burning can occur. Burning a flag could also be cited as a violation of these ordinances.

25. 538 U.S. 343 (2003).

26. See, for example, West's Georgia Code Annotated Section 16-ll-37(a) and Nebraska Revised Statute Section 28-311.01 (1995).

27. *United States v. Dysart,* 705 F.2d 1247 (1983); *United States v. Turner,* 2013 WL 3111139 (2nd Cir. 2013).

28. 626 N.W.2d 725 (Wis. 2001).

29. 70 Cal. Rptr.3d 535 (Cal. App. 2008).

30. 603 S.E.2d 86 (Ga. App. 2004).

31. *United States v. Corum,* 362 F.3d 489 (8th Cir. 2004).

32. *United States v. Floyd,* 458 F.3d 844 (8th Cir. 2006), *cert. denied,* 549 U.S. 1236 (2007).

33. *United States v. Jeffries,* 692 F.3d 473 (6th Cir. 2012).

34. 144 S.W.3d 210 (Tex. App. 2004).

35. 109 S. Ct. 2746, 2756 (1989).

36. 631 F.3d 1 (1st Cir. 2011).

37. 336 U.S. 77 (1949).

38. 391 U.S. 367 (1968).

39. 385 U.S. 39 (1967).

40. 408 U.S. 104, 92 S. Ct. 2294 (1972). The U.S. Supreme Court held:

    The nature of a place, "the pattern of its normal activities, dictates the kinds of regulations of time, place, and manner that are reasonable." Although a silent vigil may not unduly interfere with a public library, making a speech in the reading room almost certainly would. That same speech should be perfectly appropriate in a park. The crucial question is whether the manner of expression is basically incompatible with the normal activity of a particular place at a particular time. Our cases make clear that in assessing the reasonableness of regulation, we must weigh heavily the fact that communication is involved; the regulation must be narrowly tailored to further the State's legitimate interest. "Access to [the streets, sidewalks, parks, and other similar public places] for the purpose of exercising [First Amendment rights] cannot constitutionally be denied broadly." Free expression "must not, in the guise of regulation, be abridged or denied."

41. Ku Klux Klan demonstrations and parades cost local communities a lot of money. Fewer than two dozen Ku Kluxers generally show up, but many more people will appear to protest against the Ku Klux Klan. The likelihood of violence and disorderly conduct is very great. Therefore, adequate police protection must be provided, which means allocating sufficient money for the necessary extra law enforcement and other costs.

Because of such additional expenses, some communities passed laws and ordinances permitting the imposition of a fee, based on anticipated costs. This would mean that a local administrator would have to estimate the costs for a specific group. The U.S. Supreme Court struck down an ordinance that provided for a fee in the case of *Forsyth County v. Nationalist Movement* (a Ku Klux Klan group), 112 S. Ct. 2395 (1992). The U.S. Supreme Court pointed out that to estimate the fee, the local official had to consider who the group was and the contents of the message they were communicating.

Requiring prepayment of an $85 fee for the processing of a parade permit application and the cost of traffic control was upheld by the courts in the case of *Stonewell Union v. City of Columbus,* 931 F.2d 1130 (6th Cir. 1991), *review denied* U.S. Supreme Court 112 S. Ct. 275 (1991).

42. 118 S. Ct. 805 (1998).

43. States generally statutorize the crime of unlawful assembly, as does Florida in Section 870.03 of the Florida Criminal Code. But some states provide that the crime of unlawful assembly is committed when the person gathered in the unlawful assembly fails to leave the area after law enforcement declares the gathering to be an unlawful assembly and orders the group or crowd to disperse and leave the area.

44. Under the old common law, if a number of people met together and suddenly quarreled and fought among themselves, this would constitute an "affray." An affray differs from a riot in that an affray is not premeditated. Under the old common law, a riot required three or more people, whereas an affray required two or more.

45. Under New York statutes, four or more people plus the person charged are needed for the crime of "unlawful assembly." To convict a person of any of the riot offenses, it must be shown that there were ten or more people gathered, plus the person charged.

46. 978 F.2d 786 (2nd Cir. 1992).

47. *Hiibel v. Sixth District Court of Nevada,* 542 U.S. 177 (2004).

48. In the case of *Bennis v. Michigan,* 134 L. Ed. 2d 68 (1996), Mr. Bennis's vehicle was forfeited after he was convicted of this offense. But Mrs. Bennis was an innocent co-owner of the car and appealed to the U.S. Supreme Court. The Supreme Court held that as the vehicle was an abatable nuisance, it could be forfeited without an offset for the innocent co-owner and without a showing that the innocent co-owner knew or consented to the public misuse of the vehicle.

49. California's stalking statute, Penal Code Section 646.9, reads: "Any person who willfully, maliciously, and repeatedly follows or harasses another person, and who makes a credible threat with the intent to place the person in reasonable fear of death or great bodily injury is guilty of the crime of stalking."

50. 625 F.3d 1209 (9th Cir. 2010).

51. 60 Cal. Rptr. 2d 423 (Cal. App. 2d 1997).

52. *Employment Division v. Smith,* 494 U.S. 872 (S. Ct. 1990).

53. The Freedom of Religion Clause could not be used as a defense for destroying government property (760 F.2d 447); extortion and blackmail (515 F.2d 112); racketeering (695 F.2d 765, review denied, 460 U.S. 1092); refusal to testify before a grand jury (465 F.2d 802; see 409 U.S. 944); refusal to be photographed after being arrested (848 F.2d 113); putting a logging road through an area sacred to Native American tribes (108 S. Ct. 1319); refusal to have children vaccinated (25 S. Ct. 358); and refusal to participate in the Social Security system (102 S. Ct. 1051), although in 1988 Congress enacted 26 U.S.C. § 3127, which permits members of certain religious groups, such as the Amish people, to elect to opt out of the employee portion of Social Security taxes.

54. According to the New Testament in Mark 16:16-18, "He that believeth and is baptized shall be saved. . . . [T]hey shall speak with new tongues; they shall take up serpents; and if they drink any deadly thing, it shall not hurt them." In *State v. Massey,* the defendant was convicted of handling poisonous snakes in a religious ceremony, taking literally these words from the New Testament. The Court ruled that the state law forbidding the handling of poisonous snakes was a valid use of the police power of the state of North Carolina and held that the public safety factor outweighed the right to religious freedom.

55. 381 U.S. 479 (1965).

56. 123 S. Ct. 2472 (2003).

57. 410 U.S. 113 (1973).

10

Homicide

LEARNING OBJECTIVES

In this chapter we discuss the various kinds and degrees of criminal homicide. The learning objectives for this chapter are

LO 1. Explain the meaning of corpus delicti and its role in criminal prosecutions.

LO 2. State the current status of the year-and-a-day rule and why its acceptance has waned.

LO 3. Articulate the elements of the "born alive" requirement.

LO 4. Explain the doctrine of transferred intent.

LO 5. List the homicides that do not require proof of intent to kill.

LO 6. Identify which deaths that occur during the commission of a felony qualify as felony murder.

LO 7. Describe the difference between voluntary and involuntary manslaughter.

LO 8. List circumstances that could be sufficient to reduce a charge of murder to manslaughter.

LO 9. Explain why the U.S. Supreme Court upheld the Oregon Death with Dignity Law.

David Eisenhauer is pictured in this undated handout booking photo provided by the Montgomery County Sheriff's Office in Virginia, January 31, 2016. Eisenhauer, an engineering student at Virginia Tech, has been charged with the abduction and murder of a 13-year-old girl whose remains were found in North Carolina. Police say Eisenhauer lured the girl through exchanges on a social media site.

Montgomery County Sheriff's Office/Handout/Reuters

William Melchert-Dinkel visited an on-line suicide web site, where he posed as a female nurse with advice for those contemplating suicide. He responded to posts by Mark Drybrough, a man living in Coventry, England, and Nadia Kajouji, a student in Ottawa, Canada. They each expressed a wish to commit suicide, and Melchert-Dinkel responded with advice about how to accomplish suicide, as well as false statements that he would also commit suicide with them. He encouraged both to commit suicide by hanging, and to let him watch via webcam. In each case, shortly after internet communications with Melchert-Dinkel, Drybrough and Kajouji committed suicide; Drybrough by hanging and Kajouji by jumping into a frozen river.

Melchert-Dinkel was convicted of assisting suicide under a Minnesota statute making it a crime to "advise, encourage, or assist" another to commit suicide. He appealed, and in 2014 the Minnesota Supreme Court reversed his conviction, holding the statute's use of "advise" and "encourage" as elements of the crime of assisting suicide violated the First Amendment. Since it was not clear on what basis the trial court convicted Melchert-Dinkel (jury was waived) it remanded the case to the trial court to determine if Melchert-Dinkel should be convicted of "assisting" suicide. In 2015 the trial court convicted Melchert-Dinkel of assisting suicide.

As a review of what we learned in Chapter 9, is the Minnesota statute a "content-based" prohibition? If so, why didn't the Minnesota Supreme Court uphold the statute under the "speech integral to criminal conduct" exception to the First Amendment? Is suicide illegal in England, Canada, or Minnesota? What about the "incitement" or fraud exceptions to the First Amendment? Would it help the state's argument for the fraud exception if either or both of the victims (they didn't) had acquiesced in Melchert-Dinkel's request that they use a web-cam to permit him to witness their deaths? See

State v. Melchert-Dinkel, 844 N.W.2d 13 (Minn. 2014).

Finally, what must the state prove on remand to convict Melchert-Dinkel of assisting suicide? To see how it did, see 2015 WL 9437531 (2015).

In this chapter we learn the various charges that may be brought against a person or persons when a homicide occurs and what the prosecution must prove in order to obtain a conviction on those charges. We learn what different mental states and circumstances can surround a particular homicide that could result in a charge of murder, of voluntary manslaughter, or of involuntary manslaughter. We will also learn about the evolving treatment of cases such as assisted suicide and euthanasia.

HOMICIDE IN GENERAL

homicide The killing of one human being by another. There are three types of homicide: justifiable, excusable, and felonious.

Homicide the killing of one human being by another, is not always criminal. Sir William Blackstone wrote in the eighteenth century that there were three kinds of homicide—justifiable, excusable, and felonious. He wrote that the first involved no guilt, the second involved little guilt, and the third was the worst crime that humans were capable of committing against the law of nature.

Justifiable homicide is defined in the common law as an intentional homicide committed under circumstances of necessity or duty without any evil intent and without any fault or blame on the person who commits the homicide. Justifiable homicide includes state executions, homicides by police officers in the performance of their legal duty, and self-defense when the person committing the homicide is not at fault.

Excusable homicide is the killing of a human being, either by misadventure or in self-defense, when there is some civil fault, error, or omission on the part of the person who commits the homicide. The degree of fault, however, is not enough to constitute a crime.

Criminal (or *felonious*) *homicide* occurs when a person unlawfully and knowingly, recklessly, or negligently causes the death of another human being. The common law and the states have divided criminal homicide into the crimes of murder, manslaughter, and negligent homicide.

This chapter deals with criminal homicide and the circumstances that give rise to specific charges. Criminal homicide encompasses a wide variety of acts. The acts and the intent with which they were committed determine whether the homicide is intentional or unintentional. Such determination is relevant, because penalties are more severe when the killing was intentional rather than as a result of recklessness, negligence, or carelessness.

The Corpus Delicti Requirement

Corpus delicti means the body or substance of the crime (proof that a crime has been committed). The prosecution must prove in all criminal cases that the crime charged has been committed. For example, if the prosecution cannot prove a fire was deliberately set or that a building actually burned, it cannot prove arson. If it cannot prove a death was not accidental, it cannot prove murder. If both parties were competent adults and consented to sex, rape or sexual assault has not occurred.

In some cases the principal evidence against the defendant is a confession. If no other evidence exists to corroborate the confession, courts often hold that the defendant cannot be convicted of the crime that is charged. Court decisions have noted that confessions can be the result of mistake, mental problems, coercion, or even a friend trying to take the blame for another person.

The corpus delicti rule is often court created, and as a result the rule can be changed by a court, without legislative action. This was the case in Colorado, where in 2013 the Colorado Supreme Court abandoned the 100-year-old court-created corpus delicti rule that out-of-court confessions alone could not support a criminal conviction. In *People v. LaRosa*[1] the defendant confessed over the telephone to police officers that he had sexually assaulted his infant daughter. The only evidence at his trial was his out-of-court confession. He was convicted of sexual assault crimes, and appealed. The Colorado Supreme Court said that the corpus delicti rule, which would ordinarily apply in this situation, no longer played a useful role, and should be abandoned. The court noted that in many kinds of crimes, like sexual assault on a young child, direct evidence of the crime might not exist. In future prosecutions, out-of-court confessions alone may be sufficient, if the confessions are proved by the prosecution to have trustworthiness.[2]

In states where corroborating evidence is required, courts differ on the kind and quality of the evidence sufficient to corroborate a confession and prove that the crime charged did occur. See *People v. Jennings*,[3] where the court held that the state had produced sufficient corroborative evidence to verify "bragging" by the defendant that he had murdered prostitutes and then took back the money he had given them.

Proving Corpus Delicti in "No Body" Cases

Virtually every American city has active cases of persons reported missing. In 2009 the U.S. Department of Justice launched the NamUs (National Missing and Un-identified Persons System) database. In its June, 2013 NamUs Fact Sheet, NamUs reported that at any given time over 90,000 people are missing in this country, and that each year over 4,400 unidentified human remains are discovered. About 1000 remain unidentified after one year.

Usually, if no body is found, there is no criminal case to prosecute, because evidence needed to prove corpus delicti is ordinarily proved in homicide cases by evidence obtained from the body of the victim or from witnesses to the crime. The corpus delicti rule requires that the prosecution prove (1) that the missing person is dead and (2) that the defendant killed that person. In "no-body" cases, corpus delicti can be proved by circumstantial evidence or by confessions that have been corroborated and affirmed by other evidence.

In the following two "no body" cases, the body of the victim was not found, but corpus delicti was proved by circumstantial evidence. In each case, a murder conviction was affirmed.

Tetso v. State

Maryland Court of Appeals, 45 A. 3d 788 (2012), *cert. denied* 52 A.3d 979 (Md. 2012)

On March 6, 2005, Tracey Tetso was to attend a Motley Crue concert with a man with whom she was having an affair. She did not attend the concert, and was never seen again. In 2010 her husband, Dennis, was tried and convicted of second-degree murder of Tracey, based only on circumstantial evidence. On appeal, the court affirmed his conviction, stating there was sufficient evidence to support the jury verdict of guilty. The court pointed to the fact that Tracey was excited to go to the concert, that her dogs were left alone in her house, that she normally was in constant contact with her friends and family, and that her credit cards had not been used since her disappearance, was evidence sufficient to prove she was dead, the first corpus delicti requirement.

The court said defendant's knowledge of the affair and that Tracey wanted a divorce, that he was seen driving Tracey's car after March 6, that he was unwilling to help in the search for Tracey, and that a short time after her disappearance he made plans to buy a boat, telling others he would use money from a life insurance policy on Tracey, supported the jury finding that he killed Tracey, the second corpus delicti requirement.

State v. Watkins

New Jersey App. Court, 2011 WL 5573771, *cert. denied*, 43 A.3d 1168 (N.J. 2012)

On February 23, 1990, Craig White disappeared, and was never seen again. His body was never found, and no physical evidence surrounding his disappearance was discovered. Nineteen years later a jury convicted his cousin, Jesse Watkins, of murdering him. Watkins appealed that conviction, claiming insufficient evidence existed to support the jury's verdict.

On appeal the court affirmed his conviction. It held sufficient circumstantial evidence was introduced to support the jury verdict. The victim had a young son he was caring for, and the court said that it would be unlikely the victim would disappear without any communication with the son. The fact that the defendant's girlfriend had an affair with the victim, that the defendant had previously assaulted the victim over the affair, that the defendant was the last person to be seen with the victim on the day he disappeared, that the defendant left his home state right after the victim disappeared and did not return, and told a subsequent wife and girlfriend he had killed the victim, was sufficient to support the jury verdict of guilty of murder, the court held.

Body Without Proof of the Cause of Death Cases

The body of the deceased is available in most criminal homicide cases. But if doctors are not able to testify specifically that the cause of death was an unlawful act, corpus delicti has not been proved. Unexplained deaths are unusual but not rare in medical history. If doctors are unable to determine the cause of death, or if they are

---

 ## ATTEMPTS TO IDENTIFY AND MINIMIZE VIOLENCE AGAINST CHILDREN

The 2011 report of The National Centers for Disease Control, based on the 2011 National Health Survey, produced these statistics on child (ages 1–14) deaths: in 2010, 34,181 children in this age group died. Of that number, 957 died from assaults listed as homicides, about 40 percent of which involved victims under 1 year old. It is likely many other deaths were the result of abuse or neglect, but not reported as homicides.

The following systems have been created to deal with violence against children.

Child Death Review Teams

The United States (all fifty states), Australia, and Canada now have child death review teams to review deaths of children from violence, child abuse or neglect, motor vehicle accidents, child suicide, and natural or undetermined causes.

Safe Haven Laws for Unwanted Babies

For years, tragic stories of illegally abandoned babies found dead or in unsafe places have appeared in the news. Because of the continuing, sad, attention-getting cases, states began to enact safe haven laws to save the lives of babies. These laws allow a person (usually the mother) to leave an unwanted baby, anonymously and without fear of prosecution, at a hospital, fire station, or other designated place. Most states (if not all) have now enacted safe haven laws.

Mandatory Child Abuse Reporting Laws

Most states have laws that require persons who "know or have reasonable cause to suspect" child abuse, abandonment, death, or neglect to report that information to authorities. Under the Florida statute, for example, hotlines are established for communicating the information, and failure to do so is punishable as a misdemeanor.

uncertain and unable to state whether the death resulted from criminal acts or from natural causes, then a reasonable doubt may have been created.

Corpus delicti has historically been difficult to prove in sudden infant death syndrome (SIDS) deaths of babies between 2 months and 1 year old because doctors did not know the reason for the cause of death in many of the cases. Today, with more medical knowledge, physicians and medical journals have called into question the SIDS explanation for the deaths of some infants, particularly when multiple deaths occurred in one family. Prosecutors in many states reopened the death investigations of some infants that earlier had been classified as SIDS. For example, a woman in New York was convicted of the murder of five babies, which earlier had been classified as SIDS deaths, and in Philadelphia a woman was charged with the deaths of eight babies, which had earlier been thought to be SIDS deaths.[4]

The testimony of doctors that they "suspected" or had a "hunch" that a criminal act was the cause of death is not sufficient to prove corpus delicti. The *People v. Dendel* case illustrates how the corpus delicti requirement that proof of the cause of death must be established can be met.

People v. Dendel

Michigan Court of Appeals, 797 N.W.2d 645 (2010), *review denied,* 802 N.W.2d 618 (Mich. 2011)

The defendant was the long-time domestic partner of Paul Burley. Burley suffered from many medical problems, including dementia, and was HIV positive. The defendant was the sole caregiver for Burley. When Burley died, the medical examiner initially ruled the death was from "natural causes," since tests conducted on the body showed no presence of foreign substances. Although the defendant insisted on an immediate cremation, police investigators ordered an autopsy before the body could be cremated. Autopsy results showed damage to brain cells brought on by hypoglycemic shock, which can be caused by an injection of insulin in a person without diabetes. Defendant was then charged with murder. After a bench trial (one in which the judge finds the facts) she was convicted of second-degree murder and sentenced to 7–15 years in prison.

On appeal, the court affirmed her conviction. It held that sufficient circumstantial evidence supported the verdict of guilty. The court said that evidence included the following: the victim was not diabetic, and thus would not have insulin-related body signs; the victim was unable to give himself medication, so it was unlikely he committed suicide; the defendant was a diabetic, and knew insulin could not be discovered in a body after death; the defendant stated a week before the victim's death, "I feel like giving him a shot of insulin"; the defendant did not tell the victim's family he had died, and pushed for immediate cremation; the defendant objected to conducting an autopsy. The defendant's conviction for second-degree murder was affirmed.

The Common Law "Born Alive" Requirement and the Crime of Feticide (Fetal Murder)

Under the common law, the killing of a fetus (unborn baby) was not a homicide. Because most criminal homicide statutes prohibited only the killing of a "person" or a "human being," these statutes did not include the killing of a fetus, which was not a "person" under the common law. In the leading case of *Keeler v. Superior Court*[5] the California Supreme Court said the "born alive" rule prevented a conviction for the death of a fetus. After the *Keeler* decision California statutes were amended to define murder as the "unlawful killing of a human being, *or a fetus*, with malice aforethought" (Title 8, Section 187). This statute made the killing of a fetus in California "with malice aforethought" murder and changed the common law.[6]

In response to cases like *Keeler*, as of 2015 thirty-eight states have abandoned the **"born alive" requirement**, and make the death of a fetus in a mother's body a homicide. The question of whether or not the fetus must be "viable" for conviction under such a statute often depends on the statutory scheme adopted. For example, Ind. Code § 35-42-1-1 (4) defines "murder" to include killing a fetus "that has attained viability." It is a Class A felony. Ark. Code Ann. § 5-1-102 defines "person" for all classes of homicides as a fetus "in utero at any stage of development." Twenty-three states have no requirement of a showing of viability.

Many states have adopted **"feticide"** statutes, which treat the death of an unborn fetus outside the usual definitions of homicide. Under these statutes, there is no requirement that the fetus be born alive, or in most cases even be viable. The Arizona statute, for example, punishes for manslaughter anyone who "(k)nowingly or recklessly causes the death of an unborn child by any physical injury to the mother." A.R.S. § 13-1103.

In 18 U.S.C. § 1841, passed in 2004, the federal "Protection of Unborn Children" statute makes it a crime separate from murder to unlawfully take the life of a child that is *"in utero."* A child that is *in utero* is defined as "a member of the species homo sapiens, at any stage of development, who is carried in the womb." However, if the circumstances show an intention to kill the fetus, the defendant can be charged under the general murder statute, 18 U.S.C. § 1111.

About twelve states still have the "born alive" rule, and in most of those jurisdictions some showing that the fetus was alive when it left the mother's body must be made. In *State v. Lamy*, 969 A.2d 451 (N.H. 2009), the court reversed a manslaughter conviction because the state could not show the fetus displayed any signs of living on its own without life-support machines, and thus the state did not prove the fetus was born alive. In *State v. Courchesne*, 998 A.2d 1 (Conn. 2010), the Connecticut Supreme Court remanded a capital murder conviction for a determination of whether an infant kept alive for 42 days on life support after the defendant stabbed her mother to death was "alive."

"born alive" requirement To be able to charge homicide of a newborn baby, the prosecution must be able to prove that the child was living at the time it was killed.

feticide Murder of an unborn child.

PROOF THAT THE VICTIM WAS ALIVE AT THE TIME OF THE DEFENDANT'S UNLAWFUL ACT

Because criminal homicide is the unlawful killing of a living human being, the state has the burden of showing that the victim was alive at the time of the unlawful act. All people have a right to life, and whether they have 10 minutes or 10 years left to live makes no difference in the eyes of the law.

Whether or not the victim was alive when a sexual assault occurred is sometimes an issue in felony murder cases. In felony murder, discussed in more detail later in this chapter, a defendant convicted of one crime can also be convicted of murder if a person dies as a result of the crime. In such cases, it is necessary for the prosecution to prove the original crime, usually called the "predicate" crime. If for some reason the defendant cannot be convicted of the predicate crime, he or she cannot be convicted of felony murder.

In sexual assault cases, some jurisdictions hold that one cannot be guilty of sexual assault if the victim was dead at the time the assault occurred. See *People v. Hutner*,[7] where a conviction for first-degree felony murder was reversed because the victim was dead when sexual penetration occurred. Other jurisdictions hold that so long as the victim was alive when a sexual assault began, it does not matter for felony murder purposes whether the person was alive when sexual penetration occurred. See *State v. Jones*,[8] where a felony murder conviction was affirmed even though the victim may have died before sexual penetration occurred.

When Is a Person Legally Dead?

Until the 1950s and 1960s, the heart was considered the body's most vital organ, and therefore death was defined in terms of cessation of heart and respiratory functions. When doctors became able to keep the heart and other organs alive for transplanting to other patients, medical science recognized that the body's real seat of life is the brain.

Court and state legislative bodies followed the medical profession in defining death in terms of "brain death." For example, the Indiana Supreme Court has defined death as the "permanent cessation of all brain function" and joined other states in holding that "for the purposes of the law of homicide proof of the death of the victim may be established by proof of the irreversible cessation of the victim's total brain function."[9]

End-of-Life Decisions   On an average day in the United States, more than 6,000 people die. Doctors estimate that at least several hundred of these deaths occur after doctors, patients, and family members agree to withhold life-sustaining treatment and allow the inevitable to occur.

To stay within the law and to avoid criminal prosecution, the decision to withhold treatment or to "pull the plug" on persons in deep continuous comas (persistent vegetative states) should be made only when the following can be shown:

1. Terminally ill patients who are mentally competent can instruct that treatment or life-support systems be withdrawn. Courts have held that the individual's right to refuse treatment must come before the interests of the state in keeping the individual alive.

2. Life-support systems or treatment may be withheld from patients who are comatose or in a persistent vegetative state if one of the following is clearly shown:

   (a) That the patient left prior explicit written instructions that this be done (a *living will*) or

   (b) That the patient had legally appointed another adult to make such health care decisions, should the patient be unable to do so (*medical power of attorney*), or

(c) Clear and convincing evidence is presented to a court showing that the withdrawal of treatment or of a life-support system is in accordance with the patient's own wishes or best interests.[10]

The population in the United States is growing older. The Census Bureau estimates that between the years 2000 and 2050 the percentage increase in the number of people over 65 will be 147 percent, compared to the estimated overall population increase of 49 percent. Aging diseases such as Alzheimer's and dementia can cause many older people to suffer conditions that are not comas, but are nonetheless destructive of the quality of life. For example, many people with these diseases have lost their ability to swallow food, and as a result they are required to be fed by tubes inserted in their bodies, much the same as those actually in a vegetative state. The application of the criminal laws to decisions shortening or prolonging life in this complex, unsettled, and controversial area remains unclear.

THE CAUSATION REQUIREMENT

Causation and Proximate Cause

Causation and proximate cause are discussed in Chapter 3 of this text. Causation is an essential element of all crimes that have a result as an element of the crime. The state must show that what the defendant did (or failed to do) was the direct and proximate cause of the harm that occurred. The following two examples illustrate the law of causation:

EXAMPLE After loading a gun with live ammunition, X points the gun at Y and pulls the trigger. The firing pin comes down hard on the back of the live cartridge that X has placed in the chamber of the gun. The blow of the hammer detonates the primer in the cartridge, and the primer detonates the powder in the cartridge. The powder burns so rapidly that hot gases immediately build up tremendous pressure in the chamber of the gun. This pressure forces the propellant (the bullet) out of the muzzle of the gun at a high rate of speed. Because of rifling in the barrel of the gun and the direction in which X is pointing the gun, the bullet travels through the air and strikes Y in the head, killing Y immediately.

EXAMPLE After being shocked by seeing the defendant smash her door open and then rip her telephone cord out of the phone, an elderly woman dies of a heart attack. The defendant argues that he wanted to burglarize the woman's home but had no intention of harming her.

A jury can easily conclude in Example 1 that X intended the natural and probable consequences of the deliberate act; it would then find that X intended to kill Y.

In Example 1, X's acts were the direct and proximate cause of Y's death. The chain of events that occurred after X pulled the trigger was expected and desired by X. Therefore, X can be held criminally responsible for Y's death.

In Example 2, the Nebraska Supreme Court affirmed the defendant's conviction for felony murder in the case of *State v. Dixon*[11]:

> Dixon admitted to Detectives Circo and Wade that Jourdan was alive when he entered the house. The implosion of window glass and part of the wooden kitchen door would startle the most imperturbable individual. Seeing Dixon coming through the doorway into the kitchen probably would stir one to "stare" at him, visual fixation founded in fear intensified by Dixon's ripping the "cord out of the phone." All that unfolded before Susan Jourdan, 76 years old and living alone. What total terror likely seized and constricted Susan Jourdan's heart may be beyond another's comprehension. What the jury did understand was Dr. Roffman's explanation of the cause of Susan Jourdan's death, "emotional trauma of having her door kicked in and stimulating her heart to beat abnormally, causing her collapse and ultimate death."

When there is a substantial time gap between an injury and the victim's death, causation may become contested based on actions of the victim after the injury. For example, in the case of *Brown v. State*[12] the defendant doused his girlfriend with gasoline and started her on fire. After months in the hospital to treat her severe burns, the victim returned home. After 2 weeks at home she developed pneumonia. She refused to go to the hospital, and died within a few days. The Georgia Supreme Court affirmed the defendant's murder conviction and life imprisonment sentence. The court said expert medical testimony established that the pneumonia was the result of the burns inflicted by the defendant, and that the victim would have died even if she had gone to the hospital as directed by her physician. The court therefore held the defendant was the proximate cause of the death.

The Year-and-a-Day Rule

The year-and-a-day rule is also discussed in more detail in Chapter 3. The common law rule stated that a person could not be convicted of a murder unless the victim died within a year and a day from the time of the wrongful act. The Michigan Supreme Court pointed out that the year-and-a-day rule dates back to 1278 and that the "original rationale for the rule was probably tied to the inability of 13th century medicine to prove the cause of death beyond a reasonable doubt after a prolonged period of time."[13]

Common law rules became part of a new state's criminal law because virtually all states included in their constitution a clause that adopted the "common law of England" in place when the United States was formed. Subsequent changes to that common law, usually by state legislatures, were called "abrogation" of the common law. Courts also possess the power to abrogate a common law rule, which many have done in the case of the year-and-a-day rule.

The Michigan Supreme Court, in the case cited above, and many other state courts or legislatures, have abolished this rule. In *State v. Fairbanks*, 842 N.W.2d 297 (Minn. 2014), the Minnesota Supreme Court rejected the year-and-a-day argument of a defendant convicted of murdering a police officer who died 18 months after being shot by the defendant. The court said that even if the rule was ever a part of the common law of Minnesota, the criminal code adopted by the legislature clearly rejected the rule.

When the common law rule is abrogated by a state supreme court, the court must determine whether to make the abrogation retroactive, or only prospective. In *State v. Picotte*,[14] the Wisconsin Supreme Court abrogated the common law year-and-a-day rule but made the abrogation prospective. As a result, the defendant's conviction for reckless homicide of a victim who died more than one year after the crime occurred was reversed.

A few courts have not abolished the rule. In *Ex Parte Key*,[15] the Alabama Supreme Court reversed a conviction of a defendant for murder of a victim who died 18 months after the injury. The court held that the year-and-a-day rule was still part of the common law in Alabama.

Some states continue to use a variation of the rule. For example, Title 8, Section 194 of the California Penal Code provides that "To make the killing either murder or manslaughter, it is not requisite the party die within three years and a day after the stroke received or the cause of death administered. If death occurs beyond the time of three years and a day, there shall be a rebuttable presumption that the killing was not criminal." In *People v. Moncada*, 149 Cal. Rptr.3d 1 (Cal. App. 2012) the court affirmed a conviction for involuntary manslaughter and child abuse homicide, where the defendant caused injury to his child that resulted in brain damage, and the child died 8 years later. The court said that although the child died from a ruptured stomach, evidence showed children suffering brain damage often develop complications, and that the complication of a ruptured stomach in this case was the proximate result of the original injury.

MURDER

The first murder to be reported in the American colonies occurred 10 years after the Pilgrims landed at Plymouth Rock. In 1630, John Billington, one of the original band of 102 Pilgrims to come over on the *Mayflower*, fired his blunderbuss at a neighbor and killed the man at close range. John Billington was charged with the common law offense of murder under the English law and, after a prompt trial and conviction, was hanged.[16]

Only one degree of murder existed under the common law, and it was punishable by death. After the American Revolution, some state legislative bodies began creating other degrees of murder, perhaps motivated by a desire to separate homicides to be punished by death from homicides that they believed did not warrant a sentence of death. In addition, there was distrust of adoption by the new states of the harsh English criminal penalty rules. The first Pennsylvania state constitution, adopted in 1776, included the statement that penal laws should be reformed, and that punishment should be proportionate to the crime. Pennsylvania was the first state to have degrees of murder based on culpability.

By the year 1900, virtually all the states had two or three degrees of murder. At that time, the degree system was a useful and meaningful method of distinguishing murder that was punished by capital punishment and that which was not. With the decline in the use of the death penalty in this century and its virtual nonuse in the 1960s and 1970s, the utility of the degree system declined considerably.

The degree system is still meaningful today, when first-degree murder carries a mandatory life imprisonment sentence or the death penalty. The degree system is also used as part of plea-bargaining when the state finds advantage in allowing the defendant to plead guilty to second-degree murder or to some other lesser offense if a reduction is appropriate.

State murder statutes vary in how they define first- and second-degree murder. An example of a first-degree murder statute that incorporates the common law "malice" requirement is Nebraska Revised Statutes § 28-303: "A person commits murder in the first degree if he kills another person (1) purposely and with deliberate malice. . . ." Second-degree murder is defined in § 28-304: "A person commits murder in the second degree if he causes the death of a person intentionally, but without premeditation."

The Illinois statute is an example of a statute that has a broader definition of first-degree murder:

> (a) A person who kills an individual without lawful justification commits first degree murder if, in performing the acts which cause the death, (1) he either intends to kill or do great bodily injury to that individual or another, or knows that such acts will cause death to that individual or another; (2) he knows that such acts create a strong probability of death or great bodily harm to that individual or another, or (3) he is attempting to commit a forcible felony other than second degree murder.[17]

Second-degree murder is defined as doing an act that constitutes first-degree murder, but under intense passion caused by serious provocation, or under an unreasonable belief that the killing was justified.

Intent-to-Kill and Premeditated Murder

The unlawful, intentional, premeditated killing of another human being is considered the most serious criminal offense. It is in most states called first-degree or capital murder. The weapon used to implement the murder can be anything from a firearm to bare hands. The type of weapon used or the manner in which the fatal blow is delivered is not necessarily significant. Rather, the presence or absence of the specific intent to take the life of another human being separates this crime from all

---

 CLASSIFICATIONS OF COMMON LAW MURDER

- *Intent-to-kill murder:* The most common murder, the intentional killing of another human being, is considered the most serious offense in the criminal law.
- *Intent-to-do-serious-bodily-harm murder:* In this type of murder, the defendant intended to do serious bodily harm short of death, but his or her acts resulted in death.
- *Depraved-mind or depraved-heart murder:* When a death results from conduct that shows a wanton disregard for human life and when there is a high probability the conduct will result in death, the homicide is classified as this type of murder.
- *Felony murder:* At common law, one who caused another's death while committing a felony was guilty of felony murder. However, when the doctrine was created, only eight felonies were recognized, and all were punished by death. Because states now have many felonies that do not carry the death penalty, the felony murder rule is generally limited to crimes of violence.

other degrees of homicide. The type of weapon and the manner in which it is used, however, may give rise to the legal inference that a person intends the natural and probable consequences of his or her deliberate acts.

murder Unlawful homicide with malice aforethought.

Murder under the common law and as enacted by the statutes of many states as first-degree murder is often defined as an "unlawful homicide with malice afore-thought." The phrase *malice aforethought* signifies the mental state of a person who voluntarily, without legal excuse or justification, does an act that ordinarily will cause death or serious injury to another. Although the word *malice* ordinarily conveys the meaning of hatred, ill will, or malevolence, it is not limited to those meanings in "malice aforethought" but can include such motives as a mercy killing, in which the homicide is committed to end the suffering of a loved one. *Aforethought* has been interpreted to mean that the malice must exist at the time of the homicidal act. Courts have held that if the design and intent to kill precede the killing for even a moment, the person can be convicted of first-degree murder.[18]

Other states have defined first-degree murder as causing "the death of another human being with intent to kill that person." The American Law Institute Model Penal Code, § 210, uses the words *purposely* and *knowingly* causing the death of another person as the basis for a charge of murder.

A federal criminal statute, 18 U.S.C. § 1111, defines "murder" as follows: "Murder is the unlawful killing of a human being with malice aforethought." If the killing is done by poison, during the commission of certain identified crimes, or is "willful, deliberate, malicious and premeditated," it is murder in the first degree. All other murders are murder in the second degree. The meaning of "premeditated" was the issue in the following case.

In the 2011 case of *United States v. Begay*[19] the Ninth Circuit Court of Appeals, sitting *en banc*,[20] reversed a decision of a circuit court panel and affirmed the first-degree murder conviction of the defendant, Begay. A Ninth Circuit Court of Appeals panel of three judges had agreed with Begay's claim that the prosecution had failed to prove he killed the victim with premeditation. That court said the statute requires that "at some point *after* the defendant forms the intent to kill the victim, he has the time to reflect on the decision to commit murder, that he in fact does reflect on that decision, and that he commits the murder with a 'cool mind' after having engaged in such reflection."[21]

The panel had concluded the evidence did not support the jury finding of premeditation. It noted that Begay had no previous relationship with either victim, he had no shown motive for the killings, he engaged in no planning activity, and he didn't have a "cool head," because even though he was a skilled marksman, he missed with many of the rifle shots from a short range, which showed he was agitated and excited.

The *en banc* court held the evidence was sufficient to prove premeditation. That court thought it significant that after deciding to kill the victim, Begay walked back to his car, got his rifle, walked back to the car in which the victim was a passenger, walked around to the passenger window, and shot the victim at close range. A jury could reasonably conclude Begay had time then to consider the nature of his conduct, and still went through with the killing. The *en banc* court thus reversed the panel decision, and affirmed the jury verdict of guilty of first-degree murder. The U.S. Supreme Court denied certiorari, 132 S. Ct. 754 (2011).

The "Deadly Weapon" Doctrine

Committing a crime by use of a "deadly weapon," such as assault with a deadly weapon, is commonly a separate and more serious crime. In a murder case, the use of a deadly weapon can also be used to prove "malice" or other intent. Because direct evidence is rarely available to show the actual intent of a person charged with a crime, the fact finder, judge or jury, must draw inferences about intent from the conduct of the accused and the circumstances surrounding the crime to determine if the intent to kill existed. The use of a deadly weapon creates an inference of the user's intent. For example, if a defendant pointed a weapon he or she knew to be loaded at another person and pulled the trigger, no direct evidence of intent exists, but intent can be inferred by the defendant's conduct.

The "deadly weapon" doctrine is related to and part of the inference that a person intends the natural and probable consequences of his or her deliberate acts. A loaded revolver is certainly a deadly weapon when aimed and fired at close range. Under such circumstances, a jury can easily infer an intent to kill, because the natural and probable consequences of this act are death or serious bodily harm.

Determining what constitutes a deadly weapon depends on the object used and the circumstances that existed at the time of the homicide. One area where courts are split on this question involves whether human body parts—fists, feet, or teeth—can be deadly weapons. See *Parts of the Body as Dangerous Weapons*, 8 ALR 4th 1268 (1981; 2010 Cum. Supp.). Some jurisdictions hold that parts of the body cannot be a deadly weapon for purposes of conviction of crimes requiring the presence or use of a deadly weapon. For example, in the 2010 case of *McMillian v. State*,[22] the defendant used his teeth to bite out his girlfriend's left eye. The court held that using teeth to injure another cannot be "use of a deadly weapon" for purposes of a domestic assault statute. That appears to be the position of the Model Penal Code, § 210.0 (4).

On the other hand, in the 2009 cases of *Dasher v. State*[23] and *State v. Wallace*,[24] the courts held that fists or feet could be deadly weapons depending on how they were used, and the relative size of the assailant and victim. Most courts do agree that if an assailant is wearing heavy boots during an assault, the boots themselves are an extra-bodily object and can thus be a deadly weapon.[25]

Therefore, in determining what a deadly weapon is, a jury considers the instrument used, who used it, and how it was used. Some items, such as knives, clubs, or guns, are almost always considered deadly weapons because of the potential harm they can cause. Other instruments, such as automobiles, have to be viewed in light of their uses. The U.S. Supreme Court ruled in the early case of *Allen v. United States* that a lower court erred when it withdrew the question of self-defense from a jury on the ground that sticks and clubs were not deadly weapons.[26] Sticks and clubs can be deadly weapons, depending on their size, who is using them, and how they are used. The same is true for boots used to kick a victim in the head, a hardwood floor on which an infant's head was battered, and a nail gun.

Transferred Intent

If a killer is a poor shot and misses the intended victim but hits and kills another person, he or she could argue that there was no intent to kill that person. If there was a mistake of identity and the killer kills the wrong person, the same argument could be made. Defense lawyers have used these arguments for hundreds of years, arguing that because there was no ill will and malice toward the victim killed by accident, the defendant should not be convicted of intent-to-kill murder but, at the most, negligent or reckless homicide.

To accept such arguments would allow killers to benefit because of their poor marksmanship or because they killed the wrong person in a mix-up. The common law rejected that argument by creating the doctrine of **transferred intent**. This doctrine became part of the common law before the American Revolution and was recognized as early as 1766 by Blackstone in 4 *Commentaries* 200–201.

The transferred intent doctrine rests on the sensible foundation that where one has demonstrated the intent to take another person's life, it should not matter whose life is taken. The culpability of the killer remains the same: a life was taken intentionally. The law achieves this result by "transferring" the intent to kill the intended victim to the victim that actually is killed.

It does not alter the "transferred intent" doctrine if the killer manages to kill both the intended victim and another person. In the 2011 case of *Henry v. State*,[27] the defendant fired several rifle shots into a group of men fighting each other. The defendant hit the intended victim seven times, killing him. He also hit a bystander, killing her as well. The Maryland Supreme Court held that even if the defendant succeeded in killing his intended target, the doctrine of transferred intent would apply to the other person killed.

The transferred intent doctrine also may be used to prove the required "premeditation" for a first-degree murder conviction. Thus, if A aims a gun at B in a premeditated act to kill B, but instead strikes C, A can be convicted of the **premeditated murder** of C. See Wayne R. LaFave, 2 *Substantive Criminal Law*, § 14.7(a) (2nd Ed. 2003). However, the transferred intent doctrine *by itself* cannot be used to prove premeditation if the defendant in fact intended to kill the person who died. In such a case, the defendant's premeditated intent to kill another person does not "transfer," because the defendant had some kind of actual intent with respect to the actual victim. The nature of that intent must be proved by the prosecution. In the case of *State v. Hall*,[28] the defendant left an apartment with a gun, saying he planned to kill three unidentified people. In fact, the defendant walked to a gas station and fired four shots point-blank at the station clerk. The trial court instructed the jury that under the transferred intent doctrine the premeditation to kill the three unidentified people satisfied the premeditation requirement for the killing of the clerk. The Minnesota Supreme Court reversed, saying that because there was no evidence the clerk was an unintended victim, the prosecution needed to prove the defendant premeditated the clerk's death.

Finally, transferred intent cannot be used to make one person's death sufficient to sustain two murder convictions, at least one court has held. In *People v. Dubarry*, 31 N.E.3d 86 (N.Y. 2015) the defendant engaged in a gunfight on Brooklyn city streets with a rival. He fired at the rival, but missed and struck the victim, who was standing in front of a building near the shooting. The victim died, and defendant was charged with both depraved indifference murder and intentional murder, under the transferred intent doctrine. A jury convicted the defendant on both charges. On appeal, the court ordered a new trial, holding that while the transferred intent doctrine applied to make the killing of the victim an intentional murder, the defendant

transferred intent A doctrine used when the intention to harm one individual inadvertently causes a second person to be hurt instead. The individual causing the harm will be seen as having "intended" the act by means of the "transferred intent" doctrine.

premeditation Mental determination to unlawfully kill another person after planning or reflection on actions causing death.

could not also be convicted of depraved indifference murder, even though that is a separate crime.

Intent-to-Do-Serious-Bodily-Harm Murder

English courts under the common law long ago decided that a death at the hands of one who intended to do only serious bodily harm was nevertheless murder. The following famous English cases illustrate this type of murder:

Rex v. Errington
2 Lew. C.C. 148, 217 (1838)

The defendants covered a drunken man, who was sleeping, with straw, on which they threw a shovel of hot cinders. The man burned to death in the fire that resulted. The court instructed the jury that if they found that the defendants intended to do any serious harm to the deceased, the crime was murder under the common law; if the defendants' only intent was to play a joke or frighten the deceased, the crime was manslaughter.

Holloway Case
79 Eng. Rep. 715 (K.B. 1628)

The defendant tied a boy to a horse's tail and hit the horse to make it run. The boy was killed. The defendant was convicted of murder even though it was found that there was no intent to kill.

Many states follow this common law approach, and include "intent-to-do-serious-bodily-harm" as a class of murder. For example, Tex. Penal Code Ann. § 19.02(b)(2) includes in the definition of murder a person who "intends to cause serious bodily harm and commits an act clearly dangerous to human life that causes the death of an individual." In the 2012 case of *Cavazos v. State*,[29] the Texas Court of Criminal Appeals held that a man who pulled a gun at a party, pointed it at a person taunting him, and pulled the trigger twice could be found guilty of murder, even though no evidence of intent to kill was presented. Pointing a gun at another person and pulling the trigger is "clearly dangerous" the court held, even if no intent to kill was shown. The court affirmed the jury verdict of guilty of murder.

State murder statutes vary on the inclusion of "serious bodily injury" as a class or type of murder. Those that retain that class generally include it as second-degree murder, although Illinois continues to include it in the first-degree murder statute, 720 ILCS 5/9-1. The Model Penal Code, § 210.2 omits any reference to "intent to do serious bodily harm" in the classification of murder. Rather, the fact that a defendant intended to inflict serious harm would be a factor in showing the kind of "extreme indifference to the value of human life" that is included in the definition of murder.

Depraved-Mind or Depraved-Heart Murder

"Depraved heart" murder, which in some states is called second-degree murder, is similar in some aspects to intent-to-do-serious-bodily-harm murder. The primary difference is that depraved-heart murder includes no specific intent to injure or harm. However, if the conduct of the defendant were so reckless as to create a high risk of death, he or she would, in many instances, be found guilty of depraved-heart murder.

Since intent to kill is not an element of depraved-heart murder, the crime can be proved by evidence of extremely reckless actions. The distinction between "recklessly causing a death," which in most cases would be classified as involuntary manslaughter, and "depraved heart" murder, is not always clear. "Reckless" homicide generally means acting without regard to a substantial risk that death could ensue. "Depraved heart" homicide, similar to the Model Penal Code's definition of murder, means acting with "extreme indifference to the value of human life."

In the 2012 case of *Hawkins v. State*[30] the Mississippi Supreme Court affirmed a jury verdict of "depraved heart" murder under Miss. Code § 97-2-19(1)(b), which defines depraved heart murder as taking a life with actions "evincing a depraved heart, regardless of human life." The defendant got in a fight with his girlfriend, and struck her forcefully in the head at least once. Medical experts testified the victim had severe heart disease, and died from a trauma-induced heart attack. It was not clear if defendant was aware of the victim's heart condition. The court said defendant's actions satisfied the definition of depraved heart murder, and affirmed the jury verdict.

California is one of the states that define extremely reckless homicides as second-degree murder, not "depraved heart" murder. In the 2012 case of *People v. Cravens*[31] the California Supreme Court stated that this kind of murder requires a showing of "implied malice," which has both a physical and mental component. The physical component is "an act, the probable consequences of which are dangerous to life." The mental component is acting "with a conscious disregard for life." In that case the defendant struck a violent fist-blow to an impaired victim, causing the victim to hit the concrete pavement with his head, causing his death. The court said that while a blow with a fist would not ordinarily show implied malice, it did here. The court noted the victim was intoxicated, and was reeling from blows administered by defendant's friends. After knocking the helpless victim to the ground the defendant laughed, and made no attempt to summon medical help. The court affirmed the jury verdict of guilty of second-degree murder.

felony murder Most states and the federal government have felony murder statutes that punish as murder the causing of death of another while the defendant is committing a felony of violence. A felony murder conviction does not require a showing of malice or deliberate intent to kill.

Felony Murder

The **felony murder** rule became part of the common law of England many years ago. The rule initially stated that if a death occurs while a person is committing or attempting to commit any felony, the person could be convicted of felony murder even if the death was unintended and accidental. The theory behind the rule was that the intent to commit the underlying felony sufficed to show the intent to kill.

In the United States, courts and legislatures have limited the scope of the felony murder rule. The most frequent method of limiting the rule is illustrated by the federal murder statute, 18 U.S.C. § 1111. That statute includes as murder only a killing that occurs during the commission of certain enumerated crimes, such as arson, robbery, or sexual assault. If a person is killed during the commission of a felony not listed in § 1111, it is not murder *solely* because of the felony committed. In such a case, the prosecution would need to prove the required intent.

Other methods of determining when the felony murder rule is appropriate include a requirement that the killing was the "natural and direct consequence" of the felony, or that the act that caused the death occurred while the felony was in progress. In *People v. Klebanowski,*[32] the Illinois Supreme Court held the felony-murder rule, which applied to killings that occurred "during the commission" of a felony, applied when one of two robbers was killed by the victim (an off-duty police officer) during the robbers' attempt to escape. In *State v. Beach,*[33] the Kansas Supreme Court held that unless the defendant showed that an intervening force caused a death during the commission of a crime, there was no duty on the prosecution to prove otherwise that the death was a "direct result" of the commission. The court reasoned that the absence of an intervening force by itself established the causal connection between the felony and the killing.

Many states also have a version of the "continuous transaction" doctrine. Under that doctrine, a death triggers the felony murder rule only if the death was part of a continuous transaction with the underlying felony. In the 2013 case of *People v. Wilkins*, 295 P.3d 903 (Cal. 2013), the California Supreme Court reversed the conviction of a burglar who was found guilty of felony murder. The defendant had stolen several large appliances from a construction site, loading them in the back of his pickup, but forgot to shut the tailgate. While he was driving on the interstate sixty miles away from the burglary site an appliance fell off the pickup, causing an accident where a motorist was killed. A jury convicted the defendant of first-degree

YOU BE THE JUDGE

The defendant before you has been charged with second degree murder under the felony-murder rule. Defendant left her 5-year-old daughter unsupervised at home while she went to the grocery store. Upon her return, the defendant discovered her daughter had found a loaded gun kept in defendant's home by defendant's boyfriend, and accidently shot herself in the head. Defendant knew the gun was kept at her home. The daughter died from the gunshot wound a few days later.

The state charged the defendant with murder under the felony murder statute. The predicate crimes listed for the felony murder rule to apply include "cruelty to juveniles." The defendant has filed a motion in your court to quash (dismiss) the indictment, contending she cannot be convicted as a matter of law under the felony murder statute. What should you rule on her motion? What if you were a judge in Louisiana, where the Louisiana Supreme Court had earlier decided *State v. Small*, 100 So.3d 797 (La. 2012)? (Discussed in Chapter 3.) Would that case affect your decision? See *State v. Smith*, 156 So.3d 1227 (La. App. 2014).

felony murder. The California Supreme Court reversed, holding that under the "escape" rule, once the burglar had reached a "place of safety" away from the crime scene, any subsequent death could not be part of a continuous transaction with the burglary.

The Model Penal Code's definition of murder in section 210.2 omits any reference to the felony murder rule. Instead, that section states that if a homicide occurs during one of the listed crimes (e.g., robbery, rape, arson, or kidnapping) it is presumed that it was the result of "extreme indifference to the value of human life" and thus constitutes murder under § 210.2(b). Some state murder statutes, such as the statute in Kentucky, K.R.S. § 507.020, follow the Model Penal Code and drop the felony murder rule, instead using the "extreme indifference" language of the MPC.

In most states, though not all, it has been held that the death of a person, including a co-felon, that occurs during a felony but is caused by a third person—such as a person who was the intended victim, a passerby, or a police officer who confronts a felony in progress—does not qualify as felony murder. These states subscribe to what has been called the "agency" foundation of the felony murder rule. That is, if one of several persons committing a felony causes a death, the "malice" of that person is imputed to the others. However, where the death is caused by a third person, there is no "malice" to impute to the persons committing the felony.

Thus, if the police confront two robbers, and kill one of the robbers, the other robber is not guilty of felony murder. In New York, Penal Law § 125.25 states the felony murder rule applies when the defendant or "another participant" in the crime kills another person "other than a participant." In the 2012 case of *Davis v. Fox*[34] the West Virginia Supreme Court held that the killing of one of two persons committing a burglary by the owner of the building did not subject the surviving burglar to the felony murder rule. The court said that the purpose of the felony murder rule was to substitute the "malicious" intent underlying the felony for the "malicious" intent for the killing. When two defendants are involved in the felony, and one kills a third party, the malicious intent of the killer is transferred to the other defendant. However, when a death occurs that is not caused by either of the defendants, the requisite malice needed for a murder charge is not present, the court held. Citing other cases, the court said that "the thing that is imputed to a felon for a killing incidental to his felony is *malice and not the act of killing*." It ordered the dismissal of the felony murder charge. In the 2015 case of *Commonwealth v. Tejeda*, 41 N.E.3d 721 (Mass. 2015) the court rejected the state's argument it should adopt the "proximate cause" theory in felony murder cases, noting that the majority of states follow the agency or malice theory for the application of the rule to deaths caused by third parties.

In the minority of states, as the *Klebanowski* case discussed earlier shows to be the result in Illinois, the death of a co-felon makes the remaining felon guilty of felony murder. These courts follow the "proximate cause" theory of the felony murder rule, not the "agency" theory of implied malice illustrated above.

The Oklahoma Appellate Court reached that conclusion in *Kinchson v. State*.[35] The court affirmed the murder conviction of one of two robbers when the other robber was killed by the intended victim of the robbery. The court said that the felony murder rule applies because it was foreseeable that committing the crime of armed robbery could result in death of a person, including one of the perpetrators of the robbery. This also appears to be the rule in prosecutions under 18 U.S.C. § 1111. In

United States v. Garcia-Ortiz, 528 F.3d 74 (1st Cir. 2008), *cert. denied* 129 S. Ct. 254 (2008), the court held that a defendant could be convicted of felony murder when an accomplice was killed by a third party.

In those states that do not apply the felony murder rule to the killing of a co-felon by a third party, a co-felon could be charged with provocative act murder. That doctrine applies if the co-felon took some action that was likely to provoke the third party into using deadly force. For example, in *People v. Concha,*[36] the California Supreme Court held a defendant could be convicted of first-degree murder under the "provocative act" murder doctrine when the victim of an attempted murder killed a co-felon. The court stated that in California even though a co-felon could not be guilty of felony murder in connection with either the death of another felon or death caused by a third party, if the underlying crime was the proximate cause of the death, the provocative act murder doctrine applied. Moreover, rejecting the defendant's argument to the contrary, the court held that if a jury found the attempted murder was premeditated, then the resulting death of the co-felon would be first-degree murder.

MANSLAUGHTER

Definition of Manslaughter

manslaughter Criminal homicides other than murder. Most states provide for two degrees of manslaughter: voluntary and involuntary.

Manslaughter was defined by common law as a classification of criminal homicide that is less than murder. The common law divided manslaughter into two categories: voluntary and involuntary. Most U.S. jurisdictions follow the common law classifications, but a few states have created three categories. For example, Section 192 of the California Penal Code creates the three classifications of voluntary, involuntary, and vehicular manslaughter. A few states have only one degree of manslaughter. Another form of classification identifies manslaughter by degrees (first, second, and so on)[37] rather than voluntary and involuntary.

Reasons given for a manslaughter conviction rather than a murder conviction are as follows:

1. The victim may have provoked the killing, or his or her unlawful conduct set into motion a chain of events that resulted in the killing.

2. The circumstances of the killing are not bad enough to be charged as murder, but the defendant's criminal conduct should be punished.

3. In some cases, the jury cannot unanimously agree on a finding of murder, and compromises on a manslaughter conviction.

Manslaughter is a crime that is generally considered to be separate and distinct from murder. Because the penalties are less severe than for murder, defense lawyers who are unable to obtain an acquittal for clients seek a conviction of manslaughter rather than murder.

Voluntary Manslaughter

The crime of voluntary manslaughter requires proof of an intentional killing. It differs from murder in that the killing is not accompanied by premeditation or malice. Thus, in any case where the defendant intentionally killed another person, circumstances must be examined to determine if the defendant lacked the required malice for a murder charge. Absence of malice can be shown in most states by either evidence of a "sudden quarrel" or "heat of passion" that directly preceded the intentional killing, or evidence of "imperfect" self-defense.

Heat of Passion Manslaughter

All states provide for lesser charge of voluntary manslaughter where an intentional killing occurs in the "heat of passion." This crime is commonly charged when the actions of the victim cause the defendant to become enraged and angered to the point of losing normal self-control and, in the heat of passion, kill another person.

 ## EXAMPLES OF MANSLAUGHTER

Heat of Passion Manslaughter

EXAMPLE: D and V, a married couple, are separated. D arrives at V's residence and observes V having sex with another man. D becomes enraged, and kills V. Although D's actions show an intentional killing, the "heat of passion" likely would be seen as eliminating the "malice" need for a murder conviction.

Heat of passion manslaughter would be likely because

1. There was adequate provocation, which caused
2. Extreme anger and rage in a reasonable person,
3. There was no opportunity to cool off, and
4. There was a causal connection between the provocation, anger, and the fatal act.

Imperfect Self-Defense Manslaughter

EXAMPLE: Defendant unlawfully started a fistfight with another person. The other person pulled out a knife, which under the circumstances was excessive force. Seeing the knife, the defendant pulled a gun and shot the other person, killing him. Since defendant was the wrongful aggressor, his claim of self-defense is "imperfect": self-defense only applies if the other person is the wrongful aggressor. However, even though the killing was intentional, it lacks the "malice" required for a murder conviction, because the defendant was responding to excessive force.

EXAMPLE: Defendant honestly but unreasonably believed a person approaching him was about to strike him with a knife. In fact, the person was holding a flashlight. Defendant shot the person, causing his death. If the defendant actually had the mistaken belief, the killing was intentional, but the defendant lacked the malice required for murder. The defendant would not be entitled to claim self-defense, because he used unlawful force under the circumstances. His belief about the attack would permit the imperfect self-defense to lower the killing to manslaughter.

Involuntary Manslaughter (Also Called Unintended Manslaughter)

EXAMPLE: A defendant repeatedly allowed vicious dogs to run loose, even though the dogs had on past occasions attacked people they encountered. If the dogs attacked and killed a person, the killing would not be murder, because the defendant did not intend the killing to occur. However, because allowing the dogs to run loose created an unusually high risk of injury or death, involuntary manslaughter could be charged.

In 2 Wayne R. LaFave, *Substantive Criminal Law,* § 15.2(A), at 492 (West 2003) it is said,

> There are four obstacles for the defendant to overcome before he can have his intentional killing reduced from murder to manslaughter: (1) There must have been a reasonable provocation. (2) The defendant must have been in fact provoked. (3) A reasonable man so provoked would not have cooled off in the interval of time between the provocation and the delivery of the fatal blow. And (4), the defendant must not in fact have cooled off during that interval.

In the 2012 case of *United States v. Jack*[38] a defendant convicted of murder appealed, contending the jury should have been given instructions on "heat of passion" manslaughter. The defendant killed his wife, but contended it occurred in a heat of passion brought on by her admission she was having an affair with another man. The appeals court held that although under some circumstances knowledge of an affair can be sufficient provocation for a heat of passion claim, those circumstances were not present here. The court noted that no evidence linked the time defendant found out about the affair to the killing, and in any case the evidence established that after arguing with his wife the defendant's father calmed him down, and the killing occurred several hours later. The court affirmed his murder conviction.

Sufficient and Adequate Provocation   Sufficient provocation naturally and instantly produces in the mind of an ordinary person the highest degree of exasperation, rage, anger, sudden resentment, or terror. The provocation must be of such a nature and be so great as to overcome or suspend an ordinary person's exercise of good judgment. The provocation must be such as to cause the person to act uncontrollably. The killing must occur immediately during or after the provocation and during the intense heat of passion. Only a few categories of provocation have been recognized by the law as legally sufficient and adequate to justify reduction of a murder charge to that of manslaughter.

In the United States, there is an almost uniform rule that words and gestures are never sufficient provocation to reduce a charge of murder to that of manslaughter. The U.S. Supreme Court stated in the early case *of Allen v. United States* that "mere words alone do not excuse even a simple assault. Any words offered at the time [of the killing] do not reduce the grade of the killing from murder to manslaughter."[39]

Although words and gestures alone are never sufficient provocation, if other acts, such as a battery, accompany the verbal provocation, then it might be held to be sufficient. In *People v. Rice,* the deceased slapped the defendant's child and a quarrel resulted.[40] This was held to be sufficient provocation. In the Georgia case of *Lamp v. State,* a minor and technical battery accompanied by words was held to amount to a sufficient provocation to justify reducing the conviction from murder to manslaughter.[41] But in *Commonwealth v. Cisneros,* the Pennsylvania Supreme Court arrived at an opposite conclusion.[42]

Many U.S. courts have held that when a married person finds his or her spouse in an act of adultery, this amounts to sufficient provocation if it causes a genuine heat of passion.[43] In the 2014 case of *Lynn v. State*[44] the Georgia Supreme Court reversed a murder conviction because the trial court refused to permit evidence that at the time of her death the victim told the defendant, her husband, that she was being unfaithful to him. The court said that while words are not normally sufficient provocation to reduce murder to manslaughter, "words that disclose the adulterous conduct of a spouse are not *just* words," the court said.

Trespass, like battery, depends on the facts and circumstances in each particular case. A homeowner certainly does not have sufficient and adequate provocation to kill someone who walks across a lawn, yard, farm, or field in the middle of an afternoon. But snowmobilers who broke onto a farmer's land in Wisconsin and were circling the farmhouse at midnight caused a Wisconsin prosecutor to charge manslaughter when the farmer, in a terrible anger and rage, shot and killed one of the trespassers.

Courts often hold that mercy killing is not a defense to a murder charge (see the euthanasia section in this chapter). In a similar way, courts have also held that a request by a dying person to be killed is not adequate provocation to support the reduced charge of manslaughter. In the 2011 case of *State v. Goulding*[45] the court held that killing the victim at the victim's request, because the victim failed in an attempt to take his own life, was murder, not manslaughter or assisted suicide.

Heat of Passion and the Test of the Reasonable Person

The test of sufficiency or adequacy of provocation must be made in view of how the average or reasonable person would react to such provocation. Some people have extraordinary self-control and could endure much provocation before an uncontrollable rage would cause them to use deadly force. Others have short tempers and fly into a rage with little provocation.

A jury cannot give any special considerations to a defendant who has an extraordinarily bad temper. If the provocation is such that it would not cause the average reasonable person to explode in a sudden outburst of rage, it is not adequate or sufficient provocation to reduce murder to manslaughter. California courts have quoted with approval the statements of the court in the case of *People v. Logan*:

> The fundamental . . . inquiry is whether or not the defendant's reason was, at the time of his act, so disturbed or obscured by some passion—not necessarily fear and never of course the passion of revenge—to such an extent as would render *ordinary men of average disposition* liable to act rashly or without due deliberation and reflection, and from this passion rather than from judgment.[46] [Emphasis added.]

In the 2013 case of *People v. Beltran*, 301 P.3d 1120, the California Supreme Court, again basing its reasoning on the *Logan* decision, held that "heat of passion" requires only a showing that a reasonable person would under the circumstances act without rational thought but in response to the provocation. The court rejected the state's argument that the provocation must be such that it would move an ordinary person to *kill* another person. All that must be shown, the court said, is provocation that would "cause an emotion so intense that an ordinary person would simply react, without reflection." The focus of heat of passion must be on the mental state, not the act, the court said.

The case of *Bedder v. Director of Public Prosecutions* received considerable attention throughout the English-speaking world.[47] The defendant, who knew that he was impotent, attempted to have sexual intercourse with a London prostitute in a quiet courtyard. She jeered when he was unsuccessful and attempted to get away from him. He tried to hold her, and she slapped him in the face and punched him in the stomach. When he grabbed her shoulders, she kicked him in the groin. He took a knife from his pocket and stabbed her twice, killing her. The House of Lords affirmed both the finding of the jury that there was not sufficient or adequate provocation and the following jury instruction given by the trial court:

> The reasonable person, the ordinary person, is the person you must consider when you are considering the effect which any acts, any conduct, any words, might have to justify the steps which were taken in response thereto, so that an unusually excitable or pugnacious individual, or a drunken one or a man who is sexually impotent is not entitled to rely on provocation which would not have led an ordinary person to have acted in the way which was in fact carried out.

Cooling of the Blood   Cooling of the blood, also known as *cooling time* or *reasonable time to cool off*, is a factor that must be considered if there is an interval between the provocation and the killing. Assume that after Y provokes X into a heat of passion, X, who has lost his self-control, runs to get his gun. If it took X two minutes to get his gun, was this sufficient time for X to cool off? If it took X a half hour or an hour to obtain his gun, was this sufficient time for the heat of passion to cool off? These questions would have to be answered by a court and jury that would consider the type and degree of the provocation that caused the heat of passion.

Third-Party Provocation   Under the common law, the heat-of-passion/provocation claim could be asserted to reduce a murder charge to manslaughter only if the victim was also the one doing the provocative acts. This was explained as the requirement that there be a "causal" connection between the provocation and the fatal acts.

EXAMPLE   Defendant and his estranged wife were arguing. The wife's brother intervened and fought the defendant to the ground. The defendant became enraged, and got away. He ran into his house, grabbed a knife, came outside, and stabbed his wife, who died. The court held the defendant was not entitled to a manslaughter instruction, because the victim, his wife, did not supply the provocation. *Commonwealth. v. LeClair*[48] (Mass. 2006).

The Model Penal Code, § 210.3 (Comment 5), would make provocation by a third party sufficient to reduce a murder to manslaughter, if the other requirements have been met. Under the MPC approach, it is the extreme mental state of the defendant, not the source of the provocation, which is important. Only a few states have adopted the MPC's approach. One is Minnesota, where in the case of *State v. Stewart*[49] the court held that the provocative action of a third party—telling defendant she was HIV positive—could be used to reduce a charge of murder to manslaughter of another victim. However, the court held in that case that the defendant killed the

perfect self-defense A homicide in which the killer subjectively believes that his or her conduct was necessary and reasonable and that, by objective standards, a reasonable person would believe it was lawful and complied with the requirements of the law. The homicide is either justifiable or excusable, and it carries no criminal liability.

imperfect self-defense A homicide in which the killer subjectively, but unreasonably, believes that his or her conduct was necessary. It may be unlawful if the killing was done with excessive or unnecessary force. An unnecessary killing in self-defense, in defense of another, or to prevent or terminate a felony of violence could be imperfect self-defense.

victim, a child, in order to keep his crying from alerting the police. Thus, the victim was not killed as part of the rage brought on by the news the defendant's girlfriend was HIV positive. It affirmed the defendant's murder conviction.

Imperfect or Unlawful Force in Self-Defense Charged as Manslaughter

Homicide in **perfect self-defense** is either justifiable or excusable, and it carries no criminal liability. Perfect self-defense not only requires that the killer subjectively believe that his or her conduct was necessary but also that, by objective standards, a reasonable person would believe it was lawful and complied with the requirements of the law.

To use deadly force in self-defense, a person must reasonably believe he or she is (1) under threat of *imminent* death or great bodily harm, from (2) unlawful deadly force, and (3) that use of deadly force is necessary. If the belief in the imminent threat is not reasonable, and the person has other options available, deadly force is not legally justified.

If deadly force is used but not justified, and results in a death, the death could be treated as murder. However, one who kills with an actual, but unreasonable, belief that one is acting in self-defense differs from other intentional murders: "malice" is not present. That difference led many courts and legislatures to develop the mitigating doctrine known as **imperfect self-defense**.

In imperfect self-defense, the killer subjectively believes that his or her conduct was lawful and necessary, but that belief is unreasonable. If the killing was done with excessive or unnecessary force in self-defense, it is unlawful. An unnecessary killing in self-defense, in defense of another, or to prevent or terminate a felony of violence could be imperfect self-defense.

In imperfect self-defense cases the belief that use of deadly force was justified can occur in two types of situations, illustrated by the following two examples:

EXAMPLE D actually believes V is attacking him with deadly force, and D responds by using deadly force in "self-defense," killing V. In fact, D's belief that V was attacking with deadly force was unreasonable (either because the attack was not imminent, or because the force used was not deadly). D's claim of perfect self-defense will fail.

EXAMPLE D attacks V with non-deadly force. V responds with deadly force. To counter V's threat of deadly force, D uses deadly force and kills V. Because D was the initial aggressor, and didn't retreat or use all efforts to avoid using deadly force, in most states his perfect self-defense claim would fail.

In the first example most states would permit the defendant to raise imperfect self-defense to mitigate a murder charge to manslaughter. For example, in *State v. Head*[50] the Wisconsin Supreme Court said that under W.S.A. § 940.01, a defendant who actually but unreasonably believed she needed to use deadly force to defend herself from her husband's physical abuses could raise imperfect self-defense to reduce the crime from first degree intentional homicide (murder) to second degree intentional homicide (manslaughter):

> We conclude in this case that [defendant's] offer of proof established a sufficient factual basis for a claim of unnecessary defensive force (imperfect self-defense), and that she should have been allowed to present evidence of [the victim's] violent character and past acts of violence at trial in an effort to mitigate the charge of intentional first degree homicide.

In the 2012 case of *People v. Lopez*[51] the California appeals court reached a similar result. It said that imperfect self-defense is permitted under California law:

> Manslaughter is an unlawful killing without malice. (Citation omitted). The element of malice is negated, and a killing reduced from murder to voluntary manslaughter, when a defendant kills in the actual but unreasonable belief that he or she is in imminent danger of death or great bodily injury.

In the second example given above, where the defendant was the initial aggressor, some state courts have held imperfect self-defense is not available. Illinois is such a state.[52] However, even courts that have held that imperfect self-defense is not available in this situation note that some situations where the defense is claimed are situations where the prosecution may be unable to prove the malice required for a murder conviction, resulting in a manslaughter conviction without imperfect self-defense. For example, in the 2012 case of *People v. Reese*, the Michigan Supreme Court said,

> Although we reject the doctrine of imperfect self-defense, many circumstances that involve what the Court of Appeals called "imperfect self-defense" can nevertheless provide grounds for a fact-finder to conclude that the prosecution has not proved the malice element that distinguishes murder from manslaughter.[53]

Involuntary Manslaughter

Involuntary manslaughter—sometimes called *unintentional* or *unlawful act manslaughter*—was discussed in Chapter 3 in relation to proximate cause or causation.

Involuntary manslaughter is often charged when extreme negligence or wanton or reckless conduct by the defendant brings about an unintended or accidental death. Two examples of cases in which defendants were charged and convicted of involuntary manslaughter follow. (For further cases on involuntary manslaughter, see Chapter 3.)

- *Extreme negligence and failure to act:* In the 2010 case of *Whitfield v. Commonwealth*[54] the Virginia Court of Appeals affirmed a conviction of involuntary manslaughter when a day-care driver placed a 13-month-old child in a van to go to the day care, but left the child in the van the entire day while he went home to sleep. The outside temperature reached 84 degrees, and all the van windows were closed. The child died before anyone discovered the child was in the van.
- *Reckless conduct:* A congressman from South Dakota with a history of careless driving was convicted of involuntary manslaughter when, traveling 16 miles per hour over the speed limit, he ran a stop sign and struck and killed a motorcyclist.

Most states have a vehicular manslaughter/homicide statute that can be used to charge a person who operates a vehicle in a grossly negligent manner and people are killed as a result. These statutes usually distinguish ordinary automobile-accident deaths from homicide crimes by requiring the prosecution to prove aggravating circumstances, such as intoxication or extremely reckless driving. In the 2012 case of *Otuwa v. State*[55] the Georgia appeals court affirmed a defendant's conviction for first-degree vehicular homicide. The defendant drove his car on a residential road at speeds up to 93 miles per hour. He lost control of the car and rolled it, killing two passengers. The defendant's blood alcohol level was twice the legal limit. The court said that under the Georgia statute, a person is guilty of first-degree vehicular homicide if he is (1) driving while intoxicated or (2) driving recklessly, and causes a death. Second-degree vehicular homicide requires only a showing the defendant committed some other traffic offense, such as speeding.

SUICIDE, ASSISTING SUICIDE, AND EUTHANASIA

In common law, suicide was considered to be self-murder and was a felony. Because the person who committed such a crime was beyond the reach of the law, the punishment was forfeiture of the deceased person's estate to the king and burial off the highway.

Assisting a suicide is a crime in most states. A person could assist another to commit suicide by conduct (or words) that a trial judge or a jury finds to amount to "assisting."

euthanasia A killing of a terminally sick or injured individual with only a short time to live. Also called mercy killing.

Euthanasia—or mercy killing—is murder. However, the motive for the murder is love, or concern for the suffering of the victim. In the case of *State v. Forrest*[56] the defendant was convicted of first-degree murder and sentenced to life imprisonment for the mercy killing of his terminally ill father, who was suffering from a number of untreatable illnesses. In such cases, appeals are made to the governor of the state for clemency, which is frequently granted after a number of years.[57]

Murder, Suicide, or Neither?

When one person participates in the death of another, that participation may constitute the crime of murder or assisted suicide. It may not be a crime at all, depending on the degree of participation and the laws of the state having jurisdiction over the acts.

assisting suicide The act of furnishing the means of a suicide, pursuant to a statute that permits such assistance.

The difference between murder and **assisting suicide** was explained by the California Supreme Court in *In re Joseph G.* as follows:

> The key to distinguishing between the crimes of murder and of assisting suicide is the active or passive role of the defendant in the suicide. If the defendant merely furnishes the means, he is guilty of assisting a suicide; if he actively participates in the death of the suicide victim, he is guilty of murder.[58]

The difference between participation that constitutes the crime of assisting suicide and participation that is not criminal is harder to draw. A doctor who, at the patient's or family's request, removes a life-support machine obviously hastens death but does not furnish the means of that death. On the other hand, a doctor who, like Dr. Jack Kevorkian, furnishes a person with a "suicide machine" clearly does furnish the means. Kevorkian admitted in 1997 to "being present" at more than 100 deaths.[59]

So-called passive euthanasia in hospitals does not fall easily into either category. A doctor who "sends a patient home" with a morphine drip and stops all other treatment is, in one sense, only letting nature take its course. On the other hand, the doctor knows that the morphine will shorten the patient's life, so that in prescribing large doses of the morphine he or she is providing the means for death.

Because of the ambiguities surrounding physician-assisted suicide, and because many patients have asserted a "right" to choose physician-assisted suicide, various constitutional attacks on state assisted-suicide statutes have been made. In *Washington v. Glucksberg*[60] and *Vacco v. Quill*,[61] the U.S. Supreme Court upheld the constitutionality of statutes in New York and Washington making physician-assisted suicides criminal. The Court rejected the contention that the Fourteenth Amendment prohibited states from making such conduct criminal. The concept of "liberty" in the Constitution, which spawned the right to marry, to have children, and to an abortion, does not, the Court held, include a right to assistance in choosing the time and manner of one's death.

The Internet has played a role in this controversy. Among the many "chat rooms" accessible on the Internet are sites where groups provide information and assistance on both sides of the assisted-suicide issue. Some "rooms" provide information about preventing suicide, while others share thoughts and information about suicide.

In the 2012 case of *State v. Melchert-Dinkel*[62] the Minnesota appeals court affirmed the conviction of William Melchert-Dinkel of two counts of "urging suicide." Dinkel, a former nurse who had his Minnesota license revoked in 2009, was obsessed with suicide, and under various identities participated in suicide chat rooms. While there, he often both provided information on committing suicide, and encouraged others to commit suicide. He was charged in the deaths of Mark Drybrough, 22, of Coventry, England, and Nadia Kajouji, 18, of Brandon, Ontario. Dinkel urged both people to commit suicide by hanging, and in the case of Kajouji attempted to convince her to do so with a webcam filming the event. Kajouji instead drowned herself in a river in Ontario. Dinkel told investigators he was a party to at least ten suicide "pacts," and that to his knowledge five of the other participants actually killed themselves. (See the chapter-opening discussion of the Minnesota Supreme Court's reversal of the court of appeals' decision.)

In the case *of Baxter v. State*, 224 P.3d 1211 (Mont. 2009), the Montana Supreme Court held that it was not a criminal homicide for a physician to assist a terminally ill patient by giving him a prescription for a lethal drug. Because suicide is not a crime in Montana, the court said assisting the patient to do so was not a crime. Although section 45-5-102(1) MCA made it a crime to unlawfully "cause" another person's death, section 45-2-211(1) provided that consent of the "victim" was a defense, unless such consent was against public policy. The court held consent of a mature, aware, terminally ill patient was not against public policy.

The Oregon "Death with Dignity" Law

Most states make assisting a suicide a crime. Oregon, however, enacted a "death with dignity" law, which became effective in November 1997. The controversial law, which permits assisted suicides, is the first of its kind in the United States. The state of Washington followed with a similar law in 2008.

To qualify under either state's law, a patient must be found to be terminally ill and have less than six months to live. Patients must have the mental capacity to fully understand the situation that confronts them. There is a 15-day waiting period after the patient applies and is found to have qualified for physician-assisted suicide. A physician may then prescribe drugs to end the patient's life, but the physician does not administer the drugs. The physician is granted immunity from liability for her or his role in the process. Since it was enacted, about thirty people a year have used the provisions of the Oregon law. Each year about 30,000 people die in Oregon. There have been no serious efforts to repeal the law.

The Clinton administration decided not to challenge the Oregon "death with dignity" law, but the Bush administration moved to overturn it, contending physicians acting under the law were doing so in violation of the Federal Controlled Substances Act (CSA). In 2004, the Ninth Circuit Court of Appeals upheld the law, noting that the CSA was designed to fight drug abuse, not to regulate medicine and physicians.[63] On review, the U.S. Supreme Court upheld the Oregon law, reasoning that the CSA was directed at drug abuse and that treating a physician writing a prescription for a mercy killing as "drug abuse" was unreasonable.[64]

★★★
LEARNING OBJECTIVES SUMMARY

LO 1. Explain the meaning of corpus delicti and its role in criminal prosecutions.
Corpus delicti means the body of the crime. It must be proved by the prosecution before a defendant can be convicted of a crime.

LO 2. State the current status of the year-and-a-day rule and why its acceptance has waned.
The year-and-a-day rule was adopted as a "bright line" rule of causation in homicide cases. A death beyond that period was not "caused" by the criminal acts. Today, medical science makes proving the connection between actions and a resulting death much easier and clearer, so most states have dropped the year-and-a-day rule.

LO 3. Articulate the elements of the "born alive" requirement.
The "born alive" requirement under the common law excluded the death of unborn children as murder. Many states have dropped the requirement, and make the death of an unborn child a crime separate from murder. In those states that still have the requirement, a fetus must be born "alive," that is, show some signs of brain function, before its death can be murder.

LO 4. Explain the doctrine of transferred intent.
Under the doctrine of transferred intent, the intention formed by the perpetrator of a homicide as to an intended victim is "transferred" to the killing of an unintended victim, thereby satisfying the intent requirement of the applicable homicide statute.

LO 5. List the homicides that do not require proof of intent to kill.
Involuntary manslaughter and reckless homicide do not require proof of intent to kill. Second-degree murder based on intent to do serious bodily injury does not require specific intent to kill. In felony murder convictions, the intent to commit the underlying crime satisfies the intent requirement for murder.

LO 6. Identify which deaths that occur during the commission of a felony qualify as felony murder.
In all states, the death of the victim of a listed felony, and that of a third person killed by the felon, constitute felony murder. In some, but not all, states, the death of innocent persons killed by a third party or co-felons killed by a third party do not constitute felony murder.

LO 7. Describe the difference between voluntary and involuntary manslaughter.
In voluntary manslaughter, the killing was intended, but occurred under circumstances where the defendant, though not excused, is not as culpable as in murder. In involuntary manslaughter the death was not intended, but arose out of severely reckless conduct.

LO 8. List circumstances that could be sufficient to reduce a charge of murder to manslaughter.
A charge of murder could be reduced to manslaughter if provocation existed to cause the criminal conduct, or if insufficient evidence exists to prove malice or premeditation.

LO 9. Explain why the U.S. Supreme Court upheld the Oregon Death with Dignity Law.
The state of Oregon has the power to determine what conduct is criminal in that state, unless it contravenes some federal law. The U.S. Supreme Court held that the Death with Dignity Law did not violate the Federal Controlled Substance Law, and thus was a permissible exercise of state power.

KEY TERMS

homicide, p. 268
"born alive" requirement, p. 273
feticide, p. 273
murder, p. 279

transferred intent, p. 281
premeditation, p. 281
felony murder, p. 283
manslaughter, p. 286

perfect self-defense, p. 291
imperfect self-defense, p. 291
euthanasia, p. 293
assisting suicide, p. 293

CASE ANALYSIS AND WRITING EXERCISES

1. New York is a state that defines "person" as a human being who has been born alive. A fetus in utero is thus not a" person," and one cannot be guilty of a homicide by causing the death of the fetus. However, the death of a fetus intentionally injured in utero, but who is born alive and subsequently dies, can be classified as a homicide. Using this distinction, the state charged a mother with second degree manslaughter after the child she was carrying was injured by her reckless driving, and died a few days after an emergency cesarean operation. Under New York law, second degree manslaughter requires only that the death result from reckless conduct. Should the mother be convicted? Do you see some problems with such a conviction? See *People v. Jorgensen*, 41 N.E.3d 778 (N.Y. 2015).

2. Defendant, while not a member of the New York street gang "Latin Kings," regularly transported gang members and drugs in illegal drug transactions. In one incident, she was told to be available to drive a gang member away from a crime after the gang member finished the job. She was not told the crime included killing a rival gang member. At the appointed spot the gang member got in her car, and she drove him away. The gang member was convicted of murdering the rival gang member. Can the defendant be convicted of murder? If not can she be convicted of being an accessory after the fact to murder under the federal accessory after the fact statute, 18 U.S.C. § 3? What must the prosecution prove for such a conviction? See *United States v. Calderon*, 785 F.3d 847 (2nd Cir. 2015), *cert denied* 136 S. Ct. 252 (2015).

3. Defendant, an occasional drug dealer, kept a stash of cocaine hidden in a hole in a living room couch. His 1-year-old daughter found the cocaine, ingested it, and died. The defendant has been charged with felony murder under the Georgia felony murder law, which includes as predicate crimes intent to distribute illegal drugs and deprivation of a minor resulting in death. Which felony, intent to distribute or deprivation of a minor, will be sufficient to invoke the felony murder rule? If it is the former, what is the causal relationship between the felony of drug distribution and the victim's death? If it is the latter, deprivation of a minor, is the case different from the Louisiana case discussed in the You Be the Judge box in this chapter? See *Williams v. State*, 779 S.E.2d 304 (Ga. 2015).

4. Defendant fatally stabbed a woman. At his trial he asked the court to instruct the jury on manslaughter/imperfect self-defense, claiming he heard voices telling him to protect himself from danger presented by the victim. No other defenses were raised by the defendant. Should the judge give the imperfect self-defense instruction? Did the defendant raise the wrong defense? See *People v. Elmore,* 325 P.3d 951 (Cal. 2014).

ENDNOTES

1. 293 P.3d 567 (Colo. 2013).

2. The court gave the change only prospective effect, and reversed the defendant's conviction under the corpus delicti rule that was in force when he was convicted. It also said the trustworthiness could be shown by proof of facts that corroborated the confession.

3. 807 P.2d 1009 (Cal. 1991).

4. See the *Newsweek* article "Death of the Innocent," August 17, 1998; the *New York Times* article "Mother Goes from Martyr to Defendant in Infanticides," August 7, 1998; and the *Chicago Tribune,* p. 20, September 25, 1997.

5. 470 P.2d 617 (Cal. 1970).

6. In 1994, the California Supreme Court held that the state could punish fetal murder without regard to the viability of the fetus. *People v. Davis,* 872 P.2d 591.

7. 530 N.W.2d 174 (Mich. App. 1995).

8. 705 A.2d 805 (N.J. App. 1998).

9. *Swafford v. State,* 421 N.E.2d 596 (Ind. 1981).

10. Of the many court cases involving brain-dead victims, two young women received a great amount of public attention. Nancy Cruzan received severe injuries in an auto accident, and Karen Ann Quinlan was brain dead because of a drug overdose. After years in vegetative states, the parents of both young women went into courts to obtain permission to withdraw life-support systems. In both cases, the parents carried the burden of showing that their incompetent daughters would not have wanted to go on living in vegetative states. See *In re Quinlan,* 70 N.J. 10, 355 A.2d 647 (1976), *review denied,* 429 U.S. 922, 97 S. Ct. 319 (1976) and *In re Cruzan,* 497 U.S. 261, 110 S. Ct. 2841 (1990).

    In the 1990 *Cruzan* case, the U.S. Supreme Court held that states could establish standards such as the Missouri "clear and convincing" evidence requirement showing that Nancy Cruzan would have wanted to die. The state of Missouri, which was paying about $112,000 per year to keep Cruzan alive in a "persistent vegetative state," had opposed efforts by her parents to have life-support systems withdrawn. In a hearing after the Supreme Court's decision, a Missouri court heard new evidence presented by three of Cruzan's co-workers, who testified that Nancy had stated she would never have wanted to live "like a vegetable." Cruzan's doctor testified that her existence was a "living hell." After eight years on life-support systems, the feeding tube was removed, and Nancy Cruzan died.

11. 387 N.W.2d 682 (Neb. 1986).

12. 703 S.E.2d 609 (Ga. 2010), *cert. denied,* 131 S. Ct. 2454 (2011).

13. *People v. Stevenson,* 416 Mich. 383, 331 N.W.2d 143 (1982). See also *State v. Hefler,* 60 N.C. App. 466, 299 S.E.2d 456 (1983), *affirmed* 310 N.C. 135, 310 S.E.2d 310, 34 CrL 2374 (1984), in which the North Carolina court stated: "For the courts to remain judicially oblivious of these advances [in medical science] when considering whether to extend an ancient common law rule would be folly."

14. 661 N.W.2d 381 (Wis. 2003).

15. 890 So.2d 1056 (Ala. 2003).

16. See Jay Robert Nash, *Bloodletters and Badmen: A Narrative Encyclopedia of American Criminals from the Pilgrims to the Present* (New York: M. Evans & Co., 1974).

17. 720 ILCS 5/9-1.

18. In a case in which the defendant shot a 15-year-old gasoline service station attendant in the head, neck, and back six times, the Minnesota Supreme Court held:

    Extensive planning and calculated deliberation need not be shown by the prosecution. The requisite "plan" to commit a first-degree murder can be formulated virtually instantaneously by a killer . . . . Moreover . . . premeditation can be inferred from either the number of gunshots fired into the victim . . . or the fact that a killer arms himself with a loaded gun in preparation. State v. Neumann, 262 N. W.2d 426 (Minn. 1978).

19. 673 F.3d 1038 (9th Cir. 2011).

20. Federal Circuit Courts of Appeal hear cases in panels of three judges. When there is disagreement with a panel decision a request can be made for the case to be reheard in front of all the judges in that circuit. When this rehearing is held it is called *en banc.*

21. 567 F.3d 540, 546 (9th Cir. 2009).

22. 58 So.3d 849 (Ala. App. 2010).

23. 676 S.E.2d 181 (Ga. 2009).

24. 676 S.E.2d 922 (N.C. App. 2009).

25. See, e.g., *Commonwealth. v. Rumkin,* 773 N.E.2d 988 (Mass. App. 2002).

26. 157 U.S. 675, 15 S. Ct. 720 (1895).

27. 19 A.3d 944 (Md. 2011).

28. 722 N.W.2d 472 (Minn. 206).

29. 382 S.W. 3d 377 (Tex. Crim. App.).

30. 101 So.3d 638 (Miss. 2012).

31. 267 P.3d 1113 (Cal. 2012).

32. 852 N.E.2d 813 (Ill. 2006).

33. 67 P.3d 121 (Kan. 2003).

34. 735 S.E.2d 259 (W. Va. 2012).

35. 81 P.3d 681 (Okla. Crim. App. 2003).

36. 218 P.3d 660 (Cal. 2009).

37. See the New York Penal Code, Section 125.20.

38. 483 F. Appx. 427 (10th Cir. 2012).

39. 157 U.S. 675, 15 S. Ct. 720 (1895).

40. 351 Ill. 604, 184 N.E. 894 (1933).

41. 38 Ga. App. 36, 142 S.E. 202 (1928). In this case, the deceased used profane and insulting language and made threats to cut the defendant's throat.

42. 381 Pa. 447, 113 A.2d 293 (1955).

43. Years ago, Texas, New Mexico, and Utah enacted laws that provided that if a husband killed a man caught in an act of adultery with his wife, the killing was a justifiable homicide. Critics of these statutes argued that this permitted an "open shooting season" on paramours if they were caught by husbands in the act of adultery. Women's groups in these states angrily demanded that the statutes be either repealed or amended to give wives the same rights. All three states have repealed these statutes and probably have gone back to the common-law rule.

44. 765 S.E.2d 322 (Ga. 2014). Other courts disagree. In a case where a fiancée was killed after she admitted infidelity, and in another case where a spouse was killed after confessing to adultery, the question before two state supreme courts was whether "mere words" justified reducing murder charges to voluntary manslaughter. Neither the Ohio Supreme Court nor the Michigan Supreme Court would reduce the murder charges to manslaughter because of mere words. See for Ohio *State v. Shane* 590 N.E. 2d 272 (Ohio 1992) and for Michigan *State v. Pouncey* 471 N.W. 2d 346 (Mich. 1991).

45. 799 N.W.2d 412 (S.D. 2011).

46. 175 Cal. 45, 164 P. 1121 (1917).

47. House of Lords, 2, All Eng. R 801 (1954).

48. 840 N.E.2d 510 (Mass. 2006).

49. 624 N.W.2d 585 (Minn. 2001).

50. 648 N.W.2d 413 (Wis. 2002).

51. 132 Cal. Rptr. 3d 248 (Cal. App. 2012).

52. *People v. Morgan*, 719 N.E.2d 681 (Ill. 1999).

53. 815 N.W.2d 85, 99 (Mich. 2012).

54. 702 S.E.2d 590 (Va. App. 2010).

55. 734 S.E.2d 273 (Ga. App. 2012).

56. 362 S.E.2d 252 (Ga. 1987).

57. The *Roswell Gilbert* case caused a national debate on euthanasia in 1985. Mr. Gilbert killed his wife, who was suffering from terminal debilitating diseases. He was 76 years of age at the time and received a sentence of 25 years' imprisonment without parole. After serving 5 years, he was granted clemency by the Florida governor and returned to Fort Lauderdale.

58. 667 P.2d 1176 (1983). In the case of *In re Joseph G.,* a minor (Joseph G.) and his friend made a mutual suicide pact. The two males drove a car over a cliff to carry out the suicides. Joseph G. survived, but his passenger was killed. The California Supreme Court reversed the first-degree murder conviction, holding that Joseph G. should be charged with assisting a suicide.

59. In April 1999, when he was 70 years old, Dr. Kevorkian was convicted of the crime of murder by a Michigan jury and sentenced to 10–25 years in prison, with the possibility of parole after 6 years and 8 months. He was released in 2007.

60. 117 S. Ct. 2258 (1997).

61. 117 S. Ct. 2293 (1997).

62. 816 N.W.2d 703 (Minn. App. 2012).

63. *Oregon v. Ashcroft,* 368 F.3d 1118 (9th Cir. 2004).

64. *Gonzales v. Oregon,* 546 U.S. 243 (2006).

11

Assault, Battery, and Other Crimes Against the Person

LEARNING OBJECTIVES

In this chapter we examine assaults and
related crimes against the person. The
following are the learning objectives for
Chapter 11:

LO 1. Identify the different elements that must
be proved for conviction of an assault or
a battery.

LO 2. Explain what kind of nonconsensual
touching constitutes an assault or a
battery.

LO 3. Describe circumstances that warrant a
charge of aggravated assault or battery.

LO 4. List the various laws designed to protect
children from assaults and other similar
crimes.

LO 5. List some of the defenses available to a
charge of assault or battery.

LO 6. Identify the "movement" requirement for
a kidnapping conviction.

LO 7. Explain how the crime of hostage taking
differs from kidnapping.

AP image/Paul Chiasson/The Canadian Press

The Montreal Canadiens hockey player Max Pacioretty is wheeled off the ice after taking a severe hit from a Boston Bruins player. Physical contact in athletic contests, even that which causes severe injury, is generally not a crime unless the contact falls dramatically outside the kind of physical contact normally encountered in the athletic contest.

18 U.S.C. § 1589, the federal forced labor statute, makes it a crime to compel a person to perform services by force or threats of force. In 2006 the defendant, who immigrated to this country from Togo, illegally brought four children from Togo to live with him in Michigan. For the next several years the defendant, through "reprehensible, abusive force," compelled the children to perform household tasks. Failure to complete the task or violation of any of defendant's many rules was met with violent beatings with fists, broomsticks, and bathroom plungers. Ultimately, the children's teachers became concerned about the abuse, and informed Michigan investigators. They removed the children from defendant's home. Homeland Security Agents also investigated how the children entered this country, and discovered false immigration documents in defendant's home.

A grand jury indicted the defendant on immigration charges and forced labor under the federal statute. The defendant pled guilty to the immigration charges, but went to a jury trial on the forced labor charge. The jury found him guilty, and he appealed. Should he have been convicted under the forced labor statute? What might be some of the repercussions of such a conviction? Does the decision of the U. S. Supreme

Court in *Bond v. United States*, discussed in Chapter 2, influence your decision? See *United States v. Toviave*, 761 F.3d 623 (6th Cir. 2014).

In this chapter we will study the rules governing assault, as well as other crimes against the person such as kidnapping and domestic violence.

THE CRIME OF ASSAULT

assault In many instances, an assault is an attempt to commit a battery, but many states also make other conduct an assault. It could be combined with a charge of battery to constitute the crimes of "assault and battery."

battery A successful assault, in which the victim is actually and intentionally (or knowingly) struck by the defendant.

Under common law, **assault** and **battery** were two separate crimes. Today, however, the phrase *assault and battery* is sometimes used to indicate one offense. Because an assault is often an attempt to commit a battery, the California courts point out that an assault is an attempt to strike, whereas a battery is the successful attempt. A battery cannot be committed without assaulting a victim, but an assault can occur without a battery.

States have codified the common-law crime of assault. Included in the crime of assault today are (1) an attempt to commit a battery in which no actual battery or physical injury resulted and/or (2) an intentional frightening (such as pointing a loaded gun at a person or menacing with a fist or knife). Generally, in an assault, the state must show apprehension or fear on the part of the victim if no blow, touching, or injury occurred.

In many states, the crime of assault also includes battery. For example, the state of New York does not have a crime of battery.[1] Therefore, in New York, a person who swings a knife at another with intent to cause serious physical injury is guilty of first-degree assault if successful but is guilty only of attempted assault if no injury occurs. (See New York *Commentaries,* Art. 120, p. 331.)

Section 240 of the California Penal Code (enacted in 1872) defines *assault* as "an unlawful attempt, coupled with a present ability, to commit a violent injury on the person of another." Chapter 38, Section 12-1, of the Illinois Statutes provides that "a person commits an assault when, without lawful authority, he engages in conduct which places another in reasonable apprehension of receiving a battery."

In some states (including California), the lack of "present ability" to commit the injury or battery is a defense to an assault charge.[2] The defendant in the case of *People v. Miceli* attempted to use this defense.[3] He used a semi-automatic rifle to club a victim. When charged with "assault with a firearm," the defendant contended he could not be guilty of an assault, because the firearm was not loaded, and as a result he lacked the "present ability" to injure that victim. The court disagreed, both because evidence existed that the firearm might have been loaded, and because the firearm was used as a club, which satisfied the "present ability" requirement.

Other, perhaps most, states, and the Model Penal Code § 211.1, have adopted the common-law definition of assault. Under that definition, an assault occurs *either* when one does an overt act that is intended to inflict bodily harm (the "attempted battery" assault), *or* when the overt act is intended to put another person in fear of bodily harm (the "reasonable apprehension of fear" assault).

The 2012 case of *United States v. Acosta-Sierra*[4] illustrates both these aspects of the common-law meaning of assault. The defendant was walking across the border from Mexico to the United States. A U.S. Customs officer passed the defendant as he walked on the other side of the walkway. The defendant picked up a baseball-sized rock and threw it at the officer, missing him by two feet. The officer did not see the defendant throw the rock, but heard it land behind him. The defendant was charged with assault against a federal officer. Based on the judge's understanding of assault requirements, the defendant was convicted of "reasonable apprehension of fear" assault.

On appeal, the court held the government had failed to prove the customs officer had a reasonable fear of injury, since the officer did not actually see the defendant throw the rock. It therefore reversed the trial judge's verdict of guilty on the assault charge. However, the court held that sufficient evidence existed to convict the defendant under the "attempted battery" prong of assault, and remanded the case for a new trial.

Under the present Federal Criminal Code, the crime of assault is directed toward certain situations over which the federal government has jurisdiction, such as assaults on a federal officer or assaults on a federal reservation. 18 U.S.C. § 111 covers assaults on federal officers. In the most general assault statute, assault within the territorial jurisdiction of the United States, assault also includes an actual battery; 18 U.S.C. § 113(a)(4) forbids "assault by striking, beating, or wounding." Thus, in addition to the two common-law aspects of assault discussed above (present ability or fear of infliction), the statute includes a third aspect, in which the crime of assault is committed by actually inflicting injury on another person. The following two cases illustrate application of the assault against a federal officer statute and the general federal assault statute:

United States v. Janis
U.S. Court of Appeals, 810 F.3d 595 (8th Cir. 2016)

An Oglala Sioux tribal police officer went to defendant's house, based on a complaint the defendant was disturbing the peace. The defendant refused to allow the officer to enter, and the officer pushed back the door. The defendant then struck the officer with his fist before being subdued by the officer. The court affirmed a conviction for assault under the federal assault statute, 18 U.S.C. § 111. It held the federal law applicable because the tribal officer was exercising powers under contracts with the Bureau of Indian Affairs.

United States v. Lewellyn
U.S. Court of Appeals, 481 F.3d 695 (9th Cir. 2007),
cert. denied, 128 S. Ct. 154 (2007)

Defendant spit in the face of a patient at a Veterans Administration Hospital, a "federal reservation" and thus governed by federal law. The court affirmed the defendant's conviction for "simple assault" under 18 U.S.C. § 113, holding that spitting on another person constituted "offensive touching" under the common law, and thus violates the statute. The court noted that because section 113 does not define "assault," the common-law meaning of the term is followed in federal courts, and includes "offensive touching." In *United States v. Stoddard*, 407 Fed. Appx. 231 (9th Cir. 2011) the 9th Circuit court stated that spitting that actually hits a federal officer can also be a felony assault under 18 U.S.C. § 111.

Assault with a Deadly or Dangerous Weapon

A simple assault is a misdemeanor or ordinance charge. The criminal charge of assault with a deadly or dangerous weapon is a felony charge. A gun or a dangerous knife is certainly a deadly weapon if it is used to threaten or harm.

As pointed out in Chapter 10, the issue of what is a dangerous or deadly weapon is a question of fact for the fact finder (jury or judge). New York courts have held that something as common as a handkerchief can, under certain circumstances, be a deadly weapon, and many courts have also held that hands can be dangerous or deadly weapons, even if the assailant has no training in martial arts or boxing.

The relative size and strength of the assailant as compared with the victim, the manner and duration of the assault, and the severity of the injuries are all facts that must be taken into consideration in determining whether hands are dangerous or deadly weapons. Fact finders would surely find the hands of an adult man who punched a baby to be dangerous or deadly weapons under the circumstances.[5]

The defendant in *State v. Zangrilli* broke his ex-wife's jaw in two places, grabbed her by the throat and strangled her until she could feel her "eyes bulge," dragged her through several rooms in her house, punched her several times in the face and neck, and shoved her into a bathtub.[6] The Rhode Island Supreme Court affirmed his conviction of assault with a dangerous weapon, quoting the trial judge's holdings:

> The manner in which he used his hands on her throat constituted use of his hands in such a way that it could easily have led to her death.
>
> For that reason, I have concluded that his assault upon her was done with a dangerous weapon. As I say, hands are not *per se* dangerous weapons, but they are a means to produce death. And they were used, even though briefly, in a manner and in such circumstances as could be reasonably calculated to produce death.

Some things, such as guns or large knives, are treated as "inherently" deadly weapons. The "dangerousness" of other things depends on their use. For example, while a rock is not inherently a deadly weapon, it can become one. In the 2011 case of *State v. Baranovich*[7] the defendant and her 13-year-old brother attacked a former roommate of the defendant. The brother hit the female victim on the head with a rock, causing the victim to fall to the ground. The court affirmed the defendant's conviction for assault with a dangerous weapon.

Some states have created a separate crime of committing a felony while armed with a dangerous weapon, whereas other states enhance (increase) penalties of people who commit a felony while armed. What constitutes "armed" is most often a question of law.

A person who actually carries a pistol on his or her person is armed. However, it is less clear if one who commits a felony with a pistol in his or her *vicinity* is armed. The following two Illinois cases illustrate this problem.

In *People v. Board*[8] an appeals court upheld a conviction for armed violence in which the defendant was sitting on a sofa that had a gun under one of the cushions.

DANGEROUS WEAPONS UNDER FEDERAL ASSAULT STATUTES

Both the assault on a federal officer statute, 18 U.S.C. § 111 and the general assault statute, 18 U.S.C. § 113, impose increased penalties for an assault with a deadly weapon. In addition to weapons such as guns or knives, the following two cases illustrate assaults by other means that come within the definition of "forcible assault with a deadly weapon":

United States v. Hurry, 569 Fed. Appx. 796 (11ᵗʰ Cir. 2014): Defendant charged a federal officer by driving his car in reverse down a steep hill aimed at the officer. The car's side view mirror "brushed" the officer's arm, and then struck the officer's parked vehicle. Defendant was convicted under 18 U.S.C. § 111(b) for forcibly assaulting the officer with a deadly weapon. On appeal, the court stated that "forcible assault" required the prosecution to prove the defendant made a "willful threat or attempt to inflict bodily injury," with the apparent present ability to do so. The defendant's car was a deadly weapon, because it was intended to cause "death or danger" to the officer. It affirmed the conviction.

United States v. Watts, 798 F.3d 650 (7ᵗʰ Cir. 2015): Defendant intentionally threw a wooden chair at a state police officer in a federal courtroom, striking the officer and causing bodily injury. The defendant was charged and convicted under 18 U.S.C. § 113 (a) (3) for assault with a deadly weapon. On appeal the court affirmed his conviction, stating that while section 113 does not define "assault" or "dangerous weapon" ("This is a badly drafted statute"), the common law meanings of those terms can supply meaning. A chair, the court said, can be a dangerous weapon if used in an attempt to inflict serious bodily injury. That was the case here, the court said, and the conviction was affirmed.

Although the defendant made no attempt to get the gun, the court held that its accessibility sufficed to support the armed violence conviction. Conversely, in *People v. Shelato*,[9] the court reversed a conviction for armed violence when the defendant's gun was in the same room with the defendant but hidden in a zippered bag underneath sixty bags of marijuana. The court stated that it "defied common sense" to believe the defendant could have gotten this gun under the "watchful eyes of several police officers," and vacated the conviction.

BATTERY

For an offense to constitute assault, the victim must ordinarily be apprehensive of the impending harm or danger. This is not necessary in a battery. A blow from behind is a battery whether or not the victim is aware that it is coming. Battery is a crime that, like murder and manslaughter, is defined in terms of the conduct of the offender and also in terms of the harm done.

Most state battery statutes define battery to include either physical conduct or actual bodily injury. For example, Florida's battery statute, F.S.A. § 784.03, states a person commits battery if he either (1) "actually and intentionally touches or strikes another person against the will of the other" or (2) "intentionally causes bodily harm." Many other states have a statute similar to the Kansas battery law, K.S.A. § 21-3412. It includes as a battery "intentionally or recklessly" causing bodily injury. However, the "physical contact" form of battery must be done in "a rude, insulting or angry manner." Thus, if one intentionally causes another bodily harm, whether by directly striking the person, or indirectly doing so by acts like throwing an object at the person, the crime of battery has been committed. Batteries can be committed with fists, feet, sticks, stones, or other objects used to inflict injury. Under some circumstances, dogs or other animals can be used to commit a battery if they are used to injure another person illegally.[10] If there is physical contact without bodily injury, the contact must be offensive or unwanted.

Section 211 of the Model Penal Code combines the common-law crimes of assault and battery under the crime of assault. That section does not include "offensive touching" without bodily injury. The MPC limits simple "physical contact" to sexual offenses, as discussed below.

All states that make battery a crime require that the act to commit a battery must be intentional (or must be done knowingly), because an accidental physical contact or injury is not a battery. However, most states, as in the Kansas statute quoted above, include recklessly causing bodily injury in the definition of battery.

Offensive Touching Under Sexual Assault and Sexual Battery Statutes

Many states have enacted sexual assault statutes to replace or add to their old rape statutes. These statutes generally provide three or four degrees of sexual assault. In addition to defining sexual intercourse broadly, these statutes also forbid and punish **offensive touching**.

offensive touching
Unpermitted physical contact with another person, usually limited to "private" or genital parts.

Before the enactment of the sexual assault statutes, offensive touching was ordinarily charged under the general assault statute or as a battery or disorderly conduct. Although offensive touching may continue to be charged under the old statutes, the sexual assault statute is now available. However, under the sexual assault statutes, the offensive touching generally must be of an "intimate part" or "private part" of the body and for the purpose "of arousing or gratifying sexual desire of either party" (§ 213.4 Model Penal Code).

The rape charge in the case of *People v. Margiolas* was dropped because of lack of evidence of resistance. However, the defendant admitted that he unbuttoned the victim's blouse, despite her verbal as well as physical objections. The defendant was convicted of sexual battery in forcibly unbuttoning the blouse.[11] Under such a statute, a prosecutor with a weak case might also issue a sexual battery charge when it is apparent that the rape charge has defects that might be insurmountable. (See Chapter 12 for more material on sexual assault and sexual battery statutes.)

Sports Injuries When Force Exceeds the Rules of the Game

A hard tackle in football or a blow to the jaw in boxing would be within the rules of the sport being played. Players in body contact sports consent to such conduct as part of the game. This is commonly referred to as the "voluntary participant" rule.

But if the conduct is beyond the rules of the game—such as a deliberate elbow to the face or a knee to the groin in basketball, the deliberate use of spikes by a runner in baseball, eye gouging in football, or other violence that causes unnecessary injuries—is it a battery or an assault? In one recent case, the Washington Court of Appeals held that an assault was committed when, during a game, one basketball player intentionally punched another player.[12] In the 2004 case of *State v. Guidugli*[13] the court upheld the conviction for assault where the defendant, the starting quarterback for the University of Cincinnati football team, hit an opposing player in the head with a fist during an intramural basketball game. The court noted that the defendant "wound up" before delivering the punch, which caused some harm to the other player's face. That was enough, the court said, to support the conviction.

Spectator violence and parental rage are occasionally a problem at sporting events. During a July 6, 2012, Little League game in Georgia that became well known on YouTube, two dads got into a fight during the game, and both were charged with disorderly conduct.

Other Physical Contact Without Consent

Pushing, pinching, biting, scratching, touching, kissing, punching, spitting, and tackling are all forms of physical contact in which the person initiating the contact could be acting in a friendly, joking, or loving manner. Alternatively, the contact could be hostile, angry, or belligerent.[14]

If such contact were intentional (not accidental) and done without any legal justification, it could cause a great amount of anger or concern in the person not consenting to such physical contact. If the physical contact were made in an obviously hostile or belligerent manner, the physical contact could also provoke a verbal or physical reaction.

If it is shown that the conduct provoked or tended to provoke a disturbance or a disorder, the offender could be charged with disorderly conduct.

EXAMPLE	A strange man roughly grabs a woman or a girl in a public place and kisses or touches her in the presence of her husband, boyfriend, other member of her family, or friends. Because such conduct is highly likely to cause a public disturbance or disorder, it can be charged as disorderly conduct (or disorderly person).

One defense to a charge of touching or physical contact could be that the touching was accidental. Implied consent could also easily be inferred if the touching was done to pull a victim away from danger or if mouth-to-mouth resuscitation was necessary to restore breathing to a victim of an accident. The defense of necessity could also be used if the physical contact was necessary to prevent and avoid a greater harm.

menacing Intentionally placing or attempting to place another in fear of immediate serious physical injury.

Some states have enacted the crime of **menacing**, which is defined as follows in Public Law 120.15 of New York:

> [P]hysically menacing, intentionally placing or attempting to place another person in fear of imminent serious physical injury. (New York class B misdemeanor)

Other states have extended the scope of the crime of assault to include intentional scaring or menacing if a victim is apprehensive of immediate bodily harm.

A fierce look with intent to frighten would not amount to menacing or intentional scaring. Section 211.1 of the Model Penal Code provides,

(1) Simple Assault … (c) attempts by physical menace to put another in fear of imminent serious bodily injury.

New York City has passed a "jostling" law in response to the pickpocketing problem that exists in crowded public places such as subways. The procedure used by most pickpockets is to bump or shove the victim (or have a partner distract the victim by bumping and shoving) to permit entry into a pocket or purse for the theft. Jostling is defined by New York Public Law 165.25 as follows:

In a public place, intentionally and unnecessarily:

1. Placing one's hand in the proximity of a person's pocket or handbag, OR
2. Jostling or crowding another person at a time when a third person's hand is in the proximity of such person's pocket or handbag.

FELONIOUS AND AGGRAVATED ASSAULTS AND BATTERIES

aggravated assault
Assault made more serious by presence of a firearm or as part of intent to commit a felony.

aggravated battery
Battery that causes serious bodily injury or is committed with a deadly weapon.

Misdemeanor assault and misdemeanor battery are classified as class A or B misdemeanors in most states. The degree of these crimes and the penalties are increased by aggravating factors used by state legislatures. All states have enacted **"aggravated assault"** or **"aggravated battery"** statutes, which increase an assault or battery from a misdemeanor to a felony. In the case of assaults, the aggravating factors usually are (1) use of a firearm or (2) intent to commit a felony. See F.S.A. § 784.021.

The most common aggravating factors for battery charges are (1) causing serious bodily injury or (2) using a deadly weapon in the battery. Vernon's Texas Penal Code § 22.02 is an example of such a statute. In some states circumstances in addition to the two just stated constitute aggravated battery. For example, in Florida, F.S.A. § 784.045 makes it aggravated battery if the victim of a battery is pregnant and the defendant knew of or should have known that fact. In Kansas, K.S.A. § 21-3414 makes it aggravated battery to cause physical contact in a rude or insulting manner with a deadly weapon. Oregon's statute, O.R.S. § 163.175, adds as an aggravating circumstance "recklessly" causing serious physical injury under circumstances that demonstrate "extreme indifference to human life."[15] In applying that statute to injuries arising out of an automobile accident, the Oregon Supreme Court stated:

Witnesses testified that prior to the accident defendant was swerving across the road, tailgating so closely he almost hit the car in front of him and passing on a curve. The overwhelming weight of the evidence indicated that the accident occurred because defendant was across the center line in the oncoming lane of traffic. He sideswiped the first oncoming vehicle, bounced or swerved into his own lane and then swerved back across the center line into the second oncoming vehicle, causing serious injury to the passenger. Defendant had a blood alcohol content of .24 percent two hours after the accident. He was belligerent at the scene of the accident, threatening to hit the passenger of the first car he sideswiped. Because of his intoxication he was not only unable to assist the victim, but at

DEFENSES TO AN ASSAULT OR BATTERY CHARGE

The Aggressor Defense

The defendant may assert that the other party was the aggressor, and the defendant acted in self-defense. Perfect or imperfect self-defense can then be argued by attempting to show that force was necessary and the amount of force used was reasonable.

Lack of Specific Intent

Although assault is usually regarded as a general intent crime, in some states the "intent to cause fear" form of assault requires the specific intent to cause the result, that is, fear or apprehension in the victim. In such prosecutions, it would be a defense that a defendant did not intend his acts to cause fear or apprehension. In the 2012 case of *State v. Fleck*[16] the Minnesota Supreme Court held that the "assault-fear" form of assault was a specific intent crime, and intoxication could be used to prove lack of specific intent. "Assault-harm" was a general intent crime, and required only a showing the defendant intended to do the act constituting the assault, the court held. Thus, intoxication was not relevant to a conviction.

Other Defenses

- That the other party consented within the rules of the sport being played.
- That it was reasonable discipline of a child by a parent, guardian, or a person acting in place of the parent.
- That in an "offensive touching" battery, the touching was accidental, or consented to, or necessary under the circumstances.
- That the conduct was necessary and lawful:
  - in the accomplishment of a lawful arrest
  - when necessary to lawfully detain or hold a person in custody
  - when necessary to prevent an escape of a person lawfully in custody
  - when necessary to prevent a suicide
  - for any other reason when the conduct is privileged by the statutory or common law of that state

one point interfered with the assistance. The degree of intoxication, defendant's erratic driving and his conduct at the scene of the accident are circumstances the jury could properly consider in determining whether defendant was extremely indifferent to the value of human life.

We hold that the circumstances which exist in this case suffice to establish defendant's extreme indifference to the value of human life.[17]

Aggravated assault/battery cases often are complicated by an assertion of self-defense. Using force is justified for self-defense purposes, but only under certain circumstances. A person is not entitled to use force for self-defense if he is engaged in a crime when confronted by force. This has sometimes led to confusion in aggravated assault cases. For example, in the 2005 Florida case of *Williams v. State*,[18] a defendant charged with aggravated battery under the Florida statute cited above

YOU BE THE JUDGE

Should you grant the defendant's motion? **See State v. Miland, 858 N.W.2d 328 (S.D. 2014)**

The defendant before you was charged with aggravated assault and tried before you in a bench trial. The charge was based on the following agreed facts: Defendant was seated in the passenger seat of a police cruiser after his car was stopped for a traffic offense. One officer, the victim of the assault, was seated in the driver's seat, and the other officer was outside the police cruiser. Without warning, defendant began striking the victim in the face, and did so several times before the other officer entered the cruiser and subdued him. The victim was not seriously injured, but did require medical attention to his injuries. At the close of the prosecution's case the defendant moved for a judgment of acquittal, contending the state failed to prove he caused serious bodily injury, or if he did, that the circumstances manifested extreme indifference to the value of human life.

The assault statute in your state defines aggravated assault as an assault by a person who: "Attempts to cause serious bodily injury to another, or causes such injury, under circumstances manifesting extreme indifference to the value of human life." The statute does not define "circumstances manifesting extreme indifference." Defendant contends (1) he did not seriously injure the victim; (2) that the state did not prove he acted intentionally or knowingly to take the victim's life; and (3) "extreme indifference" applies only when the injuries posed a threat to the victim's life, which these did not.

contended he struck the victim in self-defense. The trial court instructed the jury that self-defense was not available if the defendant used force while committing an aggravated battery. The Florida appeals court reversed the conviction, stating that the instruction negated the self-defense claim, because if self-defense was proper, the defendant was not guilty of aggravated battery.

Mayhem and Malicious Disfigurement

mayhem and malicious disfigurement Willfully inflicting an injury on another so as to cripple or mutilate the person.

Mayhem and malicious disfigurement (or malicious wounding) have been distinguished by federal courts as follows: "[M]ayhem involves disablement of normal functioning of a human body, by contrast with malicious disfigurement which focuses on willful permanent disfigurement."[19]

Lorena Bobbitt was convicted of malicious wounding in Virginia when, in a rage, she cut off her husband's penis and threw it in a field. Believing Mrs. Bobbitt to be a battered woman, a Virginia jury found her not guilty under Virginia's insanity test. She spent four weeks in a Virginia mental hospital and was released on the condition that she receive therapy.

States also follow the common-law definition of mayhem, which is the unlawful and violent depriving of the victim of full use of any functional member of the body (hand, arms, feet, eyes, legs, and so on) that would make the victim less able to defend himself or herself.

Article 1166 of the Texas Penal Code provides that "whoever shall willfully and maliciously cut off or otherwise deprive a person of the hand, arm, finger, toe, foot, leg, nose, or ear, or put out an eye or in any way deprive a person of any other member of his body shall be confined in the penitentiary not less than two nor more than ten years."[20]

Hate Crime Laws

The U.S. Supreme Court has repeatedly held that states may not silence "speech on the basis of its content,"[21] as was done in the flag-burning and cross-burning U.S. Supreme Court cases (see Chapter 9). But states may enact hate crime laws that enhance and increase penalties for crimes if it is proved that the defendant intentionally selected the victim because of the victim's race, religion, color, disability, sexual orientation, national origin, or ancestry. Thus, while the First Amendment protects biased thoughts or speech, however repugnant they are viewed, it does not apply when those thoughts or speech are the motivation for a criminal act.

An example of a hate crime law is the New York Hate Crime Act of 2000, N.Y. Penal Law § 485.05. That act makes it an enhanced crime with added penalties to commit any of several specified crimes if the defendant "intentionally selects" the victim "in whole or in substantial part" because of the defendant's "belief or perception" of the victim's race, religion, gender, age, national origin, sexual orientation, or disability. The specified crimes include virtually all the crimes against the person, as well as many crimes against property.

Proving that the defendant actually "hated" the actual *victim* is not generally an element of a hate crime offense. Under the New York law cited above, the prosecution must only prove that the race, religion, or one of the other listed characteristics was a "substantial" factor in the decision to commit the crime. In this general sense, the New York statute makes the "hate" feature part of the elements of the crime, which under the *Apprendi* decisions discussed in Chapter 8 means the prosecution must prove the "hate" element beyond a reasonable doubt.

Section 485.05(2) states that proof that the victim possessed one of the listed characteristics does not by itself satisfy the "people's burden" to prove the elements of a hate crime. Some other corroborating evidence is thus required. In *People v. Fox*,[22] the court found the required corroborating evidence in the fact the defendants used Internet chat rooms used by gay men to lure a victim to the robbery location.

Many other states have similar hate crime laws. In the 2010 case of *State v. Hennings*[23] the Iowa Supreme Court upheld a defendant's conviction for assault intended as a hate crime. The Iowa hate crime statute requires that the prosecution prove that the crime, here assault, was committed "because of the race" (or other listed factors, such as religion, gender, or sexual orientation) of the victim. The defendant, after an expletive-filled exchange with five African-American boys walking on a street, drove his vehicle at the boys, severely injuring one of them. The defendant, a member of a family well known in the community for its racist views, contended the mere fact that he held those views did not satisfy the hate crime requirements. The Iowa Supreme Court agreed, but held there was ample evidence to support his conviction of the hate crime. The court noted that in his statements to police, the defendant said, "What . . . f------ N------ don't have enough sense to stay out of the f----- road . . . they deserve to get hit." These comments showed the defendant targeted the boys because of their race, the court held.

The statutes discussed above all require the prosecution to prove the defendant committed the crime, at least in part, because of the victim's status. In the 2015 case of *State v. Pomianek*, 110 A.3d 841 (N.J. 2015) the New Jersey Supreme Court struck down part of the New Jersey hate crime statute. N.J. Stat. 2C:16-1(a)(3) makes a crime subject to the hate crime sentence enhancement provision if the **victim** "reasonably believed" the offense was committed because of race, religion, or other specified characteristics of the victim. The Court said that part of the statute was void for vagueness, because a person holding no hate bias against the victim could not always know if the victim believed such bias existed. The court noted that no other state hate crime law made the victim's perception of bias the basis of conviction.

If a defendant selects a victim based on a prejudice against the perceived race of the victim, it is not necessary that the victim in fact be a member of that race. In *Martinez v. Texas*,[24] the court affirmed a hate crime sentence enhancement of a defendant who killed a child, believing the child to be part African American. The court said if prejudice against a particular race of people caused the defendant to select the child as a victim, it did not matter that the child was in fact not a member of that race.

On October 28, 2009, President Obama signed the Matthew Shepard and James Byrd, Jr. Hate Crimes Prevention Act. This Act was named in honor of Matthew Shepard, pictured above, a gay man, and James Byrd, Jr., a Black man, who were killed in separate hate crimes in 1998 that received national attention. The act makes it possible for federal prosecutors to expand the use of existing hate crime laws. The HCPA makes several additions to the federal hate crime laws, among them removing the previous requirement that the victim be engaged in some federally protected activity, like voting or attending school. It also gives federal prosecutors the ability to investigate suspected hate crimes that local authorities may not want to pursue. Finally, it requires the FBI to maintain statistics on hate crimes involving transgender victims.

HATE CRIMES 2014

In 2015 the Justice Department published the Hate Crime Statistics for 2014 by the Federal Bureau of Investigation's Uniform Crime Reporting Program. Law enforcement agencies stated that in 2014 there were 5,479 reported single-bias incidents, involving 6,418 criminal offenses. 4,048 of these offenses were crimes against a person, and 2,317 were crimes against property, such as destruction or defacement. The statistics showed the following:

Why? (Motivation)	Type of Crime Committed	Victims' Characteristics
Race 48.3%	Intimidation 43.1%	Black 63.5%
Religion 17.1%	Simple assault 37.4%	White 22.8%
Sexual orientation 18.4%	Aggravated assault 19.0%	Asian 5.5%
Ethnicity 12.2%	Murder, rape 0.3%	Multiple race 3%
Victim disability 1.5%	(4 murders, 9 rapes)	Native American 4.6%
Gender-identity 1.7%		
Sexual Orientation Crimes (1,178 victims)		
Anti-male homosexual 58%		
Anti-homosexual 23.6%		
Anti-female homosexual 14.3%		
Anti-bisexual 2.6%		
Anti-heterosexual 1.5%		
Religious Bias Crimes (1,092 victims)		
Anti-Jewish 58.2%		
Anti-Islam 16.3%		
Anti-Catholic 6.1%		
Anti-Protestant 2.6%		
Multiple religions 4.7%		
Anti-atheists 1.2%		

Source: U.S. Department of Justice, 2012.

CASE CLOSE-UP

United States v. Miller

Sixth Circuit Court of Appeals
767 F.3d 585 (2014)

In 2001, Samuel Mullet established the Bergholz Amish community in Ohio, when a sufficient number of ordained ministers qualified the group as a separate Amish Community. Mullet was elected Bishop of the community. In that capacity he was solely responsible for rules governing the lives of members in the community, including the right to excommunicate (called "shunning" in Amish communities) members who fail to adhere to the rules.

In 2006, Mullet shunned several Bergholz community members because of their criticism of his rules. Many of those shunned left the community, resulting in a separation between parents and children, and in one case divorce of a husband who left Bergholz but whose wife and children stayed behind. Notwithstanding the usual Amish custom that other communities recognize the shunning by Bergholz, those other Amish communities rejected the shunning and accepted the members who left Bergholz.

The divorced husband then brought appropriate actions in Pennsylvania courts to regain custody of his children. Ultimately, the court ordered a SWAT team to go to Bergholz and get possession of the children. The order also stated that the children may not return to Bergholz for parental visits.

Believing the loss of the children was a sign of spiritual weakness, many Bergholz residents as penance took the unusual step of trimming their beards or, in the case of women, cutting their hair. Not content to cut only their own hair and beards, Bergholz members executed 5 "raids" on other Amish communities, and forcefully cut hair and beards of members of those communities.

The raiding Bergholz members were charged with hate crime assaults under the federal Hate Crimes Prevention Act, 18 U.S.C. § 249(a)(2)(A). That law makes it a crime to willfully cause bodily injury to another person "because of the actual or perceived . . . religion . . . of [that] person." (The statute includes other characteristics, such as race or sexual orientation.) The trial judge instructed the jury that they could convict the defendants if they found the religion of the victims was a "significant motivating factor" in the assault, even if not the only factor. The jury returned guilty verdicts, and the defendants appealed.

During the appeal process the U.S. Supreme Court decided *Burrage v. United States*, 134 S. Ct. 881 (2014) (discussed more fully in Chapter 16). There, the Court said that the words "because of" in a federal statute linking a person's death to distribution of illegal drugs to that person required the prosecution to prove that "but for" the illegal drug distributed, death would not have occurred. The Court rejected the government's argument that it was sufficient under the statute to prove that use of the illegal drug contributed to the death.

The court of appeals in *Miller* concluded that the *Burrage* decision applied to the Hate Crimes Prevention law, since it included the term "because of" the characteristic of the victim. Since the trial judge permitted the jury to reach a guilty verdict if the religion of the victims was only a "significant motivating factor" in the attacks, the court of appeals held the instruction was in error. Noting that there were a number of other potential motivations for the attacks, such as the parent-child animosity, or the custody of the children in Pennsylvania, the court reversed the conviction and remanded the case for a new trial.

Miller is a decision under a federal statute, and is not directly binding on state statutes. However, to the extent, as the Sixth Circuit Court suggested, the decision has First Amendment overtones, it could provide a basis for attacking state hate crime laws that do not require a "but for" connection between the bias of the defendant and the motivation for the crime.

CHILD ABUSE AND NEGLECT

Child abuse, child neglect, and sexual abuse are serious problems throughout the United States. Based on statistics compiled by the U.S. Department of Health and Human Services, the national ChildHelp Foundation reported in 2011 that 3.3 million child abuse cases are reported each year, involving over 6 million children; 78.3 percent were neglect cases; and 80 percent involved children under the age of four. The report noted the dramatic increase in child abuse or neglect deaths. In 1998, 3.13 child abuse deaths occurred each day. In 2012, more than five such deaths occurred each day. According to the report, the United States has the worst child abuse/neglect record of any industrialized nation. Moreover, estimates of child deaths were probably low, because many child deaths are not reported as resulting from abuse or neglect.

Thousands of children in the United States suffer head injuries; broken bones from beatings; burns from cigarettes, stoves, and hot liquids; ruptured internal organs (such as liver, spleen, kidneys, and bowels) from blows to the abdomen; missing teeth; multiple scars; knife and gunshot wounds; and bruises and lacerations.

People who inflict such injuries on children may be charged with assault, battery, assault with a dangerous weapon, aggravated battery, and other offenses under the criminal code of the state in which the offense occurred. Criminal codes also have child abuse statutes and statutes forbidding the neglect of children. These statutes seek to protect children from injury and trauma inflicted on them by parents, stepparents, paramours, relatives, babysitters, and other adults.

Parents and others responsible for children have a duty to protect children and provide food, clothing, shelter, medical care, education, and a reasonable physical and moral environment for them. Child neglect is the failure to provide adequate food, clothing, shelter, sanitation, medical care, and supervision for a child. In extreme cases of child neglect, criminal laws are violated.

Religious beliefs that cause parents to refuse to obtain medical treatment for a child are controversial. In some states, parents can be charged under criminal homicide laws. For example, in 2009 a Wisconsin couple was convicted of reckless homicide in the death of their 11-year-old daughter. The child was suffering from diabetes, but rather than obtain medical treatment the parents relied on "faith healing." The parents appealed their convictions, relying on Wisconsin Statute 948.03(6), which they contended made them immune from prosecution.

The Wisconsin statute, like similar statutes in some other states, carves out an exception to prosecutions for neglect of a child for circumstances where the parents had

CRIMINAL AND CIVIL LAWS THAT SEEK TO PROTECT CHILDREN

Under early Roman law, children were considered to be the property of their father, who could discipline them as he saw fit: he could sell them or even condemn them to death.

This law changed slowly over the years, and by the early 1800s, mothers were the primary custodians of their children when a divorce occurred. The *tender years presumption* held that only a mother has the nurturing qualities needed to love and care for a child through the early part of the child's life, or the tender years.

The tender years presumption also changed, and today more than thirty states offer joint custody and shared parenting arrangements to parents who are divorcing or have never married. Most criminal laws seek to protect all parties (children and adults alike). States have sought to provide additional protection to children by the enactment of most (if not all) of the following statutes:

(Students should complete blanks)

Laws Forbidding	Statute # in Your State
• child abuse	_____
• child neglect	_____
• abandonment of a child	_____
• contributing to the delinquency of a child	_____
• child snatching from the lawful custody of a guardian of the child	_____
• child endangerment	_____
• child enticement	_____
• exposing children to sexually harmful material	_____
• sexual exploitation of a child	_____
• statutory rape (children cannot consent to sexual intercourse or sexual contact) under age is (*crime*)	_____
• other	_____
Compulsory School Attendance Laws	
• imposing duty on parents until age	_____
• making student offense of skipping school truancy	_____
• authorizing police to take truant into custody	_____

a good-faith belief in healing by spiritual means or prayer. See, e.g., Minn. Stat. Ann. § 609.378, but even in those states the exception does not apply if the child dies. See *State v. Beagley*, 305 P.3d 147 (Or. App. 2013), construing Oregon R. Stat. § 163.206.

The parents convicted of reckless homicide of their 11-year-old daughter in the case discussed above initially appealed their convictions to the Wisconsin Court of Appeals. In 2012 the Wisconsin Court of Appeals certified the question of the application of the "faith-healing" exception to cases of death of a child to the Wisconsin Supreme Court. In a 2013 decision, the Wisconsin Supreme Court affirmed the reckless homicide convictions of the parents of the 11-year-old girl. *State v. Neumann*, 832 N.W.2d 560 (Wisc. 2013), *cert denied* 134 S. Ct. 544 (2013).

The child abuse that often appears in courts is physical abuse, such as deliberate injuries inflicted on children. Such injuries may result from excessive and unreasonable force used in disciplining children. The U.S. Supreme Court pointed out in *Ingraham v. Wright* that parents and people taking the place of parents may use force "reasonably believed to be necessary for [the child's] proper control, training, or education."[25] What is "reasonable" is determined in view of the child's age and sex; the physical, emotional, and mental health of the child; and the conduct that prompted the punishment.

Unfortunately, most children who are victims of abuse are under age 5 and are helpless to protect themselves.

Child abuse as a crime has both an active and a passive element. Physical abuse—hitting, burning, cutting, kicking—of children is obviously the active part of child abuse crimes. But action is not always required for child abuse convictions. Most states have statutes making it a crime for one responsible for a child's welfare to endanger the life of the child. This can be done by failing to adequately feed or clothe a child, by leaving a child unattended at home, by leaving a child in an automobile on a hot day, or by failing to intervene when the child is being sexually molested.[26]

In response to the national problem of child abuse, the following have occurred:

- *Mandatory reporting laws* have been enacted by all states to require doctors, nurses, teachers, day-care workers, and other people coming in contact with children to report suspected child abuse. It is likely there is still tremendous underreporting of abuse.
- *Increased authority has been given to social workers* by some states to permit them to interview children without notifying their parents. Increased numbers of trained social workers are needed to handle growing caseloads.
- *New criminal laws* have been enacted, such as Washington's homicide by abuse statute, which makes child abuse resulting in death the equivalent of first-degree murder. Under this statute, prosecutors no longer have to prove premeditation or intent to kill for a conviction. Instead, the state must show that the defendant displayed "extreme indifference to human life." The writer of the bill stated, "Premeditation in child abuse cases is almost impossible to prove. This [law] gets around that oft-heard defense—I didn't mean to kill the boy; I just wanted to discipline him."

Sexual abuse and sexual exploitation of children are discussed in Chapter 12. Sexual abuse may be combined with physical abuse or child neglect. Abuse or neglect in any form may have a severe emotional and psychological effect on a child, causing behavioral problems that could have great impact on the child's life.

OFFENSES AGAINST THE LIBERTY OF A PERSON: KIDNAPPING

Kidnapping and Hostage Taking

Kidnapping was a crime at common law, punishable by life imprisonment. All states and the federal government, with some variations, have enacted statutes making kidnapping a crime. Section 212.1 of the Model Penal Code defines **kidnapping** in part as follows:

kidnapping False imprisonment coupled with movement of the victim.

> A person is guilty of kidnapping if he unlawfully removes another from his place of residence or business, or a substantial distance from the vicinity where he is found.

Kidnapping normally requires "moving" the victim. As discussed below, the meaning of "movement" under state kidnapping statutes varies from state to state. Under the federal kidnapping statute, 18 U.S.C. § 1201, kidnapping requires that the victim be "transported in interstate commerce." Thus, the focus in the federal statute is not on "movement" of the victim, but on "transported in interstate commerce." In *United States v. Singh*[27] the court held that "transported" begins when the victim is first abducted. Thus, even if the victim is killed before being taken across state lines, the federal kidnapping statute applies if the victim was alive when first abducted, the court said.

Just as the MPC section quoted above provides, most states' kidnapping statutes require that the victim unlawfully be "removed" from a residence or place of business, or a "substantial distance" from where the victim was found. This "moving" aspect of the kidnapping crime has frequently been an issue in kidnapping prosecutions, as the cases discussed here illustrate.

A 2015 California case involved one aspect of the "movement requirement" in kidnapping statutes, that is, what it means to "move" a victim. In *People v. Simmons,*[28] the California Court of Appeals affirmed the kidnapping conviction of 2 defendants who committed multiple home invasions in the Oakland, California area. The kidnapping charge arose out of a home invasion where the residents of the home were accosted outside their home at gunpoint, and forced to go inside the home so the robbery could take place. The court said this satisfied the "moving" requirement of the kidnapping statute. It was not just incidental to the robbery, but undertaken to make the robbery harder to detect by passers-by, the court said.

In *State v. Latham,*[29] the Arizona Court of Appeals held that the "moving" requirement under the Arizona kidnapping statute, A.R.S. § 13-1304, was satisfied even though the kidnapper did not physically move the victim. The defendant entered a married couple's home and held a gun on the husband until the man's wife returned from work. The defendant then said he would shoot the husband if the wife did not go to the bank and cash a check for $10,000. The wife did so, and after arrest the kidnapper was charged with several crimes, including kidnapping the wife. The court of appeals affirmed the conviction, noting that no other case had been found with similar facts, but that the concept of "moving" the victim under the kidnapping statute applied when the victim "moved" because of the kidnapper's threat to kill her husband if she did not "move."

OFFENSES AGAINST THE LIBERTY OF A PERSON

Offense	Usual Definition	Usual Motivation and Use of Offense
False imprisonment	False imprisonment is the unlawful restraint of another and is committed when a person is detained unlawfully.	False imprisonment most often occurs when a retail store employee makes an improper detention for shoplifting or a peace officer makes an improper arrest. These incidents are brought in civil courts and often are called "false arrest" lawsuits.
Kidnapping	Kidnapping is a false imprisonment that is aggravated by the movement of the victim to another place.	Motives could be to obtain ransom or as part of rape, robbery, or murder; to terrorize; to blackmail, and so on. Kidnapping is punished severely, as it is one of the most serious crimes against a person.
Hostage taking	Used to gain an advantage and compel others to comply with demands.	"Taking hostage" is often a tactic used as part of an escape attempt. The crime does not require forcible movement of the victim "some distance."
Parental kidnapping or child snatching (includes former live-ins, lovers, and family)	This crime is often a kidnapping by a parent who has lost (or will lose) custody of the kidnapped child.	This serious crime is committed to retaliate, to harass, to use as leverage in determining support payments, or to control and maintain custody of the child. Some children are never seen again by the other parent.
Abduction	The English enacted the first abduction statute in 1488. For many years, the crime forbade taking a female for any sexual purposes.	States using abduction as a crime generally limit it to a natural parent taking a child from a person having lawful custody.
Slavery and involuntary servitude	The Thirteenth Amendment forbids "slavery … [and] involuntary servitude, except as a punishment for crime."	Slavery, serfage, peonage, debt bondage, and exploitation of children still exist in parts of the world. In 2008 a federal court upheld the involuntary servitude convictions of a man who forced mentally retarded "patients" into working on his farm in the nude. *United States v. Kaufman*, 546 F.3d 1242 (10th Cir. 2008), *cert. denied*, 130 S. Ct. 1013 (2009).

Another aspect of the "movement" requirement that has come before many courts is whether movements of short distances incident to the commission of such crimes as rape or robbery constitute kidnapping. A summary of this issue's development in California courts is instructive. According to California Jury Instruction 652,

> To constitute the crime of simple kidnapping, . . . there must be a carrying, or otherwise forceful moving, for some distance of the person who, against his will, is stolen or taken into custody or control of another person, but the law does not

require that the one thus stolen or taken be carried or moved a long distance or any particular distance.

In interpreting "some distance," the California courts have held that "movement across a room or from one room to another" is not sufficient movement to justify a kidnapping conviction.[30] The general rule seems to be that movement "merely incident to the commission of the robbery [or rape]" is not kidnapping.[31]

In *People v. Washington,*[32] the court reversed a conviction for kidnapping during a bank robbery. The defendant took the teller and bank manager away from their posts to the bank vault room, distances of 15 and 25 feet, respectively. The manager opened the vault, and the robbers took the money and left the bank. The court said that under the California kidnapping statute, Cal. Penal Code § 209, the movement of a victim in a robbery must be more than incidental to the commission of the robbery, and must increase the risk of harm to the victim. Here, the court said, the only reason the manager and teller were moved to the vault area was to enable them to gain access to the cash in the vault. Moreover, the risks to the victims were not increased by this movement. However, in the 2010 case of *People v. Hernandez,*[33] the court affirmed a conviction of kidnapping during the robbery of a Chevron station. The court found the requirements of § 209 were satisfied by the movement of the store clerk to a back room, because there the robbers assaulted the clerk and robbed him of his personal money. Taking the clerk to the back room, which could not be seen by the public, dramatically increased the risk that harm would come to him, the court said.

Other state courts have reached similar conclusions. In the case of *State v. Masino,* the defendant dragged his victim from her car and down an embankment, out of sight from passersby, before sexually assaulting her.[34] The New Jersey Supreme Court affirmed the convictions of sexual assault and kidnapping.

The Florida Supreme Court has stated that there is a "definite trend" toward allowing a kidnapping conviction "where the purpose in confining or moving another person is to use that person as a hostage." In *Mobley v. State,* the defendants were inmates in a jail.[35] They took two guards and an attorney captive in the course of an escape attempt. In affirming the convictions of the defendants for kidnapping and other offenses, the Florida Supreme Court held that the "confinement was not incidental to the attempted escape once [defendants] began using [the victims] as hostages and threatening physical harm."

In a 2013 case, *Castro v. State,* 122 So.3d 912 (Fla. App.), the Florida Court of Appeals held that under the Florida kidnapping statute, which includes "confining" a victim as well as moving a victim, armed robbers who tied a store clerk's hands and left him tied after the robbery were properly found guilty of kidnapping as well as armed robbery.

Because kidnapping usually requires a forcible movement of the victim "some distance" or a "substantial distance," some states have created the crime of **"hostage taking"** to eliminate those requirements. A movement of the victim is not required to prove this offense. In creating this new offense, the state legislature can require all the elements of the serious felony of kidnapping except movement of the victim. They can require the state to prove "intent to use the person as a hostage."[36]

Because hostage taking is a serious and dangerous offense, it is often made a class A or B felony. To encourage offenders to release victims unharmed, some states

hostage taking The use or threat of use of force to restrain or confine a person with the intent to use the person as a hostage to compel another person to perform some act.

reduce the offense to a class B or C felony if the hostages are released "before the actor's arrest." In *State v. Warfield*,[37] the Wisconsin Court of Appeals held that a defendant who held four children hostage in an attempt to compel their mother to assist in a robbery of the check-cashing business where she worked was not entitled to the benefit of the "release" provision of the Wisconsin Hostage Statute. It rejected the defendant's arguments that he "released" the boys when he escaped from the house when police arrived. The court said the decision to escape was not the same as releasing the hostages.

Finally, under the federal robbery statute, 18 U.S.C. § 2113(e), there is an enhanced penalty if the robber in the course of fleeing the robbery scene "forces any person to accompany him" without consent of that person. In *Whitfield v. United States*, 135 S. Ct. 785 (2015), the U. S. Supreme Court held that "accompany" means only forcing the victim to move a short distance, even if it occurs in the same building. There, a fleeing robber entered the victim's home and forced the 79-year-old female occupant to take him from the hallway to the computer room of her house, a distance of 4-9 feet. There, the victim suffered a fatal heart attack. The Court held that it is not the distance moved but the forced accompanying that is the harm addressed by the statute. It affirmed the defendant's conviction and sentence.

False Imprisonment

false imprisonment
Unlawful restraint or detention of a person.

Under the common law, **false imprisonment**[38] was a crime that, like kidnapping, was punishable by life imprisonment. Many states have enacted statutes making false imprisonment a crime. The usual elements are as follows:

1. The defendant must have confined or restrained the liberty or freedom of movement of another.

2. Such act must have been intentional and without the consent of the victim.

3. The defendant had no lawful authority to confine or restrain the movement of the victim.

False imprisonment differs from kidnapping in that, in kidnapping, the victim must be moved to another place. In false imprisonment, the confinement or restraint may be at the place of the false arrest or unlawful detention of the victim. Under the old common law, it was also required that kidnapping be done secretly; this is not required for false imprisonment. However, the requirement of secrecy for kidnapping has probably been eliminated by most state statutes.

Many false imprisonment actions today are civil actions alleging false arrest or the improper detention of a person. Law enforcement officers and retail store employees should not interfere with the liberty of a person unless authority exists that justifies the restraint of a person. Many civil false imprisonment lawsuits concern detention of people believed to be shoplifters. Chapter 13 presents the law governing detentions and arrests in shoplifting cases.

Parental Kidnapping or Child Snatching

Child snatching is the abduction of a child by one parent without the consent of the other parent. It may occur before the parents have commenced a divorce action, while a divorce action is pending, or after a divorce judgment has been granted. Child snatching is also known as parental kidnapping, child abduction, and child stealing.

Thousands of children disappear each year as a result of parental kidnapping. Although the offending parent may state that he or she seeks to protect the child's welfare, other motives for child snatching are

- Retaliation against and harassment of the other spouse
- As a means to bargain for reduced child support or reduced division of property in the divorce settlement
- An attempt to bring about a reconciliation of the marriage

Children who are kidnapped by a parent experience changes that may lead to emotional damage. First, the child is often told that the parent who had custody is either dead or no longer loves the child. Second, in most instances, the child begins a lifestyle in which he or she grows up with only one parent. Third, the child is frequently exposed to life on the run, because parental kidnapping is a felony in most states. The pain, fear, guilt, anger, and anxiety from these experiences can cause severe, irreparable psychological harm.

Most states are generally prepared to extradite the offending parent back to the state in which the offense was committed, if he or she can be located. Before the passage of the Uniform Child Custody Jurisdiction Act (UCCJA), a fleeing child snatcher could run to another state, establish residence there, and seek a custody order from the courts of the new state. Under UCCJA, the home or resident state would continue to have jurisdiction.

Because the federal kidnapping statute (the Lindbergh Act)[39] specifically excludes parents from its scope, a federal Parental Kidnapping Prevention Act was passed by Congress in 1981. This act facilitates interstate enforcement of custody and visitation determinations. The act also declares that the Fugitive Felon Act applies in state felony parental kidnapping cases, giving the FBI jurisdiction when the child snatcher crosses state lines.[40]

The National Child Search Assistance Act

Because of increasing concern about child kidnapping by strangers, there are voluntary programs to fingerprint children for identification throughout the nation. The

---

 MISSING CHILDREN IN THE UNITED STATES

The FBI maintains a database of annual reports of missing persons. The National Crime Information Center published these missing-person statistics for 2014: 445,045 children (persons under age 18) were reported missing, about an equal number of male and female children. Of those reported missing, 4,806 were missing under circumstances the FBI classifies as "involuntary," meaning the person was either abducted or kidnapped.

parents or legal guardians retain the fingerprint cards for use if the child, at a later date, gets lost or becomes missing.

The National Child Search Assistance Act of 1990[41] requires all federal, state, and local law enforcement offices to maintain reports of missing children, and transmit any information relating to missing children to the National Crime Information Center computer system, so that information can be exchanged with the National Center for Missing and Exploited Children. The act thus gives parents, legal guardians, or next of kin access to the information in the FBI National Crime Information Center's (NCIC) missing persons file.

The parental kidnapping act does not confer on the FBI any new investigative jurisdiction. The FBI can participate in investigation of parental kidnapping cases through the Fugitive Felon Act if the following conditions exist:

1. A state arrest warrant has been issued charging the parent with a felony violation.

2. Law enforcement officers have evidence of interstate flight.

3. A specific request for FBI assistance has been made by state authorities, who agree to extradite and prosecute.

4. A U.S. attorney authorizes issuance of an unlawful flight warrant.

The National Center for Missing and Exploited Children coordinates efforts to recover missing children. A telephone hotline and other facilities are available to aid in these efforts.

FAMILY VIOLENCE AND DISTURBANCES

A study conducted for the National Institute of Mental Health concluded that "physical violence occurs between family members more often than it occurs between other individuals or in any other setting except wars and riots." The disturbance is often a quarrel between family members. It may start with a few angry words, or it could be a simmering dispute that explodes into violence. Destruction, damage, or taking of property may occur. One or both (or all) the parties may be under the influence of alcohol or drugs. Job stress or unemployment may contribute to the situation.

Hitting, pushing, choking, or wrestling, combined with other abusive behavior, may occur. Insulting and offending language is almost always used. Injuries can range in severity from minor to critical and life threatening.

Both parties could be at fault, or one party could be the agitator and the offender. The offender may have a prior record of violence and may be under a court order (divorce) or restraining order (criminal) forbidding such conduct. The offender may be on probation or parole, and his or her domestic conduct may violate the terms of that probation or parole. The offender's presence on the premises may be in violation of a court order or a condition of probation or parole. In addition to these violations, the offender may also be a trespasser.

Family units include not only male–female relationships (married or unmarried) but also homosexual relationships (married or unmarried), and single-parent and multigenerational households. The disturbance or violence could include not only adults but also children within the family unit.

RESPONSES TO DOMESTIC VIOLENCE

The following are some of the responses available to violent family situations:

1. Arrest of the offending person (or people)
   - If the state or city has a mandatory arrest law
   - Or at the discretion of the officer (or under the policy of the officer's department)
2. Obtaining a protective court order under the statutes of that state
3. Seeking shelter for the victim (spouse, children, parent, or others) under the shelter program available in that community
4. Commencing a divorce action and obtaining temporary or permanent court orders that could protect by
   - Removing offending spouse from premises
   - Forbidding communication or contact by offending spouse
   - Restricting visitation rights with children and enforcing other restrictions
5. Issuance (or threatened issuance) of a civil citation with a substantial money fine
6. Use of the emergency detention section of the state mental health act (if applicable) to place the offending party into custody for observation
7. Revocation of probation or parole if the offender has violated terms of a probation or parole agreement

Past experience has demonstrated that family-trouble calls can be dangerous for law enforcement officers. Approximately one-fifth of police deaths and almost one-third of assaults on officers occur when they respond to family quarrels and domestic disputes in which a weapon is used.

In past years, unless serious injury occurred or a clear violation of a court order or probation (or parole) existed, an arrest would ordinarily not be made. Police officers would attempt to mediate the dispute. However, studies by the Police Foundation have shown that police arrests sharply reduce violence in the home. The police commissioner of New York City stated that because of these studies and because of his own experience as a "cop on the street," he concluded that past police efforts to mediate have done little to stop a growing problem.

The commissioner stated that arresting violent members of a household would be more effective than attempts at mediation in protecting other family members and would help to safeguard police officers who are called to intervene in situations where violence could occur.

Some states have responded to domestic violence by passing criminal laws that address domestic violence directly. The terms of these statutes vary, but the following three state laws are representative. Nevada's domestic violence statute, N.R.S. 200.485, makes it a misdemeanor for a person to commit an assault or battery against a spouse, a former spouse, a person living with him or her, or a person in a dating relationship with him or her. The first offense is a misdemeanor with limited penalties; the second offense within 7 years is also a misdemeanor, but penalties are enhanced. The third and subsequent offenses within 7 years are felonies. The statute also provides that if the penalty is greater under the general assault and battery statutes—for example, because of the seriousness of the injury—the defendant can be sentenced under those statutes.

Indiana Code § 35-42-2-1.3 incorporates common-law assault and battery language, and it defines domestic violence to include "touching" in a "rude or insulting manner" that causes bodily injury. Persons covered by the statute include spouses, former spouses, persons who are cohabiting, or a person with whom the person charged has had a child. First-offense domestic violence is a misdemeanor. Subsequent offenses are class D felonies. It is also a class D felony if the domestic violence occurs in the presence of a child under 16 years of age.

Idaho Code § 18-918 defines domestic violence as committing an assault or battery as defined in the general criminal statutes for those crimes against a "household member," which includes a spouse, a former spouse, a person living with the person charged, or a person with whom the person charged has a child. Assaults are punished as misdemeanors. If a battery results in a "traumatic injury," it is a felony. If not, it is a misdemeanor. "Traumatic injury" means any wound, or any "external or internal injury," regardless of how serious the injury is, caused by physical force.

In past years, it was not uncommon for police departments to receive calls from women asking for protection from men who had threatened them or from wives who expected to be beaten by their husbands when they came home from a tavern. Threats to injure can be the basis of a criminal charge. If the threat was made over a telephone, the charge of unlawful use of a telephone may be made.

Because of the battered woman problem, crisis counseling centers and shelters have been established throughout the United States to assist victims and their families. These centers provide shelter when needed, counseling, support, and emergency food and clothing. Shelter locations are generally not disclosed to the public, to prevent further confrontation of the victim by the offender.

Domestic Violence and Women

Physical abuse of women, usually by husbands, ex-husbands, or boyfriends, is a crime that is likely to go unreported and, if reported, is rarely prosecuted. Frequently, the victim refuses to press charges against the abuser. Although in theory the prosecutor may continue to prosecute a case even after the complainant wants charges dropped, in practice such cases become hard to prove and are usually dismissed.

FBI studies show that a refusal by the battered spouse to cooperate with prosecutors rarely leads to better relations with the abusive spouse. This is because domestic abuse follows a familiar cycle of violence. In the first phase, the tension-building phase, the abusive spouse becomes hostile and belligerent and heaps verbal abuse on the partner.

This phase almost always leads to the next phase, the acute-battering phase. Injury and death can be the result in this phase. Following a severe battering, the abusive spouse will shower the partner with flowers, affection, and contrite behavior. This is called the honeymoon phase, but like all honeymoons, it always ends. The next phase is the tension-building phase, and the cycle continues from there.[42]

In 1994, Congress passed the Interstate Domestic Violence Act (IDVA), as part of the Violence Against Women Act (VAWA).[43] The VAWA and IDVA created new federal domestic violence crimes and also provided millions of dollars for battered women's shelters and child care. The IDVA applies when any person forces a "spouse, intimate partner, or dating partner" to travel across state lines, and commits a crime of violence against that person. The following cases illustrate prosecutions under the Interstate Domestic Violence Act:

- *United States v. Larson:*[44] The defendant beat his ex-wife in his home in Wisconsin, stuffed her in a garbage can filled with snow, took her to Illinois, and left her in an unheated self-storage facility. She was found near death the next day. In 2010 a court of appeals affirmed his conviction and sentence of life imprisonment.
- *United States v. Dowd:*[45] In 2005 a defendant was convicted under the interstate domestic violence statute for forcing his girlfriend to accompany him on an extended three-state trip during which he abused her both physically and psychologically.

SCHOOL SHOOTINGS

From 1966 to 2015 there have been several instances of school-related shootings in the United States. While schools at all levels have generally been safe for students and faculty members, these events are especially tragic because of the children involved. The following list chronicles the major fatal shootings in the past 50 years:

- *1966—Austin, Texas:* In an incident known as the Texas Tower killings, a recent graduate of the University of Texas barricaded himself in a tower on the UT campus, and for 96 minutes fired his rifle at passing pedestrians, killing fourteen and injuring thirty-one before being killed by police.
- *1997—Paducah, Kentucky:* A 14-year-old boy killed three classmates and injured five others at a high school prayer meeting.
- *1998—Jonesboro, Arkansas:* Two cousins, ages 13 and 11, dressed in camouflage, killed four girls and a teacher, and wounded eleven other people, outside a middle school. The killers were released from juvenile corrections in 2005 and 2007. The older boy was recently arrested for carrying a loaded weapon (a pistol).
- *1998—Springfield, Oregon:* After being suspended from school for bringing a gun to school, a 15-year-old boy killed three and wounded twenty-three other students before other students subdued him, and the police arrested him.
- *1999—Littleton, Colorado:* Two Columbine High School students, ages 17 and 18, killed twelve students and a teacher and wounded twenty-three other individuals before killing themselves.
- *2005—Red Lake, Minnesota:* A 16-year-old boy killed his grandparents, five fellow students, a teacher, and a security guard before killing himself on a Native American reservation.
- *2006—Nichol Mines, Pennsylvania:* A 32-year-old man entered an Amish school and shot eleven girls—killing four and wounding seven—before killing himself.
- *2007—Blacksburg, Virginia:* A Virginia Tech student killed thirty-two students and teachers in a university building on the 26,000-acre campus of Virginia Tech. The student then killed himself. This was

Abuse of the Elderly

The National Center on Elder Abuse within the Bureau of Justice Statistics reported that for 2010, there were 5,961,568 reported cases of elder abuse, or about 9.5 percent of the elder population of the United States. Neglect accounted for 58.5 percent of the reported cases, and physical abuse 15.7 percent. About 66 percent of the abusers were adult children or spouses.

A July 2001 report of federal and state inspections of the nation's 17,000 nursing homes showed that 30 percent were cited over a two-year period for physical, sexual, or verbal abuse of residents. About one in ten of the citations was a serious incident that either put the victim at great risk of harm or killed the patient. The report contained examples of nursing home residents being punched, choked, or kicked by staff members or by other residents.[46]

Under the assault statutes in many states, felony elder abuse is treated as a separate offense. For example, in the 2011 case of *People v. Gross*,[47] the defendant walked down a city street, randomly striking others with his fist. He knocked down a female

---

the worst mass shooting in the United States since 1991, when George Hennard killed twenty-three people in a cafeteria in Killeen, Texas.

- *2008—DeKalb, Illinois:* A 27-year-old student at Northern Illinois University killed himself and five other students, and wounded sixteen others. In the same year in *Baton Rouge, Louisiana,* a nursing student opened fire in a classroom at a technical college, killing two students before killing herself.
- *2009—Coral Gables, Florida:* A 17-year-old student was stabbed to death at 9:00 a.m. in the school courtyard by another student. In *Tyler, Texas,* a 16-year-old student stabbed to death a special education teacher in the classroom.
- *2010—Madison, Alabama:* A ninth-grade student was shot and killed in the school hallway by another ninth-grade student.
- *2010—Huntsville, Alabama:* A female faculty member who was bitter at being denied tenure at the University of Alabama killed three colleagues at a faculty meeting, and wounded three others.
- *2011—Omaha, Nebraska:* Two school administrators were shot by an expelled student. One died, and the student killed himself.
- *2012—Oakland, California:* A student at Oikos College ordered a class of nursing students to line up against a wall in a classroom and shot them. Seven died before the shooter fled. One L. Goh subsequently surrendered to police.
- *2012—Newtown, Connecticut:* After first killing his mother, Adam Lanza killed twenty children and six other adults at the Sandy Hook Elementary School before taking his own life. It was the second worst school massacre, after the killings at Virginia Tech in 2007.
- *2014—Isla Vista, California:* Just outside the main campus of the University of California, Santa Barbara, Eliot Rodger killed three people in an apartment, drove to a campus sorority house and killed two people there, and killed a student at a nearby deli. Rodger killed himself after crashing his car in a police chase.
- *2015—Roseburg, Oregon:* Student Christopher Harper-Mercer killed 8 students and 1 teacher at Umpqua Community College. After a gunfight with police, Harper-Mercer killed himself.

victim, age 84, causing severe injuries. He was convicted of felony elder abuse under California law and sentenced to 9 years in prison. The California Court of Appeals affirmed his conviction and sentence.

Because elder abuse frequently involves abuse by caregivers charged with caring for an elderly person, many states have enacted laws aimed at elder abuse committed by caregivers. An example of these laws is the Nebraska Adult Protective Services Act (Neb. Rev. Stat. § 28-348-387). This act broadly defines *elder abuse* as an act or omission by a caregiver that causes physical injury, cruel punishment, sexual abuse, confinement, or denial of essential services to a vulnerable adult. The act treats violations as class V felonies. It also requires those who treat elderly people, such as physicians and nurses, to report evidence of abuse. Law enforcement agencies are then required to investigate such reports and take steps to protect the elderly person being abused.

California has been a leader in responding to elder abuse. Its law states that it is a crime—a misdemeanor or a felony, depending on the dangerousness of the situation—for any person charged with the duty of caring for an elder person to "willfully cause or permit the elder or dependent adult to be placed in a situation such that his or her person or health is endangered."[48]

In *People v. Heitzmann*[49] the California Supreme Court reversed the conviction of a daughter under this statute. Her 68-year-old father died from neglect while the father lived with the defendant's brothers. The court held that the filial relationship between the daughter and the father was not by itself enough for conviction under the statute. The state needed to prove the daughter had some legal duty to control the actions of the brothers who were neglecting the father, which the court said the state failed to do.

VIOLENCE IN THE WORKPLACE

The U.S. Department of Justice reports that each year 1 million people become victims of violent crimes while at work. Most of such victims are robbed, are victims of felonious assault, or are raped.[50]

While newspapers and television depict scenes of crazed co-workers or fired employees coming back to wreak carnage, statistics show that about a thousand people are killed by violence in the workplace each year.

Is the workplace violent? Should we fear our fellow workers? Statistics show that we have little to fear. In 2011, the Occupational Safety and Health Administration (OSHA) reported that 780 occupational deaths occurred from workplace violence. Most assailants were not co-workers of the person killed. For example, 39 percent of women killed at work were killed by relatives; 36 percent of men killed at work were killed by robbers. Only a small number were killed by co-workers.

ROAD RAGE: VIOLENT AGGRESSIVE DRIVING

Vehicle traffic-related injuries and deaths are the ninth leading cause of death worldwide, and combined with the crime of driving while under the influence of alcohol they are the leading cause of criminal homicide in the United States. Moreover, common driving violations have led to the greater frequency of aggressive driving, known as "road rage."

The National Highway Traffic Safety Administration reported to the U.S. Congress that "violent aggressive driving" had increased 7 percent a year during the late 1990s. Violent aggressive driving was described as aggressive behavior like tailgating, weaving through busy traffic lanes, honking, screaming at other drivers, exchanges of insults, gunfire, and even murder.

Driving violations lead to accidents, which often can help trigger road rage. For example, a 2006 study by the University of Wisconsin showed that in the city of Milwaukee there were more than 1,000 vehicle accidents caused by drivers running stop signs or traffic lights. To combat this problem, about one-half the states have laws permitting red-light cameras, which photograph vehicles and their license plates.

In the 2002 Texas case of *Feldman v. State* (71 S.W.2d 738), a motorcyclist became enraged when a trucker passed him on the highway and nearly hit him. The motorcyclist chased the trucker, pulled up alongside the truck, and shot the driver. The motorcyclist was convicted of murder.

In 2007 motorists became so enraged at delays caused by construction work on a California state highway that they began verbally abusing, throwing objects, and even firing BB guns at the workers. The state highway department finally closed the highway until completion of the construction.[51]

LEARNING OBJECTIVES SUMMARY

LO 1. Identify the different elements that must be proved for conviction of an assault or a battery.

An assault conviction requires acts intended to cause bodily injury, or instill fear of such injury. Using a weapon to cause fear is an assault. A battery conviction requires intentional infliction of bodily harm or unlawful touching in a rude or offensive manner.

LO 2. Explain what kind of nonconsensual touching constitutes an assault or a battery.

Virtually any kind of physical contact can constitute a battery, so long as it is done in a manner that is non-consensual and in a hostile or belligerent manner.

LO 3. Describe circumstances that warrant a charge of aggravated assault or battery.

An assault or battery becomes aggravated if a deadly weapon is used to commit an assault or a battery, or there is an intent to commit a felony. In the case of a battery, if serious

bodily injury results it is aggravated battery. Sometimes other circumstances, such as the fact that the victim is pregnant, make a battery aggravated.

LO 4. List the various laws designed to protect children from assaults and other similar crimes.

All states have laws that focus on child abuse, neglect, or endangerment. It is also a crime to expose a child to sexually harmful material, or involve a child in sexual activities. Contributing to the delinquency of a child can be used as the basis of prosecution for other forms of child neglect.

LO 5. List some of the defenses available to a charge of assault or battery.

Self-defense is a common defense asserted in assault and battery charges. Under some circumstances, the conduct may be justified, as in the case of a law enforcement officer using force. In some activities, like sports, consent is given to some use of force.

LO 6. **Identify the "movement" requirement for a kidnapping conviction.**

Most states require that a kidnapping victim be "moved" as part of the crime. Generally, the movement must be substantial, and not just moving a person from one room to another. However, where it is clear the purpose of the action was to constrain the victim against that person's will, any movement of the victim will suffice.

LO 7. **Explain how the crime of hostage taking differs from kidnapping.**

Hostage taking differs from kidnapping in that it lacks a "movement" element. The crime does require that a victim be held against his will in some fashion, and that the purpose of doing so is to force another to take some act, like pay a ransom, or allow the criminals to escape.

KEY TERMS

assault, p. 302
battery, p. 302
offensive touching, p. 306
menacing, p. 307

aggravated assault, p. 308
aggravated battery, p. 308
mayhem and malicious disfigurement, p. 310

kidnapping, p. 318
hostage taking, p. 320
false imprisonment, p. 321

CASE ANALYSIS AND WRITING EXERCISES

1. At the beginning of this chapter we examined the case of *United States v. Toviave*, where the court reversed a conviction under the federal forced labor statute. That same court decided *United States v. Callahan*, 801 F.3d 606 (6th Cir. 2015), another prosecution under the federal forced labor statute, 18 U.S.C. § 1589. Both cases involved defendants who forced other persons to work in the defendants' homes. Why were the convictions affirmed in *Callahan*? How was that case different from *Toviave*? What gives Congress the power to enact the forced labor statute?

2. Many states have recently passed legislation making "texting" while driving a minor misdemeanor. See *e.g.* Ohio R.S. § 4511.204, effective March of 2015. If an accident occurs while a defendant is texting and driving, can the defendant be convicted of assault under a state's general assault statute? The New Hampshire second degree assault statute, § 631.2, makes it a class B felony to "knowingly or recklessly" cause serious bodily injury to another. The defendant while texting and driving hit another car, causing serious injury to a passenger in that car. What must the state prove to convict the defendant of second degree assault? See *State v. Belleville*, 88 A.3d 918 (N.H. 2014).

3. "Road rage" by itself is not a crime. It can, of course, lead to violence that would be a crime. However, it is not always easy to determine who

was the "victim" and who was the "aggressor" in road rage cases, though that is often necessary to find criminal violations. What should happen in this case: Driver 1 cuts off Driver 2, and Driver 2 "tailgates" Driver 1. Driving beside Driver 1's car, Driver 2 pulls up next to Driver 1 and (according to passengers in Driver 1's car) waves a gun in the air. Driver 1 stops at the next stop light, exits his car, and pulls out a handgun which he holds by his side while standing next to Driver 2. When the light changed, Driver 1 returned to his car and drove away, followed by Driver 2, who called 911. Driver 1 was charged with aggravated assault with a deadly weapon. Should he be convicted? Did he "assault" Driver 2, as you now understand that term? If so, what are his defenses? See *State v. Almeida*, 356 P.3d 822 (Az. App. 2015).

4. It is common for state statutes involving crimes committed while using a "deadly weapon" or a "dangerous weapon" to specify certain kinds of weapons (pistol, rifle, long knife, and so forth) and leave it to courts to determine when other instruments qualify as "deadly or dangerous" weapons. Is a BB gun a "deadly weapon"? How did the court answer that in *People v. Ackah-Essien*, 874 N.W.2d 172 (Mich. App. 2015)? Is that the right answer?

ENDNOTES

1. A few states (including Wisconsin) have not statutorized the common-law crime of assault. Disorderly conduct and attempt to commit a battery are substituted for assault in charging.

2. Most states have passed statutes that criminalize the conduct of pointing an unloaded gun at a victim who does not know if the gun is loaded or unloaded and becomes apprehensive and frightened. The New York crime of menacing (§ 120.15) by placing "or attempting to place another in fear of imminent serious physical injury" is an example of such a criminal statute.

3. 104 Cal. App. 4th 256, 124 Cal. Rptr. 2d 888 (2002).

4. 690 F.3d 1111 (9th Cir. 2012), *cert. denied* 2013 WL 140373.

5. In the 1991 case of *Ray v. State* (580 So. 2d 103), the Alabama Court of Appeals quoted another court as to an adult man's fists being used to beat a baby:

   Certainly the use of an adult man's fists to beat a seventeen-month [old] child may appropriately allow those fists to be classified as a deadly weapon or a dangerous instrument.

6. 440 A.2d 710 (R.I. 1982).

7. 249 P.3d 1284 (Ore. App. 2011).

8. 534 N.E.2d 312 (Ill. App. 1989).

9. 592 N.E.2d 585 (Ill. App. 1992).

10. Other batteries and assaults include a running leap onto a woman's back as assault in *Russell v. State*, 814 S.W. 2d 871 (Tex. App. 1991); poking a teacher in the chest as assault in *People v. Dunker*, 577 N.E.2d 499 (Ill. App. 1991); a profane threat of physical violence as assault in *Wells v. State*, 418 S.W.2d 437 (Ga. App. 1992); grabbing the victim by his coat and punching him in the face as assault in *State v. Waltrip*, 484 N.W.2d 831 (Neb. 1992); holding the victim against her will as battery in *Bamette v. State*, 217 S.W.2d 20 (1949); head-butting the victim as disorderly conduct and assault in *State v. McKenzie*, 605 A.2d 72 (Maine 1992); attempting to film under victim's dress with camcorder as simple battery in *Fitzgerald v. State*, 411 S.E.2d 102 (Ga. App. 1991); and throwing rocks at moving cars on highway as several counts of assault, battery, and malicious destruction in *Ford v. State*, 603 A.2d 883 (Md. 1992).

11. 117 Ill. App. 3d 363, 73 Ill. Dec. 17, 453 N.E.2d 842. The Illinois Appellate Court cited the following:

    Other instances of conduct held to be simple battery based solely on insulting or provoking physical contact [include]: *People v. Hamilton*, ... 401 N.E.2d 318 ... (where defendant reached around the female complainant and placed his hand over her mouth); *People v. Siler*, ... 406 N.E.2d 891 ... (where defendant lifted up complainant's dress during a confrontation having sexual overtones).

12. *State v. Shelly*, 929 P.2d 489 (Wash. 1997).

13. 811 N.E.2d 567 (Ohio App. 2004).

14. The Federal Aviation Act of 1958, 49 U.S.C.A. § 1472(j), forbids assault, intimidation, or threatening of a flight crew member and punishes such conduct by imprisonment for up to 20 years.

    In the 1991 case of *U.S. v. Tabacca,* 924 F.2d 906 (9th Cir.), the defendant continued to smoke a cigarette after airline flight attendants requested that he extinguish the cigarette. After addressing vulgar language to the attendant, Tabacca grabbed her arm "and jerked and twisted her arm, causing her to strike the bulkhead of the seat across the aisle." The defendant's conviction was affirmed.

15. *State v. Boone,* 294 Or. 630, 661 P.2d 917 (1983).

16. 810 N.W.2d 303 (Minn. 2012).

17. *Id.*

18. 901 So. 2d 899 (Fla. App. 2005).

19. *Whitaker v. U.S.,* 616 A.2d 843 (D.C. App. 1992).

20. Vernon's Penal Code of the State of Texas Annotated.

21. 508 U.S. 476 (1993).

22. 844 N.Y.S.2d 627 (Sup. Ct. 2007).

23. 791 N.W.2d 828 (Iowa 2010).

24. 980 S.W.2d 682 (Tex. 1998).

25. 429 U.S. 975, 97 S. Ct. 481 (1976). The 1997 U.S. Department of Justice publication *In the Wake of Child Abuse and Childhood Maltreatment* states that more than 3 million children are reported to Child Protective Services each year as being abused. Of these 3 million reported cases, 1 million are found to be abused children. The majority of abused children (85 percent) are under age 5, and nearly half of the victims (45 percent) have not reached their first birthday. More than three children die each day as a result of parental maltreatment. Abuse is the most common cause of death (48 percent), followed by neglect (37 percent), and a combination of abuse and neglect (15 percent). Child abuse is a crime that cuts across all walks of life and all social classes.

26. In *Commonwealth v. Miller,* 600 A.2d 988 (Pa. Super. 1992), the court discussed the endangerment statute's requirement that the defendant "knowingly" endangered a child's welfare. The court said the defendant must know he or she has a duty to care for the child, be aware the child is in a dangerous situation, and have either failed to act or acted in so meager a way that it could not reasonably be believed the actions would be effective. Thus, a mother who leaves her child unattended while she goes out to a nightclub can be convicted of endangerment of a child, but a mother who believes, wrongly and perhaps unreasonably, her boyfriend's statement that another person is watching her child probably would not.

27. 483 F.3d 489 (7th Cir. 2007).

28. 183 Cal Rptr.3d 597 (Cal. App. 2015).

29. 219 P.3d 280 (Az. App. 2009).

30. See *People v. Daniels,* 71 Cal. 2d 1119, 80 Cal. Rptr. 897, 459 P.2d 225 (1969).

31. See *People v. Williams,* 2 Cal. 3d 894, 88 Cal. Rptr. 208, 471 P.2d 1008 (1970).

32. 127 Cal. App. 4th 290 (Cal. App. 2005).

33. 2010 WL 2857046 (Cal App. 2010).

34. 94 N.J. 436, 466 A.2d 955 (1983).

35. 409 So. 2d 1031 (Fla. 1982).

36. Section 940.305, Wisconsin "taking hostage" felony.

37. 728 N.W.2d 374 (Wis. App. 2007).

38. The tort of false imprisonment is sometimes called *false arrest.* False arrest is a wrongful arrest made either by a law enforcement officer or by a private person. Arresting, detaining, and holding a person in custody without authority is false imprisonment and gives the victim the basis for a civil lawsuit to recover for the false arrest and false imprisonment. In a civil lawsuit (tort action) for false arrest, the plaintiff alleges that there was no authority or legal justification for the defendant to interfere with the plaintiff's freedom of movement.

39. 18 U.S.C.A. § 1201.

40. 18 U.S.C.A. § 1073.

41. In October 1984, President Ronald Reagan signed the Missing Children's Assistance Act, now amended and known as the National Child Search Assistance Act of 1990, 42 U.S.C.A. § 5779, which provides for the operation of a national toll-free telephone line for exchanging information on missing children through a national resource center and clearinghouse. The administrator of the program will "facilitate effective coordination among all federally funded programs relating to missing children." Section 5775 of the act provides,

> The Administrator is authorized to make grants to and enter into contracts with [National Center for Missing and Exploited Children] and public agencies or non-profit private organizations, or combination thereof, for research, demonstration projects, or service programs designed—

(1) to educate parents, children, and community agencies and organizations in ways to prevent the abduction and sexual exploitation of children; (2) to provide information to assist in the locating and return of missing children; (3) to aid communities in the collection of materials which would be useful to parents in assisting others in the identification of missing children; (4) to increase knowledge of and develop effective treatment pertaining to the psychological consequences, on both parents and children.

42. *FBI Law Enforcement Bulletin,* July 1, 1996, p. 15.

43. 18 U.S.C.A. §§ 2261–2266. The Act incorporates the criminal violations parts of the Violence Against Women Act of 1994. In the May 2000 case of *U.S. v. Morrison,* the U.S. Supreme Court declared the civil remedy provisions of the Violence Against Women Act unconstitutional. Just as in the Gun-Free School Zones Act case of *U.S. v. Lopez* (115 S. Ct. 1624), violence against women and firearms in a school zone do not affect interstate commerce, and therefore the federal government has limited authority to enact the civil law portions of laws. Courts commonly upheld the criminal portions of the VAWA, which specifically require movement of the victim in interstate commerce. The VAWA expired in 2011. In March of 2013 the law was reauthorized by Congress and signed by President Obama. All states have criminal laws forbidding violence against women, and most states have gun-free school zone laws.

44. 615 F.3d 780 (7th Cir. 2010), *cert. denied,* 131 S. Ct. 681 (2010).

45. 417 F.3d 1080 (9th Cir. 2005), *cert. denied,* 126 S. Ct. 816 (2005).

46. See *Milwaukee Journal Sentinel* article, "30% of Nursing Homes Cited for Abuse," July 31, 2001.

47. 2011 WL 4357778 (Cal. App. 2011).

48. California Penal Code § 368(a).

49. *People v. Heitzmann,* 886 P.2d 1229 (1994).

50. NCJ 148199, U.S. Department of Justice, July 1994.

51. See *Milwaukee Journal Sentinel* article, "Road Rage Closes California Highway," July 27, 2007.

12

Sexual Assault, Rape, Prostitution, and Related Sex Crimes

LEARNING OBJECTIVES

In this chapter we discuss sexual assault crimes and crimes related to sexual conduct. The learning objectives for Chapter 12 are the following:

LO 1. Identify the degrees of sexual assault and the conduct that distinguishes them.

LO 2. Discuss the areas of questioning of a sexual assault victim that are prohibited by the rape shield law.

LO 3. List two exceptions to the rape shield law's prohibitions.

LO 4. Discuss the *mens rea* requirement for a conviction for statutory rape.

LO 5. Explain the conditions that must be shown for civil commitment of a sexual predator.

LO 6. Explain the reasons child pornography laws have been found unconstitutional.

LO 7. Explain the current status of federal acts such as the Child Online Protection Act.

Lance King/Getty Images

Jack Montague, a Yale basketball player, was expelled from Yale in 2016 after a campus discipline committee decided "sufficient evidence" existed to conclude he sexually assaulted a fellow student. College and university committees adjudicating sexual assault cases are increasingly criticized for the unfairness of their procedures.

Nonconsensual sex is virtually always a crime. Even consensual sex can be criminal under certain circumstances. One such circumstance is the age of the "victim" of the sexual acts. If that person is a child under a specified age, ranging from 12 to 16 in most statess, consent of the child is not a defense.

What if both parties to the sexual act are both children under the specified age? If a 10-year-old boy engages in consensual sexual acts with a 10-year-old girl, can they both be guilty under a statute that makes it a crime for "any person" to engage in sexual acts with "another person" who has not attained the age of 12 years? Courts are split on the answer to that question.

In *United States v. J.D.T.*, 762 F.3d 984 (9th Cir. 2015), *cert denied* 136 S. Ct. 400 (2015) the court affirmed a decision finding a 10-year-old guilty of violating 18 U.S.C. § 2241, the federal sexual assault statute.[1] The juvenile engaged in sexual acts with younger boys, who were not prosecuted. He contended application of the sexual assault statute (which has language similar to the quoted words in the previous paragraph) to him violated due process because (1) the statute is vague and gives the prosecution too much discretion on who to prosecute when both parties are under 12 years old, and (2) he lacked the capacity to have the mens rea required under the sexual assault statute, which applies only to one who "knowingly engages in a sexual act with another person" under 12 years. The appeals court rejected those arguments. Based on the knowledge you have acquired about vagueness and mens rea, do you agree with the court or the juvenile?

Some courts view the question differently. The Ohio Supreme Court held the Ohio statutory rape statute inapplicable to a 12-year-old boy who had non-forceful sex with another 12-year-old boy. The court said that one cannot be both a victim and the offender. *In re D.B.*, 950 N.E.2d 528 (Ohio 2011). Is this a better approach to the question?

In this chapter we will study the elements of sexual assault crimes, in particular the rape of women. We will also learn about the rules and procedures put in place to preserve the reputation and emotional well-being of the victim, such as the rape shield laws.

SEXUAL RELATIONS IN THE UNITED STATES TODAY

Sexual relations (non-marital) become a crime in the United States if

- There is a lack of consent.
- They are with a minor incapable of legally consenting.
- They are with a mentally deficient person or an adult otherwise deemed by the law to be incapable of consenting.
- They are performed in public.
- They are performed for profit (prostitution).
- They are between a therapist and a patient and in violation of the laws of that state.

RAPE OR SEXUAL ASSAULT

Sex crimes occur often in the United States. The term *sex crime* includes a broad classification of offenses that range from serious offenses to nuisance offenses and private offenses between consenting adults. Historically, the term *rape* was used to identify the crime of non-consensual sexual relations obtained by force or threat of force. The National Institute of Justice (NIJ), the research and development branch of the U.S. Justice Department, defines **rape** as vaginal, oral, or anal penetration achieved through the use of force or threat of force. Rape includes penetration of the vagina or anus by penis, finger, tongue, or some other object manipulated by the rapist. Many state criminal codes use a similar definition.

rape Anal, vaginal, or oral penetration by force or threat of force.

The criminal codes of the fifty states use the terms *rape, sexual assault,* or *sexual battery* when dealing with what the common law called rape and do so in a variety of ways. All the states probably treat "ordinary" rape in much the same way as did the common law, though often listing ordinary rape as a second-degree offense and punishing it as a class B felony.

Aggravated rape, however, is handled differently in different states. For example, gang rape, which is rape committed against a single victim by multiple offenders, is an aggravated offense under the Florida sexual battery statutes. Section 794.0233 of the Florida Statutes provides for enhanced penalties and punishes the offense as a first-degree felony (life felony). Other states simply classify gang rape as a first-degree felony.

Other factors that states use as aggravating factors to elevate a rape or sexual assault to a first-degree or class A felony include inflicting serious bodily harm on the victim, using a deadly weapon such as a knife or gun in the rape, causing the victim to become pregnant, infecting the victim with AIDS or another sexually transmitted disease, anal penetration, or raping a very young child.

sexual assault The crime in most states that includes the crime of rape, as well as other lesser degrees of assault.

The NIJ has estimated that rape (or first-degree **sexual assault**) with female victims occurs over 300,000 times each year, and nearly 93,000 times with male victims. In the 2006 National Violence Against Women Survey, the results of which were published by the NIJ,[2] telephone interviews conducted nationwide with 8,000 women and 8,000 men disclosed the following information:

- In the United States, one out of every six women has experienced either rape or attempted rape at some time in her life; one out of every thirty-three men has experienced either rape or attempted rape at some time in his life.
- Rape or attempted rape frequently involves young victims, with most victims being under the age of 12 when the rape occurred.
- Most rape victims are women, and most offenders are men.
- When the victim of rape or attempted rape is 18 years of age or older, physical injury is caused to 31.5 percent of female victims and 16.1 percent of male victims.
- Only 19.1 percent of the female victims of rape or attempted rape, and 12.9 percent of male victims, over the age of 18, reported the incident to the police.
- The reasons given for failure to report a rape or attempted rape were "fear of retaliation by the offender," "too ashamed or embarrassed," "thought the matter was a minor incident," or "not a police matter."
- Where female victims reported the rape or attempted rape, 37 percent resulted in prosecutions, with convictions in 46.2 percent of the prosecutions. Thirteen percent of the female victims sought and obtained restraining orders against the offenders; 69.9 percent reported that the restraining order was violated.

In a December 2015 report by the Federal Bureau of Justice Statistics, National Crime Victimization Survey, it found that in 2014 there were 284,350 reported rapes/sexual assaults in the United States. The report also estimated that more than 50 percent of sexual assaults go unreported to law enforcement authorities.

The Importance of Corroborative Evidence in a Rape Case

corroborative evidence Physical evidence or witness testimony other than from the victim that supports the claim that a crime occurred.

Today, in virtually every state, a rape conviction can rest solely on the uncorroborated testimony of the victim.[3] However, **corroborative evidence** (evidence affirming and supporting statements of the victim) is very important in most cases.

Statistics show that in as many as 40 percent of the cases that come into the offices of prosecutors in large cities, rape charges are not issued. Lack of corroborating evidence is probably the principal reason. Statements of the complaining witness can be corroborated and affirmed by the following:

- Scratches, bruises, injuries, torn clothing, or blood stains from either the victim or the suspect.

- Witnesses who heard screams or the sounds of a struggle, or observed either party before, during, or immediately after the assault.
- Color photographs of bruises, black-and-blue marks, lacerations, cuts, scratches, or other injuries to either party, as these injuries will disappear within a few days through the healing process.
- Blood, semen, saliva, or nail scrapings taken from the victim or suspect, as well as pubic and head hair obtained at the scene of the crime and from the bodies of the victim and suspect. Such genetic material may result in a positive DNA identification of the offender.
- Weapons or instruments that may have been used to force the victim to submit to the assault.
- Buttons, torn clothing, or other items that the victim or suspect may have lost in the struggle.
- Soiled or stained clothing of the suspect and victim that contains blood, seminal stains, or other evidence of the crime.
- Fingerprints found at the scene of the sexual assault or elsewhere that can be used to corroborate or to identify the suspect.
- Observations by doctors and nurses and samples of fluids from vagina, rectum, or oral cavity showing that forcible intercourse had occurred.
- If DNA evidence from blood, semen, saliva, and so forth is available, it could prove the identity of the offender almost conclusively.

In a rape case, whether the state has a strong or a weak case in going to trial depends on the physical evidence available and the ability of the complaining witness to testify. Lack of corroborative physical evidence and/or the inability of the complaining witness to testify effectively could cause the case to be viewed as weak.

Possible Responses to a Threat of Rape

Studies show that most women, especially young women, fear rape more than any other crime. How should a woman respond to an imminent threat of rape?

- *Should she scream, fight back, and try to escape?* Studies show that women who resist decrease the odds of completed rape by 80 percent. But they increase the likelihood of being physically injured. Experts say that it is better to be raped than to risk being permanently injured or killed.
- *Should she try to talk the man out of it?* Women have tried many different tactics in trying to avoid rape. They have pretended to be pregnant, or have stated they have a sexually transmitted disease, or have AIDS. They have fainted, cried hysterically, acted insane or vomited, urinated, or acted very ill.
- *Should she grit her teeth and bear it?* This is an available option that the victim might choose. Or the victim may be able to combine one or both of the above two in an effort to avoid being raped.

The "Force" Required in Rape or Sexual Assault

William Blackstone, the author of the famous "Commentaries on the Laws of England," published in 1895, said the English common law defined rape as "the carnal knowledge of a woman forcibly and against her will." When the American states adopted their own criminal laws, virtually all defined rape in a similar manner. As a result, rape statutes required a showing of both lack of consent ("against her will") and physical force. Early on, most statutes were amended to include the "threat of force" as a substitute for the "forcible compulsion" element, where actual force was not present.

Forcible Compulsion   In many states the prosecution was required to prove force "compelled" the victim to engage in the sexual acts, by introducing proof the victim "resisted" the acts. Absence of proof of resistance by the victim was fatal to the prosecution's case. That has changed dramatically. Sexual assault and rape statutes in the fifty states are worded in many different ways, but in most states that require proof of "forcible compulsion," there is no need to prove resistance by the victim, and the force used need only be sufficient to "overcome" the victim's will. Even where "resistance" is part of the definition of forcible rape, courts usually require only proof that the victim voiced her objection to the acts but was forced to comply.

In some states, sexual assault is defined generally to include any sexual penetration obtained "against the will" of the victim. If force is used, the sexual assault is classified as a more serious felony. The Colorado sexual assault statute, Col. Stat. § 18-3-402(4)(a), is such a statute. In *People v. Keene*, 226 P.3d 1140 (Colo. App. 2009), the court held that the defendant's own body weight can be the "physical force" that triggers the increased severity of the assault, if in fact the victim struggled and the weight prevented her from escaping.

Case and State	Facts of the Case	Requirement of the State Statute
People v. Griffin, Supreme Court of California, 94 P.3d 1089 (2004).	The defendant told the victim to lie down on the floor. She did, and he held her wrists while he sexually penetrated her. The victim did not otherwise resist. The conviction for forcible rape was affirmed.	The California forcible rape statute, which had been amended to eliminate any need of showing resistance by the victim, required only a showing that the rape was "accomplished against a person's will by means of force, violence, or fear of immediate and unlawful bodily injury," the Court held.
State v. Jones, 299 P.3d 219 (Idaho 2013).	Defendant was charged with two counts of forcible rape of the victim. In one, the only force by the defendant was pushing the victim off her elbows and putting his body on her back. In the other, the victim pretended to be asleep, and offered no resistance. The court affirmed the conviction in count I but reversed the conviction in count II.	The Idaho rape statute defined forcible rape as occurring when the victim "resists, but her resistance is overcome by force or violence." The court said that under this type of forcible rape statute, some "extrinsic force" beyond the physical act of intercourse must be proved, though it need not be of any specific kind or degree. Since no extrinsic force was shown in the second rape, it was not forcible rape.

Non-Consent   There has long been a demand by rape victims and groups supporting them for reform of the traditional forcible rape laws. Reform groups sought the elimination of any requirement of force or threat of force, and instead urged legislators to make rape a purely "consent/non-consent" question. In a 2011 article in the *Journal of Criminal Law and Criminology*[4] the authors suggest that this reform movement has been only partially successful. They note that while twenty-eight states have true "non-consent" rape statutes, which require no proof of "forcible compulsion," only seventeen of them apply that standard to sexual penetration rapes. The other eleven states limit true "non-consent" sexual assaults to crimes involving sexual contact, without penetration. Sexual penetration rapes still must be accompanied by force. Fifteen states have no form of "non-consent" sexual assault, and the remaining states have statutes that incorporate force or threat of force into the meaning of "consent."

Threats of Force   Where force is still part of the rape requirement, threats or fear of force will normally serve as a substitute for actual force. The Maryland Court of Appeals has noted that the "vast majority of jurisdictions have required that the victim's fear be reasonably grounded in order to obviate the need for either proof of actual force on the part of the assailant or physical resistance on the part of the victim."[5] Pointing out that the reasonableness of a victim's apprehension or fear was plainly a question of fact for a jury to determine, the Maryland Court of Appeals held,[6]

> It was for the jury to observe the witnesses and their demeanor, and to judge their credibility and weigh their testimony. Quite obviously, the jury disbelieved Rusk [defendant] and believed Pat's [victim] testimony.

> * * *

> Just where persuasion ends and force begins in cases like the present is essentially a factual issue, to be resolved in light of the controlling legal precepts. That threats of force need not be made in any particular manner in order to put a person in fear of bodily harm is well established. . . . Indeed, conduct, rather than words, may convey the threat.

> * * *

> That a victim did not scream out for help or attempt to escape, while bearing on the question of consent, is unnecessary where she is restrained by fear of violence.

The Report of Rape Rule and the Effect of Delay in Reporting

After a sexual assault, the victim may be confused and fearful of her assailant. This could result in a delay in reporting the crime. A long delay could raise questions of the credibility of the victim, it could substantially diminish the possibility of obtaining physical evidence of the rape, and it could prevent the person receiving the report of rape from testifying as to the statements and circumstances. The Model

Penal Code, § 213.6(4) (the report of rape rule)[7], states that no prosecution may be brought if the complainant fails to report the sexual assault within three months of its occurrence or, if the victim is less than 16 years old, within three months of the time a parent or other competent adult learns of the assault.

A person to whom a rape victim has excitedly reported a rape can testify as to the statements and circumstances under the report of rape or excited utterance exceptions to the hearsay rule.[8] Such testimony is important corroborative evidence in proving a rape charge. It also counteracts what has been called the "timing myth" that assumed rape victims who do not immediately "cry out" and alert others have not been raped.

In many states the "fresh complaint" rule permits the prosecution to introduce evidence the victim spontaneously reported the rape within a reasonable time. In the case of children, courts generally permit, as a reasonable time, a much longer interval between the rape and the report than found in the MPC section discussed above.

For example, in the 2011 case of *State v. W.B.*[9] the New Jersey Supreme Court affirmed a conviction for aggravated sexual assault on a child. The court held the trial court was correct in admitting under the "fresh complaint" rule evidence that the child victim, 14 years of age when the sexual assault occurred, spontaneously reported the sexual assault 15 months after it occurred. That period was reasonable, the court held, given the age of the victim, and her fear of the defendant, her stepfather.

It is true that a significant number of reports of rape or sexual assault turn out to be unfounded, though that is true of other crimes as well. Where the alleged victim has made prior false reports of sexual assaults, defendants often try to introduce evidence of those false reports, to attack the credibility of the complainant. These attempts raise an issue under rape shield laws, which are discussed in the next section.

Rape Shield Laws

rape shield laws Laws passed by many states to limit the extent to which defense attorneys in a rape case can inquire into the victim's past sexual life.

Most states have enacted **rape shield laws** that forbid the use of evidence of a rape victim's past sexual conduct with others and evidence of her reputation. Under the protection of rape shield laws, victims appearing as witnesses in a sexual assault case therefore do not have to defend their reputations or past sexual conduct.

Rule 412 of the Federal Rules of Evidence is an example of a rape shield law and is similar to many such laws adopted by states. It provides that in a criminal trial of a sexual assault charge, evidence (1) offered to prove the victim engaged in other sexual behavior, or (2) offered to prove the victim's sexual predisposition, is inadmissible. There are three exceptions to this rule: evidence is admissible if it is (1) evidence of specific sexual behavior of the victim offered to prove another person was the source of semen or other physical evidence; (2) evidence of specific past sexual contact between the victim and the accused, if offered to prove consent; or (3) evidence the exclusion of which would violate the constitutional rights of the accused. In *United States v. Pumpkin Seed*[10] the court upheld a trial court's decision to exclude evidence that the defendant was not the source of semen and pubic hair found on the victim. The court reasoned that since the prosecution did not offer the semen or pubic hair as evidence of the rape, that evidence was not relevant to any issue in the trial.

Before rape shield laws, defense lawyers deemed a victim's reputation "fair game," and the victim could be forced to defend her entire sexual history. Rape shield laws were enacted to encourage the reporting of sexual assaults and to forbid introduction of evidence that would prejudice a jury. Such evidence is also irrelevant to the issue of guilt or innocence before the court. Rape shield laws apply to male victims as well as female victims. Evidence offered to prove that the victim was a homosexual, or had engaged in past homosexual acts, would be inadmissible under most rape shield laws.[11] In the 2010 case of *State v. Rackliffe*,[12] the court rejected the contention of a defendant convicted of sexual assault on a male victim that proof of the victim's sexual orientation was relevant on the issue of consent to the sexual assault.

However, exceptions are made in rape shield laws to allow the introduction of relevant, probative evidence at trial. In the U.S. Supreme Court case of *Olden v. Kentucky*,[13] the defendant sought to prove that the victim made up her charge of sexual battery against him in order to protect her relationship with her boyfriend. The U.S. Supreme Court reversed the defendant's conviction, holding that his Sixth Amendment right to conduct reasonable cross-examination had been violated.

The presence or absence of consent by the victim is an important issue in a rape case. As a result, almost all rape shield laws permit defendants to introduce evidence of "past sexual contact between the victim and the accused, if offered to prove consent." The fact that an alleged victim had sexual contact with the defendant in the past can support the inference that the claimed sexual assault was consensual. However, it does not always follow that any past sexual contact is admissible. In the 2014 case of *State v. Sarfraz*, 851 N.W.2d 235 (Wisc. 2014) the Wisconsin Supreme Court affirmed a conviction for sexual assault. The trial court refused to admit evidence offered by the defendant that on past occasions he and the victim engaged in mutual masturbation. While the Wisconsin rape shield law permits evidence of past sexual contact to show consent, the Supreme Court said that when the sexual assault is based on forcible rape involving sexual penetration, the probative value of other kinds of past sexual contact is lessened. Since the purpose of the rape shield law is to avoid the humiliation of the victim, the prejudicial effect of the evidence of prior sexual contact like masturbation greatly outweighed its probative value, the court held.

In the 2012 case of *Perry v. Commonwealth*[14] the Kentucky Supreme Court stated that under the Kentucky rape shield law, as in the majority of state courts, a defendant in a rape case is permitted to offer evidence that the victim had in the past made false rape claims against others. Such evidence is not about past sexual behavior, the court said, and thus the rape shield law was inapplicable. However, the court also said evidence of false reports is potentially very prejudicial, and as a result the defendant wishing to introduce such evidence must make a preliminary showing that the prior reports were "demonstrably false." Colorado's Rape Shield Law, C.R.S.A. § 18-3-407, specifically provides that evidence of past false reports is admissible. However, in *People v. Weiss*,[15] the Colorado Supreme Court held that the defendant must "by a preponderance of the evidence" show the past rape reports were "in fact" false. It reversed the decision of a trial court that permitted a defendant to introduce evidence of previous rape reports by the victim, holding that just because no charges were filed based on the reports did not make them "in fact" false under the rape shield exception.

Exceptions vary from state to state, and the rape shield law of each state must be consulted to determine the exact nature of the exceptions.

OLD RAPE LAWS AND NEW SEXUAL ASSAULT LAWS

Under Old Rape Laws and the Common Law	Statutory Changes Enacted in Most States Since the 1970s
• Only females could be the victims of rape.	• Any person (male or female) may be a victim.
• Only a male could directly commit the crime.	• Any person (male or female) can directly commit the crime. See the 1986 case of *State v. Stevens*, 510 A.2d 1070 (Me.), in which the court held that an adult woman could be charged with having sexual intercourse with a 13-year-old boy.
• A husband could not rape his wife. (Under the common law, however, the husband could be charged with assault and battery.)	• A husband can be charged with the rape of his wife under the law of states that have made this change from the common law.
• Rape was defined in one degree (or at most a few degrees).	• A variety of degrees of criminal conduct are defined in more specific language. "Ordinary" rape, which is often second-degree rape, is the most common criminal charge, while "aggravated" rape, such as gang rape or rape with use of a deadly weapon, or rape resulting in physical injury or pregnancy, is usually first-degree sexual assault.
• Rape was defined only as the insertion of the penis into a vagina by force and against the will of the female.	• Sexual intercourse is broadly defined not only as vaginal intercourse but also as "cunnilingus, fellatio, anal intercourse, or any other intrusion, however slight, of any part of a person's body or of any object into the genital or anal opening of another, but emission of semen is not required." See Section 940.225(5)(c) of the Wisconsin Criminal Code.
• Common law rape did not include the crime of offensive touching (however, this could be charged either as disorderly conduct or as assault and sometimes battery).	• Many modern sexual assault laws include the offense of offensive touching in that they forbid "sexual contact" (intentional touching of an intimate part of another person's body without consent for sexual gratification). (See, e.g., Neb. Rev. Stat. § 28-319.)
• "Utmost resistance" and resistance were required under the old common law.	• "Utmost resistance" is no longer required for the crime of rape. Instead, many states require proof that the sex act was done "without consent" and "against the will" of the victim. Wisconsin, for example, eliminated the requirement of utmost resistance in the 1970s.
• Rape was classified as a crime against sexual morality.	• Sexual assault is more often classified as a crime against a person.

statutory rape Sexual intercourse with a minor under a certain age, usually 16–18. Consent and, generally, mistake as to age are not defenses to this crime.

STATUTORY RAPE

All states have statutes that make sexual intercourse with a person who is not the spouse of the perpetrator a criminal offense if the person is under the age stated by the state criminal code. This crime is called **statutory rape**.

The origin of current U.S. statutes goes back to the English statute of 1275, when the age of consent was set at 12 years. In 1576, the age was reduced to 10 years. California, for example, enacted its first statute in 1850 making the age 10. In 1913, it was fixed at 18, where it remains.

Honest mistake as to the age of the minor is not permitted as a defense in virtually all states that forbid statutory rape. See, for example, the case of *State v. Jadowski*,[16] where the court held that even if the child intentionally misled the defendant about her age, it is no defense to a charge of statutory rape. Nor is consent by the child a defense, even if investigation shows that the child was a willing participant in the sex acts.

There are a few exceptions to the honest mistake rule. Some decisions by courts in California have said that in some circumstances a good-faith belief in the age of the child is a defense to statutory rape, but it is questionable if that is still the law.[17] Tennessee has a "criminal intent" statute that appears to require proof of intent in statutory rape. As a result, it has been held that failure to permit a jury to consider a mistake-of-age defense is reversible error.[18] At least one state, Washington, has a statute that allows a good-faith mistake in the age of a child as a defense, but only if (1) the defendant's belief was based on "declarations as to age by the alleged victim" and (2) the defendant proves the defense by a preponderance of the evidence.[19] Under 18 U.S.C. §2243, the federal sexual abuse statute of a minor over 12 but under

OTHER TYPES OF RAPES OR SEXUAL ASSAULTS

Type of Rape	Characteristics	Most Common Defense Used
Rape in which the victim was mentally defective or diseased and incapable of giving consent	This type of criminal statute seeks to protect people who are mentally incompetent and incapable of giving consent to sexual acts. The offense usually requires that the state show that the defendant knew or had reason to know of the mental incapacity of the victim. See, e.g., *Comm. v. Fuller*, 845 N.E.2d 434 (Mass. App. 2006), *cert, denied* 848 N.E.2d 1211 (2006).	Defendant denies that he knew of the mental incapacity of the victim or that any sex act occurred.
Rape by use of a date rape drug	Rohypnol ("roofies") and GHB are odorless, nearly tasteless, and potentially lethal to a victim. They are slipped into a drink to drug and sexually assault women.	The woman has no memory of what happened, and most often there are no other witnesses. With no witnesses, it is important to obtain a urine sample immediately to prove the presence of a date rape drug.
Sexual intercourse obtained by threats other than threats of violence, which would be forcible rape	In the few states that have enacted a statute such as this, the threat might be to disclose information that the victim did not want disclosed, or it could be a job-related threat that the victim would be fired or lose a promotion if she refused to have sex. Employment and sexual harassment laws also provide civil remedies for such acts.	No threat was made or implied, or no sexual act occurred.

16 years of age, it is a defense if a defendant reasonably believed the minor had attained the age of 16 years. It should be noted that under that statute the prosecution has no duty to prove the defendant knew the minor was under 16; the defendant has the burden to prove the reasonable belief defense.

THE CRIME OF INCEST

incest Sexual relations between persons closely related.

The crime of **incest** may be committed by adults within a family, but the public concern and prosecution are generally for cases involving children. Like statutory rape, the crime does not require a showing that force was used (or threatened) or that the victim did not consent.

Incest was not a crime under common law, nor was it made a statutory crime in England until 1908. Before that time, the offense was dealt with by ecclesiastical (religious) courts. Today, all the states have statutes making the offense a crime. Generally, incest in the first degree involves sexual intercourse. Incest in the second degree involves sexual contact without penetration. Under most state statutes, incest is limited to sexual relations with a descendant, ancestor, brother, or sister of the offender. The category of "descendant" usually includes adopted children or stepchildren.

Most experts believe that an estimated 60,000 to 100,000 female children are sexually abused annually and that 80 percent of sexual abuse is not reported. It is believed that incest affects more than 10 percent of all American families, with at least 5,000 cases of father-daughter incest.

Penalties for incest range from 90 days to life imprisonment. Enforcement, however, is practically impossible unless a member of the family cooperates. Unfortunately, the credibility of the child victim is often attacked and severely questioned.

In 90 percent of cases, the victim is female, and the abuse may commence while the child is too young to realize the significance of the problem. When the child becomes knowledgeable about what has happened, or is happening, the child is apt to feel guilt, betrayal, confusion, and fright.

As stated above, incest is similar to statutory rape in that consent is not a defense, nor is use of force required for conviction. Unlike statutory rape laws, however, in most states the incest statute requires proof that the defendant knew the person was related to the defendant in the statutorily proscribed manner. Thus, a reasonable belief that the other person is not related to the defendant would be a defense to a charge of incest. This belief must relate to the absence of a biological relationship between the defendant and the other person.

In *State v. Hall*,[20] 48 P.3d 350 (Wash. App. 2002), the court affirmed a conviction for second-degree incest of the defendant with his biological daughter. The court rejected the defendant's argument that because he had surrendered his parental rights when the girl was 4 years old, he did not believe she was his daughter, and thus he lacked the knowledge required by the incest statute. The court said all the statute required was knowledge that the girl was his biological daughter, because that fact made her the defendant's descendant.

HIV AND AIDS-RELATED CRIMES

HIV is the virus that causes acquired immune deficiency syndrome (AIDS). When AIDS first became known to the medical establishment in the 1970s, there were few medications or treatments for AIDS patients, and in most cases death occurred within a few months of diagnosis of the disease. During the AIDS epidemics of the 1980s and 1990s, widespread fear of the spread of this disease led many states to enact criminal laws specific to the spread of the disease.

However, in the past 10 to 15 years, knowledge and treatment of AIDS and HIV have improved substantially, and the fear of infection has subsided somewhat. Notwithstanding those medical changes, the criminal laws adopted by more than thirty states remain on the books and continue to be enforced.

In virtually all states, knowingly, recklessly, or (in some) negligently exposing a person to or infecting a person with the AIDS virus is a felony. This is often charged under a specific AIDS or HIV statute; an example is the Missouri statute, V.A.M.S. 191.677. In the 2012 case of *State v. Sykes,*[21] an HIV-positive defendant was convicted under the Missouri statute of knowingly exposing his girlfriend to the HIV virus without telling her he was HIV-positive. The defendant had previously been convicted of the same offense, but did not tell his girlfriend about that conviction. The girlfriend became HIV-positive. The defendant was sentenced to life in prison as a repeat offender, and the appeals court affirmed his conviction and sentence.

The U.S. Center for Disease Control and Prevention states in its publication "*Basic Information About HIV and AIDS*" that HIV is primarily spread through sexual contact or the exchange of blood. That publication states that the virus cannot be transmitted through tears, sweat, or saliva. It also states that as of the publication date of March 2010, "There has been no documented case of HIV being transmitted by spitting." Severe bites can transmit the virus, but only if the bites involve severe trauma and include the presence of blood. The publication states that HIV cannot be spread if the skin is not broken. In the 2012 case of *State v. Ingram*[22] the court of appeals reversed a conviction for criminal exposure to HIV based on the defendant's spitting in the face of a police officer. The court said the state failed to prove spitting created a significant risk of HIV infection, which is a required element of the offense.

LAWS THAT REQUIRE REGISTRATION FOR SEX OFFENDERS (MEGAN'S LAW)

In the case *McKune v. Lite,* the U.S. Supreme Court stated,

> Sex offenders are a serious threat in this nation. . . . Between 1980 and 1994 the population of imprisoned sex offenders increased at a faster rate than for any other category of violent crime. . . . Victims of sexual assault are most often juveniles . . . nearly four in ten violent sex offenders said their victims were 12 or younger. [When released from prison] sex offenders are more likely than any other type of offender to be rearrested for a new rape or sexual assault.[23]

Megan's laws Laws passed in many states requiring convicted sex offenders to register with a state or local registration office. Named after a young girl killed by a convicted sex offender.

In response to these grim statistics, in the 1990s states began passing registration laws for sexual offenders. These laws, called **Megan's laws** after the name of a child killed by a sexual offender in 1994, require sex offenders to register their name and address when released from prison. In 2006 Congress passed the federal Sex Offender Registration and Notification Act (SORNA), 42 U.S.C. § 16913; additionally, 18 U.S.C. § 2250 authorizes up to a 10-year prison sentence for failure to register.

State laws usually list offenses for which registration is mandatory and those for which registration is within the discretion of a sentencing judge. Such laws commonly include some or all of the following features:

- Sex offenders are prohibited from living in a residence located within a specified distance from schools, day-care facilities, or other places where children gather; zoning or other local laws might have a similar restriction.
- Sex offenders are required to personally notify authorities when they change their place of employment or change their address. Failure to give this notification is a crime.
- Sex offenders are required to provide a DNA sample to authorities to be placed in a state and national DNA database.
- A website is to be accessible to the public that includes current information about sex offenders registered in the system. In 2006 Congress created the National Sex Offender Registry, 42 U.S.C. § 16919. This law requires the FBI to maintain a national registry available to law enforcement and the public that contains the names and addresses of all persons required to register in any state's sex offender registration system.

At least one state, Utah, includes in the sex offender registration requirements that a sex offender must list all "Internet identifiers" used by the offender in any "Internet communication," such as a chat room. Utah Code § 77-27-21.5(14)(i)(j). In the 2010 case of *Doe v. Shurtleff*,[24] a federal court upheld this part of the Utah sex offender registration law against a claim it violated the First Amendment, noting that information placed in the registry could only be used in investigation of sex offenses.

In the 2015 case of *State v. Packingham*, 777 S.E.2d 738 (N.C. 2015) the North Carolina Supreme Court upheld the constitutionality of a state law that prohibited registered sex offenders from using social network sites like Facebook that permit children to join. It rejected the defendant's argument that the law arbitrarily inhibited his right to exercise free speech in an important area for communication, social networking. In March of 2016 the defendant filed a petition for certiorari in the U.S Supreme Court.

In hearings on the National Sex Offender Registry Act, the House Judiciary Committee of the U.S. Congress reported that there were 500,000 convicted sex offenders in the United States but that 100,000 of these offenders were not currently registered or were missing and could not be located.[25] Some prosecutors have stated that state registration laws have caused an increase in the number of sex offenders who disappear, leaving no information about their whereabouts. This creates an increased burden for law enforcement agencies, which must under state and federal laws track down released sex offenders and obtain the required information.

When a sexual offender has registered in a state where the offender resides, but then moves to a foreign country without informing the state where registration occurred, courts have split on whether this is a violation of the federal SORNA law. In the 2016 case of *Nichols v. United States,* 136 S. Ct. 1113, the U.S. Supreme Court held that SORNA requires a sex offender to register, when he moves from one jurisdiction, in the jurisdiction where he "resides." A foreign country, the Court said, is not a "jurisdiction" under SORNA, and thus a failure to register there does not violate the federal statute. The Court noted that legislation passed by Congress in 2016, titled "International Megan's Law to Prevent Child Exploitation and Other Sexual Crimes Through Advanced Notification of Travelling Sex Offenders," codified at 42 U.S.C. §16914(a)(7), addresses this problem. The Court reversed a conviction of a registered sex offender who registered in Kansas, but moved to the Philippines without giving notification to Kansas.

CIVIL COMMITMENT OF SEXUALLY DANGEROUS OFFENDERS

For many years states have had in place laws that permit the state to bring civil commitment proceedings for the involuntary, temporary commitment of persons who pose a threat to themselves or others. For example, a man who attempted suicide could be temporarily held for mental observation based on the demonstrated danger to his own life. If long-term civil commitment were needed, these laws required a court hearing to determine the need and justification for such commitment.

As an additional response to the threat posed by sexual predators, in the 1990s some states enacted sexual predator laws. These laws permitted the state to obtain civil commitment of convicted sexual offenders after the offenders were released from prison.[26] In *Kansas v. Crane,*[27] the U.S. Supreme Court held that before a state may commit a sex offender under a civil commitment statute, it must prove that not only was the offender dangerous and likely to commit more sex crimes but also that the offender had "serious difficulty in controlling [his] behavior." The Court noted that pedophilia was a mental abnormality that made it difficult for an offender to control his behavior and would thus properly be a basis for civil commitment.

In 2006 Congress passed 18 U.S.C. § 4248, which authorizes civil commitment of sexually dangerous federal prisoners following the expiration of their prison sentence. That section was upheld by the U.S. Supreme Court in the 2010 case of *United States v. Comstock,* 130 S. Ct. 1949.

It is estimated that about 2,700 pedophiles, rapists, and other sexual offenders are being held indefinitely under sexual predator laws enacted in twenty states. Because the goal of civil commitment is to furnish treatment to the sex offender, rather than punish the offender for criminal conduct, it is generally held that these civil commitments do not violate the Double Jeopardy Clause or Ex Post Facto Clause of the U.S. Constitution.[28]

Once committed under these programs, many sex offenders are never released. In a study of these programs published in the *New York Times,*[29] it was reported that virtually all those committed were men; only three women have been committed to date. The costs of commitment under these programs averaged more than four times the cost of keeping an inmate in prison. Ages of those committed varied greatly; under Wisconsin's sexual predator law, the youngest of the 283 persons committed was 18, and the oldest 102.

Critics of the need for civil commitment of sexual offenders have offered statistical support for their criticism. They note that only about 5.3 percent of sexual offenders commit sexual offenses within three years after release from prison. As of August 2012, the federal government has sought certification of sexually dangerous prisoners in only 136 cases, and 61 of them have been dropped. Only fifteen prisoners have been certified. Graydon Comstock, the prisoner involved in the Supreme Court case discussed above, was determined not to be sexually dangerous, and was released in 2011.[30]

PROSTITUTION

prostitution
Providing sex for money or other value.

The crime of **prostitution** can be one of at least three non-marital acts:

1. Engaging in sexual relations with another person for a fee or something of value

2. Offering (or soliciting) to engage in sexual relations with another person for a fee or something of value

3. Requesting (or agreeing) to pay a fee or something of value to another person for sexual services and acts

The fee or something of value is most often money. Members of either sex may now be convicted of prostitution, as distinguished from in the past, when only women could be convicted. Most (if not all) state prostitution statutes forbid males from selling sexual services to other males. Males who offer to pay a woman to engage in sex acts may also be charged with the crime.

Prostitution is often referred to as the world's oldest profession and is described in history's earliest written records. The Bible, for instance, makes many references to whores and whoremongering. Prostitution is an activity that grows and recedes, depending on the changing mores and morals of a particular civilization. Many believe that, like the poor, it will always be with us.

Throughout the world, efforts have been made to suppress, control, organize, or discourage prostitution, with varying degrees of success. Prostitutes range from the common streetwalker to the privately kept woman or man. In the United Kingdom and France, prostitution is legal, but publicly soliciting customers is against the law. In some countries, particularly in Asia, government-inspected houses of prostitution are allowed.

Efforts to decriminalize prostitution in the United States have met with little success. Only one state (Nevada) has legalized prostitution. In Nevada, each county has the option to legalize prostitution. Fifteen of Nevada's seventeen counties have decided to remove the legal restraints against prostitution.

The Crimes of Procuring, Promoting, and Pimping for the Practice of Prostitution

Many prostitutes operate without pimps or other people procuring or promoting for them. Some prostitutes, however, have pimps, who procure customers and provide protection and bail as needed. In addition to pimps, other people obtain money by procuring and promoting prostitution.

procuring, promoting, and pimping Actions taken to provide services of a prostitute.

Procuring, promoting, and pimping for prostitution are forbidden by state criminal codes. However, because of the potential financial gains, these people have a motive to encourage and coerce young people into prostitution. They increase the volume and extent to which prostitution is practiced and often gain a vicious hold over the prostitutes who work for them.

Most state procurement statutes apply to persons who "promote" prostitution, that is, engage in acts designed to aid unlawful sexual acts between prostitutes and third parties. As a result, some courts have held these laws do not apply to "consumers" of prostitution. In the 2010 case of *State v. Varga-Torres*[31] the court reversed a conviction under the Oregon "compelling prostitution" statute, which makes it a

JUVENILES WHO COMMIT SEX OFFENSES AGAINST CHILDREN

A 2009 Department of Justice Juvenile Bulletin reported statistics from recent studies of sex offenses generally and sex offenses targeting children. Children, boys and girls, are the victims of nearly 70 percent of all sex crimes committed each year. Older children commit more than 25.8 percent of all reported sex offenses, and 35.6 percent of sex offenses against children. The report also stated:

- The criminal incidents in the study were rape (26.4 percent), sodomy (11.9 percent), sex assault with object (4.2 percent), fondling (47.2 percent), and non-forcible sex offenses (10.5 percent).
- 88 percent of the offenders were between the ages of 12 and 18.
- The offenses occurred mostly in a home/residence (68.1 percent); 12.1 percent occurred at a school.
- Of the victims, 64.5 percent were acquainted with the offender; 23.8 percent were family members.
- The juvenile offenders differed from the adult offenders in that (1) they were more likely to offend in groups, 24 percent versus 14 percent; (2) more likely to have male victims, 25 percent versus 19 percent; and (3) more likely to target younger children as victims, 59 percent versus 39 percent.
- Most juvenile offenders were male; only 7 percent of juvenile offenders were female.
- Juvenile offenders commit more than one in four of all sex offenses, and more than one in three of sex offenses against children.

crime to "induce or cause a person under 18 years of age to engage in prostitution." The defendant gave car rides, cigarettes, and alcohol to a young girl in exchange for sex. The court said that since none of these "payments" were intended to induce the girl to have sex with others, the statute did not apply.

The federal government has a statute similar to state procuring laws, called the "2000 Trafficking Victim Protection Act." It prohibits sex trafficking in interstate commerce, including enticing minors to engage in commercial sex acts. It applies to any person who "entices . . . or obtains . . . any person" under the age of 18 who is caused to engage in a "commercial sex act." While the law is aimed at commercial sex ventures, those people who would be called "procurers" in similar state laws, the federal statute has a broader scope. In a 2013 case the law was held to apply to "consumers" as well as "providers" of child prostitution. In *United States v. Jungers*[32] the court held that a defendant who tried to "buy" time with a child for sexual acts in an FBI sting operation could be convicted under the trafficking act.

Crimes That Require Proof that the Crime Was Committed in a Public Place

Private sex acts between consenting adults are rarely charged as crimes, even if they violate specific sections of criminal codes. In the case of *Lawrence v. Texas,* 539 U.S. 558, the U.S. Supreme Court struck down a Texas statute that made it a crime for two male adults to have prohibited sex acts in the privacy of their home.

Public sex acts, however, can be charged as criminal conduct. The statute defining the crime often requires proof that the crime was committed in a public place, as well as some intent to obtain sexual gratification. For example, in the 2010 case

OLD OFFENSES THAT ARE NO LONGER CRIMES OR ARE SELDOM CHARGED

Offense	Definition	History
Bigamy (or polygamy)	Marriage to two or more spouses at the same time.	Statutorized in 1604 (prior to that time, it was an ecclesiastical crime in England). In recent years, it has seldom been prosecuted in the United States.[a]
Adultery[b]	Voluntary sexual intercourse in which one or both parties are married to another person (parties not married to each other). About half the states continue to make adultery a crime, but these old laws are rarely enforced.	Goes back in history to old Roman law. A Wisconsin woman admitted in a contested divorce hearing in 1990 that she had an affair; she received national attention when she was charged with the felony crime of adultery, which carried a possible two-year prison sentence as punishment. Charges were later dropped.
Homosexuality	Sexual relations between persons of the same sex.	For many years, this was a crime in all states. In *Lawrence v. Texas*, 123 S. Ct. 2472 (2003), the U.S. Supreme Court held a Texas sodomy statute unconstitutional because individuals have a right to engage in private consensual sexual conduct without government intervention.
Fornication	Voluntary sexual intercourse between two unmarried people.	Formerly a crime in all states. Most states have removed this offense from their criminal codes.
Seduction	Enticement by a male of an unmarried woman of prior chaste character to have sexual intercourse.	Was a crime in early English law and in many states.
Miscegenation	Intermarriage (and in some states living together) of people of different races (generally white and black).	Was a crime in some of the states. Such statutes were declared unconstitutional by the U.S. Supreme Court. See the case of *Loving v. Virginia* in Chapter 1.
Buggery (or sodomy)	Any type of sexual intercourse with an animal.	A statutory offense in England until 1967.
Abortion	Causing the expulsion of a human fetus prematurely.	Previously a crime in all states. States may not now make abortion a crime until the third trimester of pregnancy. Some states no longer have a crime of abortion.
Blasphemy, profanity, and indecent language	Cursing or reviling God; unbecoming, indecent, impious language.	Can no longer punish for language violations unless the language falls within one of the crimes listed in Chapter 9.
Crimes against transgender people	The term *transgender* covers cross-dressers, homosexual drag queens, and persons who believe they are both male and female.	An assortment of criminal laws was used in past years against transgendered persons (persons who either believe they were born in the wrong body or are intersexed).

[a] Utah banned polygamy as a required precondition to becoming a state in 1890, but over the years the practice of polygamy in Utah has failed to completely disappear. An estimated 37,000 fundamentalist Mormons still practice polygamy.

[b] Adultery remains a crime in the U.S. armed forces, Art. 134 U.C.M.J. Dismissal from the service is often the punishment. In U.S. v. Orellana, 62 M.J. 595 (N.M. Ct. Crim. App. 2005), review denied, 63 M.J. 295 (2006), a Marine corporal was convicted of adultery for having consensual sex with a woman while married to another woman. The court rejected the defendant's argument that Lawrence v. Texas (cited above) rendered Art. 134 of the U.C.M.J. unconstitutional.

A young woman, perhaps only a teenager, engages in the dangerous business of street prostitution.

Sean Murphy/Getty Images

of *People v. Honen*[33] a California Court of Appeals distinguished the elements of the crimes of indecent exposure and lewd conduct under California statutes. While both crimes require proof that they were committed in "public view," "lewd conduct," such as sexual intercourse in public, has no requirement that the acts be done with the intent to have the public see them. Indecent exposure, the court said, requires proof that the person's private parts were exposed for sexual gratification with the intent they would be seen by the public.

TOUCHING OR OTHER CONDUCT DONE TO AROUSE SEXUAL DESIRE

Touching a private part of another person's body could be (1) accidental, (2) consented to by the other person (children are not capable of consenting to sexual touching), or (3) necessary in the care of the person or for medical reasons. Touching could be in a friendly, joking, or loving manner, or the contact could be to discipline a child (spanking) or in a hostile or angry manner.

Most states have degrees of "sexual assaults," with the most serious involving sexual penetration. Sexual contact without penetration ("sexual touching") generally requires the state to show that the touching was done on "sexual or intimate parts," and for the purpose of sexual gratification. Lewd and lascivious conduct or behavior with a child statutes often require showing that the defendant "had the specific intent to arouse or gratify either child's sexual desires or his own."[34]

Following are examples of crimes that require showing that the conduct was intended to arouse sexual desire:

- The California lewd and lascivious acts with a child statute requires that the touching be done "with the specific intent to arouse, appeal to, or gratify the sexual desire of either party"; see *People v. Carson*, 890 P.2d 1115 (1995).

REGULATION OF NUDITY BY STATES OR MUNICIPALITIES

Nudity by itself is not obscene, lewd, or indecent but may be regulated by specific statutes and ordinances as follows:

Place of Nudity	Manner in Which Nudity May Be Regulated
Public nudity (public beach or public place, such as street)	May be forbidden or regulated by a specific statute or ordinance.
Nude entertainment or nudity in a place licensed to serve alcoholic beverages	May be forbidden or regulated under the authority given to states by the Twenty-First Amendment to the U.S. Constitution to regulate the sale and use of alcohol. The U.S. Supreme Court stated that "the broad sweep of the 21st Amendment has been recognized as conferring something more than the normal state authority over public health, welfare, and morals"; see *California v. LaRue*, 409 U.S. 109, 93 S. Ct. 390 (1972).
Nudity in a private place (a nudist camp, for example), a stage play, or a movie (the musical *Hair*, the play *Oh! Calcutta!*, and the opera *Salome* have nude performers)	May not be regulated unless the conduct or display is obscene. Nudity, by itself, is not obscene, lewd, or indecent.
Nudity used for sexual gratification	For example, see the case of *People v. Garrison*, 82 Ill. 2d 444, 45 Ill. Dec. 132, 412 N.E.2d 483 (1980), in which the defendant stood behind a storm door in his home exposing his penis to a woman standing outside. The Supreme Court of Illinois held that this was not private conduct and that the defendant had no right of privacy. If a jury found that the defendant exposed his body "with intent to arouse or to satisfy (his) sexual desire," the defendant could be found guilty of the Illinois public indecency statute.

The California Supreme Court also held that lewd touching can occur through the victim's clothing and does not require contact with the bare skin or with "private parts" of the defendant or victim. See *People v. Martinez*, 1995 WL 641969 (1995).

- Most state statutes include the buttocks as an intimate part of a person's body. To be a sexual battery or disorderly conduct or another sex crime, it must be shown that the touching was intentional, was without consent, and was for purposes of sexual gratification. See, for example, *State v. Osborne*, 808 P.2d 624 (N. Mex. 1991).
- The defendant offered a teenage boy a ride, made sexually suggestive inquiries of the boy, and then pressed his entire hand on the inner thigh of the boy in a manner suggestive of an intimate massage. The Massachusetts Court of Appeals affirmed the conviction of the defendant for indecent assault and battery. See *Commonwealth v. Lavigne*, 676 N.E.2d 1170 (1997).

PROTECTING CHILDREN AGAINST SEXUAL EXPLOITATION: CHILD PORNOGRAPHY

The U.S. Supreme Court has repeatedly held that states have a compelling interest in "safeguarding the physical and psychological well-being of a minor" and that "the use of children as subjects of pornographic materials is harmful to the physiological, emotional, and mental health of the child."[35]

child pornography Movies, pictures, or drawings that depict children in explicit sexual relations. Unlike adult pornography, child pornography need not be obscene to be criminal.

pornography Movies, pictures, writings, and other expressions that are intended to arouse sexual incitement and have no artistic merit or redeeming social value.

Because of these reasons, **child pornography** is treated differently from adult **pornography**. Adult pornography is sold openly in many communities throughout the United States, but child pornography is outlawed by the federal government and most states.

The child pornography laws of the majority of states and the federal government do not require obscenity as an element of the crime.[36] If an actual child or children are depicted in a photograph or video as engaged in sexually explicit conduct, possession of such material is a crime under the federal pornography law and the laws of most states, even if the photograph or video would not meet the obscenity test applicable to adult pornography. In this sense, child pornography laws are viewed as outside the usual protection for "content-based" laws given by the First Amendment.

Five categories of conduct and attempted conduct are made crimes under the federal law and the laws of most states. The crime of child pornography broadly includes the following:[37]

- Production of child pornography (for example, filming a child or children engaged in sexually explicit conduct)
- Advertising child pornography
- Possession of material, knowing that it depicts minors in sexually explicit conduct
- Trafficking in child pornography (importation, distribution, sale, loan, gift, exchange, receipt, or transportation of material, knowing that it depicts minors engaged in sexually explicit conduct)
- Procurement of child pornography (buying, selling, or transporting child pornography or inducing, coercing, or kidnapping a minor for the purposes of producing child pornography)

Child pornography includes depictions in magazines, books, motion pictures, and videos, and by other means. Most state statutes forbid live performances, and some specifically forbid the use of computers. The federal government and some states forbid visual depictions or advertisements of child pornography "by any means including by computers."

Schools and libraries using federal funds are obligated to use computer filters to block pornographic material available on the Internet. Such filters are also available for parents to use on computers used by children. Child pornography from many countries, including the United States, Russia, and others, is available on websites and can be accessed from anywhere in the world. The National Center for Missing and Exploited Children estimates that the number of child pornography websites increased by 400 percent between 2001 and 2005.

Prosecutions for child pornography have also increased dramatically because of Internet sites. In a February 2013 report to Congress the U.S. Sentencing Commission said that in the year 2000 there were 700 federal child pornography prosecutions; in 2010 there were over 2,000. The Commission report also noted that the average sentences for convictions—5 years for possession and 11 years for distribution—had doubled during that same 10-year period. The Commission report expressed doubt about the fairness of sentences given in federal courts. It noted that in 2004, only a few child pornography sentences (16 percent) fell outside the sentencing guidelines. In 2010, over 50 percent of the sentences were outside the guidelines. The Commission believed this indicated federal judges were not satisfied with the weighted factors in the guidelines for sentencing child pornography defendants, mainly because the culpability of those defendants varied so greatly. The Commission advised Congress to amend the child pornography laws and sentences to take into account the traffic volume of a child pornography website, the images depicted, the ages of the child victims depicted, and how long the defendant has had a child pornography collection. In a July 29, 2014 letter from the U. S. Department of Justice to the Sentencing Commission, the Justice Department stated it agreed with the Commission that the sentencing guidelines for child pornography crimes should be reviewed and rewritten, in light of the massive influence of computers and the Internet.

In a related manner, prosecutions under 18 U.S.C. 2251-2252 and 2252A, the federal statutes making criminal the possession and distribution of child pornography, are complicated by evolving Internet and computer technology. For example, in *United States v. Anderson*, 759 F.3d 891 (8th Cir. 2014), *cert denied* 135 S. Ct. 2309 (2015), the court held that digitally morphing a child's face onto an adult's body in sexually graphic acts, and then posting the image on the child's Facebook page violated section 2252A. It rejected the defendant's argument that because no actual child suffered sexual abuse, his actions were protected under the holding in *Ashcroft v. Free Speech Coalition* (discussed below). The court reasoned that children such as the child whose Facebook page was "targeted" by the defendant suffered serious traumatic injury by the morphed photograph. That injury justified applying the child pornography statutes to the defendant, the court held.

In *United States v. Grzybowicz*, 747 F.3d 1296 (11th Cir. 2014) the court struggled with a charge of distribution of child pornography under section 2252A. There, the defendant took four pictures of a small child's genital area with his cell phone, and then downloaded the photographs to his home computer. They were then stored in a "secret" file where he stored other child pornographic images. After his spouse discovered the images, and showed them to a police officer (with whom she was having an affair, the court noted), the defendant was arrested, charged, and convicted in a jury trial under sections 2251 and 2252A for possession and distribution of child pornography.

On appeal, the court noted that Congress had not defined distribution under section 2252A, nor had the court done so. It concluded that distribution occurs when photographs are sent from a cell phone to a computer and stored in a computer file "that makes it accessible to others through a file-sharing website or a peer-to-peer network." Since the defendant had not done so with the photographs in his computer, the court reversed his conviction for distribution of child pornography. (It affirmed the possession convictions.)

Federal legislation directed at use of the Internet to exploit children has met with attacks on the legislation's constitutionality. In response to the use of the Internet

FIGHTING THE INTERNATIONAL CHILD SEX TRADE

Representatives of 134 countries met in Yokohama, Japan, in December 2001 to fight the fast-growing world sex trade in children. The first international meeting was held in Stockholm in 1996. UNICEF estimates that every year 1 million children (girls and boys) are forced into the sex trade.

Most of these children are from poor countries or are poor illegal immigrants living in industrial countries. Using the Internet and cell phones, pedophiles can reach the children online. The governments of the 134 countries pledged increased efforts to stamp out the thriving sex trade by tougher laws and by coordinating police efforts against the child sex trade.

In the United States, in 2003 Congress passed as part of the PROTECT Act (discussed in this chapter) 18 U.S.C. §§ 1591 and 2423, which are directed at international "sex trafficking" and "sex tourism." Section 1591 is aimed at "trafficking" and makes any person guilty of the crime that entices or transports a child under 18 in interstate or foreign commerce knowing the child will be forced to engage in a commercial sex act. In *United States v. Chang Da Liu*, 538 F.3d 1078 (9th Cir. 2008) the federal government used this statute to shut down a "teahouse" operated by the defendants in the Northern Mariana Islands, a territory within the jurisdiction of the federal government by virtue of an agreement between the United States and the Islands. The defendants lured Chinese girls to the Islands, promising them work as waitresses, and charging each one $6,000 in "broker fees." When the girls arrived, they were forced to engage in commercial sex. The Ninth Circuit upheld their conviction.

Section 2423 identifies three so-called sex-tourism crimes. Subsection (a) applies to a person who knowingly "transports" a child under 18 across state or international borders for the purpose of engaging in "illicit sexual conduct," which means sex with a child under 18 that would be illegal under federal law, or any commercial sexual act with a child under 18. Subsection (b) applies to persons who travel in interstate or foreign

for dissemination of pornography and the effect of such pornography on children, Congress passed two significant pieces of legislation in 1996: the Communications Decency Act (CDA) of 1996 (47 U.S.C. § 223) and the 1996 Child Pornography Prevention Act (CPPA) (18 U.S.C. § 2256). The CDA prohibited any use of the Internet to post material that was "indecent" or "patently offensive" and made available to children. The CPPA prohibited Internet use to post any picture "that appears to be" of a minor engaged in sexually explicit conduct. Both laws were found to be unconstitutional by the U.S. Supreme Court:

- In *Reno v. American Civil Liberties Union*, 521 U.S. 844 (1997), the Court held that the CDA was unconstitutional because it failed to clearly identify what constituted "indecent" or "patently offensive" material and as a result prohibited speech that was protected under the First Amendment.
- In *Ashcroft v. Free Speech Coalition*, 122 S. Ct. 1389 (2002), the Supreme Court held that the CPPA was overbroad and unconstitutional. The Court concluded that the CPPA did not limit its prohibition to only obscene materials but included all depictions of sexual conduct between children, including depictions of "simulated sex" between children. It noted that the movie *Traffic*, which won an Academy Award, had depicted sexual conduct of a 16-year-old girl.

commerce with the purpose of engaging in illicit sexual conduct with a child under 18. Subsection (c) applies to any U.S. citizen who travels interstate or to a foreign country and engages in illicit sexual conduct with a child under 18. Subsections (a) and (b) are similar to prior law and require only that the defendant have the purpose of engaging in illicit sexual conduct. It is not a defense to prosecutions under either section that the individual the defendant intended to have illicit sex with was not under 18; it is enough the defendant believed that was the case. *United States v. Spurlock*, 495 F.3d 1011 (8th Cir. 2007), *cert. denied*, 552 U.S. 1054 (2007).

Section 2423(c) represents a change from former law and is expressly directed at "sex tourists." Under subsection (c), the government need not prove the defendant traveled to a foreign country for the purpose of having illicit sex. Thus, in the 2011 case of *United States v. Pendleton*, 658 F.3d 299 (3rd Cir. 2011), the defendant was convicted under § 2423(c) when he traveled to Germany from the United States, and while in Germany he was arrested for having sex with a 14-year-old boy. When the defendant finished a 2-year prison sentence in Germany, he was deported to the United States in January 2008; in March 2008 he was arrested and charged under § 2423(c) and was convicted.

The section also has what is called an "extraterritorial" effect on U.S. citizens. In *United States v. Clark*, 435 F.3d 1100 (9th Cir. 2006), a retired U.S. military member who resided in Cambodia but traveled between the United States and Cambodia was charged under § 2423(c) when he was arrested by Cambodian police for having sex with two 14-year-old boys and extradited to the United States. The court held that under the statute, all the government needed to prove was the illicit sexual conduct and the citizenship of the defendant.

More than two dozen states have passed criminal laws aimed at local brothels and sweatshops that bring people into the country, including children, and force them to work as sex slaves or in sweatshops. Most federal legislation in this area is directed at organized trafficking rings.

In response to these decisions, Congress passed legislation designed to eliminate the problems in the earlier legislation. The Child Online Protection Act (47 U.S.C. § 231 of 1998) (COPA) prohibits any commercial Internet communication that is "harmful to minors." *Harmful to minors* is defined in a manner that tracks the obscenity test of *Miller v. California* (discussed in Chapter 9), including the "community standards" test. In *ACLU v. Gonzales,* 478 F. Supp. 2d 775 (E.D. Pa. 2007), a federal judge held that the COPA statute was unconstitutional because it did not use the least restrictive means to achieve the desired result. The Third Circuit affirmed that decision in 2008 (534 F.3d 181), and the U.S. Supreme Court denied certiorari, 129 S. Ct. 1032 (2009).

In 2003 Congress passed the PROTECT Act, 18 U.S.C. § 2252A(a)(3), which included several specific crimes directed at children through the Internet. In *United States v. Williams,* 444 F.3d 1286 (11th Cir. 2006), a federal court of appeals held the "pandering" provision of the PROTECT Act unconstitutional because it was vague and overbroad and did not solve the problems presented by the earlier statutes. The U.S. Supreme Court granted review of this decision, 127 S. Ct. 1874 (2007). In *United States v. Williams,* the subject of the following Case-Close Up, the Supreme Court upheld the child pornography provisions of the PROTECT Act.

CASE CLOSE-UP

United States v. Williams

Supreme Court of the United States,
553 U.S. 285 (2008)

18 U.S.C. § 2252(A) of the 2003 PROTECT Act added a new pandering and solicitation section to the child exploitation provisions of that act. It makes it a crime for any person to knowingly advertise, promote, present, distribute, or solicit through the mails or the Internet any material in a manner "that reflects the belief, or that is intended to cause another to believe" that the material contains (a) an obscene visual depiction of a minor engaged in sexually explicit conduct, or (b) a visual depiction of an actual minor engaged in sexually explicit conduct. In other words, the Act made it a crime to "pander" *obscene* child sexual depictions, regardless of whether the child pictured was an actual child or a simulated child. It also made it a crime to "pander" *any* image of a child, actual or simulated, engaged in sexually explicit conduct if the person pandering the image believes it to be an actual image of a child, or intends another to have such a belief.

The legislative history of the Act made it clear Congress was concerned that the decision in *Ashcroft v. Free Speech Coalition*, which seemed to limit non-obscene child pornography prosecutions to material that involved only actual children, would make it impossible to prosecute many pornographers who would allege their "depictions" were made by "virtual" imaging. To address this concern, Congress did not in the Act attempt to prohibit the possession of "virtual" child pornography. Rather, it prohibited a person from "pandering" material he believed to be either *obscene* virtual child pornography (which can always be prohibited) or depictions of *actual* children engaged in sexually explicit conduct (which can be prohibited only if not

overbroad). It was the pandering provision that was under review in this case.

The defendant Williams conducted an online conversation in an Internet chat room with a person calling herself "Lisa n Miami." Lisa was in fact a Secret Service Agent working undercover. Williams posted a message that said, "Dad of toddler has good pics of her" for swap of "your toddler pics, or live cam." The agent exchanged some non-pornographic pictures with Williams. After some discussion, in which Williams demanded proof in the form of additional pictures which the agent refused to furnish, Williams posted a message stating "I CAN PUT UP CUZ IM FOR REAL" that contained a hyperlink that when followed led to seven pictures of actual children engaging in explicit sexual conduct. The Secret Service then obtained a warrant, seized Williams's computer, and found at least twenty-two pornographic images of actual children. He was charged with possession of child pornography under § 2252A(a)(5) (B) and pandering under § 2252A(a)(3)(B). After conviction under both statutes, Williams appealed only the pandering conviction, alleging the statute was overbroad. The court of appeals agreed, and reversed his conviction under that section.

On review, the Supreme Court upheld the statute, and reversed the court of appeals. It said that the pandering section is directed at persons who are attempting to engage in an illegal transaction, and such conduct is not protected by the First Amendment:

Offers to engage in illegal transactions are categorically excluded from First Amendment protection . . . . One would think that this principle resolves the present case, since the statute criminalizes only offers to provide or requests to obtain contraband—child obscenity and child pornography involving actual children, both of which are proscribed and the proscription of which is constitutional, see Free Speech Coalition, *553 U.S., at 245–246, 256.* Williams, *553 U.S. 285, at 297.*

Since the conduct proscribed (distributing or soliciting material believed to be depictions of actual children) was not protected, the Supreme Court said the circuit court was wrong to hold the statute up to the "strict scrutiny" test. That test only applies if a statute attempts to regulate protected speech or conduct. The Supreme Court also stated that the statute does not, unlike the statute in *Ashcroft v. Free Speech Coalition,* impinge on legitimate depictions of child sexual conduct, such as advertisements for mainstream Hollywood movies that depict underage characters having sex. The Court thought it "implausible" that either the producers or the distributors either "believed" the scenes depicted actual children having sex, or "intended to cause" others to believe that was the case. The Court stated that the "average person" knows sex scenes in movies use non-child actors or depict sex scenes in a way that does not rise to the explicit level covered by the statute. Id. at 301, 302.

The Federal Enticement Statute   Concerned with the use of the Internet to engage in online enticement of children to engage in sexual activity, in 2006 Congress passed 18 U.S.C. §2422(b). That section makes it a crime, punishable by 10 years to life in prison, to use a communication to entice an individual under 18 years old to engage in sexual activity, if such activity could be charged as "a criminal offense" under federal or state law. The following cases illustrate the application of that statute:

United States v. Roman, 795 F.3d 511 (6th Cir. 2015): The defendant, believing he was exchanging emails with the father of an 11-year-old girl, attempted to convince the father to make his daughter available for sexual activity. The "father" was a Secret Service agent on a special task force seeking to find persons using the Internet to entice children into sexual activity. There was no "daughter." They arranged to meet in a store parking lot, where the defendant was arrested and charged under §2422(b).

The defendant moved to dismiss the case, contending he never communicated with a child. The trial court rejected that contention, and the defendant was found guilty. On appeal, the court said § 2422(b) applies so long as the defendant was attempting to use the adult to entice the child into performing sexual activity. It affirmed the conviction.

United States v. Shill, 740 F.3d 1347 (9th Cir. 2014), *cert denied* 135 S. Ct. 147 (2014): The defendant sent a Facebook "friend" request to a 16-year-old high school student, asking her to not to disclose his request. She told her father, who informed the police. With the girl's consent, an FBI agent took over her Facebook account, and established an account to exchange instant messages with the defendant. In these messages the defendant attempted to entice the agent, who he believed was the girl, into having sexual contact with him. The agent arranged a meeting place, and there the defendant was arrested and charged under §2422(b).

Defendant was indicted under §2422(b). Defendant's communications would have been a violation of Oregon's sexual abuse in the third degree statute, a misdemeanor. Under the enticement statute, the prosecution contended that was the "criminal offense" that makes the enticement statute applicable to the defendant's actions. The defendant contended that a state misdemeanor could not be the predicate offence under the enticement statute, because it carries a 10-year minimum sentence, which misdemeanor crimes do not. The trial court rejected that argument, and sentenced the defendant to the 10-year minimum prison term.

On appeal the court affirmed the conviction. It said that the enticement statute makes no distinction between felony and misdemeanor sexual offences. All that is required to trigger the federal enticement statute is communications that would be a "criminal offense," whether a felony or a misdemeanor. It affirmed the conviction and sentence.

United States v. Howard, 766 F.3d 414 (9th Cir. 2014), *cert denied* 135 S. Ct. 1015 (2015): Defendant responded to a government sting operation designed to find adults attempting to entice children for sexual purposes. A police officer posed as a mother of young girls interested in making them available to adults. The defendant and the "mother" exchanged emails, and ultimately the defendant stated he wanted to have sex with her "14-year-old daughter." In several conversations and messages the defendant suggested ways of "grooming" the daughter, but despite the officer's attempts to get the defendant to commit to a trip to Corpus Christi (where the fictional family supposedly resided), the defendant would not commit to the trip. Ultimately the defendant was arrested at his home in California, and charged under §2224(b).

Defendant contended his actions did not constitute a substantial step toward having sexual contact with the supposed 14-year-old. The trial judge rejected that contention, and in a bench trial convicted defendant under the enticement statute. On appeal the court held that the statute includes attempted enticement of a minor, and it was not essential that the defendant actually make plans to have a physical meeting with the minor child. The fact that the defendant suggested ways of "grooming" the supposed minor was enough to constitute attempted enticement under the statute, the court held. It affirmed the conviction.

MOVIES, VIDEOS, AND PHOTOGRAPHS

X-rated videos are a multibillion-dollar business in the United States. European and Asian producers also have large sales throughout the world. Are producers of X-rated videos and films, who pay adults to perform sexual acts that are filmed for movies and videos, engaged in the business of prostitution? This issue was before the courts in the case of *California v. Freeman*.[38]

Freeman was convicted of pandering under the California Criminal Code for hiring adults to perform sex acts, which he filmed and sold. The Supreme Court of California reversed the conviction, holding that Freeman's conduct was not prohibited by the California prostitution and pandering laws. The court held that hiring actors to perform sexual acts to be filmed in a private place is not "procuring" prostitution, because the payment to the actors was not made for the purpose of sexual gratification, a necessary part of the definition of prostitution. The court also noted that the film made was not obscene, and thus the prosecution under the pandering statute amounted to an improper "end run" around the First Amendment.

Because a new law expanding the California pandering and prostitution statute has not been enacted, California has become the capital of the United States for the production of X-rated and pornographic films and videos.[39]

"Sexting," and Nude Photos of Children Taken by Family Members

Many family photo and video collections have pictures of young nude children. But when children are no longer babies and have begun to develop sexually, is photography of them by parents and stepparents sexual abuse? This question has been before a number of U.S. courts, with results similar to the following case.

The defendant took color photos of his physically mature 14-year-old stepdaughter, showing her fully exposed breasts. He was convicted in a jury trial and sentenced to 10 years in prison. The Massachusetts Supreme Judicial Court reversed the conviction, holding the statute to be overbroad. The U.S. Supreme Court vacated the Massachusetts Supreme Court ruling and remanded the case for further hearings. On remand, the Massachusetts Supreme Judicial Court upheld the defendant's conviction, holding that although his photographs were not obscene, the state had a legitimate interest in protecting minors from such practices and that interest was more compelling than the defendant's "restrictive speech" interest under the First Amendment.[40]

Convictions of other defendants in similar situations have been affirmed. In *Perry v. State*, 568 So. 2d 339 (Ala. Cr. App. 1990), the defendant photographed not only his 15-year-old daughter but also her 14-year-old friend. In *Brackins v. State*, 578 A.2d 300 (Md. App. 1990), the court affirmed defendant's conviction for child sexual abuse based on the semi-nude photographing of a 12-year-old stepdaughter.[41]

Nude home photos can also result in prosecution under the federal child pornography statutes, including the PROTECT Act. In a 2010 case the Sixth Circuit Court of Appeals upheld the conviction under 18 U.S.C. §§ 2251 and 2252 of a defendant charged with possession of child pornography based on home pictures. The defendant took nude photographs of his 10-year-old daughter and her friends. He did not distribute the photographs or show them to other people. Because the pictures showed actual children in sexually suggestive positions, the court said the pictures were child pornography and violated the statutes. The court also held that Congress had power to regulate the activity under the Commerce Clause because of the possibility that homemade child pornography would hinder the purpose Congress has in regulating national child pornography.[42]

In the July 2010 issue of the *FBI Law Enforcement Bulletin,* an article entitled "Sexting: Risky Actions and Overreactions" discusses the problems related to juveniles "sexting" naked or near-naked pictures of themselves to others. Sexting is defined as "sending or posting sexually suggestive messages and images, including nude or semi-nude photographs, via cellular telephones or over the Internet." The article suggests that juveniles consider the consequences of sexting, and offers this advice:

> Before hitting send, remember that you cannot control where this image may travel;
>
> If you forward a sexual picture of someone underage, you are responsible for this image as the original sender.

YOU BE THE JUDGE

With modern technology like "smart" phones, taking photographs can be both easy and secretive. "Upskirting," in which a person surreptitiously takes photographs of the female anatomy visible under skirts being worn by the females, has regrettably become a practice using cell phones as cameras. Two cases have come before you, where defendants are charged with violation of statutes making it a crime to secretly photograph a person who is "nude or partially nude," or to secretly photograph the "uncovered genital area" of a person.

In one case, the defendant was seated on a public trolley, and bending over, used his cell phone to "upskirt" women standing in the trolley. In the other case, the defendant attached a cell phone to his shoe, and walking through a mall, stood behind females wearing dresses and used his cell phone to photograph their anatomy under their skirts.

Both defendants have moved to dismiss the charges filed against them. The first defendant contends he took the photographs in a public place. The second defendant contends none of the photographs he took showed "uncovered genitalia."

Should you dismiss the charges? Assume in the first case the statute is identical to the one at issue in **Commonwealth v. Robertson, 5 N.E.3d 522 (Mass. 2014).** ***Assume in the second case the statute is identical to the one at issue in*** **Delagrange v. State, 5 N.E.3d 354 (Ind. 2014).** ***What is your decision?***

Think about the consequences of taking, sending, or forwarding a sexual image of yourself or someone else under age.

One of those consequences could include criminal charges. In the 2009 case of *State v. Canal*, 773 N.W.2d 528 (Iowa 2009), the Iowa Supreme Court upheld the conviction of an 18-year-old man who sent a cell phone picture of his erect penis to a 14-year-old girl. He was convicted under a statute that made it a crime to send obscene material to a minor.

VOYEURISM AND OTHER CRIMINAL INVASIONS OF PRIVACY

Until recent years, Peeping Toms who trespassed or were not in a public place were often charged as a disorderly person (or with disorderly conduct). Many states now have voyeurism or invasion of privacy laws in their criminal codes. An example of such law is Ohio Criminal Code Section 2907.08(A), which reads:

No person, for the purpose of sexually arousing or gratifying himself or herself, shall commit trespass or otherwise surreptitiously invade the privacy of another, to spy or eavesdrop upon another.

These laws have been toughened in many states by provisions forbidding video voyeurism or video stalking. The terms *upskirting* and *downblousing* describe offenses that are charged under invasion of privacy statutes. Examples of conduct charged under these laws are as follows:

- A California man videotaped three different women at three different times as he had sex with them. The women did not know and did not consent to the filming.

Police learned of the tapes when the man showed the videos to friends. He was convicted under California's invasion of privacy law, which forbids filming or recording confidential communications without the consent of participants. See *People v. Gibbons,* 263 Cal. Rptr. 905 (1989).

- An apartment manager secretly installed a video camera in a shower used by college women living in his building. After several months of filming the women taking showers, the camera was discovered, and the man was criminally charged under the Wisconsin Criminal Code.

★★

LEARNING OBJECTIVES SUMMARY

LO 1. Identify the degrees of sexual assault, and the conduct that distinguishes them.
Most states divide sexual assault into two or more degrees. Factors that can increase the degree of the crime include force used, a weapon used, or bodily injury inflicted.

LO 2. Explain the areas of questioning of a sexual assault victim that are prohibited by the rape shield law.
Rape shield laws prohibit questioning of a rape victim if the purpose of the questions is to expose the victim's previous sexual history.

LO 3. List two exceptions to the rape shield law's prohibitions.
Rape shield laws do not prevent the introduction of evidence of past sexual conduct of the victim if it is offered to prove either consent of the victim, or that another person was the source of semen or other physical evidence used as part of the case against the defendant.

LO 4. Discuss the *mens rea* requirement for a conviction for statutory rape.
Statutory rape requires no specific intent to have sex with a minor. It is not a defense to the charge that the defendant reasonably believed the person was not a minor.

LO 5. Explain the conditions that must be shown for civil commitment of a sexual predator.
Civil commitment is permissible only if it can be shown the person is a dangerous sexual predator who poses a substantial threat to commit sexual offenses in the future, and that the person cannot control his behavior.

LO 6. Explain the reasons child pornography laws have been found unconstitutional.
Child pornography can be regulated either because it is obscene, and thus prohibited even if it did not involve a child, or because it depicts actual children in sexually explicit conduct. The federal and state governments have a legitimate interest in keeping children away from such sexual conduct.

LO 7. Explain the current status of federal acts such as the Child Online Protection Act.
The Child Online Protection Act has been found unconstitutional by a circuit court of appeal, and the Supreme Court has denied review of that decision. Provisions of the PROTECT Act that apply to child pornography have been upheld by the Supreme Court.

KEY TERMS

CASE ANALYSIS AND WRITING EXERCISES

1. In cases of alleged sexual assault where there is no evidence of bodily injury or forcible rape, such as "date-rape" cases, the non-consent of the victim establishes the sexual assault. This is particularly true in the (relatively few) jurisdictions that have no requirement of force or compulsion. Is non-consent an element of the crime? If so, is evidence offered by the defendant to prove consent an affirmative defense? Who has the duty to prove consent or non-consent, the prosecution or the defendant? If it is the prosecution, what duty if any does the defendant have? See *State v. W.R.*, 336 P.3d 1134 (Wash. 2014).

2. 18 U.S.C. § 2423(a) makes it a crime to transport a minor across state lines with the intent to have the minor engage in any sexual activity that would be a criminal offense. Thus, the transportation with the requisite intent is the crime, not the sexual activity. Indeed, courts routinely hold that no illegal sexual activity need occur for the crime to be committed. What "intent" is required under the statute? If a 25-year-old army soldier pays a friend to give his 15-year-old girlfriend a ride from Pennsylvania to Texas, where the soldier is stationed, has he violated the statute? What if his motivation is allegations by the girl that she is being abused at her home, and he wants to protect her from that abuse? See *United States v. Kearns*, 73 M.J. 177 (C.A.A.F. 2014)

3. The defendant in *United States v. Husmann*, 765 F.3d 169 (3rd Cir. 2014) stored multiple child pornographic photographs in a file stored on a 360 Share Pro program installed on his computer. The Share Pro program enabled others to access the files directly in a peer-to-peer network without going through a server. Other members of the network can download files available on the shared network. Husmann was charged and convicted under 18 U.S.C. § 2252(a)(2) for distributing child pornography. On appeal, the issue was the meaning of "distribute" under the statute. Compare the result in *Husmann* with the court's decision in *Grzybowicz*, discussed in this chapter. Which decision do you think is better reasoned? Which decision do you think is closer to Congress's intent in drafting these child pornography/computer statutes?

4. SORNA has what is called the "Romeo-and-Juliet" exception to the sex offender registration requirements under the law. A sex offender cannot be convicted of a failure to register as a sex offender if at the time of his conviction for a sex offense the sex was consensual and if "the victim was at least 13 years old and the offender was not more than 4 years older than the victim." In *United States v. Brown*, 740 F.3d 145 (3rd Cir. 2014) the defendant was charged with failing to register as a sex offender under SORNA. The sex offense the defendant was convicted of occurred when he was 17, and involved consensual sexual contact with a victim aged 13. The trial judge dismissed the charges, holding that even though the defendant was born 52 months before the victim, a person is not more than 4 years older than another until that person is 5 years older. The prosecution appealed the dismissal. It contends "more than 4 years" means more than 48 months or 1461 days (365X4 plus a leap year). Who is right? Should the court look at the birth certificates of both parties? How exact must "4 years" be?

ENDNOTES

1. The defendant was adjudicated a delinquent under the Federal Juvenile Delinquency Act; the federal court had jurisdiction because the sexual acts occurred on a military base, and no state agency had asserted jurisdiction over the juvenile. Under the FJDA the court, after finding delinquency, may suspend the finding of delinquency so as to encourage rehabilitation. The district court refused to do so, and the court of appeals remanded the case for reconsideration on that question.

2. The title of this report is "Extent, Nature, and Consequences of Rape Victimization: Findings from the National Violence Against Women Survey," NCJ 210346 (2006).

3. See *Gilmore v. State*, 855 P.2d 143 (Okla. Cr. 1993); *Cole v. State*, 818 SW.2d 573 (Ark. 1991); *Wealot v. Armontrout*, 740 F. Supp. 1436 (W.D. Mo. 1990); and *Case v. State*, 458 N.E.2d 223 (Ind. 1984).

4. John Decker and Peter Baroni, *"No" Still Means "Yes": The Failure of the "Non-Consent" Reform Movement in American Rape and Sexual Assault Laws,* 101 JCRLC 1081 (2011).

5. *State v. Rusk,* 289 Md. 230, 424 A.2d 720 (1981).

6. See also *State v. Reinhold,* 123 Ariz. 50, 597 P.2d 532 (1979); *People v. Hunt,* 72 Cal. App.3d 190, 139 Cal. Rptr. 675 (1977); *State v. Dill,* 3 Terry 533, 42 Del. 533, 40 A.2d 443 (1944); *Arnold v. United States,* 358 A2d 335 (D.C. App. 1976); *Doyle v. State,* 39 Fla. 155, 22 So. 272 (1897); *Curtis v. State,* 236 Ga. 362, 223 S.E.2d 721 (1976); *People v. Murphy,* 124 Ill. App.2d 71, 260 N.E.2d 386 (1970); *Carroll v. State,* 263 Ind. 86, 324 N.E.2d 809 (1975); *Fields v. State,* 293 So. 2d 430 (Miss. 1974); *State v. Beck,* 368 SW.2d 490 (Mo. 1963); *Cascio v. State,* 147 Neb. 1075, 25 NW.2d 897 (1947); *State v. Burns,* 287 N.C. 102, 214 S.E.2d 56 (1975), *cert, denied* 423 U.S. 933, 96 S. Ct. 288 (1975); *State v. Verdone,* 114 R.I. 613, 337 A.2d 804 (1975); *Brown v. State,* 576 SW.2d 820 (Tex. Cr. App. 1978); *Jones v. Commonwealth,* 219 Va. 983, 252 S.E.2d 370 (1979); *State v. Baker,* 30 Wash. 2d 601, 192 P.2d 839 (1948); *Brown v. State,* 581 P.2d 189 (Wyo. 1978).

7. MPC section 213. Not all states have formal report of rape rules like the MPC rule, though failure to make a prompt report of a sexual assault may be a factor in a prosecution.

8. Report of rape could also be made to a medical professional and be admissible under statements for the purposes of medical diagnosis or treatment. Report of rape is also known as the *fresh complaint* or the *outcry rule.*

9. 17 A.3d 187 (N.J. 2011).

10. 572 F.3d 552 (8th Cir. 2009).

11. See, e.g., *Comm. v. Battista,* 1995 WL 864097 (Pa. App. 1995).

12. 1 A.3d 438 (Me. 2010).

13. 488 U.S. 227 (1988).

14. 2012 WL 5274733 (Ky. 2012).

15. 133 P.3d 1180 (Colo. 2006).

16. 680 N.W.2d 810 (Wis. 2004).

17. See *People v. Branch,* 109 Cal. Rptr. 3d 412 (Cal. App. 2010).

18. *State v. Ballinger,* 93 S.W.3d 881 (Tenn. App. 2001).

19. Wash. RCWA 9A.44.030.

20. 48 P.3d 350 (Wash. App. 2002).

21. 372 S.W.3d 33 (Mo. App. 2012).

22. 2012 WL 5355694 (Tenn. App. 2012).

23. 536 U.S. 24, 32 (2002).

24. 628 F.3d 1217 (10th Cir. 2010).

25. See the *Milwaukee Journal Sentinel* article, "Sex Offender Database Passes House," July 26, 2006.

26. U.S. Supreme Court cases on sex offenders found to be sexual predators include *Kansas v. Crane,* 122 S. Ct. 867 (2002); *Kansas v. Hendricks,* 521 U.S. 346 (2002); *Conn. v. John Doe,* 123 S. Ct. 1160 (2002); *Foucha v. Louisiana,* 112 S. Ct. 1780 (1992); *Smith v. Doe,* 538 U.S. 84 (2003).

27. 534 U.S. 407 (2002).

28. *Hendricks v. Kansas,* 521 U.S. 346 (1997).

29. *New York Times,* March 4–March 6, 2007.

30. *Prison Legal News,* Vol. 23, No. 8 (August 2012).

31. 242 P.3d 619 (Ore. App. 2010).

32. 702 F.3d 1066 (8th Cir. 2013), *cert denied* 134 S. Ct. 167 (2013). While the statute is aimed at sexual exploitation of children, at least one court has held it is applicable to exploitation of adults as well. In *United States v. Afyare,* 632 Fed. Appx. 272 (6th Cir. 2016) the court held that because the title of 18 U.S.C. § 1591 states that it covers "Sex trafficking of children or by force, fraud or coercion," sex trafficking of adults is also a crime under the statute.

33. 111 Cal. Rptr. 3d 351 (Cal. App. 2010).

34. *State v. Rollins,* 581 So. 2d 379 (La. App. 1991).

35. *Osborne v. Ohio,* 110 S. Ct. 1691 (1990).

36. In 1977, the U.S. Congress enacted the Protection of Children Against Sexual Exploitation Act (18 U.S.C.A. § 2252). The federal child pornography law was upheld as constitutional by the U.S. Supreme Court in the case of *U.S. v. X-Citement Video, Inc.,* 115 S. Ct. 464, and the state of New York child pornography law was upheld in the case of *New York v. Ferber,* 458 U.S. 747, 102 S. Ct. 3348 (1982).

37. This material is adapted from the U.S. Department of Justice publication entitled *Child Sexual Exploitation: Improving Investigations and Protecting Victims* (1995).

38. 758 P.2d 1128 (Cal. 1988), *cert. denied,* 109 S. Ct. 1133 (1989).

39. In the 1990 Arizona case of *State v. Taylor* (808 P.2d 314), the Arizona courts distinguished between "prostitution and theatre." The defendant was convicted of four counts under the Arizona prostitution statute for paid performances in which "sexual contact" occurred. The Arizona case distinguishes this case and statute from the California *Freeman* case.

   In defending a criminal or civil obscenity case, defense counsel often use pay-for-view sex movies available at local hotels, erotic films available from cable or satellite providers, the number and location of X-rated video stores, X-rated material available on the Internet, and local nightclubs that feature nude or semi-nude entertainment as a way to prove the "contemporary community standards" requirement.

40. *Massachusetts v. Oakes,* 109 S. Ct. 2633 (1989); *on remand* 551 N.E.2d 910 (1990).

41. See the *New York Times* article, "Family Photos or Pornography? A Father's Bitter Legal Odyssey," January 30, 1995, which tells of a 45-year-old businessman who was arrested, handcuffed, and taken from his home. The man took 110 photographs of his nude 6-year-old daughter for an art class he was taking. The article tells of similar incidents in Ohio and California.

42. *United States v. Bowers,* 594 F.3d 522 (6th Cir. 2010).

13
Theft

OUTLINE

LEARNING OBJECTIVES

In this chapter we discuss the various forms of larceny or theft. The learning objectives for Chapter 13 are the following:

LO 1. List the property concepts that underlie property theft crimes.

LO 2. Explain the "money" rule and why it is an exception to general property rules.

LO 3. List four ways the taking element can be proved.

LO 4. Define "property of another" as it applies to theft of jointly owned property.

LO 5. Identify ways the taking requirement can be met in shoplifting.

LO 6. Advise a hypothetical merchant on how best to proceed when a suspected shoplifter is identified.

LO 7. Explain the ways credit card theft can be proved.

LO 8. Distinguish between forgery and uttering a forged instrument.

LO 9. Describe how a check-kiting scheme works.

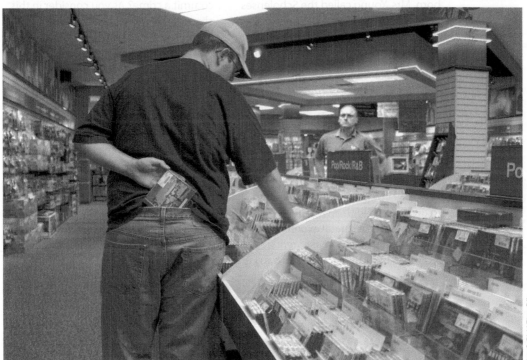

Someone forgot to tell this shoplifter about the surveillance camera.

The crime of theft can be committed in a wide variety of ways, as this chapter discusses. Some kinds of actions, however, are more easily shown to be crimes than other kinds. Opening a car door, and taking the wallet lying on the front seat, is clearly theft. But what should happen in the following situation?

Mr. and Mrs. Young had three children (boys) they were raising. Some years ago, they agreed with Mr. and Mrs. Scholens for the adoption of another child, and that adoption occurred. When Mrs. Young became pregnant for the fifth time in the summer of 2009, the couple decided to place the baby up for

adoption when it arrived in February of 2010. They contacted a Boston adoption agency to begin the process of an adoption, and as part of that process began receiving pre-natal expense funds from the agency. In September of 2009 they also contacted the Scholenses about a potential private adoption, and in the course of these discussions the Scholenses began paying pre-natal expenses to the Youngs, totaling about $6000.00 between September of 2009 and February of 2010. The Youngs did not immediately inform the Scholenses about their dealings with the Boston adoption agency. In early February Mrs. Young did tell the Scholenses they were working with an adoption agency, and receiving expense money from that agency as part of a planned adoption.

In February of 2010 the baby was born. Mrs. Young called the Scholenses and left a voice message saying they no longer planned on putting the baby up for adoption because, contrary to what they were told, the baby was a girl and not a boy. Dismayed by this message, the Scholenses gave these facts to the Kentucky State Police. The Youngs were ultimately indicted and charged with theft by deception, a felony.

The Youngs contend they have committed no crime, because under Kentucky law they were not required to go through with an adoption even if they received pre-natal expenses from the prospective adoptive parents. That is correct: In most states after a baby is born the mother (or both parents) has the right to change her mind and keep the baby. As a result, they contend, the expense money they received from the Scholenses was always subject to the chance they would not get to adopt the baby when it was born, and that is exactly what happened. Do you agree with the Youngs? Or did they commit a crime? As you consider in this chapter the elements of the various forms of theft, see within which, if any, of the forms of theft the Youngs' behavior might fall, and what would have to be proved to convict them. Then read *Commonwealth v. Young*, 2015 WL 9242558 (Ky. 2015).

In this chapter we will learn about several property crimes committed against individuals, government, and businesses, such as shoplifting, fraudulent use of credit cards, and check forgery. We will also learn about the rise of computer-related crimes and the use of computers in committing crimes. In shoplifting cases we will learn the rules that determine when a business is justified in detaining and questioning a suspected shoplifter and the risks associated with such a decision that turns out not to be justified.

GENERAL PROPERTY CONCEPTS

Understanding the criminal law as it relates to property or interests in property requires some understanding of property law concepts. The following paragraphs illustrate some of these concepts.

- *Property* is divided into two types: real property and personal property. Real estate is real property; everything else is personal property.
- Two important rights to property are (1) the right of ownership and (2) the right of possession of the property. A person may have the lawful possession of property but not necessarily be its owner. Possession of personal property is presumptive evidence of ownership if no evidence to the contrary is shown. Possession accompanied by the exercise of the complete acts of ownership for a considerable period is strong evidence of the ownership of property.[1]
- Property ownership may be in the form of sole ownership. It could also be in the form of joint ownership, as between husband and wife, business partners, or friends or relatives. The property may be owned by a corporation or a business partnership. Property ownership may be vested in a government unit, such as a city, a county, a state, or the national government.

- Lawful possession of property takes many forms. The owner may have the possession of property or may permit another person to have lawful possession and use of the property. An employee or agent of the owner of the property may have possession.

  Bailees and pledges also have the lawful possession of property that belongs to others. A bailment exists, for example, when people take their car into a garage for repairs. The owner of the car retains title and ownership to the vehicle but gives possession to the garage so the repair work may be done. State statutes give the garage a right to a lien on the vehicle in the amount of the work that was done on the car. The garage then has a superior right of possession of the vehicle until the owner satisfies the amount lawfully due to the garage. In many states, the owners of the property can be charged with theft if they intentionally and unlawfully take possession of such property from a pledgee or bailee who has a superior right of possession.[2]

- A thief lacks the lawful right either to possession or to ownership of stolen property. Therefore, in almost all situations, a thief cannot convey lawful title to stolen property to another person, even if that person is an innocent good-faith purchaser of the property. Known by the Latin phrase *nemo dat quod non habet* ("one cannot give what one does not have"), this principle, together with the phrase *caveat emptor* ("let the buyer beware"), requires the innocent purchaser to be very wary of buying from strangers.

- One exception to the *nemo dat* rule involves the transfer by a thief of stolen money or negotiable securities, such as bearer bonds, which are securities payable to any person in possession of the bonds. Called the "money" rule, it provides that a person who receives money in good faith and for value given takes title to the money. For example, in *City of Portland v. Berry*,[3] a thief stole nine $1,000 bills and eighteen $500 bills from her employer and took them to her bank, where she converted the large bills to bills of smaller denomination. When the theft was discovered, the bank still had possession of the large bills, and the owners sought their return. The court said no, because the bank had given value for the bills in good faith; that is, it had no reason to suspect the bills were stolen.

Bakalar v. Vavra

Court of Appeals of the United States for the Second Circuit, 500 Fed. Appx. 6 (2nd Cir.2012), *cert. denied*, 133 S. Ct. 2038 (2013).

During the 1930s and early 1940s the Nazi government in Germany "confiscated" hundreds of millions of dollars of property from Jewish owners who had the misfortune to be under Nazi control. This included some of the great works of art in Europe. Following the war, the owners and the heirs of many other owners who perished in Nazi death camps sought return of the stolen art. This was sometimes possible, because the art-collection world has long been accustomed to carefully mark the "provenance" of important artworks, detailing the purchase and sale of the art. These attempts continue today, as this case shows.

Fritz Grunbaum, an Austrian art collector, owned several drawings made by the artist Egon Schiele. In 1941 Grunbaum was seized by the Nazis, and he died at the Dachau death camp. In 1942 his wife died in another concentration camp in Minsk. Grunbaum's art collection disappeared.

In 1956 one drawing appeared in a Swiss art gallery. In 1963 the drawing was sold to a New York gallery, who sold it to David Bakalar for $4,300 in 1963. In 2005, Bakalar consigned the drawing to Sotheby's auction house, where it received a bid of $675,000. However, before the sale could close, the Grunbaums' heirs brought an action to determine the ownership of the drawing.

The trial court found that under New York law, which applied, it was Bakalar's duty to prove the drawing had not been stolen by the Nazis. If the drawing was stolen, he did not get title when he bought it, even if he acted in good faith. Bakalar was able to show that Grunbaum's sister-in-law sold the drawing in 1956, but was unable to show how she acquired it from her sister, Grunbaum's wife. However, the court nonetheless awarded the drawing to Bakalar, holding the heirs failed to assert their claim in a timely manner once they were aware Bakalar possessed the drawing. The Court of Appeals affirmed the decision and the U.S. Supreme Court denied review.

THEFT OR LARCENY[4]

theft or larceny
Stealing property of another with the intent to deprive the owner of possession.

Historically, the common law recognized a broad and often confusing number of theft of property crimes. Today, virtually all states have consolidated these many crimes under the heading of **theft or larceny**.[5] A great number of these crimes remain, however. The federal government alone has more than 100 separate statutes in Title 18 of the U.S. Code that deal with theft or theft-related activity.[6]

A typical theft or larceny statute today would require an unlawful (1) taking of (2) property of another with (3) intent to deprive the owner of possession thereof. In this section, these requirements are discussed in detail.

The Taking

taking The act of obtaining physical possession or control of another's property. The key to taking is that the thief exercises unauthorized dominion over the property.

Taking refers to the act of obtaining physical possession or control of another's property. A taking can occur by acts of a stranger, by a trusted employee, or even by a spouse. It can be by one having no right to possess the property or by one with limited rights to that possession. The key to taking is that the thief exercises unauthorized dominion over the property.

Direct Taking The most easily understood taking is direct taking, where the thief directly takes physical possession of another person's property. Examples of this include purse snatching, pickpocketing, shoplifting, and car theft. This kind of taking requires the thief to obtain actual physical possession of the property, even if for a short time.

EXAMPLE   A stranger walks into your backyard and up to your locked bike. He attempts to break the lock, but before he can do so, he is stopped by a passing police officer. He has not yet taken the bike and is not guilty of theft.

EXAMPLE   The same facts, except that the stranger breaks the lock. While he is turning to wheel the bike out of your yard, the police stop him. Even if he has moved only a few feet, he has taken the bike and is guilty of theft.

The common law and some states today require both a taking ("caption") and carrying away ("asportation") of the stolen property. Carrying away requires that the property be moved in some manner. However, even the slightest change of position of the property satisfies this requirement. Thus, in the example, in a state that retains a carrying away requirement, the smallest movement of the bike would be sufficient.[7]

The Taking of Lost and Mislaid Goods or Goods Delivered by Mistake

A taking may also occur where the initial physical possession of the property of another is not unlawful but where the person in possession acts in a manner showing an intent to deprive the owner of ownership rights.

EXAMPLE   A woman found a purse under a bush near a walking path. Inside the purse she found $500 in cash. The woman put the cash in her pocket. At this point, she had not taken the cash, because her possession was not yet unlawful. Later, she used the cash to buy herself a new coat. At this point, she had taken the cash.

EXAMPLE   A man deposited a federal income tax return check in the amount of $1,907 into his checking account. His bank mistakenly credited his account in the amount of $10,907. When he discovered the mistake, the man withdrew over $7,000 of the money. He was convicted of theft.[8]

EXAMPLE   A man leaving the U.S. Army was to receive a severance check for $183.00, but to his surprise, the check he received was for $836,728.19. The man immediately deposited the money and began spending it. After the error was discovered, legal action was taken against the man.[9]

Sometimes in situations like these examples, the person in possession of lost or misdirected property does nothing about it. For example, the owner of a checking account may do nothing when he discovers that his bank has credited his account with too much money. Proving a taking in those cases may be difficult, even though the account's owner plans to wait and see if the bank discovers the mistake and, if not, keep the money. Some states have followed the Model Penal Code's approach to this problem. Section 223.5 makes one guilty of theft if "with purpose to deceive the owner thereof, he fails to take reasonable measures to restore the property to a person entitled to it." Other states, following the common law rules, find the person guilty of theft only if at the time the person learned of the mistake he or she formed the intent to appropriate the funds. In those states, the taking must occur at the same time the intent to steal is formed.[10]

A person who finds lost property and promptly makes an attempt to return it to the true owner is not guilty of theft, even if a reward is asked for the return of the property. However, at some point failure to make the return would become "appropriation" for the finder's own purpose, and a taking would occur. In the 2010 case of *People v. Zamani*[11] a company lost two valuable circuit boards while they were in transit in California. A buyer bought the boards on eBay for $74.95, though he knew they were worth "thousands." The defendant acquired the boards from that buyer, ostensibly to return them to the owner. When the defendant contacted the owners, he demanded a "reward" of $10,000, and refused repeated requests for their return for a smaller reward of $1,000. Finally, the owners turned the case over to the police. The defendant was arrested, charged with, and convicted of felony theft of lost property. The California appeals court affirmed the conviction.

If property is not lost, and a person takes it and subsequently demands a reward for its return, a taking does occur. For example, in *People v. Stay,*[12] a defendant was convicted of theft when he collected shopping carts owned by various supermarkets that customers had removed from the owners' premises. The defendant then offered to return the carts upon payment of a "finder's" fee. As the fee was not paid, the defendant sold the carts. The court held that because the carts were left within a few blocks of each store, in front of customers' houses, the markets knew where they were and routinely collected them. The carts were not lost, and therefore the defendant had no right to a finder's fee. The defendant was convicted of grand theft.

Taking by Trick, Deception, or Fraud   Taking has been achieved by the use of many tricks, deceptions, and **fraud**. The owner of the property may be deceived by false representations that cause the owner to give up possession of the property. Con games fall into this category. Modern theft and larceny statutes specifically define these forms of taking as elements of the crimes of theft and larceny.

Confidence games and schemes (con games) have been used for hundreds of years. The pigeon drop was reportedly used more than 1,000 years ago in China. The deception has always been the same. The con man or woman wins the confidence of the victim, talking fast enough to keep the victim confused while dangling enough temptation to appeal to the victim. Unfortunately, a large percentage of the victims are elderly.

Phone call thefts are also common in the United States. The Federal Trade Commission (FTC), which monitors and investigates interstate telemarketing scams,

fraud Use of deceit or trickery to obtain profit or advantage.

reported that Americans lose nearly $1 billion each year in phony telemarketing schemes. The FTC reported that telephone swindlers are increasingly defrauding the elderly in telephone frauds. The chance of victims' recovering their money from con games and phone call thefts, unfortunately, is low.

The following cases illustrate two examples of theft by fraud or deception: insurance fraud and deceiving buyers of goods.

State v. Penalver
New Jersey Superior Court, 2006 WL 709839 (2006)

Defendants, mother and son, filed an insurance claim for $160,000, based on a fire that destroyed a residence owned by the mother. The fire insurance company paid the defendants $10,000 for living expenses while the fire was investigated. The insurance company concluded the cause of the fire was arson, denied the claim, and turned the case over to the police. The defendants ultimately were convicted of arson for starting the fire and theft by deception for taking the $10,000 from the insurance company. (On review by the N.J. Supreme Court the convictions were affirmed, but the case was remanded to cure some sentencing irregularities. 901 A.2d 953 (N.J. 2006).)

Commonwealth. v. Pappas
Pennsylvania Superior Court, 845 A.2d 829 (2004), *appeal denied*, 862 A.2d 1254 (2004)

Defendant, a used car dealer, bought used cars, repaired them, and sold them to buyers. Many of the cars had undergone substantial (and faulty) repairs, and this was known to the defendant. However, when the cars were sold to buyers, the defendant stated that the cars had never been repaired and were as good as new. He was charged with theft by deception, based on his false statements about the fact of repair, and the appeals court held this was sufficient to support his conviction.

Embezzlement[13] Many employees have money and property that belong to their employer. Lawyers, stockbrokers, business partners, and bailees also have money or property that belongs to clients and business associates. Because bank clerks and cashiers in restaurants and stores already have possession of money belonging to their employers, they do not have to take the money in the physical sense in order to steal.

embezzlement To wrongfully appropriate money or property entrusted to one for one's own use.

To fill in this large gap left in the criminal codes, the crime of **embezzlement** was created by statutes in England and the United States. It forbids a person already in lawful possession of money or property from fraudulently converting the money or property to his or her own use.

Many states have also solved this problem by expanding the "taking" in their theft or larceny statutes to include use, transfer, concealment, and/or retaining possession. Under such a statute, a stockbroker, lawyer, or cashier who stole money could be charged with theft or larceny.

Defining What Property Can Be Stolen

Under the common law, only tangible personal property could be stolen. Real estate and items attached to the land could not be stolen, because of the "asportation," or "carrying away" requirement. Documents such as stocks, bonds, checks, or promissory notes were not subject to theft, because they are intangible personal property.

All states and the federal government have broadened the original common law definition of property that can be stolen. Some modern criminal codes include any sort of property of value that can be moved. Illinois defines *property subject to theft* as "anything of value," including real estate, money, commercial instruments, tickets, and written documents.[14] Minnesota defines *property* to include documents and things growing on or affixed to land.[15] Section 223.2 of the Model Penal Code defines "theft by unlawful taking or disposition" as

1. *Movable Property:* A person is guilty of theft if he takes, or exercises unlawful control over, movable property of another with purpose to deprive him thereof.

2. *Immovable Property:* A person is guilty of theft if he unlawfully transfers immovable property of another or any interest therein with purpose to benefit himself or another not entitled thereto.

As the above definition of "immovable property" suggests, in order to convict a person of theft of real estate there must be a "transfer" of the property, or of an interest in the property. Because an interest in real estate is transferred by the owner signing a deed, the theft offense is usually committed by the thief deceptively persuading the owner to sign a deed transferring the property. For this reason, most state theft statutes that include theft of real estate define theft to include obtaining property by deception. See, *e.g.*, Cal. Penal Code § 484(a). However, executing a purported deed by forging the owner's signature and recording the deed is not theft, since absent a lawful deed nothing has been taken. The California Court of Appeals reversed a conviction under the theft statute based on a forged deed, holding that a forged deed cannot convey title. The person forging the deed could be charged with forgery, or fraudulently recording a forged deed, the court said.[16]

In addition to documents, information from computers, files, and other places may be stolen.[17] Under fraud statutes and other specific statutes, telephone and computer services may be stolen. In a 2008 case, the Wisconsin Court of Appeals held that the Wisconsin theft statute, WSA 943.20(2)(b), applied to theft of phone services. An inmate serving a 133-year term in a Wisconsin prison set up several telephone accounts in fictitious names and then used the telephone numbers to make collect calls totaling over 40,000 minutes. The court held that the definition of "property" in the theft statute included "electricity," and that electricity includes telephone service. The court also held that the defendant could be prosecuted under the general theft statute, even though Wisconsin has a specific statute, WSA § 943.45, for telecommunications theft.[18]

Contraband, such as illegal drugs, can be stolen, even though people losing such property are not likely to report such thefts to the police. In *Ceballos v. State*,[19] the Arkansas Court of Appeals held that the Arkansas theft statutes included contraband. The defendant broke into a residence to steal illegal marijuana held there by the residence's owner. When charged with theft, the defendant argued illegal contraband is not "property of another," because no one can own contraband. The court disagreed, stating that the theft statutes define "property" as anything of value that can be possessed, and that illegal marijuana satisfies both of those requirements.

Value of Property   If the property has no intrinsic value, a prosecution for theft or larceny would be hard to sustain. A single sheet of paper worth a penny or less has little intrinsic value. If, however, a signed promissory note for $1,000 were on the sheet of paper, the value of the paper would increase considerably. In charging theft or larceny, the state must introduce evidence showing the value of the property alleged to have been stolen.

The value of the property stolen, in most instances, determines whether the charge is a misdemeanor or a felony. The value of the property must be determined by the court or jury. Statements by the owner concerning what he or she paid for the property, how long it was possessed, its replacement cost, and its condition are admissible in determining value. Evidence of the value of comparable property in comparable condition is admissible to show the value of the property at issue. Experts and appraisers may, in some instances, be called into court to testify as to value. (Sentimental value can generally not be considered.)

In the New York case of *People v. Harold*, the defendant was convicted of grand larceny for the theft of a water pump that had been purchased five days before the theft. However, the pump had been damaged before the theft by two men, Crego and Terpening, who had attempted to install the pump. In ordering a new trial, the court stated:

> The question presented by this appeal pertains to the value of the stolen pump . . . [T]he market value of a stolen item is to be measured by what the thief would have had to pay had he purchased the item instead of stealing it. . . . In the instant case, the value of the pump must be reduced to reflect the mechanical prowess of Crego and Terpening. Additionally, an allowance must be made for the fact that the pump, when taken, was no longer new.
>
> Many state statutes provide that *value* means the market value at the time of the theft or the cost to the victim of replacing the property within a reasonable time after the theft. The replacement value to a retail store is the replacement cost to the store, not the retail price of the item.[20]

As the New York court pointed out in the *Harold* case, the value in New York would be "market value" or "what the thief would have to pay had he purchased the item instead of stealing it." Colorado[21] and many other states also follow this rule

FORMS OF TAKING AND TYPES OF THEFT

Shoplifting (Retail Theft) or Price Altering

- Shoplifting—the most common form of theft in retail stores—is the taking by concealment to avoid payment for goods.
- Price altering avoids payment of the full price of an object by lowering the amount on the price tag.

Taking by Employee, Bailee, or Trustee

- Employee theft of money and other objects from business premises causes large losses.
- Embezzlement of funds or negotiable securities that are in the custody of employees, bailees, or trustees.

Snatch and Run

- The taking is observed, and the offender flees to avoid apprehension.

Till Tap

- The thief opens a cash register unobserved and takes cash and coins.
- While store employee has cash drawer open, thief grabs money and flees (snatch and run).

Taking by Trick, Deception, or Fraud (Stings, Scams, and Swindles)

- Con games and operations.
- Deceptions and tricks to obtain property illegally.
- Obtaining property by false pretenses.

Taking from a Person

- Purse snatching (a form of snatch and run).
- Pickpocketing.
- Rolling a drunk (taking from a person incapacitated by alcohol, drugs, or other means).

Taking of Lost or Mislaid Goods or Money
Taking of Objects or Money Delivered by Mistake

- Example: a check for too much money is mailed to a person by mistake.

in determining value. Other states use the replacement value rule—the replacement cost to a retail store to replace a stolen item.

Property of Another

To prove theft or larceny, the state must show that the property belonged to another, whether that is an individual, a corporation, or a governmental unit. Because the consent of the owner would constitute a total defense to a theft or larceny charge, the owner (or a representative of the owner) must testify that the taking was without

Looting

- Taking property from or near a building damaged, destroyed, or left unoccupied following a tornado, fire, physical disaster, riot, bombing, earthquake, or similar event.

Taking by Failure to Return a Leased or Rented Object

- Example: failure to return a rented car or DVD within the time specified by state statutes or city ordinance.

Taking by Illegal Entry into Locked Coin Box

- Vending machine, pay telephone, parking meter, and so on.

Smash and Run

- A store or other window is broken, and after snatching objects, the thief runs to avoid apprehension. (This can also be charged as burglary.)
- Women drivers waiting at stoplights are sometimes subjected to this tactic. The thief breaks the car window, takes the woman's purse from the front seat, and runs.[a]

Taking by Illegally Obtaining or Using Information

- Stock market insider trading scandals are examples of illegally using information.

Taking by Illegal Use of a Credit Card or Credit Card Number

Taking from a Person with a Superior Right of Possession

- People may acquire a superior right of possession over the owner of property because of a bailment, pledge, or contract. State criminal codes may make taking from a person with a superior right of possession a crime.

Theft by Possession of Stolen Property

- A person who receives stolen property, knowing it was stolen, commits theft.

Ordinary Theft

- Taking occurs observed or unobserved by owner or other people.

[a]The "bump" technique is also used. An expensive car occupied only by its driver is usually targeted. While the victim is waiting at a stoplight, the victim's car is bumped intentionally. When the victim gets out of the car to view the damages, one of the thieves distracts the victim while the other thief sneaks around to get into the victim's car. Because the victim generally leaves the keys in the ignition, the thief drives off in the victim's car. The other thief jumps in his or her car and also speeds away, leaving the victim stranded.

his or her consent. A showing that the owner did not consent to the conduct of the defendant is also necessary in criminal damage to property, in trespass, and in arson of either real property or personal property.

Under modern law, a husband and wife are not treated as a single entity for many purposes, including the criminal law of theft. As a result, in most states one spouse can be guilty of theft of the other spouse's property, because that property qualifies as "property of another." However, the property must belong to the spouse from whom it is taken, and it cannot be the kind of property that is "normally accessible" to both spouses. A refrigerator, for example, even if bought by one spouse, cannot be stolen by the other spouse if the couple is still living together.

An example of theft by a spouse is *State v. Krinitt*,[22] a decision of the Supreme Court of Montana. In *Krinitt*, a husband was convicted of stealing his wife's trust fund check. The husband had a history of wasting the couple's finances, so the wife instructed the trust fund to send the check to her attorney. When the check was delivered to their home by mistake, the husband cashed it and spent the money. He was convicted of theft because the trust fund check was not "accessible" to both spouses.

In some states "property of another" is defined to exclude property owned by a spouse or owned jointly by a husband and wife. That is the case in Georgia under Ga. Code Ann. § 16-8-1. In the 2010 case of *Keathley v. State*[23] a husband was convicted of burglary when he broke into his estranged wife's apartment and stole some of her jewelry and a television set they jointly owned. The appeals court reversed the conviction, holding that burglary requires proof of intent to commit theft, and the husband could not have that intent because he intended to take only property of his wife or jointly owned property.

Many people hold property jointly with others. Suppose a business partner steals $1,000 from the partnership checking account and uses it for his personal needs. Or suppose a wife runs off with another man and takes $500 out of a savings and loan account that is in the name of her husband and herself. Is this stealing the property of another? Whether this constitutes theft or larceny would be determined by how the statutes of that jurisdiction define "property of another."

The Model Penal Code Section 233(7) defines "property of another" to include property in which the defendant has an interest, so long as the interest of the other person is one the defendant "is not privileged to infringe." Although each partner in a partnership, or each holder of a joint checking account, may have access to partnership funds or the checking account, they are not privileged to infringe on the others' rights and can be guilty of theft. In *State v. Mora*,[24] the court upheld a conviction for theft of funds in a checking account. The defendants convinced the mother of one of them to place their names on her checking and savings accounts. They then withdrew more than $50,000 from those accounts. When charged with theft, they contended that they did not steal property of another, because they were authorized to make the withdrawals. The court rejected their defense, stating that while a good-faith belief that a person had a right to take property was a good defense, the defendants could not have that belief based only on the fact their names were on the accounts. They knew the funds belonged to the mother, and that she had no intention of giving them any interest in the funds.

The question of the meaning of "property of another" also came up in the 2011 Hawaii case of *State v. Taylor*.[25] The defendant dug up some graves on public land, which contained artifacts of Native Hawaiians that had been repatriated by the state and reburied. He was charged with theft, and defended by contending the artifacts were not "property of another" because they were owned by no one. The appeals court affirmed his theft conviction, holding that under Hawaii law, all "historic property on lands and under the waters" was the property of the state, and thus the artifacts were the property of another under the theft statute.

Difficulties in Identifying Property   Some property is difficult for owners to identify. Diamonds and other valuable stones are an example. Valuable stones may be easily identified by their settings, but once they are removed, they are difficult to distinguish. The four Cs of the diamond business—cut, clarity, carat, and color—provide only the roughest means of identification. An owner's testimony of "it looks like my property, but I am not sure" is not sufficient identification. Because of the difficulty of identification, in some situations the police have been forced to return property to a known thief because of lack of evidence that the property was stolen.

The stolen property must be identified by introducing evidence showing no reasonable doubt as to its identity. For this reason, law enforcement agencies urge marking property in such ways that the identification marks cannot be easily removed or obliterated.

Abandoned Property   If the property has been abandoned or if the owner of the property cannot be located, then theft or larceny cannot be proved. *Abandonment* has been defined as the relinquishment or surrender of property or the rights to property. Most states permit the defense if in fact the property was abandoned, or the defendant had an honest, reasonable belief the property was abandoned. That was the reasoning of the U.S. Supreme Court in the case of *Morissette v. United States*,[26] discussed in Chapter 7.

Whether property is abandoned can depend on the way a state defines that term. In the 2009 case of *Hamilton v. Noe*[27] the defendant was arrested taking scrap metal from a demolition site. The city had torn down the pool house at a city pool, and the debris was left on the site. The defendant entered the site and carried away some of the scrap metal found in the debris. He was charged with theft, and contended the scrap metal was abandoned property. The city parks director testified the city planned to "junk" the debris. The appeals court affirmed the defendant's theft conviction, holding that under Ohio theft law, abandoned property requires a showing of intent by the owner to abandon *and* actions implementing that intent. The parks director's testimony showed intent to abandon, but no actions were taken to implement that intent.

In the 2014 case of *Hawkins v. United States*, 103 A.3d 199(D.C. 2014), the court reversed a conviction for theft of a bicycle. Police had left a bicycle on a public bike rack as part of a sting operation to catch bike thieves. Defendant saw the bike and took it from the rack. He was then arrested. At his trial he contended he believed the bike was abandoned by its owner. The judge, in a bench trial, stated she did not believe the defendant could reasonably believe the bike was abandoned and found him guilty. On appeal, the court said that the trial judge erred. Theft is a specific intent crime, the court said, and if the defendant in fact believed the bike was abandoned, even if that belief was unreasonable, he lacked the required mens rea. It remanded the case for a new trial to determine if in fact the defendant had a genuine belief the bike was abandoned.

Intent to Steal

Theft or larceny requires a specific intent to deprive the owner of possession of the property. The intent to steal may be proved by direct evidence or by circumstantial evidence. Generally, the fact finder (jury or judge) concludes and infers an intent to steal from the conduct and acts of the defendant.

Frequently, defendants attempt to defeat the intent to steal requirement by contending that they intended only to borrow the property. In many cases, the jury gives little credence to this defense, sensibly concluding that the defendants' actions show a different intent. However, if proved, an intent to return the property negates guilt of theft, unless the return date is unusually far in the future. For example, taking a neighbor's lawn mower in April and intending to return it in November may be enough to prove theft, unless the theft statute of that state requires a showing that the taker intended to permanently deprive the owner of possession.

In some states, the "borrowing" problem has been solved by establishing a separate theft offense for taking property without the intent to deprive the owner of "permanent" possession. For example, the Kansas "Criminal deprivation of property" statute, KSA § 21-3705, makes a theft crime of any "obtaining or exerting unauthorized control over property of another, with the intent to deprive the owner of the temporary use thereof." In Texas, VTCA Penal Code § 31.01 includes within the meaning of "deprive another" of property keeping the property for "so extended a period of time that a major portion of the value . . . of the property is lost to the owner."

In some cases, even short-term borrowing can be a crime. Many states have statutes that make it a crime to use or operate another person's automobile, motorcycle, or other motor-propelled vehicle without permission of the owner, even if the person intends to return the vehicle after a short joyride. The Model Penal Code, Section 223.9, makes this conduct a misdemeanor.

SHOPLIFTING

Theft has always been a problem for retail stores in the United States. Annual studies done jointly by the National Retail Federation and the University of Florida indicate that the cost of retail theft and fraud every year in the United States runs into billions of dollars. Preliminary results from the most recent survey, released by the National Retail Federation on June 22, 2012, show national retail inventory "shrinkage" (inventory losses) was $34.5 billion for 2011, down from $37.1 billion in 2010. Of that total, employee theft accounted for 43.9 percent of the total. Shoplifting was responsible for 35.7 percent. The balance of the shrinkage was due to administrative error (12.1 per cent), and vendor fraud (5.0 per cent).[28]

The most common form of employee fraud and theft is called "sweethearting," which occurs when cashiers fail to scan goods or ring up sales for goods brought through a checkout line or to a register by friends or relatives. Stealing from the till continues to be a problem, as does manipulation of store computers to issue gift cards or other fraudulent schemes. When stolen or fake credit cards are used to purchase inventory, the retail store owner can suffer losses if the credit card company does not honor the credit card.

shoplifting Stealing goods from retail stores by concealment, generally on the person of the defendant. Commission does not require removal of the goods from the store.

The crime of **shoplifting**, or retail theft, is a form of theft and larceny. Shoplifting has the same essential elements as theft and larceny: (1) a taking and carrying away (2) of the property of another (3) without consent and (4) with intent to steal and deprive the owner of possession of the property.

Taking and Carrying Away in Shoplifting

In modern self-service stores, customers are invited to examine merchandise on display. Garments may be taken to dressing rooms and tried on. Customers carry about merchandise either in their hands or in shopping carts provided by the store. The New York Court of Appeals pointed out in the case of *People v. Olivo* that stores therefore consent "to the customer's possession of the goods" for limited purposes.[29]

Stores do not consent, however, to concealment of their merchandise by customers. The merchandise is offered for sale, and if customers are not going to purchase an object, they are obligated to return the merchandise to the display counter in good condition.

If customers take the merchandise, they have a legal obligation to pay the purchase price. The highest court in New York State held in the *Olivo* case:

> If the customer exercises dominion and control wholly inconsistent with the continued rights of the owner, and the other elements of the crime are present, a larceny has occurred. Such conduct on the part of a customer satisfies the "taking" element of the crime.

> * * *

> A taking of property in the self-service store context can be established by evidence that a customer exercised control over merchandise wholly inconsistent with the store's continued rights. Quite simply, a customer who crosses the line between the limited right he or she has to deal with merchandise and the store owner's rights may be subject to prosecution for larceny. Such a rule should foster the legitimate interests and continued operation of self-service shops, a convenience which most members of the society enjoy.[30]

Proving the Crime of Shoplifting When the Suspect Has Not Left the Store

There is a common belief that shoplifting has not occurred until the merchandise has been taken from the store premises. The Criminal Court of the City of New York discussed this belief in *People v. Britto:*

> There are a number of myths about the criminal law, comfortably shared and nourished by those in the street, the business community and sometimes, the courts. One of these is the belief that an observed shoplifter acts with impunity unless and until he or she leaves the store with the goods. So strong is this belief that the majority of store detectives are instructed to refrain from stopping the suspect anywhere inside the premises; although the likelihood of apprehension is thus enormously decreased.[31]

Courts are virtually unanimous in holding that goods need not leave the store for theft to occur. The New York Court of Appeals explained that result as follows:

> Case law from other jurisdictions seems unanimous in holding that a shoplifter need not leave the store to be guilty of larceny. . . . This is because a shopper may treat merchandise in a manner inconsistent with the owner's continued

THE HOME DEPOT SCAM

The "big box" stores, like Home Depot, process hundreds, even thousands, of transactions a day. Many of these transactions involve the return of merchandise by customers, with a resulting payment of cash or credit from the store. Since some customers returning merchandise will fail to keep the store receipt, stores must have a procedure to deal with such returns. They must also have a procedure to deal with returns where the buyer shows a store receipt that the buyer paid cash for the merchandise, since that buyer will usually expect to get cash back on the return.

Home Depot had such policies. For cash sales with receipts, Home Depot returned cash to the customer. For returns without a receipt, Home Depot required the customer to show a driver's license (or other government-issued identification), which Home Depot scanned to an Internet service that determined if that person had made previous returns without a receipt. If the person had exceeded the permitted number of non-receipt returns, the transaction was declined by Home Depot. If not, the person was given a store credit card to be used for other purchases at Home Depot.

James Dabney used the Home Depot procedures to steal from Home Depot. He did this in two ways: First, he supplied confederates with counterfeit bills, which they used to purchase goods for "cash" at Home Depot. Later, armed with the cash receipt, the individuals returned the merchandise and received genuine cash back from Home Depot.

Second, Dabney, and five others he recruited, stole merchandise from Home Depot, then returned the merchandise without a receipt for the store credit card. Dabney himself engaged in 47 such "return" transactions, for more than $12,000.00 in stolen merchandise. After the return process started declining his return attempts, he recruited the five other individuals. They would return stolen goods, obtain the Home Depot credit card, and transfer it to Dabney for a fee.

In *State v. Dabney*, 2015 WL 5833934 (Ohio App 2015), *rev. denied* 45 N.E.3d 245 (Ohio 2016) the court affirmed Dabney's convictions for money laundering and theft. The transfer of the counterfeit bills for genuine cash violated the Ohio money laundering statute, the court held. The exchange of stolen goods for store credit was theft by deception, the court said. (Based on his method of recruiting others into the scheme, Dabney was also convicted of several counts of telecommunications fraud under an Ohio statute, as well as counts of receiving stolen property.)

rights—and in a manner not in accord with that of a prospective purchaser—without actually walking out of the store.[32]

Inconsistent actions might include hiding the goods under the shopper's coat or other clothes. As the Maryland Court of Special Appeals held in *Lee v. State,* if merchandise is secreted under clothing, it meets the requirement of concealment, and it does not matter if the concealment was for a short time or the shopper did not leave the store.[33]

The Requirement of Probable Cause Based on Personal Knowledge

probable cause
Reasonable grounds to believe.

Private security officers and retail store employees are often told, "If you have not seen it, it has not happened." Customers are not to be treated like shoplifters until hard, firsthand information demonstrates that shoplifting has occurred. The Criminal Court of New York emphasized the **probable cause** requirement in *People v. Britto:*

It must be emphasized that this court's holding in no way lessens the burden of proof on the People in shoplifting cases. On the contrary, there is, and should be, a higher standard of proof upon the People in self-service situations than in other larceny cases, because the mere fact of possession may not be used to demonstrate larceny. This remains true even when such possession is accompanied by suspicious or equivocal actions, such as placing unpaid goods directly into the defendant's shopping bag (citation omitted). It is only when the trier of fact concludes, beyond a reasonable doubt, that defendant's actions were totally inconsistent with and clearly adverse to the owner's interests that a conviction may lie. If the facts are sufficient to support such a conclusion *before* the defendant leaves the store, the fact that he has not left is wholly irrelevant and should not absolve him from the consequences of his acts.[34]

The U.S. Supreme Court defined *probable cause* as "facts and circumstances within their knowledge and of which they had reasonable trustworthy information [that] were sufficient in themselves to warrant a man of reasonable caution in the belief that the suspect had committed a crime."[35] The Supreme Judicial Court of Massachusetts has held:

Historically, the words "reasonable grounds" and "probable cause" have been given the same meaning by the courts.

* * *

The Oregon Supreme Court construed the meaning of the words "reasonable grounds" in its "shoplifting statute" as having the same meaning as they have in a statute authorizing arrest without a warrant and applied the probable cause standard to the facts before it.[36]

EXAMPLE

On a hot July day, a woman customer stated to a clerk in a large food store, "I suspect that young man of shoplifting." She pointed at a young man wearing a jogging suit. The clerk relayed the statement to the assistant manager of the store, who confronted the young man, accusing him of shoplifting in a voice overheard by other people. The young man was detained, and the police were called. Did probable cause exist to justify this action?

When the police arrived, they questioned the store employees and the woman customer. The woman customer stated that she had not witnessed a shoplifting but had only "suspected" that a theft had occurred. The police then realized that probable cause did not exist from the facts known to the store employees, and they released the young man. In the civil lawsuit that followed, a jury awarded the young man money damages for false imprisonment and **defamation** (slander).

Defamation Wrongful injury to another's reputation.

Criminal or Civil Prosecution of Shoplifters?

Shoplifting cases can be handled in a variety of different ways, depending on the circumstances of the case. Following are some of the alternatives for handling shoplifting cases:

- When the amount stolen is very small or the offender is very young or very old, a scolding and warning might be used. Parents of children could be called, or the police could take the child home and inform the parents of the problem. Many states have laws making parents liable in a civil action for goods damaged or taken by a minor in a theft.
- More than thirty states have passed laws giving merchants and retailers authority to extract payments and fines from thieves they catch in the act. The offender could sign an agreement under a civil settlement of shoplifting law, acknowledging guilt and agreeing to make the payments to the merchant. In this way, the merchant can save time and expenses by bypassing the police and the courts. The advantages to the shoplifter are that a criminal record is avoided and the incident is taken care of without a court appearance.
- Because criminal courts are very crowded, shoplifting cases are not ordinarily charged criminally unless the amount taken is very large. Civil citations are issued in many cases, and offenders can pay the fine in the same way as parking tickets are paid. Or the offender can be ordered to appear in a municipal court, where the case will be heard by a judge in the same way speeding and other traffic violations are heard.

 ## HANDLING A SHOPLIFTING INCIDENT

1. Make sure you have probable cause and a good solid case before you restrain the freedom of movement of a person for shoplifting. Probable cause (or "reasonable grounds to believe") must be based on personal knowledge (firsthand information)—either yours or that of another reliable adult employee. Remember: "If you did not see it, it did not happen. When in doubt, let them go."
2. Observing a person concealing "something" or putting "something" in his or her pocket or purse is not sufficient to establish probable cause. The person may be putting a handkerchief or glasses back in a pocket. You must have "reasonable grounds to believe" (probable cause) that the object is unpaid-for merchandise and that the item belongs to the store. If you do not have probable cause, you may
   - Keep the person under observation.
   - Engage in voluntary conversation ("May I help you?" and "Are you looking for something?").
   - Ask the person what they put in his or her pocket, or whether the person has a receipt for merchandise in his or her possession, under circumstances in which there is no restraint of their freedom of movement.
3. After a person is observed shoplifting, the following options are available to store employees or a security officer:
   - Confront the person immediately, and ask that he or she produce the item. Always ask if the person has a receipt showing that he or she paid for the item. Under these circumstances, you may seek only recovery of the item and deterrence, rather than prosecution in court.
   - You may be under instructions to allow the person to go beyond the last pay station (or, in some cases, even out of the store). Under these circumstances, the person should be kept under surveillance. A person who becomes aware of your surveillance may attempt to discard the shoplifted item or pass it onto another person. If you fail to observe the "discard" or "pass-on," you may then

- Criminal charges are likely to be issued in shoplifting cases when
  - The shoplifter commits a serious assault or battery in resisting detention or in attempting to escape. Assault on a law enforcement officer is a felony in probably all states.
  - Escape is made from a law enforcement officer while the defendant is in custody, which is a crime. Some states also forbid escape from a merchant who has lawfully detained a shoplifter. See Ohio R.C. 2921.34.
  - The shoplifter has a concealed weapon or illegal drugs on his or her person, or is in possession of a criminal tool or a shoplifting device. See *State v. Lee* 2012 WL 5333542 (Ariz. App. 2012), where the court held a reusable shopping bag was a shoplifting device under the Arizona shoplifting statute.
  - The shoplifter causes considerable damage to the merchant's property in an effort to escape. Many states make criminal damage to property a crime if the damage is done either "intentionally" or "recklessly."
  - The shoplifter obstructs and hinders a law enforcement officer by giving the wrong name and date of birth, as in the 2012 case of *State v. Collins*.[37]
  - The shoplifter has a long prior record of theft and/or has a serious drug or alcohol problem, which the person is stealing to support. (Prosecutors can encourage such people to enter drug treatment programs by threatening jail sentences.)

---

be unable to explain why the stolen property was not recovered. If it appears that the person may outrun you and other store employees, it may be wise to position yourself between the exit door and the person.

4. If your state has a civil settlement of shoplifting law, you should know the requirements of this law and also any guidelines that your employer has established for using the law.
5. Shoplifting cases are handled by your local law enforcement agency (police or sheriff), prosecutor, and judges. Consult a knowledgeable official to determine whether any specific standards are required, such as
   - Whether the local judges require that the person observed shoplifting be allowed beyond the pay station (or out of the store) before being detained. (A young man in gym shoes who gets near a door or out of the store is going to outrun most store security people.)
   - Whether cases will be prosecuted when
     - The value of the merchandise stolen is small. (What is the minimum for prosecution?)
     - The merchandise or item stolen has not been recovered.
     - The offender is very young or very old.
     - Other factors are considered.
6. Absolute defenses to civil suits are
   - That the person either voluntarily stayed in the area or that the restraint of movement was made in good faith on probable cause based on personal knowledge.
   - That if any force was used, it was necessary and reasonable either
   - In self-defense.
   - To detain the person.
   - To prevent the theft of the property.

Other Retail Theft Crimes

- *Tag Switching:* A lower price tag is placed on a store item.
- *Undercharging by Checkout Clerk* (under ringing schemes): The checkout clerk undercharges a friend or co-conspirator.
- *"Storming" or Mass Shoplifting:* Two or many more people storm an all-night or late-night convenience store, take items, and then leave. If force is used or threatened, this could be charged as robbery.
- *Till Tapping:* A person reaches into a cash register after distracting the employee, or grabs money from an open cash register ("snatch and run").
- *Boosting:* This is an organized form of shoplifting used by gangs, in which goods in large quantities are placed in booster bags (ordinary bags lined with aluminum foil to avoid store detectors) and then sold by the gangs at huge discounts.

FRAUDULENT USE OF CREDIT CARDS

Credit cards are a means of extending short-term credit. The three parties ordinarily involved in a credit card transaction are (1) the issuer of the credit card, which could be a bank or an organization, such as American Express or MasterCard; (2) the credit card user, who is the holder of the card and the person purchasing the merchandise or service; and (3) the seller of the merchandise or provider of the services.

A person holding a valid credit card signs for the receipt of the goods and commits himself or herself to pay for the service or the property that has been received. The merchant or business organization supplying the goods or services is then reimbursed for the amount of the billing by the issuer of the credit card. The credit card issuer then bills the credit card holder.

Credit Card Theft and Obtaining Credit Cards and Bank Cards for Fraudulent Use

Credit card theft occurs when a credit card is stolen, and every state has a statute directed at such theft. The Maryland statute is illustrative of these credit card theft statutes. Section 8-204 of the Maryland Code (2002) makes it a crime to either (1) take a credit card from another without the owner's consent or (2) receive a credit card knowing it was stolen and with the intent to use the card.

The methods of obtaining credit cards for fraudulent use are many and varied. They can be stolen by burglars, pickpockets, or robbers. They can be retained by workers in gas stations or restaurants or stolen from the mail. They can be counterfeited or altered. In the 2009 case of *Gheorghiu v. Commonwealth,*[38] the Virginia Court of Appeals upheld the conviction under the credit card theft statute of a defendant who produced fake credit cards using a laptop computer and a "remagger" device. The device enabled the defendant to place stolen credit card numbers on a fake card, and encode the number onto the magnetic bar used when a credit card is swiped.

The credit card itself need not be stolen; if a thief uses the card number unlawfully, it is credit card theft.[39] Many states have credit card abuse laws that make it a crime to use a revoked or canceled credit card to fraudulently obtain property.[40]

Thieves obtain credit cards to commit crimes in the following ways:

- Counterfeiting cards (29 percent)
- Stealing credit cards (22.4 percent)

- Obtaining lost or mislaid credit cards (16.4 percent)
- Theft from the mail (13.7 percent)
- Making fraudulent applications for credit cards (3.2 percent)
- Placing telephone and mail orders with false cards (9.3 percent)[41]

It is generally held that a defendant can be convicted under a credit card fraud statute even without possession of the credit card. In *Robinson v. State*,[42] the defendant handed an invalid credit card to a merchant to swipe in the card reader. When the card would not register, the defendant took the card back and "read" the numbers to the merchant. In fact, the defendant was reading numbers from credit cards the defendant had seen being used by their owners. The court held that the defendant could be convicted under the credit card statute even though he never had the credit card in his possession.

It is also generally held that possession alone of a stolen credit card constitutes credit card theft, even if the card had not been used. In the 2009 case of *State v. Jernigan*,[43] the court upheld a credit card theft conviction even though the prosecution offered no proof the defendant used or intended to use the cards. The defendant knowingly had lost or stolen cards in his possession for over two weeks, which the court said satisfied the "appropriating" requirement of the statute, ARS § 13-1802, since the defendant was both depriving the true owner of possession, and was holding the credit cards for his own use, whatever use that was.

The meaning of "misrepresentation" under a fraudulent use of a credit card was the issue in the 2013 case of *State v. Borquez*.[44] In that case the defendant stole a credit card and called the clerk of a criminal court to use the card to pay his court fines of over $5000.00. The clerk asked the defendant if he was the cardholder whose name appeared on the card, and the defendant said yes. The clerk then charged the court fines to the card. The actual cardholder discovered the theft of the card and the charge against the card for the court fines. She then informed the police and the card issuer, and the defendant was charged with theft of the card and obtaining property by fraudulent misrepresentation. He was convicted and appealed.

On appeal the defendant contended he could not be convicted of fraudulent misrepresentation because (1) he did not make the misrepresentation to the victim (the card company; the cardholder is not normally responsible for fraudulent use of the card) with intent to obtain property by deception and (2) the victim did not rely on the misrepresentation. The appeals court rejected that argument, holding that the theft statute requires only that a fraudulent misrepresentation be made to obtain property with the intent to deprive the true owner of the property. The misrepresentation need not be made directly to the victim (here, the credit card company) whose property is being taken, the court said. Moreover, the credit card company relied on the misrepresentation by processing the transaction concluded by the court clerk. It affirmed the defendant's conviction.

One leading commentator appears to question decisions like the one in *Borquez*. In Wayne R. LaFave, 3 *Substantive Criminal Law* §19.7 (2nd Ed. 2011) the author expresses doubts about prosecuting a person who steals and misuses a credit card (by, for example, going to a store and charging items on the card) on the theory of theft by deception:

> The usual three-party arrangement is that the creditor collects from the credit-card issuer, who assumes the risk of misuse of credit cards to encourage creditors to honor cards promptly. Under these circumstances it is difficult to convict the misuser of a credit card of the crime of false pretenses, for the person deceived (the creditor) loses nothing, and the person who loses something (the issuer) is not the one deceived.

CHECK VIOLATIONS

Most checks that bounce are the result of negligence, mistakes, or bad bookkeeping. Persons writing NSF (nonsufficient funds) or ISF (insufficient funds) checks generally make the checks good within the period provided by the statutes of that state. For example, Florida Statutes, Section 832.07, require that a bad check be made good within seven days or a criminal prosecution may be commenced, and further make the writer of the check liable in a civil action for triple the amount of the check.

Bad checks are a constant problem for retail businesses and banks, as the crime is easy to commit and the money losses are huge.[45] Not only are the money losses growing every year, but an *FBI Law Enforcement Bulletin* article of 1996 pointed out that half of all check fraud in the United States is committed by professional and organized groups.[46] The article pointed out that even street gangs are using sophisticated means to commit check fraud.

The problem of bad checks overwhelms most local law enforcement agencies. The sheer volume of bad checks limits the number that can be investigated and prosecuted.

Debit cards, which are used to take funds directly out of the card owner's bank account, are similar to both checks and credit cards. Theft and use of a debit card can be prosecuted under many states' credit card theft statutes, though in some states existing credit card theft statutes had to be amended to cover debit cards. For example, the Arkansas "theft by receiving" statute, ARS §5-36-106, was amended in 2011 to add "debit cards" to the kinds of stolen property covered by the statute. Earlier, in *Withers v. State*,[47] the Arkansas Court of Appeals held the defendant could not be convicted of theft of a debit card under the existing credit card statute.

The Crime of Uttering

forgery Wrongfully signing a writing or instrument in the name of the person who issued the writing or instrument, or to whom it was payable.

uttering Putting into circulation a check known to be worthless.

When a person signs a false name in the presence of a bank clerk to a check that does not belong to him or her, the felony crime of **forgery** has been committed. The bank clerk can then testify in court that he or she witnessed the forgery. When a forged check is presented for payment, the felony of **uttering** has been committed. The Supreme Court of Virginia defined the crime of uttering:

> Under our bad-check statute, the gravamen of the offense is the intent to defraud, and the offense is complete when, with the requisite intent, a person utters a check he knows to be worthless. . . . A check is uttered when it is put into circulation; for example, when it is presented for payment. . . . The presentment is more than a request for payment; it constitutes an implied representation that the check is good. The statute itself dispenses with proof of an extrinsic representation.
>
> ★ ★ ★
>
> It need not be shown that the implied representation was relied upon or that anything was received in return for the check; indeed, the discovery by a payee that a check is worthless before a purchase transaction is completed does not preclude a conviction under the statute. . . . And, while we have stated that the statute is "specifically aimed to discourage the giving of bad checks for what purports to be a cash purchase," . . . such a purchase is not the only transaction proscribed; the statute clearly encompasses a worthless check given to obtain cash.[48]

The crime of uttering a forged instrument is most often committed when a person presents a forged instrument for payment. In the case of *England v. State,* the defendant handed a forged check to a bank teller without saying anything.[49] In affirming the defendant's conviction for uttering a forged instrument, the Supreme Court of Indiana held: "We conclude the offering of the check to the teller with no instructions, when this act is generally construed in the banking industry as a request to exchange said check for cash, is sufficient conduct to warrant the jury to believe that the appellant intended to cash a forged instrument." In the case of *State v. Tolliver,*[50] the defendant deposited a forged check into his own checking account through the use of an ATM. A Wisconsin Court of Appeals affirmed his conviction for uttering, holding that the defendant's act introduced the forged check "into the stream of financial commerce." The crime of uttering can be committed with a forged check or with a bad check that is not forged but is known to be worthless.

The crime of uttering can also be committed with counterfeit money or "raised" bills. In the case of *United States v. Brown,*[51] the defendant was convicted of connecting parts of different denominations of bills and uttering the altered bills. (Defendant "raised" $1 bills to $20 bills and then uttered them.)

In the 2014 case of *United States v. Powell,* 767 F.3d 1026 (10th Cir. 2014), a prosecution under the federal uttering statute, 18 U.S.C. § 513(a), the court held that the prosecution must prove that the forged checks deposited into a defendant's account were property "of" an organization affecting interstate commerce. The prosecution there proved only that the depository banks into which the forged checks were deposited affected interstate commerce. It did not prove the banks issuing the checks affected interstate commerce. The court said the federal statute makes it a crime to utter securities "of an organization." The forged checks were not "securities of" the depository banks, the court held. It reversed the defendant's uttering convictions as to those checks.

The Crime of Forgery

Documents and writing are important in the functioning of a modern society. The crimes of forgery and uttering are offenses created primarily to safeguard confidence in the genuineness of documents and writing. Forgery is committed when a person with an intent to defraud falsely makes or alters a writing or document. Forgery may be committed by

- Creating a wholly new false writing or document
- Altering an existing document (raising the amount of a check, e.g.)
- Endorsing a check or other instrument with another person's name (example: X steals Y's check and cashes the check by endorsing Y's name on the back of the check)
- Filling in blanks over a signature of another, either without authority or with unauthorized terms

When a check is presented either for cash or in payment for goods, there is an implied representation that the check is good. A common business practice is to request people presenting a check to either endorse or sign the check in the presence of the person who is about to honor the document. If the presenters of the check (the bearers) know that the check is forged, they have committed the crime of uttering in presenting the forged document. If they sign a false name to the check, they have then committed the crime of forgery in the presence of the person who is about to honor the check.

The many types of forged documents include driver's licenses, identification cards, credit cards, passports, and residency cards for people illegally in the United States.

With checks, the forgery could be done by hand. However, the many desktop computers have created a new industry. Forgery and counterfeiting of documents, including checks, is a fast-growing problem throughout the United States. The American Bankers Association states that desktop counterfeiting is the number-one crime problem facing banks.[52]

Operations of Check-Forging Rings

Check-forging rings operate in all large cities in the United States. Some of their blank checks are obtained as the result of burglaries or thefts from business firms. Other checks are the product of a computer, which is a new tool for making false copies of checks and other documents.

Checks are often forged by using names found on stolen identification cards and papers. Such identification can be obtained by purse snatching and pickpocketing. The thief looks for a victim with the same general appearance as the person who will utter (pass) the check. With a good set of identification cards and with checks that have all the appearance of payroll checks, the check-forging ring goes to work.

To minimize the possibilities of being apprehended, professional criminals often recruit other people to commit the actual uttering and passing of the checks. This can be done by selling the checks, made out in whatever amount and name the person wishes, or by making an agreement with the recruited people to share the criminal loot.

If a criminal is apprehended while attempting to pass a forged check, he or she is likely to attempt to eliminate the evidence of the crime by eating the check or destroying it in some other way. Should the offender be successful, he or she can then be charged with the offense of destroying (or attempting to destroy) evidence of a crime.

Passing Forged Checks and Other Counterfeit Securities in Interstate Commerce

In the 1930s, the U.S. Congress became concerned about the use of fraudulent securities in interstate commerce. The Congress amended the National Stolen Property Act (58 Statute 1178) by also forbidding "falsely made, forged, altered or counterfeit

---

 ## SAFEGUARDS IN HANDLING CHECKS

- Do not endorse checks in blank (with just your name), as the check then becomes a bearer instrument that can be cashed by any person obtaining possession.
- Do not sign blank checks, as any person obtaining possession of the checks could fill in the amount and cash the checks.
- In sending checks through the mail, make the checks payable to a specific person or corporation. Make bank deposits payable to "deposit only" or "for deposit to account number."

securities" to be used and passed in interstate commerce. The U.S. Supreme Court recognized that the "general intent" and "broad purpose" of Congress was to "curb the type of trafficking in fraudulent securities that often depends for its success on the exploitation of interstate commerce."[53]

The National Stolen Property Act, therefore, makes it unlawful to transport not only stolen property in interstate commerce but also fraudulent securities, which include forged or "falsely made" checks. The following U.S. Supreme Court cases illustrate the enforcement of the law:

United States v. Sheridan
Supreme Court of the United States (1946), 329 U.S. 379, 67 S. Ct. 332

The defendant was convicted under the National Stolen Property Act for cashing checks at a Michigan bank, drawn on a Missouri account, with a forged signature. The Supreme Court held:

Drawing the [forged] check upon an out-of-state bank, knowing it must be sent there for presentation, is an obviously facile way to delay and often defeat apprehension, conviction, and restoration of the ill-gotten gain. There are sound reasons therefore why Congress would wish not to exclude such persons (from the statute's reach), among them the very case with which they may escape the state's grasp.

McElroy v. United States
Supreme Court of the United States (1982), 455 U.S. 642, 102 S. Ct. 1332

The defendant used blank checks that had been stolen in Ohio to buy a car and a boat in Pennsylvania. The Supreme Court held that the defendant circulated fraudulent securities in violation of the National Stolen Property Act and that Congress's general purpose was "to combat interstate fraud."

check kiting Creating multiple checking accounts at multiple banks for the purpose of writing fraudulent checks from one account and depositing them in another, and then withdrawing funds from the deposit bank.

Check Kiting

Check kiting can be compared with a shell game at a carnival, in that manipulations are used in both to deceive. The most common reason for the deception in check kiting is to create a false bank balance from which to draw and run off with money that does not belong to oneself. The U.S. Supreme Court used the following example to explain a check-kiting scheme in the case of *Williams v. United States:*

> The check kiter opens an account at Bank A with a nominal deposit. He then writes a check on that account for a large sum, such as $50,000. The check kiter then opens an account at Bank B and deposits the $50,000 check from Bank A in that account. At the time of deposit, the check is not supported by sufficient funds in the account at Bank A. However, Bank B, unaware of this fact, gives the check kiter immediate credit on his account at Bank B. During the several-day period that the check on Bank A is being processed for collection . . . the check kiter writes a $50,000 check on his account at Bank B and deposits it into his account at Bank A. At the time of the deposit of that check, Bank A gives the check kiter immediate credit on his account there, and on the basis of that grant of credit pays the original $50,000 check when it is presented for collection.
>
> By repeating this scheme, or some variation of it, the check kiter can use the $50,000 credit originally given by Bank B as an interest-free loan for an extended period of time. In effect, the check kiter can take advantage of the several-day period required for the transmittal, processing, and payment of checks from accounts in different banks.[54]

A check kiter can build up a big "float" by using many accounts in different banks and then running off with all the money. In *United States v. Payne,*[55] used car dealers exchanged checks for the sale of automobiles between themselves and used the immediate credit to operate their businesses. One nonexistent car was sold seven or eight times a week for a four-month period. The Court concluded:

> Payne and Fountain successfully managed a kite for four months with a float that rose to $178,000. They obtained that credit, advance, and loan only by falsely representing the worthless checks as worth their face value. 18 U.S.C. § 1014 makes their misrepresentation a federal offense when the injured bank is insured by the FDIC.

The banking system in the United States has begun the process of electronically debiting checks, rather than sending the paper through the banking system. This results in an immediate debit on the account on which a check is drawn, rather than the three- to seven-day wait to send a check through the system. "Floats" are likely to become a thing of the past when full electronic debiting comes into existence, and crimes such as check kiting may also decrease.

★★

LEARNING OBJECTIVES SUMMARY

LO 1. List the property concepts that underlie property theft crimes.

The owners of property hold both the right to title and possession of the property. Therefore, when a thief takes possession of the property the owner's rights have been violated. Because one cannot acquire rights in property except through consent of the owner, a thief generally

acquires no rights in stolen property, and cannot transfer rights in that property.

LO 2. Explain the "money" rule and why it is an exception to general property rules.

The "money" rule, which permits good-faith purchasers for value of money or certain negotiable securities to obtain title unless they knew or should have known the money was stolen, is necessary to make sure money is freely negotiable.

LO 3. List four ways the taking element can be proved.
Taking can occur by direct acts, by appropriating lost or mislaid goods, by deception, or by embezzlement.

LO 4. Define "property of another" as it applies to theft of jointly owned property.
A joint owner "takes" the property of the other joint owner if the taker had no right to use or keep the property and doing so infringes on the rights of the joint owner.

LO 5. Identify ways the taking requirement can be met in shoplifting.
Hiding retail goods on one's person, taking the goods out of the store, or otherwise exercising control over the goods inconsistent with the right of a shopper to possess goods prior to sale can constitute taking in a shoplifting crime.

LO 6. Advise a hypothetical merchant on how best to proceed when a suspected shoplifter is identified.
A suspected shoplifter in the store may be stopped and questioned, and a shoplifter outside the store may be followed to discover the person's identity. In some states, a merchant or security officer with probable cause can detain a suspected shoplifter and search for stolen goods.

LO 7. Explain the ways credit card theft can be proved.
Credit card theft can be proved by showing the defendant was in actual possession of a stolen card, or by showing the defendant caused purchases to be made with the number taken from another person's credit card.

LO 8. Distinguish between forgery and uttering a forged instrument.
Forgery occurs when, with the intent to defraud another, a person creates or alters an instrument or document by signing with a fictitious name or another person's name. Uttering occurs when a forged instrument is presented for payment.

LO 9. Describe how a check-kiting scheme works.
A check-kiting scheme works by establishing an account at one bank, and then writing a large check on that account, which is deposited in a second account at another bank. While the check is going through the clearing process, which can take days, money is fraudulently withdrawn from the second account.

KEY TERMS

theft or larceny, p. 370
taking, p. 370
fraud, p. 372
embezzlement, p. 374

shoplifting, p. 380
probable cause, p. 382
defamation, p. 383
forgery, p. 388

uttering, p. 388
check kiting, p. 391

CASE ANALYSIS AND WRITING EXERCISES

1. When a person rents furniture for home use from a rent-to-own company, the rental agreement states that unless the renter elects to purchase the furniture, it must be returned at a stated period, or at once in the event of a default in rental payment. If a renter misses several payments, but does not return the rented furniture to the rental company, can the renter be prosecuted for theft? If so, what must the prosecution prove? Do you think the prosecution proved its case in *State v. Latham*, 970 N.E.2d 1169 (Ohio App. 2012)? Or do you think the dissenting judge was correct?

2. If an elderly father puts his daughter's name on his accounts at a bank and an investment company as a "joint owner," with instructions that she may deposit and withdraw funds from the accounts, can the daughter be convicted of theft for such withdrawals? If so, under what circumstances? See *Wagner v. State*, 128 A.3d 1 (Md. App. 2016).

3. In *Boyd v. Commonwealth*, 357 S.W.3d 216 (Ky. App. 2011) the defendant was convicted of possession of counterfeit currency under Kentucky law. (The federal crime of counterfeiting is discussed in Chapter 15.) The elements of that crime include proof that the bills possessed were counterfeit, and that the defendant possessed the bills with the intent to pass the bills and defraud another person. Defendant had two counterfeit hundred-dollar bills in her purse. How did the state prove the required "intent to pass" element? If you were the judge, would you have reached the same result as did the court?

4. Degrees of theft often depend on the value of the stolen items. The higher the value, the greater the offense and punishment. How is value to be determined? It is the state's burden to prove value, and a failure to do so will normally result in a not guilty verdict. If the owner of the stolen goods must establish the value (as is often the case), how does he or she do that? Consider the failure of proof of value of the prosecution in *State v. Sanchez*, 101 So.3d 1283 (Fla. App. 2012). What should it have done?

ENDNOTES

1. A 22A *Corpus Juris Secundum* (Criminal Law), Section 597.

2. For cases in which the owners of cars were convicted of theft when they took their car from a person with a superior right of possession, see *State v. Pike*, 826 P.2d 152 (Wash.1992) (car taken from mechanic without paying for repairs, but the conviction was reversed when it was shown that a written repair estimate was not provided as required by state law); see also *Courtney v. Rice*, 546 N.E.2d 461 (Ohio App. 1989) (car towed to police lot after a parking violation; defendant was convicted of theft and the parking violation, but both convictions were reversed on appeal).

3. 739 P.2d 1041 (1987).

4. *Theft* and *larceny* are interchangeable terms for the crime of stealing. Some states use the term *theft;* other states use *larceny.* The Model Penal Code uses *theft* (Article 223).

5. Nebraska Revised Statutes Section 28-510.

6. "Working Papers of the National Commission on Reform of Federal Criminal Laws," 2: 913.

7. See *State v. Johnson*, 432 So. 2d 758 (Fla. App. 1983), where forcing the store clerk to put money in a paper bag and place it on the store counter satisfied the carry-away requirement.

8. *People v. Schlicht*, 709 P.2d 94 (Colo. App. 1985).

9. See the *Chicago Tribune* article, "$836,000 Check for GI Triggers Row," October 23, 1993. For criminal cases on the taking of mislaid or lost property, see *State v. Evans*, 807 P.2d (Idaho App. 1991) and *State v. Getz*, 830 P.2d 5 (Kan. 1992).

10. See LaFave, *Criminal Law*, 4th ed., pp. 930–931 (Belmont, Calif: West, 2003).

11. 107 Cal. Rptr. 3d 608 (Cal. App. 2010).

12. 96 Cal. Rptr. 651 (Cal. App. 1971).

13. LaFave and Scott, in *Criminal Law*, 2nd ed. (Belmont, Calif: West/Wadsworth, 1986), discuss the following on pp. 729–739: (a) Embezzlement by a person in lawful possession of money or property (an employee; a person who found the money or property; or a person who obtained it by mistake), (b) what is called fraudulent embezzlement, and (c) embezzlement by public officials.

   The crime of "breaking bulk" is sometimes classified as an embezzlement crime. It is committed when a person takes a portion of goods that have been temporarily placed in his or her custody by the owner. This could be done by a warehouse employee or a common carrier in charge of transporting a shipment of goods. (For example, dockworkers loading cases of beer into a railroad car remove many bottles from cases for their own consumption.) Some states have statutorized the common law crime of breaking bulk (or breaking bale). Other states have made the offense that of larceny or embezzlement; still others include it as larceny by bailee.

14. Illinois Revised Statutes, Chapter 38, Section 15-1.

15. Minnesota Statutes Annotated Section 609.25.

16. *People v. Sanders*, 79 Cal. Rptr. 2d 806 (1998).

17. See *U.S. v. Riggs*, 739 R Supp. 414 (N.D. 111. 1990).

18. *State v. Howard*, 760 N.W.2d 183 (Wis. App. 2008), *review denied*, 775 N.W.2d 100 (2009).

19. 2009 WL 1478000 (Ark. App. 2009).

20. 22 N.Y.2d 443, 293 N.Y.S.2d 96, 239 N.E.2d 727 (1968).

21. See *People v. Schmidt* (1996 WL 350878), in which the Colorado Court of Appeals pointed out that Colorado has a statute that makes price tags attached to a stolen item prima facie evidence of the item's value in a theft prosecution, unless the price is commonly subject to negotiation, as a motor vehicle would be.

22. 823 P.2d 848 (1991). Also, in the case *of People v. Wallace*, 434 N.W.2d 423 (Mich. 1989), a Michigan Court of Appeals

held that a chain given to a wife during the marriage was her property and not the jointly owned property of the husband and wife.

23. 699 S.E.2d 765 (Ga. App. 2010).

24. 43 P.3d 38 (Wash. App. 2002).

25. 269 P.3d 740 (Hawai'i 2011).

26. 342 U.S. 246, 72 S. Ct. 240 (1952). This case is also discussed in Chapter 7.

27. 2009 WL 1655486 (Ohio App. 2009).

28. The preliminary results from the survey may be viewed online at http://www.ncf.com/lpl0.

29. 420 N.E.2d 40 (1981).

30. In affirming the convictions of three different defendants in the *Olivo* case, the New York court held:

> In *People v. Olivo*, defendant not only concealed goods in his clothing, but he did so in a particularly suspicious manner. And, when defendant was stopped, he was moving towards the door, just three feet short of exiting the store. It cannot be said as a matter of law that these circumstances failed to establish a taking.
>
> In *People v. Gasparik*, defendant removed the price tag and sensor device from a jacket, abandoned his own garment, put the jacket on, and ultimately headed for the main floor of the store. Removal of the price tag and sensor device, and careful concealment of those items, is highly unusual and suspicious conduct for a shopper. Coupled with defendant's abandonment of his own coat and his attempt to leave the floor, those factors were sufficient to make out a prima facie case of a taking.
>
> In *People v. Spatzier*, defendant concealed a book in an attaché case. Unaware that he was being observed in an overhead mirror, defendant looked furtively up and down an aisle before secreting the book. In these circumstances, given the manner in which defendant concealed the book and his suspicious behavior, the evidence was not insufficient as a matter of law.

31. 93 Misc. 2d 151, 402 N.Y.S.2d 546 (1978).

32. 438 N.Y.S. at 246 (1981).

33. 59 Md. App. 28, 474 A.2d 537 (1984).

34. 402 N.Y.S.2d at 548 (1978).

35. *Carroll v. United States,* 267 U.S. 132, 45 S. Ct. 280 (1925).

36. *Coblyn v. Kennedy's, Inc.,* 359 Mass. 319, 268 N.E.2d 860 (1971).

37. 2012 WL 589527 (Ohio App. 2012).

38. 682 S.E.2d 50 (Va. App. 2009).

39. In *State v. Morgan,* 985 P.2d 1022 (Alaska App. 1999), a man gave his former girlfriend's credit card number to the defendant, who used it to place $3,669 worth of long-distance calls. The court held his use of the card number was obtaining a credit card by fraudulent means.

40. See *Nolan v. State,* 629 S.W.2d 940 (Tex. App. 1982).

41. MasterCard International and the *New York Times* article, "Guarding Credit Cards from the Latest Scams," July 2, 1994.

42. 780 N.E.2d 849 (Ind. App. 2002).

43. 209 P.3d 153 (Ariz. App. 2009).

44. 307 P.3d 51 (Az. App. 2013)

45. Even the Congress of the United States had a "bad check" scandal in 1992. More than 100 members of the House of Representatives had written bad checks in a year's time on the House bank. One member of Congress wrote 996 bad checks in a three-year period. See the *New York Times* articles, "Adding Up the Casualties in the House Bank Scandal" and "The House Is Getting Jittery over Bad-Check Disclosures," March 12, 1992. All the bad checks were made good, but at the time they were written there were insufficient funds to cover the checks.

46. See the *FBI Law Enforcement Bulletin* article, "Check Fraud: A Sophisticated Criminal Enterprise," August 1996.

47. 218 S.W.3d 386 (Ark. App. 2005).

48. *Warren v. Commonwealth,* 219 Va. 416, 247 S.E.2d 692 (1978).

49. 249 Ind. 446, 233 N.E.2d 168 (1968).

50. 149 Wis. 2d 166, 440 N.W.2d 571 (Wis. App. 1989).

51. 938 F.2d 1482.

52. See the *New York Times* article, "New Breed of Check Forgers Exploit Desktop Publishing," August 15, 1994.

53. See *Moskal v. United States,* 111 S. Ct. at 466 (1990).

54. 458 U.S. 279, 102 S. Ct. 3088 (1982).

55. 602 F.2d 1215 (5th Cir. 1979), *review denied,* 445 U.S. 903, 100 S. Ct. 1079 (1980).

14

Robbery, Burglary, and Related Crimes

LEARNING OBJECTIVES

In this chapter we discuss the theft crimes of robbery and burglary, as well as the related crimes of extortion and trespass. The learning objectives for Chapter 14 are

LO 1. Describe what facts separate robbery from common theft.

LO 2. Articulate when robbery becomes armed or aggravated robbery.

LO 3. List the requirements for home invasion robbery.

LO 4. Articulate when purse snatching or pickpocketing can become robbery.

LO 5. Distinguish robbery from extortion.

LO 6. List the elements of the general burglary offense under the common law.

LO 7. Describe ways current state criminal codes modified the common law burglary offense.

LO 8. Distinguish criminal trespass from defiant trespass.

Bank robbers come in all sizes and disguises. Here, Darth Vader demands cash from the bank teller. Unlike most robbers, however, this bank robber brandishes a weapon. Most bank robberies do not involve weapons but only notes to the cashier demanding cash.

Gary Coleman walked into a bank, approached a teller, and handed the teller a clear plastic bag. He then said, "I need you to do me a favor. Put the money in this bag." The teller put $1472.00 in the bag. An assistant manager approached the teller's location, and Coleman said, "Ma'am stop where you are and don't move any farther." She did, and Coleman ran out of the bank. The incident lasted about 45 seconds.

Coleman was arrested and charged with bank robbery under the Missouri robbery statute. It defines robbery as "forcibly" stealing property. Coleman was convicted of robbery, and appealed his conviction, contending he did not "forcibly" steal anything. What should the result be on appeal? What does "forcibly" mean in this context? What circumstances support the use of force by Coleman? What circumstances point the other way? If Coleman "forcibly" robbed the bank, does it follow that every theft is robbery? See *State v. Coleman*, 463 S.W.3d 353 (Mo. 2015).

In this chapter we learn the elements of many of the crimes involving theft or other taking of property.

Crimes against property occur in a variety of ways, with or without the presence of violence. The manner in which the crime occurs can change the name of the crime or the punishment for it.

For example, the value of the property taken is often important in determining if the crime is a felony or misdemeanor. In the case of burglary, the time when the crime occurs (night or day), or the manner of gaining entry to the premises where the burglary occurs (breaking a door or window or walking through an unlocked door) can aggravate the crime and resulting punishment.

We will study many of these different elements in this chapter.

ROBBERY

Robbery Forcible stealing.

Robbery is forcible stealing. It is one of the most frequent crimes of violence in the United States. The common law crime of robbery was defined before the early English courts had defined larceny. The Model Penal Code, § 222.1, defines robbery as follows:

1. Robbery Defined. A person is guilty of robbery if, in the course of committing a theft, he:

(a) inflicts serious bodily harm upon another; or

(b) threatens another with or purposely puts him in fear of immediate serious bodily injury; or

(c) commits or threatens immediately to commit any felony of the first or second degree.

An act shall be deemed "in the course of committing a theft" if it occurs in an attempt to commit theft or in flight after the attempt or commission.

The usual elements incorporated into robbery statutes by the states include

- A taking and carrying away (only a slight movement of the property is needed)[1]
- of the property of another
- with intent to steal
- from the person or from the presence of the victim
- by the use of force against the person, or
- with the threat of the use of imminent force, to compel the victim to acquiesce in the taking and carrying away of the property.

Simple robbery, also called strong-arm robbery or mugging, is distinguished in most state statutes from the aggravated form of robbery, commonly called **armed robbery**. Armed robbery carries penalties that are more severe than those for simple robbery. Some of the statutory distinctions various states use in distinguishing between armed robbery and simple robbery are the following:

armed robbery Forcible stealing combined with the use of a deadly or dangerous weapon, or which results in serious bodily injury to another.

- That the perpetrator was armed with a "dangerous" or "deadly" weapon
- That the perpetrator intended to kill or wound if the victim resisted
- That the perpetrator did actually inflict a bodily injury[2]

State statutes differ on what is required for a conviction of armed robbery or aggravated robbery, where the presence or use of a "weapon" or "deadly weapon" is the basis for increasing the crime from simple robbery to armed robbery. The issue arises when a robber either (1) brandishes a toy or simulated weapon, like a starter pistol or (2) states that he has a weapon, but does not actually show the weapon, and it later turns out the robber did not have a weapon.

One approach, called the objective approach, requires that the defendant actually possessed a deadly weapon during the robbery. An example of that approach is the definition *of weapon* for purposes of the Montana armed robbery statute, MCA § 45-2-101(76). That section has been interpreted as requiring proof that the defendant actually possessed a weapon, something "readily capable of producing death or serious bodily injury." See *In re L. S.*[3] A similar result was reached by the New York Court of Appeals in the 2011 case of *People v. Grant,*[4] where the court held that simply saying, "I have a gun. Fill the bag. Don't say anything or I'll shoot" did not satisfy the New York first-degree (armed) robbery statute. Such a threat would satisfy the requirements for a third-degree (simple) robbery conviction, but not a first-degree conviction, the court held.

More commonly, states have adopted the subjective approach, which requires proof only that the defendant appeared to have a deadly weapon, such as a firearm. The Georgia armed robbery statute, Ga. Code Ann. § 16-8-41(a), states that the crime occurs if the defendant has a weapon, or "any replica . . . or device having the appearance of such a weapon." In *Kirk v. State,* 610 S.E.2d 604 (Ga. App. 2005), the court held that the defendant must give some physical manifestation of a weapon, but it was the reasonable apprehension by the victim that determined if it appeared a weapon was being used. In *State v. Wren,* 32 P.3d 717 (Kan. App. 2001), the Court interpreted the Kansas armed robbery statute, KSA § 21-3427, as requiring that the victim reasonably believed the robber had a firearm or dangerous weapon.

It is generally held that some indication or representation of a weapon is needed to make a crime armed robbery. In *State v. Muldrow,* 559 S.E.2d 847 (S.C. 2002), the defendant walked into a convenience store and handed the clerk a note that said "give me all your cash or I'll shoot you." He did not show a gun. The court reversed his conviction under the South Carolina armed robbery statute, which defined armed robbery as "alleging . . . he was armed while using a representation of a deadly weapon." The court said, "[w]ords alone are not sufficient" to support a conviction for armed robbery.

The Illinois legislature resolved the "actual" weapon problem by enacting both an armed robbery statute, 720 ILCS 5/18-2(a), which requires carrying an actual weapon, and an aggravated robbery statute, 720 ILCS 5/18-5(a), which only requires that the robber "indicate" he has a weapon, whether or not he actually does. See *People v. Gray,* 806 N.E.2d 753 (Ill. App. 2004), *appeal denied,* 823 N.E.2d 694 (Ill. 2004).

Finally, it is clear that the fact that a firearm used by a robber is unloaded is not relevant to a conviction for armed robbery. In *McLaughlin v. United States,*[5] the U.S. Supreme Court held that the "dangerous weapon" requirement in the federal bank robbery statute, 18 U.S.C. § 2113(d), was satisfied by an unloaded gun.

Changes in Bank Robbery

In 2014, 3961 bank robberies occurred in the United States, which was about a 10% decrease from 2011. The great majority of the 4347 persons participating in the bank robberies were male; only 349 were female. The predominant method was presentation of a demand note (2179), accompanied by the threat of the use of a weapon (1666). However, in only 930 cases was a weapon actually brandished by a robber. There were 63 people injured in bank robberies, and 13 people died. Ten of those deaths were perpetrators, two were bank employees, and one was a customer. See *Crime In America, FBI Bank Crime Statistics for 2014*, March 9, 2015.

The image of the gun-wielding, masked bank robber forcing all the bank employees to lie on the floor while the bank vault is opened is one of the most common images of the crime of robbery. In fact, as a method of bank robbery, that image has changed, as the statistics stated above show. Most bank robberies are "note" jobs, where the robber presents a note to a bank employee demanding money under a threat of violence.

The identity of the robber also has changed from the classic image of a violent, career criminal. Perpetrators of note jobs have included a New York housewife, a 91-year-old man in Texas, a Florida golf pro, and a former college basketball player and his pre-med student girlfriend. Law enforcement officers have speculated that these "amateurs" have turned to bank robbery as a way to solve financial problems because they know bank tellers have been told to surrender money from their cash drawers on demand. The average take in a bank robbery is between $5,000 and $7,000; banks lose about $30–40 million a year to bank robbers. By contrast, banks lose about $700 million each year to check fraud schemes.

More than half of all bank robbers are apprehended each year. Better bank surveillance cameras, more undercover guards, and dye packs that explode and color stolen money have all contributed to the increased number of bank robbers captured. The most recent advance has been the implantation of global positioning devices in the money given to robbers, which enables investigators to follow the money with their laptops. These devices were used in only 558 of the 2011 robberies.

The *Chicago Police Department Training Bulletin* lists the following factors that favor a robber:

- He or she can carry out the crime swiftly.
- He or she will usually leave few clues that would lead to his or her arrest.
- The robbery is committed in such a short period that the victim and witnesses sometimes do not have sufficient time and composure to view the offender so as to furnish an accurate description to the police.
- The probability of interruption is limited because of the short time.[6]

Distinguishing Robbery from Theft or Larceny

Under the common law, robbery was distinguished from theft or larceny by reference to the use of force, or the threat of force, in the "taking" of the property. Thus, in charging the crime of robbery, under the common law it must be shown that (1) property was taken from the victim or taken in the presence of the victim and (2) the use of force or the threat of force was used in the taking.

In the 2011 case of *Spencer v. State*[7] the Maryland Supreme Court held that under the common law definition of robbery, still used in Maryland, a defendant did not use the "threat of force" when he said to a Jiffy Lube cashier, "Don't say nothing." In response to this statement the cashier handed the defendant the cash drawer and the defendant left the premises. The court said that if this statement, without any other expressed or implied threat of force, satisfied the robbery definition, the distinction between theft and robbery would virtually be eliminated. The court reversed the defendant's conviction for robbery.

The common law "taking" requirement for a robbery conviction has been changed by many state statutes. A 2012 Michigan case illustrates what is called the "course of conduct" definition of robbery. The defendant entered a tobacco store with his hand in his pocket and told the clerk "You know what this is, just give me what I want." The clerk refused to give the defendant any money, and the defendant fled the store without taking anything. The defendant was convicted of armed robbery.

On appeal the Michigan Supreme Court affirmed the conviction, stating that while the common law required a completed theft, the Michigan robbery and armed robbery statutes defined robbery to include use of force or threat of force "during the course of committing" a larceny. Under this statute, it is not a requirement that the robbery be successful, the court held. The court stated that the legislature clearly recognized that the use or threat of force during a larceny were harms independent of the larceny, and thus treated it as severely as a completed larceny. The court noted twenty-three states have similar provisions, as does the Model Penal Code in § 222.[8]

The timing of the "force" used in a theft remains an issue. In some states, the required force must be part of the "taking," that is, the force must occur during the period the property is taken from the victim. For example, in the 2010 case of *Hobson v. Commonwealth,*[9] the Kentucky Supreme Court reversed a robbery conviction where the only force used by the defendant was in an attempt to escape from the robbery scene. The court held that under the Kentucky statute the force must be part of the "taking."

Florida's robbery statute applies to a theft if force is used (or threatened) at any time during the taking of the property or in flight after the taking. In *Rockmore v. State*, 140 So. 3d 979 (Fla. 2014), the Florida Supreme Court affirmed a robbery conviction where the defendant displayed a weapon to pursuing security officers who observed defendant steal property from a store. The court rejected the defendant's argument that because he had thrown the stolen property to the ground while running away, his display of the weapon was not part of the robbery. The court said that the defendant's actions were a "continuous series of events" under the robbery statute, and thus showing the weapon was part of the robbery transaction.

Many states and the MPC follow the "transactional" theory of robbery. Under this theory, the "force" needed to make a theft crime robbery could be present during any part of the "transaction," and would include force used to either retain the property or escape after the "taking" had occurred. In the 2011 case of *Commonwealth v. Rogers,* the Massachusetts Supreme Judicial Court held that force used in escaping from a robbery scene satisfied the force requirement for robbery.[10]

Carjacking: A New Name for an Old Crime

Thieves have been stealing cars from their owners or occupants by force or fear of force for years. These cases did not fit easily into theft or robbery criminal statutes because the thief often did not intend to keep the car permanently. (Figure 14.1 describes the various types of car and vehicle theft.) It is generally true that in most years more than 90 percent of the vehicles taken in carjackings were returned.

Broken Up By
- chop-shop operations, in which professionals cut up the vehicle for parts. Because nothing is left of the vehicle, the criminals are called "buzzards." Chop-shop operations are generally believed to be under the control of organized criminal groups.
- strippers, who "strip" cars for some of the easily resalable parts, such as tires, wheels, doors, fenders, hoods, radios, stereos, and spark plugs. Strippers are considered semi-professional; some are drug addicts who sell car parts to finance their habits. Stripped cars are generally recovered by owners.

Exported from the United States
200,000 vehicles are exported to other countries, where the vehicles or the parts sell at prices much higher than in the United States.

Abandoned/Returned/Recovered
- after use by a joyrider (once the biggest offender but now estimated to be responsible for 10 percent of missing cars)
- after being used for a crime
- after being stripped
- after a breakdown or being damaged

What Happens to Stolen Cars and Vehicles?
In 2014, 689,527 cars were stolen in the United States. This is a marked decline from the highest reported year, 1991, when 1,661,738 cars were stolen.

Phony Car Thefts
Car owners hide or abandon their vehicles and then falsely report them stolen in hopes of collecting insurance. Estimates range that from 15 percent to as high as 30 percent of reported thefts are phony.

Used on Streets and Highways of the United States
- with original VINs and different plates
- with identification numbers salvaged from similar make and model cars in junkyards ("salvage and switch" operations)

FIGURE 14.1 Car and Vehicle Theft in the United States

Source: The National Insurance Crime Bureau, 2015.

carjacking Forcibly taking possession of a motor vehicle in the possession of another against his or her will with intent either to permanently or temporarily deprive the person of possession.

To remedy the limited applicability of standard theft statutes, most states and the federal government passed statutes making **carjacking** a separate offense. Congress passed the Anti-Car Theft Act of 1992, 18 U.S.C. 2119, in response to the more than 35,000 carjackings completed or attempted each year in the United States. An example of a carjacking statute is the following California law:

Carjacking is the felonious taking of a motor vehicle in the possession of another, from his or her person or in the immediate presence . . . against his or her will and with the intent to either permanently or temporarily deprive the person . . . of his or her possession, accomplished by force or fear.[11]

Carjacking statutes raise several problems not found in standard theft statutes concerning the requisite elements of the offense. Some of these are the following:

- A taking occurs even if the true owner of the car remains in the car during the carjacking.
- The true owner is in "possession" of the car even if he is alighting from the car when the carjacking occurs or outside the car. In the 2009 case of *People v. Magallanes*[12] the owner was standing outside her car attempting to put her child in a car seat when the defendant stole her car. The court affirmed his conviction for carjacking.
- Where the defendant entered the victim's car and sat in the passenger seat and gave her directions on where to drive her car, the court in *Corbin v. United States*, 120 A.3d 588 (D.C. 2015), held the elements of carjacking had not been proved. Since the driver willfully followed the defendant's directions, he did not at any time take possession of the car, as required by the D.C. carjacking statute.
- In *People v. Lopez*, 79 P.3d 548 (Cal. 2003), the California Supreme Court reversed earlier decisions under the carjacking statute and held that movement of the car, however slight, was an element of the crime. Florida's statute, FSA § 812.133, has been interpreted as not requiring movement of the car. See *Price v. State*, 816 So. 2d 738 (Fla. App. 2002).[13]
- A carjacker may also be convicted of kidnapping if the owner of the car is purposely kept in the car and the car is moved a substantial distance from the vicinity of the carjacking. In the 2012 case of *People v. Ortiz*[14] the court affirmed a kidnapping conviction because the purpose of the carjacking and kidnapping was to use both crimes to force payment of an illegal drug sale debt. However, movement of the car owner merely as "incidental" to the carjacking is not kidnapping. See *People v. Medina*, 161 P.3d 186 (Cal. 2007).

HOME INVASION ROBBERIES

home invasion robbery Robbery of persons inhabiting a dwelling.

Home invasion robbery differs from similar crimes, such as burglary or breaking and entering, in how the crime is defined. For example, the Illinois Criminal Code defines home invasion as an unlawful entering of a dwelling by a person who knows someone was present therein, and armed with a dangerous weapon either uses or threatens use of force or injures someone inside the home.[15]

In some states, this difference means that a defendant can be convicted of both home invasion and another crime, such as armed violence during residential burglary, based on one unlawful entry. See *People v. Cunningham*, 851 N.E.2d 653 (Ill. App. 2006). Other states hold that conviction of home invasion bars conviction of related crimes such as residential burglary based on one unlawful entry. See *State v. Tuttle*, 177 So.3d 1246 (Fla. 2015). Florida courts also hold that only one conviction on a count of home invasion may be obtained, even if more than one person is in the home. See *Schulterbrandt v. State*, 984 So. 2d 542 (Fla. App. 2008). Other courts have reached the opposite result. See, for example, *Commonwealth. v. Antonmarch*, 874 N.E.2d 665 (Mass. App. 2007), which upheld convictions on two counts of home invasion based on the presence of two people in the home.

Purse Snatching, Pickpocketing, and Other Thefts from a Person

The crimes of robbery and theft have many common elements, such as the requirement that there be a "taking" with intent to deprive the owner of the property stolen. One principal difference between the crimes is, of course, the use of force to accomplish the "taking." Force is not part of theft, but it is part of robbery. Another difference is the penalty that results from the crime. Robbery is typically a felony, while theft can be a misdemeanor, depending on the value of the property. Those distinctions are important in crimes where some force must be used to take property from another person, but the force does not go beyond that needed to accomplish the taking. Purse snatching and similar crimes are examples of this distinction.

The majority rule in the United States is that crimes like purse snatching are not robberies unless some force is used that is greater than that needed to take the purse. In the case of *State v. Sein*,[16] the Supreme Court of New Jersey stated the majority rule as follows:

> [A] simple snatching or sudden taking of property from the person of another does not of itself involve sufficient force to constitute robbery, though the act may be robbery where a struggle ensues, the victim is injured in the taking, or the property is so attached to the victim's person or clothing as to create resistance to the taking.

An example of force in a purse snatching sufficient to satisfy a robbery conviction is *Jones v. Commonwealth*.[17] There, the court held that grabbing a woman's shoulder to jerk her around so that the defendant could snatch her purse was enough force to constitute robbery.

A few courts have adopted the rule that the snatching of a purse without the use of any other force is sufficient to permit a jury verdict on the charge of robbery. The Supreme Judicial Court of Massachusetts adopted this rule in the case of *Commonwealth v. Jones*.[18] In affirming the defendant's conviction of unarmed robbery for a purse snatching, the court stated:

> The question whether the snatching or sudden taking of property constitutes robbery has arisen in other jurisdictions although not in Massachusetts. In Kentucky, the rule is that snatching, without more, involves the requisite element of force to permit a jury verdict on a charge of robbery. (Citations omitted.) According to the rule prevailing in most jurisdictions, however, snatching does not involve sufficient force to constitute robbery, unless the victim resists the taking or sustains physical injury, or unless the article taken is so attached to the victim's clothing as to afford resistance. . . .

> We prefer the Kentucky rule on purse snatching. The majority jurisdiction rule, in looking to whether or not the victim resists, we think, wrongly emphasizes the victim's opportunity to defend himself over the willingness of the purse snatcher to use violence if necessary.

sudden snatching A form of robbery where force is not used beyond that needed to take property from another person.

In some states this issue is resolved by adding **"sudden snatching"** to the general robbery statute. Georgia's robbery statute, Ga. Code Ann. § 16-8-40, defines robbery in the usual manner as taking by use of force, but includes a taking "by sudden snatching." Florida addressed the force issue by passing a "robbery by sudden snatching" statute, FSA § 812.131, which explicitly does not require any use of force beyond that needed to take the property, and does not need any showing the victim resisted the taking. It is a third-degree felony, unless the perpetrator carried a firearm, in which case it is a second-degree felony. In *Walker v. State,* 933 So. 2d 1236 (Fla. App. 2006), the court reversed a conviction under the robbery by sudden snatching statute, holding that a conviction under the statute required that the victim knew her purse was being snatched.

Even if not treated as a robbery, theft from the person is punished more severely than ordinary theft, and it is a felony in most states, whether the amount taken is very small or very large. State legislative bodies and courts are well aware that injury can easily occur to a victim who is often startled by the theft and may seek to protect his or her property.

Common forms of theft from a person are pickpocketing and purse snatching. However, theft of a purse from a shopping cart was also held to be theft from the person when the victim's hand was on the cart.[19]

Extortion

extortion Obtaining property by threats of future harm. It differs from robbery in that robbery requires threat of immediate harm.

Extortion is a crime of threatened force, fear, or violence. The name comes from the Latin *torquere,* which means "to wrench or twist." The term *torture* also can be traced to this Latin root. State statutes have different definitions of extortion, but they all make it a crime to obtain "property" (usually money) of another by causing that person to consent to transfer the property because of fear or threats that the extortionist will take some action in the future. The nature of the threat varies from state to state. New York's extortion statute, McKinney's Penal Law § 155(e), lists nine kinds of threats used in "instilling a fear" of extortionate acts. The most common kinds of threats listed in state statutes are bodily injury or death, damage to property, false criminal accusations, exposure of a secret that would subject the victim to contempt or ridicule, or economic harm.

Robbery and extortion are similar in that they are both methods used to obtain money or property illegally. Extortion differs from robbery in these ways:

- There is a threat to inflict a future harm (extortion) rather than an immediate harm (robbery).
- In robbery, the victim must immediately comply with the criminal demand, or violence will immediately occur. In extortion, future compliance is demanded to avoid future harm to a third party or to the victim.
- Robbery must be committed in the presence of the victim, whereas extortion can be committed over the telephone or by mail (such conduct, however, immediately makes the offense also a federal violation).

The harm that is threatened differs also. In robbery, immediate force is threatened or used against the owner or victim to compel the victim to acquiesce in the taking of the property. In extortion, the victim must pay the amount demanded to avoid or prevent

- Destruction of property. (Bombing a restaurant or business place is a standard practice of organized crime, which could result in a serious loss of life and injuries if the restaurant or business place were open for business.)

- Kidnapping or injuries to the victim or the victim's family or friends.
- Accusations of crime, and so forth.
- Damage to the good name or business reputation of the victim or the victim's family.
- Exposure of a secret or failing of the victim or family.[20]

The U.S. Congress has passed a federal extortion act. The Hobbs Act (18 U.S.C.A. 1951(b)(2)) defines extortion as "the obtaining of property of another, with his consent, induced by wrongful use of actual or threatened force, violence, or fear." When Congress enacted the Hobbs Act, the statute was aimed primarily at gangsters who were extorting protection money from businesses. That is, the business would not be bombed or receive other violence if the protection money was paid.

The Hobbs Act also covers other kinds of threatened violence. For example, in the 2010 case of *United States v. Markle*[21] a federal court of appeals upheld the conviction under the Hobbs Act of a member of a labor union who threatened members of a rival union in order to keep the other union off a job site the defendant's union wanted to work on exclusively. While the court recognized the Supreme Court had carved out an exception to the Hobbs Act for union violence used to obtain legitimate labor objectives, the court held that the exception did not apply to illegitimate objectives.[22]

In *Sekhar v. United States*, 133 S. Ct. 2720 (2013) the U.S. Supreme Court held that a conviction under the Hobbs Act for extortion requires proof that the defendant made threats to obtain "property of another." Property under the Hobbs Act, the Court said, must be something of value that can be transferred from one person to another. The defendant in *Sekhar* made threats in anonymous emails sent to the general counsel of a retirement program with the intent to coerce him into recommending to the retirement program that it invest in the defendant's company. Whatever crime that was, the Court concluded, it was not extortion under the Hobbs Act. It reversed the defendant's conviction for extortion.

Extortion by Intimidation

Extortion is often accomplished by threats of violence, but other kinds of threats or coercive tactics can constitute extortion. For example, in *State v. Gant*,[23] a defendant was charged with extortion under the Iowa extortion statute, Iowa Code Section 711.4(6). That section states that a person commits the crime of extortion if the person takes certain actions for the purpose of obtaining anything of value from another person. Among the prohibited actions is "threaten[ing] to testify or provide information or to withhold testimony or information with respect to another's legal claim or defense." In *Gant,* a garage owner had tools and equipment stolen. Gant told the owner he could provide information concerning the location of the stolen goods but would do so only if the owner paid him $200. The court found this to be a threat to withhold information about the owner's claim to the stolen goods and affirmed the defendant's conviction for extortion.

The threat must be wrongful; that is, it must threaten some action that is not legally protected. It would not be extortion, for example, to threaten to sue a debtor if the debtor did not pay a debt on time. However, if the person making the threat is not privileged to do so, it can be extortion. In *State v. Pauling*,[24] the court held that a man who threatened to publish nude photographs of his former girlfriend if she did not repay a debt could be charged with extortion. Publishing the photographs was not protected as free speech, because its only purpose was to threaten the girlfriend.

The crime of extortion does require a threat, and the receipt of property from another without a threat is not extortion. For example, in *People v. Hesslink*[25] the court reversed the conviction of a defendant who, posing as a police officer, forced a prostitute to perform oral sex on him. The prostitute also gave the defendant money in the hope he would not arrest her, and based on that payment he was charged with extortion. The court held that because the defendant did not demand money under threat of "arrest," the money paid by the prostitute was not the result of a threat and could not sustain a conviction for extortion.

In some states extortion can be charged based on threats of future economic harm. In the 2009 case of *State v. Hynes*[26] the New Hampshire Supreme Court upheld the extortion conviction of a lawyer who threatened to bring a civil action based on a "gender discrimination" claim against a beauty salon. The New Hampshire extortion statute, like the New York statute discussed earlier, contained a listing of eight specific kinds of extortionate acts, plus a "catch-all" provision based on threatened acts that would not benefit the person making the threats but would harm the person threatened. The lawyer demanded $1,000 to avoid filing the action. The court said that the lawyer's threatened claim was groundless, because the lawyer had not himself used the salon, and he didn't have a client who had been discriminated against by the salon. As a result, the defendant would not benefit from the threatened action, and the salon would be harmed. This made the lawyer's actions extortion, the court held.

Other courts have reached a different conclusion. In the 2008 case of *Rendelman v. State*,[27] the Maryland Supreme Court held that under the Maryland extortion statute, CL § 3-701(a), threatening to file a lawsuit unless a "settlement" payment was made on a "claim" was not extortion, even if the claim was made in bad faith. The court reasoned that while a threat to file a meritless lawsuit is a threat to inflict economic harm, the extortion statute states that the threat must be "wrongful." Because it is not illegal to file a lawsuit, even in bad faith, the court concluded that the threat to do so cannot be a "wrongful threat of economic injury." The court noted that this is also the result reached by federal courts in prosecutions under the Hobbs Act based on filing frivolous civil lawsuits, citing *United States v. Pendergraft*,[28] 297 F.3d 1198 (11th Cir. 2002).

Burglary

burglary Unlawful entry into the premises of another with intent to steal or commit a felony. Two hundred years ago in England, an illegal entry into the home of another by force and at night was punishable by death if the entry was done to steal or commit a felony.

Burglary is among the most frequently committed major crimes in the United States, with more than 3.5 million burglaries committed every year. Because burglary is a crime of stealth and opportunity, the national clearance rate, as reported by the Uniform Crime Report, is low, at approximately 15 percent. (That is, arrests are made in only approximately 15 percent of the burglaries reported.)

Burglary is a crime committed by both amateurs and professionals. It is committed against residences (homes and apartments) and commercial premises (offices, business places, and so on). It is committed not only at night but also during the day.

Under the old common law, burglary was punished by death. Because of the severe penalty, burglary required a breaking under the common law. It was also limited to the dwelling house of another, at night, and with intent to commit a felony.

All states have modified and changed the definition of burglary in their jurisdictions, resulting in differences in the definitions of burglary in the United States.[29] The Uniform Crime Reporting Program defines burglary as "the unlawful entry of a structure to commit a felony or theft. The use of force to gain entry is not required to classify an offense as burglary."

Breaking

Under common law, a "breaking" or a "breach" was required to constitute the crime of burglary. An entry through an open door or window without the consent of the person living in or controlling the building was not a breaking. All states have abolished the requirement of breaking in their general burglary statutes. For example, the Texas burglary statute, VTCA Penal Code § 30.02, defines burglary as "entry" into a residence or building that is not open to the public without consent and with intent to commit a felony, theft, or assault. In *Clark v. State,*[30] the court held that entry through an open door can be burglary, if not open to the public and occurs without the owner's consent. In the 2010 case of *Martinez v. State,*[31] the court said the "entry" occurs as soon as some part of the burglar's body, such as a hand or a foot, crosses the home's threshold.

Some states, however, continue to use an act of "breaking" to gain entry as an aggravated form of burglary in addition to their regular or simple burglary statutes.

Unlawful Entry into Premises

Because burglary is a form of trespass, an unlawful entry into the premises must take place. An entry could be made by inserting a hand or arm (or even the tip of a screwdriver) into the premises. For example, suppose X threw a brick through a jewelry store window and then inserted his hand and arm through the broken window to obtain watches and rings from the window display. This would be an unlawful entry that would justify a conviction of X for burglary of the jewelry store.

Suppose that instead of using his arm, X inserted a cane and began removing watches and rings by hooking them with the cane. Would this be an entry that justifies a conviction of burglary? Most courts would hold that this was an entry, because the cane was an extension of X's body inserted into the store to carry out a criminal purpose.[32]

Entry does not require a substantial movement into the home's interior. For example, in the 2016 case of *State v. Holt*, 368 P.3d 409 (N.M. 2016) the court held that a defendant "entered" a residence for purposes of the breaking and entering statute once his fingertips entered the space between an outer window screen and the interior window.

Any element of a crime may be proved by circumstantial evidence. In the U.S. Supreme Court case of *United States v. Edwards,* someone burglarized a U.S. post office using a pry bar on a window.[33] The defendant had in his possession property stolen from the post office. Direct evidence of the break-in could not be shown, because no witnesses were available. However, crime lab tests showed paint and wood fragments on the defendant's clothing similar to the paint and wood on the post office window. A jury held that this evidence proved unlawful entry, and the defendant's conviction was affirmed.

In the case of *State v. Tixier,* police officers responded to a triggered burglar alarm within a minute.[34] They found a small hole near the door-opening mechanism of a

EXAMPLES OF DIFFERENT THEFT CRIMES

- Theft: A man lays his ring on the edge of a sink while washing his hands. Another man takes the ring and runs off while the owner is not looking (felony if ring's value is more than the amount determined by state statute).
- Theft from Person: A ring is taken from a pocket by a pickpocket or taken in a purse by a purse-snatcher (felony in most or all states, regardless of value of ring).
- Simple Robbery (Mugging): A woman is accosted in an alley by a menacing robber who threatens to beat her if she does not give the thief the ring on her finger (felony regardless of value of ring if she gave up the ring out of fear).
- Armed Robbery: A woman is held at gunpoint by a robber who demands that she give him the ring on her finger (higher-degree felony than mugging).

garage. The defendant was found hiding among tires stacked near the door. The piece of the door that had been removed was found near the defendant. It was concluded that the defendant had used an instrument to penetrate the building. In affirming the defendant's burglary conviction, the court held:

> Evidence of a break-in by use of an instrument which penetrates into the building is, in our opinion, evidence of entry into the building. The sufficiency of this evidence is not destroyed by a failure to prove that the instrument was used to steal something from the building or to commit another felony. Such proof is unnecessary because burglary does not depend upon actions after the entry; the crime is complete when there is an unauthorized entry with the requisite intent.

In the case of *Champlin v. State,* the defendant entered a hotel lobby open to the general public 24 hours a day and removed a television set and a cash register.[35] Instead of charging the defendant with theft, a prosecutor charged the defendant with burglary. In reversing the conviction for burglary, the court pointed out that the defendant's conduct, although illegal, was not burglary, because the premises were open to the general public.

The Dwelling House of Another

A "dwelling house" is a place where people live and sleep. Under the common law, unlawful entry into and theft from a business place would not be a burglary, because a business place is not a dwelling house. Hotel rooms and apartments are dwelling houses, because people live and sleep in such places. A new building into which no one has yet moved has been held not to be a dwelling house.[36]

All the states and the federal government have changed the common law restricting burglary to only dwelling houses. Today, virtually all buildings are contained within the scope of the crime of burglary (and some states, such as California, also include vehicles). Under Model Penal Code § 221.1 it is a felony of the third degree if one unlawfully enters any building with the intent to commit a crime. It is felony of the second degree if the unlawful entry occurs "in the dwelling of another at night."

Many states also punish the burglary of an inhabited building more severely than that of an uninhabited building. In the case of *People v. Lewis,* the court held that the question of "inhabited" or "uninhabited" turns not on the immediate presence or absence of people in the building but rather on the character of the use of the building.[37] In the 2010 case of *State v. Jackson*[38] the court reversed a burglary conviction under the Ohio burglary statute, which applied to a break-in of a building where inhabitants are "present or likely to be present." In that case, the defendant broke into a mobile home, but the owner had not regularly used the mobile home as a residence for several weeks, because he was away caring for his ailing parents. The court stated that just because a building is a "residence" does not mean persons are "likely to be present" in the building.

Nighttime

The common law required that burglary be committed at night, which was defined as the time between sunset and sunrise. An entry into a dwelling house with an accompanying theft during the day could not be charged as a burglary under this definition. The defendant, however, could be charged with the separate crimes of trespass, stealing, and, depending on the circumstances, criminal damage to property. Today, about half the burglaries in the United States are committed during the day, and all jurisdictions recognize daylight burglaries. Some states impose more severe penalties for nighttime burglaries.

Intent to Commit a Felony

Common law burglary required proof of intent to commit a felony. Most states and the federal government have broadened this element of burglary. Some states now

YOU BE THE JUDGE

Should you grant the motion? Or does "any house" actually mean "any house of another"? See **State v. White, 330 P.3d 482 (Nev. 2014)**

You are a Nevada trial judge. The defendant has been charged with various crimes, based on the following facts: He and his wife were separated. They agreed the couple's children would live with the wife in the marital house, which was owned by the defendant, during the week, and that the defendant would spend the weekends at the house. However, this arrangement broke down when another man began living with the wife at the house. After making threats, in the early morning hours on a Friday, defendant entered the house, and shot his wife and the other man. The wife died from the gunshot wounds.

One of the charges against the defendant is burglary, under the Nevada burglary statute. It defines burglary as entering "any house or building" with intent to commit a crime. Defendant has filed a pretrial motion to dismiss the burglary charge, contending one cannot be guilty of burglary of one's own house. The state contends the statue says "any house," and that is what it means.

INTENT TO STEAL IN A BURGLARY CHARGE

The general rule of law is that intent to steal cannot be inferred from the single fact of an unlawful entry into a building. Additional circumstances must be considered, such as these:

- Type of Entry: Was it forcible?
- Manner of Entry: Was there a breaking or splintering?
- Place of Entry: Was it the rear or side of the building?
- Type of Building: Did the building contain items that a thief would be interested in stealing?
- Time of Entry: Was it the middle of the night or the middle of the day?
- Conduct of the Defendant When Interrupted: Did he or she attempt to hide or escape?

Source: This material is adapted from a chart originated by the Supreme Court of Wisconsin in the case of *State v. Barclay*.[39]

require that the state prove intent to steal or commit a felony. Others provide that the intent must be to commit a crime (misdemeanor or felony). Other state statutes specify crimes, whereas still others require that intent to commit a larceny, theft, or other felony be shown.

Courts have held that whether the state must prove intent to commit a specific crime depends on the language of the statute. For example, in the 2009 case of *State v. Chatelain*,[40] the Oregon Supreme Court held that the Oregon burglary statute,

WHAT IS THE STATE OBLIGATED TO PROVE?

In addition to the intent or mental element of each crime . . .			
In Order to Charge	**That There was a Stealing (Taking and Carrying Away)?**	**The Value of the Property Taken?**	**Elements Other Than the Crime of Stealing?**
Theft/Larceny	Yes	Yes	No
Robbery	Yes	Not necessary as long as the property was something of value	Yes, (1) that the taking was by force or threat of force and (2) that the taking was from the victim's person or presence
Burglary	No, only an intent to steal or to commit a felony as required by the statutes of that state	Not necessary as long as the property was something of value (or there was an intent to steal)	Yes, requires a showing of an unlawful entry into a dwelling or building (or an unlawful remaining after closing)

which requires a showing that the defendant entered with "the intent to commit a crime therein," meant that the state must prove what specific crime a defendant was intending to commit. The court said that proof of the unlawful entry by itself does not satisfy the elements of the burglary statute.

On the other hand, because a New Jersey burglary statute required only that the defendant have entered with a "purpose to commit an offense," the court in *State v. Robinson*[41] held that the state need not prove that any specific crime was intended. General intent can be inferred from the circumstances of the break-in itself. For example, a defendant who is apprehended in a warehouse in the middle of the night with an armful of merchandise leaves little question concerning intent in that particular situation.

The intent to steal is not always presumed. In the Pennsylvania case of *Commonwealth v. Muniem,* the defendant, who had been found in an empty warehouse about noon, was convicted of burglary.[42] The door was half open and the defendant was walking out when the police arrived. He was cooperative, did not run, and had nothing in his possession. The owner testified that nothing was missing. The defendant stated that he had to go to the toilet and had looked for a lavatory in the empty building. The defendant was thirty-three years old, employed, and married, and he had no prior record. In reversing the conviction and ordering the defendant discharged, the court stated:

> In the instant case, the only evidence produced against the appellant is his presence, perhaps as a trespasser, in a vacant building in daylight at about noontime. When found by the police, he was walking to the open door by which he testified he entered the building. The owner of the building testified that nothing was missing and there was no evidence of a forcible entry, or possession of any burglary tools, other tools or anything else.
>
> Each case must stand on its own facts in determining whether the Commonwealth has sustained its burden of proof. At best, the evidence of the Commonwealth may give rise to suspicion and conjecture of guilt but most certainly does not have such volume and quality capable of reasonably and naturally justifying an inference of a willful and malicious entry into a building with the intent to commit a felony so as to overcome the presumption of innocence and establish guilt beyond a reasonable doubt of the crime of burglary.

Proof of Burglary When Other Crimes Are Committed

As a trespass offense, burglary is most often committed by a defendant who steals or who has an intent to steal. Criminals, however, enter private premises for criminal purposes other than to steal. Offenders have entered the premises of others with intent to commit rape, arson, or other serious felonies. In the 2008 case of *State v. Jacobs,*[43] the court affirmed a conviction of burglary, holding that evidence showed the defendant entered the victim's hotel room with the intent to assault her and steal her purse.

The charge of burglary is sometimes one of multiple serious charges against a defendant who went on a criminal rampage in a private home or business place. In the *Jacobs* case discussed above prosecutors charged the defendant with both forcible rape and aggravated burglary, based on the unlawful entry and resulting battery of the victim, which increased simple burglary to aggravated burglary under

FORMS OF THEFT

Theft/Larceny	Theft from the Person	Robbery[a] (Theft[b] by Force or Threat of Force)	Burglary (Trespass with Intent to Steal or to Commit a Felony)
• Ordinary theft (usually done secretly) • "Snatch and run" theft • Shoplifting • Theft from autos • Theft from buildings • Theft by fraud (con game) • Embezzlement • Theft by bailee • Fraud on innkeeper, restaurant • Looting—taking property from building that has been destroyed by disaster, riot, bombing, fire, tornado, and so on	• Purse snatching • Pickpocketing • "Rolling a drunk" (taking valuables from an intoxicated person or person in a stupor) • Taking valuables from injured, dead, or disabled people	• Mugging or yoking (strong-arm robbery) • Armed robbery (weapon shown or not shown) • Carjacking • Burglaries that turn into robberies • Purse snatching and pickpocketing in which such force is used against the person that it constitutes strong-arm robbery • Home invasion robbery	• Ordinary burglary (some states punish burglary committed at night more severely) • Armed burglary • Burglary in which an occupant of the building is injured • "Break and run" burglary (breaking store window and running off with property) • Newspapers use the term car burglary. Some states do have this crime. For example, N.J.S.A. 2C:18-1 includes "car" in the burglary statute, as does the Idaho burglary statute, I.C. § 18-1401.

[a]Depending on the laws of the state, sentences could be enhanced (increased) when there is concealment of identity (mask), a bulletproof garment is used, or a police scanner radio is used during the commission of the crime.
[b]In robberies of banks and stores, the terms counter-jumpers and take-over robberies (as distinguished from "single-teller" or "single-clerk" robberies) are sometimes used to describe the methods used by the robbers.

the Louisiana statute. The court held that while the defendant could be convicted of both forcible rape and simple burglary, the forcible rape could not be used as the basis for a conviction of aggravated burglary under the Double Jeopardy Clause.

The charge of burglary also offers prosecutors an alternative charge when doubt exists as to whether the state can prove attempted rape, murder, arson, or another crime. If X broke into W's apartment with the intent to rape her but found that she was not home, X could be charged with burglary if the state could prove his intent to commit a felony.

THE CRIME OF TRAFFICKING IN STOLEN GOODS

The crimes of trafficking in stolen goods are defined by the statutes of each state and ordinarily include (1) receiving (a single act), (2) concealing and possessing (continuing acts), and, in some states, (3) buying and transferring. In determining the statute of limitations for these offenses, the Supreme Court of Minnesota held in the 1981 case of *State v. Lawrence*, 312 N.W.2d 251:

> The crime commonly known as "receiving stolen property," when used in a shorthand sense, is a misnomer, since it includes a number of different legal concepts in addition to and separate from receiving. The offense includes not only receiving, but concealing; . . . it includes buying; and . . . it also includes possessing and transferring.
>
> The issue here is whether any of these terms may be deemed continuing in nature. The two most likely descriptions of defendant's conduct are possession and concealment. Does either, or both, apply? In answering this question we should keep in mind that a crime is not continuing in nature if not clearly so indicated by the legislature. . . .
>
> Both possessing and concealing are distinguishable from receiving in that the latter connotes a single act. Behind possessing and concealing, however, is the notion that property is being kept from someone in violation of a duty to return and this duty to return continues. One of the reasons for including possessing and concealing as crimes is to be able to prosecute even though the time has run out on receiving. Surely this serves the purpose of the statute, which is to deter trafficking in stolen goods.
>
> * * *
>
> We hold, therefore, that either concealing or possessing stolen goods is a continuing offense for the purpose of the statute of limitations. We hold this defendant may not assert the statute of limitations as a bar where he kept the goods he stole in his house and garage, thereby not only possessing the goods but making their discovery more difficult for the owner.

To convict a defendant of trafficking in stolen goods, the state is ordinarily required to prove

- That the property involved was stolen property
- That the defendant received, concealed, possessed, purchased, or transferred the property as forbidden by the statutes of that state
- That the defendant knew the property was stolen. "Stolen" means that the property was obtained as a result of a theft, burglary, robbery, or any other form of theft crime, such as shoplifting or obtaining property by deception.

The Fence and Fencing Stolen Property

Fence A person who traffics in stolen property (receiving, concealing, possessing, buying, transferring, and so on).

A **fence** is a person who traffics in stolen property (receiving, concealing, possessing, buying, transferring, and so on). A fence acts as a middleperson and pays the thief for stolen property, which the fence in turn attempts to merchandise at a profit. The compensation paid by the fence to the thief is usually a small fraction of the value of the goods. The report of the President's Commission on Law Enforcement and Administration of Justice makes the following observations regarding fencing in the United States:

Nearly all professional theft is undertaken with the aim of selling the goods thereafter. Although the thief himself may retail his stolen merchandise, he probably will prefer to sell to a fence. He thereby increases his safety by reducing the risk that he will be arrested with the goods in his possession, or that they will be stolen in turn from him. He also avoids the dangers associated with the disposal process itself. In addition, large quantities of goods which may be perishable or otherwise quickly lose their value, or for which there is a specialized demand, will require a division of labor and level of organization beyond the capacity of an individual thief operating as his own retailer. The professional thief thus needs a "middleman" in the same way and for some of the same reasons as the farmer, manufacturer, or other producer.

* * *

Some fences engage in fencing as a supplement to their legitimate businesses, often on a more or less regular basis. The consultants learned of clothing and appliance dealers who regularly serve as outlets for stolen goods. The major outlets for stolen jewels in one of the cities studied were reported to be legitimate jewelry merchants. Other fences deal primarily or wholly in stolen goods and are therefore professional criminals themselves.

Some narcotics pushers act as fences, taking stolen goods instead of cash for narcotics. While dealing with addicts is generally regarded as more dangerous than dealing with nonaddicts, it is also more profitable. The addict in need of a "fix" does not bargain well.

When Property Loses Its Character as Stolen Goods

United States v. Monasterski
U.S. Court of Appeals for the Sixth Circuit
(1977), 567 F.2d 677

Three juveniles were caught attempting to steal tires from a railroad boxcar. The juveniles cooperated with FBI agents and delivered some of the tires to the defendant, whom they identified as their prospective fence. The defendant was convicted of receiving stolen property (the tires). In reversing the defendant's conviction, the Sixth Circuit Court held that once the thieves were caught, the tires lost their character as stolen goods and could no longer support the defendant's conviction. The court further held:

In accord with the common law rule, one cannot be convicted of receiving stolen goods when actual physical possession of the stolen goods has been recovered by their owner or his agent before delivery to the intended receiver. We further hold, also in accord with the common law rule, that the term "agent" means any person with a right to possession or control over the goods.

(Continued)

The Alabama Supreme Court followed the common law rule that goods that had never been stolen or goods that had lost their stolen character could not support a conviction of the crime of receiving stolen property.

Florida, however, changed the common law and enacted a law taking away this defense from a person charged with the crime of dealing in stolen property. Florida Statutes (1995), § 812.028(3), permits criminal convictions in Florida for endeavoring to traffic in stolen property without proof by the state of Florida that the property was actually stolen.

Possession of Criminal or Burglary Tools

Most states have statutes making the possession of criminal or burglary tools a criminal offense. The usual elements of this crime are as follows:

- The defendant had a device or implement in his or her possession.
- This device or implement was suitable for or was capable of being used in committing burglary.
- The defendant intended to use this device or implement to break into a building, dwelling, or depository with the intent to steal.

Like the crime of receiving stolen property, possession of burglary tools is difficult to prove. The difficult element to prove in receiving stolen property is knowledge by the defendant that the property was stolen. In possession of burglary tools, the difficult element is intent by the defendant to use the tool for purposes of burglary. Possession of ordinary work tools is not ordinarily sufficient to justify a conviction for possession of burglary tools; there must be additional evidence of intent to use them to commit burglary.

Cases in which most convictions have been obtained can be divided into the following categories:

- The defendant was apprehended while committing or attempting to commit a burglary with the tool or had the tool in his or her actual or constructive possession.
- The defendant was in the possession of a specifically designed or adapted tool under circumstances in which a judge or jury could infer the tool's use for an illegal purpose of entry.

DESTROYING OR DAMAGING THE PROPERTY OF ANOTHER

No U.S. city, town, or village escapes the physical and psychological disfigurement vandalism brings to public and private property. Vandalism is a serious problem in most public transport systems, and it costs millions of dollars in large cities. Schools are often hit hard, with broken windows, break-ins, damaged property, and spray-painted walls.

Veteran law enforcement officers observe that vandalism (criminal damage to property) occurs in cycles. In the summertime, public parks are hit. Benches are piled up, debris is thrown into lagoons, and beaches are littered. If buildings are left vacant, they sometimes are vandalized to the point where they must be razed. Criminal damage to private property varies considerably and is a constant source of citizen complaints to law enforcement agencies.

Many states and cities have passed laws making parents of minors responsible for damage their child causes. Kansas imposes liability on the homeowner's insurance company, which gives the owner of damaged property the right to collect damages from the insurance company.

In 1990, one 18-year-old did more than $500,000 in damage by graffiti vandalism in Los Angeles. The Los Angeles city attorney said that it was "the worst case of graffiti vandalism we have seen in Los Angeles . . . or anywhere else in the nation [by a single individual]." Near Tampa, Florida, three teenagers pulled down more than a dozen traffic stop signs for kicks one night. Other teenagers driving home after bowling were killed when their car drove into an intersection and was hit broadside, killing the occupants. The teenagers who took down the stop sign were convicted of three counts of manslaughter.

Trespass

In its broad sense, the word *trespass* means an unlawful act against a person, property, or right of another. For example, court decisions today continue to speak of the trespassory taking of property, meaning that the property was wrongfully taken. Murder, assault, and battery are trespassory acts because they are wrongful and unlawful acts that violate the rights of other people.

trespass A wrongful intrusion on the land or into the premises of another person.

However, in its usual and more common use, **trespass** refers to a wrongful intrusion on the land or into the premises of another person. All states have statutes that reflect this usual and common concept of the offense, and when newspapers use the word, they usually mean it in this limited sense. The Washington statute, RCWA 9A.52.070, defines criminal trespass as follows: "a person is guilty of criminal trespass in the first degree if he knowingly enters or remains unlawfully in a building."

A variety of trespass statutes can be found in criminal codes and municipal ordinances. The trespass to land statutes make the unlawful entry on land (when the land has been posted or the person notified to stay off) a criminal offense if the entry or the remaining on the land is without the consent of the owner or the person in lawful possession. Trespass to dwelling statutes and ordinances forbid entry into homes and residences without the consent of an occupant.

Other trespass statutes and ordinances forbid entry into specific places, such as schools with classes in session, unless the person has legitimate business or is a parent. Trespass statutes generally have a section dealing with entry and also a section pertaining to "failure to depart."

The Crime of Defiant Trespass

defiant trespass Remaining in a place where one is not privileged to be even after notice of trespass is given.

The crime of **defiant trespass** occurs when a person remains in a place where he is not privileged to remain after notice of trespass is given. In most states, the offense is defined by statute similar to the following definition:

(b) Defiant trespasser.—(1) A person commits an offense if, knowing that he is not licensed or privileged to do so, he enters or remains in any place as to which notice against trespass is given by: (i) actual communication to the actor; or (ii) posting in a manner prescribed by law or reasonably likely to come to the attention of intruders; or (iii) fencing or other enclosure manifestly designed to exclude intruders.

In the 2004 case of *State v. Hamilton*,[44] a New Jersey appeals court upheld the conviction for defiant trespass of a protester who trespassed on a county roadway providing access to a municipal plant. A police officer told the protesters not to stand on the roadway to block entrance to the plant, but the defendant entered nonetheless. The court said that the defiant trespass statute applied when a person entered premises as to which notice against trespass was given by "actual communication" of such notice. It didn't matter under the statute, the court held, that the premises were on public land.

LEARNING OBJECTIVES SUMMARY

LO 1. **Describe what facts separate robbery from common theft.**
Robbery differs from common theft in that force or threat of force must be used to take property from the victim. Theft can occur without force and outside the victim's presence.

LO 2. **Articulate when robbery becomes armed or aggravated robbery.**
Armed or aggravated robbery occurs when a deadly weapon is used in a robbery, or when a victim suffers serious bodily injury. In most states, the threat of the presence of a deadly weapon satisfies the statute, though in many the weapon must in some manner be shown.

LO 3. **List the requirements for home invasion robbery.**
Home invasion requires unlawful entry of the dwelling of another with intent to commit a crime, with persons present in the home, and the use of force or threat of force to commit a crime. In most states, a home invasion while armed with a dangerous weapon carries an increased penalty.

LO 4. **Articulate when purse snatching or pickpocketing can become robbery.**
Purse snatching becomes robbery when force more than that needed to take the property is used in the crime. Grabbing the victim and turning her around to get at the purse is sufficient to make the crime robbery.

LO 5. **Distinguish robbery from extortion.**
Robbery involves a taking of property by the present threat of use of force; extortion is the unlawful taking of property by threat of force or other harm in the future, if the victim does not comply with the demand.

LO 6. **List the elements of the general burglary offense under the common law.**
Under the common law, burglary was defined as breaking into a residence of another at night with the intent to commit a felony.

LO 7. **Describe ways current state criminal codes modified the common law burglary offense.**
Under modern statutes, burglary is usually defined as the unlawful entry, with or without a breaking, of a residence or building, either during the day or at night, with the intent to commit a crime therein. In some states the statute requires the intent to commit a felony; in others, specific crimes are listed.

LO 8. **Distinguish criminal trespass from defiant trespass.**
Criminal trespass occurs when a person unlawfully and knowingly enters the land or building of another. Defiant trespass occurs when the person unlawfully entering is given notice of the trespass, but refuses to leave the premises.

KEY TERMS

robbery, p. 398

armed robbery, p. 398

carjacking, p. 402

home invasion robbery, p. 403

sudden snatching, p. 404

extortion, p. 405

burglary, p. 407

fence, p. 414

trespass, p. 417

defiant trespass, p. 417

CASE ANALYSIS AND WRITING EXERCISES

1. Robbery requires a "forcible" taking of property. We saw in this chapter that states have gone beyond a strict definition of "taking" as meaning the actual act of theft, and have also included in the definition of "forcible" under a robbery statute the force used in flight after the theft. Was force used in the theft that occurred in *People v. Williams*, 305 P.3d 1241 (Cal. 2013)? There, the defendant used fraudulent credit cards to buy gift cards at a Wal-Mart store. Store security officers discovered the fraud while the defendant was still in the store, and attempted to block his exit from the store. The defendant struggled with the officers, and was held for the police to arrive. He was convicted of robbery, and appealed. Should his conviction be reversed? Why or why not?

2. In addition to the Hobbs Act, discussed in this chapter, Congress also enacted 18 U.S.C. §876. That statute makes it a crime to use the U.S. Mail for the purpose of communicating threats to extort property from a person. Has the statute been violated when a defendant mails threatening letters, demanding money or other property, to businesses located near the veterinary business operated by a woman the defendant wished to harm, and to which the defendant signed the veterinarian's name? Is it a defense under the statute that the defendant never intended to obtain the extorted property for herself? Should it be? See *United States v. Carlson*, 787 F.3d 939 (8th Cir. 2015).

3. In early morning a police officer observed the defendant leaning on a porch at a community center. The building had a sign that clearly said "No Loitering." The officer approached the defendant and arrested him for trespass. A resulting search found crack cocaine on the defendant's person. He was charged with possession of the cocaine, and pled guilty reserving a right to appeal.

    On appeal he contends that if he was not properly arrested for defiant trespass, the resulting search by the arresting officer was illegal. (He is right about that.) Did he commit the crime of defiant trespass? See *State v. Gibson*, 95 A.3d 110 (N.J. 2014).

4. Defendant entered a Wal-Mart store and placed two television wall-mount kits in her cart. She then went to the customer service counter and "returned" one of the kits for a gift card. She used the gift card to purchase the other kit, which she returned the next day for cash. The state has charged her with "trafficking in stolen goods" under the Washington statute, which applies to one who "disposes of stolen property to another person." Is the defendant guilty as charged? See *State v. Graham*, 327 P.3d 717 (Wash. App. 2014).

ENDNOTES

1. The asportation or carrying away requirement in robbery is usually easily met. For example, in *State v. Johnson*, 432 So. 2d 758 (Fla. App. 1983), the court found asportation complete when the defendant forced a store clerk to put money in a paper bag and set it on the counter near the defendant, even if the defendant never touched the bag. In *Lattimore v. U.S.*, 684 A2d 357 (D.C. 1996), asportation was found when the defendant took a wallet from the victim, saw only a payroll check in the wallet, and threw the wallet back at the victim.

2. Many states also make concealing identity while committing a crime such as robbery conduct for which the degree of the crime and the penalty may be increased. The Supreme Court of Wisconsin has held that if one robber concealed his identity and the other did not, the second robber could be a

party to the crime of concealing identity: *Vogel v. State*, 96 Wis. 2d 372, 291 N.W.2d 838 (1980).

3. 977 P.2d 967 (Mont. 1999).

4. 959 N.E.2d 479 (N.Y. 2011).

5. 476 U.S. 16 (1986).

6. Volume IX, No. 27, July 1, 1968.

7. 30 A.3d 891 (Md. 2011).

8. *People v. Williams*, 814 N.W.2d 270 (Mich. 2012).

9. 306 S.W.3d 478 (Ky. 2010).

10. 945 N.E.2d 295 (Mass. 2011).

11. West's Annotated Penal Code, § 215.

12. 92 Cal. Rptr. 3d 751 (Cal. App. 2009).

13. Courts facing the movement or asportation question under the general robbery statute have reached a different answer. In *State v. Johnson*, 558 N.W.2d 375 (Wis. 1996), the Wisconsin Supreme Court held that the robber must move the car to be guilty.

14. 145 Cal. Rptr. 3d 907 (Cal. App. 2012).

15. Illinois Revised Statutes 1983, Chapter 38, paragraphs 12-11.

16. 590 A.2d 665 (1991).

17. 496 S.E.2d 668 (Va. App. 1998).

18. 362 Mass. 83, 283 N.E.2d 840 (1972).

19. See *Alfred v. State*, 659 S.W.2d 97 (Tex. App. 1983).

20. In 1997 Autumn Jackson attempted to extort $40 million from actor Bill Cosby. Jackson alleged she was Cosby's illegitimate daughter, and she threatened to make her claim public if he did not pay her the $40 million. After she began writing letters to companies whose products Cosby endorsed, he went to the FBI and then began tape recording conversations between himself and Jackson. Jackson was subsequently found guilty of extortion. See the *New York Times* articles, "Cosby Describes Requests for Money from 2 Women," July 16, 1997, and "To Ask Is Not Always to Extort: In the Case Involving Bill Cosby, a Troubling Legal Issue," July 18, 1997.

21. 628 F.3d 58 (2nd Cir. 2010).

22. *United States v. Enmons*, 410 U.S. 396 (1973).

23. 597 N.W.2d 501 (Iowa 1999).

24. 69 P.3d 331 (Wash. 2003).

25. 213 Cal. Rptr. 465 (Cal. App. 1985).

26. 978 A.2d 264 (N.H. 2009), *cert denied* 130 S. Ct. 1083 (2010).

27. 947 A.2d 546 (Md. 2008).

28. 297 F.3d 1198 (11th Cir. 2002).

29. Florida's burglary statutes, adopted in 1975, provide that "burglary means entering or remaining in a structure or conveyance with the intent to commit an offense therein, unless the premises are at the time open to the public or the defendant is licensed or invited to enter or remain."

30. 667 S.W.2d 906 (Tex. App. 1984).

31. 304 S.W.3d 642 (Tex. App. 2010).

32. The New Mexico Court of Appeals held in the 1976 case of *State v. Tixier*, 89 N.M. 297, 551 P.2d 987, that "A one-half inch penetration into the building is sufficient. Any penetration, however slight, of the interior space is sufficient. The fact that the penetration is by an instrument is also sufficient. 2 *Wharton's Criminal Law and Procedure* (1957) § 421; Clark and Marshall, *Crimes*, 6th ed., § 13.04."

33. 415 U.S. 800, 94 S. Ct. 1234 (1974).

34. See note 15.

35. 84 Wis. 2d 621, 267 N.W.2d 295 (1978).

36. *Woods v. State*, 186 Miss. 463, 191 So. 283 (1939).

37. 274 Cal. App. 2d 912, 79 Cal. Rptr. 650 (1969).

38. 937 N.E.2d 120 (Ohio App. 2010).

39. 196 N.W.2d 745 (Wis. 1972).

40. 220 P.3d 41 (Ore. 2009).

41. 673 A.2d 1372 (1996).

42. 225 Pa. Super. 311, 303 A.2d 528 (1973).

43. 987 So.2d 208 (La. App. 2008), *writ denied*, 6 So.3d 769 (La. 2009).

44. 845 A.2d 669 (N.J. Super. 2004).

15

White-Collar Crime, Cybercrime, and Commercial Crime

LEARNING OBJECTIVES

In this chapter we discuss nonviolent, mainly economic theft or harm crimes. The learning objectives for Chapter 15 are

LO 1. Define white-collar crime.

LO 2. Explain why fraud convictions require action done knowingly.

LO 3. Describe the elements of a "scheme or artifice" under federal criminal statutes.

LO 4. Explain the status of the "quid pro quo" requirement in federal bribery charges.

LO 5. List the laws protecting intellectual property.

LO 6. Name two federal criminal statutes frequently used to convict white-collar criminals.

LO 7. Identify one element making wire fraud different from bank fraud, and state why the element exists.

LO 8. Define insider trading.

LO 9. State the elements of identity theft crimes.

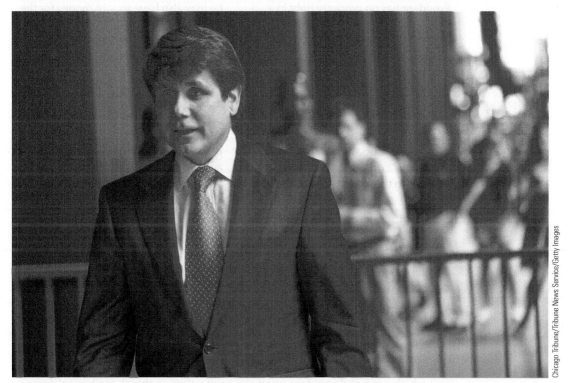

Former Illinois Governor Rod Blagojevich, who was convicted of various federal crimes including wire fraud, bribery, and extortion. While some of these convictions were overturned on appeal, his conviction for attempted bribery was affirmed.

After one mistrial and a second jury trial, Rod Blagojevich, former governor of Illinois, was convicted of multiple federal crimes based on FBI wiretaps, and other evidence, showing that he used promises or threats of official acts to obtain property from various persons. Included were convictions for attempted extortion under the Hobbs Act, and wire fraud (use of a telephone in his attempts to deal with President Obama). These convictions were based on Blagojevich's efforts to get then-President-elect Obama to name him to a cabinet post in exchange

for his appointment of an Obama associate to the U.S. Senate seat Obama held when he was elected president. Sentenced to 168 months in prison, Blagojevich appealed his convictions.

The appeals court vacated Blagojevich's conviction for attempted extortion and wire fraud. It held that the Hobbs Act requires proof that the official attempted to extort "property from another," which the U.S Supreme Court said meant something of value that could be transferred or sold. (See the discussion of the *Sekhar* case in Chapter 14.) The court said Blagojevich's offer to exchange the Senate appointment for a cabinet post was not an attempt to obtain "property" from President Obama, because the President has no property right in a cabinet post to transfer. Rather, the court said, Blagojevich's actions were "logrolling," a legal practice politicians use to exchange votes or other official acts between one and the other.

The court affirmed Blagojevich's convictions for attempted bribery of persons to whom he made threats or promises of official actions for cash "campaign" contributions. It remanded the case to the district court for

resentencing; it also noted that if the prosecution chose to proceed against Blagojevich for attempted extortion under the Hobbs act based on evidence he may also have sought money for the Senate appointment, double jeopardy would not be a problem. In March of 2016 the U.S. Supreme Court denied certiorari in the case.

In this chapter we will learn about many crimes that focus on schemes or plans designed to fraudulently deprive another person of money or other property, as well as crimes like arson and trespass that directly injure another person's property.

WHITE-COLLAR CRIME

white-collar crime A class or type of criminal conduct whose only goal is the criminal's economic gain.

The term **white-collar crime** is generally understood to refer to a class or type of criminal conduct whose only goal is the criminal's economic gain. While the "white-collar" language suggests the status of the wrongdoer, most definitions of the term focus on the kind of behavior made criminal, not the identity of the criminal. The U.S. Department of Justice, in its 1989 FBI report entitled *White-Collar Crime: A Report to the Public,*[1] defined white-collar crime as "those illegal acts which are characterized by deceit, concealment or violation of trust and which are not dependent upon the application or threat of physical force or violence."

The economic cost of white-collar crimes and the other commercial crimes discussed in this chapter is enormous and greatly outstrips the cost of many other crimes. For example, in the 2012 FBI report *Crime in the United States: 2011,*[2] it was estimated that the total economic cost of all robbery, burglary, theft, and car theft crimes in 2011 was $15.6 billion. By contrast, the estimated loss in 2009 suffered by investors in the Bernard Madoff Ponzi scheme was $65 billion.

In this chapter we focus on the many forms of commercial, business, financial, and fraudulent conduct that are made criminal under state and federal laws.

FRAUD AND FRAUDULENT PRACTICES

fraud Deceitful means or acts used to cheat a person, corporation, or governmental agency.

Fraud consists of deceitful means or acts used to cheat a person, corporation, or governmental agency. Theft by fraud or larceny by fraud is often the criminal charge used, as fraud can be a form of theft and larceny. Fraud convictions require some form of specific intent, such as acting knowingly or willfully, as distinguished from negligent conduct. In the following materials this chapter examines some of the key criminal laws that target white-collar crimes of fraud.

Bank Fraud

The federal government has an important interest in fraud aimed at banks and other financial institutions. Most of these institutions are federally insured, so that losses suffered by them caused by fraud can end up being paid for by the federal government. Because of this, Congress passed the bank fraud statute, 18 U.S.C. § 1344, which makes it a federal crime to defraud a financial institution that is federally insured. Examples of **bank fraud** that would fall under this statute are check kiting (discussed in Chapter 13), check forgery, false statements on loan applications, unauthorized use of ATM machines, credit card fraud, and student loan fraud. These crimes all require proof that the defendant knowingly executed or attempted to execute a "scheme or artifice" to defraud, or, through false statements, obtained money or property from a federally insured financial institution.

The statute does not define "scheme or artifice," but 18 U.S.C. § 1346 states that a "scheme or artifice" includes a scheme to deprive another of the intangible right to honest services (discussed later in this chapter). The federal fraud statutes otherwise leave it to courts to determine whether "a scheme or artifice" exists. A definition that is too specific makes it possible for criminals to manipulate their scheme so that it falls outside the definition. The U.S. Supreme Court has held that any such scheme must include a "material falsehood," that is, one that a person would understand to be important and relied on by another. See *Neder v. United States,*[3] where the holding was made applicable to mail fraud and wire fraud statutes as well. These statutes also require proof of a "scheme or artifice."

One aspect of the bank fraud statute had split the federal courts: Does a conviction under 18 U.S.C. §1344 (2) require proof that the defendant had the specific intent to defraud a financial institution? §1344 states that whoever "knowingly" executes a "scheme or artifice" to "(1) defraud a financial institution; or (2) obtain moneys. . . under the control of a financial institution" by false representation violates the statute. While all the federal courts agreed that a conviction under 1344 (1) required proof the defendant intended to defraud a financial institution, they disagreed about whether a conviction under 1344 (2) also required proof of that specific intent.

In the 2014 case of *Loughrin v. United States*[4] the U.S. Supreme Court resolved that question. The following Case Close-Up highlights that decision.

Health Care Fraud

Health care costs in the United States in 2014 reached nearly $4 trillion; by comparison, in 2014 the gross domestic product of the United States was about $17.3 trillion. The federal government has many health care programs, most notably Medicare and Medicaid. These programs rely on statements, claims, and bills sent to program administrators by health care professionals, as well as persons served in the programs. False claims under these programs cost the federal government huge amounts each year. The 2014 FBI *Health Care Fraud Report* estimates that the yearly cost of health care fraud is more than $100 billion.

Congress has passed various statutes that address this problem, among them the Medicaid False Claims Statute, 42 U.S.C. § 1320a-7b(a), and the Medicaid

bank fraud Fraud aimed at banks and other financial institutions.

CASE CLOSE-UP
Loughrin v. United States
Supreme Court of the United States
134 S. Ct. 2384 (2014)

Kevin Loughrin concocted a "scheme" to forge and cash checks. He roamed neighborhoods in Salt Lake City, posing as a Mormon missionary. Going door-to-door, he rifled individuals' mailboxes, and stole any checks he found in the mail. He altered the checks by "washing" them to remove lettering, or simply crossing out the named payee and adding another name. As part of the scheme, Loughrin presented the altered checks to merchants for a "cash" purchase transaction. He then returned the merchandise to the seller for a cash return. (Recall the Home Depot Scam discussed in Chapter 13.) The merchant in turn presented the checks to the payor banks for payment.

Loughrin was caught operating this scheme at a Target store. He was arrested, and charged under §1344 (2) (the theft and forgery crimes would be prosecuted in state court; violation of the bank fraud statute is a federal crime and prosecuted in federal court). He was convicted, and on appeal his conviction was affirmed by the court of appeals. The U.S. Supreme Court granted review to resolve the split in the lower courts on the specific intent required under 1344 (2).

Loughrin contended 1344 (2), like 1344 (1), required proof that he had the specific intent to deceive a financial institution, since it was the involvement of financial institutions that made his actions a federal crime. Loughrin said there was no proof he had such intent; his only intent was to deceive Target, which by itself would not be a violation of the federal bank fraud statute, he argued.

The Supreme Court rejected that argument. It agreed that 1344 (1) required proof of an intent to defraud a financial institution, since that was the "whole sum and substance" of 1344 (1). However, the Court said, the elements of 1344 (2) require only proof that the defendant intended a scheme to obtain money under the control of a financial institution and did so by false misrepresentations, whether made to the bank or to a person (like Target) that takes the altered check based on the false representation, and then presents the check to the bank. Congress clearly intended to protect banks from "fraudsters" like Loughrin, the Court concluded, and thus 1344 (2) does not require proof that Loughrin also had the specific intent to defraud a financial institution.

The Court also rejected Loughrin's argument, relying on the decision in *Bond v. United States*, 134 S. Ct. 2077 (2014) [discussed in Chapter 2], that the Court should reject an interpretation of 1344 (2) that would make every "garden-variety" scheme involving checks a violation of federal law. The Court said a scheme like passing off a "cheap knock-off as a Louis Vuitton handbag" and getting paid by check, would not violate the statute even though the check would be cashed to obtain "moneys under the control" of a bank. The statute requires that deceiving the bank be part of the "means" to obtain the funds, the Court said. Here, unlike the Louis Vuitton example, the false representations concerning the checks passed at Target were part of the mechanism that resulted in the bank paying out funds it controlled, the Court said. It therefore affirmed Loughrin's conviction under 1344(2).

Anti-Kickback Statute, 42 U.S.C. § 1320a-7b(b). The false claims statute makes it a crime for any person to knowingly and willfully make a false statement in any application for a federal health care benefit. An example of a crime falling within this statute includes submitting a bill for services or tests that were not performed. The anti-kickback statute is aimed at those who promise or receive payments based on referrals of patients for services paid under federal health care programs. An example of a crime coming under this statute includes accepting a fee for sending a patient to a physician or other provider for medical services. It also includes sending a patient to a health care provider with whom the referring physician has a financial relationship. Violation of these laws can lead to massive fines. In 2001 TAP Pharmaceutical Products, Inc. was fined $875 million, the largest fine ever for health care fraud.

The federal government also has a general health care fraud statute, 18 U.S.C. § 1347, which makes it a crime to willfully execute a "scheme or artifice" intended to defraud a "health care benefit" program. One typical prosecution under this statute is found in the 2009 case of *United States v. Franklin-El*.[5] The defendants ran an alcohol and drug addiction counseling clinic, which received reimbursement payments under Medicaid for qualified patients. Only diagnosed addicts were qualified patients. The defendants filed 1,331 false claims for reimbursement from Medicaid that totaled over $1.2 million, listing as "addicts" persons who were not addicts, were not enrolled in the defendant's program, or in some cases were children only a few weeks old. The court affirmed their convictions on fifty-two counts of health care fraud.

Convictions under the health care fraud statute carry both a prison sentence and a fine. In extreme cases, the prison sentence can be for life. In *United States v. Martinez*,[6] a physician operated a "pain management clinic." Some of the medical services he provided were paid for under Medicaid, Medicare, and the Ohio Bureau of Workers Compensation, each of which qualifies as a "health care benefit" program. Martinez gave his patients "nerve-block" injections, for which he billed these programs. The average number of "nerve-block" injections patients usually received was 2.5 per year; Martinez gave his patients an average of 64 injections per year, with the result that many became addicted to the medication and incurred serious bodily injury. Two patients died as a result of Martinez's treatments. He was convicted of health care fraud for claiming reimbursements of more than $14 million for improperly administered treatments and improper medical services. Because his actions resulted in the deaths of two patients, he was sentenced to life in prison under § 1347(2). In 2010 the U.S. Supreme Court denied certiorari.[7]

The Meaning of "Willful" Many of the federal statutes that are directed at criminal conduct of the type included in this chapter have a "scienter" requirement that the defendant act "knowingly," and/or "willfully." The Medicaid False Claims Statute, discussed above, is an example of such a requirement. It makes it a crime for one to "knowingly and willfully" make a false claim. The federal criminal copyright statute, 17 U.S.C. § 506 (a), which makes it a crime to "willfully infringe" a copyright, is another example. (Discussed in next section.)

What does "willfully" mean in these statutes? Is it enough that the defendant knew he was making a false claim or statement, or in copyright infringement, that he was copying another person's work? In other words, is it enough to prove that the defendant's actions were intentional rather than accidental or negligent? Or, must the government also prove that the defendant knew that making the false claim or statement, or copying the work, was illegal? (Not every false thing we say or do violates the criminal law.) Federal courts have split on the meaning of "willful" in these contexts.

As a background, the U. S. Supreme Court has observed that the word "willfully" can be a "word of many meanings." *Bryan v. United States*, 118 S. Ct. 1939, 1944 (1998). In general, the term used in a criminal statute requires proof that a defendant acted "with knowledge his conduct was unlawful." 118 S. Ct., at 1945. However, there is some older Supreme Court authority that in the context of these kind of statutes, "willful" means only acting "deliberately and with knowledge." *Browden v. United States*, 312 U. S. 335 (1941).

Health Care Fraud The cases in *United States v. Russell*, 728 F.3d 23 (1st Cir. 2013) and *United States v. Ajoku*, 718 F.3d 882 (9th Cir. 2013) involved prosecutions under the health care false statements statute, 18 U.S.C. § 1035. That statute makes it a crime to "knowingly and willfully" make a false statement to a health care benefit program in the delivery of or payment for health care. In *Russell* the defendant applied for subsidized health insurance from a state agency and in his application misrepresented his employment and income. In *Ajoku* the defendant filed an application with a state agency to act as an "exemptee" for a pharmacy company. The position required the "exemptee" to monitor and distribute medical devices for the pharmacy. The defendant stated in his application that he would actively be present at the pharmacy performing those services; in fact, he and his employer knew Ajoku would almost never be present at the pharmacy when medical devices were dispensed.

The trial judges in each trial instructed the jury that the prosecution was not required to prove the defendants knew their false statements violated the law. "Willfully" only required the prosecution to prove the defendants acted intentionally in making the false statements, the court said. Both Russell and Ajoku were convicted, and on appeal the courts in both cases held that "willful" did not require proof the defendant knew his actions violated the law. As the trial judge instructed the jury, all the government had to prove was that the defendants acted intentionally.

Both defendants filed petitions for certiorari in the U.S. Supreme Court. In an unusual action, the U. S. Solicitor General (who appears for the United States in the Supreme Court) conceded in the government's brief opposing review that "willful" in the false statement statute should require proof the defendants knew their actions violated the law. *Brief for the United States in Opposition*, p. 11, filed March 10, 2014. Following this, the Supreme Court vacated the convictions and remanded the cases to the court of appeals for further consideration "in light of the confession of error by the Solicitor General." 134 S. Ct. 1872 (2014)

Intellectual Property Fraud

intellectual property fraud Theft, piracy, or counterfeiting of ideas, inventions, artistic works, and the like.

Intellectual property generally means property rights in ideas; inventions; artistic works such as books, movies, and songs; and the like. The theft, piracy, or counterfeiting of intellectual property costs its owners billions of dollars each year and has become even more damaging with the rise of Internet theft. The primary criminal laws aimed at **intellectual property fraud** are the federal copyright and patent acts and federal and state trade secret acts.

Copyright   The copyright act, 17 U.S.C. § 506, protects books, movies, and songs once they have been published. Any person who willfully infringes a valid copyright for economic gain violates the statute, and can be sentenced to up to 5 years in prison. "Infringing" means reproducing or distributing the work without permission. Thus, while it is permitted to use a copyrighted song in a free school production, it is not permitted to use the same song in a production that charges admission. Questions about the permissible use of copyrighted material are decided under the "fair use" doctrine, 17 U.S.C. § 107. "Fair use" includes classroom use, scholarship use, research, teaching, and related uses of the copyrighted materials.

The Internet has presented a great challenge to the "fair use" doctrine. Many software programs available on the Internet enable users to "share" files with other users on a "peer-to-peer" basis, meaning that the users' computers communicate directly with one another without using an Internet server. If these files contain copyrighted works, such as songs downloaded from a CD to the user's computer, the songs are being distributed and such distribution may be a violation of the copyright law. Individual criminal prosecutions for copyright infringement have not been found. However, courts have found Internet servers to be in civil violation of the copyright laws, based on the actual "sharing" done by their Internet customers.

In *M.G.M. Studios v. Grokster, LLC,* 545 U.S. 913 (2005), the Supreme Court held that two Internet companies that distributed software to their customers that enabled the customers to share copyrighted works could be found to be in violation of the copyright laws. The software created a network that allowed users to access other computers using the same software program, find designated files, and download them. Since about 90 percent of the files included copyrighted songs, the Court held that the Internet companies could be found in violation of the copyright owners' exclusive distribution and reproduction rights.

The Internet sharing of copyright materials also makes application of the "first sale" defense questionable. It has long been recognized that one who purchases a copyrighted work is entitled to sell that very work without violating the copyright act. That is because after this "first sale," the seller no longer has the work to sell and cannot use it for the kind of economic gain the copyright laws are intended to punish. However, if a computer file is "sold" or traded, the seller/trader keeps the file and can do it again. The "first sale" defense does not seem appropriate in that case.

In a 2013 decision, the U.S. Supreme Court held that the "first sale" exception to the copyright acts applied to the sale in the United States of books published in Europe or Asia. In *Kirtsaeng v. John Wiley & Sons, Inc.*[8] a student from Thailand studying in the United States had his family buy used books in Thailand and send them to him in the United States, where he sold them at a profit. The court held the first sale doctrine applied to the sales by the student because the books had been "lawfully" published outside the United States.

Criminal Copyright Infringement   In *United States v. Liu,* 731 F.3d 982 (9th Cir. 2013) the court held that a conviction under the criminal copyright infringement statute required proof not only that the defendant knew his actions were copying another person's work, but also that doing so violated the law. There, the defendant operated a "replication" business that produced CD's and DVD's that replicated copyrighted works like songs and movies. He was charged and convicted under the criminal copyright infringement statute. At his trial the judge instructed the jury that "willful" meant acting intentionally and knowingly, but did not include the requirement that the defendant knew his actions violated the law. The court of appeals reversed his conviction, holding that the criminal copyright statute required proof not only that the defendant knowingly copied the works, but also that in doing so he knew his acts violated the copyright laws.

Trade Secrets   The federal government and every state have trade secret laws that make it a crime to steal a trade secret. Generally, trade secrets are property characteristics that have been kept a secret by the owner of the property, which property is made valuable because of the trade secret. The best example of a trade secret is the recipe for Coca-Cola, which is aggressively kept secret by the Coca-Cola Company. The federal government makes it a crime under the Economic Espionage Act, 18 U.S.C. § 1831–1839, to convert a trade secret for economic gain.

Fraud and Corruption in Government

Fraud against government is as old as government itself. Reports of fraud and corruption date back to biblical times and early civilizations. The U.S. government spent over $3.8 trillion in 2014 as provided in the U. S. budget, so it is not surprising that it has serious fraud and corruption problems.

Losses through fraud and corruption occur in many ways. Fraud can be charged criminally in federal courts as mail fraud (when the U.S. mails are used); wire fraud (when interstate or international communications are used); racketeering, bribery, and theft of public funds; fraud and conspiracy to commit fraud; false entries or false statements; fraud in connection with government contracting; equity skimming; false statements and misappropriation of funds; conspiracy to defraud the United States; and interstate transportation of funds obtained by fraud.

The following areas account for many of the fraud losses in the federal government.

Contract Fraud and the False Claims Act   In the procurement of arms and military supplies, the federal government spends more than $600 billion yearly. Fraud in military procurement contracts has been discovered in the selling of inside information on contract bids, bid rigging, bribes and kickbacks, double billing, falsifying test results or failure to conduct tests, and overcharging for materials and services. The False Claims Act, 18 U.S.C. § 287, makes it a crime to present a claim to the U.S. government that is false or fraudulent and known to be false or fraudulent. The statute was first passed during the Civil War, because of the rampant fraud practiced by contractors providing goods and services to the Union Army.

The False Claims Act applies to any kind of false claim, if its purpose is to obtain payment from the government. For example, in the 2009 case of *United States v. Saybolt,*[9] defendants were convicted under § 287 for filing false income tax returns with the IRS and seeking refunds. They were also convicted under 18 U.S.C. § 286, which punishes conspiracies to defraud the government by false claims.

Program Frauds   Billions of dollars are dispersed every year through programs such as Medicaid, Medicare,[10] the Supplemental Nutrition Assistance Program (food stamps),[11] small business loans, subsidy programs, HUD (U.S. Department of Housing and Urban Development), Social Security, and various aid programs. Persons who make false claims for benefits under these programs can be prosecuted under the False Claims Act or, in some cases, under statutes directed at specific programs such as Medicaid, discussed earlier.

In many federal programs, funds are disbursed by city or state granting agencies to be used for appropriate purposes under the federal funding legislation. The federal program theft statute, 18 U.S.C. § 666, applies to theft or bribery by persons who are agents for organizations that receive in one year more than $10,000 of federal funds. A conviction under this statute requires (1) that the defendant be an agent of the organization and (2) that the theft involve property of the organization. For example, an independent contractor providing services to a regional airport that received federal funds was convicted under § 666 for overbilling the airport for services allegedly provided to the airport. The court held the contractor was an "agent" of the airport and thus was guilty of theft from the organization that received the federal funds. *United States v. Vitillo.*[12] However, not every theft of federal program funds is covered by § 666. In *United States v. Abu-Shawish,*[13] the court held that a defendant who was given a "block" grant of HUD funds by a Milwaukee city agency for development of a community organization could not be convicted for theft of property under § 666. It was not enough that the defendant defrauded the Milwaukee "organization" that disbursed the federal funds; the court said the defendant must be an agent of that organization as well, which the defendant was not. The court stated that the defendant should have been prosecuted under the federal mail or wire fraud acts.

bribery Offering a gift or payment to another with the specific intent to obtain some unlawful particular *quid pro quo* for the gift or payment.

Bribery of agents of an organization that receives federal funds is also covered by § 666. In *United States v. Caro-Muniz,*[14] the mayor of Rincon, Puerto Rico, was convicted for taking bribes to award contracts that were funded by federal grants.

In *United States v. Ganim,*[15] the mayor of Bridgeport, Connecticut, was convicted of accepting illegal "gifts" from persons who received city contracts. Often, as was the case in *Ganim,* defendants convicted under § 666 are also charged under the RICO statutes, discussed in Chapter 18. Moreover, public officials like the defendant in *Ganim* could also be prosecuted under state bribery laws such as § 53(a)-148 of the Connecticut General Statutes.

Bribery   Bribery of federal officials is covered by 18 U.S.C. § 201(b). Federal officials include everyone from members of Congress to food inspectors. In *United States v. Alfisi,*[16] produce inspectors for the U.S. Department of Agriculture were convicted for taking bribes from wholesale produce sellers in exchange for higher quality produce-inspection receipts.

Bribery prosecutions under 18 U.S.C. § 201(b) often are coupled with extortion charges under 18 U.S.C. § 872. A federal officer that "solicits" a bribe in exchange for some official act may also threaten to use his official position to prevent the official act from occurring. The former is a "bribe" under § 201, and the latter is "extortion" under § 872. Moreover, there are similarities between extortion and bribery offenses, as the Supreme Court noted in *Evans v. United States,* 504 U.S. 255 (1992).

KICKBACKS

It is not unusual, and often not illegal, for one person to compensate another person for that person's help in arranging a transaction, employment contract, loan, or other service. In some areas, however, this compensation is called a "kickback," and made a crime. The federal government has several "anti-kickback" statutes; the cases that follow illustrate some issues that arise under those statutes:

United States v. Shoemaker, 746 F.3d 614 (5th Cir. 2014): The owner of a nurse staffing company that provided nurses to area hospitals paid the chairman of a board of trustees that supervised a hospital $5 for every billed nursing hour for nurses provided to the hospital by the staffing company. The board chairman in turn induced the hospital administrative officer to use nurses from the staffing company at the hospital and authorized a $50,000 raise for the administrator. Both the company owner and the administrator were convicted under the anti-kickback provisions of 42 U.S.C. §1320a-7b(b), which makes it a crime to pay another person money to induce that person to arrange for services for which payment would be made under a Federal health care program (here Medicare and Medicaid). The appeals court affirmed the convictions, noting that while the board chairman (who cooperated with the government investigation) did not decide which nurse staffing company would supply nurses to the hospital, he had enough influence to be a "relevant decision-maker" under the act.

United States v. Patel, 778 F.3d 607 (7th Cir. 2015): A Chicago physician was convicted under the anti-kickback provisions of 42 U.S.C. § 1320 discussed above for "referring" patients to a company that provided home health care services to those patients. The patients, after the physician prescribed home health care services, were shown brochures from several home health care providers, including the Grand Company. If they selected Grand, the physician would then sign a medical certification form (known as Form 485) agreeing with the proposed treatment plan. Form 485 was required for payments under Medicare and Medicaid. Each time he signed a form the physician was paid cash by Grand. On appeal, the physician contended the statute did not apply to him because he did not "refer" patients to Grand as required by §1320. The court disagreed. It said that each time the physician signed an initial Form 485 or a recertification Form, he effectively referred the patients to Grand. It affirmed his conviction under the statute.

The Court said in *Evans* that while conviction of an official for extortion "under color of law" under the Hobbs Act, 19 U.S.C. § 1951, requires proof of an exchange of payment for an agreement to perform an official act, it does not require proof that the official took affirmative steps to "induce" the payment. And even if the official did solicit the payment, the Court stated that it is no defense to an extortion charge that the facts would also support a bribery conviction.

A case illustrating bribery and extortion charges under the federal statutes discussed above is *United States v. Valle*.[17] In that case, an Immigration and Customs agent approached a Mexican national being held in a detention facility pending deportation. The agent told the detainee that there were pending criminal charges against the detainee but that the agent would remove them for a payment of $20,000. The detainee told other federal officers about the conversation, and ultimately an undercover FBI officer gave the agent the $20,000 and then arrested the agent. The court affirmed his convictions under both the bribery statute and the extortion statute. It rejected the agent's defense that he never intended to remove any criminal charges because they didn't exist, stating that all either statute required was that the official enter into a "corrupt" agreement to use his official position.

quid pro quo Giving something of value ("quid") for something else.

Bribery and, to some degree, extortion crimes usually involve a **quid pro quo,** that is, an exchange of some official act for some promised payment. (See the discussion of *quid pro quo* for Hobbs Act [extortion] violations in Chapter 14.) The nature of the *quid pro quo* requirement in the federal bribery statutes was described in the U.S. Supreme Court case of *United States v. Sun-Diamond Growers of California,* 526 U.S. 398 (1999). In that case the defendant was prosecuted under 18 U.S.C. § 201 (c), the crime of giving an official an illegal gratuity. The trial court had instructed the jury that the crime included giving an official a gift "simply because of his position," without tying the gift to any particular official act. The Supreme Court reversed the conviction, holding that § 201(c) required proof of a link between the gratuity and some official act.

In the course of its decision in *Sun-Diamond,* the Supreme Court made this statement about the federal bribery statute, § 201(b): "[b]ribery requires intent to 'influence' an official act (the bribe-giver) or to be 'influenced' in an official act (the public official bribe receiver). . . . In other words, for bribery there must be a *quid pro quo*—a specific intent to give or receive something of value in exchange for an official act." 526 U.S. at 404–405.

Bribery convictions under § 201(b) thus have as an element of the offense a showing that the bribe was given or solicited as part of an agreement to exchange some official action for the bribe. Courts addressing the *quid pro quo* issue in prosecutions under 18 U.S.C. § 666, the federal program bribery statute, have reached a different conclusion. Those courts hold that there need be no showing of payment for a particular official act, but only that the payment was made to influence the official "in connection" with transactions under the federal programs. *United States v. McNair,* 605 F.3d 1152 (11th Cir. 2010). The U.S. Supreme Court denied review in the *McNair* case: 131 S. Ct. 1600 (2011).

Bribery was traditionally a crime committed by or with officials, and as a result many state bribery statutes are specifically addressed to official misconduct. The Georgia bribery statute, OCGA § 16-10-2, makes it a crime to (1) offer to give an official anything of value in order to influence the official in performance of official acts and (2) solicit anything of value from another by "inducing the reasonable belief" that giving the thing of value will result in influencing the performance of official actions.

Most states also have bribery statutes that are directed at persons other than public officials. One example is in sports bribery cases. As a result of famous "point-shaving" basketball scandals and other sports bribery incidents, many states have passed bribery statutes aimed directly at sports participants. Louisiana's statute, LSA-RS 14-118.1, and North Carolina's NC GSA § 14-373 are examples of these statutes.

Stock Market and Financial Market Frauds

The stock markets and financial markets of the United States and other industrial countries are important to their economic development in creating jobs and providing for economic security. Among the crimes that infect this field is insider trading.

YOU BE THE JUDGE

Should you dismiss the charges? See **Commonwealth v. Moran, 104 A.3d 1136 (Pa. 2014)**

The defendant before you has been charged with bribery under state law. The law includes in the meaning of bribery any attempt by a public official to solicit anything of value in exchange for the promise of official action for the benefit of the person solicited. The defendant was a member of a county Board of Commissioners. The county needed funds to pay expenses, and the defendant suggested he approach a potential buyer of land owned by the county, and promise the buyer expedited actions on zoning changes in exchange for a payment of $500,000.00 to be used for county expenses. The defendant made that offer, but the buyer did not accept.

Later, the defendant was charged with bribery under the state bribery statute. He has moved for a dismissal of the charges, contending that he could not be convicted of bribery because he never intended to get anything of value for himself under the offer to the buyer. He also contends making his actions criminal would make every attempt by a county commissioner to obtain funds for payment of county expenses criminal.

People who obtain inside information on the plans of large corporations can often make huge profits by insider trading or by selling the information illegally.

The federal criminal securities laws applicable to crimes like insider trading are generally contained in regulations promulgated in Section 10(b) of the Securities Exchange Act of 1934, 15 U.S.C. § 78j. Section 78j makes it a crime for any person to use a "manipulative or deceptive device or contrivance" in connection with the purchase or sale of a security, such as a share of stock. This includes insider trading.

Insider trading often involves a person with some fiduciary responsibility, such as a corporate officer, using information known only to corporate "insiders" to profit from the information by buying or selling corporate stock in advance of public acquisition of the information. Insider trading also includes the so-called tippee situation, where an "outsider" acquires information from an insider and uses it to his advantage. If the tippee knew the information came from an insider in breach of a fiduciary duty, the tippee could be convicted under § 78j. See *United States v. Evans.*[18]

In a decision of potentially significant importance, the Second Circuit Court of Appeals held in *United States v. Newman*, 773 F.3d 438 (2014) that a tippee could not be convicted of insider trading without proof the tipper committed a breach of fiduciary duty by communicating nonpublic information to the tippee. There, a group of hedge fund managers, calling themselves "The Fight Club," exchanged bits of information they obtained from various sources with each other, including nonpublic inside information. When prosecuted for insider trading, however, the government did not prove the defendant-tippees knew if the person disclosing the information (the "tipper") did so to obtain any personal benefit from the disclosure. The court of appeals held that because a breach of fiduciary duty only occurs if the fiduciary seeks some personal benefit, the absence of proof the defendants knew about such a benefit meant the prosecution did not prove they knew of a breach of fiduciary duty by disclosure of the information. The court reversed the convictions for insider trading, and ordered the charges to be dismissed. The U.S. Supreme Court denied review; 136 S. Ct. 242 (2015).

Determining exactly what constitutes a "manipulative" device under the securities laws can be difficult. In *United States v. Finnerty*,[19] the court held that the so-called inter-positioning practice used by a trader on the New York Stock Exchange did not violate the securities laws. "Inter-positioning" refers to the practice of a trader taking a position in a stock transaction between two customers, one wishing to buy a stock and one wishing to sell. Stock Exchange rules state that in such a case, the trader is required to "match" the buyer with the seller. In inter-positioning, the trader trades separately with each customer, thereby taking advantage of any gap that existed between the two orders. The court said that while the trader was acting wrongly for his own gain, he did not deceive or manipulate his customers.

Stock market and corporate fraud reached unprecedented heights during the period 1990–2004. Although there have been previous instances of scandal and greed in American economic markets, nothing comes close to those in recent years. The bankruptcy of the energy giant Enron Corporation alone cost investors and employees billions of dollars. In February 2001, Enron stock sold for

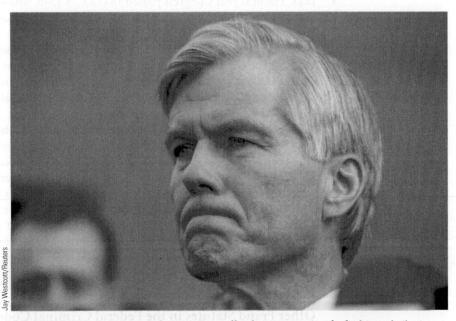

Jay Westcott/Reuters

Former VIrginia Governor Robert McDonnell, who was convicted of taking a bribe in 2015. In 2016, the U.S. Supreme Court reversed his conviction, in the process narrowing the meaning of the "official act" requirement under the federal bribery statute.

$90 per share; when it filed for bankruptcy 10 months later, those same shares were selling for pennies. Many of Enron's executives made millions of dollars selling their shares at a time when the company's employees were unable to sell their shares. In 2006 Jeffrey Skilling and Kenneth Lay, chief executive officers of Enron during the period Enron misrepresented its financial condition to investors and banks, were convicted of fraud and conspiracy. Skilling was sentenced to 24 years in prison; Lay died before he could be sentenced. Skilling appealed his conviction on various grounds; the court of appeals affirmed his convictions in 2009, but the U.S. Supreme Court reversed and remanded the case in a 2010 decision.

Skilling was charged with violations of federal fraud statutes, including "honest services" fraud under the mail and wire fraud acts. The term "honest services" was derived from federal court cases where courts interpreted the "scheme or artifice" language of the mail and wire fraud statutes as including actions that didn't directly deprive a victim of money or property, but were nonetheless fraudulent. An example would be a mayor who takes a bribe or kickback to give a city contract to a friend. Even if the contract price were fair, so that no money was fraudulently "taken" from the city, the city would have been deprived of the "honest services" of the mayor. Federal courts were frequently affirming convictions under the mail and wire fraud statutes for bribery and kickback schemes.

In 1987 the U.S. Supreme Court held in *McNally v. United States*, 483 U.S. 350, that the "scheme or artifice" language of the wire and mail fraud acts applied only to direct frauds, where victims were deprived of money or other property by the fraudulent actions. "Honest services" fraud was not covered by the statutes, the Court held. The next year Congress passed 18 U.S.C. § 1346, which stated that for the mail and other fraud statutes a "scheme or artifice" included depriving another of the "intangible right of honest services."

Courts began applying § 1346 to various kinds of fraudulent actions, if, as the result of these actions, a defendant acted dishonestly. For example, making false representations about a company's financial situation, as in the Enron case, or acting with a conflict of interest were actions treated by federal prosecutors and courts as covered by the mail and wire fraud statutes.

In *Skilling v. United States*, 130 S. Ct. 2896 (2010), the Supreme Court held that Section 1346 didn't include under the language "honest services" fraudulent actions that didn't directly deprive a victim of money or property, except for bribery or kickback schemes. Since Skilling had been convicted of "honest services" fraud without any evidence he took a bribe or received a kickback, the Court reversed and remanded his case for consideration of whether he should receive a new trial on all of the counts of his indictment. On remand, the court of appeals held in 2011 that ample evidence supported the other convictions, and affirmed those convictions. In 2012, the U.S. Supreme Court denied review of that decision.[20]

Other Fraud Statutes in the Federal Criminal Code

Each state has fraud statutes in its criminal code to punish fraudulent conduct that takes place within that state. Because most large fraud schemes involve criminal

NATIONAL FRAUD FACTS

Which fraud case is the largest on record?	The 2009 conviction of Bernie Madoff marked the end of a $64.8 billion Ponzi scheme that defrauded hundreds of investors. Madoff maintained elaborate books that showed investment returns on his clients' money, when in fact those investments did not exist. The 1998 accounting fraud on the Cendant Corporation, by Walter Forbes, is believed to be the next largest fraud on record, at $19 billion. After lengthy litigation, Forbes was convicted of securities fraud in 2007. See *United States v. Forbes*, 2007 WL 141952. It is likely the Enron collapse cost shareholders and other investors more than that amount. The WorldCom accounting fraud in 2004, in which the CEO, Bernard Ebbers, received a 25-year prison sentence, cost investors $11 billion.
Which fraud case led to the most criminal convictions?	The Enron case resulted in the convictions of ten executives and guilty pleas from sixteen others. Only one executive was acquitted, and one trial resulted in a hung jury.
What were the most common charges in the largest fraud cases?	Securities fraud, wire fraud, conspiracy, false statements, mail fraud, bank fraud, insider trading, and theft were the criminal charges in these frauds.
How often are government employees convicted of corruption charges?	While most government employees are honest, the FBI reports that about 500 city, state, or federal employees each year are convicted of corrupt practices. Former Illinois Governor George Ryan, former Congressman Randall Cunningham, and mega-lobbyist Jack Abramoff were among those convicted. See the *New York Times*, "FBI Focus on Public Corruption Includes 2000 Investigations," May 11, 2006.
Which computer-related crimes are prosecuted in state courts?	The type of crimes prosecuted, from the highest number to the lowest, are credit card fraud; bank card fraud, identity theft, child pornography; computer forgery (altering documents); cyberstalking (sending threatening or harassing e-mails); hacking (unauthorized access); computer sabotage (placing worms, viruses, or logic bombs—hidden programs "detonated" by a specific date or event); and theft of computer data (copyright infringement).

conduct that crosses state lines, Congress has power to punish these crimes under the Commerce Clause. Also, because many fraud schemes use the banking system, the stock market, or other large financial institutions regulated by federal law, Congress has passed several federal fraud crime laws, and violators are frequently charged under these laws.

Many federal crimes have a broad scope and are used in prosecutions for violations of the particular statute and also in both fraud and RICO violations (see Chapter 18). They include the following:

Fraudulent Schemes Under State Law   Every state has enacted statutes that make fraud a crime under certain circumstances. In many states, the general

Mail Fraud Act	
18 U.S.C. § 1341. This act has been amended to include all interstate carriers, such as FedEx and UPS.	"To prove mail fraud, the government must show that the defendant (1) intentionally participated in a scheme to defraud, and (2) used the mails to execute the fraudulent scheme; . . . conviction for mail fraud need not rest on the success of the fraudulent scheme." *United States v. Bailey*, 123 F.3d 1381 (11th Cir. 1997). The scheme need not be such as to deceive a reasonable person; even one directed at the naive or ignorant is a violation. *United States v. Svete*, 556 F.3d 1157 (11th Cir. 2009).
Wire Fraud Act	
18 U.S.C. § 1343	The same elements as mail fraud, plus the wire communication must cross state lines. The Commerce Clause gives the federal government jurisdiction over wire communications, whereas the mail fraud statute stems from the Constitution's grant of power to Congress over the postal service.
Travel Act	
18 U.S.C.A. § 1952	To prove a violation of the Travel Act, the government must show "(1) travel in interstate or foreign commerce, or use of telephone, mail, or other facility in interstate or foreign commerce; (2) with intent to facilitate the promotion, management, establishment, or carrying on of any unlawful activity, and (3) thereafter performs an additional act in furtherance of the specified unlawful activity." *United States v. Long*, 949 F.2d 1370 (5th Cir. 1991). In 2007 the football player Michael Vick was charged with violation of the Travel Act, as well as other crimes.
Major Fraud Act	
18 U.S.C. § 1031	Any person who executes a scheme or artifice to defraud the United States or obtain property under false pretenses based on a contract or grant from the United States in excess of $1,000,000 is guilty of major fraud.

fraud statute follows the language of the federal acts, such as mail or wire fraud. Arizona's statute, ARS § 13-2310, makes it a crime to execute a "scheme or artifice" intended to deprive another person of property fraudulently. Some states also have specific statutes aimed at "confidence games" or related trickery. New York's statute, titled "Fraudulent accosting," Penal Law § 165.30, is an example of such a statute. It makes it a crime to obtain property of another by trick, deception, or confidence game. Finally, many states have statutes aimed at schemes to obtain money by false pretenses. See, e.g., W. Va. Code § 61-3-24.

The Crime of Identity Theft and False Identification Documents

In a report issued November 30, 2011, the Department of Justice Bureau of Justice Statistics stated that in 2010, 8.6 million households were victims of some form of identity theft, causing direct losses of $13.3 billion. Total costs of identity theft are likely greater than $50 billion.

identity theft Theft
based on stealing a real
person's identification
information (true
name) or theft based
on creating a fictitious
person's identification
(synthetic identity).

Identity theft can be both "true name" and "synthetic identity" theft. In true name theft, an actual person's identity—his or her name, address, Social Security number, or credit card number—is stolen. In synthetic identity theft, a fictitious person's name or Social Security number are used to commit the theft. It is reported that the number of synthetic identity thefts exceeds the number of true name thefts.

Because it is common to use stolen identity documents or numbers in computers, the mail system, or over telephone lines, many identity theft prosecutions are under federal laws. The principal federal statutes are 18 U.S.C. § 1028, identity theft; and 18 U.S.C. § 1028(A), aggravated identity theft. Section 1028 makes it a crime to "knowingly" possess, transfer, use, or produce a false identification document or authentication feature of a document, or use, possess, or transfer an identification document of another person. Section 1028(A) makes it an aggravated offense punishable by an additional 2-year prison term to use or possess the identification document of another person as part of any of the crimes listed in § 1028(a).

Prosecutions under § 1028 include production of false identification documents, as well as theft of identification documents. The statute prohibits production of identification documents that appear to be issued by an agency of the United States. However, it is not necessary for the prosecution to prove that a false document makes reference to an actual U.S. agency, like the FBI or the U.S. Marshal's Office. In *United States v. Fuller*,[21] the court upheld the conviction of a defendant who produced an identification allegedly issued by the "United States Special Response Department Anti-Terrorism Unit." The court stated that the statute is violated when a false identification appeared to be issued by an agency of the United States, whether or not such an agency actually exists.

Prosecutions for theft of an identification document or number, at least under § 1028(A) for aggravated identity theft, require the prosecution to prove the defendant knew that the document or number used belonged to an actual person. In *United States v. Flores-Figueroa*, 129 S. Ct. 1886 (2009), discussed in Chapter 3, the U.S. Supreme Court held that a conviction for use of the identification document of another required proof the defendant knew the identity card belonged to another person. This may also be the case for a conviction under § 1028, which employs the same "knowingly" language, though the Court did not expressly consider the requirements under that statute.

Flores-Figueroa, a Mexican citizen, unlawfully entered the United States. In order to secure employment, Flores-Figueroa presented an employer with a counterfeit Social Security card and alien registration card ("green card"). The cards used his real name, but the numbers on the documents belonged to other people. Flores-Figueroa was charged with various immigration crimes, and was also charged with "aggravated identity theft" under 18 U.S.C. §1028A(a)(l), which upon conviction provides for a mandatory two years of imprisonment to be added to the sentences for the underlying crimes. Section 1028A(a)(l) states that it is a crime if one "knowingly transfers, possesses, or uses, without lawful authority, a means of identification of another person."

Flores-Figueroa was convicted of all charges, and he appealed the conviction and increased sentence under the aggravated identity theft statute. He alleged the prosecution failed to prove that he knew the numbers on the counterfeit cards belonged to "another person." Flores-Figueroa contended that §1028A(a)(l) required the government to prove he "knowingly" violated every element of the statute, including the use of a number belonging to another person. The trial court and court of appeals disagreed, and the Supreme Court granted review on that specific question. The Supreme Court agreed with Flores-Figueroa, and it reversed his conviction under the aggravated identity theft statute.

The government contended that "knowingly" modified only the actions of transferring or possessing counterfeit documents, and that Flores-Figueroa did so without lawful authority. It did not require, the government contended, knowledge that the counterfeit numbers belonged to "another" person. The Court rejected the government's position, mainly based on the way the statute was worded:

> There are strong textual reasons for rejecting the Government's position. As a matter of ordinary English grammar, it seems natural to read the statute's word "knowingly" as applying to all the subsequently listed elements of the crime. . . . In ordinary English, where a transitive verb has an object, listeners in most contexts assume that an adverb (such as knowingly) that modifies the transitive verb tells the listener how the subject performed the entire action, including the object as set forth in the sentence. (129 S. Ct. at 1890)

Since the object of the sentence was the means of identification of "another person," the Court concluded the government must prove Flores-Figueroa knew the documents he used belonged to "another person." Since it did not, the conviction was reversed.

Justice Alito, in a concurring opinion, expressed concern that the majority decision was an "overly rigid rule of statutory construction." He identified some statutes where the lower federal courts had interpreted statutes differently, because of the context of the statute. For example, 18 U.S.C. § 2423(a), which makes it a crime to "knowingly" transport an individual under 18 years of age across state lines for the purpose of prostitution, has uniformly been interpreted by the federal courts of appeals as not requiring proof the defendant knew the individual transported was under 18 years of age. In the appropriate context, Justice Alito stated, such an interpretation would be correct. He concluded, however, that the present case did not have such a context, and thus agreed with the result.

At least one lower federal court has adopted Justice Alito's understanding of the limited holding in *Flores-Figueroa*. In *United States v. Cox*, 577 F.3d 833 (7th Cir. 2009), decided shortly after *Flores-Figueroa*, the Seventh Circuit Court of Appeals held that 18 U.S.C. § 2423(a) does not require proof that the defendant knew the individual transported was under the age of 18.

The prosecution may prove the knowledge requirement under § 1028(A) by inference. In *United States v. Holmes*, 595 F.3d 1255 (11th Cir. 2010), the court held that the fact the defendant had previously successfully used another person's name to obtain a driver's license and passport was sufficient evidence for a jury to infer she knew the name belonged to an actual person. Nor does the name have to belong to a living person. In the 2012 case of *United States v. Zuniga-Artaga*,[22] the court held that the prosecution need not prove that "another person" under § 1028(A) was living at the time the defendant used that person's identification documents.

In the 2012 case of *United States v. Hilton*[23] a federal court of appeals held that corporations are not "persons" under the federal aggravated identity theft statute. Though the term "person" usually includes corporations, the court held the identity theft statutes were vague on this issue, since those statutes also referred to means of identification of "a specific individual." It therefore held the statute should not be read to include theft of a corporation's identity.

In the 2013 case of *United States v. Lombard,*[24] the court held that identity theft included use of information about "another person" to obtain false identification documents, even though the "other person" sold that information to the defendant. There, the defendant paid another person to use his birth date and social security number to get a false driver's license and U.S. passport. He then left a fake suicide note by a bridge in Illinois, and left a voice mail at the local sheriff's office stating they would find his body and could then "kiss my cold, white, wet a***." The defendant left the country, and was arrested in Burma in 2011. He was returned to the United States and convicted of identity theft. The court of appeals affirmed his conviction, holding the federal identity theft statutes applied whenever a person used another person's identity to obtain false identification documents, since those documents were obtained "without lawful authority" under the statute.

In *United States v. Reynolds*, 710 F.3d 434 (D.C. Cir. 2013) the court held that improper use of a person's signature, even if some use was authorized, violated the aggravated identity theft statute. There, a church financial officer, who had access to the digital signatures of other church officers, used the signatures to swindle the church out of $850,000. The court also rejected the defendant's argument that under the identity theft statute the government must prove the individual whose signature was improperly used suffered economic harm. The court said all the government had to prove was the unlawful use of the signatures.

However, "use" of another person's name or signature violates the identity theft statute only when that use involves impersonation of that person, one court has held. In *United States v. Miller*, 734 F.3d 530 (6th Cir. 2013) the court reversed a conviction under section 1028A where the defendant signed a loan application, listed his partners by name, and falsely represented his partners had all authorized him to use partnership property as security for the loan. The court said the defendant did not "use" the partner's identities because he was not impersonating them or purporting to act on their behalf.

Most states have identity theft statutes similar to the federal statutes, though often with broader definitions of the crime. The Wisconsin identity theft statute, Wis. Stat. § 943.201(2)(c), includes using another person's identification information to cause harm to that person's reputation. In *State v. Baron,*[25] the court held the statute applied to a defendant who gained access to his employer's e-mail account and learned the employer was having an extramarital affair. The defendant sent out an e-mail to several persons, purporting to come from the employer, which made the affair public. The next day, the employer committed suicide. The court rejected the defendant's argument that the statute violated his First Amendment rights.

In *State v. Hardesty,*[26] the Kansas Court of Appeals held that "another person" in the Kansas identity theft statute, KSA 21-4018, includes a deceased person. Perhaps in response to that decision and the U.S. Supreme Court's decision in *Flores-Figueroa,* the Kansas legislature amended the identity theft statute in 2010 to state expressly that (1) theft of a deceased person's identification is covered by the statute and (2) it is not a defense that the thief did not know the identification belonged to an actual person.

⚖ IDENTITY THEFT

Identity theft has grown rapidly to the point where, according to the U.S. Federal Trade Commission, over 15 million people were victims of identity theft in 2010. These thefts cost the victims and businesses an estimated $50 billion.

To commit the crime a thief needs
Your name, date of birth, Social Security number, and an estimate of your annual income.

How would a thief obtain this information?
Steal (or find) a purse or wallet, steal your mail, or go through your trash looking for credit or bank card statements. Old or recent tax returns also have this information. It can be obtained from the databases of some businesses.

A thief can then
Open a new credit card account or bank account in your name. Use the credit card (or cards) to obtain goods. Write bad checks on your bank account. Open charge accounts with retail stores. Establish telephone or wireless service in your name. Use your identity and credit to obtain many items of value.

To avoid immediate detection, the thief can
Use a change-of-address form and divert your mail and the bills to another address.

To protect your family and yourself, take the following precautions: (1) Keep an eye open for missing mail, as a change of address filed by a clever thief will send bills and credit card statements to another address; (2) reveal only such personal information as is necessary; and (3) check your credit file every year or two to make sure a thief is not borrowing money in your name.

In theft of identity, thieves seek to profit in the following ways:

COUNTERFEITING OF MONEY AND COMMERCIAL PRODUCTS

Counterfeiting of Currency

Counterfeiting of currency is a serious federal offense that could have a severe economic impact on society. The history of counterfeiting in the United States can be summarized as follows:

- Until and during the Civil War, counterfeiting was a serious problem. Thousands of various legitimate bills were being printed by more than 1,500 state banks. Therefore, counterfeiting was easy during that period. An estimated one-third of the currency used during the Civil War was counterfeit.
- Establishment of a single national currency in 1863 and the creation of the U.S. Secret Service immediately made counterfeiting harder. Counterfeiting the new currency required skilled people with sophisticated equipment. The diligent efforts of the Secret Service made the pooling of the necessary material and equipment plus the necessary highly trained skills difficult. Counterfeiting and alteration of currency were kept at a minimum over the following years.
- Today, sophisticated color copiers allow what law enforcement officers call "casual counterfeiters" to print thousands of crude bills. However, the principal problem is professional craftspeople, many of whom live in foreign countries and are producing counterfeit money that is difficult to detect.

In response to the growing problem of counterfeiting, the United States began issuing new folding money that is much harder to counterfeit. The introduction of new $100 bills began in 1996 and that of $50 bills began in 1997. The $20 bill, which most Americans use in their daily lives, began to be replaced in 1998. The $10 and $5 bills also have been replaced, and a "more modestly redesigned" $1 bill is to follow. Amateur counterfeiters such as high school students using school computers and color printers continue to be a problem to merchants and other people who do not look closely at the paper money they receive.[27]

Other Counterfeiting Problems

Counterfeited designer jeans, compact discs, recordings of movies, electronic components, computers, books, circuit relays, and drugs are sold extensively in the United States. Many of the counterfeited products are manufactured in foreign countries, and also sold there. Usually, the counterfeit product is a cheap or inferior copy of the real thing. However, the phony label deceives many dealers and consumers, who believe that they are buying the name-brand product.

Importation, manufacture, or sale of a counterfeit product in the United States could result in (1) prosecution under the criminal code of a state, which would probably treat the offense as a misdemeanor; (2) civil suit and sanctions in federal or state civil courts; or (3) federal prosecution under the mail fraud statute (18 U.S.C.A. § 1341), the wire fraud statute (18 U.S.C.A. § 1343), the Food, Drug and Cosmetic Act (21 U.S.C.A. §§ 301, 321, and so on), or other federal statutes.

Counterfeiting of driver's licenses and other documents has become a serious problem in the United States. This crime is committed not only by private individuals, both within and outside of the United States, but sometimes also by state employees, who have access to the necessary forms for counterfeiting official documents.

The state of New York announced in March 2013 that in July 2013 it would begin issuing driver's licenses made of rigid polycarbonate, with identification information imprinted on the card with laser technology, and a black-and-white photograph of the license holder. State officials believe such a card would make counterfeiting of driver's licenses impossible.[28]

COMPUTER CRIME OR CYBERCRIME

The rise of computer use and ownership has seen a corresponding rise in the use of computers in criminal activity. Using computers as tools in crime makes many aspects of criminal behavior easier and more efficient. Even an illegal drug gang must keep records of sales and purchases, and computers make that task easier.

Computers can also be the object of criminal activity, such as where computer hardware or software is stolen. Finally, computers can be the subject of a crime, such as where information on a computer file is stolen or damaged. The phrase **cybercrime** generally refers to the last two kinds of crimes involving computers, where computers are used to access, or are accessed through, the Internet.

The earliest forms of Internet attacks on computers involved amateur hackers who invaded a computer just to prove they could. Most states have "unauthorized access" statutes that make it a crime to "knowingly" access another person's computer or computer accounts. In the 2011 case of *Muhammed v. State*[29] the court held that the Texas computer access statute requires that the prosecution prove the defendant accessed another person's computer knowing that he was doing so, and that he did so knowing he did not have that person's permission. This appears to be the majority view on the *mens rea* for unlawful computer access.

As use of the Internet exploded, computers began being used in a wide variety of crimes, including fraud, money laundering, extortion, software theft, corporate espionage, and child pornography (discussed in Chapter 12).

Most states have modified their criminal codes to account for the rise in computer use in criminal behavior. Many states have, for example, made it a crime to use computers for online harassment; see Texas Penal Code § 42.07(a)(2) (Vernon 2003). Some states have passed specific statutes making it a crime to use a computer to obtain money or property unlawfully. For example, in *Damaio v. Commonwealth*,[30] a defendant was convicted under the Virginia computer theft statute, § 18.2-152.3. The defendant quit his job as human resources director and transferred over 829 employee files to a third-party server only he could access. He told his employer he would return the files only if a debt he owed the employer were canceled. He was convicted of computer theft under the statute.

California has passed a law, California Penal Code § 502(c)(1), directed at unlawful access to a computer system for altering or using data on the system for the purpose of advancing a scheme to fraud or extort money or property.

Most states have a statute similar to § 9A.52.110 of the Washington Criminal Code, which prohibits computer trespass. **Computer trespass** is defined as unlawful access to a computer or computer system with intent to commit a crime or unlawful access to a computer or computer system maintained by a government unit. Most states also have a statute similar to the Maryland Code, Criminal Law, § 7-302, the "anti-hacking" statute. This law makes it a crime to enter a computer system without permission with intent to alter or damage the system or data stored in the system.

cybercrime Criminal acts implemented through use of a computer or other form of electronic communication.

computer trespass Unlawful access to a computer or computer system with intent to commit a crime, or unlawful access to a computer or computer system maintained by a government unit.

CYBERCRIMES IN THE NEWS

The F.B.I. has created an organization, the Internet Crimes Complaint Center (called "IC3") to receive reports of cybercrime, and begin investigation of the crimes. In its 2015 report, covering the period from April, 2014 to June, 2015, IC3 reported that 269,422 complaints of cybercrimes were reported to IC3. Economic losses during that period from these crimes were estimated at $800,492,073.00. Some of the leading cybercrimes included:

- Cryptowall Ransomware: Victims click into an infected internet ad or website; the infection spreads to the victim's computer, encrypting all the computer files. The victim is then told (via e-mails or calls) to pay a sum of money (or often Bitcoin) to "ransom" the files and eliminate the encryption.
- Real estate fraud: Criminals take a post from a legitimate website, such as house rentals, and repost it with a different payment address. The victim agrees to rent the house, and sends a deposit or other payment to the fraudulent location.
- Auto fraud: Criminal lists non-existent auto for sale on legitimate website, drops price, and states a fast sale is needed because the seller is leaving the country, or something similar. Often lists payment to what looks like a legitimate site, such as a bank name or dealer name, but criminal controls the site.
- Government Imposter: Criminal poses as government employee, such as an IRS Agent, and sends emails informing victim they have been audited and owe back taxes. Directs payment to a post office box controlled by criminals.
- Extortion: Criminals hack into a "pay day" loan company and acquire personal information on borrowers. They then harass the borrowers, threatening legal action or public disclosure of personal information if loan not "repaid" at once.
- Business emails: Criminals hack into a business computer and obtain identities of vendors who will be making payments to the business. They then send emails in the business name to the vendors redirecting those payments to a new location controlled by the criminals. This scam caused over $226 million in 2014, IC3 reports.
- Social Media: Concealed hyperlinks in social media sites send users to fraudulent websites when they "click," "Like," or "Share" on the social media site. Called "clickjacking" or "pharming," it then becomes possible to defraud the victims who unknowingly visit the fraudulent website.

The federal government uses the Computer Fraud and Abuse Act, 18 U.S.C. § 1030 (CFAA), to target computer crime. Under this statute, a wide variety of cybercrimes is prohibited, from unlawfully accessing computers (the anti-hacking law) to unlawfully obtaining information from a financial institution, as the following cases illustrate.

In *Musacchio v. United States*, 136 S. Ct. 709 (2016) the U.S. Supreme Court affirmed the conviction of Michael Musacchio for violation of the CFAA. Musacchio was the CEO of Excel Transportation Services Inc., a logistics company. After Musacchio resigned to form a new company he "hacked" into Excel's computers to pirate company information. He was caught, and charged under the CFAA with unlawful access to the Excel computers. At his trial the trial judge instructed the jury (without an objection by the government) that the prosecution needed to prove Musacchio both unlawfully accessed the Excel computers, and exceeded his authority to access those computers. This instruction was incorrect; in fact, § 1030 states that it is a violation to unlawfully access a computer *or* exceed one's authorized access. Musacchio was convicted, and sentenced to 60 months in prison. The Fifth Circuit affirmed his conviction.

 ## EMPLOYEES AND UNAUTHORIZED COMPUTER ACCESS

Employees use their employer's computers at work, and are often privileged, by use of a password, to access employer or client records. Is it a violation of an applicable federal or state unlawful computer access statute for an employee to access an employer's computer for purposes other than work? That is, does "unauthorized access" include unauthorized "use" of an employer's computer or accounts? That was the issue in the following state and federal cases:

- In *Willoughby v. State*, 84 So.3d 1210 (Fla. App. 2012) an employee was convicted of violations of the Florida unlawful computer access statute and the improper acquisition of confidential information statute. The employee accessed her employer's computer at home using her laptop, and downloaded confidential information. The appeals court reversed the conviction under the "unlawful access" statute, stating the employer had given permission to the employee to use her laptop at work because it was faster than the employer's computer. However, it affirmed the conviction for improper acquisition of confidential information.
- In *United States v. Teague*, 646 F.3d 1119 (8th Cir. 2011) an employee of a company working under contract with the U.S. Department of Education was convicted of violating the CFAA. The employee had access to the National Student Loan Data System records as part of her position as an advisor on student loan debt collection. She improperly used her access privilege to acquire information on President Obama's student loan history. The court of appeals affirmed her conviction, stating the CFAA applied to computer access that exceeded lawful permission to access a computer.
- In *United States v. John*, 597 F.3d 263 (5th Cir. 2010), the court considered another violation of the CFAA. In *John* an employee of Citigroup Company accessed computer accounts of customers of Citigroup. She then gave the information gained from that access to confederates, who made fraudulent charges against those accounts. She was arrested and charged with violating CFAA, convicted on several counts, and sentenced to 108 months in prison. On appeal she contended she could not be convicted of unauthorized access under § 1030, because in her position at Citigroup she was authorized to access the accounts and view the information in the accounts. As a result, she argued, her access was not "unauthorized." The court disagreed, and it affirmed her conviction. It stated that "unauthorized access" includes accessing a computer with the fraudulent intent to take information from the computer and use it in a scheme to defraud the computer account holders.
- In *United States v. Nosal*, 676 F.3d 854 (9th Cir. 2012) the court sitting *en banc* disagreed with the Fifth Circuit's interpretation of the CFAA in *John*, discussed above. In *Nosal* employees with authorized access to an employer's computer and client files did so in order to acquire information to give to Nosal, a former employee. Nosal was charged, among other crimes, with aiding and abetting those employees in violations of the CFAA. The trial court dismissed those charges, holding the CFAA did not apply to unauthorized use of information contained on an employer's computer, but only to unauthorized access.

On appeal to the Supreme Court Musacchio contended the government introduced insufficient evidence to satisfy the elements of the crime as instructed to the jury. The Supreme Court held that so long as the evidence supported the actual elements of the statute, here that Musacchio unlawfully accessed the Excel computers, there was no need to prove the alternative elements. It affirmed the conviction and sentence.

In *United States v. Phillips*, 477 F3d 215 (5th Cir. 2007), the court affirmed a conviction of a University of Texas student under the CFAA. The student was granted access to the UT computer system when he enrolled as a freshman. He then used a technique called "port scanning" to find other computers on the network that could easily be accessed. The student gained access to many computers this way, and he stole information. He also found a secure UT web server called "TXClass" and, by using a "brute force" attack (a program that sends multiple possible passwords to enter a computer), was able to make multiple entries into the TXClass server. Once there, he collected sensitive data such as Social Security numbers of students and faculty. The Secret Service investigated the intrusions into the UT system, which were damaging the system and making it crash repeatedly. The student was arrested and charged with a violation of the CFAA. He was convicted, sentenced to 5 years' probation and 500 hours of community service, and ordered to pay $170,000 in restitution to UT.

The student appealed, contending the prosecution had not proven "unauthorized access" under § 1030. The court of appeals rejected his contention, stating that, under § 1030, "unauthorized access" included accessing a computer without authorization, such as hacking, and also exceeding authorized use. While the student did have authority to access the UT computer system, the court held he clearly did not have authority to use a brute force attack to gain entry to a secure server, and the court affirmed his conviction.

ARSON

One of the first concerns of a fire investigator is the fire's origin. Fires can be classified by their causes as accidental fires, natural fires (caused without human intervention), **arson** (fires of incendiary origin), and fires of unknown origin.

Arson A person's deliberate, willful, and malicious burning of a building or personal property.

Many fires are started accidentally, when children play with matches or people are careless with cigarettes, cigars, or pipe ashes. Some fires are of natural origin and occur without human intervention because of spontaneous combustion, defective heating units, faulty electrical appliances or wiring, and the like.

Arson is a person's deliberate, willful, and malicious burning of a building or personal property. Arson is the easiest of the major crimes to commit, the most difficult to detect, and the hardest to prove in court.

In most states, arson has several degrees or grades of commission, with gradations depending on whether the property destroyed is a residence or other kind of structure. An example of a common form of arson statute is Idaho Code § 18-802-805. First-degree arson under § 802 includes unlawfully and willfully damaging by fire or explosives a dwelling or a structure where people are commonly present or any structure in which the arsonist has reasonable grounds to believe a person might be present. Second-degree arson under § 803 is damaging any structure not covered in § 802. Third-degree arson under § 804 is damage to any other real or personal property. Finally, Idaho, like most states, has an "aggravated arson" statute, § 18-805, under which the penalty for arson is greatly increased if a person, including a firefighter, is killed or suffers serious bodily injury as a result of the fire.

The United States has an arson statute, 18 U.S.C. § 844(f), that applies to any malicious damage by fire or explosives to any property owned by or leased to the United States, an agency of the United States, or any organization receiving financial assistance from the United States. In the 2009 case of *United States v. Hersom*,[31] the court held that the federal arson statute applied to arson of four buildings owned by a private company that were undergoing renovations with financial assistance provided by block grants from HUD.

Essential Elements of Arson

All states have enacted statutes that define arson. In general, most statutes require that the state prove the following elements:

- That there was a fire and that some part of the building or personal property was damaged. Some courts require an actual burning of part of the property. In the case of *State v. Williams,* the Indiana Court of Appeals held that soot and smoke constituted "damage" within the meaning of the Indiana arson statute. Attempted arson or conspiracy to commit arson may also be possible criminal charges.[32]
- That the fire was of incendiary origin and was willfully and intentionally set. This is the required proof of corpus delicti (that a crime was in fact committed). For a fire inspector to testify in court that he or she "suspected" arson or that the fire was of "unknown origin" is insufficient to prove corpus delicti.[33] An expert witness is usually required to testify that arson did occur and support the statement with specific evidence.
- That the accused committed or was party to the crime of arson charged. Like all other crimes, the evidence required to convict a person of arson is proof beyond a reasonable doubt.

PRODUCT TAMPERING

Since 1982, product tampering has cost the lives of at least twelve people in the United States. The offense of poisoning over-the-counter drugs and food products was described by a high-ranking federal official as "an insidious and terrible crime. It is a form of terrorism not unlike planting a bomb in some public place to gain media attention, notoriety, or some sick sense of control over human life."

Although it is rare that a product is actually contaminated or poisoned, crimes related to product tampering include the following:

- *Extortion:* After seven people died in the Chicago area in 1982 from cyanide-laced Extra-Strength Tylenol, James Lewis tried to use the killings in attempting to extort $1 million from the manufacturer of Tylenol. Lewis was convicted in a federal court in 1983. The FBI continues to investigate the Tylenol killings, but as of 2013 the perpetrator had not been found. The Tylenol killings led to Congress enacting the federal Anti-Tampering Act discussed below.

- *Threats to Tamper and/or Threats to Allege Tampering:* Another form of extortion attempts to obtain money from manufacturers, who incur huge costs and loss of market and sales in tampering cases. In March of 2013 the makers of Red Bull announced there was a threat to place fecal matter in cans of the popular drink if the company did not pay a money demand.
- *Attempts to Create the Basis of a Civil Lawsuit:* A person fakes a tampering case to make it appear that a person in a family has been the victim of random tampering.

The Federal Consumer Tampering Act, 18 U.S.C.A. § 1365, forbids tampering with consumer products "with reckless disregard" that another person will be placed in danger of death or serious injury. In the 2011 case of *United States v. Wilson*[34] an ambulance paramedic developed a morphine addiction when he began using morphine stored in a safe at the premises of his employer, the rescue company. Initially he took only morphine vials marked "expired," since those would not be missed and were routinely destroyed. At some point, he began emptying unexpired vials of morphine and replacing the morphine with saline solution. He also took steps designed to limit the risk that the tampered vials would be used by other paramedics when helping injured persons. He argued he should not be convicted under the federal consumer tampering statute because he lacked the required *mens rea*: "reckless disregard." The court rejected that argument, noting that the defendant knew he did not eliminate altogether the risk of exposure of the tampered vials to injured persons, and that was enough to prove reckless disregard. He was convicted under the statute.

The federal statute also includes as product tampering actions that reduce the efficacy of a drug designed to save a life or alleviate bodily injury, as well as tampering that turns a drug into a poison. In the 2014 case of *United States v. Lyle,*[35] the defendant opened boxes stored in a secure narcotics safe that contained fentanyl patches, a narcotic much more potent than morphine. He took out the patches, and then re-secured the box. He was charged with violation of the federal anti-tampering statute but contended the statute did not apply to his actions because he didn't substitute another substance for the drug that was stolen. The court rejected that argument, noting that § 1365 applied to tampering with the container in which drugs are stored. The defendant clearly did that, because he removed the drug listed on the container as being inside. The Ninth Circuit affirmed his conviction; the U.S. Supreme Court denied certiorari: 135 S. Ct. 110.

The crime of consumer product tampering receives a great deal of attention and concern because all societies are vulnerable to such acts. Millions of dollars have been invested in tamper-proof packaging. Most consumers are well aware of the remote possibility that the product they purchase may have been tampered with in a way that could seriously hurt them or someone in their family.

Federal statutes and the laws of most (if not all) states also make the following conduct criminal:

- Tampering with (altering) or destroying evidence of a crime
- Tampering with (altering) a financial document such as a check or another document such as a will or a mortgage
- Tampering with (altering) an odometer of a motor vehicle that is to be sold to another person
- Tampering with a witness or potential witness by telling the witness what to say or what not to say

ENVIRONMENTAL CRIMES AND CORPORATE RESPONSIBILITY

On April 20, 2010, a massive explosion struck the *Deepwater Horizon* oil rig, which was drilling for oil 70 miles off the Louisiana coast. Eleven workers were killed in the blast, which resulted in the release of over 4.9 million barrels of oil into the Gulf of Mexico. The Macondo well site where the blowout explosion occurred was finally capped in July 2010, after causing enormous damage to the ocean, ocean floor, migratory birds, ocean mammals, and the economic vitality of the Gulf Coast. BP Company was the company responsible for the well site, and Transocean owned the oil rig that exploded.

BP faced massive civil responsibility for the damages to the workers, their families, and the environment. It immediately set up a $20-billion-dollar fund to address civil claims, and reached an agreement with the Justice Department to administer those funds under the Deepwater Horizon Court-Supervised Settlement Program. As of the end of 2012, over $8.2 billion had been paid under that settlement.

BP also faced criminal prosecution for violating the criminal provisions of several federal statutes passed to protect the environment. The Clean Water Act, the Migratory Bird Act, the Marine Mammal Protection Act, the Endangered Species Act, and the Outer Continental Shelf Lands Act all have criminal penalties for harm caused to the environment by the oil spill. In addition, BP could also have been prosecuted under the Seaman's Manslaughter Statute for the death of the eleven workers. The environmental crimes acts generally apply to any knowing violation of the statute, though some federal courts have applied the criminal provisions to negligent acts. See e.g., *United States v. Ortiz*, 427 F.3d 1278 (10th Cir. 2005). Violation of the Migratory Bird Act is a strict liability crime.

In December of 2012 BP agreed to plead guilty to eleven felony charges, including violations of the Clean Water Act and obstruction of justice, and manslaughter charges for the deaths of the oil workers. A federal judge approved a fine of $4.5 billion, and 5 years of probation in oil exploration ventures, where BP's actions will be monitored. Transocean, which owned the oil rig, agreed to pay criminal fines of $1.4 billion.

In the Gulf oil spill, the corporation incurred criminal liability. In environmental crimes, many federal statutes such as the Clean Water Act (CWA); the Clean Air Act (CAA); the Reserve Conservation and Recovery Act (RCHA); and the Comprehensive Environmental Response, Compliance, and Liability Act (CERCLA) also provide for criminal liability of corporate officers.

Beginning with the case of *United States v. Dotterwich*[36] the U.S. Supreme Court has held that "responsible" corporate officers may be criminally liable for actions taken by the corporation. Subsequently, Congress amended the CWA and CAA to specifically provide for "responsible corporate officer" (RCO) criminal liability for violations of those statutes. Courts have incorporated RCO criminal liability for violations of other environmental criminal provisions in a similar manner.

Virtually all the environmental criminal statutes require a showing of a "knowing" violation of the statute. Thus, in criminal suits against a corporate officer the prosecution cannot simply prove the officer is an RCO. It must also show the officer knew the corporation was taking actions that created the risk of harm addressed by the statute. In a leading case, *United States v. Hansen*,[37] corporate officers were convicted of violations of the CWA, RCRA, and CERCLA. They argued they could not be convicted because they did not personally oversee the actions of the company that violated the statutes. The court of appeals affirmed the convictions, stating that all the prosecution need prove is that the officers were aware violations were occurring, based on their knowledge of plant operations.

Finally, both the CWA and the CAA acts provide that "knowingly" can be proved by evidence an RCO took affirmative steps to shield himself from knowledge of actions that violated the statutes.

★★★
LEARNING OBJECTIVES SUMMARY

LO 1. Define white-collar crime.

White-collar crime refers to criminal offenses in which the criminal's only goal is economic gain.

LO 2. Explain why fraud convictions require action done knowingly.

Fraud is in essence a crime of deceit, and therefore it must be shown that the defendant's actions were intended to be deceitful. One cannot normally be negligently deceitful.

LO 3. Describe the elements of a "scheme or artifice" under federal criminal statutes.

A "scheme or artifice" in federal criminal statutes is an intentional act that has as a goal fraudulent and unlawful gain, and includes a material falsehood one would understand to be important and would be relied on by others. It specifically includes depriving another of the intangible right to honest services.

LO 4. Explain the status of the "quid pro quo" requirement in federal bribery charges.

Bribery under the federal statute requires proof that the person making the bribe and the official taking the bribe had the "specific intent" to exchange something of value for the official's act.

LO 5. List the laws protecting intellectual property.

The principal laws protecting intellectual property are the federal copyright, patent, and trademark laws, as well as state trade secret laws.

LO 6. Name two federal criminal statutes frequently used to convict white-collar criminals.

The federal bank fraud act and the wire fraud act are frequently used to convict white-collar criminals.

LO 7. Identify one element making wire fraud different from bank fraud, and state why the element exists.

A communication under the wire fraud act must cross state lines. This is necessary to give Congress jurisdiction over the crime under the Commerce Clause. By definition, use of the U.S. mails involves interstate commerce. Because the federal government insures bank deposits, it has jurisdiction over bank fraud without any interstate commerce requirement.

LO 8. Define insider trading.

Insider trading includes using information not available to the public acquired by an insider who owes a fiduciary obligation to an employer, and profit from the use of the information. It also includes use of such information by a person not an insider, if the person acquired the information knowing it came from an insider and was not available to the public, and involved a breach of a fiduciary obligation.

LO 9. State the elements of identity theft crimes.

A conviction under the federal identity theft statute requires proof that a person produced a false identification document or possessed or used an identification document that belonged to another person. The federal statute requires that the defendant know the identification document belongs to another person, though some state statutes do not have this requirement.

KEY TERMS

white-collar crime, p. 424
fraud, p. 424
bank fraud, p. 425
intellectual property fraud, p. 428

bribery, p. 431
quid pro quo, p. 433
identity theft, p. 439
cybercrime, p. 444

computer trespass, p. 444
arson, p. 447

CASE ANALYSIS AND WRITING EXERCISES

1. Woody and Kathy Medlock ran a medical ambulance company. They transported patients to and from hospitals and clinics for treatments like kidney dialysis, where use of an ambulance was required. Medicare reimbursed them for such transportation. The Medlocks made several billings to Medicare for transportation of named patients that misrepresented the nature of the transportation, e.g. saying a stretcher was used when it wasn't, or "double loading" patients but billing for two ambulance runs. They were charged with both health care fraud and aggravated identity theft under federal statutes. Should they be convicted of both crimes? See *United States v. Medlock*, 792 F.3d 700 (6th Cir. 2015), *cert denied* 136 S. Ct. 601 (2015).

2. Carlos Ezeta was a professor and student advisor at a Las Vegas community college. As part of his position he advised Hispanic students on enrollment and curriculum choices. He also helped these students apply for federal financial aid by making false statements on FAFSA forms. He did not receive any payment for his actions, and any financial aid went to the students. Ezeta was indicted under 20 U.S.C. § 1097(a) for making false statements to the government to "obtain federal financial aid money." He moved to quash (dismiss) the indictment, contending he could not violate the statute because he did not "obtain" any financial aid for himself. The trial judge agreed, and dismissed the indictment. The government appealed. What should the appeals court decide? Why? See *United States v. Ezeta*, 752 F.3d 1182 (9th Cir. 2014).

3. The two top executives of Executive Recycling Inc. (ERI) were convicted of violating the federal Resource Conservation and Recovery Act, which was applicable through adoption by the EPA of the Colorado Hazardous Waste Management Act. ERI was a recycling company that recycled electronic waste (computer keyboards, monitors, television tubes, and so forth). Because some computer parts, like Cathode Ray Tubes (CRT) contain lead, e-waste must be disposed of as a hazardous material. ERI collected e-waste from its customers in Colorado, promising to dispose of the waste in compliance with environmental laws. However, ERI resold 142917 CRTs to buyers in China, for incorporation into electronic devices made in China. The government contended those sales violated the environmental laws, because any electronic part that could not be resold or refurbished "for its original intended purpose" must be destroyed under the state and federal acts. The executives contended the state statute, which the EPA adopted in lieu of the federal act, did not say "original intended purpose," and thus it was not a violation to sell the e-waste for another purpose. How did the court of appeals receive those arguments? If the government was correct, why were some of the convictions reversed? See *United States v. Richter*, 796 F.3d 1173 (10th Cir. 2015), *cert denied* 2016 WL 2842489 (2016).

4. As we saw in the *Skilling* case discussed in this chapter, the "honest services" fraud statute was interpreted by the U. S. Supreme Court to apply only to "core" corruption actions like "bribery and kickbacks." Lower courts were then left to figure out when a "bribe or kickback" occurred. Why did the courts in the following two cases conclude neither a bribe nor a kickback took place, and reversed convictions for honest services fraud? *United States v. Aunspaugh*, 792 F.3d 1302 (11th Cir. 2015). [Defendant made secret payments to key employee of company defendants were negotiating with for business]; *United States v. Hawkins*, 777 F.3d 880 (7th Cir. 2015). [Defendants, county employees, accepted gratuity from undercover agent posing as taxpayer seeking review of the assessed value of real estate.]

ENDNOTES

1. U.S. Department of Justice, 1989, p. 3.

2. U.S. Department of Justice, "Crime in the United States: 2011."

3. 527 U.S. 1 (1999).

4. 134 S. Ct. 2384 (2014).

5. 554 F.3d 903 (10th Cir. 2009).

6. 588 F.3d 301 (6th Cir. 2009).

7. 131 S. Ct. 538 (2010).

8. 2013 WL 1104736 (2013).

9. 577 F.3d 195 (3rd Cir. 2009).

10. Investigating fraud in Medicaid and Medicare programs is discussed in two *FBI Law Enforcement Bulletins:* "Medicaid Fraud Control" (October 1992) and "Health Care Fraud" (October 1992).

    See the *New York Times* editorial, "Fraud and Waste in Medicare" (August 1, 1997), and other news articles reporting that federal auditors estimate $23 billion in fraud and mistake loss in Medicare payments in 1996. These losses fell into the following categories: (1) "raw fraud," which for the most part was services not provided; (2) a gray area requiring the exercise of judgment; and (3) violations of the anti-kickback provision, which forbids payment for referrals.

11. See the *New York Times* article "Agents Uncover Rampant Food Stamp Fraud," September 11, 1994, which estimates that in a $24 billion program, $2 billion is used for fraudulent purposes.

12. 490 F.3d 314 (3rd Cir. 2007).

13. 507 F.3d 550 (7th Cir. 2007).

14. 406 F.3d 22 (1st Cir. 2005).

15. 510 F.3d 134 (2nd Cir. 2007).

16. 308 F.3d 144 (2nd Cir. 2002).

17. 538 F.3d 341 (5th Cir. 2008).

18. 486 F.3d 315 (7th Cir. 2007).

19. 533 F.3d 143 (2nd Cir. 2008).

20. *United States v. Skilling,* 638 F.3d 480 (5th Cir. 2011), *cert. denied,* 132 S. Ct. 1905 (2012).

21. 531 F.3d 1020 (9th Cir. 2008).

22. 681 F.3d 1220 (11th Cir. 2012).

23. 701 F.3d 959 (4th Cir. 2012), *cert. denied,* 133 S. Ct. 1839 (2013). State identity theft statutes may have different interpretations. In *State v. Evans,* 298 P.3d 724 (Wash. 2013) the court held theft of a corporation's identity violated the Washington identity theft statute.

24. 706 F.3d 716 (6th Cir. 2013).

25. 769 N.W.2d 34 (Wis. 2009).

26. 213 P.3d 745 (Kans. App. 2009).

27. See the *New York Times* article "Teens Accused of Using Computers to Counterfeit," February 17, 1997.

28. *New York Times,* March 16, 2013: "Black and White, Wallet Size, Unfit for Faking."

29. 331 S.W.3d 187 (Tex. App. 2011).

30. 621 S.E.2d 696 (Va. App. 2005).

31. 588 F.3d 60 (1st Cir. 2009).

32. 600 N.E.2d 962 (Ind. App. 1992). If the completed crime of arson cannot be proved beyond a reasonable doubt, the state may then consider charging attempt to commit arson (or in an appropriate situation, conspiracy to commit arson).

33. See *Hughes v. State,* 6 Md. App. 389, 251 A2d 373 (1969), in which the court pointed out that mere presence of the accused at the scene of a fire is not proof beyond reasonable doubt that the fire was willfully and maliciously set. In *Hughes v. State,* a fire chief testified that he could not determine the cause of the fire. The court reversed the defendant's conviction, holding that the evidence was legally insufficient to establish the corpus delicti of the crime of arson.

34. 2011 WL 3876949 (C.D. Cal. 2011).

35. 742 F.3d 434 (9th Cir. 2014).

36. 320 U.S. 277 (1943).

37. 262 F.3d 1217 (11th Cir. 2001), *cert. denied,* 535 U.S. 1111 (2002).

16

Drug Abuse and Alcohol-Related Crimes

LEARNING OBJECTIVES

In this chapter we discuss crimes related to drugs, drug abuse, and alcohol abuse. The learning objectives for Chapter 16 are

LO 1. List the ways a person can violate the Uniform Controlled Substances Act.

LO 2. Identify the elements of the crime of possession of an illegal drug with intent to deliver.

LO 3. State the current status of state medical-use-of-marijuana statutes.

LO 4. Explain the rationale of the Supreme Court's holding in Gonzales v. Raich.

LO 5. Identify the elements that must be proved for a conviction under a state drug-induced death statute, as compared to the federal drug-induced penalty statute.

LO 6. State the basis of the argument a state's "booze it and lose it" implied consent law violated the U.S. Constitution.

LO 7. Identify what must be shown to prove a person was operating a motor vehicle.

Police administering an alcohol breath test using a Breathalyzer device. In 2016, the U.S. Supreme Court held that states could lawfully require suspected drunk drivers to consent to a breath test or suffer penalties if they refuse consent. The Court said blood tests of suspected drunk drivers require consent, and, if consent is not given, a warrant must be obtained to take a blood sample without consent.

Most states have statutes making it a crime to cause another "person" to ingest a controlled substance. Many other states have statutes aimed specifically at "chemical endangerment" of a "child" by causing the child to ingest a controlled substance. How, if at all, do these statutes apply to pregnant women who use a controlled substance during the pregnancy, thereby causing the unborn fetus to receive the controlled substance in the mother's blood supply to the fetus?

In *Ex parte Ankrom*, 152 So.3d 397 (Ala. 2013) the court affirmed a conviction under the Alabama child endangerment statute. In *Arms v. State*, 471 S.W.3d 637 (Ark. 2015) the court reversed a conviction under the Arkansas statute making it a crime to cause another "person" to ingest a controlled substance. What are the issues in prosecutions such as these? What should "person" or "child" mean in these criminal cases? What should "ingest" mean? Which court gave better answers to these questions?

In this chapter we will study the many ways the criminal laws are used to combat the illegal drug problem in the United States. We will also study the relationship of the abuse of alcohol to criminal behavior and government's attempts to control that behavior.

DRUG ABUSE

The Frightening Drug Problem

The possession, sale, and use of illegal drugs is a problem of epic proportion in the United States. Illegal drugs have shattered many lives, led to suicides and murders, and caused serious health problems in many people. Sections of many American cities where illegal drugs are readily available have become seriously disrupted; where drugs are available, other crimes follow.

Drug lords all over the world have become rich and powerful. Gangs and organized criminals in the United States find selling drugs to be an easy way to make money and gain power, which in turn leads to even greater lawlessness. For example, where criminals have huge amounts of cash available, the crime of bribery becomes more common. A March 14, 2016 report by the Homeland Security Advisory Council disclosed extensive corruption in the U.S. Customs & Border Protection Agency (CBP). The CBP has over 60,000 employees; 44,000 are sworn officers. Since October 1, 2004, 170 CBP officers and agents have been charged with corruption, including bribery and allowing illegal drugs to be brought into the United States. The report identifies multiple attempts by drug cartels to infiltrate the CBP. Since 2010, when the CBP began giving polygraph tests to all applicants, 75 percent of the applicants have been rejected because they either failed the polygraph or did not show up to take the test. In response to this problem, the FBI has several task forces operating along the U.S. southwest border with Mexico, investigating corruption and other problems in the CBP.

Illegal smuggling goes both ways on the United States–Mexico border. Going north is the largest constant flow of illegal drugs in the world. In a March 2016 report the Drug Enforcement Agency (DEA) stated that in 2014 33,770 kg of cocaine, 74,225 kg of marijuana, and 2,946 kg of meth were seized in the United States. This is likely a small percentage of the total volume of illegal drugs smuggled into the United States in any year.

Going south are smuggled American dollars for the purchase of illegal drugs. The Drug Enforcement Agency (DEA) estimates that $18 billion to $39 billion crosses the border each year. More than 16,000 vehicles cross the border each day in Laredo, Texas, alone, making policing the border almost impossible.

Also going south are smuggled firearms. Mexican drug gangs are a fertile market for sales of illegal weapons. There reportedly are about 6,600 American gun dealers along the Mexican border, and these dealers sell high-powered pistols and military rifles to the drug gangs. Data released by the Bureau of Alcohol, Tobacco and Firearms (ATF) on April 26, 2012, show that from 2007 to 2011 96,691 firearms seized in Mexico crime scenes were traced back to their manufacturer. Of those, 66,161 came from a source in the United States. In the failed "Fast and Furious" campaign conducted between 2008 and 2009, federal officials allowed over 2,000 automatic weapons to "walk" in to Mexico so that U.S. agents could follow the weapons to their purchasers. However, most of the guns were "lost," and the plan was scrapped. The "lost" guns later turned up at several crime scenes, including the murder in December 2010 of Border Patrol agent Brian Terry.

The year 2006 marked renewed efforts in the "war on drugs." In the United States, billions of dollars were allocated to increasing border security and hiring more border and customs agents. In Mexico, then-President Felipe Caldron launched a "federal assault" on drug cartels, using federal police to attack drug cartels in areas of Mexico where they operated.

The results on illegal drug smuggling and production since 2006 are mixed. While marijuana is harder to smuggle across the border with Mexico, the increase in production in the United States is dramatic. The Drug Enforcement Agency (DEA) reports that Mexican drug cartels are now sending members to the parks and forests of the United States to plant and harvest the drug. The DEA also reports that 80 percent of the marijuana grown in the United States is grown on state or federal land.

The production and import of methamphetamine has also increased over 2006 levels, according to the Justice Department's 2015 National Drug Threat Assessment Summary. The Methamphetamine Threat Assessment report stated that the supply of methamphetamine was the highest since 2005, the quality was the best, and the price was the lowest. Although domestic manufacture in small "one-pot" operations is also at a high level, domestic production has declined. The report states that in 2010 the DEA seized 10,520 small-pot domestic meth production operations. In 2014, the number of such seizures declined to 5935.

The largest percentage of methamphetamine comes from Mexico. Mexican drug cartels are frequently producing methamphetamine using non–ephedrine-based methods. Both the United States and Mexico have passed laws making it harder to obtain ephedrine and pseudoephedrine, the preferred base chemicals used in the manufacture of methamphetamine. This method produces drugs with the highest potency. Mexican drug cartels are now producing the drug by the "P2P" method, which produces drugs with lower potency, and then using other chemicals, such as tartaric acid, to increase the potency.

Heroin smuggling and use in the United States, which had been declining, appears to be on the rise, the Drug Threat Assessment summary stated. In 2010 the DEA seized 2763 kg of heroin; in 2014 this amount doubled to 5013 kg. Heroin overdose deaths also have increased. In 2007 there were 2402 reported heroin overdose deaths. In 2013 that number increased to 8257.

Heroin production has increased since 2005. Opium, a product derived from certain kinds of poppy plants, was produced in amounts significantly greater than previous years starting in 2006. Afghanistan, which produces about 90 percent of the world's opium, produced about 6,100 metric tons of opium in 2006, a 49 percent increase over the previous year. The 2007 crop was about 8,300 metric tons. The volume dropped in 2008, when opium having a value of about $3.4 billion was exported from Afghanistan. In 2009 exported opium dropped again, when $2.8 billion worth was exported. Based on crops planted in 2010, the United Nations believed opium production would drop again in 2010, which would mean a one-third drop since the highs of 2007.[1] Of the opium grown in Afghanistan, 80 percent comes from villages controlled by Taliban forces, according to the United Nations.

Most of the opium crop grown in Afghanistan (and other Asia locations) ends up in Europe; only about 10% goes to the United States, the 2015 Drug Threat Assessment reported. However, South America, mainly Colombia, and Mexico have dramatically increased heroin production for shipment to the United States.

The "war on drugs" has had tragic consequences for Mexican border towns. Since the crackdown efforts commenced in late 2006, more than 25,000 people have been killed by drug cartel gunmen, or in gunfights between federal police and drug cartels. One border city, Ciudad Juarez, which shares a border with El Paso, Texas, has been especially hard hit by the killings. On July 17, 2010, the Mexican drug gang La Linea exploded a car bomb in a trap set for federal police, killing three officers. In the weeks preceding the car bomb attack, fourteen police officers were killed by drug gunmen. In Juarez alone, 4,000 people have been killed since 2006 in drug cartel-related killings.

With virtually unlimited sources, illegal drugs have become readily available to anyone seeking them. Not only are the drugs available, but they are cheaper and of a better quality, making them attractive to the poor and the young. The Partnership for a Drug-Free America points out that

- Americans spend billions of dollars yearly for the purchase of illegal drugs.
- Many organized criminal groups, gangs, and terrorists depend on drug money. Police surveys show that there are now more than 30,000 gangs in the United States, with more than 800,000 members. (See Chapter 18.)
- Each year, more than 25 million Americans use illegal drugs.

Illegal Drug Users

The war against illegal drugs is being fought on both the supply side and on the demand side. Most cocaine, heroin, crack, and marijuana are produced outside the United States. Great efforts are being made to prevent illegal drugs from entering the United States. Efforts to win the supply-side war have been going on since the 1950s, but an estimated 90 percent of these illegal drugs get into the United States.

The demand-side problem is that millions of Americans are willing to pay billions of dollars yearly for illegal drugs. More money is spent annually in the United States on illegal drugs and legal alcohol than is spent for clothing.[2] The United States is the biggest market in the world for illegal drugs and the profits are huge; therefore, criminals take great risks to bring the illegal drugs into the country. The users of illegal drugs can be classified as follows:

- *The "Situational" Drug Abuser:* A person who uses illegal drugs for a specific or "situational" purpose, such as to accomplish some other objective. A person who is under a great deal of stress or tension might use a drug such as marijuana to relax. A performer or a truck driver might use a stimulant, or an upper, to stay awake.
- *The "Party" or "Weekend" User:* A drug abuser who might use drugs for kicks or just for the experience. These users are great sources of profits for drug pushers.
- *The Drug Addict:* A person who is physically and/or psychologically dependent on drugs. He or she cannot perform daily without drug support. Addicts have a "monkey on their back," which can be very expensive to support. To raise the money for their daily supply of drugs ($50, $100, or even $150 per day), addicts steal, break into cars, commit burglaries, rob, snatch purses, or push drugs.

Women and men who trade sex for drugs are among those most susceptible to disease, including AIDS.

Today, common forms of drug abuse include so-called street drugs, such as marijuana, cocaine or crack, methamphetamine, heroin, and other drugs; prescription drugs, whether obtained legally through a prescription or by theft of either the drugs or a prescription slip to obtain the drugs; and over-the-counter substances that produce a "high," such as cold medicines and inhalants. Combining any of these drugs with each other, or with alcohol, creates the risk of stroke, seizure, coma, or even death. Accidental drug overdoses doubled in the period from 1999 to 2004 and in 2007 became the nation's second leading cause of accidental deaths, behind only automobile accidents. The National Center for Health Statistics reported over 46,000 deaths from drug overdose in 2013. Prescription drug overdose accounted for much of the increase in fatalities, causing considerably more deaths than cocaine or heroin.

Prescription Drugs   Abuse of prescription drugs, mainly painkillers, has also risen markedly over the past few years. A July 15, 2010, report by the Substance Abuse and Mental Health Services Administration concluded that prescription painkiller abuse increased by 400 percent in the 10 years prior to the report. The percentage of hospital admissions for substance abuse of painkiller medications increased from 2.8 percent in 1998 to 9.8 percent in 2008. Admissions for cocaine and alcohol abuse during the same period went down, the report stated.

In a June 3, 2010, report the Centers for Disease Control stated that in 2009 it conducted its National Youth Risk Behavior Survey, and for the first time it obtained data on high school students' use of prescription drugs without a prescription. It found that one in five high school students has used prescription drugs like OxyContin, Percocet, Vicodin, or Adderall.

Adderall is a prescription psychostimulant that is commonly prescribed for persons with attention deficit hyperactivity disorder. It has become popular on college campuses as a stimulant used during exam and "cramming" periods. While college students generally regard the drug as harmless, it is a Schedule II drug under the Controlled Substances Act, which means that while it has accepted medical usages it carries a high potential for addiction.

There is some good news. In a March 2016 study by the DEA Resources Center of drug use during the period 2000–2015, data (collected by a University of Michigan research institute) indicated that in 2015 meth use among teenagers decreased 80%; cocaine use was down 59%.

DRUG LAWS IN THE UNITED STATES

The first law enacted in the United States was an anti-opium smoking ordinance passed in San Francisco in 1875 because of the opium problem there.[3] This was one of the few restrictions on drugs in the United States at that time.

In the 1880s and 1890s, people in the United States could still concoct and sell to the American public practically any drug or drug compound they wished. Drugs were available in stores, through mail-order catalogs, and from traveling vendors and peddlers. Little was known at that time about the effects of drugs on human beings. Drug promoters claimed their drugs cured sickness and other human problems.

A German firm, for example, marketed a newly discovered drug in the 1890s as a cough suppressant. The name the firm gave the drug is well known today—heroin.

Heroin did a wonderful job of suppressing coughs, but years passed before people realized the terrible problems of addiction to heroin. Other drugs and compounds, which often contained either cocaine or heroin, were advertised and promoted as cures for everything from ingrown toenails to cancer. Medications were sold that guaranteed sex rejuvenation, new hair for bald people, breast enlargement, a cure for arthritis, and more.

Cocaine was used in Coca-Cola®, a very popular soft drink even in those days. Cocaine was not replaced by the drug caffeine in Coca-Cola until 1906.

Responding to the use of cocaine and heroin in some everyday products, U.S. President William Howard Taft stated in 1910 that "the misuse of cocaine is undoubtedly an American habit, the most threatening of the drug habits that has ever appeared in this country." In 1906, the federal Pure Food and Drug Act was enacted because of the concern over heroin addiction. In 1914 the federal Harrison Narcotics Act was passed.

The Food and Drug Administration (FDA) now requires a firm or person who wishes to market and sell a drug in the United States to show that

- The drug or medication is not harmful to humans.
- The drug or medication will do what it is advertised to do.

The Uniform Controlled Substances Act

Uniform Controlled Substances Act Model act identifying illegal drug crimes, drafted by a national conference of uniform law commissioners and adopted by the states and the federal government.

Today, the federal government and all of the states have enacted the **Uniform Controlled Substances Act**, which was approved by the National Conference of Commissioners on Uniform State Laws in 1970.[4] The purposes of this act have been stated as follows:

> This Uniform Act was drafted to achieve uniformity between the laws of the several States and those of the Federal government. It has been designed to complement the new Federal narcotic and dangerous drug legislation and provide an interlocking trellis of Federal and State law to enable government at all levels to control more effectively the drug abuse problem. (Uniform Controlled Substances Act, 9 U.L.A., Commissioners' Prefatory Note, 1979, p. 188)

controlled substance A drug that may be possessed or sold only as permitted by state or federal law.

In their **controlled substance** acts, most states forbid and make it criminal conduct to

- Manufacture[5] or deliver a controlled (forbidden) substance.
- Possess with intent to manufacture or deliver a controlled substance.
- Create, deliver, or possess with intent to deliver a counterfeit substance.
- Offer or agree to deliver a controlled substance and then deliver or dispense a substance that is not a controlled substance.
- Possess a controlled substance.
- Knowingly keep or maintain a store, dwelling, building, vehicle, boat, or aircraft, or other place resorted to by persons illegally using controlled substances.
- Acquire or obtain possession of a controlled substance by misrepresentation, fraud, forgery, deception, or subterfuge.

The Uniform Controlled Substances Act has five schedules of controlled substances according to their potential for abuse, degree of accepted medical use, and relative physical danger to the abuser. These schedules were summarized by the U.S. Bureau of Justice Statistics in its 1992 *Report on Drugs, Crime and the Justice System* (see box).

Types of Possession of Controlled Substances

The most common criminal (or ordinance) illegal drug charge is that of possession of a controlled substance.[6] Possession must be proved to sustain an arrest and conviction. The federal Controlled Substances Act (21 U.S.C. § 841(a)(1)) defines the possession offenses to include a *mens rea* requirement: that the person knowingly or intentionally possessed the controlled substance. See *United States v. Abdulle*, 564 F.3d 119 (2d Cir. 2009). As a result, when states adopted their own controlled substances acts, they usually included the requirement that the possession be done "knowingly." For example, the Texas statute, VTCA § 481.115, states, "Except as authorized by this Chapter, a person commits an offense if the person knowingly or intentionally possesses a controlled substance listed in Penalty Group I. . . ."

FIVE SCHEDULES OF CONTROLLED SUBSTANCES

Schedule	Abuse Potential	Examples of Drugs Covered	Some of the Effects	Medical Use
I	Highest	Heroin, LSD, hashish, marijuana, methaqualone (Quaalude), "designer drugs"	Unpredictable effects, severe psychological or physical dependence, or death	No accepted use; some are legal for limited research use only
II	High	Morphine, PCP, codeine, cocaine, methadone, Demerol, Benzedrine, Dexedrine	May lead to severe psychological or physical dependence	Accepted use with restrictions
III	Medium	Codeine with aspirin or Tylenol, some amphetamines, anabolic steroids	May lead to moderate or low physical dependence or high psychological dependence	Accepted use
IV	Low	Darvon, Talwin, phenobarbital, Equanil, Miltown, Librium, diazepam (Valium)	May lead to limited physical or psychological dependence	Accepted use
V	Lowest	Over-the-counter or prescription compounds with codeine, Lomotil, Robitussin A-C	May lead to limited physical or psychological dependence	Accepted use

Some states make the simple fact of possession a crime. The Washington Supreme Court held in *State v. Bradshaw*[7] that because the Washington state legislature omitted the "knowingly" language when it adopted its controlled substances act, mere possession of a controlled substance is a criminal offense. The *Bradshaw* court stated that there is "no *mens rea*" in RCWA 69.50.4013, the Washington illegal possession statute.

It is uniformly held in both state and federal courts that as long as a defendant knew he possessed *some* kind of controlled substance, the prosecution need not prove he knew the exact nature and kind of drug possessed. For example, in the 2010 case of *United States v. De La Torre*,[8] the court held that a defendant carrying a backpack that he knew contained marijuana could be convicted of possession of methamphetamine that was also in the backpack, whether or not the defendant knew that fact.

For some kinds of controlled substances, which are not as well-known as marijuana or cocaine, proof of knowledge of possession can be more difficult. Khat is the name of an African plant commonly chewed in African countries as a stimulant. Khat is not a controlled substance. After harvest, khat contains a chemical called catherinone, a Schedule I controlled substance. However, over a short time, the plant decays and the catherinone is replaced by a different substance, cathine, a Schedule IV controlled substance. A person in possession of khat may thus be in possession of either catherinone or cathine, depending on how much the plant has decayed. In *United States v. Hassan*,[9] the court reversed a conviction of a defendant charged with conspiracy to possess catherinone with intent to distribute. The court said that it was not enough to prove the defendant intended to import khat. The government needed to prove the defendant knew khat contained catherinone, and that he intended to import khat that had catherinone.

Proof of possession may be satisfied by either of the following:

- *Actual possession,* which is possession on the person of the defendant, or within an area of his or her immediate control and reach. Actual possession may be within a container (e.g., purse, package, or suitcase) that the defendant may be carrying or has within reach. Actual possession may also occur in a vehicle when the controlled substance is under the seat of the person or in the glove compartment of the vehicle owned or driven by the defendant.
- *Constructive possession* of a controlled substance, which occurs when illegal drugs are in a place immediately accessible to the accused and subject to his or her domination and control. Examples of constructive possession would be drugs found in the trunk of a car the defendant owned or was the driver of, or in a home or business place controlled and dominated by a defendant, to such an extent that a strong inference of possession could be drawn by a judge or jury.

To Convict of Possession of an Illegal Drug, Must the State Present a "Usable Amount" as Evidence?

State courts differ on the question as to whether a "trace" amount of an illegal drug (that is, an amount so small that it is unusable) will sustain a conviction for possession of that drug.

In the case of *People v. Mizell*,[10] the highest court in the state of New York followed the majority of the states and held that "any amount of an (illegal drug) is sufficient to sustain a conviction for possession." In the *Mizell* case, cocaine residue found on the sides of vials was used to support the criminal charge and conviction for possession. The conviction was affirmed, with the court holding that "cocaine residue—though unusable—is nevertheless a controlled substance" under the criminal code of the state of New York.[11]

In *Beeler v. State,*[12] the court found that possession of an electronic scale with minute quantities of cocaine residue satisfied the requirements for illegal "possession" of a controlled substance. The defendant contended that he could not "knowingly" possess a miniscule amount of a drug and thus could not be convicted under the Indiana statute, Ind. Code § 35-48-4-6. That statute, like other possession statutes in most states, prohibits one from "knowingly or intentionally" possessing a controlled substance. The court said that circumstantial evidence, such as the admitted use the defendant planned for the scale, was sufficient to prove he "knew" the residue was a controlled substance.

usable amount In contrast to a useless trace amount, a quantity of an illegal drug sufficient to be used.

However, other courts follow the "usable quantity" rule and hold that a blackened residue or a useless trace amount is not a **usable amount** and will not sustain a criminal conviction for possession of an illegal drug. Courts holding that a usable quantity of drugs must be presented include California[13] and Florida, at least where

---

YOU BE THE JUDGE

The federal Controlled Substance Analogue Enforcement Act of 1986 (CSAE) makes it a crime to possess for distribution designated substances that are similar to those listed in the Controlled Substances Act (CSA), if the substances are intended for human consumption. If a substance is similar to a controlled substance listed in the CSA, it is prosecuted as a controlled substance under the federal CSA statute. That statute makes it a crime to "knowingly" possess with the intent to distribute a controlled substance.

You are the trial judge in a CSA prosecution. The case before you involves the sale of analog chemical substances that were similar to drugs listed in the CSA. Stephen McFadden sold so-called "bath salts" to various merchants for resale, advertising them as having effects similar to cocaine or crystal meth. McFadden also said that the substances were "not for human consumption," although he was aware the merchant would sell the substances to customers for just such use. McFadden sold the substances to the merchants for $15 a gram, who then resold them to customers for $30-70 per gram.

Evidence was admitted, and the case is now ready to go to the jury. The prosecutor and defendant cannot agree on what you should instruct the jury on the question of McFadden's "knowledge" of his actions. Since the CSA is violated only by "knowingly" possessing with the intent to distribute a controlled substance, the issue is, what must the prosecution prove the defendant did "knowingly"? Sell a substance intended for human consumption, and that is all? Sell a substance that creates an effect similar to cocaine or crystal meth? Sell a substance having the chemical composition sufficient to create such effects? Sell a substance that is a "controlled substance"?

Draft your instruction to the jury. Then, compare it to the jury instruction a majority of the U.S. Supreme Court adopted in *McFadden v. United States,* 135 S. Ct. 2298 (2015). Do you prefer the instruction suggested by Chief Justice Roberts in his concurring opinion?

the trace amount of the substance is found on a commonly exchanged object, such as a dollar bill.[14]

The "knowing" element of the federal Controlled Substances Act may also be satisfied by "deliberate ignorance" on the part of the person in possession of illegal drugs. The 2012 case of *United States v. Vasquez*[15] illustrates this rule. The defendant worked in Laredo, Texas, but walked across the border to Nuevo Laredo, Mexico on a regular basis. His employer stated that the defendant did not drive a car, and was not believed to own a car. The defendant was stopped at a border patrol inspection station in the United States. He was driving a Chevrolet Suburban. Officers searched the vehicle, and under the hood found two car batteries. Since vehicles usually have only one battery, officers dismantled the batteries. Inside they found small motorcycle batteries used to start the car, and 5 kilograms of cocaine in each battery. The defendant admitted he owned the car, but stated that another unidentified man bought the car for him, placing defendant's name on the title. The defendant stated he did not know the batteries had cocaine inside. The court of appeals upheld his conviction, stating that the circumstances of the purchase of the car, the presence of the two batteries, and the request to disassemble the batteries under the front seat put the defendant on notice something was wrong. His refusal to discover what was actually in the batteries was an example of "deliberate ignorance," the court held.

Delivery of Controlled Substances

The acts that are prohibited under the Uniform Controlled Substances Act, as illustrated in Florida's Criminal Code Section 893.13, include the following:

> [I]t is unlawful for any person to sell, purchase, manufacture, or deliver, or possess with intent to sell . . . a controlled substance.

Delivery of an illegal drug can be either an actual delivery, or the crime of possession of a controlled substance with intent to deliver (sell or transfer).

In most of the actual delivery cases that come into criminal courts throughout the United States, the government presents evidence showing that the accused sold (delivered) illegal drugs to an undercover law enforcement officer. In other actual delivery cases, the state proves its case by producing a witness to the illegal drug transaction (either the receiver of the drugs or an observer of the delivery). Videotapes or a film of the delivery can also be used as evidence.

possession with intent to deliver A criminal case in which the state presents evidence showing that the accused had possession of a large amount of an illegal drug, meaning more than the accused would personally use.

In the typical criminal case of **possession with intent to deliver**, the state presents evidence showing that the accused had possession of a large amount of an illegal drug (more than he or she would personally use). A combination of the following evidence is also generally presented: that the accused also possessed scales and/or small plastic bags with evenly weighed-out illegal drugs, a large amount of money, a pager, or a cellular phone.

The evidence presented by the government must be sufficient to justify a conclusion by the fact finder (jury or judge) that the accused possessed the illegal drug with intent to deliver (sell or transfer) it to another person. To do this, the U.S. Supreme Court requires that there must be a "rational connection"[16] between the facts presented and the conclusion drawn by the fact finder.

Drawing that connection may be difficult, as the following case shows. In *Commonwealth v. Ilya I*, 24 N.E.3d 1048 (Mass. 2015), the court affirmed a trial court's

POSSESSION OF A SMALL AMOUNT OF MARIJUANA

The offense of possession of a small amount of marijuana is charged in different ways throughout the United States.

Criminal Offense

If the person is charged and convicted under a statute and could receive a jail sentence, the conviction is a criminal conviction and the person has been convicted of a crime.

Civil Offense

If the only penalty that can be imposed after conviction is a monetary fine, the conviction is for a civil offense and is similar to a speeding ticket or a parking ticket. Under these circumstances, the offense of possession of a small amount of marijuana has been "decriminalized," as it is no longer charged as a crime.

Legalized Conduct

If neither criminal nor civil punishment is imposed for possession of a small amount of marijuana, the conduct has then been legalized and is no longer a crime or a civil offense. The Alaska Supreme Court has held that under the Alaska Constitution's right of privacy, adults may possess up to four grams of marijuana in their homes. See *State v. Crocker,* 97 P.3d 93 (Alaska App. 2004).

dismissal of a charge of possession with intent to deliver. There, a 16-year-old juvenile was arrested with 13 individually wrapped "small" baggies of marijuana in his pocket. (The quantity in each bag was not established.) Arresting officers found no smoking paraphernalia on the juvenile, and had earlier observed him in "furtive" conversations with others on the street. The prosecution contended these factors were enough to infer the intent to distribute the marijuana. The trial court disagreed, and dismissed the charge. On appeal, the Massachusetts Court of Appeals reversed the trial court. The Massachusetts Supreme Judicial Court granted review, and reversed the court of appeals. It concluded possession of 13 small bags of marijuana was not inconsistent with personal use. It noted the drugs were not bagged in a manner similar to bags that are intended for distribution.

State–Federal Clash over the Medical Use of Marijuana

As of 2016, 24 states and the District of Columbia had adopted some type of "Compassionate Use Medical Marijuana" statute. Under these statutes, doctors may prescribe the personal use of marijuana for pain management for people with serious illnesses who do not respond to other treatments. These laws, such as the California Compassionate Use Act of 1996 (California Health & Safety Code, Section 11362.5), created what is termed a "medical use" exception to the state's drug laws.

The federal government did not initially challenge these laws, but beginning with President George W. Bush's first administration, the attorney general began directing federal prosecutors to prosecute, under the federal Controlled Substances Act (CSA), persons distributing prescribed marijuana. In *United States v. Oakland Cannabis Buyers' Cooperative,*[17] the Supreme Court held that the CSA had no "medical use" exception and that as a result manufacturers and providers, such as the cooperative, of marijuana for medical use could be prosecuted under the CSA. The Court did not specifically hold that *users* of marijuana for medical purposes could be prosecuted under the CSA, but it did suggest as much in a footnote: "nothing in our analysis, or the statute, suggests that a distinction should be drawn between the prohibition on manufacturing and distributing and the other prohibitions in the Controlled Substances Act" (532 U.S. at 495).

After *Oakland,* several seriously ill persons using marijuana brought an action to declare the CSA unconstitutional, alleging that prosecutions of *users* of marijuana was not permitted because their use did not affect interstate commerce. That being so, they alleged, Congress had no constitutional authority to prohibit the medical use of marijuana.

In *Raich v. Ashcroft,*[18] the Ninth Circuit Court of Appeals agreed, holding that medical use of marijuana "does not have any direct or obvious effect on interstate commerce." (See Chapter 2 for a discussion of the Commerce Clause as authority for federal laws.) In 2005 the U.S. Supreme Court reversed the Ninth Circuit Court, holding that because the in-state use of marijuana might have an effect on the interstate market for marijuana, the federal government had the power under the Commerce Clause to prohibit the use of marijuana for medical purposes. See *Gonzales v. Raich.*[19]

In the years immediately following the decision in *Raich* federal law enforcement agencies conducted many "raids" on medical-use marijuana suppliers and users. On October 19, 2009, U.S. Attorney General Eric Holder announced that prosecutions of medical-use marijuana suppliers and users would be relaxed, with law enforcement focusing on large-scale marijuana operations. In 2011, federal drug agents conducted raids on medical dispensaries in several states, raising questions about the continued force of the 2009 Holder statement. Since Washington and Colorado legalized the recreational use of marijuana in 2012, state governors and some members of Congress have pushed the Justice Department for a determination of how marijuana users in states that permit marijuana use will be treated. In August 2013, the Justice Department advised all 94 U.S. Attorney offices that states will be permitted to pass recreational-use of marijuana laws, so long as they have strict regulatory policies to protect public health and safety.

Many states have passed laws regulating the production, use, and physician prescription for use of marijuana. An example is the Montana Marijuana Act, which limits the number of patients a physician may certify for medical marijuana use to no more than 25 per year, prohibits marijuana providers' advertising, bans commercial sale of marijuana by limiting the number of patients (3) a provider may "assist" at any given time, and authorizes warrantless inspections of providers' businesses. In *Mont. Cannabis Indus. Ass'n v. State*, 368 P.3d 1131 (Mont. 2016) the court upheld these regulations over the marijuana providers' arguments they were unconstitutional.

Congress has considered several bills intended to address the relationship of state marijuana laws and the Controlled Substances Act; to date none have been enacted into law. As a result, in theory at least, all state laws making possession of marijuana legal, for medical reasons or otherwise, run afoul of federal law.

In July 2010 the House of Representatives passed a bill that changes the sentencing structure for "crack" cocaine convictions. Under the present law, possession of 5 grams of crack triggers the mandatory 5-year prison sentence rule, while for powder cocaine the triggering amount is possession of 500 grams. Because crack convictions overwhelmingly involve black defendants, many persons and organizations objected to the sentence disparity on grounds that it led to racial distinctions in sentencing decisions. Under the new law, which the Senate passed earlier in 2010, the amount of crack needed to trigger the 5-year mandatory sentence has been raised to 28 grams. The powder cocaine amounts remain the same.

Controlled Substances Used in Religious Ceremonies

When Congress adopted the Controlled Substances Act, the issue of religious use of substances included in the schedules of controlled substances arose. An immediate exception to the Act's prohibitions was made for the use of peyote by members of the Native American Church. In 1994, Congress passed 42 U.S.C. § 1996a(b)(l), which made this exception applicable to all Indian tribes.

Other religious groups had no specific exception to the Controlled Substances Act's prohibitions. Moreover, the Supreme Court had held that the Free Exercise Clause of the Constitution did not require judges to consider the burden placed on religious exercise by facially constitutional laws, such as the Controlled Substances Act. See *Employment Div. Dept. of Human Resources of Ore. v. Smith*, 494 U.S. 872 (1990). However, in 1993 Congress passed the Religious Freedom Restoration Act, 42 U.S.C. § 2000bb. Section 2000bb-l(a) of the Act prohibits the government from placing a "substantial burden" on the exercise of religion, even if the "burden results from a rule of general applicability" (such as the drug laws), unless the government can show a compelling interest in doing so. This section has been used by religious groups to resist federal prosecutions under the Controlled Substances Act.

The U.S. Supreme Court considered the application of the Religious Freedom Restoration Act in *Gonzales v. O Centra Espirita.*[20] In that case the government sought to use the Controlled Substances Act to prohibit a practice followed by a religious sect located in the United States but with ties to a Christian Spiritist sect in Brazil, with origins in the Amazon rainforest. That sect uses a ceremonial drink called *hoasca*, made from plants that contain a Schedule I controlled substance called DMT. The Supreme Court said that since the government agreed the group using the *hoasca* was sincere in its religious significance, it could prohibit that use only if it could show some "compelling interest" for doing so. The Court rejected the government's argument that the fact DMT was a controlled substance by itself justified the prohibition. Because the government made no other showing of a compelling interest, the Court said it was barred from prosecuting the religious sect.

The original Religious Freedom Restoration Act applied to the states as well as the federal government, but in *Boerne v. Flores*,[21] the Supreme Court held that Congress lacked the power to make the law effective against the states. As a result, state prosecutions for use of a controlled substance in a religious ceremony are possible, unless the state has made its own exception to state controlled substances laws. Some have: Arizona has a statute, ARS § 541-1493.01, that is similar to the federal Religious Freedom Restoration Act. Other states have specific exceptions for the Native American Church for use of peyote; Wis. Code § 161.115 is such a statute. The Utah Supreme Court has held that the federal exception for the Native American Church was incorporated into the Utah Controlled Substances Act. See *State v. Mooney.*[22]

Drug Rip-Off Cases and Simulated Drugs

In *State v. Glover*,[23] the defendant planned to "rip off" a buyer of illegal drugs. Instead of cocaine, the defendant delivered two bags of baking soda to the buyer, at $50 a bag. His conviction for attempted trafficking in cocaine was affirmed. Glover's buyer was an undercover police officer.

Other states, among them Iowa, have statutes that make the delivery or possession of a "simulated controlled substance" a crime. A simulated controlled substance is a substance "represented to be [an illegal drug]... [that] because of its nature, packaging, or appearance would lead a reasonable person to believe it to be a controlled substance" (Iowa Statute 204.401(1)).

Georgia has a similar statute, which makes it a crime to sell an uncontrolled substance that the seller has represented to be a controlled substance. (See Georgia Code Annotated § 16-13-30.1.) In *Brown v. State*,[24] the court held that a defendant who sold a fake "rock" of crack cocaine to an undercover agent could be convicted under the statute.

Criminal Liability for Drug-Induced Deaths

Drug overdose cases occur regularly in every city in the United States, as drugs have become purer, cheaper, and easier to obtain. Cocaine is particularly dangerous because it is an unpredictable killer that can cause life-threatening complications that are not related to the dose taken, the length of use, or the manner in which the drug is taken. Swallowing an "eight-ball" of cocaine (one-eighth of an ounce) can easily cause acute cocaine intoxication and death.[25]

A number of states have enacted laws that make people who illegally manufacture, distribute, or dispense illegal drugs strictly liable for a death that results from the injection, inhalation, or ingestion of such a drug.[26] Such laws are often called *Len Bias laws*. Len Bias was a basketball star at the University of Maryland. Shortly after being drafted by an NBA team, he died as the result of using cocaine.

An example of a prosecution under a drug-induced statute is *People v. Kidd*, 997 N.E.2d 634 (Ill 2013). Illinois's drug-induced death statute, 720 ILCS 5/9-3.3(a), applies if a defendant delivered a controlled substance to another person and "any person's death is caused by" ingestion or other use of the controlled substance. Kidd "delivered" some cocaine to his girlfriend, which they both used. Later in the evening, Kidd found his girlfriend lying dead on the floor of her bedroom. Kidd was charged under the drug-induced death statute, and convicted.

On appeal, Kidd contended he did not "cause" the victim's death under the statute, because the victim also used morphine the night of her death, and he did not supply her with that drug. The appeals court rejected that argument, stating that since Kidd knew the victim had morphine in her possession, it was foreseeable by him that she might take that drug as well as the cocaine he provided. Therefore, the court held, Kidd's delivery of the cocaine was the "proximate cause" of the victim's death. (The conviction was reversed for other reasons.)

The causation analysis under the federal drug-induced death statute appears to be different from the interpretation given the Illinois statute. In *Burrage v. United States*, 134 S. Ct. 881 (2014) the U.S. Supreme Court considered the causation question under the CSA, specifically § 841(b)(1)(C). That section adds a sentence enhancement of 20 years if "death results from" the use of a controlled substance delivered by the defendant. In *Burrage* the defendant sold heroin to the victim, who injected the heroin on top of using a variety of other drugs. The victim died after injecting the heroin and using the other drugs.

Burrage was convicted of selling the heroin to the victim, and the trial judge sentenced Burrage to the 20-year minimum under the "results from" enhancement section. The court of appeals affirmed the conviction and sentence. The Supreme Court reversed. It held that a death "results from" use of a controlled substance only if it is proved the victim would not have died "but for" the use of the substance. Here, the Court said, experts testifying at Burrage's trial could not say the victim would have lived had he not ingested the heroin. The other drugs could have caused the respiratory failure that caused his death, the experts said, but heroin likely "contributed" to the death. The Court rejected the government's argument that "results from" is satisfied if the use of the controlled substance is a substantial, contributing factor in the death. It therefore reversed the conviction and sentence enhancement for "death resulting" from the sale of the controlled substance. (As a review, do you think the *Burrage* court would agree with the conclusions drawn in the Multiple Causes of Death in Homicide Prosecutions box in Chapter 3, p. 75)

Possession or Sale of Drug Paraphernalia

drug paraphernalia
Objects that are primarily intended or designed for use with illegal drugs.

State criminal codes and the federal government make the possession or sale of **drug paraphernalia** a crime. The Federal Criminal Code defines *drug paraphernalia* as "any equipment, product or material of any kind which is primarily intended or designed for use" with illegal drugs.[27]

Some products have only one use, and that is as drug paraphernalia. For example, bongs, which are water pipes used for the smoking of marijuana, were called "hardcore paraphernalia by virtue of (their) physical features . . . (because bongs have) no alternative uses."[28]

An example of an item that has more than one use is inositol, an optically inactive alcohol. Inositol is a common cocaine-cutting ingredient. Because inositol has dual purposes, the government must establish that the inositol was "primarily intended" as drug paraphernalia in order to convict a defendant under the statute.[29]

Drug paraphernalia charges and convictions are most often obtained when the item or paraphernalia is seized along with drugs such as marijuana and cocaine. In the 1994 case of *People v. Veld* (641 N.E.2d 924), an Illinois appellate court held that the state failed to establish that boxes and small wooden pipes were drug paraphernalia. The defendant, a manufacturer, was not apprehended using the boxes and wooden pipes for illegal drug use.

The federal Mail Order Drug Paraphernalia Control Act (21 U.S.C.A. § 857) was upheld in *Posters V Things Ltd. v. United States,* 969 F.2d 652 (1992), *affirmed,* 511 U.S. 513 (1994). The defendant in the *Posters* case sold scales and substances commonly used by cocaine dealers to dilute cocaine. The defendant advertised the products for such use, and purchases were made in such large quantities that it showed that dealers rather than other users were buying the items.

SNIFFING, BAGGING, AND HUFFING INHALANTS

Inhalants are chemicals that give off fumes or vapors that slow the body's reactions and cloud thinking when breathed in. Many common household products are inhalants. Common products available to children that will produce a high include glue, gasoline, correction fluid, and felt-tipped markers. The Partnership for a Drug-Free America estimates that more than 1,200 products available to kids are capable of producing highs, and states that the use of inhalants has become an "epidemic."

Inhalants can be "sniffed" (inhaling the substance into the nose directly from the container); "bagged" (dumping the substance into a bag and inhaling the fumes); or "huffed" (soaking a rag with a mixture, putting the rag to the mouth, and inhaling the fumes).

Inhalants can cause suffocation, heart attack, or even death. Common symptoms in a child (or an adult) of inhalant use are staggering gait and uncoordinated walk and movement; delirium; slurred speech; chemical odor on breath, body, or clothes; loss of appetite; intoxication; nausea or vomiting; belligerence; and impaired hearing.

Making methamphetamine in a "mom and pop" meth lab.

Thierry Falise/Getty Images

ALCOHOL-RELATED CRIMES

Alcohol is a drug used by an estimated 95 million Americans in some form and in varying amounts. It is a mood-altering drug that many people use as a tranquilizer. It has been observed that if alcohol were discovered today for the first time, the FDA would be obligated by law to forbid its over-the-counter sale without prescription. Alcohol is an addictive drug, and it is toxic—it is a poison. However, alcohol has, for a long time, been part of our economic, social, and cultural environment. Because of the beverage's long history of social acceptance and our society's economic dependence on it, it continues to be sold openly on the market.

Alcohol's Relation to Crimes and Deaths

British and U.S. studies of accidental deaths in the 1980s and a National Institutes of Health study in 2002 showed that alcohol has a high relationship to deaths caused by drowning, choking, burns and fires, and falls.[30] A pedestrian who is intoxicated was reported 3.5 times more likely to be killed or injured in a traffic accident.

Alcohol is the most widely abused and misused drug in America and in many other countries. Alcoholism is one of the biggest health problems in the United States, just behind heart disease and cancer. Excessive use of alcohol is also a factor causing heart disease and cancer.

 ## OTHER STATUTES AND LAWS USED IN THE WAR ON DRUGS

Subject Matter of Law	Problem Addressed by Law
"Drug kingpin" statutes	The federal government and many states have created a separate crime of being the leader of a narcotics trafficking network. Many criminal codes punish this offense with life imprisonment. New Jersey is one of the states that does, and defines the leader's role as follows in New Jersey Statute 2C-35-3: A person is a leader of a narcotics trafficking network if he conspires with others as an organizer, supervisor, financier or manager, to engage for profit in a scheme or course of conduct to unlawfully manufacture, distribute, dispense, bring into or transport in this State any substance classified in Schedule I or II, or any controlled substance analog thereof.
Additional imprisonment for using or carrying a firearm during and in relation to a drug-trafficking crime	The Federal Criminal Code (18 U.S.C.A. § 924(c)) and the statutes of most (if not all) states provide for additional punishment for a person using or carrying a firearm during and in relation to a drug-trafficking crime.[a]
Nuisance laws and drug house abatement statutes and ordinances	Landlords are often warned that if they allow tenants to sell drugs from the landlord's property, an abatement or nuisance proceeding could be started against the property. Drug houses could also be taken over by a state or local government because of failure to pay taxes, or they could be condemned because of fire or code violations.

(Continued)

Forfeiture of property	Under the Controlled Substances Act and other forfeiture statutes, the following may be seized under court order: (1) instruments of the crime (such as vehicles or watercraft used to commit the crime); (2) profits of the crime (money from drug dealing, stolen goods, and so on); and (3) proceeds of the illegal act (houses, condos, yachts, farms, or other luxury goods purchased from profits of the crime). If the offender did not pay taxes on the profits of drug dealing, the Internal Revenue Service may take action against drug traffickers.
Use of communications facility to further a drug violation	The use of a communications facility to commit or facilitate a drug violation is a crime under federal law if the defendant has a prior conviction for a felony drug violation.
Possession of wiretapping devices, illegal bugs, and eavesdropping equipment	Title 18, Chapter 119 of the Omnibus Crime and Safe Streets Act makes it illegal to own, manufacture, or sell eavesdropping and wiretapping equipment specifically designed for "the surreptitious interception of wire, oral or electronic communications." Only law enforcement agencies are permitted to buy or use such devices and then only with a court order. Some drug dealers and other criminals illegally possess and use these devices.
"Schoolyard" or "Schoolhouse" laws	In an attempt to keep drugs from schoolyards and neighborhoods, "schoolyard" laws were passed that increase jail time for dealing drugs within 1,000 feet of an elementary or secondary school.
Loss of financial aid and student loans for a year for students who are found guilty of simple possession of an illegal drug such as marijuana	Under federal law, 20 U.S.C.A. § 1091(r)(1), a student convicted of sale or possession of illegal drugs while receiving federal student aid funds is ineligible for financial aid for either one year (possession) or two years (sale).
Laws punishing the sale of counterfeit medical drugs	Medical personnel report an increase in counterfeit drugs for the treatment of diseases such as tuberculosis, AIDS, and malaria as well as antibiotics. The World Health Organization has reported that labs in China produce most of these counterfeit drugs, which cause thousands of unnecessary deaths each year.[b]
"Doctor shopping" as violation of Controlled Substances Act	Doctor shopping is obtaining multiple prescriptions from different doctors for the same drug. Police affidavits state that Rush Limbaugh, the radio commentator, received 2,000 painkillers from four different doctors in a 6-month period.

[a]In 1998 Congress amended § 924(c) to add "possession" to "uses or carries" a weapon under the statute. This was done to change the Supreme Court's decision in 1995 that "use" did not include mere possession. Now, simple possession of a firearm during a drug trafficking crime violates the statute. See *United States v. O'Brien*, 130 S. Ct. 2169 (2010).

[b]See *The New York Times*, "In the World of Life-Saving Drugs: A Growing Epidemic of Deadly Fakes," March 15, 2007.

When public drunkenness was prosecuted as a crime throughout the United States, it was always high on the yearly list of crimes.[31] Alcohol continues to be an important factor in many disorderly conduct, battery, assault, rape, child abuse, domestic relations disputes, and criminal damage to property cases in the United States every year. The movement from other drugs to alcohol is sometimes condoned by parents who, in their relief that their children are not involved in the use of other forms of drugs, do not recognize the dangers of alcohol.

The January 2016 report of the National Institute on Alcohol Abuse and Alcoholism reported these statistics for 2014: 37.9% of college students aged 18–24 indulged in "binge drinking" (5 or more drinks) within the past month of a survey; 1,825 college students died in 2014 from alcohol-related causes; 97,000 reported a sexual assault related to alcohol use.

Drunk Driving: The Criminal Homicide Causing the Most Deaths

About twenty-seven people are killed every day in the United States because of driving under the influence of drugs or alcohol, the Centers for Disease Control and Prevention reported in 2016. In 2014, 9,967 people died in alcohol-related motor vehicle traffic accidents, accounting for about 31 percent of all traffic deaths. This number is down from 10,228 in 2010, and reflects a steady decrease in alcohol-related traffic deaths. In 1982, by comparison, 26,173 people died in alcohol-related motor vehicle traffic accidents. About 18 percent of all motor vehicle traffic deaths involved drug use. In addition, about 1 million people are injured annually. The National Highway Traffic Safety Administration estimates the yearly costs of drunk driving to be $51 billion. In 2014, over 1.1 million people were arrested for driving under the influence of alcohol or drugs. It is estimated that each year there are as many as 112 million episodes of drunk driving.

Tougher laws and enforcement, taking more blood alcohol tests of suspected drunk and drugged drivers, and increased efforts to educate students and the public on the dangers of drunk and drugged driving are being used to decrease the dangers on our streets and highways. The punishment for drunk driving has been increased, and some states have enacted laws forbidding or curbing happy hours by taverns and clubs. Victims of drunk driving are reminded that they may commence lawsuits in most states under "dram shop"[32] laws (a dram being a small drink of liquor) that permit civil lawsuits under some circumstances against bars and individuals who furnish or sell the alcoholic drinks.

All fifty states have now set the blood-alcohol content (BAC) limit for operating a motor vehicle at .08 percent. That limit is still higher than in most European countries and Japan. Insurance companies and the American Medical Association join in noting that alcohol can unravel driving skills subtly and insidiously, long before people look and act drunk.

Experts now point out that it is the driver with a drinking or drug problem who is the problem. Too many people with severe alcohol and/or drug problems continue to drive while impaired and under the influence. Problem drinkers continue to drink and drive even after their licenses have been revoked. They are generally the danger on the highway.

Elements and Defenses in Drunk-Driving Prosecutions

Drunk driving statutes differ from state to state, but most follow a format similar to the following statute, Neb. Rev. Stat. § 60-6,196:

It shall be unlawful for any person to operate or be in the actual physical control of any motor vehicle:

(a) While under the influence of alcoholic liquor or of any drug;

(b) When such person has a concentration of eight-hundredths of one gram or more by weight of alcohol per one hundred ten liters of his or her blood; or

(c) When such person has a concentration of eight-hundredths of one gram or more by weight of alcohol per two hundred ten liters of his or her breath.

Most states also increase the penalty for a conviction based on a blood-alcohol count appreciably higher than the statutory limit, and for subsequent convictions.

DRIVING AND ALCOHOL

Does your state regulate the following conduct or have the following laws?

Conduct	Statute
Driving a vehicle while under the influence of alcohol or drugs. (Does "vehicle" include watercraft, aircraft, moped, etc.?)	
First offense	_____
Second offense	_____
Third offense	_____
The legal drinking limit is	_____
Drinking and driving age is	_____
"Booze it and lose it" statute (administrative license revocation laws that give police the right to seize licenses of drivers who fail or refuse sobriety tests)	_____
Punish refusal of driver to take Breathalyzer or other test when lawfully requested	_____
Ban open containers of alcoholic beverages in motor vehicles	_____
While driving under the influence:	_____
• causes property damage	_____
• causes serious injury to another person	_____
• causes the death of another person	_____
Leaving scene of accident (failing to stop and report):	_____
• property damage	_____
• injury to person	_____
• fatal accident	_____
Can law enforcement agencies in your state set up sobriety checkpoints?	_____

See, e.g., NJSA § 39:4-50(a)(1), (2), and (3). At some point, repeated violations can be treated as felonies.

Under the most common type of statute, the prosecution can prove the violation either by evidence the driver was under the influence of alcohol or drugs, or by use of a blood or breath test. Blood tests are more reliable, but they are more expensive, time-consuming, and not always available. As a result, breath tests on a Breathalyzer® or similar machine are often used to prove the violation.

A prosecution based on evidence of impairment due to drugs or alcohol, where no results from breath or blood tests are available, usually includes police evidence from **field sobriety tests**. These tests, done according to guidelines established by the National Highway Traffic Safety Administration (NHTSA), are given by officers in the field who suspect a motorist they have stopped is impaired by alcohol or drugs. Because alcohol can cause **nystagmus**, a condition in which the eye demonstrates abnormal and involuntary movement, horizontal gaze nystagmus (HGN) testing can be used as evidence of alcohol impairment. While there has been some controversy about the reliability of HGN testing, most courts conclude the results are admissible. See, e.g., the 2010 case of *People v. McKown*.[33] Observation of the other two field tests can be combined with results from the HGN testing and can be used as evidence of impairment if the tests are conducted according to NHTSA guidelines. Most states require that the NHTSA guidelines be strictly or substantially followed for the test results to be admitted. See, e.g., *State v. Boczur*.[34] Prosecutors will usually have additional observed evidence of impairment, such as the suspect's physical condition, the smell of alcohol on the breath, slurring of words, and so forth. This evidence can be sufficient to convict a defendant of driving while intoxicated, or driving while impaired as it is called in some states.

Breath testing results are also generally admissible, so long as the person administering the test follows proper procedures. Currently, two machines, the Datamaster and the Intoxilizer, are commonly used by law enforcement agencies. The sophistication of breath testing machines has increased over the years. In 2003 New Jersey began using a new computer-operated machine called the Alcotest. In a 2008 decision, *State v. Chun*,[35] the New Jersey Supreme Court upheld the reliability of the machine and stated that results from the machine could be used to prove a drunk driving charge, if the machine's procedures were followed.

With all breath testing machines, defenses in DUI cases can turn on the operation of the machine and how the machine has been maintained. Procedures for routinely checking the machine for reliability are required to guarantee its accuracy, and law enforcement agencies must keep detailed records of maintenance checks. Many DUI defense arguments are based on the absence of such records or checks. See, e.g., *Blazier v. Vincent*.[36]

"Booze It and Lose It" Laws

More than thirty states have passed **"booze it and lose it" laws** (usually called "implied consent" laws), which give the police the authority to immediately seize the driver's licenses of people who fail or refuse sobriety tests. In addition to the administrative sanction of a loss of license, many states have attached criminal penalties for refusal to consent to a blood or breath test if a driver fails the field sobriety tests. After these new laws became known to the drinking public, nighttime fatal crashes

field sobriety tests
Field tests used to evaluate a motorist's alcohol or drug impairment. They include HGN testing, the walk-and-turn test, and the one-leg stand test.

nystagmus A persistent, rapid, involuntary, side-to-side eye movement.

"booze it and lose it" laws Laws, enacted in more than thirty states, that give the police the authority to immediately seize the driver's licenses of people who fail or refuse sobriety tests.

dropped dramatically. The National Safety Board estimated that if all fifty states adopted such laws, 2,000 lives could be saved in the United States each year.

As a result of the U.S. Supreme Court's decision in *Missouri v. McNeeley*, 133 S. Ct. 1552 (2013), state laws punishing motorists who refuse blood or breath tests have come under scrutiny. *McNeeley* held that absent exigent circumstances, a warrant is required before a blood sample can be taken from a DUI suspect without consent.

Some courts have held that, consistent with *McNeeley*, administrative or criminal penalties for refusing to consent to a blood or breath test violate the Fourth Amendment. An example is *State v. Ryce*, 368 P.3d 342 (Kan. 2016), where the court held the Kansas implied consent law was unconstitutional. The Hawaii Supreme Court held in *State v. Yong Shik Won*, 2015 WL 10384497 (Haw. 2015) that a consent to a breath test in a DUI arrest after police gave the suspect the choice to consent to the test or be sent to jail for 30 days was involuntary, and reversed a DUI conviction.

Other courts have upheld the implied consent laws. The Nebraska Supreme Court in *State v. Modlin*, 867 N.W.2d 609 (Neb. 2015) refused to find consent given by a DUI suspect to a blood test violated the holding in *McNeeley*. In *State v. Bernard*, 859 N.W.2d 762 (Minn. 2015) the court affirmed a conviction under the state implied consent law of a defendant who refused to take a Breathalyzer test after being arrested for DUI. The U.S. Supreme Court granted review of the Minnesota case (as well as a similar decision by the North Dakota Supreme Court) in December 2015. In *Bernard v. Minnesota*, 136 S. Ct. 615, (2016), the Court held that requiring suspected drunk drivers to take a blood/alcohol test without consent violated the Fourth Amendment. Police must obtain a warrant to take blood from a motorist if the motorist does not consent.

When Is a Person Driving, Operating, or "In Physical Control" of a Vehicle?

States forbid operating motor vehicles, watercraft, snowmobiles, and aircraft while under the influence of alcohol or of a controlled substance. In most drunk driving cases, either a police officer or a witness testifies to seeing the defendant drive a vehicle while intoxicated. However, when no witnesses are available to testify about the driving, courts must decide when a person is driving, operating, or "in physical control" of a vehicle.

It is not a crime to be intoxicated inside a motor vehicle. Leaving a party or bar and deciding to "sleep it off" in one's car by itself is not a violation of the law. However, though these laws are referred to as "drunk driving" laws, in fact courts find violations whenever an intoxicated person "operates" a motor vehicle. One can be "operating" a motor vehicle without actually driving the motor vehicle. As a result, courts have generally rejected the defense of defendants who admitted being in their cars with the motor running, but who claimed they were not driving the car. Sitting intoxicated behind the wheel of a running car with the key in the ignition, with the potential to drive it, is exactly the harm the statutes are designed to avoid, courts uniformly hold.

What actions, short of placing the key in the ignition and turning on the car's engine, constitute "operating"? For most courts, the question is whether some action has been taken to initiate the sequence of acts that activate the motor vehicle. The following cases are examples of courts considering when a person has begun that sequence. In each example the defendant was intoxicated:

- *State v. Fitzgerald*, 63 So.3d 75 (Fla. App. 2011): Defendant was behind the wheel of the parked car at intersection. Motor was not running, and keys were in defendant's right hand. Court held this constituted "physical control" under the Florida statute.
- *State v. Haight*, 903 A.2d 217 (Conn. 2007): Key was in the ignition with the defendant sitting in the driver's seat. The court held this constituted "operating" whether or not the key was turned to the "on" position.
- *Nelson v. Commonwealth*, 707 S.E.2d 815 (Va. 2011): The court held the ignition key must be turned to the "on" or "accessory" position, but need not be turned to the position that starts the engine.
- *State v. Cyr*, 967 A.2d 32 (Conn. 2009): Defendant started car's engine by remote device, but had not placed key in ignition, which was required to move car. The court held starting the car began the sequence leading to activate the motor vehicle.
- *State v. Rogers*, 224 S.W.3d 564 (Mo. App. 2007) (contrasting result): Operating is not begun until keys are in the engine, even though engine has been started by remote control device.

LEARNING OBJECTIVES SUMMARY

LO 1. **List the ways a person can violate the Uniform Controlled Substances Act.**
All states and the federal government have enacted the Uniform Controlled Substances Act of 1970. Under this law, which is part of the criminal code of your state, the following are crimes:

1. *Manufacture or delivery of an illegal drug*
2. *Possession with intent to deliver an illegal drug*
3. *Delivery or possession with intent to deliver a counterfeit substance*
4. *Offering or agreeing to deliver an illegal drug and then delivering a substance that is not a controlled substance*
5. *Possession of an illegal drug*
6. *Knowingly allowing a store, dwelling, building, vehicle, boat, aircraft, or other place to be used by people using illegal drugs*
7. *Obtaining possession of an illegal drug by misrepresentation, fraud, forgery, deception, or subterfuge*

LO 2. **Identify the elements of the crime of possession of an illegal drug with intent to deliver.**
Intent to deliver illegal drugs can be proved by showing a "rational connection" between the facts of possession, such as a large quantity of the drug, and an intent to sell the drugs.

LO 3. **State the current status of state medical-use-of-marijuana statutes.**
Medical use of marijuana is permitted in 24 states, if done as prescribed treatment for listed illness or conditions. While medical users can be prosecuted under federal laws, in 2013 the Justice Department stated it would not do so in states that have sufficient regulation procedures for use of marijuana.

LO 4. **Explain the rationale of the Supreme Court's holding in Gonzales v. Raich.**
In Gonzales v. Raich *the court reasoned that private use of marijuana might have an adverse impact on federal drug laws, and thus Congress had the power under the Commerce Clause to regulate even purely intrastate use of marijuana.*

LO 5. **Identify the elements that must be proved for a conviction under a state drug-induced death statute, as compared to the federal drug-induced penalty statute.**
The state must show only that the defendant provided the drugs to the victim, and that the victim died as a proximate result of the defendant's actions. That means no other intervening event must have caused the death. Under the federal statute, the prosecution must show use of the illegal drug was the "but-for" cause of death, not just a contributing cause.

LO 6. **State the basis of the argument a state's "booze it and lose it" implied consent law violated the U.S. Constitution.**
Defendants argue implied consent (implied when motorists use public highways) laws that make it a crime to refuse to consent to blood or breath tests in traffic stops where officers suspect the driver is intoxicated violate the Fourth Amendment. Because the U.S. Supreme Court has said taking such samples is a seizure which requires a warrant, penalties for refusal to consent to a test, it is argued, are also unconstitutional.

LO 7. **Identify what must be shown to prove a person was operating a motor vehicle.**
An intoxicated suspect can be found to have been operating a motor vehicle by simply being behind the wheel of a car with the keys in the ignition, though in some states the key must be turned to the "on" position.

KEY TERMS

CASE ANALYSIS AND WRITING EXERCISES

1. Is a driver suffering from "sleep driving" because of a reaction to the prescription sleep aid Ambien guilty of DUI? If so, does the sleep driving constitute a defense under the DUI statute? Do DUI statutes have a mental state requirement? See *Leeka v. State*, 461 S.W.3d 331 (Ark. 2015). Is the dissent right?

2. Some states have a state statute similar to the federal Religious Freedom Restoration Act, discussed in this chapter. Idaho is such a state: The Idaho Free Exercise of Religion Protection Act (FERPA) states that government may not substantially burden the exercise of religion by laws of general application (like criminal laws) unless there is a "compelling state interest" in having the law. In *State v. Cordingly*, 302 P.3d 730 (Idaho App. 2013) the court found that the state's controlled substances law "substantially burdened" defendant's actions as a member of the "Church of Cognitive Therapy." Why didn't the court reverse the defendant's conviction? Was he "exercising" a religion when he used controlled substances (marijuana)?

3. In every state, the penalty for possession of controlled substances with the intent to deliver (sell) is much greater than possession for personal use. As noted in this chapter, proof of intent to deliver is frequently done by circumstantial evidence. Is there sufficient evidence for proof of intent if: (1) the police observe a "frantic" woman flag down defendant's SUV, reach into the SUV and hand something to the driver, and take something from the driver? The driver is subsequently stopped and police find 2.5 grams of crack cocaine hidden in the ceiling of the SUV. (2) The police search the SUV and find neither cash nor packaging, nor do they find drug paraphernalia like a crack pipe. If this isn't enough proof, what additional factors convinced the court the defendant intended to sell the crack cocaine in *State v. Stewart*, 2015 WL 4714829 (Minn. App. 2015)?

4. Most states have statutes permitting the seizure and forfeiture of contraband, including money related to the illegal sale of controlled substances. Texas has a forfeiture statute for contraband, including cash used in drug trafficking. Was the trial court correct to order seizure of cash found in defendant's possession in *Approximately $31,421.00 v. State*, 2015 WL 7730827 (Tex. Crim. App. 2015)? What, in your view, was the most significant fact pointing to the cash being part of drug trafficking? What facts needed under the statute seemed to be missing?

ENDNOTES

1. See the February 10, 2010, report of the United Nations Office of Drug Control.

2. A UN report in 1997 estimated that the illegal drug trade makes up 8 percent of world trade. This illegal industry is estimated at between $400 billion and $1 trillion worldwide. It is as large as the worldwide trade in textiles and bigger than the sales of iron or steel. See the *Pensacola News Journal* article "UN Report: Social Costs of Drug Abuse About $120 Billion," November 16, 1997.

3. The "Opium War," which Great Britain waged against China from 1839 to 1842, was conducted to force China to permit the importing of opium into China. China had silk and many other goods to sell to the world but would not buy goods from Britain and other nations. As a result, the British ran up a huge trade deficit. To pay off this deficit, the British commenced selling opium to the Chinese and established a British colony at Hong Kong. When the Chinese government tried to stop the sale of opium, the Opium War began.

   To supply the opium trade, opium was grown in the British colony of India and shipped to China to be traded for Chinese exports. By 1850, India's largest export was opium, exceeding the export of Indian cotton textiles.

   American shippers also brought opium into China to sell in exchange for goods from China. The biggest American trader was Warren Delano (the grandfather of President Franklin Delano Roosevelt). Delano became a very wealthy man in the trade with China. But this trade created thousands of opium addicts and was denounced in churches and in newspapers throughout the United States. After trading in opium was forbidden, illegal shipping and trading in opium continued to supply this deadly drug. See the *New York Times* articles "The Opium War's Secret History" and "Hong Kong's Colonial Ghosts," June 22, 1997. Also see Martin Booth, *Opium: A History* (New York: St. Martin's Press, 1998).

4. This act replaced the 1933 Uniform Narcotic Drug Act and the 1966 Model State Drug Abuse Control Act.

5. A designer drug is a drug that is cheaply made from chemicals and is sometimes similar to a commonly known illegal drug. New designer drugs come on the market regularly. To prevent the invention, manufacturing, and distribution of designer drugs before they are permanently scheduled in the Uniform Controlled Substances Act, the U.S. Congress enacted a law permitting the quick and temporary placement of a new designer drug in the federal Controlled Substances Act. If this law had not been passed, a new designer drug could be sold throughout the United States for up to a year before it was permanently made a part of the Uniform Controlled Substances Act. The U.S. Supreme Court unanimously upheld the quick scheduling of new designer drugs in the 1991 case of *Touby v. U.S.* (111 S. Ct. 1752).

6. Many courts hold that a person cannot be convicted of possession of a drug solely because the drug is in the person's body. See *State v. Thronsen*, 809 P.2d 941 (Alaska App. 1991) and *State v. Vorm*, 570 N.E.2d 109 (Ind. App. 1991). However, people with an illegal drug in their bodies may be charged with the crime of "being under the influence of a controlled substance." See *Junior v. State*, 807 P.2d 205 (Nev. 1991).

7. 98 P.3d 1190 (Wash. 2004), *cert. denied,* 544 U.S. 922 (2005).

8. 599 F.3d 1198 (10th Cir. 2010).

9. 542 F.3d 968 (2nd Cir. 2008).

10. 532 NE.2d 1249 (N.Y. 1988). Surprisingly, tests done by the Argonne National Laboratory in 1997 showed that many $1 and $2 bills circulated in Chicago, Miami, and Houston were tainted with microscopic traces of cocaine. The chemists conducting the tests stated that $1 and $2 bills are used to wrap "rocks" (chunks of solid cocaine chipped off a cocaine brick). The rock is then sold. Paper money is used instead of newspaper because the money does not transfer ink to the cocaine as newspaper does. Dollar bills are also rolled into tubes and used to snort cocaine powder.

    Defense lawyers have used these findings in cocaine possession cases. The report also states that people who handle cocaine-tainted money do not show traces of cocaine on their person except when money comes into contact with large amounts of cocaine immediately before a person handled it. See the *New York Times* article "Cocaine Turns Up in Many $1 and $2 Bills," September 23, 1997.

11. The Court of Appeals of South Carolina held that ordinarily a measurable quantity is necessary, but when the cocaine was the "remnant of a larger amount previously possessed in the past," the conviction was affirmed. The cocaine residue was in a crack pipe; *State v. Robinson,* 411 S.E.2d 678 (1991). In *State v. Wood,* 1994 WL 250015 (N.M. App. 1994), the cocaine residue was in syringes (conviction sustained).

12. 807 N.E.2d 789 (Ind. App. 2004).

13. *People v. Rubacalba,* 859 P.2d 708 (Calif. 1993).

14. *Lord v. State,* 616 So. 2d 1065 (Fla. App. 1993). In *Gilchrist v. State,* 784 So. 2d 624 (Fla. App. 2001), the court suggested that the holding in *Lord* applied only to common objects like dollar bills. Where the trace amounts are on a device used to ingest the drug, as was the case in *Gilchrist,* the usable quantity rule does not apply.

15. 677 F.3d 685 (5th Cir. 2012).

16. See *County Court of Ulster County v. Allen,* 442 U.S. 140, 99 S. Ct. 2213 (1979).

17. 532 U.S. 483 (2001).

18. 352 F.3d 122 (9th Cir. 2003).

19. 545 U.S. 1 (2005). A spokesperson for the California attorney general's office stated in 2005 that there was now "a sort of detente" between federal and state law enforcement agencies over medical use of marijuana. He stated that federal law enforcement agencies for the most part are targeting individuals who seem clearly to be using marijuana for purposes other than medical treatment, something the state of California was doing also. As of July 2013, eighteen other states and the District of Columbia had passed laws permitting the medical use of marijuana.

20. 546 U.S. 418 (2006).

21. 521 U.S. 507 (1997).

22. 96 P.3d 420 (Utah 2004).

23. 594 A.2d 1086 (Me. 1991).

24. 581 S.E.2d 35 (Ga. 2003).

25. See the *Harvard Medical School Heart Letter* article "Cocaine: An Unpredictable Killer" (April 1992). The article points out that until 1914, cocaine was an ingredient in many cough syrups and home remedy medications sold in the United States. The article also notes that cocaine was used in Coca-Cola until it was replaced by caffeine in 1906. The Harrison Narcotics Act of 1914 classified cocaine as a narcotic in 1914 and limited its use to prescription medical purposes. The article states that cocaine "then went underground, where it remains (today)."

26. If a person was committing a felony in supplying an illegal drug that directly caused a drug-induced death, a prosecutor could issue a criminal charge of felony murder in addition to other criminal charges if the case met the requirements of the felony murder law of that state. (See Chapter 10 of this text for a discussion of the crime of felony murder.)

27. 21 U.S.C.A. § 863(d).

28. *U.S. v. Dyer,* 750 F. Supp. 1275 (E.D. Va. 1990).

29. *United States v. Mishra,* 979 F.2d 301 (3d Cir. 1992).

30. *Harvard Medical School Health Letter* (September 1993) citing *British Medical Journal* and *Southern Medical Journal.* The April 2002 report is entitled *A Call to Action: Changing the Culture of Drinking at U.S. Colleges.* The study was done by the National Institute of Alcohol Abuse and Alcoholism, which is a branch of the National Institutes of Health. (See the *New York Times* article, "Study Calculates the Effects of College Drinking in U.S.," April 10, 2002.)

31. Although many states have decriminalized public drunkenness, other states continue to make public drunkenness a crime. In cities and states where public drunkenness is not a crime, a person who is intoxicated in a public place is often ignored if not getting into trouble or endangered. If such people are a problem, they could be taken to a detoxification center (if available) or a homeless shelter. Such people could also be arrested for disorderly conduct or another offense.

32. Most states have dram shop liability laws under which taverns and bars can be liable to innocent victims of alcohol-related accidents and crimes. Social hosts who provide alcohol can also be liable under the laws of some states. Providing alcohol to an intoxicated minor creates the greatest dram shop liability.

33. 924 N.E.2d 155 (Ill. 2010).

34. 863 N.E.2d 155 (Ohio 2007).

35. 943 A.2d 114 (N.J. 2008).

36. 204 S.W.3rd 658 (Mo. App. 2006).

17

Terrorism

OUTLINE

LEARNING OBJECTIVES

In this chapter we discuss criminal statutes aimed at punishing and preventing terrorism. The learning objectives for Chapter 17 are as follows:

LO 1. Construct a working definition of terrorism.

LO 2. Explain why federal criminal statutes must define terrorism.

LO 3. Explain one method by which a group can be identified as a terrorist group.

LO 4. List the elements of the crime of terrorism under most state laws.

LO 5. Define a terrorist threat under state criminal laws.

LO 6. Explain the concept of the rules of war.

LO 7. List ways terrorists obtain financial support for their terrorist actions.

LO 8. List ways money is sent into and out of the United States by terrorist supporters.

LO 9. Identify when a seizure is an extraordinary rendition.

This drawing depicts Khalid Sheik Mohammed, the alleged organizer of the 9/11 attacks. Mohammed has been detained for more than nine years at the Guantanamo Bay detention center, where he waits for trial on terrorism charges.

Christopher Gillette was a U.S. Army veteran with a grievance. He believed he suffered from serious injuries incurred while he was in the military, and that he was not receiving proper care from the Veteran's Administration and military hospitals. He therefore wrote a letter to his Texas Congressman, in which he made demands for proper treatment, and an apology from the federal government. Gillette also made various statements concerning the consequences if his demands were not met. When the police were given copies of the letter, Gillette was arrested and charged under the Texas "terrorist threat" statute, TEX PENAL CODE § 22.07(a)(5), (6). That statute makes it a crime to make threats intended to (5) place the public in fear of serious injury, or (6) influence the actions of a branch of government.

What was it in Gillette's letter that the prosecution alleged violated the statute? Do you agree with the result in his trial and appeals? See *Gillette v. State*, 444 S.W.3d 713 (Tex. Crim. App. 2014).[1]

In this chapter we will study the many forms terrorism takes and the criminal laws passed by governments to punish terrorism. We will learn the criminal laws enacted to address both terrorist acts committed by U.S. citizens and those committed by citizens of other countries.

TERRORISM

Terrorists are criminals who use force and violence in the pursuit of extreme political, ideological, or religious goals. They are willing to take innocent lives to make their statements. Terrorists may be domestic or international. They may be stateless (acting on their own), or they may be domestic (homegrown) acting against their own people and government. They might be acting for a nation, backed by a nation, or supported by people within a nation.

terrorism The use of force and violence in the pursuit of extreme political, ideological, or religious goals, without regard to the innocent lives that may be lost.

Terrorism can be cheap and relatively easy. Terrorists use surprise and vulnerability to their advantage. A handful of dedicated individuals can cause great harm. Timothy McVeigh and Terry Nichols killed 168 people in seconds by blowing up the Alfred P. Murrah Federal Building in Oklahoma City. Fewer than 100 foreign terrorists killed thousands on September 11, 2001.

Terrorism has existed for ages. The term *terrorism* comes from the Latin word *terere*, which means "to frighten." The word *zealot* originated as a term for militant Jews who used terrorism to fight the Roman occupation of Israel in the first century. The word *assassin* comes from the name of a group of Shiite Muslims who used terrorism against Persia in the twelfth century. In 1901 an American president, William McKinley, was killed by an American terrorist. Four European heads of state were assassinated by terrorists between the years 1894 and 1900.

Terrorists can be religious or ethnic zealots. They might be people seeking to avenge a perceived wrong or maniacs who get their kicks out of violence. They are sometimes oppressed people angry or desperate enough to use bombs and guns.

Terrorism is a tactic—a means of striking out suddenly, using surprise. The goal is to intimidate and coerce a civilian population, or influence or punish a government. It has put governments around the world on the defensive, forcing them to spend billions of dollars to protect their civilian populations.

While terrorism has existed for centuries, the international community has yet to agree on a definition of the term. The term first appeared during the French Revolution in 1789 and was used to describe the actions of the republican government, mainly Prime Minister Robespierre, in executing more than 17,000 people. In subsequent years the term came to be applied to specific kinds of crimes in which the criminal had a political motivation.

The United Nations has never defined international terrorism. Rather, it has adopted several international agreements, called "conventions," which member nations must follow. For example, after the bombings of civilian aircraft in the 1960s and 1970s, the UN adopted the Tokyo and Montreal Conventions against attacks on civilian aircraft. As part of these Conventions, every member nation was required to make the specified acts criminal under their domestic law.

Similar conventions have been adopted to deal with nuclear terror, financing terrorists, holding hostages, and bombing. These conventions are aimed at individual terrorists, not at member nations. Their goal is not to identify international terrorism as a specific offense, but rather to identify various kinds of conduct used by terrorists or that supports terrorists and to require member nations to make such conduct criminal.

The United States has a definition of international terrorism in 18 U.S.C. § 2331(1). International terrorism is defined as violent acts that would be crimes in the United States, and are intended to

1. Intimidate or coerce a civilian population,
2. Influence government by intimidation or coercion, or
3. Affect government by mass destruction, assassination, or kidnapping.

Because of the constitutional prohibition against vagueness (see Chapter 1), terrorism as an offense must be clearly defined under U.S. law.

Terrorists differ from other criminals because they commit their crimes to send a political or ideological message or to retaliate for a wrong that they believe has occurred. They may seek a change, such as people who wanted to stop abortions by burning down abortion clinics and shooting doctors.

Terrorism is also a form of warfare that has existed since wars have been waged and conducted. Northern Ireland witnessed terrorism for more than a half century. To people who are believers in the cause of the terrorist, the terrorist may be viewed as a hero. However, to the great majority of the civilized world, terrorists are criminals.

EARLY TERRORIST ACTS

Anarchists (people who oppose organized government) historically have used terrorism to convey their political message. In May 1886, after local anarchists printed and distributed fliers calling for workers to arm themselves, a bomb exploded at a Haymarket Square rally in Chicago. It killed a policeman and wounded several other people. Two editors of an anarchist newspaper and six other men were convicted of conspiracy in the bombing; four were hanged.

In the years between 1894 and 1900, four European heads of state (the president of France, the prime minister of Spain, the empress of Austria, and the king of Italy) were assassinated by anarchists. President McKinley's assassin, an anarchist, stated in 1901 before his execution, "I don't believe we should have any rulers. It is right to kill them."[2]

World War I was started, in part, by the assassination in Sarajevo (now part of Bosnia) of Archduke Franz Ferdinand, the heir to the Austrian throne, by a terrorist in 1914. That war, which lasted for four years, caused the deaths of more than 20 million people.

INTERNATIONAL AND DOMESTIC TERRORISM IN RECENT YEARS

Terrorism has become a global problem, and all nations have become vulnerable to terrorist attacks. In September 2004, more than 300 people, mostly children, were killed by terrorists in Beslan, Russia, in a protest against Russian policy in Chechnya. In Madrid, Spain, in March 2004, more than 200 people were killed when terrorists exploded bombs on crowded city commuter trains. In London, England, in July 2005, 52 people were killed by terrorist bombs in subway cars. In Paris,

France, in November 2015, 129 people were killed by terrorist attacks in theaters and restaurants. In the Middle East, the ISIS or Islamic State group executes people under circumstances that can only be called terrorism.

Because of these and other terrorist attacks, police all over the world are on almost constant alert for suspected terrorist activities. The United States in particular is a stated target of the terrorist group al-Qaeda, a radical Islamic fundamentalist group.

In 2004 the U.S. government created the National Counterterrorism Center (NCTC) to act as a clearinghouse on international terrorism intelligence and information. In a report published in July 2012, the last date for which statistics were available, the NCTC gave these statistics on international terrorism:

- In 2011 there were 10,283 terrorist attacks worldwide.
- 12,533 people were killed in these attacks.
- Afghanistan, Iraq, and Pakistan accounted for 64 percent of attacks worldwide.
- Sunni Muslim extremists accounted for 56 percent of all attacks, and 70 percent of all fatalities.
- Al-Qaeda and its affiliates caused almost 2,000 deaths in 688 attacks, while the Taliban caused about 1,900 deaths in over 800 attacks.
- The Nigeria-based Boko Haram increased its attacks in 2011 to 136, up from 31 in 2010.
- More than one-half of the victims killed were civilians, and 755 were children. However, the percentage of governmental employees and contractors killed in 2011 marked an increase over previous years.

Recent domestic terrorist acts include these:
- During the 1980s and 1990s antiabortion extremists bombed, shot at, and torched abortion clinics in the United States and Canada, killing six people.
- The Unabomber (Theodore Kaczynski), during a 17-year period, killed three people and injured 28 others by sending letter bombs through the mail.
- Deadly anthrax spores were sent through the mail in many eastern U.S. cities in 2001, killing five people.
- In 1995, the Alfred P. Murrah Federal Building in Oklahoma City was destroyed by a massive bomb, killing 168 people and injuring more than 500 others. Timothy McVeigh received the death sentence for this crime and was executed in 2001. Terry Nichols was sentenced to life in prison for his role in the bombings.[3]
- In 2007, six Muslim men were arrested and charged with planning an attack on Fort Dix, a federal military base in New Jersey. Using automatic weapons and hand grenades, they planned "to kill as many soldiers as possible." Authorities also thwarted a 2003 plot to blow up the Brooklyn Bridge.[4]
- In January 2011 a lone gunman killed six people in a Tucson, Arizona, shopping mall.
- In April 2013 terrorist bombers attacked the Boston Marathon, killing 4 people and injuring 183.
- In July 2015 a gunman attacked a Navy operations center in Chattanooga, Tennessee, killing 4 Marines and 1 Navy sailor.
- In December 2015, in San Bernardino, California, two terrorists attacked an office party where one of the terrorists worked, killing 14 and injuring 21.

- In February 2016 a terrorist wielding a machete attacked customers in a Columbus, Ohio, restaurant, injuring 4 people.
- In June 2016 a terrorist armed with an assault rifle killed 49 people in an Orlando, Florida, night club. In a 911 call to police during the rampage, Omar Mateen declared his allegiance to the Islamic State, the terrorist group fighting in Syria, Iraq, and Libya. Police officers shot and killed Mateen in a gun battle to free hostages he was holding at the club.

The Council on Foreign Relations reported on February 7, 2011, on trends in domestic terrorism in the United States. It stated in part:

- *Leftist Groups:* Weather Underground, Black Liberation Army, and Black Panther Party terrorist acts peaked in the 1980s, and have declined dramatically since.
- *Antigovernment and White Supremacist Groups:* Terrorist acts by white supremacist groups and conservative militia groups have increased in recent years.
- *Single-Issue Groups:* Terrorist acts by groups of extremists tied to a single issue, such as the environment or abortion rights, peaked in 2004, when the FBI named them the number-one threat of domestic terrorism.
- *"Lone Wolf" Terrorists:* By far the greatest increase in terrorist acts was by individual, "lone wolf" terrorists, who are not affiliated with any group. Before the Oklahoma City bombing in 1995, only about 6 percent of domestic terrorist acts were committed by a sole terrorist. Since 1995, more than 30 percent of domestic terrorist acts have been committed by a "lone wolf."

The Antiterrorism and Effective Death Penalty Act (AEDPA), 18 U.S.C. § 1332, and the USA Patriot Act, 18 U.S.C. § 2239, make it a federal crime to provide "material support or resources" to an organization that has been designated and named as a foreign terrorist organization in the United States by the State Department. The penalty for violation of these statutes is imprisonment for up to 15 years or, if a death occurs, for life. In addition, triple civil damages may be recovered from any organization that provides support to a terrorist organization that injures or kills a U.S. citizen.[5]

As the statistics above state, Muslim extremists were responsible for the majority of terrorist attacks worldwide. The following are some of the terrorist acts that were committed by Muslim extremists against the United States:

- Pan Am World Airways Flight 103 was blown out of the sky over Lockerbie, Scotland, killing all 259 on board the aircraft and 11 people on the ground.
- Seven U.S. overseas buildings were bombed between 1985 and 1998. More than 150 people were killed and more than 2,000 injured. Many of the dead and injured were foreign nationals working for the United States. The locations were U.S. Air Force bases in Spain and Germany, a military training center and barracks in Saudi Arabia, and the U.S. embassies in Kenya, Tanzania, and Peru.
- A truck bomb damaged the New York World Trade Center in 1993, killing 6 people and injuring more than 1,000. Sheik Omar Rahman and nine other militant Muslims were convicted of this attack and of a conspiracy which, if carried out, would have destroyed the United Nations building and many other New York City landmarks.

- The U.S. naval ship *U.S.S. Cole* was seriously damaged in a suicide bombing in the Middle Eastern country of Yemen, killing seventeen sailors and injuring thirty-nine.
- On September 11, 2001, four U.S. commercial aircraft were hijacked by nineteen terrorists. Two planes loaded with jet fuel were deliberately flown into the 110-story twin towers of the New York World Trade Center, causing the towers to collapse. One aircraft was flown into a section of the Pentagon in Washington, D.C., while passengers in the fourth aircraft fought with the hijackers, causing the plane to crash in Pennsylvania. More than 2,800 people died in these attacks. In 2006, Habib Zacarias Moussaoui was convicted in federal court of conspiring with and aiding the 9/11 attackers and was sentenced to life in prison without parole. He is currently incarcerated at the Federal ADX Supermax prison in Florence, Colorado. Khalid Sheikh Mohammed, believed to be the ringleader of the 9/11 terrorists, is being detained at the U.S. detention center in Guantanamo Bay, Cuba, awaiting trial on terrorist charges. Because of the complexity of the case and the number of parties involved (about 150 lawyers, officials, and court personnel play a role in the case), as of May 24, 2016 Mohammed has not been tried. He has been detained at Guantanamo for over 9 years.

THE TORTURE ACT

In 1988 President Reagan signed the United Nations Convention against Torture (CAT). This international agreement was aimed at persons who, under color of law, torture individuals for political or other reasons. Nations who sign the convention agree to prosecute persons who violate international law by torturing others. In 1994 Congress passed the Torture Act, 18 U.S.C. § 2340–2340A, which punishes any person who subjects another person to torture, defined as the intention, under color of law, to inflict severe pain or suffering. Federal courts are given jurisdiction to try persons charged under this statute for torture that occurred outside the United States if they are U.S. nationals or were arrested within the United States.

The first person charged under the Torture Act was Charles Arthur Emmanuel, a/k/a Charles Taylor, Jr. Emmanuel was the son of Charles Taylor, a Liberian citizen living in the United States, where Emmanuel was born. In the 1990s Taylor led a revolt that ended with his election to the Liberian presidency in 1997. From 1999 to 2003, when Taylor was forced out of Liberia, Emmanuel was his father's security chief. In that position he tortured and killed Liberian citizens, and he was known as "the demon." After his father left Liberia, Emmanuel returned to the United States in 2006, where he had lived with his mother under the name of Belfast. He was arrested in Florida that year and charged under the Torture Act. He was convicted and sentenced to 97 years in prison. His conviction and sentence were affirmed in *United States v. Belfast*, 611 F.3d 783. (11th Cir. 2010).

Emmanuel's father, Charles Taylor, was extradited to The Hague, Netherlands, where in April 2012 he was convicted of multiple war crimes for aiding and inciting the rape and murder of thousands of civilians. He was sentenced on May 30, 2012, to 50 years in prison. Taylor's conviction is the first conviction of a former head of state for international war crimes since the Nazi trials after World War II.

CRIMINAL CHARGES AGAINST TERRORISTS

After the 1995 terrorist attack that destroyed the Oklahoma City Federal Building, Congress enacted the Federal Antiterrorism Law, 18 U.S.C.A. § 1331, which gives the federal government jurisdiction to act against terrorism toward the United States, whether it occurs in the United States or elsewhere in the world. 18 U.S.C. §2332 and other statutes address various ways terrorist activities are made crimes under federal statutes. Many of those statutes are listed in the "Antiterrorism Laws" insert found later in this chapter.

Because the federal government lists thousands of crimes in the Federal Criminal Code, terrorists have been and will generally be charged under existing federal or state criminal law. In addition to crimes of general applicability, such as assault with a deadly weapon, murder, and arson, the following materials discuss possible criminal charges that could be brought against those committing terrorist acts.

treason Acting to overthrow one's government, or in violation of allegiance to one's country.

Treason   **Treason** is the only crime defined in the U.S. Constitution. Article III, Section 3, provides:

> Treason against the United States, shall consist only in levying War against them, or in adhering to their Enemies, giving them Aid and Comfort. No Person shall be convicted of Treason unless on the Testimony of two Witnesses to the same overt Act, or on Confession in open Court.

Treason is a difficult crime to prove. In the history of the United States, treason has been charged only some thirty times. Aaron Burr was charged with treason in 1807 and, after a trial, was acquitted on a technicality. After World War II, Tokyo Rose, among others, was convicted of treason and served 7 years in prison for urging American military personnel to desert during World War II.

sedition The crime of advocating the forceful overthrow of the established government. In this country, the Smith Act makes such advocacy a crime.

Sedition   All democratic countries have had to pass laws to protect their governments from overthrow by the use of force and violence. The **sedition** law now in effect in the United States is the Smith Act of 1940, 18 U.S.C. § 2385. It forbids advocating the forceful overthrow of the U.S. government, distributing with disloyal intent materials teaching and advising the overthrow of the government by violence, and organizing or helping to organize any group having such purpose.

The seditious conspiracy statute, 18 U.S.C. § 2384, makes it a crime to conspire with another person to destroy by force the government of the United States. In *United States v. Rodriguez*,[6] the court upheld the conviction under the seditious conspiracy statute of a member of FALN, a terrorist group seeking the independence of Puerto Rico. The court rejected the defendant's argument that the statute violated the Treason Clause of the U.S. Constitution, which is Article III, Section 3. That clause limits convictions for treason by requiring proof of overt acts and corroboration by two witnesses in open court. The defendant contended the seditious conspiracy act was "constructive treason," but the court disagreed, finding it served a different interest than the Treason Clause. The purpose of the conspiracy statute, the court said, was to combat "urban terrorism" and make government property and officials safe. It was not simply directed at those making war on the United States.

The U.S. Supreme Court affirmed the conviction of an officer in the American Communist Party in the case of *Dennis v. United States*.[7] At that time, Communist

Anwar al-Awlaki, a suspected terrorist, killed by a U.S. drone aircraft in 2011.

Osama bin Laden, killed in 2012 by U.S. Navy Seals.

Taliban leader Mulah Akhtar Mohammad Mansour, killed by a U.S. drone attack in 2016.

ANTITERRORISM LAWS ENACTED BY U.S. CONGRESS

Year	Popular Name/ Citation	Purpose of Law
1903 and 1918	Immigration Act of 1903 and Act of 1918	Permitted exclusion of aliens advocating overthrow of government or affiliated with organizations who did so.
1940	Alien Registration Act and Smith Act of 1940	Requires deportation of aliens violating Act of 1918. Forbids advocating the forceful overthrow of the U.S. government, distributing with disloyal intent materials teaching and advising the overthrow of government by violence, and organizing any group having such purpose.

(Continued)

Year	Popular Name/Citation	Purpose of Law
1950	Internal Security Act of 1950, 50 U.S.C.A. § 402	Further regulated actions of resident aliens.
1976	Foreign Sovereign Immunities Act, 28 U.S.C.A. § 1602	Permits civil lawsuits by persons injured by terrorists against nations supporting those terrorists.
1978 and 2000	Foreign Intelligence and Surveillance Act of 1978 as amended by the Act of 2000	Gives government broad power to conduct electronic and other surveillance of suspected terrorists.
1984	Hostage Taking, 18 U.S.C.A. § 1203	Makes it a federal crime to take an American citizen hostage anywhere in the world if purpose is to coerce person or government.
1996	Antiterrorism Act of 1996, 18 U.S.C.A. § 2332(d)	Makes it a crime for U.S. citizens to support any group listed as a foreign terrorist organization by either money or with other meaningful assistance. Also makes it a crime to enter into a financial transaction with a nation designated as a supporter of terrorism.
1996	Iran and Libya Sanctions Act of 1996, 50 U.S.C. § 1701	Places sanctions on persons or nations that engage in trade with Iran or Libya.
2001	USA Patriot Act of 2001, 18 U.S.C. § 1993 Title III	Criminal penalties and forfeiture rules for money laundering by or for terrorist organizations.
	Title IV	Establishes new rules for protecting U.S. borders.
	Title V	Removes obstacles to investigating terrorism; pays rewards and uses DNA to identify terrorists.
	Title VI	Payments to victims of terrorism.
	Title VIII	Strengthens criminal laws against terrorism. New crimes governing attacks against mass transportation systems, harboring terrorists, or providing support to terrorists.
2006	18 U.S.C. § 2709 (as amended in 18 U.S.C. § 3511)	Requires communication systems, such as Internet servers, to give FBI access to records of communications by suspected terrorists.
2006	Animal Enterprise	Prohibits acts of violence against animal enterprises and persons associated with such enterprises.
2011	Terrorism Act, 18 U.S.C. § 43 National Defense Authority Act of 2012, 125 Stat. 1298	Permits federal government to detain indefinitely enemy combatants who have given material aid to al-Qaeda or the Taliban. In a 2013 decision, *Hedges v. Obama*, 2013 WL 3717774 (2nd Cir. 2013), the court held the Act did not apply to U.S. citizens or individuals arrested in the United States, and thus did not change the existing law on detention of citizens or others arrested in the United States, which generally does not permit such detention.

literature distributed in the United States urged the violent overthrow of the U.S. government. Following the conviction of defendant Dennis, the Communist Party stopped urging the violent overthrow of the U.S. government and now advocates change through peaceful and lawful means.

Sabotage The crime of damaging or injuring national defense material or utilities with the intention of interfering with national defense.

Sabotage   **Sabotage** is made a crime by 18 U.S.C.A. § 2155. The offense forbids damaging or injuring national defense material or national defense utilities "with intent to injure, interfere with, or obstruct the national defense."

A person can be convicted under 18 U.S.C. § 2155 for any acts that obstruct or interfere with any national defense installation or material. In *United States v. Platte,* [8] three Sisters of the Dominican Order were convicted under the statute for breaking into

---

 ## THE CONTINUING BATTLE AGAINST TERRORISM

The many national and international incidents of terrorism, both attempted and successful, force authorities all over the world to maintain a constant state of vigilance against these attacks. The following reports show some of the incidents that received national and international coverage, the ways terrorists can be prosecuted, and international concerns about future terrorist attacks:

Failed Attempts to Ignite Explosives

In 2010 a terrorist parked a van loaded with explosives in New York's Times Square, and triggered the device. The explosives smoldered, but did not ignite. Nearby vendors noticed the van and informed police, who broke into the van and disarmed the explosives. The driver of the van was quickly apprehended, and after talking freely to the police about his terrorist goals, pled guilty to criminal charges.

In 2009 a passenger on a commercial airplane attempted to ignite explosives he had concealed in his clothing. Although other passengers heard a series of loud pops, the explosives did not ignite.

In 2008 a passenger traveling by airplane from Europe to New York attempted to trigger explosives concealed in his shoes. There was smoke but no explosion.

Incidents of International Terrorism

Nations all over the world have been the victims of attacks by terrorist groups. In one of the most deadly since 9/11, in 2008 ten Pakistani terrorists attacked India's largest city, Mumbai (formerly called Bombay), illustrating the brazen and deadly tactics terrorists employ. Armed with assault rifles and grenades, the terrorists entered the city on small boats, and for 3 days launched attacks against hotels and other targets in the city, killing as many as 164 people, including 6 Americans, before 9 of the terrorists were killed by police. A Chicago man, David Headley, pled guilty in March 2010 to providing surveillance support to the terrorists. In exchange for an agreement not to seek the death penalty or extradite Headley to India, prosecutors obtained his cooperation in investigations of other terrorist actions.

In one of the longest, costliest, and most serious trials in English history, in 2008 a London jury convicted three terrorists of plotting to use liquid explosives to bring down in one day at least seven airliners traveling from England to the United States or Canada. Other members of the conspiracy were convicted in 2010. The suicide bombers planned to carry "liquid bombs" made by injecting liquid explosives into soft drink containers to be carried onto the airplanes. London police discovered the plot only days before the men planned the attacks. Worldwide airport security was changed to adjust to this new threat.

a Minuteman III missile site in Colorado. The defendants cut through a chain fence surrounding the property, and using ball-peen hammers they pounded on the rails that held the blast doors on nuclear missile silos. The court rejected their contentions that they did nothing that would have prevented the missiles from launching, stating that the statute required only that their actions interfere with or obstruct the national defense. Because the national defense includes training, the fact that the defendants' actions forced the virtual shutdown of the missile base for a period meant that their actions violated the statute.

The sabotage statute requires the prosecution to prove that destructive actions taken against military bases or materials were intended to "injure, interfere with,

Prosecuting Terrorists

Both federal and state courts could have jurisdiction to try a terrorist, if the terrorist's conduct were a violation of their respective criminal codes. Most terrorist crimes are tried in federal courts, since federal procedures offer more flexibility in determining venue and bringing in witnesses. Moreover, because federal courts have a long and successful history of trying difficult and complex cases such as espionage or those involving highly classified information, federal officials believe federal courts to be a "good fit" for these cases.

Military courts may also be used to try these cases when they involve a member of the military. Nidal Hasan, the army major charged with killing thirteen people at Fort Hood in 2009, will be tried in military courts. That trial is scheduled to begin in August 2013. Prosecutors have indicated they will seek the death penalty. Military commissions created to try "enemy combatants" may also try these kind of cases, but not if the defendant is a citizen of the United States.

Placing Terrorists on the "Kill List"

The Central Intelligence Agency is permitted under federal law to maintain a list (called the "kill list") of enemy targets, and is authorized to mount attacks against those targets. This list includes names of persons found to be enemies of the United States. If the person placed on the list is a U.S. citizen, the CIA must get approval from the White House. Anwar al-Awlaki, an American-born cleric hiding in Yemen, was placed on this list, based in part on his statement that "it is a religious duty to attack the United States." Anwar al-Awlaki was believed to have actively plotted and supported violence against the United States, and has been involved in more than a dozen terrorist plots, including the recent failed Times Square bombing plot. He is known to have had contact with Nidal Hasan, the army major discussed above, and in a statement posted on the Internet he praised Hasan's actions. In September 2011 a CIA drone fired a rocket into vehicles holding al-Awlaki and Samir Khan, an American living in Yemen who founded the militant, anti-American Internet magazine "Inspired," killing them both. In 2012, a U.S. Navy Seal team found and killed Osama bin Laden.

Concern over Future Terrorist Attacks

The National Intelligence has stated that the United States, and other democracies, face an enemy that has "no scruples about employing any weapon or tactic." This could include nuclear weapons. At a 2010 nuclear summit meeting President Obama and other world leaders voiced great concern about the prospect of terrorists using stolen or homemade nuclear devices to kill thousands of civilians in major cities.

or obstruct" the national defense of the United States. Not every intentional act causing destruction or damage of buildings or material at a military base meets that requirement. In *United States v. Walli*, 785 F.3d 1080 (6th Cir. 2015) three protesters broke through a fence surrounding a Department of Energy facility that stored enriched (weapons grade) uranium. Once inside the fence they spray-painted anti-war slogans on the facility. They were convicted under § 2155, which carries a maximum sentence of 20 years in prison. On appeal, the court of appeals reversed the convictions, holding that "interfere or obstruct" the national defense requires proof that the actions taken were intended to "impair the nation's capacity to wage war or defend against attack." No evidence existed to prove the defendant's conduct was intended to cause such a result, or would likely lead to such a result, the court concluded.

TERRORISM, TERRORIST THREATS, AND SUPPORT OF TERRORISM

crime of terrorizing A crime that creates a state of extreme fear, dread, or fright.

The term *terror* means a state of extreme fear, dread, or fright. Crimes that create such a condition are sometimes labeled "terrorist" crimes or the **crime of terrorizing** in state criminal codes. (See discussion of assault crimes in Chapter 11.)

Over the years, in addition to the federal statutes discussed earlier, states have enacted many of their own antiterrorism laws, and other laws protecting the state and the state government. At least twenty-four states have adopted antiterrorism statutes. An example of a state statute is Florida Statutes Annotated, § 775.30. That statute defines the crime of terrorism as an act or acts intended to

(a) Intimidate or coerce a civilian population.

(b) Influence the policy of a unit of government by intimidation or coercion.

(c) Affect the conduct of a unit of government by murder, assassination, or kidnapping.

Many states have passed statutes similar to the Florida statute, punishing terrorist threats that are directed at civilian populations or governments. Michigan's terrorist threat statute, MCL 750.543m, makes it a crime to threaten to perform a "terrorist act." A terrorist act is defined as a (1) violent felony that (2) is dangerous to human life and (3) is intended to intimidate or coerce a civilian population or influence a government by coercion or intimidation. In *People v. Osantowski*,[9] the Michigan Supreme Court upheld the conviction under § 750.543m of a high school student who sent e-mails to his 16-year-old girlfriend threatening to commit "mass murder" at his high school with guns and explosives.

States also have enacted statutes making it a crime to make a false report of a bomb or explosive threat with the purpose of either frightening a group of people or causing the evacuation of a building. In *State v. Tanis*,[10] the court upheld a conviction under the Missouri terrorist threat act, V.A.M.S. 574.115, of a man who falsely told police he had explosives in his truck and would use it to blow up a college building. The police evacuated the building, but a search of the truck revealed no explosives. The court affirmed his conviction, stating that the statute is aimed at actions that are intended to cause fear, and the evidence showed that was the intent of the defendant in making the false report.

YOU BE THE JUDGE

Should you grant the motion to dismiss? What does "by any means" refer to in the statute; actions taken or threats made? How should you treat the phone call from Smoak's wife? Is it a "communication" under the statute? When would it be a communication? See Smoak v. State, 186 So.3d 493 (Ala. App. 2015)

You are an Alabama state trial judge. The defendant, Thomas Smoak, has been charged with making terrorist threats under the Alabama Terrorist Threat statute, Ala. Code § 13A-10-15. That statute states that a person makes a terrorist threat if "by any means" the person threatens to commit a crime of violence by "(a) Terrorizing another person, or (b) Causing the disruption of school activities."

The parties agree that Smoak, angry that his son had been expelled from his high school, put his shotgun in his car and drove to the school. Concerned about what might happen, Smoak's wife called the school and alerted the school staff to Smoak's actions. The school officials "locked down" the school buildings, and called the police. When Smoak arrived, he drove unto school property, but seeing the police already there, attempted to drive away. He was stopped, and arrested. When stopped, he had his shotgun on the seat beside him.

Smoak has moved for a dismissal of the terrorist threat charge. He contends he never made a threat that was communicated to any person, and did not intend to disrupt school activities. The prosecution contends the statute says "by any means," and that showing up with the shotgun, coupled with the call by his wife, made Smoak's actions a terrorist threat.

Prosecutions for making terrorist threats under state criminal codes generally require proof that the defendant threatened violence against another person, with the purpose of terrorizing that person. An example of the application of a terrorist threat statute in a terrorist threat prosecution is *Cobble v. State*.[11]

The defendant stood outside his former girlfriend's house and shouted obscenities at her, in violation of a protective order obtained by the woman. Police were called and arrested the defendant. The defendant struggled with the arresting officers and was subdued by pepper spray, which required his hospitalization. While he was in the hospital, in the presence of officers, the defendant stated that when he was released he "would kill" the woman. He was then charged with making terrorist threats and was convicted. On appeal the defendant argued that he could not be convicted under the Georgia terrorist threat statute for two reasons: first, because the threat was never communicated to the victim, and second, because the statute specifically stated a conviction could not be based solely on the uncorroborated testimony of the person to whom the threat was communicated.

The Georgia Court of Appeals disagreed. It held that it did not matter if the victim did not actually hear the threat; it was enough if the defendant made the threat under circumstances where he intended or knew the threat would be communicated to the victim. It also held that the defendant's actions in violation of the protective order were sufficient corroboration of his intent to carry out his threat.

RULES OF WAR

Rules of war are a body of customs, practices, treaties, and agreements that most nations subscribe to for the conduct of wars openly declared against sovereign nations. President Abraham Lincoln began the codification of these rules in 1864, and since that time most nations have signed the international conventions adopting these rules. Under these rules, combatants in a war are liable for violation of ordinary criminal laws, such as rape or theft, even if carried out pursuant to orders from a superior. Such combatants can be charged with violation of their own nation's laws or the laws of the nation where the crimes took place. Saddam Hussein, the former president of Iraq, was tried and convicted in an Iraqi court of murder (under Iraqi law) and crimes against humanity (under international law).

The rules of war create three categories of crimes:

- *Crimes Against Peace:* These laws forbid the planning, commencement, and conduct of an aggressive war. The United Nations recognizes only wars fought in self-defense as lawful wars. Hermann Goering and other Nazi leaders were convicted at the Nuremberg war crimes trials of violation of this law.
- *Crimes Against Humanity:* These laws forbid deportation, enslavement, persecution, and extermination of groups of people based on their race, religion, or ethnic origin. These laws were the result of the concentration camps and slave labor camps used by the Nazis during World War II.
- *Traditional War Crimes: These are traditional laws concerning rules of conduct of the combatants toward prisoners of war and toward civilians living in the war zone. After World War II, Japanese General Yamashita was convicted and executed for "failing to provide effective control" over Japanese troops who raped and killed Philippine civilians.

Most state statutes also make it a crime for a person to support a terrorist act or organization. Actions that could constitute support include providing financial support, lodging, training, safe houses, false documents, communications equipment, weapons, lethal substances, explosives, personnel transportation, and other physical assets, except religious or medical material.

The federal material support of terrorist statute is 18 U.S.C. §2339A. It makes it a crime to provide material support or resources with the intent to violate any of the many federal terrorism statutes, such as 18 U.S.C §2332(a) and (b). An example of a prosecution under the material support statute is *United States v. Hassan*, 742 F.3d 104 (4th Cir. 2014), *cert denied* 135 S. Ct. 157 (2014).

In *Hassan*, three men became friends through their contacts with Boyd, an American who at a young age converted to Islam. Boyd traveled to Afghanistan and Pakistan as a young adult, and on his return became a radical supporter of violent jihad against non-Muslims. Together the men expressed their belief in violence as part of their duty to Islam, including through posts in social media urging others to engage in violent jihad. Two of the men travelled to Kosovo and Jordan in the hopes of engaging in violent jihad, and each supported the others in these efforts. However, none of the men actually engaged in violent acts, and ultimately returned to the United States.

Upon their return the men began weapons training in preparation for a planned attack on the Marine base at Quantico, Virginia. By this time the FBI had planted informants within the group who were engaged in the weapons training and meetings to discuss violent jihad. After learning of the planned attack at Quantico the FBI arrested the men, and charged them with various crimes, including providing material support to terrorism.

The defendants contended they could not be convicted under section 2339A because they did not provide any support to terrorists, and no terrorist acts were taken by any person based on their support or encouragement. Rather, they contended, they simply expressed their political beliefs, which were protected by the First Amendment. The trial court and court of appeals rejected those contentions. The appeals court affirmed their convictions, holding that travelling to foreign countries to engage in violent jihad, obtaining weapons and training in their use, and planning the attack on the Marine Base, all in the name of violent jihad, amounted to material support of terrorism. The court also affirmed prison sentences of 180, 360, and 540 months for the three men.

THE 804 TERRORISM PROSECUTIONS FROM 2001 TO 2009

In 2010 the Center on Law and Security at New York University School of Law published an excellent study entitled "The Terrorist Trial Report Card, 2001–2009." The study analyzed the public records of 804 terrorist prosecutions conducted during that 8-year period, and reached conclusions from those records. The conclusions reached in the study likely mirror statistics from more recent prosecutions, though those statistics have not been compiled. Some of the findings of the study, used with the kind permission of the Center on Law and Security, appear here. A copy of the full study may be obtained by contacting the Center at http://www.lawandsecurity.org.

Where Did the 804 Persons Charged Come from?

The persons charged came from at least forty-seven different countries (there was no information on the home countries of about 20 percent of the defendants). The largest group indicted (273) comprised persons with U.S. citizenship. Next were Colombia, South America (98), Pakistan (60), the Palestinian Territories (22), Jordan (18), Iraq (14), Egypt (13), and the United Kingdom (12). The remainder came from a group of thirty-nine countries.

What Were the Most Common Categories of Criminal Charges Brought by the Prosecutors?

The crime of terrorism was charged in 244 of the cases, followed by racketeering (127), national security or hostage taking (102), fraud and false statements (77), drug charges (60), commercial fraud, embezzlement, and theft (54), immigration violations (43), obstruction charges (9), and violent crimes (4).

What Conduct Constituted a Violation of a "Terrorist Statute"?

Two hundred forty-four of the defendants were convicted under terrorism statutes that required proof of involvement with terrorism, which included terrorist conduct, knowingly or intentionally aiding a "terrorist organization," or acting in furtherance of a terrorist objective.

What Conduct Constituted Violation of "National Security Statutes"?

One hundred two prosecutions were brought under statutes forbidding hostage taking; sabotage (including destruction of national defense material, premises, or utilities); or possession or use of chemical weapons.

Were Terrorism Actions Used for Sentence Enhancement Purposes?

Terrorism was also used for sentence enhancement in convictions under the following principal crimes: immigration violations (1), obstruction of an investigation (1), and crimes of terrorism or against national security (20).

What Conduct Did the Study Include Under "Domestic Terrorism"?

In this study "domestic terrorism" focused on white supremacy advocates, antiabortion activists, animal liberation groups, and environmental terrorism.

How Many Prosecutions Involved Weapons of Mass Destruction?

One hundred sixty-one prosecutions alleged weapons of mass destruction (WMD) charges. Pursuant to 18 U.S.C. § 2332a, a federal statute, WMD include a broad list of weapons, such as "destructive devices" like grenades or other explosive devices, and poison gases. This list is larger than what the general public considers WMD to include, which is probably limited to nuclear, chemical, radioactive, and biological weapons. Many of the violations occurred overseas against American military targets. Groups behind these violations were al-Qaeda (22), FARC (71), Cambodian Freedom Fighters (1), the Free Papua (New Guinea) Movement (1), Ku Klux Klan (1), and Tamil Tigers (5). In fifty-seven of the cases no affiliation was found. Narco-terrorists, covered by 21 U.S.C. § 960, were briefly mentioned in the study, in connection with four persons in Afghanistan charged with narco-terrorism.

FINANCING TERRORISM: WHERE DOES THE MONEY COME FROM?

Terrorists need money to operate. INTERPOL (the International Criminal Police Organization, located in Lyon, France) has said: "The frequency and seriousness of international terrorist acts are often proportionate to the financing that terrorist groups might get."

The 9/11 Commission report[12] issued in 2004 found no evidence of any foreign government knowingly helping to finance the 9/11 attack. The 9/11 Commission found that most of the $400,000 to $500,000 used to finance that operation came from donations to "charitable organizations," which then funneled the necessary funds to the terrorists.[13] At least nineteen terrorists lived and trained in the United States for a period of 18 months to 2 years before the 9/11 attack. Organizations that knowingly provide aid to terrorists violate the Anti-Terrorism Act,[14] 18 U.S.C. § 2339B, and also can be sued for civil damages under 18 U.S.C. § 2333(a).

The shortage of financial support can affect the scope of a terrorist attack. In the February 2007 issue of the *FBI Law Enforcement Bulletin,* the 1993 attack on the World Trade Center is used to illustrate this fact. The terrorists in that first attack on the World Trade Center had plans to use larger bombs as well as chemical and biological weapons that would have hampered rescue efforts and increased fatalities. Because of a shortage of funds, they were unable to execute the attack as planned, which greatly limited the harm caused and casualties inflicted.

Terrorists frequently use other criminal activity to finance their terrorism, the FBI article states. So-called low-risk, high-reward crimes are favored by terrorists. These include drug trafficking ("if we can't kill them with guns, we kill them with drugs"); theft; and fraud crimes, such as identity theft, credit card, Social Security, welfare, and insurance fraud. In one instance, the theft of baby formula netted a terrorist ring $18 million during an 18-month period. Intellectual property crimes were also committed by terrorists, such as counterfeiting watches, selling fake driver's licenses, and pirating software. One terrorist group made $750,000 in one year smuggling cigarettes.

Stopping the flow of funds to terrorists is an extraordinarily difficult task. One major obstacle is the international source of funds. The 9/11 Commission stated that Saudi Arabian charities alone funneled hundreds of millions of dollars to jihad groups and al-Qaeda cells over the last few years. There is little the United States can do to prevent such transfers.

For groups with assets within the United States, the Trading With the Enemy Act, 50 U.S.C. § 1702(a)(1)(b), permits the president to establish a "Specially Designated Terrorist List" and freeze assets of those groups or those who contribute financial support to the groups. The USA Patriot Act, passed after 9/11, includes a provision permitting the president to block assets held by any group or person being investigated for involvement with terrorist attacks.

Moving Money into and out of the United States

Moving funds into and out of the United States happens on a massive scale each business day and can be part of a lawful banking or business activity. However, it can also be illegal money laundering, movement of funds in illegal operations, or transfer of funds to terrorist groups for future operations.

Funds can be transferred by human couriers, a time-honored custom in many parts of the world, or could be moved through high-tech electronic wire transfers. Web pages on the Internet can be used to solicit funds, which can then be sent to terrorist groups. One large fund, the Benevolence International Foundation, used a website that appealed to Muslim donors to send money to the foundation. The director of the foundation, Enaam Arnaout, pleaded guilty to a count of racketeering in 2003, admitting he sent money from the foundation to support Muslim "fighters" in Bosnia and Chechnya. He was sentenced to 10 years in prison, and the foundation has been banned everywhere in the world.

Funds can also be transferred through the use of so-called informal value transfer systems (IVTS). An example of an IVTS is the ancient system known as Hawala, which originated in India. In a Hawala transaction a person in one location gives money to a representative of the network. The money is not physically or electronically transferred. Instead, a representative of the system in the location where the sender wants the money to go gives funds to the intended recipient. The advantages of the Hawala system are that the cost of the transaction can be lower than more traditional transfer methods, and there is virtually no paper trail for the transaction. The 9/11 Commission Report stated that al-Qaeda cells used the Hawala system for moving funds in and out of Afghanistan, the headquarters of al-Qaeda.

Illegal use of the Hawala system violates many federal money-laundering laws and could also violate provisions of antiterrorism laws. The case of *United States v. Anvari-Hamedani,* 378 F. Supp. 2d 821 (N.D. Ohio 2005), illustrates use of the Hawala system in violation of these laws. An Iranian doctor living in Ohio was indicted for money laundering and violating the federal International Emergency Economic Powers Act (IEEPA) based on transfers of money and goods to Iran. In Executive Order 13059, the president had placed Iran on the list of designated countries that support terrorism and made any investment in business in Iran or commitment of funds to groups in Iran a violation. The defendant instructed Merrill Lynch to send funds from an account he had with that brokerage firm to persons in Iran. Merrill Lynch filed a Suspicious Financial Activity Report, as required under federal law, detailing the transaction. The FBI investigated and found that the defendant also sent funds to Iran through a Hawala system.

However, in the 2012 case of *United States v. Banki*[15] a federal court of appeals held that noncommercial intrafamily transfers of money to and from Iran through the Hawala system did not violate the U.S. Treasury Department's Iranian Transactions Regulations. It reversed a conviction of an Iranian national living in New York who arranged the transfer of over $3.4 million from his family in Iran to him in New York.

International Criticism of Aspects of the U.S. War Against Terrorism

The war against terrorism has been in some ways an international effort. The United Nations has adopted a number of conventions aimed at specific kinds of terrorist acts, such as attacks on civilian aircraft or kidnapping of government officers. Member nations are expected to pass local laws to implement these conventions. Prior to 9/11 the United States was mainly content to participate in these internationally sponsored efforts.

But after 9/11, the United States, together with some of its allies, began fighting terrorism without the formal cooperation of the United Nations. Some of the actions taken by the U.S. government have received criticism from other nations and their governments; chief of these is the war in Iraq. Other actions have also engendered controversy. They include these:

- Kidnapping and Abductions: In 2007 both Italy and Germany issued criminal complaints and warrants against thirty-nine Americans working in a U.S. program called "extraordinary rendition." Under this program, first used pursuant to a presidential directive by President Clinton in 1995, suspected terrorists are seized by U.S. agents and are transported to another country for interrogation.

Many of the pre-9/11 "ghost detainees" were suspected al-Qaeda operatives, and they were sent to Egypt for interrogation. Since 9/11, persons detained under this program have been sent to several countries for interrogation, including Jordan, Syria, Morocco, and Uzbekistan. Critics of the program say it permits the United States to indirectly use torture to interrogate detainees, something forbidden under U.S. law and the United Nations Convention Against Torture. Supporters of the program contend it makes sense to send detainees to countries that know the detainees' language and cultural background.[16]

- Secret Over-Flights of European Countries: A European Union Parliament committee has objected to flights by U.S. military and civilian government aircraft over European airspace without prior approval from the countries affected. The committee stated that at least 1,245 secret CIA flights were made over Europe from 2003 to 2007.

 ## LAW ENFORCEMENT NEEDS CITIZENS' HELP TO DETER HOMEGROWN TERRORISTS

Timothy McVeigh, the man who masterminded the bombing of the Alfred P. Murrah Federal Building in Oklahoma City in 1995, appeared to be a "regular guy." He was a U.S. Army veteran who served with great distinction. He held a regular job after leaving the service and seemed like a man who believed in the ideals upon which the United States was founded. In fact, McVeigh had become deeply bitter about the role of federal agents in the Waco, Texas, action against the Branch Davidians, a religious sect, in which several members died, and the Ruby Ridge action against a separatist group, which caused the death of a woman and a 14-year-old girl.

In 1995, McVeigh, with the help of Terry Nichols, constructed a massive fertilizer bomb and blew up the Alfred P. Murrah Federal Building in Oklahoma City. The attack killed 168 innocent people and injured more than 500 others. During the Vietnam War, radical students had used a similar device to blow up buildings on the campus of the University of Wisconsin.

Constructing these bombs required the purchase of large amounts of materials that were known to be capable of destructive power. Nonetheless, no one reported anything unusual to the authorities until after the bombs were detonated.

In 2006, a Circuit City employee in New Jersey became concerned about a video he saw that showed men apparently training for combat. He called the police, and the FBI were able to place an informant with the group, which was, in fact, planning a terrorist attack on the soldiers at Fort Dix. After 16 months of investigation, in 2007 the FBI arrested the men and stopped the terrorist plan before it could be executed.

Also in 2006, the FBI received a tip on its website that led it to place two New Jersey men under surveillance for suspected terrorist plans for a "jihad" against the United States. The men were arrested in 2010. Both tips were essential to the success of the investigations and demonstrate that help from the public in spotting "homegrown" terrorists is an ongoing need for law enforcement officers.

Because extremists like McVeigh can come from a large and varied pool of disaffected people, the help of the public in identifying potential terrorist threats is vital to the success of law enforcement efforts to curb "homegrown" terrorists.[a]

[a]See the *Chicago Tribune* article, "FBI Says Domestic Extremists Big Threat," May 13, 2007.

- Canadian Citizen's Treatment: Canada, historically a U.S. ally, in 2003 participated with American agents in the seizure of a Canadian citizen in New York by American agents and transferred to Syrian authorities. The man was held for more than 10 months in Syria, where he stated he was subjected to torture. Though Canadian authorities denied any knowledge that the United States was planning to send the man to Syria, Canadian intelligence officials acknowledged they sent a list of questions for the man to American agents. The man ultimately was returned to Canada, where he was awarded $9.75 million in damages for his wrongful detention.[17]

★★★
LEARNING OBJECTIVES SUMMARY

LO 1. Construct a working definition of terrorism.
Terrorism is the use of unlawful force to coerce or intimidate persons or governments in the pursuit of political, social, or religious goals.

LO 2. Explain why federal criminal statutes must define terrorism.
International law does not clearly define terrorism. When the United States became a signatory to international conventions that addressed specific terrorist acts, Congress passed laws to implement those conventions. Because of the vagueness limitation on statutes, Congress was required to clearly define the acts that constituted terrorism and were condemned under the conventions.

LO 3. Explain one method by which a group can be identified as a terrorist group.
The State Department is authorized to identify groups or organizations as terrorist organizations.

LO 4. List the elements of the crime of terrorism under most state laws.
The crime of terrorism under most state laws requires proof that a defendant took acts intended to

intimidate or coerce a civilian population, or
influence a government by intimidation or coercion, or
affect the conduct of government by intimidation or coercion.

LO 5. Define a terrorist threat under state criminal laws.
A terrorist threat is a threat to (1) commit a violent felony that (2) is a danger to human life and is made to (3) intimidate or coerce a civilian group or a government. In many states it includes actions intended to disrupt schools or other public buildings.

LO 6. Explain the concept of the rules of war.
Rules of war are customs and practices followed by most nations in wartime, and now are the subject of international conventions. They create three classes of crimes: crimes against peace, crimes against humanity, and traditional war crimes.

LO 7. List ways terrorists obtain financial support for their terrorist actions.
Terrorists raise money for their actions both directly and indirectly. Some countries contribute directly to terrorist organizations. The U.S. president has the power to identify such countries and place them on a list of countries that support terrorism. Individuals contribute indirectly to terrorist organizations by giving money and support to phony charitable groups that support terrorists.

LO 8. List ways money is sent into and out of the United States by terrorist supporters.
Money can be sent out of the United States through normal banking channels or by funneling the cash through international business organizations. It can also be sent by

human carrier, such as is done in the Hawala system used for centuries in the Middle East.

LO 9. Identify when a seizure is an extraordinary rendition.

An extraordinary rendition occurs when a person is seized in one country and then transported to another country for interrogation. The country to which the person is transported often has a relationship with the person, or the country permits interrogation procedures not permitted by the country where the seizure occurred.

KEY TERMS

terrorism, p. 484

treason, p. 489

sedition, p. 489

sabotage, p. 492

crime of terrorizing, p. 494

CASE ANALYSIS AND WRITING EXERCISES

1. One of the antiterrorism laws passed by Congress was the Chemical Weapons Act, 18 U.S.C. §229(a)(1). As we saw in Chapter 2, in *United States v. Bond*, 134 S. Ct. 2077 (2014), the U.S. Supreme Court held that the statute did not apply to a "simple assault" using household chemicals. Is the Chemical Weapons Act equally inapplicable to a disgruntled patient, a pharmacist, who spread mercury throughout a hospital in retaliation for what he believed was substandard treatment and excessive billing? If so, what separates the case from *Bond*? See *United States v. Kimber*, 777 F.3d 553 (2nd Cir. 2015), *cert denied* 136 S. Ct. 170 (2015).

2. In addition to the many federal terrorist-related statutes discussed in this chapter, Congress also passed a statute directed at threats against federal judges, 18 U.S.C. § 115(a)(1)(B). In *United States v. Turner*, 720 F.3d 411 (2nd Cir.2013), *cert denied* 135 S. Ct. 49 (2014) a man upset with a decision on gun control by federal judges put posts on his gun rights blog criticizing the judges and the decision. It is clear the First Amendment protects such speech, even if it is virulent and even violent. At what point did the man cross the line and violate section 115? How would you define that line?

3. Terrorists use social media to advance their goals. The terrorist group al-Shabab, which attacked a shopping center in Kenya, Nairobi, in 2013 killing nearly 70 civilians, used Twitter accounts to publicize the attacks, showing live films and information about the attacks. The Islamic State of Iraq is well-known for its use of social media to advance its cause. While Twitter, Facebook, and other social media monitor the use of their sites, they are not always successful at keeping terrorist-supporting posts from the terrorist accounts. Should Congress pass a law making social media companies liable if they don't monitor accounts closely enough? In *Holder v. Humanitarian Law Project*, 561 U.S. 1 (2010) there is some language that suggests the material support of terrorism statute (discussed in this chapter) might be used for that purpose. Senator Dianne Feinstein of California has introduced a bill in the U.S. Senate mandating social media to report posts that are terrorist-related. Is that a good idea? Would it lead to more intense monitoring of posts on social media? Is that a good idea?

4. There are threats, and there are terrorist threats. Many threats are not crimes, and many others are misdemeanors. Terrorist threats, however, are generally felonies, and carry substantial prison sentences as punishment. When a person makes a threat, the prosecution must decide how to frame the charges. In *State v. Yocum*, 759 S.E.2d 182 (W.Va. 2014) the defendant was arrested on a domestic disturbance call. While in the back seat of the officer's police cruiser, the defendant said, "After I get out of jail, I'll be fu*king your wife, and I will fu*k your daughters." (The officer had two step-daughters, ages 9 and 12.) He was charged and convicted under the West Virginia terrorist threat statute, W.Va. Code §61-6-24, which, like most state terrorist threat statutes,

identifies a terrorist threat as a threat of serious injury intended to intimidate or affect the conduct of a branch of government. On appeal the West Virginia Supreme Court of Appeals reversed the conviction. Why did it do so? What should the prosecution have done instead?

ENDNOTES

1. Do you think Gillette's threats to his congressman are similar to the threats the defendant posted on his blog in *United States v. Turner,* 720 F.3d 411 (2nd Cir. 2013), discussed above? Do they urge the same kind of action against the identified officials? Which would cause you more concern?

2. After McKinley's death, President Theodore Roosevelt stated that anarchism was "a crime against the whole human race." The United States passed immigration laws that excluded anarchists from entry into the country.

3. A jury found McVeigh guilty of all charges against him, which were the federal crimes of (1) conspiracy to use a weapon of mass destruction, (2) use of a weapon of mass destruction, (3) destruction by an explosive, and (4–11) the eight counts of the murders of the eight federal law enforcement officers killed in the blast. All three men were charged in federal courts for federal crimes.

   The third man, Michael J. Fortier, pleaded guilty to four federal charges and was sentenced to 12 years in prison. Because of his cooperation, this sentence was a reduction of the longer sentence he would have received. One of the federal criminal charges was "misprision of a felony." Fortier had known of the planned bombing but had not warned anyone. See Chapter 19 on the federal crime of misprision of a felony.

4. See the *New York Times* article, "Men Arrested in a Terror Plot Against Ft. Dix," May 9, 2007.

5. See *Boim v. Quranic Literacy Inst. & Holy Land Foundation,* 291 F.3d 1000 (7th Cir. 2002).

6. 803 F.2d 318 (7th Cir. 1986), *cert. denied,* 480 U.S. 908 (1987).

7. 341 U.S. 494, 71 S. Ct. 857 (1951).

8. 401 F.3d 1176 (10th Cir. 2005).

9. 748 N.W.799 (Mich. 2008).

10. 247 S.W.3d 610 (Mo. App. 2008).

11. 603 S.E.2d 86 (Ga. App. 2004).

12. *The 9/11 Commission Report: Final Report of the National Commission of Terrorist Attacks Upon the United States* (Washington, D.C., 2004).

13. See the article "Dealing with Hawala" in the February 2007 issue of the *FBI Bulletin* and the 9/11 Report.

14. See *Weiss v. Westminster Bank PLC,* 453 F. Supp. 2d 609 (E.D.N.Y. 2006).

15. 685 F.3d 99 (2nd Cir. 2012).

16. See the *New York Times* article, "Italy Indicts 26, Many From C.I.A. in '03 Abductions," February 17, 2007.

17. See the *New York Times* article, "Canadian Court Limits Detention in Terror Cases," February 24, 2007.

18

Organized Crime and Gangs

LEARNING OBJECTIVES

In this chapter we discuss organized crime and gangs and the various ways the federal and state governments combat this criminal activity. The learning objectives for Chapter 18 are the following:

LO 1. List the requirements for a RICO conviction.

LO 2. Identify the jurisdictional requirements for a federal RICO charge.

LO 3. List three ways money can be laundered.

LO 4. List four federal statutes used to combat interstate crime.

LO 5. Explain the knowledge needed for a conviction under the federal money laundering statute, specifically the section on transportation of illegal proceeds.

LO 6. Define proceeds under the money laundering statutes.

LO 7. Explain why federal and state prosecutions of organized crime figures before 1970 were generally unsuccessful.

LO 8. Describe the advantages statutes passed after 1970 gave to the prosecution.

Aftermath of a gun battle between two rival biker gangs, the Cossacks and the Bandidos, in Waco, Texas, in 2015.

The federal Racketeer Influenced and Corrupt Organizations Act (RICO) has been a valuable weapon in the fight against organized crime. It is directed at "criminal enterprises" that commit crimes in the United States as part of the criminal goals of the enterprises.

While the initial focus of RICO prosecutions was on crime organizations like the Mafia and other groups of criminals working as part of a criminal enterprise, RICO has a much broader application today. For example, the Los Angeles private detective Anthony Pellicano (the "private eye to the stars") and his cohorts were tried under RICO laws for crimes involving bribery of police officers, illegal wiretaps of individuals involved in litigation where Pellicano was hired by attorneys for one party to record phone conversations of other

parties, and illegal access to confidential telephone information used to execute illegal wiretaps.

The various members of the "enterprise," a police officer, telephone company employee, and an attorney, each assisted Pellicano in his illegal actions, though they did not always know each other or their role in the criminal actions, or work together as a group. They were all nonetheless convicted for violating RICO, and other criminal laws as well. On appeal, their convictions for RICO violations were affirmed in 2015 by the Ninth Circuit Court of Appeals.[1]

The appeals court rejected the defendants' argument that they were not a "criminal enterprise" under RICO. The court said that whether or not they knew of each other's existence and role in the enterprise, they were all aware Pellicano was taking the actions needed to make the enterprise work, and that was sufficient under RICO.

In this chapter we will study the state and federal criminal laws enacted to give prosecutors the tools to go after criminals who engage in criminal acts but who are protected by the nature of an organization engaged in a criminal enterprise. We will also see how those laws can be used to prosecute individuals like criminal gang members who commit criminal acts as part of a plan to further a criminal enterprise. Finally, we will study the limitations the Constitution places on those uses.

ORGANIZED CRIME AND CRIMINAL GANGS

Gangs of organized criminals have operated in the United States for over 200 years, and in Europe for much longer. Bands of criminals soon realized that working together greatly increased their chances of success.

In most periods of American history, the character of gangs was dictated by the environment. In the Wild West of the late nineteenth century, outlaw gangs traveling around on horseback specialized in cattle rustling or stagecoach robbery. At the same time, in the infamous Five Points section of New York (what is now Lower Manhattan's Chinatown), various gangs of Irish, Italian, and German immigrants practiced murder, prostitution, theft, and extortion. With the rise of the automobile in the 1920s and 1930s, gangs became mobile and could travel about the country, robbing small-town banks. Indeed, it was the inability of the local police to coordinate efforts to apprehend gangs like the Dillinger gang that played a significant role in the creation of the FBI as a national crime-fighting agency.

The Prohibition period helped the spread of the most notorious gang in the twentieth century, the Mafia. While the Mafia had its roots in a much earlier period in Italy and Sicily, controlling the market in illegal alcohol sales during Prohibition made it possible for the Mafia to branch out and control many other criminal endeavors.

In 2002, the U.S. Department of Justice, with the participation of about 2,000 law enforcement agencies, published a study of gangs in the United States.[2] The study, which was prompted by a 1996 report that identified more than 30,000 gangs with more than 800,000 members, focused on the nature and growth of violent gangs in the past 20 years.

The study concluded that most law enforcement agencies distinguished between "gangs" and "organized crime" associations by the nature of their organizations. Organized crime generally involved a highly structured leadership arrangement, designed in part to insulate those at the top from criminal accountability. These organizations generally have a chief or "don" who makes policy and issues orders, which are carried out by captains, lieutenants, and soldiers, all of whom are sworn career criminals.

Gangs, the study found, tended to be a far looser affiliation of criminals:

> Most gangs are loosely knit coalitions of small, autonomous cliques. Apart from a general commitment to their "hood" and the gang lifestyle, the only unifying force is combat with outsiders. Gang leadership is usually decentralized, nonhierarchical, even situational; it is more a function of individual prowess and

ATTEMPTS BY CITIES AND STATES TO REGULATE GANG ACTIVITY

Cities and states have used a variety of laws in attempts to curb gang violence:

- Nuisance laws, both civil and criminal, are used to seize and tear down crack houses and other drug houses and to prosecute landlords who permit drug use by gangs in rented premises.
- Laws against the crimes of unlawful assembly, rioting, stalking, and curfew violation (see discussion in Chapter 9) are used to curb gang activity.
- Injunction laws are used to deter gang action. Because of its serious gang problems, the city of Los Angeles is seeking injunctions (court orders) against gang members that forbid a specific gang to gather, even in groups as small as two, in specified public places. In defending these injunctions, a Los Angeles city attorney states: "People deserve protection. . . . Gang members are terrorizing our communities." Penalties for violating the injunction include up to a year in jail.[a]
- Graffiti laws, cruising laws, and laws making membership in a gang a crime (found in a few states) are used.
- If the offense was committed by gang members, laws to increase criminal penalties can be used.
- Laws punishing parents for the gang behavior of their children.
- Laws making parents civilly liable for the criminal behavior of their children may be applied.
- Laws forbidding intimidation and threats (discussed in Chapter 9).
- Forfeiture laws such as those found in the Uniform Controlled Substances Act permit the government to seize the proceeds and profits of a crime, as well as cars, boats, airplanes, or real estate used in the commission of crimes. In Los Angeles prosecutors have seized homes and businesses owned by members of the 18th Street gang which were shown to be the proceeds of or instrumentalities used in drug crimes, extortion, money laundering, and related crimes.
- Deportation of those who enter the United States illegally, or commit crimes while in the United States.
- Street gang terrorism and drug conspiracy laws may be used, such as Illinois Comp. Stat. Ch. 720, Section 5/12-6 (1998).

Many state and city loitering laws and ordinances criminalize specific acts, such as "overt acts or evidence of criminal intent" or "loitering for the purpose to engage in drug-related activities," which have been upheld in state courts. However, in *City of Chicago v. Morales*, 527 U.S. 41 (1999), the U.S. Supreme Court struck down the Chicago gang congregation ordinance as unconstitutional because it was too vague and did not give citizens fair notice of what was required of them to comply with the law. (See Chapter 1 on the "void for vagueness" doctrine.)

[a]See the *New York Times* article "Gangs Without Borders, Fierce and Resilient, Are Confronting the Law," September 26, 2004.

reputation than a formalized structure for making collective decisions. Leadership changes rapidly and may vary by activity. . . . The type of gang leadership varies from gang to gang and by geographical area.

Some gangs, and most groups of organized criminals, have long histories of criminal activities as groups. Others are recent entries into organized crime. The Russian mafia is an example of the latter group; the FBI in 2004 identified it as the fastest-growing criminal organization in the United States. Terrorist groups would

U.S. Drug Enforcement Administration

A rare published photo of Enedina Arellano-Felix (lower right), now believed to be the leader of the Arellano-Felix Tijuana drug cartel. If so, she is the first female leader of a major illegal drug cartel. Most of the male members of the family are dead or in prison.

probably be classified as criminal organizations because they generally have more structured leadership organizations.

Law enforcement agencies participating in the study reported that

the delinquent gang was the most typical gang in their jurisdiction . . . consisting primarily of juveniles who engaged in vandalism and other delinquent behavior. . . . Yet police reported that most gangs, regardless of type, participated in many different types of crimes.

The membership and location of gangs varied greatly, the report found. Street gangs made up of delinquents were found in inner cities, suburbs, rural areas, and small towns. Gangs organized along ethnic or racial lines included Asian, Hispanic, Jewish, Russian, African American, and Irish. The nature of the activity, such as drug dealing, sometimes served as the identifying feature of a gang. Shoplifting, purse snatching, check forging, insurance fraud, and identity theft are examples of these kinds of gangs.

The report found that most gangs began as local groups that, if successful, expanded to nearby cities and states. If a gang was involved with illegal drugs or weapons, expansion included violence to achieve dominance. Criminal networks crossing state lines can be formed, which the report stated could use "modern weapons, communication technology, and transportation in their operations to control and expand their operations more effectively."

The waves of immigrants coming to the United States since the 1970s, especially from Asian, Latin American, and eastern European nations, have changed the membership of old gangs and caused the creation of many new gangs.

THE LATIN KINGS

Many street gangs began as cultural groups intending to maintain their national heritage after immigrating to the United States. The gang known as the Latin Kings began in Chicago as a group with the goal of keeping alive their Hispanic heritage. It evolved, however, into one of the largest and most violent criminal street gangs in the United States, with branches located in most major cities and in most regions of the nation.

The Latin Kings have a rigid internal structure. Within each chapter the leaders (male members are named "King" and female members "Queen") are called the five "Crowns." The First Crown is the group's leader, who makes final decisions. Under the First Crown are four other Crowns, each of which has a designated function and command. The principal business of the gang is crime, mainly the illegal drug trade, though the gang also participates in illegal gun sales, and other crimes. Because so many of the gang members are incarcerated, there exists in most prisons a rigid Latin King hierarchy tied to a Latin King chapter outside the prison.

As the Latin Kings grew and became more involved in crimes, the gang became the target of RICO prosecutions, even though much of any given chapter's crimes were within one state, or even one city. A case in point is *United States v. Cornell*, 780 F.3d 616 (4th Cir. 2015). There, the leaders of a Latin King gang located in Greensboro, North Carolina were convicted under the RICO statute, based on the commission of various crimes such as armed robbery, bank fraud, and attempted murder. The First Crown, "King Jay," was sentenced to 336 months in prison; another gang member, "King Peaceful," was sentenced to 180 months in prison.

The defendants appealed, contending RICO could not be applied to them because they were not a criminal enterprise engaged in substantial interstate economic activity. They relied primarily on the *Waucaush* decision (discussed later in this chapter), which held that RICO convictions required proof that a street gang be engaged in more than minimal interstate economic activity. The court of appeals rejected that argument, noting that it was not sure the *Waucaush* was "good law" any more, and that in any case it was not the law in the Fourth Circuit. The court held that so long as any of the crimes committed by the defendants had an impact on interstate commerce, however small, the RICO statute was applicable to the enterprise. It affirmed the convictions and prison sentences. The U.S. Supreme Court denied review; 136 S. Ct. 127 (2015).

The youth gang known as the Bloods has demonstrated that recruiting new members is possible, including from the populations in prisons and jails. The name Bloods reflects the fact that blood must be spilled for one to become a new member, and blood will be spilled if a member tries to leave the gang. The blood spilled is frequently that of an innocent passerby, slashed by a gang member in a random act of violence.

Some gangs are extremely large. The Black Gangster Disciples (BGD) gang, for example, is reported to have as many as 30,000 members heavily involved in drug trafficking. The Latin Kings have an estimated membership of 5,000 to 15,000. Gangs continue to grow despite the criminal convictions or deaths of key leaders.

In the 2011 National Gang Threat Assessment, the Justice Department released information on gang membership and crimes, based on statistics gained from law enforcement jurisdictions from all fifty states. Based on those reports, the Threat Assessment concluded:

- There are about 1.4 million gang members nationwide. Of those, about 150,000 are in prison.
- In the years since the last report (2009), gang activity increased the most in the Northeast and Southeast regions of the United States.
- Gang members are moving to other crimes, including prostitution, alien smuggling, and human trafficking.
- Gangs account for 48 percent of all violent crimes nationally, and as much as 90 percent in some cities.
- Outlaw Motorcycle Gangs (OMGs) have increased dramatically since 2009. There are presently 3,000 OMGs, with more than 44,000 members.

In 2008, the city of Chicago launched a concentrated attack on gangs and gang-related crime, including the hiring of 400 officers to form a special unit to work with communities to reduce violence. While these efforts resulted in the arrest and conviction of many gang leaders, the approximately seventy gangs located in Chicago still have an estimated 100,000 members. In 2011, 435 homicides occurred in Chicago, up to 80 percent of them gang-related; 2012 had 504 homicides. The years 2013 (420) and 2014 (416) showed a decline in homicides in Chicago, but again in 2015, Chicago recorded 470 homicides, the highest number for any U.S. city. Thus, even though violent crimes have dropped nationwide since their peak in the 1990s, gang-related murders have increased in Chicago. Gang members also now tend to be younger (most under 20 years of age) and more violent.

The Police Department of the city of Los Angeles reported that from 2007 to 2009 there were 16,398 gang-related crimes committed in Los Angeles; 491 of those crimes were homicides, 98 were rapes, and 5,518 were robberies. However, in March 2016, the L.A. Police Chief reported that violent crimes have been increasing in recent years. In 2013, 251 people in Los Angeles were killed; in 2014, killings increased to 260; and in 2015, they totaled 283, the police chief reported. He estimated about 60% of those killings were gang-related.

Recruiting younger members from schools and illegal immigration has helped make the Mara Salvatruchas and the 18th Street Gang two of the fastest-growing gangs in the United States, with branches and operations as far east as Washington, D.C., New York, and North Carolina. Former L.A. Police Chief William J. Bratton refers to gangs as "domestic terrorists" and urges that gang problems receive top priority from state and federal authorities.[3]

FEDERAL AND STATE LAWS PASSED AFTER 1970 TO FIGHT ORGANIZED CRIME

Prior to 1970, federal and state criminal codes did not have effective laws to penetrate the code of silence that insulated organized crime leaders from prosecution. Because lower-ranking gang members actually committed most crimes under orders from above, the lack of success in linking crimes to the leaders meant that they were rarely prosecuted. Indeed, the long-time director of the FBI, J. Edgar Hoover, went so far as to deny the existence of the Mafia, a denial that mystified much of the population that saw and read reports of horror stories of Mafia crime.

A well-known Mafia leader, Al Capone, enjoyed a reputation as a vicious killer, yet he was ultimately convicted not of murder but of income tax evasion, and was sentenced to 11 years in prison.[4] Other crime leaders then saw the danger presented by prosecutions for tax evasion, and instituted what we now call money laundering (which was made a separate crime in 1986) to obscure or eliminate any paper trail linking illegal gains to the crime bosses who reaped those gains.

In the federal and state fight against organized crime, 1970 marked the beginning of a concentrated effort against criminal organizations like the Mafia. The most important federal statute was the Racketeer Influenced and Corrupt Organizations Act **(RICO).** The state laws often had similar titles, such as Organized Crime Control Act or Offenses Concerning Racketeering.

RICO The Racketeer Influenced and Corrupt Organizations Act. Passed by Congress to enable prosecutors to charge all people engaged in unlawful activity who own or invest in an enterprise that affects interstate commerce.

The RICO laws, and the similar state laws commonly known as "little RICO" laws, were drafted to enable prosecutors to focus on the conspiratorial nature of organized crime. That is, the statutes made individuals, groups, and organizations criminally liable for multiple criminal acts that established a pattern of criminal activity.

The federal and state RICO laws generally require the government to prove that the defendants committed or conspired to commit acts of racketeering, called "predicate acts." The list of criminal acts that qualify as predicate acts is very long in both federal and state RICO statutes, including drug trafficking, violent crimes, witness tampering, mail or wire fraud, and illegal gambling. To obtain a RICO or "little RICO" conviction, the prosecution must prove:

- That the enterprise existed and was engaged in racketeering activity
- Two or more incidents of racketeering conduct "that have the same or similar intents, results, victims, or methods of commission" (Fla. Stat. § 895.02)
- That the defendants in the criminal action were members of the racketeering enterprise
- That the racketeering conduct by the defendants was committed for the purpose of maintaining or advancing their positions in the racketeering enterprise

The RICO and the related Continuing Criminal Enterprise (CCE) laws, both federal and state, are written very broadly and permit convictions for more than a half dozen separate and distinct racketeering crimes.[5] Each year hundreds of criminal and civil prosecutions under the RICO laws are brought in the United States for a wide variety of criminal violations. RICO has been successfully used to stop illegal activities by anti-abortion groups, violations by brokers and traders on stock exchanges, Taft-Hartley violations, porn shop violations, Medicare and public assistance frauds, and many other illegal acts.

RICO laws target membership in a "criminal enterprise." In the 2009 case of *Boyle v. United States,*[6] the U.S. Supreme Court considered the meaning of "enterprise" for a conviction under the federal RICO law, 18 U.S.C. § 1962. The defendant was one of a group of criminals who robbed bank night deposit boxes. They did this over a period of several years. However, the group had no leader, no hierarchy, no long-term plan, and no formal structure. The defendant appealed his conviction under § 1962, claiming he did not belong to a "criminal enterprise."

The Supreme Court concluded he did. While the Court agreed an "enterprise" under the RICO act must have an ascertainable structure, it need not have a formal or business structure. It was enough that a group was an "association in fact" with

MAKING GANG MEMBERS PAY

Crime, it is said, doesn't pay. Most states have statutes that try to do the same for gang membership by increasing the penalty for crimes that are committed by gang members. The following cases are illustrative of these statutes:

- New York has a "gang assault" statute that elevates an assault into a class B felony if the assault is "aided by two or more persons actually present" and causes serious physical injury. In *People v. Sanchez,*[7] the court upheld a conviction under the gang assault statute even though the prosecution did not prove the persons aiding the defendant intended to cause serious bodily injury.
- Most states have statutes that elevate the seriousness of an offense if the defendant is a member of a "criminal street gang." The Texas statute, VTCA Penal Code § 71.02, elevates the offense to the next level if it is proved the defendant was a member of a criminal street gang. See the 2010 case of *Coleman v. State.*[8] California's statute, Cal. Penal Code § 186.22, provides for sentence enhancements of 1 to 10 years, depending on the nature of the underlying offense, if the defendant is a member of a criminal street gang, or acts to further the interests of a criminal street gang. Both state statutes define "criminal street gang" in a similar manner: a criminal street gang is a group of three or more persons who have a common name or symbol, have as a primary purpose the commission of crimes, and have a pattern of criminal activity. In *People v. Bragg,*[9] the court upheld sentence enhancements under the statute for a defendant who attempted to murder a rival gang member. The court said the prosecution need not prove the defendant was a current member of the gang, but only that his actions were taken to further the interests of the gang.
- Minnesota § 609.229 provides for sentence enhancements of up to 10 years if the underlying offense is a felony and was committed "for the benefit of a gang," with a definition of gang similar to the definition of a criminal street gang in the Texas and California statutes.
- Street gang membership is also relevant in juvenile courts. Under Florida law, F.S.A. § 985.433, a court making a disposition order for a juvenile adjudicated a delinquent must take into consideration the fact that the juvenile is a member of a street gang.

a common purpose, and with some longevity. The Court rejected the defendant's claim that to be an "enterprise" the group must have a leader or a manager. It compared the RICO act to the illegal gambling act, 18 U.S.C. § 1955(b) and the Continuing Criminal Enterprise act, 21 U.S.C. § 848(c), which each have a requirement that the enterprise have an owner, supervisor, or other manager. Because the RICO act says nothing about owners or organizers, the Court concluded a "criminal enterprise" includes an informal group with a common purpose, even if no structural hierarchy exists within the group.

As we saw in Chapter 4, RICO conspiracy violations do not require an "overt act" for conviction; all that is required is that the defendant agreed to participate in the "criminal enterprise." In the 2012 case of *United States v. Harris*[10] the court held that a conspiracy to violate RICO did not require proof that a "criminal enterprise" in fact existed; it was enough that the defendant agreed to participate in such an enterprise.

Limits on Federal Jurisdiction and RICO Prosecutions

The federal RICO statute permits federal prosecutions based on criminal acts that would normally fall under state criminal jurisdiction. (See Chapter 2 of this text.)

Federal jurisdiction is possible under RICO if the underlying acts affect interstate commerce, because Congress has the authority to pass laws, including criminal laws, to regulate interstate commerce. However, if the underlying predicate acts do not affect interstate commerce, the federal government has no jurisdiction over those crimes and cannot charge defendants under the RICO law. *Waucaush v. United States*[11] is an example of a case where a federal court of appeals held the predicate acts did not affect interstate commerce.

The defendant Waucaush was a member of a Detroit, Michigan street gang called the Cash Flow Posse (CFP). In CFP's effort to control its turf from encroachment by rival gangs, the government alleged that members of the CFP murdered members of those other gangs. Waucaush and other gang members were charged with violation of the RICO laws. The indictment identified the gang as the criminal enterprise but included only the murders and other acts of violence as the predicate acts.

Waucaush initially pleaded guilty to the RICO charges, but after his conviction, two U.S. Supreme Court decisions were announced that potentially placed restrictions on the ability of Congress under the Commerce Clause to make the RICO laws applicable to criminal acts. In *United States v. Morrison,*[12] the Court held that Congress could pass a law regulating conduct that did not have a direct interstate element only if the conduct had an economic effect on interstate commerce. In *Jones v. United States,*[13] the Court held that the arson of a private residence did not affect interstate commerce, even though it was insured by an out-of-state entity. Based on these decisions, Waucaush sought to retract his guilty plea and have the charges against him dismissed. Charges against other defendants, who had not been sentenced when these decisions came down, had already been dismissed.

The court of appeals held that the murders and other violent acts were not by themselves sufficient to sustain federal jurisdiction under the Commerce Clause. Where a gang is not involved in economic activity, RICO requires a criminal enterprise that substantially affects interstate commerce, the court held.

Violent crimes can be prosecuted under RICO only if they are done for the purpose of furthering the criminal enterprise. Because the CFP was engaged in no proven economic activity, such as drug dealing, gambling, or credit card fraud, the murders were not undertaken to further an enterprise that affects interstate commerce.

The court agreed that every person's death has an effect in some way on interstate commerce—"a corpse cannot shop"—but "we may not 'follow the but-for causal chain from the initial occurrence of violent crime (the suppression of which has always been the prime object of the States' police power) to every attenuated effect upon interstate commerce.'"

After *Waucaush* was decided, the Supreme Court issued its opinion in *Gonzales v. Raich*[14] (discussed in Chapter 2). In this decision the Court suggested that

MEXICAN DRUG CARTELS AND THEIR AFFILIATES

Since 2006, when the president of Mexico announced increased efforts to stamp out drug cartels, Mexican drug cartels have waged violent battles with one another and the Mexican government to determine who will control the lucrative drug and contraband smuggling market into the United States. The U.S. Department of Justice stated in 2009 that the Mexican drug cartels "represent the greatest organized crime threat to the United States." The Justice Department also identified 230 cities in the United States and Canada (up from 100 cities in 2006) where the Mexican drug cartels and their affiliates "maintain drug distribution networks or supply (illegal) drugs to their distributors."

The Mexican government stated in 2015 that over 164,000 people have been killed between 2007 and 2014, since the drug crackdown was started by the government in 2006. Of those killed, at least 2,076 were Mexican local, state, or federal police officers. In April 2015 the CJNG cartel (see below) killed 15 elite police officers in the city of Guadalajara. The Mexican government has offered rewards of up to $2 million for information leading to the arrest of any of the known top drug kingpins, and up to $1 million for similar information on any of thirteen named lieutenants.

Violence has spread north over the borders. Officials in Vancouver, Canada, believe that drug traffickers are responsible for the increased shootings in that city. There have also been increased kidnappings and home invasions in border states like Arizona, as well as increased violence in other American cities, such as Birmingham, Alabama, where several murders have been linked to drug cartels. In 2010, three American diplomats were murdered by drug terrorists in Ciudad Juarez, which is "ground zero" in the battle against drug cartels. See the *New York Times*, March 15, 2010.

While it is difficult to document Mexican cartels' movements, many law enforcement officials believe the cartels are sending agents into the United States to establish the cartels in American cities. In a July, 2015 DEA Intelligence Report, "Areas of Influence of Major Mexican Transnational Criminal Organizations," the DEA stated that Mexican drug cartels were the dominant illegal drug force within the United States, with cartel members present and strong in every major city and region.

The DEA identified the major Mexican illegal drug cartels as:

1. Sinaloa cartel, by far the largest and most powerful, even though its infamous leader Joaquin "El Chapo" Guzman was recaptured in January 2016.
2. Jalisco New Generation Drug Cartel (CJNG), the second most powerful cartel.
3. Los Zetas, Juarez Cartel, and Arellano Felix Organization (also called the Tijuana cartel) have markedly decreased in strength and power in recent years. Because most of the male members of the Arellano family have been killed or imprisoned, it is believed the present leader of that cartel is Enedina Anellano-Felix. She would be the first female leader of a major Mexican drug cartel.

the Commerce Clause should be read broadly to give Congress power to pass laws regulating interstate commerce. That decision has persuaded some federal circuit courts to reject the reasoning of the *Waucaush* court. In addition to the Fourth circuit's decision discussed in the Latin Kings insert earlier in this chapter, the court in *United States v. Nasceminto*,[15] upheld a RICO conviction of gang members who, like the gang members in *Waucaush*, were not engaged in economic activity but merely focused on violence against other gangs. The court held that the activities of the gang had a *de minimis* effect on interstate commerce, in part because one of the gang members bought a gun in another state and brought it into his home state, and that a *de minimis* effect was sufficient to satisfy the interstate commerce requirement. The court accordingly rejected the requirement of "substantial effect" applied by the *Waucaush* court.

THE FEDERAL WITNESS PROTECTION PROGRAM AND THE CRIME OF WITNESS TAMPERING

Organized crime leaders were often insulated from the violent crimes they ordered committed. As a result, prosecutors needed the testimony of witnesses familiar with the leaders' role in the organization to charge and convict those leaders. Moreover, the Sixth Amendment's Confrontation Clause required that a defendant be permitted to be "confronted with the witnesses against him."

Obtaining witnesses to testify against gang and organized crime figures has always been a problem, both because in many cases the witnesses were themselves gang or organized crime members who had sworn a blood oath of silence and because of real fears of reprisal against the witness or his or her family. Threats of violence, bribery of witnesses, and extortion of witnesses and their family members were common methods criminals used to prevent witnesses from testifying.

In an effort to break these barriers to prosecution, Congress passed significant legislation in 1970 and 1982. As part of the Organized Crime Control Act of 1970,[16] Congress established the **witness protection program**. This program provides new identities and relocation for witnesses and their families in both state and federal criminal prosecutions of organized crime. Since its creation, this program has protected more than 7,500 witnesses and 9,500 family members from fear of reprisals, enabling them to safely testify against gang and organized crime figures.

In 1982, Congress passed the Federal Victim and Witness Protection Act of 1982. This statute created the crime of **witness tampering** and punishes any person who by any means tampers with a witness, victim, or informant.[17] Tampering is a crime, whether the witness plans to testify in a criminal trial or a civil trial. The U.S. Supreme Court has held that the duty to testify and give information in both civil and criminal cases is inherent in being a citizen of the United States, even when witnesses fear for their lives because of such testimony.[18] These and other federal laws are designed to make it possible for witnesses to perform their duties and to convict gang and organized crime members.

One form of witness tampering under the federal statute, 18 U.S.C. § 1512 (a) (1) (A), is acts done to prevent a witness from testifying in an official proceeding. In October 2004, Dustin Honken, a methamphetamine dealer, was convicted in the U.S. District Court for Iowa of murdering five people. Two were witnesses the government planned to have testify against him in a drug charge, one was the girlfriend of one of the witnesses, and two were the girlfriend's small children. He was charged with the murders as furtherance of a continuing criminal enterprise and witness tampering, both federal laws that permit imposition of the death penalty. Even though Iowa is one of twelve states that do not have the death penalty, under

witness protection program Established as part of the Organized Crime Control Act of 1970, this program provides new identities and relocation for witnesses and their families in both state and federal criminal prosecutions of organized crime.

witness tampering Criminal interference with someone who plans to testify in either a criminal or a civil trial.

the federal murder statute the jury sentenced Honken to life imprisonment for the murders of the adults and sentenced him to death for the murders of the children. The Eighth Circuit Court of Appeals upheld his sentence, and the U.S. Supreme Court denied certiorari in December 2009.[19]

Witness tampering under 18 U.S.C. §1512 (a) also includes killing a person with the intent to prevent that person from communicating with a federal officer about the possible commission of a federal offense. Federal courts interpreted the "intent" requirement inconsistently. Some said it was enough that the defendant intended to prevent the victim from communicating with any law enforcement officer, since it is possible that officer might be a federal official. Other courts required the prosecution to prove the defendant killed the victim to prevent communication with a federal officer, not law enforcement in general.

In *Fowler v. United States*, 131 S. Ct. 2045 (2011), the U.S. Supreme Court agreed with the holdings in the latter courts. It held that if the defendant kills a person to prevent communication with any law enforcement officers, the prosecution must prove that it was likely that one of the communications would have been to a federal officer.

The "likely" will communicate with a federal official standard of proof articulated in *Fowler* may not apply to other aspects of witness tampering under the statute. In *United States v. Shavers*, 693 F.3d 363 (3d Cir. 2012) the court held that in a prosecution under section 1512 (b) for intimidation of a witness to prevent the witness from testifying in an official proceeding, it isn't enough to show the defendant should have known it was likely the witness might testify in a federal proceeding. The prosecution must prove the defendant had a particular federal proceeding in mind when he made the intimidating statements or acts, the court said.

THE CRIME OF MONEY LAUNDERING

money laundering
The crime of disguising money obtained illegally by channeling it through legitimate commercial and financial transactions.

Money laundering is defined by the U.S. Department of the Treasury as "the process by which criminals or criminal organizations seek to disguise the illicit nature of their proceeds by introducing them into the stream of legitimate commerce and finance."[20] The Bank Secrecy Act of 1970[21] was the first attempt by Congress to prevent criminals from concealing or laundering money through banks or other financial institutions. The Money Laundering Control Act of 1986 created the crimes of money laundering and knowingly helping with money laundering of the proceeds of criminal activities.[22] Because terrorists must conceal and launder money to achieve their criminal purposes, the USA Patriot Act of 2001[23] toughened laws prohibiting the concealment or laundering of money for criminal purposes. Under this statute, U.S. banks dealing with foreign customers are held accountable, sentences for cash smuggling are increased, and both civil and criminal penalties for violation of the law are enlarged.

Money laundering has been called the world's third largest business. Drug dealers, terrorists, and organized crime figures need to have money move undetected through the world's financial systems. "Following the money" is one effective way for investigators to find the criminals who made the money. The International Monetary Fund estimates that money laundering activities account for between 2 and 5 percent of the world's gross domestic product, or about $600 billion annually.[24]

In addition to laundering money through legitimate businesses owned or controlled by them, criminals use several other methods. In the July 2006 issue of the

FBI Law Enforcement Bulletin, the article "Breaking the Bank" listed the following methods of money laundering and transfer used by drug dealers:

> . . . some of the more common laundering methods include . . . the Black Market Peso Exchange, cash smuggling (courier or bulk cash shipments), gold purchases, structured deposits to or withdrawals from bank accounts, purchases of monetary instruments (e.g., cashier's checks, money orders, traveler's checks), wire transfers, and forms of underground banking, particularly the Hawala system.

The article points out that while drug money is the leading source of money laundering, persons laundering money gained from other criminal activity can also be prosecuted under federal law.

Transactions Covered by the Federal Money Laundering Statutes

Title 18 of the United States Code prohibits the following money laundering activities, among others:

- Section 1956: "intending to transport or transfer monetary funds knowing that the property represents the proceeds of unlawful activity"
- Section 1957: "knowingly engaging in a monetary transaction involving criminally derived property valued at more than $10,000"

Prosecutions under 18 U.S.C. § 1957 require only that the defendant engage in a transaction where he knew the money being transferred was over $10,000 and came from criminal activities. In *United States v. Johnson,*[25] the court affirmed the conviction of a defendant who accepted over $10,000 from a person to use as a down payment on a house, knowing the money came from illegal drug transactions.

Recent court decisions by the U.S. Supreme Court and Courts of Appeals have addressed some of the issues raised in prosecutions under 18 U.S.C. § 1956, the principal money laundering statute. In *Whitfield v. United States,*[26] the U.S. Supreme Court held that convictions for conspiracy to violate the money laundering statute did not require proof of an overt act. While the general federal conspiracy statute, 18 U.S.C. § 371, does require proof of the commission of an overt act in furtherance of the conspiracy, the Court held that when Congress leaves out that specific requirement, as it did in the money laundering statutes, it intends to exclude the necessity of proof of that element.

Prior to 2008, the federal courts of appeals were split on the elements the prosecution must prove for a conviction under the transportation part of the money laundering statute. Section 1956(a)(2)(B)(i) states that it is a crime to transport certain funds into or out of the United States with a design "to conceal or disguise the nature, the location, the source, the ownership, or the control of the proceeds of specified unlawful activity." Some courts interpreted this provision as requiring proof that the defendant intended to give the transported funds "the appearance of legitimacy." See *United States v. Morales-Rodriguez.*[27] These courts reasoned that the "classic" example of money laundering was schemes designed to make illegal money look legal, using a "disguise" of some sort.

Other federal courts disagreed. In *United States v. Ness,*[28] the court of appeals held that conviction under the "transportation" money laundering statute did not require proof that the defendant intended to give the transported funds the appearance of legitimate wealth. The defendant, who operated an armored car company, transported proceeds from illegal drug sales to persons outside the country. He contended that he made no effort to pass the money as legal wealth and thus could not be guilty of "concealing" under the statute. The court disagreed, finding that the concealment element was satisfied because the defendant used "elaborate" methods attended by a high degree of secrecy in transporting the money.

The U.S. Supreme Court settled the split in the circuits in the 2008 case of *Cuellar v. United States*.[29] There, the defendant was caught in Texas on his way to Mexico carrying $81,000 of illegal drug money in a concealed compartment of his car. He was convicted under the transportation part of § 1956. On appeal, the Fifth Circuit affirmed his conviction, concluding that evidence the defendant made an elaborate attempt to conceal the money satisfied the money laundering requirements of a "design" to transfer funds to conceal their unlawful source. The defendant appealed to the Supreme Court, contending the prosecution did not prove he made any attempt to give the money the "appearance of legitimate wealth."

The Supreme Court held the prosecution was not required to prove the defendant tried to give the money the appearance of legitimate wealth. However, it also held that the prosecution under § 1956 had to prove that the defendant knew the purpose of the transportation of the money to Mexico was to conceal its unlawful origin. Simply proving the defendant concealed the money did not suffice to prove he knew the purpose of the transportation to Mexico was to conceal its source. "There is a difference between concealing something to transport it, and transporting something to conceal it."[30] Because the prosecution offered no evidence on the defendant's knowledge of the purpose of the transportation, all the elements of § 1956 were not proved, the Court said, and reversed the conviction.

The Supreme Court also remanded the *Ness* case back to the Second Circuit Court, and in 2009 that court reversed the convictions under the money laundering statute.[31] In the later case of *United States v. Garcia*,[32] the court held that the financial transaction part of the money laundering statute, § 1956(a)(1), also required proof that the defendant knew the purpose of the transaction was to conceal the unlawful origin of the money transferred.

18 U.S.C. § 1956 expressly prohibits using the "proceeds of specified unlawful activity" in financial transactions or transportation transactions. For example, if a thief used stolen money as a down payment when buying a house, the use of the money in a "financial transaction" would be a separate crime from the theft of the money. However, in *United States v. Santos*,[33] the U.S. Supreme Court held that the term *proceeds* in the money laundering statutes covers "profits" from unlawful activity, not "gross receipts." In *Santos* a defendant ran an illegal lottery in Indiana. He used money paid by lottery players for their tickets to pay expenses of running the illegal lottery, such as making payouts on winning tickets. He kept the profits after paying all expenses. He was convicted under the federal money laundering statute based on transactions where he "used" receipts from the unlawful activity to pay expenses. The government contended these transactions qualified as money laundering because the funds transferred were "proceeds" of the illegal lottery, and thus were "proceeds" under § 1956. The Supreme Court rejected the government's position, and reversed the conviction under the money laundering

YOU BE THE JUDGE

Based on your understanding of the Cuellar decision (discussed above), has the prosecution proved the trainer was part of the money-laundering conspiracy? What must it prove? Is knowledge of the source of funds used to buy and sell the horses enough under the statute? The trainer has filed a motion for a judgment of acquittal. What is your decision? See United States v. Cessa, 785 F.3d 165 (5th Cir. 2015), cert denied 136 S. Ct. 522 (2015)

You are the federal district judge in the Western District of Texas. You have just heard the evidence in the trial of several defendants who are members of the Mexican illegal drug cartel, Los Zetas. Two of the defendants are the leaders of Los Zetas; "Zeta 40," the leader, and "Zeta 42," his second-in-command. Members of Los Zetas are given a number based on the order in which they joined Los Zetas. The original 30 members of Los Zetas were part of a Mexican special-forces military group that deserted and formed the criminal organization, taking the name "Zeta" from their military call sign. The cartel makes hundreds of millions of illegal dollars each year selling illegal drugs in the U.S.

The Los Zetas are charged with conspiracy to commit money laundering in violation of the federal statute, 18 U.S.C. §1956 (h). They did so in a scheme involving the purchase and sale of race horses stabled and trained in the U.S. In a simplified explanation, the evidence shows that the scheme worked as follows. Using illegal drug dollars, individuals hired by Los Zetas would buy a horse for a sum, and then immediately "resell" the horse to another individual working for Los Zetas, who paid the inflated price using illegal drug dollars. The sale price would be much greater than the original price. The same horse, and other similar horses, would be "sold" over and over, generating hundreds of thousands of what appeared to be legitimate funds that Los Zetas could then move in financial markets as "clean" money.

A codefendant, a reputable race horse trainer, was employed by Zeta 40 to stable and train the horses used in the scheme. The trainer admits he knew Zeta 40 was using drug money to buy the horses brought to the trainer for stabling and training. Evidence also shows that the trainer, who had moderate income from training before being hired by Zeta 40, declared income over $500,000 after being hired. Other evidence shows that the trainer did not participate in Los Zetas drug transactions or other illegal actions the Los Zetas undertook.

statute. Congress did not define "proceeds" in the money laundering statute, and the Court concluded either "receipts" or "profits" would fit within the meaning of "proceeds" as used in the statute. That being so, "Under a long line of our decisions, the tie must go to the defendant. The rule of lenity requires ambiguous criminal laws to be interpreted in favor of the defendants subjected to them."[34] The Court also reasoned that because there were 250 "predicate" offenses that could produce unlawful proceeds, every time a criminal paid the costs of committing one of those crimes (such as thief renting a car to move his stolen property) a money laundering violation would occur. The Court did not think that was the intended result of the money laundering legislation.

In 2009 Congress amended the money laundering statute to make it clear proceeds means either profits of illegal activities, or "gross receipts of such activity."

In addition, courts after the decision in *Santos* continued to hold that in illegal drug transactions, any money obtained from the sale of illegal drugs constitutes "proceeds" for purpose of the money laundering statutes. Thus, in the 2011 case of *United States v. Richardson*[35] the use of receipts from illegal drug transactions to make the down payment on a house purchase was held to violate the money-laundering act.

Currency Transaction Reports and the Crime of Smurfing

With drug-trafficking revenues as high as $300 billion a year, many drug dealers and other criminals reap huge profits. A large amount of such criminal profits is spent purchasing expensive cars, houses, condos, jewelry, furs, clothing, and other luxuries.

Businesses and financial institutions in the United States are required to report cash transactions of $10,000 or more under the Currency Transaction Reporting Act (31 U.S.C.A. § 5311). The **CTRs (currency transaction reports)** filed by businesses, banks, and other financial institutions are used to determine whether tax fraud or money laundering is occurring. Further investigation could then uncover illegal drug dealings and racketeering.

CTRs (currency transaction reports)
Reports that businesses, banks, and financial institutions are required to file for cash transactions of more than $10,000. CTRs can help determine whether tax fraud or money laundering is occurring.

Unfortunately, businesspeople who want to make profits sometimes cooperate with drug dealers and other criminals seeking to hide cash transactions. Car dealers, real estate agents, and jewelers sometimes illegally agree to structure a transaction. In a structured transaction, the buyer makes a series of payments in cash or cashier's checks of under $10,000 each over a period of weeks. When the sales price is reached, the dealer or real estate agent turns the car or condo over to the buyer. For a $50,000 car, six or seven payments under $10,000 would be the structured transaction. This illegal practice is sometimes called "smurfing" and is made a crime by the Federal Money Laundering Control Act of 1986 (31 U.S.C. § 5324).

Section 5324(a)(3) prohibits "structured transactions" involving financial institutions. It states, "No person shall, for the purpose of evading the reporting requirements of section 5313(a) . . . structure or assist in structuring . . . any transaction with one or more domestic financial institutions." The U.S. Supreme Court defined "structuring" in *Ratzlaf v. United States*[36] as any plan "to break up a single transaction above the reporting threshold into two or more separate transactions for the purpose of evading a financial institution's reporting requirement." In *United States v. Morales-Rodriguez*,[37] the court affirmed the conviction under § 5324(a)(3) of a vice president of a non-profit organization that provided benefits to police officers and fire fighters. The defendant received monthly checks from the organization's 18,000 members and deposited them in bank accounts. He then had the banks issue him hundreds of checks made out to cash for just under $10,000. Over a two-year period he received about $1.2 million dollars in this manner, none of which was reported anywhere.

Title 31 of the United States Code, which contains rules for monetary recording and reporting, requires in § 5316 that a CMIR (currency or other monetary instruments report) be filed when more than $10,000 is taken out of or brought into the United States. Because illegal drugs are a major source of profit for many criminals and criminal organizations, law enforcement officers look not only for importation of illegal drugs but also for the money making the narcotics deals possible. These statutes enable law enforcement officers to "follow the money," if it is laundered in legal entities, and prosecute those engaged in the laundering activities.

Failing to file a report, or filing a false report, is a violation of § 5316, and under § 5317 the funds taken out of the country can be confiscated.[38]

OTHER CRIMINAL LAWS USED TO FIGHT GANGS AND ORGANIZED CRIME

The Travel Act

Travel Act Legislation that can be used to prosecute those involved in criminal activities that cross state borders or involve foreign commerce.

Title 18 of the United States Code, § 1951, titled the **Travel Act,** can be used to prosecute those involved in criminal activities that cross state borders or involve foreign commerce. That act prohibits traveling in interstate or foreign commerce or use of the mail or any facility in interstate or foreign commerce with intent to:

1. Distribute the proceeds of any unlawful activity; or

2. Commit any crime of violence to further any unlawful activity; or

3. Otherwise promote, manage, establish, carry on, or facilitate the promotion, management, establishment or carrying on of any unlawful activity

Felony convictions for violations of the Travel Act have been obtained for interstate travel as part of a scheme to

- Bomb a homosexual bar.[39]
- Travel with the intent to violate state law.[40]
- Place illegal gambling wagers using telephones, which are included in the meaning of a "facility" under the act.[41]
- Use a telephone to demand the payment of a ransom for the release of a person held unlawfully.[42]
- Travel to facilitate an illegal narcotics transaction.[43]

Extortion

Both the federal government and the state governments have statutes making extortion criminal. The federal statute, known as the Hobbs Act (discussed in Chapter 14), permits prosecution under that act if the extortion can be shown to interfere with interstate commerce. The Hobbs Act defines *extortion* as "obtaining of property of another, with his consent, induced by wrongful use of actual or threatened force, violence, or fear, or under the color of official right" (18 U.S.C. § 1951). In a 2013 case, *Sekhar v. United States,* 133 S. Ct. 2720, the U.S. Supreme Court held that attempts to bully a government lawyer to give his employer favorable legal advice about the defendant so he could obtain a government contract did not constitute extortion under the Hobbs Act. The court held that a lawyer's opinion did not constitute "property" under the Hobbs Act; "property," the court held, must be something that can be transferred from one person to another.

A common example of extortion used by gangs or organized crime members is the threat of violence against a business that does not pay "protection" money. Often, a business owner is forced to pay one gang extortion money to protect the business from another gang. An example of the use of the "color of official right" is

ILLEGAL GAMBLING IN THE UNITED STATES

During Prohibition in the United States (1919–1933), organized crime made huge profits selling illegal beer and alcohol to the many people who wanted to drink.

With the legalization of alcoholic drinks, organized crime turned to other illegal activities. It is widely believed that until the 1970s, illegal gambling was the greatest moneymaker for organized crime.

With the legalization of many forms of gambling in the United States and with the effective use of RICO, profits from gambling dropped rapidly, while the risks in illegal gambling went up. Illegal gambling is no longer as attractive to criminals as it previously was. However, some forms of gambling continue to be illegal.

Distinguishing Illegal Gambling from Friendly Gambling

For a game of chance or a lottery to be illegal, it must violate a specific law or ordinance. Illegal gambling is often distinguished from legitimate commercial promotions by the fact that illegal gambling or lotteries have (1) a prize, (2) consideration, and (3) chance elements.

Therefore, a company that wishes to run a promotion can offer a prize if the customer does not have to buy anything or pay anything (no consideration). Or the contest can be legal if, instead of a chance element, there is a skill element (writing an essay or naming a new product, for example).[a]

The Federal Crime of Gambling: 18 U.S.C.A. § 1955

(b) *As used in this section—*

(1) "illegal gambling business" means a gambling business which—
(i) is a violation of the law of a State or political subdivision in which it is conducted;
(ii) involves five or more persons who conduct, finance, manage, supervise, direct, or own all or part of such business; and
(iii) has been or remains in substantially continuous operation for a period in excess of thirty days or has a gross revenue of $2,000 in any single day.

The Federal Professional and Amateur Sports Protection Act (PASPA), (Public Law 102-559) Prohibiting Sports Gambling

Section 3702 makes it unlawful for states or individuals to sponsor, operate, advertise, promote, or license a lottery, sweepstakes, or betting on one or more competitive games in which amateur or professional athletes participate.

the city health inspector who threatens to charge a business with serious sanitation violations unless the official is paid off.

Bribery

Bribery has always been a problem for society. Using money, property, or "favors" to influence a public or private official to act in some agreed manner is a crime in all the states and under federal statutes. The problem has been acute in recent years because of the huge amounts of money controlled by criminal organizations. The presence of this money not only encourages criminals to approach officials to

Several exemptions are provided, including betting on pari-mutuel animal racing and jai alai, and some casino betting.[b]

Sports Betting and States' Rights

The PASPA law, discussed above, contains exceptions for four states (Nevada, Delaware, Oregon, and Montana), where sports betting is permitted. In Nevada each year about $2 billion is wagered on sports; while "March Madness" brings in nearly $200 million each year, college and professional football produces the greatest amount of legal sports bets each year. The amounts wagered illegally on sports, especially football games, far exceeds legal betting. Experts estimate that nearly $95 billion is bet each year in illegal gambling operations.

Other states want in. In 2012 New Jersey voters passed a resolution permitting sports betting in the state's twelve casinos and four horse racing tracks. The legislature passed a bill doing so, and Governor Christie signed the bill into law. The NCAA, the NBA, the NFL, other sports institutions, and the U.S. Justice department, immediately brought a suit in federal district court challenging the law. In March 2013 a federal district judge held the law violated federal gambling laws. On appeal, the court of appeals upheld the district court and found that the New Jersey law violated the PASPA. *NCAA v. Governor of New Jersey*, 730 F.3d 208 (3rd Cir. 2013), *cert denied*, 134 S. Ct. 2866 (2014)

[a]When is gambling a "social game" between friends, between neighbors, or in an office or factory pool? The court in the 1991 case of *State v. Hansen*, 816 P.2d 706 (Or. App.), cited Oregon Statute 167.117(4)(c):

"Social game" means:

(a) A game, other than a lottery, between players in a private home where no house player, house bank or house odds exist and there is no house income from the operation of the social game; and

(b) If authorized pursuant to ORS 167.121, a game, other than a lottery, between players in a private business, private club or place of public accommodation where no house player, house bank or house odds exist and there is no house income from *the operation of the social game* ORS 167.117(13). [Emphasis added.]

Friendly gambling (office or factory football pool, neighborhood poker game, and so on) can be distinguished from commercial gambling by some or all of the following factors:

- Where the game is played and who the players are
- Size of the pot
- Whether the house takes a percentage of each pot
- Whether the players bet against the house and the house acts as the banker, and whether the house acts as the dealer in such games as blackjack and craps
- Other factors such as the type of game played

[b]Sports betting is a big business in the United States, with billions of dollars, most of it illegally, wagered each year.

---

attempt to buy their actions but also serves as an illegal incentive for corrupt officials to solicit such payments.

An example of a state bribery law is Chapter 838 of the Florida Criminal Code, which makes it a crime to offer a bribe to any state, county, or city employee or official, or any employee or official of any political subdivision in the state. Both the person offering the bribe and the person taking the bribe can be charged under the statute. It is also the crime of bribery to offer money to "fix" an athletic contest (§ 838.12). The crime of "commercial bribery" (§ 838.15) is committed when a bribe is offered to any employee or agent of a business or another person; a trustee, guardian, or other fiduciary; a lawyer, physician, accountant, appraiser, or other professional advisor; an officer, director, or manager of an organization; or an arbitrator, adjudicator, or referee.

Bribery is a specific intent crime, and to obtain a conviction the prosecution must prove the bribe was offered with "corrupt intent," that is, with intent to influence the actions of the person to whom the bribe was paid. It is not necessary that the bribe be offered to influence a specific official act, but only that its purpose is to cause favorable results in the future.

In some states the prosecution must prove the bribed official was actually influenced by the bribe. See, for instance, Nebraska Revised Statutes § 28-917 (Reissue of 1995), though even there the defendant can be convicted of attempted bribery if the official action is not in fact influenced by the bribe; see *State v. Kao.*[44] Attempted bribery is often the charge, because in many cases of bribery of officials the official is a law enforcement officer posing as the official, or the actual official is cooperating with the police.

The Federal Foreign Corrupt Practices Act of 1977, 15 U.S.C. § 78, prohibits U.S. companies and individuals from making payments to win contracts from foreign governments. This law was enacted after it was disclosed that the Lockheed Corporation had paid Japan's prime minister more than $1.9 million so that Japan would purchase Lockheed jet aircraft.

Kickbacks

It is not uncommon for parties in a sales transaction to agree that some part of the purchase price paid by the buyer will be returned to the buyer. In new car sales, for example, this practice goes under the name of a "factory rebate" or "dealer participation" bonus. A bank may agree with a car dealer that if the car dealer sends credit customers to the bank for new car loans, part of the interest charged to the customer will be returned to the car dealer. These agreements, commonly called kickbacks, are not all illegal, but many of them are.

In one famous case, Spiro T. Agnew, then vice president of the United States, was forced to resign the vice presidency because of kickback schemes he was involved in as governor of Maryland. Agnew forced engineering firms seeking government contracts to kick back a percentage of the contract amount to various people, including him. He also required every vendor selling cigarettes in the state capitol building to kick back five cents on every pack sold. In addition to being forced to resign, Agnew pleaded guilty to income tax evasion because of his failure to report the kickbacks as income.

Kickbacks can be charged under a state bribery law because the person receiving the kickback is soliciting payment to influence her or his actions. Kickbacks are also covered under the Foreign Corrupt Practices Act of 1977, discussed previously, and kickback agreements between a contractor and a federal procurement officer or other employee are prohibited under the federal bribery and anti-gratuity statute, 18 U.S.C. § 201. However, any payment received by the official must be made "for an official act." In *United States v. Valdes,*[45] the court held that a gratuity is an unlawful payment "for an official act" only if it was paid in order to influence some pending public question. In *Valdes* an FBI agent posing as a judge paid a District of Columbia police inspector $50 to run the names of four fictitious people through a law enforcement database to see if they had any outstanding warrants. The court held that the inspector's use of

THE ADVANTAGES OF FEDERAL PROSECUTION

A December 2003 publication of the U.S. Department of Justice titled "Fighting Urban Crime: The Evolution of Federal-State Collaboration" (NCJ #197040) discussed the following advantages of federal over state prosecution of criminals:

- *Federal Grand Jury:* This body can be called at any time, can be kept in action for as long as three years, can hear hearsay evidence, and is armed with national subpoena power. State grand juries have a shorter duration, "no hearsay" rules, and limited subpoena power.
- *Immunity:* Limited immunity for a grand jury witness conferred by federal prosecutors does not impede later prosecution of the witness for perjury, obstruction of justice, or contempt. Most states have only blanket transactional immunity, which provides less flexibility and leverage against potential witnesses.
- *Search Warrants:* Federal standards for obtaining a search warrant are generally lower than those of most states.
- *Preventive Detention:* The federal bail statute provides for preventive detention in a range of circumstances. State laws do not have such provisions.
- *Electronic Surveillance:* Most states require a higher burden of proof for wiretaps than the federal government.
- *Witness Protection:* In contrast to the well-developed federal witness protection program, most states do not have such a program.
- *Accomplice Testimony:* Federal rules permit conviction on the basis of an accomplice's uncorroborated testimony. State rules generally do not.
- *Discovery:* Federal rules provide that a statement by a government witness need not be made available to the defense until the witness has testified at trial. Also, the defense has no entitlement to a witness list before trial or to interview government witnesses prior to trial. Most state rules provide otherwise.

It should also be recognized that federal prosecutors generally have much more money than state prosecutors to spend on investigations and trials.

the government database was not an "official act" under Section 201(c)(1)(B), because it was not intended to have any effect on any pending charge or issue.

Mail Fraud

People who commit crimes involving fraud on another person can usually be prosecuted under state criminal fraud laws. However, when they use the U.S. mail or any other interstate delivery system such as Federal Express or United Parcel Service to defraud a victim, they can be prosecuted under the federal **mail fraud** statute (18 U.S.C. § 1341–1346). In 1994, Congress expanded the mail fraud crime to include "any matter or thing whatever to be sent or delivered by private or commercial interstate carrier." Any fraudulent scheme, whatever its purpose or method, that uses any of these delivery services can be prosecuted as a felony under the mail fraud statute.

Incidental use of the mail or other interstate carrier does not violate the mail fraud statute. For example, in *United States v. Maze,*[46] the U.S. Supreme Court held

mail fraud A fraudulent scheme, no matter its purpose or method, that uses either private or public delivery service.

the mail fraud act was not applicable to a defendant who stole his roommate's credit card and made local purchases. The merchants who sold the goods sent their invoices through the mail for payment from the credit card company, and based on this use of the mails, the federal prosecutor charged the defendant under the mail fraud statute. The Supreme Court said the merchants' use of the mail did not trigger the mail fraud statute because the mails were not used to perpetrate the theft or fraud, but were only incidental to the crime.

HONEST SERVICES FRAUD

wire fraud A fraudulent scheme that uses interstate or international wire or other electronic communications.

The **wire fraud** act (discussed in Chapter 15) prohibits any scheme to defraud another by use of wire services. A wire fraud scheme is defined to include a scheme to deprive another of the "intangible right of honest services." This definition was added to the wire and mail fraud acts because of the Supreme Court's holding in *McNally v. United States*,[47] which limited the scope of the fraud statutes to deprivations of money or property. The fraud statutes can thus be used to prosecute persons whose scheme is designed not to take money from another, but to deprive him or her of the right to the "honest services" of some person.

The U.S. Supreme Court limited the scope of honest services fraud in the 2010 case of *Skilling v. United States*,[48] discussed more fully in Chapter 15. As a result, prosecutions under the federal mail and wire fraud acts based on deprivations of the right to honest services will be limited to classic property crimes, where the defendant defrauds another out of money or property, and bribery or kickback schemes. Prosecutions for breach only of a fiduciary duty, as was the case in *Skilling*, can no longer be brought under honest services fraud.

★★
LEARNING OBJECTIVES SUMMARY

LO 1. List the requirements for a RICO conviction.
A RICO conviction requires proof that an enterprise existed that engaged in racketeering activity, that the defendants were members of the enterprise and participated in the activity, and that the enterprise had a pattern of racketeering activity.

LO 2. Identify the jurisdictional requirements for a federal RICO charge.
The federal statute adds the jurisdictional requirement that the racketeering activities affected interstate commerce. Most courts now hold that any effect on interstate commerce satisfies the jurisdictional requirement.

LO 3. List three ways money can be laundered.
Money can be laundered by transporting it to another country, buying cash or bearer

instruments, passing it through a legitimate business, or using underground banking like the Hawala system.

LO 4. List four federal statutes used to combat interstate crime.
The mail fraud act, wire fraud act, money laundering act, and the RICO act are principal federal laws that are used to combat organized crime.

LO 5. Explain the knowledge needed for a conviction under the federal money laundering statute, specifically the section on transportation of illegal proceeds.
Money laundering by transporting the proceeds of unlawful activity requires knowledge that the purpose of the transportation is to conceal the origin of the money.

LO 6. Define proceeds under the money laundering statutes.
Proceeds for purpose of the money laundering statutes means profits gained from unlawful activities, or gross receipts of such activity.

LO 7. Explain why federal and state prosecutions of organized crime figures before 1970 were generally unsuccessful.
Because lower-ranking members of crime families were the ones usually arrested with specific crimes such as murder or extortion, heads of organizations could not be prosecuted without testimony from those arrested. Such testimony was rarely given.

LO 8. Describe the advantages statutes passed after 1970 gave to the prosecution.
The grand jury system, witness protection program, immunity doctrines, and federal court discovery rules all make prosecution in federal courts advantageous.

KEY TERMS

Racketeer Influenced and Corrupt Organizations Act (RICO), p. 513
witness protection program, p. 517
witness tampering, p. 517

money laundering, p. 518
CTRs (currency transaction reports), p. 522
Travel Act, p. 523

mail fraud, p. 527
wire fraud, p. 528

CASE ANALYSIS AND WRITING EXERCISES

1. As noted in this chapter, most states have "little" RICO statutes. Oregon is such a state: ORS § 166.720 (3). What exactly is a criminal "enterprise" under the Oregon statute? Does it include two men who on several occasions enter a Safeway store, split up, and each shoplift frozen shrimp and disposable diapers? Does that sound like a RICO case? What did the Oregon Supreme Court conclude, and why? See *State v. Walker*, 333 P.3d 316 (Or. 2014).

2. This chapter notes that cities like Los Angeles, California, which has thousands of street gang members, have used nuisance laws to obtain injunctions against gang members, preventing the gang members from engaging in many legal as well as illegal activities. While this practice has existed for years, only recently has a federal court considered the propriety of such laws. In *Vasquez v. Rackauckas*, 734 F.3d 1025 (9th Cir. 2013), 115 members of the Orange Varrio Cypress street gang appealed a decision granting an injunction against the gang members from engaging in a broad range of activities-legal and illegal- within a 3.78 square mile area in the City of Orange. What do you see as the problems created by such broad, sweeping injunctions? How should the problem be resolved?

3. Notwithstanding Congress' amending of the federal money laundering statute in response to the U.S. Supreme Court's decision in *United States v. Santos*, discussed in this chapter, the reasoning of the court in Santos lives on. Courts continue to see a "merger" problem in prosecutions under the money laundering statute for using "proceeds" of criminal activities in financial transactions. To use the Supreme Court's example of "merger" in Santos, if a thief uses stolen money to rent a getaway car, the theft crime and the money laundering crime merge, which makes dual convictions almost like double jeopardy. What was the "merger" problem in *United States v. Abdulwahab*, 715 F.3d 521 (4ᵗʰ Cir. 2013)? How did the court define "proceeds" under the money laundering statute to resolve the problem?

4. This chapter discusses gambling on sports under federal anti-gambling statutes. States also have laws making illegal gambling a crime. Is this gambling ?: An owner of an Internet café rented Internet time to customers by selling cards that were "swiped" by a card reader near a computer terminal. The owner instituted a "sweepstakes" game where customers were given entries into a cash sweepstakes contest for each 10 minutes they purchased on the Internet. Drawings were held periodically, and cash prizes were awarded the winners. The owner was arrested, charged and convicted of gambling under New Mexico state law. He appealed his conviction, and the New Mexico Court of Appeals reversed his conviction. Did the court say the evidence didn't prove the owner conducted a gambling operation? Or did it say something else? See *State v. Vento*, 286 P.3d 627 (N.M. App. 2012). Does it matter that customers purchased 140,000 hours of Internet time, and 110,000 of those hours were purchased with sweepstakes winnings? Or that only 330 hours of Internet time were actually used by all those purchases? What kind of "game" does that practice resemble?

ENDNOTES

1. *United States v. Christensen,* 801 F.3d 970 (9th Cir. 2015). The court did reverse some of the convictions for violation of the computer fraud and unauthorized access provisions under the federal Computer Fraud and Abuse Act.

2. See the 2002 U.S. Department of Justice publication NCJ 190351, "Responding to Gangs: Evaluation and Research."

3. See the *New York Times*, "Gangs Without Borders, Fierce and Resilient, Confront the Law," September 26, 2004.

4. See Chapter 19 of this book for materials on tax evasion.

5. Most, if not all, state RICO statutes create three distinct crimes: (1) using or investing the proceeds of racketeering activity, (2) acquiring an interest in property or an enterprise engaged in racketeering activity, and (3) conducting or participating in the enterprise. Each of these crimes requires proof of a fact the others do not and can therefore result in multiple convictions without violating the Double Jeopardy Clause. (See Chapter 7 of this book for additional material on the Double Jeopardy Clause.)

    Courts have uniformly held not only that the substantive violations may be charged but also that the corresponding conspiracy violations may be charged. In addition, the underlying predicate offenses may also be charged. See *Iannelli v. United States,* 420 U.S. 770 (1975).

6. 129 S. Ct. 2237 (2009).

7. 921 N.E.2d 570 (NY 2009).

8. 2010 WL 2741534 (Tex. App. 2010).

9. 75 Cal. Rptr. 3d 200 (Cal. App. 2008).

10. 695 F.3d 1125 (10th Cir. 2012).

11. 380 F.3d 251 (6th Cir. 2004).

12. 529 U.S. 598 (2000).

13. 529 U.S. 848 (2000).

14. 545 U.S. 1 (2005).

15. 491 F.3d 25 (1st Cir. 2007), *cert. denied,* 552 U.S. 1297 (2008).

16. Public Law No. 91-452, 84 Stat. 938.

17. 18 U.S.C. § 1512.

18. For additional material on witnesses, see Thomas Gardner and Terry Anderson, *Criminal Evidence, Principles and Cases,* 8th ed., Chapter 5 (Belmont, CA: Wadsworth, 2013). The May 2004 *FBI Law Enforcement Bulletin* article "Hiding in Plain Sight: A Peek into the Witness Protection Program," is an excellent description of the witness protection program.

19. 130 S. Ct. 1011 (2009).

20. *U.S. Department of the Treasury,* "2000–2005 Strategic Plan," p. 1.

21. 11 U.S.C. § 5311–5332.

22. 18 U.S.C. § 1956.

23. 18 U.S.C. § 5332.

24. In what has been called the biggest drug bust in history, the United States invaded Panama in 1989 to stop the use of Panama as a money-laundering center.

25. 450 F.3d 366 (8th Cir. 2006).

26. 543 U.S. 209 (2005).

27. 467 F.3d 1 (1st Cir. 2006).

28. 466 F.3d 79 (2nd Cir. 2006).

29. 128 S. Ct. 1994 (2008).

30. 128 S. Ct., at 2005.

31. 565 F.3d 73 (2nd Cir. 2009).

32. 587 F.3d 509 (2nd Cir. 2009).

33. 128 S. Ct. 2020 (2008).

34. 128 S. Ct. at 2024.

35. 658 F.3d 333 (3rd Cir. 2011). The court reversed the conviction of the defendant, the wife of the drug dealer, because the government failed to prove she used the drug sale proceeds with the intent to conceal their source, a requirement under the statute.

36. 510 U.S. 135, 136 (1994).

37. 467 F.3d 1 (6th Cir. 2006).

38. See *United States v. United States Currency in Amount of Two Hundred Forty-Eight Thousand Dollars,* 2004 WL 958010 (E.D.N.Y. 2004).

39. *United States v. Winslow,* 962 R2d 1488 (9th Cir. 1992).

40. *United States v. Briggs,* 700 F.2d 408 (7th Cir. 1983), *cert. denied,* 103 S. Ct. 2463 (1983).

41. *United States v. Hanon,* 428 F.2d 101 (8th Cir. 1970).

42. *Mcintosh v. United States,* 385 F.2d 274 (8th Cir. 1967).

43. *United States v. Bernaugh,* 969 F.2d 858 (10th Cir. 1992).

44. 531 N.W.2de 555 (Neb. App. 1995).

45. 475 F.3d 1319 (D.C. Cir. 2007).

46. 94 S. Ct. 603 (1974).

47. 483 U.S. 350 (1987).

48. 130 S. Ct. 2896 (2010).

19

Immigration Crimes, Contempt, and Other Crimes Against Government

LEARNING OBJECTIVES

In this chapter we discuss various crimes in which a government body or court is the complaining party. The learning objectives for Chapter 19 are the following:

LO 1. List the various kinds of conduct made criminal under the immigration laws.

LO 2. Distinguish civil contempt from criminal contempt.

LO 3. Explain the connection between a gift and an official act required for conviction under the bribery laws.

LO 4. State the reason the U.S. Supreme Court declared invalid some provisions in the Arizona laws directed at illegal aliens.

LO 5. State the limits on summary contempt convictions.

The border wall divides Nogales, Arizona (left), and Nogales, Sonora, Mexico. At one time, the area was referred to as Ambos Nogales.

Foreigners who wish to immigrate to the United States must apply for and receive permission, in the form of various kinds of visas issued by U.S. consulates in the applicant's home country. Once a person comes to the United States as a lawful alien and has been granted permanent resident status, the steps toward becoming a naturalized citizen may begin.

Not every request for a visa is granted, and as a result many people resort to other means of entering the United States. The immigration laws discussed in this chapter highlight some of the many criminal laws that are tied to illegal attempts to enter or remain in this country.

One method for obtaining lawful alien presence in the United States is marriage to a U.S. citizen. If a foreign national and a U.S. citizen decide to marry, the foreign national or the U.S. citizen may either apply for a "fiancé" visa or, if the couple marry abroad, an "alien spouse" visa. If the decision to marry occurs while the alien is lawfully in the United States, the alien can apply for a change of status to a permanent resident.

The marriage exception can be abused by fraudulent marriages, and such marriages are made a criminal violation under federal immigration laws. Entering into a fraudulent marriage with a U.S. citizen is a crime for both parties to the fraudulent marriage, as well as for any "brokers" who facilitate the false marriage. An example is the 2012 case of *United States v. Adriatico-Fernandez.*[1] The defendant in that case arranged several "marriages" between U.S. citizens and foreign nationals, in which the U.S. citizen received a substantial "down payment" when the marriage occurred, plus monthly payments until the "spouse" obtained permanent resident status. Upon conviction under the immigration laws the U.S. citizens faced fines and imprisonment, and the foreign "spouses" were deported.

Many illegal aliens, such as those who enter the United States illegally across our borders, have been in this country for many years, and have entered into legitimate marriages with U.S. citizens. In the past, the only way illegal aliens could use marriage as a way to change their status to legal resident was to leave the United States, and apply for an alien spouse visa. However, once the illegal alien left the United States, immigration laws banned that person from re-entry for 10 years. In 2012, President Obama approved changes to the 10-year ban policy, effective March 4, 2013, which will permit an illegal alien in the United States to seek a waiver of the ban based on "extreme hardship" suffered by family members if the alien is forced to stay out of the country for the 10-year period. In that case, the illegal alien may seek permanent resident status without the 10-year delay.

In this chapter we will study immigration crimes, because these crimes are essentially crimes against government. We will study civil and criminal contempt and how those charges are used by government. We will also learn about other crimes directed against government, such as perjury, espionage, and tax evasion, where the criminal laws are used to protect the integrity or financial security of governments.

IMMIGRATION CRIMES

In 1997, the Center for Immigration Studies estimated that there were more than 5 million illegal immigrants in the United States. Ten years later, in 2007, the U.S. government estimated that the number of illegal immigrants living and working in the United States was over 12 million. Despite efforts to secure the borders of the United States, the wave of illegal immigrants was increasing. Most experts believed at least 500,000 and perhaps as many as 1,000,000 illegal immigrants crossed the borders each year. The U.S. Congress passed bills starting in 2006 designed to construct both actual and "virtual" barriers on the 2,000-mile U.S.-Mexico border. Actual walls, varying from chain-link fence to concrete and steel, have been constructed at key points along the border, covering perhaps one-third of the border. Virtual borders, consisting of cameras and other electronic monitoring devices, have also been put in place, though not in the quantity anticipated by sponsors of that barrier.

Comprehensive immigration reform has been debated by Congress, but no legislation has been passed. In 2010, Arizona passed a state statute aimed at illegal immigrants, which permitted police to detain persons suspected of being in this country illegally and also required aliens to carry valid immigration registration documents; failure to carry valid alien registration documents thus became a crime under Arizona law. States that pass laws aimed at immigration problems may run afoul of the Supremacy Clause of the U.S. Constitution. Under that clause, if the Constitution has expressly given Congress the power to regulate a field, such as immigration and naturalization of aliens, the power of the states to pass laws in that area is preempted by any congressional acts. In the 2012 case of *Arizona v. United States*[2] the U.S. Supreme Court held that some of the provisions in the Arizona law conflicted with federal immigration laws, and were thus preempted by federal law. It struck down the state requirement that aliens carry and produce valid alien registration papers, as well as the provision permitting law enforcement officers to make warrantless arrests of suspected illegal aliens who might be removable under federal law. The Supreme Court did uphold one provision in the Arizona law, which requires state police officers to check with Immigration and Customs Enforcement ("ICE") to determine the immigration status of persons lawfully detained. That provision does not violate federal immigration law, the Court held, since it applies only to persons lawfully stopped or detained by state police officers where the state officers have "reasonable suspicion" that the person is an illegal alien. The Court noted that under the Arizona law, "reasonable suspicion" cannot be based on the detained person's race, color, or national origin, and that the presentation of a valid Arizona driver's license creates a presumption of legality.

In a 2014 decision, *County of Maricopa v. Lopez-Valenzuela*, 770 F.3d 772 (9th Cir. 2014) the court declared unconstitutional a provision in the Arizona law that denies bail to persons illegally in the United States who are charged with felonies. The court said the law violates "substantive due process" because it was not narrowly tailored to specific serious crimes, and made assumptions about illegal aliens that punish them before trial. The U.S. Supreme Court denied review: 135 S. Ct. 2046 (2015).

Illegal immigrants enter this country through many methods. The United States has thousands of miles of borders with Mexico and Canada, and many illegal immigrants simply walk across the border into the United States. Others are smuggled in ships docking at any of the many ports on the Atlantic and Pacific oceans. Still others arrive under student, visitor, work, or business visas and remain after their visas have expired. It is estimated that 30 percent of all illegal immigrants in this country arrived here legally but then overstayed their visas. Because some of the 9/11 terrorists were in the United States under expired visas, efforts were made by the government to develop a system to monitor persons here under a visa. However, because of the prohibitive cost of such a system, and the lengthy lead time for it to become effective, there is not presently in place a reliable method to track those in the United States under an expired visa.

Illegal aliens generally come to the United States for work. Many "melt" into society and stay in the country for years. Forged green cards and other documents necessary to remain in this country are often used by illegal aliens to secure employment and housing. While many illegal aliens remain in the United States without attempting to change their illegal status, some attempt to obtain legal alien status.

The U.S. Congress has in the past granted limited amnesty to some illegal aliens. In 1986, it passed a law granting amnesty and legal resident status to persons who illegally entered the United States prior to 1982. In 2000, the INS released a report that while about 2.7 million aliens were given legal status under that law, the number of illegal aliens in the United States actually increased. This was in part because family members of those granted legal status entered the country illegally to join their relatives.

In 2013, eight members of Congress, called the "gang of eight," proposed immigration reform laws that would make it possible for many of the estimated 11.5 million illegal aliens in the United States to obtain lawful status. Under the proposals, any

APPREHENDING THE "WORST OF THE WORST" OF ILLEGAL IMMIGRANTS: THE "SECURE COMMUNITIES" PROGRAM

The "Secure Communities" program was begun under the Bush administration, and continued under the Obama administration. The purpose of the program is to help law enforcement officers identify the "worst of the worst" of violent criminals, drug traffickers, gang members, and other dangerous aliens by checking the immigration history of a person arrested. Law enforcement officers holding a person may either contact the Immigration and Customs Enforcement Department (ICE), or have the person's fingerprints run through an immigration database under the "Secure Communities" program. The latter process is much faster, and costs nothing.

As of July 31, 2012, the Immigration and Customs Enforcement Department reported that 97 percent of the 3,181 law enforcement jurisdictions in the United States have activated the information sharing system of the Secure Communities program. ICE also reported that 159,409 convicted criminal aliens have been removed from the United States under the program.

alien in the United States as of December 3, 2011, may apply for Registered Provisional Immigrant status, including the applicant's spouse and children. After 6 years, the application can be renewed, and after 10 years the applicant can apply for permanent resident status. Then, after 3 more years, the applicant may seek to become a naturalized citizen. To qualify for this program the alien must have committed no serious crimes, and must show proof of income of at least 125 percent of poverty level. In June 2013, the Senate passed an immigration reform bill based on the above model. It also contained an expedited process for the "dreamers," children brought illegally into the United States who graduated from high school or college, or served in the U.S. armed forces. The House of Representatives failed to approve the Senate bill, and the bill died. As of the end of 2015, no other comprehensive immigration reform bill was pending in either the Senate or the House of Representatives.

Illegal aliens can place significant economic pressure on state social service programs. In response to this, a few states have passed laws limiting the availability of social services to illegal aliens. Most recently, in 2006 and 2011 Georgia passed laws that declared illegal aliens ineligible for such services, required employers to verify the legal status of workers before hiring them, and required police to inform the INS when illegal aliens were arrested for crimes. It is unclear what effect the Supreme Court's decision in *Arizona v. United States* will have on these state laws, though in 2013 the Supreme Court denied review of a federal court's opinion declaring many sections of the Alabama immigration law invalid.[3]

Criminal Charges for Illegal Immigration Offenses

There are many criminal laws aimed at illegal immigration. Violators of these laws can be charged in criminal courts, or they can be deported after a hearing in an immigration court. In some cases, immigration officials may simply transport the illegal alien to a border and release that person without formal prosecution. The chart shows some of the various crimes that can be charged for immigration offenses, and the maximum punishments possible if convicted (see 8 U.S.C. § 1301 and the following).

Felonies	Misdemeanors
• Failure of alien to deport after order to do so (10 years) • Counterfeiting alien papers or application to enter (5 years) • Bringing in or harboring illegal aliens (5 years) • Illegal entry, second offense (2 years) • Reentry of deported alien (2 years) • Aiding subversive alien to enter (5 years) • Importing alien for immoral purposes (10 years)	• Failure to register (6 months) • Failure to notify of change of address (30 days) • Making false statements (6 months) • First illegal entry (6 months) • Knowingly hiring an illegal alien (6 months)

Deportation laws, now called removal laws, provide for removal of a person from the United States for a variety of reasons. Most directly, 8 U.S.C. § 1225 states that an immigration officer who inspects an immigrant at the place of entry may order the removal of the person if the person is inadmissible for any of the reasons set forth in 8 U.S.C. § 1182. In some situations an immigration judge may hold a hearing on inadmissibility, though in others the decision that a person is inadmissible is not reviewable.

A person within the United States and who is not a citizen or legal resident may be removed for any of the many reasons set forth in 8 U.S.C. § 1227. These include violation of entry conditions, overstaying a visa, helping smuggle in other illegal immigrants, commission of crimes of "moral turpitude," which carry a sentence of one year or more in prison, multiple convictions, or conviction of an aggravated or violent felony. Failing to register as a sex offender, using false documents, trafficking in controlled substances, or committing crimes of domestic violence are also reasons for removal of an illegal immigrant. During the removal process the alien may be detained pending removal, and removal is to occur within 90 days of the removal order.

Many persons removed from the United States subsequently reenter this country, usually illegally. Because of this, a federal statute, 8 U.S.C. § 1231(a)(5), permits immigration officials to reinstate former removal orders where any person reenters illegally. Such reinstatement orders are not subject to review.

Admission, Removal, and Detention

Federal immigration laws, such as 8 U.S.C. § 1231(a)(6), have always permitted immigration authorities to detain an alien after a removal order has been entered. The duration of those detentions has been considered by courts in a long history of claimed abuses of detention. In *Zadvydas v. Davis*,[4] the U.S. Supreme Court held that such a detention could not extend beyond the "reasonable time" necessary to remove the alien. In *Tuan Thai v. Ashcroft*,[5] the court found that a detention for more than 16 months, with no prospect of removal, was unreasonable, and ordered the government to release the alien. In *Suarez-Martinez v. Rozos*,[6] the U.S. Supreme Court held that the reasoning of *Zadvydas* applied also to aliens detained after having been convicted of a crime that would result in deportation, even though the home-land of the detainee would not accept the detainee's return. The Court reasoned that notwithstanding the above, a person cannot constitutionally be detained indefinitely and that a reasonable time to detain an alien while deportation is pending should not exceed six months.

When Congress in 1996 passed the Illegal Immigration Reform and Immigrant Responsibility Act (IIRIRA), the category (and thus the number) of aliens who could be denied admission, detained, and eventually removed by Immigration and Customs Enforcement (ICE) increased substantially. As a combination of the act and the increase in the number of aliens entering the U.S. (both legally and illegally), a significant number of aliens were denied admission, detained, and removed in the years after 1996. The following cases involve admission, detention and removal issues before courts in the last few years.

Vartelas v. Holder, 132 S. Ct. 1497 (2012): Vartelas became a lawful permanent resident (LPR) in 1989. In 1994 he pled guilty to passing a counterfeit security, and served 4 months in jail. In 2003, he went to Greece for a one-week visit with relatives. When he returned he was denied readmission to the U.S. under provisions of the IIRIRA, and removal was ordered. Vartelas appealed, and the Board of Immigration Appeals (BIA) and the court of appeals denied his appeal. The U.S. Supreme Court granted review.

Under the IIRIRA any reentry by an LPR is treated as an "entry," and admission can be denied for any of the many reasons stated in the immigration statutes. Conviction of the crime Vartelas pled to is one of them. However, under the law in place when Vartelas pled guilty, an LPR could leave the country for brief periods without making an "entry" upon return to the U.S. The Supreme Court concluded that the change in the incidents of "entry" created by the IIRIRA imposed a punishment retroactively, and the statute did not authorize retroactive application of the entry rules. It reversed the removal order.

Torres v. Lynch, 136 S. Ct. 1619 (2016): An alien resident, even an LPR, is subject to removal under many conditions. One condition is being convicted of an "aggra-vated felony" while in the U.S. Torres came to the U.S. as a child and lived here ever since as an LPR. In 1999, he was convicted of attempted arson under a New York third-degree arson statute. Seven years later immigration officials started removal proceedings, based on the 1999 conviction. Torres' request for cancellation of the removal was denied, and both the BIA and the court of appeals denied his appeals. The court of appeals held that the New York arson statute qualified as an "aggra-vated felony" under immigration law, though other courts of appeal had reached the opposite conclusion for similar state statutes.

The Supreme Court agreed with the court of appeals in *Torres*, and affirmed the removal order. It held that a state statute did not require as an element of the offense an effect on interstate commerce to qualify as a crime "described" in the federal statute as an aggravated felony. Although the federal arson statute includes as an element of the offense that the property burned be engaged in interstate commerce, the Court said the engaged in interstate commerce element was purely jurisdictional. The "aggravated felony" list of crimes includes any crime with the same substantive elements, the Court held.

Rodriguez v. Robbins, 804 F.3d 1060 (9th Cir. 2015): Under the detention provisions of the immigration laws, which are mandatory in the case of an alien who has committed certain listed crimes, persons subject to removal are detained pending removal. Immigration and Customs Enforcement (ICE) detained 315,943 such persons in 2014; statistics suggest that ICE detains around 429,000 persons every year. Detention periods vary; for those not contesting removal, it lasts for 4 to 6 months. For those contesting removal (about 71 % of those detained) detention can last years. In *Rodriguez v. Robbins*, 804 F.3d 1060 (9th Cir. 2016) and *Lora v. Shanahan*, 804 F.3d 601 (2nd Cir. 2016) two federal appeals courts held that any detention without a bail hearing for more than six months violated the Due Process Clause. It also held that while such detainees are not automatically released after six months, at the bail hearing the government must prove the person detained is a flight or public safety risk. The government has filed a petition for review in the U.S. Supreme Court in each case.

INTENT UNDER IMMIGRATION LAW VIOLATIONS

Many immigration crimes require the government to prove some mental state of the defendant, such as "knowingly," "deliberately," or "intentionally." Where that is the case, federal courts have sometimes reached different results on how the required mental state must be proved. The following federal statutes and decisions illustrate this problem.

Marriage Fraud

8 U.S.C. § 1325(c) makes it a criminal violation for any person who "knowingly enters into a marriage for the purpose of evading any provision of the immigration laws." What does "knowingly" require the government to prove? Some federal courts have held that the government must prove the alien defendant had no intent to "establish a life" with the U.S. citizen. Under that reading of the statute, even if the purpose of the marriage was to obtain resident status in the United States, the intent to "establish a lifetime relationship" would save the marriage from being fraudulent. See *United States v. Gonzales*, 404 F.3d 96 (1st Cir. 2005), and *United States v. Yang*, 603 F.3d 1024 (8th Cir. 2010). More recent cases have held that the government need only prove that the marriage was entered with the purpose to obtain lawful resident status. The "intent to establish a life" would only be a factor in determining the "purpose" of the marriage. See *United States v. Ortiz-Mendez*, 634 F.3d 837 (5th Cir. 2011).

Harboring Illegal Aliens

8 U.S.C. § 1324 makes it a crime for any person "knowing or in reckless disregard" of the fact a person is an illegal alien to "harbor or shield from detection" the illegal alien. Some courts have held that the statute is violated if a person takes "any means" to shield the alien from discovery by the government. See *United States v. Ye*, 588 F.3d 411 (7th Cir. 2009). Other courts have held that the government must show the defendant intended to give the illegal alien "refuge" or "safe haven" from the government. Thus, in *United States v. Costello*, 666 F.3d 1040 (7th Cir. 2012), the court reversed a conviction for harboring an illegal alien when all the defendant did was permit the alien, her boyfriend, to live with her in her home.

CONTEMPT

contempt Failure or refusal to obey a court order (civil contempt), or interfering with the functioning of a court or legislative body (criminal contempt). Criminal contempt that occurs in the presence of the court can be punished summarily; other types of criminal contempt require the normal prosecution procedures.

Contempt is the willful disregard of the authority of a court of law or of a legislative body. Acts that delay, impede, or frustrate the functioning or the dignity of a court or legislative body may be held to be in contempt of that body. The deliberate, willful, and contumacious (obstinate) disobedience of a lawful order is a common reason for finding a person in contempt. Contempt that occurs in the presence of the court, often called "direct" contempt, can be punished summarily, that is, by an immediate finding of contempt and appropriate sentence. However, courts commonly require that the contempt occur completely in the court's presence for this summary action to be upheld. That is because actions taken outside the presence of the court are not personally observed by the judge, and thus must be proved in the usual manner. In that case, the usual procedures for proving facts must be followed. An example of this principle is the 2010 case of *Scialdone v. Commonwealth*.[7] In that case, two attorneys introduced into evidence documents that appeared to have been altered. The trial judge conducted an investigation of how the documents were altered, which included questioning witnesses who may have been involved in the alteration. The judge concluded the attorneys altered the document, and that offering the altered document was criminal contempt. It summarily sentenced the attorneys to short jail terms. On appeal, the Virginia Supreme Court reversed the contempt convictions, holding that because some of the facts needed for the contempt charge did not occur in the presence of the court, the summary finding of contempt was improper.

In 2015, the Florida Supreme Court held that failure to obey a court order to appear before the court is not direct contempt, but indirect contempt. A party in a divorce proceeding was ordered by the court to give his wife custody of the family dog. He refused, and failed to appear at a hearing to show cause why he should not be held in contempt for that refusal. When the husband didn't appear at that hearing, the district judge (clearly tired of it all!) found him in criminal contempt. The husband appealed, and the Florida Supreme Court said failing to appear in court is not the same as violating a court order in the presence of the court. The conduct was thus indirect criminal contempt, not direct criminal contempt, the court said, and the husband could not be found in criminal contempt without a hearing. *State v. De La Portilla*, 177 So.3d 965 (Fla. 2015)

Civil Contempt

civil contempt This is a remedial form of contempt order used to force people to do what they are lawfully required to do (answer questions, identify themselves, pay support money as ordered by a divorce court, and so on).

criminal contempt This is a criminal charge based on a person's actions in a court case or legislative proceeding and used to punish people by a fine or imprisonment for what they have done.

Contempt is classified as either civil or criminal. **Civil contempt** is used to compel people to do something they are obligated to do. **Criminal contempt** can be used to punish people for what they have done. Civil or criminal contempt is sometimes used in divorce cases, child custody cases, and other matters to compel people to comply with court orders.

A contempt order is treated as a civil contempt if the purpose of the contempt is to compel compliance with a court order. In such a case, confinement is permitted until the person confined complies with the order. However, where it becomes clear compliance will not or cannot occur, a civil contempt order of confinement is normally lifted. An example of this kind of contempt is the 2011 case of *Warmkessel v. Heffnee*.[8] There, the defendant failed to pay child support, and was sentenced to three months in jail. Pennsylvania law provides that imprisonment for civil contempt is permitted, but requires the sentencing judge to set a "purge" amount, the payment of which will obtain release of the defendant from prison.

In the 2011 case of *Turner v. Rogers*,[9] the U.S. Supreme Court for the first time considered the question of the right to appointed counsel in civil contempt cases, where the failure of a defendant to comply with a civil order resulted in imprisonment. In *Turner* a defendant owed $5,728.76 in back child support to the mother of his child. He was brought before a judge, and because he did not pay the amount owed, was sentenced to 12 months in jail, which sentence he could "purge" only by paying the full amount due. The defendant contended his imprisonment violated the Constitution, because he was not represented by counsel at the contempt hearing. State courts disagreed, and the U.S. Supreme Court granted review.

The Court held that the Sixth Amendment, which requires appointment of counsel for indigent defendants in criminal cases, did not apply to civil contempt cases. However, under the Due Process Clause, because of the prospect of incarceration, an attorney must be provided for an indigent defendant unless certain procedural protections were provided to the defendant. Those include (1) informing the defendant his ability to comply with the court order was a "critical issue" in the contempt proceeding, (2) use of a form to determine the defendant's financial ability to comply with the order, (3) an opportunity at the hearing for the defendant to respond to questions about his financial ability, and (4) an express finding by the court that the defendant possessed the financial ability to comply with the order. Since that did not happen in this case, the Court held, the defendant's incarceration violated the Due Process Clause.

Criminal Contempt

Criminal contempt is designed to protect the public interest by ensuring the effective functioning of the judicial and legislative systems. In 1968, the U.S. Supreme Court stated in *Bloom v. Illinois* that "criminal contempt is a crime in the ordinary sense; it is a violation of the law, a public wrong which is punishable by fine or imprisonment or both."[10] The Court quoted Justice Oliver Wendell Holmes in stating that "these contempts are infractions of the law, visited with punishment as such. If such acts are not criminal, we are in error as to the most fundamental characteristic of crimes as that word has been understood in English speech."

The defendant in the *Bloom* case was sentenced to 24 months in prison for submitting a falsely prepared will for probate. His demand for a jury trial was denied. In holding that in serious contempt cases the defendant had a right to a jury, the Court stated:

> Prosecution for contempt plays a significant role in the proper functioning of our judicial system; but despite the important values which the contempt power protects, courts and legislatures have gradually eroded the power of judges to try contempts of their own authority. In modern times, procedures in criminal contempt cases have come to mirror those used in ordinary criminal cases.[11]

Criminal contempt is treated as a crime, as stated above, which includes application of the Double Jeopardy Clause. In *United States v. Dixon*,[12] the U.S. Supreme Court held that a prior conviction of a defendant on a criminal contempt charge for violation of a protection order barred subsequent prosecution by the government for the crime that constituted the violation of the order. However, in a 2010 case the U.S. Supreme Court reversed its decision to grant a petition for certiorari on the question of whether a subsequent criminal contempt charge brought by a woman who obtained a protective order violated the Double Jeopardy Clause. In *In re Robertson*,[13] a federal court of appeals upheld a criminal contempt order based on the defendant's assault on the woman who filed the action. In an earlier proceeding the woman had obtained a civil protection order against the defendant, who subsequently violated the order on more than one occasion. The defendant and the government had entered into a plea agreement on criminal charges related to those violations, and the defendant served time in prison. The defendant thus argued that under *Dixon* the criminal contempt prosecution brought by the woman was barred by the Double Jeopardy Clause. The Supreme Court initially granted certiorari on that question, 130 S. Ct. 1011, but subsequently voted to deny certiorari as "improvidently granted," 130 S. Ct. 2184 (2010). Four Justices dissented, believing the subsequent criminal contempt conviction violated the Double Jeopardy Clause.[14]

Contempt Is a Specific Intent Crime That Requires Proof of Intentional Wrongdoing

In the 1976 case of *Commonwealth v. Washington,* the Supreme Court of Pennsylvania quoted other courts, holding,

> There is no contempt unless there is some sort of wrongful intent. *Offutt v. United States,* 98 U.S. App. D.C. 69, 232 F.2d 69, 72 (1956), *cert, denied* 351 U.S. 988, 76 S. Ct. 1049, 100 L. Ed. 1501 (1956). "[A] degree of intentional wrongdoing is an ingredient of the offense of criminal contempt." *In re Brown,* 147 U.S. App. D.C. 156, 454 F.2d 999, 1006 (1971). "Willfulness is, of course, an element of criminal contempt and must be proved beyond a reasonable doubt." *United States v. Greyhound Corporation,* 508 F.2d 529, 531 (7th Cir. 1974).[15]

In the *Washington* case, the defendant overslept and failed to appear on time at his trial. In reversing his contempt conviction, the Pennsylvania Supreme Court held,

> Were we to accept the prosecution's argument, any person, judge, attorney, witness, or party, who comes into the courtroom late can be held guilty of contempt of court, regardless of the reason for the lateness. We cannot accept such a conclusion. Unless the evidence establishes an intentional disobedience or an intentional neglect of the lawful process of the court, no contempt has been proven. Such is the case here. Judgment of sentence reversed.

In the 1976 case of *People v. Harris,* the defendant failed to pay a fine imposed for a prior criminal conviction.[16] Although the defendant showed that he had no money and was unemployed, he was found in contempt for failure to pay the fine. The Illinois Court of Appeals reversed the contempt finding, holding that there was no showing that the defendant willfully placed himself in a position to be unable to pay the fine.

Language by a Witness or Attorney That Would Justify a Contempt Finding

While answering a question on cross-examination, a witness used the expression *chicken shit.* As a result, the witness was found to be in direct contempt for the use of this term in a courtroom. The U.S. Supreme Court reversed the defendant's conviction in the case of *Eaton v. City of Tulsa,* holding,

> This single isolated usage of street vernacular, not directed at the judge or any officer of the court, cannot constitutionally support the conviction of criminal contempt. "The vehemence of language used is not alone the measure of the power to punish for contempt. The fires which it kindles must constitute an imminent, not merely a likely, threat to the administration of justice." *Craig v. Harney,* 331 U.S. 367, 376 (1947). In using the expletive in answering the question on cross-examination "it is not charged that [petitioner] here disobeyed any valid court order, talked loudly, acted boisterously, or attempted to prevent the judge or any other officer of the court from carrying on his court duties." *Holt v. Virginia,* 381 U.S. 131, 136 (1965); see also *In re Little,* 404 U.S. 553 (1972). In the circumstances, the use of the expletive thus cannot be held to "constitute an imminent … threat to the administration of justice."[17]

Contempt and the Crime of Failure to Appear (Bail Jumping)

In all states and in the federal court system, a criminal defendant free on bail may be charged with criminal contempt if he or she intentionally fails to appear at a scheduled hearing in his or her criminal case. The penalty for bail jumping is generally determined by the severity of the underlying crime charged. For example, in *Curley v. Commonwealth,*[18] the court reversed a conviction of first-degree bail jumping because the underlying criminal charge had been reduced from a felony to a misdemeanor before the bail jumping occurred. Under most state bail jumping

 CONTEMPT

Classification	Type	Procedure Used to Punish
Civil contempt is remedial and is used to force people to do what they are lawfully required to do (answer questions, identify themselves, pay support money as ordered by a divorce court, and so on).	Direct contempt is committed in the immediate presence and view or hearing of the court or legislative body.	Summary process: Only direct contempt may be punished summarily. If the court or legislative body does not act at the time the contempt is committed, notice and an opportunity for a hearing must be given to the person.
"Criminal contempt is a crime in the ordinary sense; it is a violation of the law, a public wrong which is punishable by fine or imprisonment or both." U.S. Supreme Court in Bloom v. Illinois, 391 U.S. 194, 88 S. Ct. 1477 (1968).	Constructive, or indirect, contempt is committed out of the presence or hearing of the court or legislative body. Although the matter or incident does not occur in or near the presence of a court or legislative body, it obstructs or delays the functioning of the court or the legislative body.[a]	Contempt hearings: Notice and an opportunity for a hearing (plus other due process rights) must be given for constructive (indirect contempt) and for direct contempt when the court or legislative body does not act immediately.

[a]State legislatures and the U.S. Congress have the constitutional power to hold persons in contempt, as well as the authority to issue subpoenas, grant immunity from prosecution, and demand within the law that persons appearing before them answer questions.

statutes, the crime is committed if the defendant is free on bail as a result of being charged with a crime. If the defendant does not appear at a scheduled hearing on the criminal charge, he or she can be convicted of bail jumping, even if the criminal charge is subsequently dismissed.[19]

Most states provide an affirmative defense to bail jumping if the defendant can show that his or her failure to appear at a scheduled hearing was the result of "uncontrollable circumstances" not created by the defendant. Hospitalization for a serious illness would be an example of this defense.

CRIMES BY PUBLIC OFFICIALS

If all people were angels who lived in peace and harmony with one another, then, as James Madison observed in *The Federalist Papers* of the 1780s, there would be no need for governments. But people are not angels, nor are they governed by angels (as Madison also pointed out more than 200 years ago).

The U.S. Supreme Court observed that "nothing can destroy a government more quickly than its failure to observe its own laws, or worse, its disregard of the charter of its own existence."[20] In 1928, Justice Louis D. Brandeis stated in his dissenting opinion in *Olmstead v. United States:* "Our Government is the potent, the omnipresent teacher. For good or ill, it teaches the whole people by its example. . . . If the Government becomes a lawbreaker, it breeds contempt for law; it invites every man to become a law unto himself; it invites anarchy."[21]

Cicero wrote long ago in *Pro Cluentio 53* that "we are in bondage to the law in order that we may be free." While president of the United States, Calvin Coolidge observed:

> Wherever the law goes, there civilization goes and stays. When the law fails, barbarism flourishes. Whoever scorns the law, whoever brings it into disrespect, whoever connives at its evasion, is an enemy of civilization. Change it if you will . . . but observe it always. That is government.

Some Crimes Committed by Public Officials and Others

Some of the many offenses committed by public officials and private individuals are as follows:

- Unauthorized (or excessive) use of force (assault and battery)
- False imprisonment
- Unauthorized wiretapping (federal felony) or bugging (state offense)
- **Perjury**[22] or **subornation of perjury** (the crime of perjury consists of knowingly and materially testifying falsely while under oath; the crime of subornation of perjury is inducing or knowingly permitting another person to testify falsely). The federal perjury statute, 18 U.S.C. § 1623, makes it perjury to "knowingly" make a "false material declaration" to a court or grand jury. In *Bronston v. United States,*[23] the U.S. Supreme Court held that an answer that is literally true, but either unresponsive to a question or that creates a false impression, cannot be perjury. For example, if the president of a corporation is asked, "Have you ever had a Swiss bank account?" and he answered, "The company has never had a Swiss bank account," his answer cannot be perjury even though it created the

perjury The crime of knowingly and materially testifying falsely while under oath.

subornation of perjury The crime of inducing or knowingly permitting another person to testify falsely while under oath.

false impression the president did not personally have such an account. In *United States v. Thomas,*[24] the court held the "literal truth" defense was not available to a professional cyclist who gave false answers to a grand jury investigating a company called BALCO about the distribution and use of steroids by athletes. Called before a grand jury, the defendant was asked if she had ever been "given" steroids by a BALCO representative. She testified "no." She was subsequently indicted for perjury under § 1623, and she raised the literal truth defense. She claimed her answer was literally true, because she paid for the steroids, and thus they were not "given" to her. The court said the defense is not available when the witness understands the meaning of the question in the context it was asked and the answer is false as to that meaning.

- Official misconduct and misconduct in public office (using the powers of one's office to obtain a dishonest advantage for oneself, or falsifying an entry in a record or report)
- Aiding, assisting, or permitting the escape of a prisoner
- Intimidating witnesses, prisoners, or others
- **Tampering with evidence** or falsifying evidence
- **Misprision of felony**. Some states and the federal government have codified this old common law crime. In 1998, Michael Fortier pleaded guilty to misprision of a felony (and other crimes) because he failed to warn officials of the plot to blow up the Alfred P. Murrah Federal Building in Oklahoma City.[25] Federal courts define the crime of misprision of a felony as follows:

> [T]o sustain a conviction . . . for misprision of felony it was incumbent upon the government to prove beyond a reasonable doubt (1) that . . . the principal had committed and completed the felony alleged; . . . (2) that the defendant had full knowledge of that fact; (3) that he failed to notify the authorities; and (4) that he took . . . affirmative steps to conceal the crime of the principal.[26]

- Bribery. The U.S. Supreme Court held that to prove a violation of the federal gratuity statute (18 U.S.C.A. § 201(c)(1)(A)), the government must prove a link between the thing of value given to a public official and a specific "official act" for which it was given.[27]

The federal court in the case of *United States v. Arthur* described the crime of bribery as follows:

> Not every gift, favor or contribution to a government or political official constitutes bribery. It is universally recognized that bribery occurs only if the gift is coupled with a particular criminal intent. . . . That intent is not supplied merely by the fact that the gift was motivated by some generalized hope or expectation of ultimate benefit on the part of the donor. . . . "Bribery" imports the notion of some more or less specific quid pro quo for which the gift or contribution is offered or accepted.[28]

- Extortion by a public official or employee in violation of the Hobbs Act, 18 U.S.C.A. § 1951. The public official or employee obtains payment because of his or her office and by use of "force, violence or fear." In *United States v. Swift,* the defendant was a city sewer director who received payments from a contractor

tampering with evidence Knowingly altering or damaging evidence intended to be used in a court proceeding.

misprision of felony Failing to report knowledge of a felony to the appropriate authorities.

in return for approval of payments made for work done on sewage pumping stations.[29] Another example of extortion under the Hobbs Act is as follows:

EXAMPLE

A bail bond agent who was also an alderman in a small town conspired with members of the police department to extort money from travelers passing through town in exchange for dismissal or reduction of drunk driving charges against the travelers.[30]

• Fraud and corruption.

CRIMES AGAINST GOVERNMENT

Espionage

espionage Giving or selling national military or defense secrets to a foreign nation.

Spying and being a party to **espionage** are forbidden by all democratic countries. Giving or selling national military or defense secrets to a foreign nation is a serious felony. A shocking number of Americans have been charged with or convicted of spying. Most spies today sell secrets for money.

The Federal Espionage Act forbids disclosing, transmitting, stealing, or receiving information that has been classified. Experience has shown that most of the violators of this act either work for the U.S. government and have security clearances or are part of a foreign government's spy operation. Espionage cases receiving national attention include the following:

• *Aldrich Ames* was an alcoholic for years, yet he worked for the Central Intelligence Agency and received regular promotions within the organization. On a civil servant's pay, he bought an expensive home in Washington, D.C., for cash, and he drove a Jaguar. To obtain the money to live a luxurious life, Ames delivered vast amounts of highly secret documents and information to the Soviet Union, which paid Ames millions of dollars. Ames betrayed at least a dozen of the United States' best spies working within Russia. All were jailed, and most were executed. Ames and his wife were taken into custody in 1994 after nine years of espionage.
• *Robert P. Hanssen* was convicted in May 2001 of selling highly sensitive national secrets to Russia for 15 years. Hanssen was a high-ranking FBI counterintelligence agent. It is believed that Hanssen also corroborated information that Aldrich Ames provided to the Russians.
• *John A. Walker, Jr.,* headed a spy ring of family members and friends. Officials called it the most damaging espionage conspiracy in decades. Walker received life imprisonment and said the Soviet Union paid $1 million for his information on military communication codes.
• *Jonathan Jay Pollard* provided secret information to Israel that was available to him as a U.S. Navy intelligence analyst. He received a long prison sentence.[31]
• The highest-ranking military officer to be convicted of spying was German-born George Trofimoff, a retired Army Reserve colonel. He was convicted in September 2001 of selling military secrets to Russia for more than 20 years.
• *Ronald A. Pelton* was convicted of selling military secrets from the National Security Agency to Russia.

- *Richard W. Miller,* a former FBI agent, became involved with a Russian woman and provided national secrets to Russia.
- In 2010, ten people who had lived in the United States for more than 10 years as ordinary citizens working ordinary jobs were arrested as "deep-cover" Russian spies. After revealing their true identities they all pled guilty to conspiracy to commit espionage. They were then returned to Russia in a "swap" for the release of four Russian citizens who had been jailed in Russia, accused of spying for England or the United States. Two of the four Russians released under this swap were high-ranking Russian military officers. See the *New York Times,* June 29, 2010 and July 9, 2010.
- In 2013, Sixing Lin was sentenced to 70 months in prison for violation of the Arms Export Control Act. In an effort to curry favor with government officials of the People's Republic of China, Lin stole thousands of computer files from a defense contractor that contained confidential rocket guidance and missile details.

Obstruction of Justice

obstruction of justice
Intentional acts that hinder, corrupt, or impede the functioning of the judicial system.

The offense of **obstruction of justice** was a common-law misdemeanor and is now part of the criminal code of the federal government and states. The offense seeks to protect the judicial system, both civil and criminal, from intentional acts that would

Justin Sullivan/Getty Images

Barry Bonds, the former professional baseball player, entering a courthouse. Bonds was convicted of obstruction of justice in a federal investigation of use of performance enhancing drugs in professional sports. In 2016. a court of appeals reversed his conviction.

hinder, corrupt, or impede the functioning of the system. Attempting to influence a juror, destroying or suppressing evidence, and seeking to prevent a witness from testifying or from attending a trial are some of the acts that have justified charging the offense of obstruction of justice.

In the early days of the law, resisting, hindering, or obstructing a law enforcement officer was a common form of obstruction of justice. Many states, however, have made this offense a separate offense from obstruction of justice.[32] For example, Chapter 843 of the Florida Criminal Code is entitled "Obstructing Justice." Within Florida Chapter 843 are 18 separate offenses, two of which forbid "resisting an officer." Tampering with evidence (destroying, concealing, or altering) is found in Florida Chapter 918.

Police officers can also be guilty of obstructing justice. In the 2013 case of *United States v. Moore*[33] a rookie police officer was convicted of obstruction of justice when he filled out an incident report that backed up the false incident report filed by his training officer. The training officer had beaten a suspect, who subsequently died from his injuries. The training officer reported the incident as a "medical incident," and did not mention the use of force.

The federal government has several "obstruction" statutes, depending on the federal investigation or proceeding that is obstructed. 18 U.S.C. §1512 (c) makes it a crime to obstruct an "official proceeding." In *United States v. Petruk*, 781 F.3d 438 (8th Cir. 2015) the court held that, as in other alleged violations of §1512 such as witness intimidation or evidence tampering, the prosecution must show that the obstructing conduct was done with the specific intent to obstruct a particular official proceeding.

In the obstruction trial of the baseball player Barry Bonds, the jury convicted him of one count of obstruction of justice under 18 U.S.C. §1503. Bonds testified for three hours before a grand jury investigating the use of steroids in professional sports; the trial jury convicted him based on one answer to a question. On appeal, the court of appeals reversed his conviction, stating that a single "rambling, non-responsive answer" to a simple question was not enough to convict Bonds of obstruction of justice. *United States v. Bonds*, 784 F.3d 582 (9th Cir. 2015)

It is a crime under federal and state statutes to escape from lawful custody. This includes not only the classic "jailbreak" scenario, but also many other kinds of "custody." For example, in the 2010 case of *United States v. Gowdy*[34] a defendant convicted in federal court was transferred to a state prison to serve a pending state sentence. After doing so he was to be transferred back to serve the federal sentence. By mistake, the defendant was released after serving the state sentence. Federal marshals discovered the mistake, and contacted the man, who agreed to turn himself in to the U.S. Marshal's office. When he didn't show up, the marshals tracked him down, and he was charged with escape under federal law. The defendant argued he was not in custody, and thus could not illegally escape. The court disagreed, saying "custody" required only that there exist a lawful judgment of conviction and sentence ordering the defendant confined to a federal prison.

Tax Evasion

To operate and provide services, government needs money. Former U.S. Supreme Court Justice Oliver Wendell Holmes pointed out that taxes are the price we pay for civilization. Much of the money needed to fund government services and activities is obtained through taxes. Deliberate tax evasion and tax fraud are generally punished as crimes. Tax evasion cases that have received national attention include the following:

- In 1973, the vice president of the United States, Spiro T. Agnew, resigned after pleading no contest to tax evasion charges.
- Socially prominent hotel owner Leona Helmsley was convicted of failure to report and pay taxes on $1.8 million in 1990. She was sentenced to four years in prison and fined $7.1 million.
- Former baseball player and manager Pete Rose spent five months in prison in 1990 for tax charges related to gambling and other income earned but not reported. In 2003, it was reported that Rose still owed about $1 million, on which he is making monthly payments.
- In the 1920s, gangster Al Capone and his gang had an extraordinary grip on Chicago. Law enforcement officials were unable to convict Capone of any of the many felonies they believed he had committed, but they were able to convict him of income tax fraud and send him to prison. Capone was one of the first people to be convicted with the use of the "net worth" method (circumstantial evidence). The U.S. Supreme Court affirmed the use of the net worth method in the case of *Holland v. United States*.[35]
- In a 2012 case, *Kawashima v. Holder*,[36] the U.S. Supreme Court held that a conviction for tax evasion qualified as an "aggravated felony" for purpose of immigration laws, and affirmed a decision ordering deportation of two Japanese citizens lawfully.

Other Criminal Violations

The President's Commission on Law Enforcement reported that the federal government alone has more than 2,800 crimes in the Federal Criminal Code. The President's Commission also pointed out that each state has the same number of or more crimes in their state statutes. The following are a very few of the many crimes reported in daily newspapers:

- States often make the failure of an employer to withhold income taxes on employees' wages and salaries a crime. Under California law, employers who fail to withhold can be charged with a felony. (See the May 3, 2001, *New York Times* article, "California Raids a Business that Refuses to Withhold Taxes.")
- State election laws sometimes make it a felony to induce a person to vote if the inducement is worth one dollar or more. A New York woman came to Wisconsin and passed out packages of cigarettes to homeless men as an inducement to vote in the presidential election of 2000. She was fined $5,000. (See *Milwaukee Journal Sentinel*, "$5,000 Settles Election Case," May 4, 2001.)
- States often make failure to report for jury duty when summoned a crime. In Wisconsin, the misdemeanor is punished by a $40 fine, and ignorance of the law is not a defense. (*Milwaukee Journal Sentinel*, "County Prosecuting Jury Service No-Shows," October 31, 2000.)
- Bootlegging whiskey has made millionaires of some families in the Appalachian hills of Virginia and West Virginia. Cigarette smuggling is a problem in the

Detroit area. Both crimes cause federal and state government to lose tax revenue. The federal government claimed a loss of $2.9 million in unpaid federal taxes for one moonshiner alone. (See the September 9, 2001, *New York Times* article, "Alleged Bootleggers Face Sobering Case," and the May 20, 1997, *Detroit Free Press* article, "Cigarette Smugglers Busted.")

- Criminal nonpayment of child support is a crime in all states, and is frequently charged. The federal government also makes such nonpayment a crime, primarily as a way to assist states in their efforts to apprehend nonpaying defendants who flee a state to avoid prosecution.
- Criminal antitrust laws, such as the Sherman Antitrust Act (1890), the Clayton Act (1914), and the Robinson-Patman Act (1936). These laws prohibit individuals and corporations from taking actions to create monopolies or engaging in unreasonable restraints of trade, such as discriminatory pricing schemes, market allocation agreements, or agreements to restrict production, output, or competition. These laws have successfully protected consumers from many predatory practices of persons and businesses in the United States.

LEARNING OBJECTIVES SUMMARY

LO 1. **List the various kinds of conduct made criminal under the immigration laws.**
The immigration laws make it a crime to make a false entry into this country, either by illegal crossing or by using false documents, to assist others to make an illegal entry into or stay in this country, to reenter after being removed, or to harbor or hire an illegal alien. They also make the commission of certain aggravated crimes the basis for removal of a legal alien from the U.S, or the denial of reentry to the U.S.

LO 2. **Distinguish civil contempt from criminal contempt.**
Civil contempt is punishment used to coerce a defendant into obeying a lawful court order; criminal contempt is punishment for actions that constitute a "public wrong," just like ordinary criminal laws.

LO 3. **Explain the connection between a gift and an official act required for conviction under the bribery laws.**

All that is required for a gift to be an illegal gratuity is that the gift was given or received with the specific intent to obtain some favorable treatment for the giver in the future, although the exact nature of the return need not be expressed.

LO 4. **State the reason the U.S. Supreme Court declared invalid some provisions in the Arizona laws directed at illegal aliens.**
In Arizona v. United States the Supreme Court held that provisions of the Arizona law directed at alien registration and control interfered with federal laws on those subjects, and thus were preempted by the federal laws.

LO 5. **State the limits on summary contempt convictions.**
Summary contempt is proper only where all the actions making up the contempt occurred in the presence of the judge.

KEY TERMS

contempt, p. 540
civil contempt, p. 540
criminal contempt, p. 540

perjury, p. 544
subornation of perjury, p. 544
tampering with evidence, p. 545

misprision of felony, p. 545
espionage, p. 546
obstruction of justice, p. 547

CASE ANALYSIS AND WRITING EXERCISES

1. 18 U.S.C. §1326 (a) makes it a crime, punishable by up to 2 years in prison, for an illegal alien who has previously been removed or deported to be "found" in the U.S. Is such a person "found" in the U.S. under the statute if he is apprehended by border control officers while trying to leave the U.S.? In *United States v. Rojas*, 770 F.3d 366 (9th Cir. 2014), *cert denied* 135 S. Ct. 2312 (2015) the answer was "Yes." In *United States v. Vasquez Macias*, 740 F.3d 96 (2nd Cir. 2014) the answer was "No." How, if at all, are these cases different? Which seems to be the better result from an immigration policy perspective?

2. It is a federal crime for any person to enter into a marriage for the purpose of evading immigration laws. In *United States v. Sonmez*, 777 F.3d 684 (4th Cir. 2015), *cert denied* 136 S. Ct. 689 (2015) the defendant, a Turkish national, outstayed his visa and became an illegal alien in the U.S. He then married a U.S. citizen, and applied for permanent residence status under immigration rules. His application was denied, and he was charged under 8 U.S.C. §1325(c), the marriage fraud statute. What jury instructions did the defendant request at his trial? Why was the trial judge correct to refuse to give those instructions?

3. Persons with lawful permanent resident (LPR) status are subject to removal if they commit an "aggravated felony" while in the U.S. "Aggravated felony" is defined in the immigration statutes by a lengthy list of crimes, one of which is "sexual abuse of a minor." If the crime is under state law, it qualifies as an "aggravated felony" for removal purposes if a conviction under the state law "necessarily" includes facts that would be a violation of a similar federal criminal law. In *Amos v. Lynch*, 790 F.3d 512 (4th Cir. 2015) the defendant was convicted in 1990 of "causing abuse to a child" under a Maryland law. Under the Maryland statute, causing abuse included failing to prevent another from abusing a child. In 2008, immigration officials began removal proceedings against the defendant, contending his 1990 conviction was an "aggravated felony" that justified his removal. The Board of Immigration Appeals agreed, and the defendant appealed. The court of appeals reversed the removal order, holding that the conviction under Maryland's child abuse statute did not "match" the "sexual abuse of a child" crime listed in the federal statutes. What did the defendant do in the Maryland conviction? Why wasn't that a sufficient reason for removal?

4. Among the many laws passed in 2010 by the Arizona legislature that have an impact on immigration and thus pose a federal preemption problem is Ariz. Rev. Stat. §13-2929. This law makes it a crime for any person "who is in violation of a criminal offense" to harbor or transport an illegal alien. How does a person know if she is included in the class of persons covered by the statute? If she could determine the answer to that question, is the Arizona statute, like some of the other Arizona statutes the U.S. Supreme Court said were preempted by federal immigration laws, also preempted? See *Valle del Sol Inc. v. Whiting*, 732 F.3d 1006 (9th Cir. 2013), *cert denied* 134 S. Ct. 1876 (2014).

ENDNOTES

1. 2012 WL 6200276 (7th Cir. 2012).

2. 132 S. Ct. 2492 (2012).

3. *United States v. Alabama*, 691 F.3d 1269 (11th Cir. 2012), *cert. denied*, 2013 WL 210698 (2013).

4. 533 U.S. 678 (2001).

5. 366 F.3d 790 (9th Cir. 2004).

6. 125 S. Ct. 716 (2005).

7. 689 S.E.2d 716 (Va. 2010).

8. 17 A.3d 408 (Pa. Super. 2011), review denied, 34 A.3d 833 (Pa. 2011).

9. 131 S. Ct. 2507 (2011).

10. 391 U.S. 194, 88 S. Ct. 1477 (1968).

11. *Bloom v. Illinois*, 391 U.S. 194, 206 (1968). New Jersey courts have held that "before a judge makes a contempt determination the accused should be permitted to speak," 357 A.2d at 276 (1976). In the case of *In re Logan Jr.*, 52 N.J. 475, 246 A.2d 441 (1968), the court held: "The

pronouncement of guilt before according that opportunity places the defendant at the disadvantage of trying to persuade a mind apparently already made up, and also puts the judge in the possibly embarrassing position of reversing himself if such persuasion results."

12. 509 U.S. 688 (1993).

13. 940 A.2d 1050 (D.C. Cir. 2008).

14. After remand, the U.S. Court of Appeals for the D.C. Circuit held that the contempt prosecution was brought by the government, but that the contempt prosecution did not violate the earlier plea agreement.

15. 466 Pa. 506, 353 A2d 806 (1976).

16. 41 Ill. App. 3d 690, 354 N.E.2d 648 (1976).

17. 415 U.S. 697, 94 S. Ct. 1228 (1974). In a dissenting opinion, Justice William H. Rehnquist suggests "a flat rule, analogous to the hoary doctrine of the law of torts that every dog is entitled to one bite, to the effect that every witness is entitled to one free contumacious or other impermissible remark."

18. 895 S.W.2d 10 (Ky. App. 1995).

19. See *State v. Downing*, 93 P.3d 900 (Wash. App. 2004).

20. *Mapp v. Ohio*, 367 U.S. 643, 81 S. Ct. 1684 (1961).

21. 277 U.S. 438, 48 S. Ct. 564 (1928).

22. In 1968, the President's Commission on Crime noted that perjury has always been widespread and that there must be more effective deterrents against perjury to ensure the integrity of trials. Another writer commented that few crimes "except fornication are more prevalent or carried off with greater impunity." See "Perjury: The Forgotten Offense," *Journal of Criminal Law & Criminology* 65 (1974).

23. 409 U.S. 352 (1973).

24. 612 F.3d 1107 (9th Cir. 2010), *cert. denied*, 131 S. Ct. 1836 (2011).

25. See the *New York Times* article, "Sentencing the Man Who Failed to Warn of a Fatal Conspiracy," May 13, 1998.

26. Court in *U.S. v. Stuard*, 556 F.2d 1, 22 CrL 2337 (6th Cir. 1977), quoting *Neal v. U.S.*, 102 R2d 643 (8th Cir. 1939). See also *Pope v. State*, 284 Md. 309, 396 A.2d 1054 (1979).

27. *U.S. v. Sun-Diamond Growers of California*, 119 S. Ct. 1402 (1999). In other criminal cases concerning the biggest sting operation conducted by the FBI, more than sixty lawyers, bailiffs, judges, and other people in the Chicago court system were indicted for bribery. Operation Greylord was conducted because money was used to buy and fix criminal and civil Chicago court cases. Other criminal charges resulting from Operation Greylord included mail fraud, racketeering, and obstruction of justice.

28. 544 F.2d 730 (4th Cir.). The decision of the court continues as follows:

This requirement of criminal intent would, of course, be satisfied if the jury were to find a "course of conduct of favors and gifts flowing" to a public official in exchange for a pattern of official actions favorable to the donor even though no particular gift or favor is directly connected to any particular official act. *U.S. v. Baggett* (4th Cir. 1973) 481 F.2d 114, *cert. denied*, 414 U.S. 1116 (1973) (Travel Act prosecution involving alleged bribery of Maryland County Commissioner). Moreover, as the Seventh Circuit has held, it is sufficient that the gift is made on the condition "that the offeree act favorably to the offer or when necessary." *U.S. v. Isaacs* (7th Cir. 1974) 493 F.2d 1124, 1145, *cert. denied*, 417 U.S. 976 (1974) (construing Illinois statute in a Travel Act prosecution). It does not follow, however, that the traditional business practice of promoting a favorable business climate by entertaining and doing favors for potential customers becomes bribery merely because the potential customer is the government. Such expenditures, although inspired by the hope of greater government business, are not intended as a quid pro quo for that business: they are in no way conditioned upon the performance of an official act or pattern of acts or upon the recipient's express or implied agreement to act favorably to the donor when necessary.

29. 732 F2d 878 (11th Cir. 1984). In the 1992 case of *Evans v. U.S.* (504 U.S. 255, 112 S. Ct. 1881), the U.S. Supreme Court held that a demand or other act of inducement by the public official was not necessary to convict of extortion under the Hobbs Act.

30. See *United States v. Stephens*, 964 F.2d 424 (5th Cir. 1992).

31. See *United States v. Pollard*, 959 F.2d 1011, *review denied*, U.S. Supreme Court, 52 CrL 3033 (1992).

32. An example of "resisting law enforcement" is *Jackson v. State*, 576 N.E.2d 607 (Ind. App. 1991), in which the defendant refused to provide identification under circumstances that obligated him to do so. An example of "interfering with an officer" is *State v. Peruta*, 591 A.2d 140 (Conn. App. 1991), in which a jury found that the defendant, a news cameraman, interfered with law enforcement officers at the scene of a fatal automobile accident.

33. 708 F.3d 639 (5th Cir. 2013).

34. 628 F.3d 1265 (11th Cir. 2010).

35. 348 U.S. 121 (1954).

36. 132 S. Ct. 1166 (2012).

Appendix

Sections of the U.S. Constitution Related to Criminal Law

(RATIFIED IN 1788)

Preamble

We the People of the United States, in Order to form a more perfect union, establish Justice, insure domestic Tranquility, provide for the common defense, promote the general Welfare, and secure the Blessings of Liberty to ourselves and our Posterity, do ordain and establish this Constitution for the United States of America.

Article I

Section 1   All legislative Powers herein granted shall be vested in a Congress of the United States, which shall consist of a Senate and House of Representatives. . . .

Article II

Section 1   The executive Power shall be vested in a President of the United States of America. . . .

Article III

Section 1   The judicial Power of the United States, shall be vested in one supreme Court, and in such inferior Courts as the Congress may from time to time ordain and establish. . . .

Article IV

Section 4   The United States shall guarantee to every State in this Union a Republican Form of Government, and shall protect each of them against Invasion; and on Application of the Legislature, or of the Executive [when the Legislature cannot be convened] against domestic Violence. . . .

Article VI

This constitution, and the Laws of the United States which shall be made in Pursuance thereof; and all Treaties made, or which shall be made, under the Authority of the United States, shall be the supreme Law of the Land; and the Judges in every State shall be bound thereby, any Thing in the Constitution or Laws of any State to the Contrary notwithstanding. . . .

AMERICAN BILL OF RIGHTS (RATIFIED IN 1791)

Amendment 1

Congress shall make no law respecting an establishment of religion, or prohibiting the free exercise thereof; or abridging the freedom of speech, or of the press; or the right of the people peaceably to assemble, and to petition the Government for a redress of grievances.

Amendment II

A well regulated Militia, being necessary to the security of a free State, the right of the people to keep and bear Arms, shall not be infringed.

Amendment III

No Soldier shall, in time of peace be quartered in any house, without the consent of the Owner, nor in time of war, but in a manner to be prescribed by law.

Amendment IV

The right of the people to be secure in their persons, houses, papers, and effects, against unreasonable searches and seizures, shall not be violated, and no

Warrants shall issue, but upon probable cause, supported by Oath affirmation, and particularly describing the place to be searched, and the persons or things to be seized.

Amendment V

No person shall be held to answer for a capital, or otherwise infamous crime, unless on a presentment or indictment of a Grand Jury, except in cases arising in the land or naval forces, or in the Militia, when in actual service in time of War or public danger, nor shall any person be subject for the same offence to be twice put in jeopardy of life or limb; nor shall be compelled in any criminal case to be a witness against himself, nor be deprived of life, liberty, or property, without due process of law; nor shall private property be taken for public use, without just compensation.

Amendment VI

In all criminal prosecutions, the accused shall enjoy the right to a speedy and public trial, by an impartial jury of the State and district wherein the crime shall have been committed, which district shall have been previously ascertained by law, and to be informed of the nature and cause of the accusation; to be confronted with the witnesses against him; to have compulsory process for obtaining witnesses in his favor, and to have the Assistance of Counsel for his defence.

Amendment VII

In suits at common law, where the value in controversy shall exceed twenty dollars, the right of trial by jury shall be preserved, and no fact tried by a jury, shall be otherwise reexamined in any Court of the United States, than according to the rules of the common law.

Amendment VIII

Excessive bail shall not be required, nor excessive fines imposed, nor cruel and unusual punishments inflicted.

Amendment IX

The enumeration in the Constitution, of certain rights, shall not be construed to deny or disparage others retained by the people.

Amendment X

The powers not delegated to the United States by the Constitution, nor prohibited by it to the States, are reserved to the States respectively, or to the people....

14TH AMENDMENT, RATIFIED 1868

Amendment XIV

Section 1   All persons born or naturalized in the United States, and subject to the jurisdiction thereof, are citizens of the United States and of the State wherein they reside. No State shall make or enforce any law which shall abridge the privileges or immunities of citizens of the United States; nor shall any State deprive any person of life, liberty, or property, without due process of law; nor deny to any person within its jurisdiction the equal protection of the laws....

accomplice One who aids another in the commission of a crime. An accomplice is generally treated the same as a principal.

actus reus The criminal act.

administrative crime Crime created by government administrative agencies under specific authority and guidelines granted to the regulatory or administrative agency by law of that state or the federal government.

affirmative defense A defense to a criminal charge in which the defendant generally admits doing the criminal act but claims an affirmative defense such as duress (he or she was forced) or entrapment.

aggravated assault Assault made more serious by presence of a firearm or as part of intent to commit a felony.

aggravated battery Battery that causes serious bodily injury or is committed with a deadly weapon.

aggravating circumstances A consideration in imposing the death penalty that judges and juries must make a finding of statutory aggravating circumstances to justify the penalty.

aider and abettor One who provides help to the person who commits a crime, either before or after the crime is committed.

alibi A defense to criminal prosecution on the grounds that the defendant physically could not have committed the crime because at the time the crime was committed, he or she was at another place.

armed robbery Forcible stealing combined with the use of a deadly or dangerous weapon, or which results in serious bodily injury to another.

arson A person's deliberate, willful, and malicious burning of a building or personal property.

assault In many instances, an assault is an attempt to commit a battery, but many states also make other conduct an assault. It could be combined with a charge of battery to constitute the crimes of "assault and battery."

assisting suicide The act of furnishing the means of a suicide, pursuant to a statute that permits such assistance.

attempt crimes Acts that are a substantial step toward the commission of a crime that is not yet completed.

bank fraud Fraud aimed at banks and other financial institutions.

battered woman defense Evidence of past abuse offered by women charged with violence against their abusers to show its psychological effects as part of their claim of self-defense.

battery A successful assault, in which the victim is actually and intentionally (or knowingly) struck by the defendant.

benefit of clergy A medieval limit on capital punishment. People convicted of a capital crime entitled to claim the benefit of clergy (by the fifteenth century, anyone who could read) could not be executed for their offense. By the end of the eighteenth century, the privilege had been eliminated for most crimes.

bill of attainder Legislative act that inflicts punishment without trial; prohibited by Article I, Sections 9 and 10, of the Constitution.

"booze it and lose it" laws Laws, enacted in more than thirty states, that give the police the authority to immediately seize the driver's licenses of people who fail or refuse sobriety tests.

"born alive" requirement To be able to charge homicide of a newborn baby, the prosecution must be able to prove that the child was living at the time it was killed.

bribery Offering a gift or payment to another with the specific intent to obtain some unlawful particular *quid pro quo* for the gift or payment.

burglary Unlawful entry into the premises of another with intent to steal or commit a felony. Two hundred years ago in England, an illegal entry into the home of another by force and at night was punishable by death if the entry was done to steal or commit a felony.

capital punishment Inflicting deadly injury as punishment for criminal conduct.

carjacking Forcibly taking possession of a motor vehicle in the possession of another against his or her will with intent either to permanently or temporarily deprive the person of possession.

"castle" doctrine The doctrine permitting people who have been assaulted in their homes by a trespasser to stand their ground and use such force as is necessary and reasonable to defend themselves.

certiorari A form of review of lower court decisions by the U.S. Supreme Court. Certiorari is discretionary with the Court, and most petitions requesting it are denied. Traditional legal doctrine is that no conclusion can be drawn from a denial of certiorari.

check kiting Creating multiple checking accounts at multiple banks for the purpose of writing fraudulent checks from one account and depositing them in another, and then withdrawing funds from the deposit bank.

child pornography Movies, pictures, or drawings that depict children in explicit sexual relations. Unlike adult pornography, child pornography need not be obscene to be criminal.

civil contempt This is a remedial form of contempt order used to force people to do what they are lawfully required to do (answer questions, identify themselves, pay support money as ordered by a divorce court, and so on).

"clear and present danger" test One of the tests used to judge government restrictions on speech.

coercion A person who forces (coerces) another to commit a crime can be charged and convicted of the crime committed in addition to other offenses.

common design or plan Scope of liability of persons who are party to a conspiracy or other agreement to do an unlawful act.

common law The earliest type of law. Common law was created by judges based on custom, usages, and moral concepts of the people. Most law today is statutory law enacted by legislative bodies.

common law crimes Crimes created by judges.

competency to stand trial Defendants must have the ability to cooperate with their attorneys and the ability to understand the charges and proceedings against them.

computer trespass Unlawful access to a computer or computer system with intent to commit a crime, or unlawful access to a computer or computer system maintained by a government unit.

concurrence The requirement in crimes requiring proof of mental intent that the forbidden act and guilty mind must occur at the same time or otherwise be linked. For example, trustees, guardians, or lawyers might have possession of another person's money (physical act). However, for the crime of embezzlement to occur they must intentionally and wrongfully misappropriate this money (forbidden act and guilty mind).

conspiracy An agreement between two or more persons to engage in unlawful acts.

conspirator A person who is a party to an agreement to commit an unlawful act.

contempt Failure or refusal to obey a court order (civil contempt), or interfering with the functioning of a court or legislative body (criminal contempt). Criminal contempt that occurs in the presence of the court can be punished summarily; other types of criminal contempt require the normal prosecution procedures.

controlled substance A drug that may be possessed or sold only as permitted by state or federal law.

corporal punishment Inflicting nondeadly physical injury as punishment for criminal conduct

corpus delicti In all criminal cases, the government must prove that the crime charged was committed (corpus delicti) and that the defendant was party to the crime (committed the crime or was an accomplice).

corroborative evidence Physical evidence or witness testimony other than from the victim that supports the claim that a crime occurred.

crime of terrorizing A crime that creates a state of extreme fear, dread, or fright.

criminal contempt This is a criminal charge based on a person's actions in a court case or legislative proceeding and used to punish people by a fine or imprisonment for what they have done.

criminal liability of corporations The rules for making corporations liable for actions taken by officers, directors, or employees. Corporations can be vicariously criminally liable for actions of their agents if the offense is minor, a duty is specifically assigned to a corporation, a statute explicitly creates vicarious criminal liability, or the person committing the crime is acting in the interest of the corporation and is a high managerial agent.

criminology The sociological and psychological study of the causes, development, and control of crime, as well as the conditions under which criminal law developed.

cruel and unusual punishment Under the Eighth Amendment, a limitation on punishment for criminal conduct.

CTRs (currency transaction reports) Reports that businesses, banks, and financial institutions are required to file for cash transactions of more than $10,000. CTRs can help determine whether tax fraud or money laundering is occurring.

cybercrime Criminal acts implemented through use of a computer or other form of electronic communication.

deadly force Force that is likely to cause or is capable of causing death or serious bodily injury.

defamation The offense of injuring the character or reputation of another by oral or written communication of false statements. Defamation consists of libel (written offense) or slander (oral offense).

defense of another The elements to evaluate whether an act of force for defense of another is justified include the unlawfulness of the action toward the other, the necessity to defend the other

immediately, and the reasonableness of the act of defense under the circumstances.

defiant trespass Remaining in a place where one is not privileged to be even after notice of trespass is given.

diminished capacity defense A defense for criminal responsibility based on the fact that because of mental or emotional conditions, the defendant did not possess the required *mens rea* for conviction of crime charged.

disorderly conduct Loud, obnoxious, or other offensive conduct in a public place.

double jeopardy A defense, stated in the Fifth Amendment, to prosecution on the grounds that the defendant has been tried before on the same charge, and acquitted.

drug paraphernalia Objects that are primarily intended or designed for use with illegal drugs.

Dual Sovereignty Doctrine A doctrine that different governments may each file separate criminal actions for the same criminal act.

due process The constitutional guarantee that criminal arrests and trials must meet certain minimum standards of fairness (procedural due process) and that laws not violate constitutional rights (substantive due process).

duress A defense to criminal prosecution on the grounds that the defendant was forced to commit the criminal act.

embezzlement To wrongfully appropriate money or property entrusted to one for one's own use.

entrapment The defense that a law enforcement officer used excessive temptation or urging to wrongfully induce the defendants to commit a crime they would not have ordinarily committed.

espionage Giving or selling national military or defense secrets to a foreign nation.

euthanasia A killing of a terminally sick or injured individual with only a short time to live. Also called mercy killing.

ex post facto Criminal law made retroactive to punish prior conduct not criminal when done. Prohibited by Article I, Sections 9 and 10, of the Constitution.

extortion   Obtaining property by threats of future harm. It differs from robbery in that robbery requires threat of immediate harm.

extradition   The surrender of an accused criminal under the provisions of a treaty or statute by one authority to another having jurisdiction.

false imprisonment   Unlawful restraint or detention of a person.

federal enclaves   Federally owned and controlled lands.

felony   The most serious grade of crime; usually includes possibility of prison sentence.

felony murder   Most states and the federal government have felony murder statutes that punish as murder the causing of death of another while the defendant is committing a felony of violence. A felony murder conviction does not require a showing of malice or deliberate intent to kill.

fence   A person who traffics in stolen property (receiving, concealing, possessing, buying, transferring, and so on).

feticide   Murder of an unborn child.

field sobriety tests   Field tests used to evaluate a motorist's alcohol or drug impairment. They include HGN testing, the walk-and-turn test, and the one-leg stand test.

fighting words   Speech which, because it will likely incite immediate violence, is not protected by the First Amendment.

forensic science   scientific principles and tests used in courts of law.

forfeiture   Going back to early English law, the concept and use of seizing the property that was used to commit a crime.

forgery   Wrongfully signing a writing or instrument in the name of the person who issued the writing or instrument, or to whom it was payable.

fraud   Deceitful means or acts used to cheat a person, corporation, or governmental agency.

Good Samaritan laws   Laws that encourage people to come to the aid of another or to defend another against unlawful force or interference.

guilty but mentally ill   A defendant may be found guilty but mentally ill if all the following are found beyond a reasonable doubt: (1) defendant is guilty of the offense; (2) defendant was mentally ill at the time the offense was committed; and (3) defendant was not legally insane at the time the offense was committed.

habeas corpus   A writ that compels the authority holding a person in confinement to explain the basis for that confinement. Used frequently as a method for state and federal prisoners to attack the constitutionality of their imprisonment. Both the federal government and states have some form of habeas corpus laws, often called post-conviction relief laws.

home invasion robbery   Robbery of persons inhabiting a dwelling.

homicide   The killing of one human being by another. There are three types of homicide: justifiable, excusable, and felonious.

hostage taking   The use or threat of use of force to restrain or confine a person with the intent to use the person as a hostage to compel another person to perform some act.

identity theft   Theft based on stealing a real person's identification information (true name) or theft based on creating a fictitious person's identification (synthetic identity).

immunity   An exemption from criminal prosecution based on the U.S. Constitution, statutes, or international agreements.

imperfect self-defense   A homicide in which the killer subjectively, but unreasonably, believes that his or her conduct was necessary. It may be unlawful if the killing was done with excessive or unnecessary force. An unnecessary killing in self-defense, in defense of another, or to prevent or terminate a felony of violence could be imperfect self-defense.

incest   Sexual relations between persons closely related.

inciting   The offense of urging another to commit an unlawful act.

infant (child)   Under the civil law, a person who has not yet reached the age of majority, whether that age is 18, 19, 20, or 21, as determined by the law of each jurisdiction.

inference A conclusion or deduction that a jury or judge may draw from a fact or a group of facts presented to them.

in loco parentis (Latin; "in place of the parents") Any person taking the place of the parents has the duties and responsibilities of the parents and may reasonably discipline a child in his or her care. This category includes legal guardians, foster parents, and public schoolteachers.

insanity tests Tests to determine legal and moral liability.

intellectual property fraud Theft, piracy, or counterfeiting of ideas, inventions, artistic works, and the like.

intent The mental purpose or design to commit a specific act (or omission).

jurisdiction Power to create and enforce laws. The federal government has power to create laws under the U.S. Constitution; each state has the legislative power to create laws effective within the state; city and village police departments have the power to enforce the laws; and local and state courts have power to sit in judgment of those accused of violating the laws.

kidnapping False imprisonment coupled with movement of the victim.

Magna Carta The document signed by King John in 1215 giving certain rights to his nobles. Successive kings affirmed this charter before Parliament.

mail fraud A fraudulent scheme, no matter its purpose or method, that uses either private or public delivery service.

"make my day" rules Rules adopted by some states that put no limits on the use of deadly force by the occupant of a dwelling in response to a trespasser.

manslaughter Criminal homicides other than murder. Most states provide for two degrees of manslaughter: voluntary and involuntary.

maritime jurisdiction Jurisdiction of the United States over actions within territorial waters of the United States on U.S. ships, or stateless vessels on the high seas.

martial law A state of military control over civilian populations as declared by state or federal government.

mayhem and malicious disfigurement Willfully inflicting an injury on another so as to cripple or mutilate the person.

Megan's laws Laws passed in many states requiring convicted sex offenders to register with a state or local registration office. Named after a young girl killed by a convicted sex offender.

menacing Intentionally placing or attempting to place another in fear of immediate serious physical injury.

mens rea The criminal intent or state of mind.

misdemeanor Offenses that carry punishment of a degree less than felonies. Usually misdemeanor crimes do not involve prison sentences.

misprision of felony Failing to report knowledge of a felony to the appropriate authorities.

mistake of law A claim by a defendant that the defendant did not know the action taken violated the criminal law.

mitigating circumstances A consideration in imposing the death penalty that judges and juries must make findings of the mitigating circumstances that would weigh against the imposition of the death penalty.

Model Penal Code (MPC) Proposed criminal law developed by the American Law Institute, a group of lawyers, judges, and teachers. Many states have modeled their criminal codes on the Model Penal Code.

money laundering The crime of disguising money obtained illegally by channeling it through legitimate commercial and financial transactions.

motive The cause, inducement, or reason why an act is committed.

murder Unlawful homicide with malice aforethought.

M'Naghten rule The insanity defense rule requiring proof that because of mental disease or defect defendants did not know the scope or character of their actions.

necessity A defense to criminal prosecution on the grounds that the harm to be avoided outweighed the harm caused by the crime committed. Necessity will not justify taking another person's life.

nulla poena sine lege The principle of legality; no act should be made criminal or punished without advance warning in the form of legislative act.

nystagmus A persistent, rapid, involuntary, side-to-side eye movement.

obscenity Communication that the average person, using contemporary community standards, would find appeals to the prurient interests or depicts sexual conduct in a patently offensive manner and, taken as a whole, lacks serious artistic, literary, political, or scientific value.

obstruction of justice Intentional acts that hinder, corrupt, or impede the functioning of the judicial system.

offensive touching Unpermitted physical contact with another person, usually limited to "private" or genital parts.

"overbreadth" doctrine The constitutional law doctrine that invalidates laws that regulate conduct so broadly that they interfere with individual freedoms.

parties to the principal crime Under common law, persons who either committed the crime, or aided or abetted the commission of the crime or the persons who committed the crime.

perfect self-defense A homicide in which the killer subjectively believes that his or her conduct was necessary and reasonable and that, by objective standards, a reasonable person would believe it was lawful and complied with the requirements of the law. The homicide is either justifiable or excusable, and it carries no criminal liability.

perjury The crime of knowingly and materially testifying falsely while under oath.

Pinkerton rule The rule followed in federal courts that one conspirator is liable for crimes committed by another conspirator, if foreseeable and done in furtherance of the conspiracy.

police power The inherent power of every state and local government, subject to constitutional limits, to enact criminal laws.

pornography Movies, pictures, writings, and other expressions that are intended to arouse sexual incitement and have no artistic merit or redeeming social value.

posse comitatus Latin, meaning "power of the country." In the United States, it traditionally has referred to the military forces.

possession with intent to deliver A criminal case in which the state presents evidence showing that the accused had possession of a large amount of an illegal drug, meaning more than the accused would personally use.

post-crime offenses Actions taken after a crime has been committed, with knowledge that the crime was committed, which provide aid to the person who committed the crime.

preliminary, anticipatory, and inchoate crimes Criminal acts that lead to or are attempts to commit other crimes.

premeditation Mental determination to unlawfully kill another person after planning or reflection on actions causing death.

preponderance of the evidence The greater weight of the evidence, though not necessarily the amount needed to remove every reasonable doubt. It is proof sufficient to incline a reasonable person toward one side of an issue rather than the other.

presumption A rule of law that the trier of fact shall assume the existence of a state of facts without evidence being produced. Presumptions are either rebuttable or irrebuttable.

probable cause Reasonable grounds to believe.

procedural due process A claim under the Fourteenth Amendment that there is an absence of fair procedures regulating state conduct.

procuring, promoting, and pimping Actions taken to provide services of a prostitute.

proportionality An objective evaluation of the appropriateness of a punishment for a particular crime.

prostitution Providing sex for money or other value.

proximate cause The ordinary and probable cause of a result.

public law Laws or statutes that apply to all people within a state or nation. Criminal laws in England and the United States are examples of public law.

quid pro quo Giving something of value ("quid") for something else.

rape Anal, vaginal, or oral penetration by force or threat of force.

rape shield laws Laws passed by many states to limit the extent to which defense attorneys in a rape case can inquire into the victim's past sexual life.

reasonable doubt Proof beyond a reasonable doubt means that it is not enough to prove it was more likely than not that an element of the crime was true. The proof must be such that a reasonable person could not conclude the element was not true.

recidivist One who is a habitual criminal.

RICO The Racketeer Influenced and Corrupt Organizations Act. Passed by Congress to enable prosecutors to charge all people engaged in unlawful activity who own or invest in an enterprise that affects interstate commerce.

"right and wrong" test An insanity test that claims that defendants are not legally responsible for their acts if, due to a defect of the mind, at the time of the crime they were unable to understand the difference between right and wrong.

riot Under the common law, a tumultuous disturbance of the peace by three or more people assembled with a common purpose to do an unlawful act.

robbery Forcible stealing.

sabotage The crime of damaging or injuring national defense material or utilities with the intention of interfering with national defense.

sanctuary In the Middle Ages in England, a sanctuary was a religious place where criminals could take refuge. The concept of sanctuary later broadened to include asylum for refugees.

scienter A form of specific intent requiring a showing that the actor knew of the existence of certain facts. For example, one cannot be guilty of possession of stolen property if one does not know property is stolen.

sedition The crime of advocating the forceful overthrow of the established government. In this country, the Smith Act makes such advocacy a crime.

self-defense The elements to evaluate whether an act of force for self-defense is justified include the unlawfulness of the other's action, the necessity to defend oneself immediately, and the reasonableness of the act of self-defense under the circumstances.

sexual assault The crime in most states that includes the crime of rape, as well as other lesser degrees of assault.

shoplifting Stealing goods from retail stores by concealment, generally on the person of the defendant. Commission does not require removal of the goods from the store.

solicitation or incitement crimes Attempting to get another to commit a crime.

specific intent The intent necessary for one or more elements of an offense. Murder, for example, requires the specific intent that the act be done intentionally or purposely.

stalking A crime involving activities such as spying on the victim, following the victim, or attempting to communicate with the victim through the telephone or mail. Cyberstalking through the Internet is also a crime.

"stand your ground" laws Recent laws passed in many states that permit using deadly force in response to an unlawful attack, in contrast to the traditional "duty to retreat" policy.

status crime Criminal laws that punish a status, such as drug addiction, with no act requirement.

statute of limitations A defense to a criminal prosecution based on a statute that sets the maximum time the government has to prosecute a violation of a criminal law.

statutory rape Sexual intercourse with a minor under a certain age, usually 16–18. Consent and, generally, mistake as to age are not defenses to this crime.

strict liability crime Crime that does not require proof of the mental element essential to true crimes.

subornation of perjury The crime of inducing or knowingly permitting another person to testify falsely while under oath.

"substantial capacity" test A test to determine criminal responsibility based on whether the defendant could (1) distinguish between right and wrong or (2) conform his or her conduct to the requirements of law.

substantive due process A claim under the Fourteenth Amendment that state conduct is so brutal, demeaning, and harmful as to shock the conscience.

sudden snatching A form of robbery where force is not used beyond that needed to take property from another person.

symbolic speech Nonverbal expressions that convey a belief or idea.

taking The act of obtaining physical possession or control of another's property. The key to taking is that the thief exercises unauthorized dominion over the property.

tampering with evidence Knowingly altering or damaging evidence intended to be used in a court proceeding.

terrorism The use of force and violence in the pursuit of extreme political, ideological, or religious goals, without regard to the innocent lives that may be lost.

theft or larceny Stealing property of another with the intent to deprive the owner of possession.

threats of violence Statements or actions that unequivocally convey the message that violent actions will be taken.

"three strikes" laws Laws that impose increased penalties for multiple felony convictions.

tort A noncontractual civil wrong.

transactional immunity Total or full immunity for the criminal offense to which compelled testimony relates.

transferred intent A doctrine used when the intention to harm one individual inadvertently causes a second person to be hurt instead. The individual causing the harm will be seen as having "intended" the act by means of the "transferred intent" doctrine.

Travel Act Legislation that can be used to prosecute those involved in criminal activities that cross state borders or involve foreign commerce.

treason Acting to overthrow one's government, or in violation of allegiance to one's country.

trespass A wrongful intrusion on the land or into the premises of another person.

trial by ordeal A test used to determine criminal responsibility in ancient England involving subjecting the individual to a torturous ordeal. These ordeals were essentially appeals to God; surviving the ordeal was viewed as God's judgment of innocence.

true threat A serious expression of an intent to inflict bodily harm.

Uniform Controlled Substances Act Model act identifying illegal drug crimes, drafted by a national conference of uniform law commissioners and adopted by the states and the federal government.

unlawful assembly Under the common law, a gathering of three or more people for any unlawful purpose or under such circumstances as to endanger the public peace or cause alarm and apprehension.

unreasonable seizure A seizure made by a government officer that is unreasonable under the circumstances and thus violates the Fourth Amendment.

usable amount In contrast to a useless trace amount, a quantity of an illegal drug sufficient to be used.

use immunity Prohibits prosecutorial authorities from using compelled testimony in a criminal prosecution, but does not make the witness totally immune from prosecution based on evidence other than the witness's testimony and not derived from that testimony.

uttering Putting into circulation a check known to be worthless.

"void for vagueness" doctrine The constitutional law doctrine that invalidates criminal laws written in such a manner as to make it unreasonably difficult for a defendant to know whether or not conduct is prohibited by the law.

Wharton rule The requirement that crimes needing more than one person for commission, such as bigamy, require three or more people for a conspiracy conviction.

what one did, they all did The rule that all parties to a conspiracy or other agreement to perform an unlawful act are liable for every action taken by any party in furtherance of the conspiracy or agreement.

white-collar crime   A class or type of criminal conduct whose only goal is the criminal's economic gain.

wire fraud   A fraudulent scheme that uses interstate or international wire or other electronic communications.

witness protection program   Established as part of the Organized Crime Control Act of 1970, this program provides new identities and relocation for witnesses and their families in both state and federal criminal prosecutions of organized crime.

witness tampering   Criminal interference with someone who plans to testify in either a criminal or a civil trial.

Case Index

Subject Index